PROF. Dᴿ FREUD

Dear Mrs

I gather from your letter that your son is a homosexual. I am most impressed by the fact that you do not mention this term yourself in your information about him. May I question you why you avoid it? Homosexuality is assuredly no advantage but it is nothing to be ashamed of, no vice, no degradation, it cannot be classified as an illness; we consider it to be a variation of the sexual function produced by a certain arrest of sexual development. Many highly respectable individuals of ancient and modern times have been homosexuals, several of the greatest men among them (Plato, Michelangelo, Leonardo da Vinci etc). It is a great injustice to persecute homosexuality as a crime and a cruelty too. If you do not believe me, read the books of Havelock Ellis.

By asking me if I can help, you mean, I suppose, if I can abolish homosexuality and make normal heterosexuality take its place. The answer is, in a general way we cannot promise to achieve it. In a certain number of cases we succeed in developing the blighted germs of heterosexual tendencies which are present in every homosexual, in the majority of cases it is no more possible. It

Frontispiece. Letter to an American mother from Sigmund Freud, continued on next page and followed by a printed copy of the letter.

(The original was presented to Dr. Kinsey by the recipient, and is in the collection of the Kinsey Institute library.)

is a question of the quality and the age of the individual. The result of treatment cann. be predicted.

What analysis can do for your son runs in a different line. If he is unhappy neurotic torn by conflicts inhibited in his social life analysis may bring him harmony peace of mind full efficiency whether he remains a homosexual or gets changed.

If you make up your mind he should have analysis with me — I don't expect you will —, he has to come over to Vienna. I have no intention of leaving here. However don't neglect to give me your answer. Sincerely yours with kind wishes

Freud

P.S. I did not not find it difficult to read your handwriting. Hope you will not find my writing and my English a harder task.

April 9, 1935
Vienna, IX, Bergasse 9

Dear Mrs. _____ :

I gather from your letter that your son is a homosexual. I am most impressed by the fact that you do not mention this term in your information about him. May I question you, why you avoid it? Homosexuality is assuredly no advantage but it is nothing to be ashamed of, no vice, no degradation, it cannot be classified as an illness; we consider it to be a variation of the sexual function produced by a certain arrest of sexual development. Many highly respectable individuals of ancient and modern times have been homosexuals, several of the greatest men among them. (Plato, Michelangelo, Leonardo da Vinci, etc.) It is a great injustice to persecute homosexuality as a crime and a cruelty too. If you do not believe me, read the books of Havelock Ellis.

By asking me if I can help, you mean, I suppose, if I can abolish homosexuality and make normal heterosexuality take its place. The answer is, in a general way, we cannot promise to achieve it. In a certain number of cases we succeed in developing the blighted germs of heterosexual tendencies, which are present in every homosexual; in the majority of cases it is no more possible. It is a question of the quality and the age of the individual. The result of treatment cannot be predicted.

What analysis can do for your son runs in a different line. If he is unhappy, neurotic, torn by conflicts, inhibited in his social life, analysis may bring him in harmony, peace of mind, full efficiency, whether he remains homosexual or gets changed. If you make up your mind he should have an analysis with me—I don't expect he will—he has to come over to Vienna. However, don't neglect to give me your answer.

Sincerely yours with kind wishes

Freud

P.S. I did not find it difficult to read your handwriting. I hope you will not find my writing and my English a harder task.

THE PUZZLE

"Evolution is central to the understanding of life, including human life. Like all living things, we are the outcomes of natural selection; we got here because we inherited traits that allowed our ancestors to survive, find mates, and reproduce. This momentous fact explains our deepest strivings, why having a thankless child is sharper than a serpent's tooth, why it is a truth universally acknowledged that a single man in possession of a good fortune must be in want of a wife. . . . ."
                    --Steven Pinker, *The Blank Slate*, page 52

. . . and that's why

homosexual behavior is "a profound puzzle . . . [H]omosexual behavior is the antithesis of reproductive success."
        --Malcolm Potts and Roger Short, *Ever Since Adam and Eve*:
                    The Evolution of Human Sexuality, page 74

Gratefully dedicated
to the many hundreds of homosexual men*—
journalists, researchers, autobiographers,
interviewees, research subjects,
survey respondents, patients,
Christian strugglers, and
gay spokesmen—
whose willingness to share their recollections,
their experiences, their thoughts and feelings have made this book
possible.

*Among those authors whose courage, honesty, and hard work have advanced psychological knowledge on this special topic, the following men (listed alphabetically) deserve a special note of thanks: Robert Baumann, Roger Brown, Michael Davidson, Will Fellows, Richard Isay, Martin Levine, Francis Mondimore, Walt Odets, Gabriel Rotello, Andrew Solomon, George Stambolian, Andrew Sullivan, and Andrew Tobias.

THE PUZZLE

Exploring the Evolutionary Puzzle

of Male Homosexuality

Louis A. Berman

GODOT

GODOT

Published by the Godot Press
601 Ridge Road, Unit 101, Wilmette, Illinois
60691

First edition

Library of Congress Cataloging-in-Publication Data

Berman, Louis A., 1921-
The puzzle; exploring the evolutionary puzzle of male homosexuality

Includes bibliographical references,
subject index, authors index, and index of cases.

ISBN 0-9723013-0-5 (hardcover), ISBN 0-9723013-1-3 (pbk.)

1. Homosexuality, Male. 2. Evolutionary psychology. 3. Gay men–Psychology. 4. Homosexuality, Male–Cross-cultural studies. I. Title.

10 9 8 7 6 5 4 3 2 1

Manufactured in the United States of America
Printed on acid-free stock, sewn binding.

Acknowledgements

The fundamental purpose of copyright law is to promote and encourage the publication of literary and scientific works by protecting innovators from unfair appropriation (simple copying reproducing, stealing, plagiarizing) of one's work. Does this make the original, copyrighted work "untouchable," immune from criticism or commentary? No, copyright case law makes a careful distinction between the substitutional and complementary use of published material.

By substitutional use, we refer to simple reproduction or copying (however abridged, condensed, translated, or adapted) of a substantial portion of a published work. This could be a violation of copyright law because if permitted, authors would be discouraged from preparing work for publication. Publishers could never recoup the cost of publishing a work if it could be freely replaced by an unauthorized substitute for the original work. Complementary use, on the other hand, means that the new work serves a related though significantly different purpose than the published work.

Copyright law does not bar a copyrighted work from scholarly or research use, or make it immune from criticism, from reinterpretation, or evaluation. That is the difference between substitutional use, which copyright law protects against, and complementary use, which is recognizd as fair use. Contrary to the intent of the copyright law, some publishers (including, incredibly, some university presses) refuse to grant "permission" because the new work disagrees with their author's point of view.

Publishing custom, however, requires that an author request permission to reprint *all* quotations (exceeding more than a few words) from copyright works, a custom that may require an author to spend hundreds of hours of correspondence with publishers. Publishers can amortize the cost of this expensive (and in some cases needless) activity by charging the authors for "permission" to reprint.

When a request is for *fair use*, most publishers freely acknowledge that fact and grant the request without charge. This author thanks the publishers who did so, by placing an asterisk (*) before their name in the listing that follows. In this listing, page numbers refer to pages in this book where the "permitted" quotations appear. For briefer references to those works, and for paraphrases, which do not require "permission," see Authors Index at the end of this book.

Grateful acknowledgement is therefore made for permission to reprint the following copyrighted material. ALBOM on p. 79: *Tuesdays with Morrie*, by Mitch Albom, *Doubleday, 1997. BELL on pp. 45, 288, 298, 305: *Homosexualities: A Study of Diversity Among Men and Women*, by A.P. Bell and M.S. Weinberg. *Simon & Schuster, 1978. BLUM on pp. 102, 103: *Sex on the Brain; The Biological Differences Between Men and Women*, by Deborah Blum, copyright © 1997 by the author. *Viking Penguin. BROWN on pp. 96, 219-220, 237. *Against My Better Judgement*, by Roger Brown. *Harrington Park Press, 1996. CLARK on pp. 234, 239, 253, 268, 271, 441-442: *Loving Someone Gay*, by Don Clark, *Celestial Arts Publishing, Berkeley CA, 1997. DAVIDSON on pp. 195-

305: *The World, the Flesh and Myself*, by Michael Davidson, *GMP Publishers Ltd., London, 1962. GOULD on pp. xx, 362-363, 493: *Ever Since Darwin: Reflections in Natural History* by Stephen Jay Gould. W.W. Norton & Co. 1977, © 1973, 1974, 1975, 1976, 1977 by The American Museum of Natural History. GREVER on pp. 194, 407: *My Husband Is Gay; A Woman's Guide to Surviving the Crisis*, by Carole Grever. *Crossing Press, Freedom CA, 2001. HAMER on p. 259: *The Science of Desire: The Search for the Gay Gene and the Biology of Behavior*, by Dean Hamer and Peter Copeland, *Simon & Schuster, © 1994 by the authors. HART on p. 309: *Gay Sex; A Manual for Men Who Love Men*, by Jack Hart. *Alyson Publications, 1991. HERDT on p. 309: *Same Sex, Different Cultures*, by Gilbert Herdt. © 1997 by *Westview Press. HOCHMAN on pp. 423-424: *A Brilliant Madness; Living with Manic-Depressive Illness*, by P. Duke and G. Hochman. *Bantam Books, 1992. KAHN on pp. 55, 148, 157, 446: *The Many Faces of Gay*, by A.D. Kahn. Praeger Publishers, 1997. KIRK on pp. 237-238, 437-438: *After the Ball* by Marshall Kirk and Hunter Madsen. Doubleday, 1989. © 1989 by the authors. LE VAY on pp. 25, 109, 116: *The Sexual Brain* by Simon LeVay, *MIT Press, 1993. LE VAY on pp. 319, 344, 427: *City of Friends* by Simon LeVay and Elizabeth Nonas. *MIT Press, 1995. LEVINE on pp. 395, 396-397, 410-411: *Gay Macho: Ethnography of the Homosexual Clone* *NYU doctoral dissertation, 1990. MACCOBY on pp. 30, 52: *The Two Sexes; Growing Up Apart, Coming Together* by Eleanor E. Maccoby, *The Bellnap Press of Harvard University Press, © 1998 by the President and Fellows of Harvard College. MC COURT on p. 417, *Angela's Ashes: A Memoir* by Frank McCourt, Scribner, a Division of Simon & Schuster,© 1996 by the author. MONDIMORE on pp. 156-157: *A Natural History of Homosexuality* by Francis Mondimore. *Johns Hopkins University Press, © 1996. MONEY on pp. 254, 335, 447-448: *Gay, Straight, and In-Between* by John Money. *Oxford University Press, 1998. OUTLAND on pages 211: Coming Out; A Handbook for Men by Orland Outland. *Alyson Publications 2000, © by the author. OWENS on pp. 94-96: *Queer Kids; the Challenges and Promise for Lesbian, Gay and Bisexual Youth* by R.E. Owens, Jr. *Harrington Park Press,1998. POMEROY on pp.410, 443-444: *Boys and Sex; A Long-Needed Sexual Guide for Boys* by W.B. Pomeroy, *Dell Publishing, a division of Random House, 1963. POTTS on pp. 378-380: *Ever Since Adam and Eve: The Evolution of Human Sexuality* by Malcolm Potts and Roger Short. *Cambridge University Press, 1999. ROSS on pp. 64-65: *The Male Paradox* by John Munder Ross. *Simon & Schuster, 1992, © 1992 by the author. ROWE on pp. 158, 389: *Looking for Brothers* by Michael Rowe. *Mosaic Press, Toronto, 1999. SIGNORILE on pp. 216, 248: *Life Outside; The Signorile Report on Gay Men: Sex, Drugs, Muscles and the Passages of Life* by Michelangelo Signorile. *HarperCollins, 1997. SULLIVAN on pp.147, 159, 306, 349, 391, 402: *Virtually Normal* by Andrew Sullivan. Alfred A. Knopf, a division of Random House, 1995. © by the author. SULLIVAN pp. 225, 343: *Love Undetectable* by Andrew Sullivan, Alfred A. Knopf, a division of Random House, 1998, © by the author. TOBIAS on pp. 246, 304: *The Best Little Boy in the World Grows Up* by Andrew Tobias. *Random House, 1998. UPDIKE on page 70: An excerpt from "The Rumor," in *The Afterlife and Other Stories*. *Knopf, 1995.

Contents

The worriers   454

26 Low-Masculinized Brain (LMB) Males
        A population worth studying   459

27 From Harem Chief to Family Man; Homosexuality as a By-Product
    of the De-Dimorphism of the Species   472
        E.O. Wilson's altruism theory   473
        A by-product theory of male homosexuality   473
        Premature birth reshapes hominid society   478
        A brain wired for learning   479
        Male and female become more alike 480
        Status minimizes social conflict   483
        Man the social animal   483
        Man the hunter   484
        Nature evolves the caring husband and father   485
        Mutations gentle the male temperament   487
        The low-masculinized male brain   488
        The curve of variation   488
        Low-masculinization the by-product of a moderated male norm   489
        A prediction that comes close to the truth   489
        The LBM Puzzle   490

Epilogue: Some Practical Questions   499
            Part 1. Treatment Questions   499
                Predicting success in reorientation therapy   503
                The success rate of reorientation therapy   510

            Part 2. 18 More Questions About Homosexuality   515
                1. Can homosexuality be defined as a lifestyle?
                    from an evolutionary point of view?   515
                2. Are not homosexuals a gifted population?   516
                3. Is the tendency toward male homosexuality genetic?   516
                4. Does upbringing make a difference?   517
                5. How can parents decide what kind of sex play is good
                    for the child's development ...?   517
                6. Is man-boy sex really so harmful as to justify classifying this
                    activity as criminal conduct?   518
                7. Does adult homosexuality ever result from childhood
                    seduction?   519
                8. Why do certain young men who are not in fact homosexual
                    worry that they might be?   520

Tables and Figures

Foreword

By A. Dean Byrd, Ph.D., Clinical Professor of Medicine
Department of Family and Preventive Medicine, University of Utah

Quite by chance, I heard about Dr. Berman's manuscript on male homosexuality, and my curiosity was piqued. I offered to look it over and give the author some kind of feedback, that's all. But I was not prepared for such a challenging task, and spent about a week examining *The Puzzle*, so named because homosexuality does not obey the major principle of evolution that only those traits survive that favor reproduction.

A retired Professor of Psychology at the University of Illinois at Chicago, Dr. Berman draws upon his doctoral studies in personality theory, learning theory, social psychology, and a career in personal counseling. His by-product theory reflects his interest in evolutionary psychology, a specialty that did not exist in his student days. *The Puzzle* also reflects a passion for library research, and a talent for clear, readable writing.

The author's thesis that male homosexuality is the by-product of human evolution deserves careful scrutiny. But aside from the author's evolutionary perspective (with which you may or may not agree), here is a truly comprehensive examination of the topic of male homosexuality, both factual and theoretical. Generous use of direct quotations from gay writers, survey respondents, and patients makes the book come alive with the words of homosexual men themselves. *The Puzzle* is a pleasure to read, the result of a herculean effort to carefully examine a wide range of field observation, research and theory, and to somehow connect it to practice, to make some sense of a most controversial topic.

I approached the book from the perspective of a psychologist (Clinical Professor of Medicine at the University of Utah) who has spent almost 30 years in teaching, research, and clinical practice. Over the years, many of my patients have been men who were unhappy with their homosexual compulsions, and came with complaints like "this lifestyle just isn't working for me." Some were married, had a family and placed a higher value on their family than on following their homosexual attractions. They wanted to diminish their homosexual attractions and increase their heterosexual feelings. Most of my patients were easily engaged in therapy. They were well motivated and they worked very hard. If I were to estimate my treatment success, I would guess that my success with these men was not so different from my other patients. I therefore find it hard to justify the mental health Establishment's opposition to reorientation therapy.

The author closely examines the "nature versus nurture" issue and adopts an interactionist model, which recognizes the interplay of genetic factors, cultural influences, and individual experience in shaping one's sexual likes and dislikes. Political correctness is *not* one of this book's virtues. The author's by-product theory and interactionist model will not please gay advocates, nor will his emphasis on the genetic side of the phenomenon please those therapists who are sure that homosexuality is almost always the result of a close-binding mother and a distant father.

Ultimately, all behavior has a biological substrate. Certainly both nature and nurture play a role in the development of homosexual attractions, and the relative weight of nature and nurture varies from person to person. But to say that there is a heritable factor at work does not fix a person's sexuality. The author quotes Stephen Jay Gould's reminder that "to a geneticist, 'inherited' . . . carries no implication of inevitability or of immmutable entities beyond the reach of environmental influence. Eyeglasses correct a variety of inherited problems in vision, insulin can check diabetes" (*Ever Since Darwin*, page 245).

There is much in *The Puzzle* that is consistent with my own research and clinical experience. Certainly the routes are quite different for men and for women, which justifies the author's restriction of this study to *male* behavior. Whether or not one likes an evolutionary approach to the development of homosexuality is not critical to an appreciation of Dr. Berman's work. What is clear to me, on the basis of almost 30 years' clinical experience, is that his bio-psycho-social model fits the data.

The Puzzle is not likely to win applause from believers that homosexuality is an "innate and immutable condition," or from those who believe that homosexuality is a "fluid and flexible" phenomenon that can be learned and unlearned. Rather, the book will appeal to the reader who wants to see how biological, social, and psychological factors *interact*, to make the person what he becomes.

What if homosexuality is "what comes naturally" to a person? In *The Road Less Traveled* (pages 213-214) Dr. Scott Peck notes that it is also natural "to never brush our teeth. Yet we teach ourselves to do the unnatural until the unnatural becomes itself second nature. Indeed, all self-discipline might be defined as teaching ourselves to do the unnatural. Another characteristic of human nature—perhaps the one that makes us more human—is our capacity to do the unnatural, to transcend and hence transform our own nature." Most of the men I have treated for unwanted homosexual attractions tell me their life has been transformed.

The author boldly speaks truth to power. He does not hide his disagreement with the American Psychological Association and the American Psychiatric Association for their opposition to reorientation therapy, and argues that this position not only blocks potentially helpful treatment, but also inhibits the improvement of professional training, and blocks the kind of research that would develop better treatment strategies as it advances our basic understanding of homosexuality. I would hope that mental health professionals give this important work the attention it deserves, and reexamine their professional organizations' policies in the light of the facts and logic so clearly presented in *The Puzzle*.

Thanks to Louis Berman for writing the text I have been looking for, to serve as required reading for students in my human sexuality courses. I am a teacher, researcher, and therapist, not a salesman, but I hope this Foreword persuades my colleagues everywhere to consider *The Puzzle* as required reading for themselves and for their students. And for those whose school days are over but understand the truism that learning is a lifelong adventure, you'll find this book both challenging and enlightening.

And I totally endorse the author's view that in a decent society, persons who follow whatever sexual option deserve "compassion, understanding and good will. . . . "

Preface

Facing an Age-old Puzzle

Every thoughtful person is a psychologist in his or her own way, curious about the varieties and uniformities of human behavior. It is no wonder that, for many, the topic of homosexuality—pursued secretly or openly, professionally or casually—is an interesting, even fascinating, topic to observe, study, wonder and sometimes worry about.

To the traditionalist, homosexuality is a puzzle for various reasons. In is forbidden in the Hebrew Bible, but so are many ordinary practices of everyday life: eating pork and shrimp, cutting the corners of one's beard, using cloths made of diverse fibers, etc. Why is one taboo so tenaciously maintained by Judaeo-Christian traditionalists, while many others are regarded as no longer meaningful? Why does the New Testament explicitly denounce homosexuality, while other taboos of the Hebrew Bible are ignored?

If homosexuality is genetic, even in part, why was this "sinful" tendency implanted in man's physical nature? If homosexuality is an abomination, why is it so strongly felt, and even practiced, by some men of the most admirable character, including some priests, some ministers, and some rabbis?

These are questions that have torn apart religious councils. Religious leaders, wise and learned, express contradictory viewpoints on whether their community should condemn, tolerate, or even celebrate same-sex partnerships.

Might science throw some light on a question that has split traditionalists apart? *To the scientific community, homosexuality is also a puzzle.* According to modern evolutionary theory,[1] a trait survives if it favors reproduction. Homosexual activity does not result in reproduction, yet homosexuality can be found in human cultures of all sorts, preliterate and advanced. Biologists Potts and Short (page 74) characterize homosexuality as "a profound puzzle . . . [since] homosexual behavior is the antithesis of reproductive success." How did this trait get into the human repertory, and why does it reappear in every generation, though homosexuals themselves do not usually reproduce?

We see people around us willingly bear heavy social handicaps, physical risks to their personal safety, and grave medical risks, to follow a homosexual orientation. How did they get that way, and why do they willingly pay such a high price for this lifestyle? [2]

Thirdly, heterosexual men may have homosexual dreams, may harbor passing, recurring, surprising or annoying homosexual impulses—or feel an irrational aversion to homosexuals that suggests perhaps they are defending themselves against an unwanted temptation—*what about homosexuality and everyman?* This book explores some theoretical issues, and tries to answer some practical questions, about male homosexuality from the standpoint of evolutionary psychology.

Karl Ulrichs (1825-1895) and Magnus Hirschfeld (1868-1935), pioneers in the scientific study of homosexuality (and gay men themselves), independently concluded that homosexuality was essentially an inborn trait. On the basis of close clinical observation, Sigmund Freud arrived at four conclusions regarding homosexuality. (1) The homosexual habit, per se, is not a disorder. True, some homosexuals are so unsettled, so miserable about the direction of their sex drive that they plead with therapists to help them change it.[3] But there are also homosexual men, as Freud acknowledged, who lead sane, productive, and happy lives. (2) Those homosexuals who are anxious or distressed about their sexual habits, and plead for help in reorienting their sex life, are exceedingly difficult to "cure." (3) In those patients whose emotional problem has nothing to do with homosexuality, no matter why the patient entered therapy, long-term analysis would usually uncover some same-sex attractions. Homosexual impulses (conscious or unconscious), Freud concluded, exist throughout the human species. (4) Finally, years of experience led Freud to believe that a homosexual orientation arises from *both* a constitutional[4] predisposition, and certain experiences of infancy or childhood. (A mother who is seductive or over-controlling, a father who is distant, weak, or absent have thus become stock characters, tragicomic figures, in the formative experience of the typical pre-homosexual boy.)

Perhaps we have an unexamined faith that whatever has been learned can be unlearned, what has been acquired can be discarded, and replaced with something more satisfying, less troublesome. This makes personal experience far more manageable than a constitutional predisposition, so when psychoanalysts (and other therapists) theorize, they stress, perhaps to the exclusion of everything else, the *role of life* experience in the making of a homosexual. This tactic recalls the joke about the man who comes home drunk one night, and when he tries to unlock his front door, fumbles and drops his keys in the darkness. He then staggers down the steps and goes to the corner of the block to look for his keys under the lamp-post. Why? "Because that's where the light is."

If we delve into Freud's statement that homosexuality results from the *interaction* of constitutional factors and experience, this suggests that no two homosexual habits may be exactly alike in their underlying dynamics. One man's homosexual tendencies may arise from so strong a constitutional predisposition that a very moderate life influence was enough to trigger the habit. Another may arise from powerful and many-faceted life experiences, interacting with a modest constitutional predisposition. In-between these extremes lie the possibilities of all sorts of combinations of constitutional and environmental loadings. To complicate the picture further, the constitutional and environmental factors may vary from case to case.

Now we know we are dealing not with the simple question of "nature *or* nurture" but *with* the more complicated question of "How may heredity interact with environment?" We are faced with various possible constitutional factors, and with a multiplicity of possible environmental factors. We are challenged to evolve a theory that can systematize the diversity of our observations, to account for both constitutional and environmental factors.

What are the constitutional factors, and what are the environmental factors that lead to the formation of a homosexual habit? That is one question this book wrestles with. Most of the book summarizes what has been observed of homosexual behavior by researchers, therapists, and by gay men themselves.

Homosexuality may be usefully conceptualized as a breakaway from, or variant of, biologically functional human sexuality. A theory of homosexuality can be no better than our understanding of human sexuality in general. Therefore, this book begins with a theory of human sexuality in general. What's so special about *human* sexuality? Frank A. Beach, an experimental psychologist who spent about 40 years researching sexual behavior in animals—its neural, hormonal, and experiential control—arrived at the conclusion that human sexuality is an evolutionary emergent:

> [H]uman sexuality is about as closely related to mating behavior
> of other species as human language is related to animal com-
> munication, and that relationship is distant indeed (1978, page
> 124).

Is Homosexuality "Just Part of Nature"?

Many a reputable scientist, many a wise and experienced clinician has asserted that no single theory can explain so complex and varied a phenomenon as homosexuality. Then why don't we just relax and accept homosexual behavior as a part of the diversity of nature? To some folks this is a comfortable point of view, though it does not face up to the question, How does homosexuality fit into the theory of evolution?

It is true that same-sex activity can be found among animals of all kinds—rats, frogs, monkeys, sheep, dogs, cats, dolphins, seagulls. All sorts of creatures, it is argued, exhibit "homosexual behavior." Farm and zoo animals often exhibit "homosexual behavior" that free-ranging animals usually do not.[5] Also, acts that *look* homosexual emerge as a result of confinement, segregation, or domestication. Ethologists have even claimed that they can *induce* adult homosexuality in certain birds by exposing young males to certain treatments.[6] What looks like homosexual behavior may often be more accurately categorized as infantile play, dominance-submission behavior,[7] or poor discrimination. [For example, male and female frogs of some species look alike even to other frogs. When a male frog clasps another male, the clasped male utters a "release call" which apparently means: "Let go, and find yourself a real female" (George Williams, page 47)].

A bird story

In the 1970s, ecologists George and Molly Hunt monitored the

breeding colonies of western gulls in islands off the coast of
Southern California. Since male and female gulls look so much
alike, what led them to suspect that there were many female-
female pairs? Their curiosity was aroused by the fact that about
every seventh nest contained twice as many eggs as one female
normally lays. The pair of birds that inhabited these "supernumerary clutches" exhibited all the behaviors of a male-female
pair: they courted and remained paired for more than one season.
When they copulated, the same bird always did the mounting.
*Close examination confirmed the fact that these were indeed
female-female pairs: "lesbian seagulls."*

Both gay men and lesbians hailed the discovery of these committed "lesbian seagulls" with enduring "butch" and "femme" roles,
and their existence was widely broadcast. For example, James
Weinrich's 1987 survey of *Sexual Landscapes* documents the
Hunts' "careful observations," and suggests that the gulls indeed
"*had a choice* between same- and opposite-sex partners." (page
297, emphasis added) He concludes : "Although the causes of all
this homosexual behavior are still not well understood, one thing
is clear: *preferential* homosexual behavior is indeed observed in
natural, free-living populations in some animals" (page 298,
emphasis added).

But this celebration of the "diversity of nature" was short-lived.
Twenty years after the original discovery of these feathered
"lesbian couples," a study group of about 45 lesbians and gay
men organized a boat trip to Anacapa Island, where the Hunts
had discovered this phenomenon. Much to the disappointment of
these visitors, they found *no* supernumerary egg clutches. The
feathered "lesbian couples." had mysteriously disappeared.

Investigation led to the conclusion that during the 1960s, con-
tamination of the ocean with DDT had selectively weakened and
sterilized male seagulls, and the shortage of males at the breeding grounds had led to female-female pairings. DDT was banned
in the early 1970s, and as healthy, willing males reappeared,
"seagull lesbianism" vanished (LeVay 1996, paraphrased).

An interesting story. But an evolutionist would take seriously only the similarities between the behavior of humans and creatures, like chimpanzees, closely related to humans. Birds, frogs, sheep, and dolphins are too remote from
human origins to shed light on human predispositions.[8]

It is quite probable, as Chapter 10 suggests, that in *Homo sapiens* there is a
more-or-less stable fraction (maybe three percent) of male homosexuals in soci-

eties throughout the world, traditional and modern, ancient and contemporary. This may be what makes human male homosexuality so different.

The Author, Who He Is, and Who He Isn't

"You're not gay, are you? What business do you have writing a book about homosexuals?" (Yes, I have actually had that question put to me by a very dear friend whose son is homosexual.) As I ruminated over this question, I thought of Alexis de Tocqueville, that Frenchman who at the age of 26, spent only nine months in the United States during 1831 and 1832. His *Democracy in America* is still quoted for its insights into the American character, American society, and the American government. We recognize the special advantage of an outside observer whenever we ask: "What would a man from Mars say about this?" (To characterize this author, or anyone else, as "an outside observer" is not completely accurate since, as Chapter 5, argues, a homosexual tendency, great or small, is a tendency shared by virtually everybody.)

I am not a man from Mars, neither am I a 26-year old French tourist. I am a retired professor of psychology, a psychological counselor, and a lifelong student of what people think, feel, and do. I have been a personal counselor of college students, about a dozen of whom told me about their homosexual experience. (I found their stories more than interesting but my own training really didn't prepare me to help them.) Growing up, in civilian life and in the military, the phenomenon of homosexuality has touched my life and engaged my imagination in many ways, as it does every man.

I am now retired, after over 30 years of teaching and psychological counseling at the University of Illinois at Chicago, when I decided to do some library research, field work and writing on a topic that a working psychologist might *avoid* for practical reasons.[9] Since I am retired, I do not have access to those bright and eager student assistants who help their professor by looking up original sources and verifying page numbers. I have therefore relied to an extent on some reliable secondary sources to keep this project within manageable time limits. I hope my readers will indulge me this shortcut.

In my reading, I searched for suggestions for a theory of homosexuality that covers virtually all of the facts. If the theory disagrees with the favorite beliefs of reorientation therapists, of gay-affirmative therapists, of religious counselors, or of gay advocacy groups, perhaps it is time for all of us to have a closer look at the facts.

By professional training and experience, I felt qualified to embark on an in-depth and critical study of the psychological literature on homosexuality, including the recent output of writings by gay men and gay advocates. Writing a book and finding a publisher for it is not new to me. I have authored five books over the years, and was always able to find a publisher with or without the help of a literary agent. I did not anticipate that no publisher would take this book, even

though it was represented by a literary agent of excellent reputation, who recommended it to a dozen or more publishers.

Almost two hundred years ago, a poet could say, "Beauty is truth, truth [is] beauty."[10] But almost a thousand years ago, a Hebrew psalmist advised that we distinguish between the facts of nature and our spiritual longings: *Truth springs up from the earth; justice looks down from heaven.*[11] Reluctantly, painfully, we must concede that there may be a difference between what *is* and what *ought* to be.

When I was a graduate student, in the 1950s, psychology was under the spell of learning theory, supported by Margaret Mead's arresting message of cultural relativism. Today, our knowledge of the biological bases of behavior enables us to ask better questions about human behavior. Meanwhile, a new specialty is emerging in psychology—evolutionary psychology[12]--a specialty that fills what I sensed was lacking in the psychology of my own student days. My reading of Heinz Werner, Weston LaBarre, E.O. Wilson, Richard Leakey, Robert Wright, Harry Harlow, Frank Beach, Glenn Weisfeld and others alerted me to this emerg-ing specialty, and helped make this book what it is.

It would be possible to write a book on homosexuality that was truly com-prehensive and well organized if the topic was already covered by a well-devel-oped theory, and had been thoroughly researched. Unfortunately, neither is true. Research in homosexuality has been severely limited by a number of factors: Much research and theorizing has been based exclusively on clinical cases, on those homosexuals who felt so miserable about their sexual orientation that they sought professional help to change it, and willingly surrendered a good deal of time and money for the prescribed treatment. Gay spokesmen have protested, rightly, that this patient sample is simply unrepresentative of homosexual com-munities that therapists know little or nothing about.

Another deterrent to research in this area is a factor already touched upon: the a priori commitments of various interest groups. Gay advocates defend the posi-tion first espoused by both Ulrich and Hirschfeld, that homosexuality is inborn, "like being left-handed," or is an early and irreversible acquisition.[13] Advocates of sexual-orientation change, therapists and ex-gays alike, on the contrary, stress the proposition that homosexuality is an acquired habit, and that what has been learned can be unlearned.

Much survey research has been conducted in gay bars, and that has been sim-ilarly criticized for being unrepresentative of the vast numbers of gay men who seldom if ever set foot in gay bars.[14]

Field research conducted by "participant-observers" has yielded a more panoramic picture of homosexual life.[15] Controlled psychological studies have similarly enriched our understanding of the homosexual phenomenon. Provocative findings are now emerging from biological laboratories, pointing to brain differences between males and females, and between homosexuals and heterosexuals, a development reported in Chapter 7.

A comprehensive theory is like a well-designed and well-built house: it has a solid foundation below and a leak-proof roof above. In-between are sturdy walls and partitions, windows, doors, and a functioning network of utilities. This book is more like a stockpile of building materials: a pile of bricks here, a stack of lumber there, pipes, windows, etc., ready to be assembled when the missing parts and a working blueprint are at hand.

Why write a book that we know will be incomplete? Why not wait until enough evidence is at hand for a full and well-rounded theory? First, this book is intended as a report on where we stand *now* in our understanding of male homosexuality. Secondly, an important objective of this book is to identify and broadcast the gaps in our knowledge, to challenge a new generation of investigators to engage in needed research in an area of psychology that is largely taboo.[16] A major purpose of this book is to pinpoint these gaps in our knowledge, to guide a new generation of bold and dedicated investigators.

Male homosexuality is a phenomenon of great theoretical interest, but it is also a human experience of pride and shame, of ambivalence and confusion, of pain and suffering, an occurrence that has hobbled careers, and torn families apart. A saying goes, "The truth hurts" but civilization rests on the faith that *the truth helps*. In that spirit, I share with the reader facts about male homosexuality that may not have great theoretical importance, but have a practical significance.

Again and again, the reader is advised that knowledge of this topic is both fragmentary and contaminated by beliefs that are contrary to the evidence. Taken as a whole, this book constitutes what I believe is a comprehensive and fair-minded report on what are the facts, and what can be inferred about the origins of male homosexuality.

More Acknowledgements

My reading tapped the vast library holdings of the Health Sciences Library of the University of Illinois at Chicago, Northwestern University, Loyola Medical College, Chicago Public Library, Evanston (Illinois) Public Library, the Institute for Psychoanalysis in Chicago, the Kinsey Institute at Indiana University in Bloomington, and the Library of Congress, in Washington, DC. In my hometown of Wilmette (Illinois), I not only profited from the extensive holdings of a fine public library, but their interlibrary loan service gave me access to books not otherwise accessible to me.

In addition to my library work, I also did a considerable amount of interviewing, both in person, by telephone, by letter and e-mail. I made two field trips to ex-gay conventions, in Washington, D.C. and Auburn, Kentucky. Frank and Anita Wortham, who conduct a residential program for Christian "homosexual strugglers" in San Raphael (California), kindly consented to be interviewed by me. I made a field trip to their establishment. Unhurrried, thoughtful interviews with Mr. and Mrs. Wortham enriched my understanding of what religious counselors are like and what they say they are accomplishing.

My wife, Helga Kauf-Berman freely served as proofreader, translator, and chauffeur, gave me a generous measure of moral support, and patiently endured my neglect of ordinary household duties while I worked on a project that to her (and sometimes to me) seemed endless. Mr. Frank Oveis, Publishing Director of The Continuum Publishing Group, rejected an early draft of this book, but none the less took time, by telephone, to give me a detailed and encouraging critique of what was missing from the draft I had sent him, and how I could improve it. Marilyn A. Smith, my son Daniel Berman, and Philip Hardgrave edited portions of the manuscript. For computer help, I depended on the expertise of Marvin Schumer, Benjamin Salazar and Ken Kendzy.

On April 7, 2002, it was my good fortune to attend a lecture by Dr. Fred Goodwin at Beth Emet Synagogue in Evanston, Illinois. Senior author of the Oxford University Press textbook on bipolar disorder, Dr. Goodwin was keynote speaker at a community conference on mental illness organized by Beth Emet and The Naomi Ruth Cohen Charitable Foundation.

Friends, colleagues, and resource persons who did a critical reading of various portions of this book, or offered useful information, include Prof. Wilbert McKeachie, Prof. Allen Howard, Prof. Michael Little, Prof. Glenn Weisfeld, Prof. Ben Diamond, Prof. Louis Marder, Dr. Lawrence Hatterer, Dr. Stanley Lipkin, and Dr. James Kohlenberg. I owe them much credit for the virtues of my book, and I alone am responsible for its flaws.

Thanks to Mark H. Barinholtz, P.C., for legal counsel. Thanks to Jerry Warshaw for illustrations that appear on pages 63 and 487. Many thanks to my talented son-in-law Matt Minde (MinDesign of Xenia, Ohio) for taking my sketch for a cover and book jacket and executing it so beautifully by computer.

This book invites the reader to share a wide-ranging exploration of a significant and controversial topic of our times: faithful, we hope, to the best tradition of scholarship: to boldly pursue the facts no matter where they lead.

NOTES TO PREFACE

1. Three statements contained in a 2001 book on evolution by Ernst Mayr especially worth repeating here:

> "Evolution is not merely an idea, a theory, or a concept, but is
> the name of a process in nature, the occurrence of which can be
> documented by mountains of evidence that nobody has been able
> to refute. . . It is now actually misleading to refer to evolution as
> a theory, considering the massive evidence that has been discov-
> ered over the last 140 years documenting its existence. Evolution

is no longer a theory, it is simply a fact" (Mayr, page 275).

"What Darwin called natural selection is actually a process of elimination. The progenitors of the next generation are those individuals among their parents' offspring who survived owing to luck or to the possession of characteristics that made them particularly well adapted for the prevailing environmental conditions" (*ibid,*, page 117).

"Selection is not teleological (goal directed). Indeed, how could an elimination process be teleological? It is a process repeated anew in every generation" (*ibid,*, page 121).

The author of the above three statements, Ernst Mayr, is described by Stephen Jay Gould as "the world's greatest living evolutionary biologist. . . ."

2. How significant are the social handicaps and risks borne by gay men? The gay advocate might argue that many gay men are free of internal conflict and lead productive, satisfying lives. But to adapt to a gay lifestyle, a man must often leave his home town, move to another part of the country, and cut himself off from family and old friends. This separation from his past is for many a grave personal sacrifice and social handicap.

High risk is the price that many gay men willingly pay for sexual gratification. For some, high risk adds to the pleasure of sexual experience. One might argue that some heterosexual men also seek out sexual experiences that are dangerously risky. Common sense argues that "anything can happen to anyone." But scientific discussion focuses on norms, on the *average* situation, and on differences between the *average* situation of different known groups. There is little doubt that the search for sexual gratification is significantly riskier for the average gay man than for the average heterosexual.

3. A fundamental question is whether the misery that drives some homosexuals into therapy (or drugs, or alcoholism) is a product of inner conflict, or social oppression (to use the term that gay advocates favor). This is an issue that we will find occasion to deal with in more detail, later in this book.

4. Throughout this book, the terms *inborn* and *constitutional* are intended to refer to the inherent structure of the person's body or mind, whether the result of genetic factors or the prenatal environment.

5. It is true that elaborate forms of same-sex play have been observed in free-ranging animals. For example, Chevalier-Skolnikoff describes pairs of male

manipulates each other's penis, a small male sucks on the penis of a larger one.

6. Konrad Lorenz reported that it's easy to imprint captive male greylag geese so that they will, as adults, court other males, not females. (See Lorenz 1966/63, pp. 195-200, and Evans 1974.) Craig in 1909 suggests that by exposing a young male dove to certain vocalizations, in adulthood it will act like a female.

7. Many groups of animals maintain a dominance hierarchy. (Each animal acts as if it knows who would defeat whom in a fight.) Acts of mounting seem to assert the individual's position in the "pecking order." A naturalist reports this extreme case of dominance mounting:

> In mountain sheep, there is an important sense in which the dom-
> inance mount not only resembles sexual intercourse, but is indis-
> tinguishable from sexual intercourse. That is, when two males
> fight and one wins, the winner gets an erection, mounts the loser,
> and thrusts away very much like when a male mounts a female
> in the rutting season.

8. Even those "behavioral traits shared by humans and our closest primate rela-
tives" cannot be assumed to have a common genetic origin, warns Stephen Jay Gould (1977a, page 254). All the more unlikely is it that the social behavior of humans is genetically related to the social behavior of laboratory rats, or birds, or dolphins. Gould continues (page 254):

> [E]volutionists are so keenly aware of this problem that they
> have developed a terminology to express it. Similar features due
> to common genetic ancestry are "homologous"; similarities due
> to common functions but with different evolutionary histories,
> are "analogous" (the wings of birds and insects, for example—
> the common ancestor of both groups lacked wings.) . . . [A]
> basic feature of human biology supports the idea that many
> behavioral similarities between humans and other primates are
> analogous, [but] they have no direct genetic specification in
> humans.

In their more systematic and rigorous discourse, biologists make a clear distinc-
tion between homologous and analogous phenomena. But in more *exploratory* discussion, scientists compare human behavior with the behavior of other ani-
mals, simply to show that what is considered a human trait is not uniquely human. For example, Mayr (page 282) compares human guilt feelings with the emotional expression "a dog displays when, in the absence of its master, he has done something for which he expects to be punished." Scholars also look into the life of other creatures to get clues or ideas about human behavior. For example,

anthropologists have derived kinship systems from studies of insects and birds (Tanner and Zihlman, page 588).

9. This author recalls that back in the 1950s his director turned down a promising applicant on the basis that his research interest was aggressive behavior. The director was afraid the applicant might have "an aggression problem."
10. Quoted from "Ode on a Grecian Urn," by John Keats, 1819.

11. Quoted from Psalm 85:12, 1988 JPS (Jewish Publication Society) translation. (In the King James translation, Psalm 85:11 goes: Truth shall spring out of the earth; and righteousness shall look down from heaven.

12. Evolutionary psychology has its adherents but it still has its critics. Some biologists seem reluctant to share evolutionary theory with outsiders. Some sociologists prefer to concentrate on historical and social (including economic) forces as the ones that *really* shape human behavior. For example, in a gender studies textbook published in 2000 is a good example of what was lamented in the 1972 *American Psychologist* letter (Chapter 1, endnote 4). In that book, the author, sociologist Michael S. Kimmel (2000, page 28), suggests that a "simple economic calculation" makes it quite unnecessary to assume that there is a genetic basis for mother-infant interaction:

> "In return for taking care of our offspring when they are young
> and dependent, we expect them to take care of us when we are
> old and dependent;" a formulation that Kimmel commends as "*a
> far more compact and tidy explanation* (emphasis added)" than
> reference to genetic forces "that are empirically untestable."
> (Kimmel credits psychologists Travis and Wade with this ele-
> gantly "simple economic formulation.")

But what about the evidence of maternal behavior throughout the animal kingdom? What about the loving care that childless adults lavish on dogs and cats? Sociologists like Kimmel (and psychologists like Travis and Wade) ignore too much of the living world to make their case that historical and social forces sufficiently shape human behavior so that genetic factors can be ignored.

13. John Money's application of the imprinting model to homosexuality is discussed in Chapter 18.

14. This is a major argument of Bruce Bawer, in *A Place at the Table*.

15. An outstanding piece of participant-observer research is the 1990 doctoral dissertation of Martin P. Levine, *Gay Macho: Ethnography of the Homosexual*

Clone. Sadly, the author died of AIDS a few years later.

16. Is homosexual research taboo? Nonsense! What about the *Journal of Homosexuality*, which publishes research articles every month? But these articles are restricted to studies of homosexuality as a lifestyle. Research on the treatment of gender-discordant boys—suggesting that homosexuality might be prevented—would be out of place in that Journal. Research on the treatment of those homosexual adults who seek relief from their same-sex attractions is denounced by contributors to that *Journal.*

About 35 years ago, Evelyn Hooker (1963, page 51) lamented the career hazards of graduate students who might study homosexual behavior. However bold and courageous, graduate students need the moral support and guidance of faculty advisers, and the financial support of research funding agencies. If journals of the American Psychological Association refuse to publish announcements of the meetings of the National Association for Research and Therapy of Homosexuals (NARTH), would these journals publish the results of the kind of studies promoted by NARTH?

Introduction

An Overview of This Book

One tactic in problem-solving is to divide a problem into manageable pieces. We will begin by confining our interest to *male* homosexuality, not because we regard it as more important or more interesting, but because (as Chapter 4 makes clear) lesbianism seems to follow different rules.

Does this book offer a theory that covers *all* male homosexuality? No. The homosexual behavior of prisoners, for example, does not require much theorizing. Similarly, there are men of low frustration tolerance, whose character, personality, and experience make them rather indifferent as to just how they relieve their sexual tension, and it can be quicker, cheaper and simpler to find a willing male partner. So great is the diversity of male homosexual behavior (the topic of Chapters 10 through 25) that *no* single theory can encompass it all. Within these pages is presented a theory that accounts for *a significant portion* of male homosexual behavior.

The major thesis of this book is that male homosexuality is a by-product of human evolution. In the earliest ancestors of the human species, about eight million years ago, adult males grew to almost twice the size of adult females,[1] a gender difference (or dimorphism, as anthropologist call it) very adaptive to a species in which a dominant male defended a territory in which it kept a harem of six or so females.

Like present-day gorillas, these hominid males were not only much bigger than adult females, but no doubt much different in temperament: ferocious defenders of their harem. As evolutionary forces favored closer cooperation between adult males and females, this extreme dimorphism became maladaptive and therefore gradually decreased, until about two million years ago there was no more difference between the size (and probably no more difference in the temperament) of the average adult male and female than there is today.[2]

Why did survival favor a reduction in gender dimorphism? Why did it become adaptive for male and female become more alike, both physically and temperamentally? Upright posture[3] eventually made the hominid a good walker, even a good runner. Adaptation to an omnivorous diet freed it from a local territory with its familiar location of edible vegetation, and made it easier for it to wander into new territories and adopt new habitations.[4]

With hands free to carry objects and to handle tools, and with good eye-hand coordination, these bipedal omnivores were now free to travel and willing to eat almost anything. Worms, grubs, lizards, nestlings, and small mammals may not seem like an appetizing diet but they are all high-protein foods. Having acquired a taste for animal protein, hominids very gradually advanced from searching for worms and grubs, to hunting small and large animals in well-organized hunting parties, exercising cooperation, courage, stamina, and strategy.

1

A harem chief spent his years defending its territory and its harem, but when tribes of males and females (some of them paired) became free to travel, they cooperated for their common defense, protection, and survival. Parties of males hunted together while females stayed closer to the home base, tended to their off-spring, and gathered food. *Cooperation became a survival mechanism before it became a moral value.* To a harem chief, survival favored strong gender differences in size and strength, but to a wandering tribe of paired mates, there was survival value in near-equality.[5]

When males hunted together and protected their present territory together, success depended not so much on the ferocity and dominance of any individual but on how effectively they worked together. When many adult males were more-or-less permanently bonded with a female, success of the partnership was probably favored more by *similarity* in size, strength, and temperament than by differences.

In time, upright posture and good eye-hand coordination gave an enormous survival-value to *brain growth*. Every bit of brain growth made its owner a bit more resourceful, a bit more ingenious, a bit more likely to survive and repro-duce. Bit by bit, the hominid evolved a brain so big, it actually made childbirth painful and dangerous. The female pelvis, though larger than the male's, was simply not big enough to accommodate such bulbous-headed newborns, and an enlargement of the pelvis would compromise the mother's walking and running ability.

Nature's solution was to let the fetus emerge grossly premature; let it be born in a truly fetal state[6] and continue its fetal growth rate outside the womb. Born utterly helpless, with an enormous nutritional need, the big-brained newborn had a promising future but, unlike newborn apes, needed constant care and protec-tion. A mother so encumbered needed, in turn, someone who would feed and pro-tect *her* while she tended her helpless newborn. Mayr (page 249) comments on prematurity as the price of human brain specialization:

> If the infant had too big a head [at birth] . . . it would die owing
> to labor difficulties. It could survive only if born somewhat pre-
> maturely and if rapid growth of the brain was shifted to the
> [postnatal] period. [The human brain almost doubles in size dur-
> ing the first year of life.] *At birth, the human infant is essentially
> 17 months premature. . . .* To put this in another way, it is only at
> the age of 17 months that human infants acquire the mobility and
> independence of *newborn* chimpanzees.

Survival of the fetal offspring and its encumbered mother would be greatly enhanced if adult males were genetically predisposed to so love this mate and family, that he would care for them, protect them, and ensure their survival. Male aggressiveness could protect mother and infant, but to tend patiently to their welfare gave a survival value to a predisposition to feel compassion and tenderness.[7]

What was the genetic mechanism that reduced the temperamental differences between male and female? Looking for an answer to this question takes us into embryology and genetics. Among hominids, at conception each individual's *future* is genetically stamped as male or female, but for the first six weeks of life, there is virtually no visible difference between male and female. At about six weeks after conception, male genes activate the production of that masculinize the male embryo, mainly its sex organs and brain. If development continues *without* the intervention of those male hormones, the embryo develops into a female. *No female hormones are necessary for normal prenatal female development.* An embryo "naturally" develops into a female unless male hormones intervene. Male or female, every infant is born with a pair of nipples, a lifetime reminder that the basic body (*and brain*) plan is prototypically female. Every embryo is equipped with a "starter kit" for both male and female sex organs, and every person carries through life the vestigial remains of the "starter kit"[8] that he or she never developed.

Male and female newborns look practically indistinguishable[9] except for their sex organs. Prenatal masculinization seems to be concentrated on shaping only the male sex organs (internal as well as external.) *and the male brain.*

When they approach puberty, the production of *female* hormones will then feminize the figure of girls, and a rise in the production of male hormones will masculinize the physique of boys. It is much easier to mistake a male infant for a baby girl, than to mistake a man for a woman. To reduce gender differences (or dimorphism), nature just had to reduce the action of those male hormones. Right?

No, it's not that simple. Sexual potency is too valuable a survival trait for nature to reduce the power of male hormones to shape the male sex organs. But nature can reduce the tendency for males to grow into physical giants after the females of the species have stopped growing. *Nature can also reduce the masculinization of the male brain*, which makes the males of sexually dimorphic species so violent, so pugnacious, so aggressive, so competitive, and seems to implant other behavioral tendencies as well.

There is plenty of evidence of prenatal brain masculinization in humans and in animals. By injecting pregnant monkeys with male hormones, it is possible to produce female offspring that behave like infant males: aggressive play-mounters. There is plenty of evidence (see Chapter 7) that the brains of human males and females function predictably different. How can brain-differences between male and female fetuses be reduced, and still permit the full masculinization of the male sex organs? This is probably accomplished by making male brain tissue resistant to the influence of male hormones.[10]

Resistance to brain masculinization is probably a trait that depends not on one gene, but on dozens (perhaps hundreds) of genes. As in height, weight, or intelligence, males vary *in degree*, in how tall, or heavy, or bright, or *brain-masculinized* they are genetically predisposed to become. *Variation* is a basic fact of nature, and patterns of variation usually follow the curve of normal distribution, the familiar bell-shaped curve. This means that most men are close to average in brain masculinization. At one extreme are a small number who are very masculinized, and at the other extreme are those males who are not very brain-masculinized at all. This minority is at risk of worrying about their masculinity, at risk of feeling different from other boys, at risk of feeling that they lack something important that most other boys have.

Please note that we are dealing here with low *brain* masculinity (experienced as thought and feeling), *not* with physical low-masculinity. A boy (or man) may have a very masculine physique, but he may also have a low-masculine brain. Brain masculinity is established prenatally, unlike the outward signs of masculinity, which are developed as the boy grows into manhood. In this book we are presenting the theory that boys who are likely (but not certain) to become homosexual, *think and feel* differerent, *not* that they necessarily look different.[11]

Variation is a fact of nature. Because there are all degrees of low brain masculinization, there are also all degrees of thinking and feeling different--from having an occasional sense that one doesn't fit in, to suffering from a chronic and agonizing feeling of deficit. And this suggests that there is also a range of experience from an occasional thought or fantasy of a homosexual cast (Chapter 5), to a persistent and driving hunger for homosexual experience. This means that the genetic component of a homosexual tendency varies from very strong to very weak, and whether a man *acts* homosexually or develops a homosexual identity depends significantly on the interaction of his hereditary *tendencies* and his character, which in turn results from his personal and social experience.[12]

Why should a feeling of deficit, based on low-masculine brain function, lead to a homosexual tendency? Because the low brain masculinized boy is likely to develop a "crush" on boys who seem to have in abundance what he seems to lack. He adores and worships them and wants to be physically close to them (Chapter 9). With the onset of puberty, the penis becomes a penetrating organ, and the feeling of wanting to be close may become transformed into a wish to penetrate or be penetrated by a male partner.

Before we can fill in the details of our theory, we must get to know something about what male homosexuals are actually like, what they do, how stable their habit is, and how they vary in their behavior (Chapters 11 through 16). We want to know more about the human sex drive (Chapters 3). We want to know about homosexuality in other cultures and at other times of history (Chapter 10). We want to know more about the human brain, and about the evidence for brain gender differences (Chapter 7). We want to know what have been the results and what have been the deficiencies of research in male homosexuality (Chapter 19), and how can we do better. In the final chapter (27) we will take a closer look at our by-product theory, and judge for ourselves how well it fits a wide range of facts: laboratory evidence, anthropological evidence, experimental evidence, clinical observations, and everyday experience.

Finally, in the Epilogue we will ask, How do the facts and arguments set forth in this book bear on future research needs, on some practical problems, and on questions of public policy?

A Multidisciplinary Approach

One can study homosexuality from the standpoint of history, psychology, sociology, anthropology, or psychiatry, and each perspective sheds *some* light on the subject. But to understand the subject well enough to address the evolutionary puzzle, calls for a multidisciplinary approach. Conducting a serious multidisciplinary study is risky business. Who knows everything that there is to be known? Certain guidelines have to be followed to prevent a multidisciplinary study from getting lost. (1) The author must bring himself up-to-date in his own field. (2) He must be willing to do some serious reading in primary sources outside his field. (3) He must reach out for help from persons whose expertise he has reason to respect. Unfortunately, many experts are too busy with their own work, or fail to respond to correspondence from an outsider for whatever reason. Happily, a few scholars have been more than generous in giving various portions of this book a critical reading, in recommending source material, and in offering moral support. (4) He must be willing to use his imagination[13] to fill in the gaps between what is known and what is unknown. But he must clearly distinguish between what is fact and what is conjecture. (5) Finally, his work should be held together by a dominant discipline, the field the author knows best. Here, that field of study is psychology, a field that aims to understand the *whole* person; not just the brain, not just the nature of society, not just neuroses, but the whole person in *his environment*.

Probably specialists will find that the author has made an occasional error when he wanders outside his own field of expertise. Hopefully, these lapses will not weaken the author's basic thesis, of which I have already given the reader a foretaste: that to a significant extent, *male homosexuality is a by-product of an evolutionary process that reduced gender differences in the human species*. In the 27 chapters that follow, I will present the evidence—from anthropology, biology, psychology, sociology, and from everyday observation—that supports this thesis.

NOTES TO INTRODUCTION

1. Yale anthropologist David Philbeam estimates that male and female A. africanus weighed about 90 and 50 pounds (Gould, 1977a, page 183). If the same ratio held for present-day humans, and the average woman weighed 125 pounds, the average man would weigh 225 pounds.

2. The Cro-magnon man, who is believed to have lived 35,000 years ago, is believed to be anatomically identical with modern humans. If function follows form, it is possible that he was temperamentally identical as well.

3. Upright posture was a remarkable evolutionary change, which had important survival advantages, as well as some costs. Chapter 27 examines this topic in detail.

4. Man is a wanderer. One of the unique characteristics of the human species is that it has spread throughout the world, from polar to tropic regions, from aquatic environments to deserts.

5. Why near-equality; why not *total* (or at least, virtual) equality? Because a division of labor was part of human living for tens of thousands of years. While women bore and raised children, gathered and processed food, made clothing and utensils, men were usually the hunters, warriors, tool-makers, and builders-tasks that made greater muscle power and endurance a survival advantage.

Over the millenia, natural selection would genetically implant in each gender those traits, physical and temperamental, that favored their survival. This is true not only of hominids. Throughout the animal world, one can observe gender differences in physique and temperament. Differentiation appears to favor survival.

6. The human newborn not only *looks* fetal outwardly, but for some time after birth, continues to show some of the basic characteristics of a mammalian fetus. For example, the finger bones of a human newborn are still cartiliginous. For weeks after birth, growth proceeds at a fetal rate.

7. Animals respond to certain stimuli with a pre-programmed response of fear or aggression. It is altogether likely that other stimui evoke an unlearned nurturant response. Or as Shakespeare put it, "The quality of mercy is not strained."

8. Technical terms for the embryonic internal sex organs are the Müllerian ducts and the mesonephric ducts. Every embryo is equipped with *both*; one set develops and the other set remains in a vestigial form for the life of the individual.

9. Male and female newborns look practically alike (except for their genitals) but they are not completely alike. On the average, boys are more active prenatally and during infancy. At birth, infant girls already have a slightly larger pelvis opening. According to the 1978 finding of M.L. Hoffman, *day-old girls* respond differentially to the sound of an infant's cry, than to other noises of equal volume.

10. Francis Mondimore, in his 1996 book *A Natural History of Homosexuality*, acquainted this author with the concept of brain resistance to masculinization as a possible genetic trait.

11. Males vary, of course, in their outward, visible masculinization as well as they do in their brain masculinzation. A few men are genetically endowed to look like wrestlers, a few to look like jockeys, and the vast majority of men stand in-between. Brain masculinization and somatic masculinization are to a consider-able extent independent, but by chance a few males are genetically programmed to be low-masculine in *both* physique and temperament. Gender-discordant boys is the topic of Chapters 8 and 9.

12. Psychologists make this distinction between personal and social experience: Personal experience covers what happens in a person's unique life history. Social experience covers what he learns from the social atmosphere in which he lives. Both probably contribute, in unknown ways, to triggering an individual's homo-sexual potential.

13. Exploring a topic as vast and complex as homosexuality leads one to some facts that are so well established as to be indisputable, to some some facts that seem likely on the basis of the limited evidence available, to some "facts" that are little more than hunches or hypotheses that must be confirmed by more evi-dence before they can really be accepted as reliable knowledge. One makes con-jectures that cannot be proven but are consistent with well-established facts or with the theory of evolution, which is the foundation of biological science. Throughout this book, I have tried to separate facts from conjecture, and to indi-cate how well established, or how tentative, are the facts presented.

Leading scientific writers agree on the exercise of intuition and daring in scien-tific writing. Writes Stephen Jay Gould (1977a, page 125): "[C]reative thought in science is . . . not a mechanical collection of facts and induction of theories, but a complex process involving intuition, bias, and insight from other fields. Science, at its best, interposes human judgement and ingenuity upon all its pro-ceedings." Ernst Mayr has this to say: "To take an unequivocal stand, it seems to me, is of greater value and far more likely to stimulate constructive criticism than to evade the issue."

1 Preview and Overview of a By-Product Theory

Human Sexuality, Interactionism, and the De-dimorphism of the Species

Sex. Is it a drive? An instinct?[1] A need, like the need for air, water or food? Instinct is better reserved to describe animal behavior that is uniform for a given species, and appears without any need for either trial-and-error or guided learning. In many species of animals, copulation is stereotyped—unvarying and predictable—and fits the concept of instinct better than human love-making with its endless variations. Isn't human sexuality simply the expression of a biological drive? Of course, but like all human behavior, sexual behaviors are so diverse that they can be best understood as products of the *interaction* of a biological drive together with experience. Even a person who engages in a sex act for the very first time—masturbatory, homosexual or heterosexual—approaches it with a background of experience: fantasy,[2] knowledge, misinformation, inhibitions, expectations, and all the fears and hopes that accompany these attitudes. In human experience, as in much of the animal world, there is no such thing as the expression of a drive uninfluenced by experience. What people do makes sense when viewed as the *interaction* of nature and nurture.

The social animal

Nurture is an important component of the nature-nurture interaction because man is a *social* animal. Nothing is more typical for humans of all ages than group play, group affiliation, group activity. At work and at play, whether cooperating or competing, at leisure or in prayer, most people are happiest when they are with other people.[3] And no punishment is more severe than solitary confinement.

Nurture is an important component of the nature-nurture interaction because at the beginning of life, unlike other creatures that can fend for themselves, the human infant is completely dependent on others for survival. Unlike other creatures that reach adulthood in a few years, humans are genetically programmed to have a prolonged infancy, followed by years of childhood and adolescence, which permits the continued growth of the brain, the learning of a language and the adoption of a culture.

Sociability, referred to by the older psychologists as gregariousness, has long been recognized as an important human trait. Undoubtedly, it stems from both genetic factors and experience. For fifteen years or so, the individual's survival depends on social support. Upbringing is described as socialization. Learning to be human, absorbing a culture, proceeds from an interaction with kin, peers and

8

elders. This was especially true during those millennia when everything one knew was conveyed orally from generation to generation, if not drawn from direct experience. Man's prolonged period of dependency contributes to what makes him a social animal

The emotional comfort that comes from being part of a friendly group is probably inherited, in part, from a past when it was truly dangerous for the individual to be alone. A lone hominid was no match for a predator, but there was safety in numbers. D. Campbell observes (page 131) that "a single baboon is a dead baboon," but "three or four male baboons constitute an impressive display and can frighten any predator, even a lion."

To summarize, living inside a group had at least four advantages: (1) insuring physical safety, in a dangerous environment, and (2) promoting learning. Group living had two other survival advantages: (3) finding and sharing food (a successful hunt provided food for the entire group), and (4) participating in sexual play, and in adult sexual bonding.

What happens to be our native language is a gift (or accident) of our social environment, although it becomes truly a part of who we are. But whether we do acquire a language (or learn a new one), depends on whether we have a language-learning brain. That's what we mean by *interaction*.

The cultural climate of our times, still struggling to free itself from the instinct theory of earlier centuries[4] and guided by the optimistic belief that "man makes himself," is biased in favor of cultural relativism, and sees human differences as the outcome of custom and upbringing. We are inclined to believe that men and women differ in attitudes, interests, and thought because they are brought up differently. But the genders[5] also differ, on the average, in ways that have little to do with upbringing: stature, physique, and musculature. Almost everywhere, men are more aggressive and competitive, women are more gentle and cooperative.[6] Could gender differences in behavioral tendencies also be part of our inborn nature?

What about our sexual orientation? On this question, homosexual advocates usually insist that they were "born that way," that a homosexual orientation is part of their nature. "Homosexuality is as natural for us as heterosexuality is for you," gay advocates assert.

Opinion surveys of the general public repeatedly show that people who believe that homosexuals are born that way are the most sympathetic to homosexuals. On the other hand, those who believe that homosexuality is wrong tend to believe that it is a "bad habit," and that if a homosexual *wanted* to change and could find the right kind of help, he would change. Likewise, those homosexuals who are profoundly unhappy and blame their distress on their sexual attraction to other men, hope that change is possible, and often look for a minister or counselor or therapist who can help them change.

Religious counselors who minister to distressed, unhappy homosexuals also emphasize that homosexuality is acquired—either through prenatal influence, misguided parental treatment or other childhood experience—and with skilled counseling, support groups, residental programs[7] (milieu therapy), and prayer, can be overcome. Similarly, psychiatric and psychological counselors who offer reorientation therapy tend to believe that homosexuality is an attitude based on conditions of infancy and childhood. The homosexual habit is an acquired trait that was learned, psychotherapy is a kind of re-education by which homosexual tendencies can be unlearned and replaced with heterosexual tendencies.

Thus, there is a clear disagreement between, on the one hand, those who believe that homosexuals can and should change, and those who believe that homosexuals cannot and need not change; those who favor (or hope for) change, believe that homosexual attitudes are learned and can be unlearned, while those who are satisfied that homosexuality is a permanent condition, and believe that it is inborn.

This distinction is fairly clear but not absolute. Sigmund Freud theorized that a homosexual orientation may be implanted by the experience of an overcontrolling mother and a distant father, but Freud also believed that homosexuality was based on a constitutional predisposition.

The resistance of homosexuality to change does not necessarily mean that the person was born that way. Perhaps there is a kind of early learning that, once "stamped into the nervous system," cannot be unlearned. So argues John Money, Professor of Medical Psychology at Johns Hopkins University, and dean of sexological research.[8] Money likens the early learning of sexual orientation to the "imprinting" experience of ducklings and other baby animals. (Chapter 18 presents his theory in some detail.)

A historical approach views homosexuality as a perennial part of the human condition. Same-sex attractions are described in the hieroglyphics of ancient Egypt. The priests of ancient Israel decreed that it was a mark of paganism for one man to lie with another as with a woman, and explicitly banned it. That they banned it so explicitly implies not only that it was considered sinful, but that it was regarded as a common tendency.[9] Surely cannibalism would also have been considered sinful, but it is not explicitly banned for the simple reason that it was so rare. In ancient Greece, male (as well as female) prostitutes were available to most men. Married aristocrats were privileged to adopt handsome boys to provide sexual pleasure.

Travelers of all times have brought home tales of cultures in which a minority of men dressed like women and adopted the roles of women. More recently, anthropologists have brought back similar stories from field trips in various parts of the world.

In North America, in most native American tribes, men were trained to be fierce warriors and brave hunters. Women raised the children, prepared food, and practiced arts and crafts such as pottery, basketry, weaving, and garment making.

But a few men were recognized from boyhood as better fit for the roles of women than for hunting and warfare, and they were raised to occupy a special status in their society. Chapter 10 surveys a number of such cross-gender groups.

In recent years, scholars and writers, like other men, have been able to openly acknowledge their homosexual identity, and relate it to their work. Biologists who are also gay men have dedicated their careers to discovering biological mechanisms that underlie sexual orientation. For example, Simon LeVay compared certain brain structures of homosexuals who had died of AIDS with the brains of men who were presumed to have been heterosexual. He reported the observation of consistent differences in a tiny portion of the brain known to regulate sexual behavior. But skeptics asked: Was the reported difference the basis for sexual orientation, or was the difference the *result* of different sexual behavior? Or did the observed difference have something to do with the AIDS infection? There is more to be learned, in all likelihood, from the function of living brains than from the study of brain tissue retrieved from cadavers. But how does one study the living brain?

Researchers have begun to answer that question, as Chapter 7 reports, and animal studies demonstrate that some males do begin life with what could be called a low-masculinized brain. Studies of the living human brain use a brain-imaging machine, originally developed for medical diagnostics. This apparatus allows the researcher to "look inside the head" of their subjects, and brain scans indicate what portions of the brain are most active when subjects are given a particular task. Such studies have revealed important gender differences between how men and women think.

There is some evidence that the brain activity of homosexual males to a significant extent resembles that of females. Does this mean that homosexual males are to some extent different in their brain structure, that they think and feel more like females than like males? If so, how could this difference have developed, and how might it lead to a homosexual identity? Are we really on the trail of a genetic factor, or could this condition be the result of an identifiable prenatal condition? Is this human variant a genetic accident, or did the evolution of the human species systematically lead up to this tendency for a minority of males to be born with a low-masculinized brain? Could the male homosexual potential thus be a by-product of human evolution, as Chapter 27 proposes?

Our by-product theory of male homosexuality, set forth in the final chapter, is so named because it argues that the homosexual potential is a by-product of the evolutionary process that transformed hominids into humans. The humanization of the species was accomplished by transforming hominid (proto-human) society from harems of females and their offspring, each harem dominated by one ferocious and powerful male,[10] to tribes of male-female partners and their offspring. This transition took place over many thousands of years, and there were no doubt intermediate types of social organization between harem and tribe. Let us suppose that harem chiefs very gradually discovered that life would be less stressful, more enjoyable, and even more productive if instead of spending so much time and energy warding off male challengers, the chief would lead a platoon of other mature males who could defend their territory together, hunt together, play together, and interact (sexually and otherwise) with receptive females that wandered into their territory. Very gradually, there emerged relatively enduring male-female partnerships, and this "design for living" gave their offspring a powerful survival advantage. In a dangerous prehistoric world (far more so than today), an infant cared for by *two* parents was more likely to reach maturity than an infant cared for only by its mother and other females.

In this way, there evolved tribes whose females watched over their helpless infants while males protected their territory and hunted for food. Clearly, such a tribe would have a survival advantage over harems of females and their young defended by one ferocious leader. With this transformation from harem to tribe, males no longer needed the physical and temperamental ferocity required of a harem leader. Now ferocity was giving way to tendencies toward male bonding and teamwork, as *male and female became more alike both in physique and temperament.*

Variation is a basic characteristic of all living creatures. Variation is what makes evolution possible. In every generation, a few males are born with so low-masculine a temperament that they are temperamentally closer to the female norm than to the male norm. Chapter 9 sketches out the sequence of events from low-masculine temperament to homosexual feelings, behavior and identity. In order to be activated, this genetic tendency must *interact* with congenital or environmental forces. Male homosexuality may thus be a by-product or *overcorrection* of an important evolutionary process, one that humanized the hominid by making males and female more alike.

This theory incorporates the known facts of human evolution, as conveyed by physical anthropologists, who are guided by the fossil evidence. According to this theory, male homosexuality results from the interaction of genetic and environmental forces, environmental forces that may channel, deflect, promote, facilitate, or inhibit homosexual tendencies, large or small, that are distributed throughout the human species.

NOTES TO CHAPTER 1

1. An older definition described an instinct as "an inborn response," one that requires no learning experience. From a more modern point of view, an instinct is a habit that is easily learned and is very gratifying.

2. By fantasy, we include both private thoughts, shared fantasy (jokes, gossip, ideas shared with peers). and "structured fantasy"—legends, stories, movies, novels, TV soap operas, talk shows and comic monologues.

3. Living in a culture which encourages systematic physical exercise and "body-building," it is interesting to note that many people prefer to pay for membership in a work-out club, and travel miles to reach it, rather than exercise in the privacy of their own home. Exercise that is felt as drudgery when done alone, becomes fun when it is done in the company of others who are doing the same thing.

4. In the July 1972 issue of *American Psychologist*, official publication of the Anerican Psychological Association, appeared a letter lamenting the environmental bias of the profession. It has "required considerable courage" to emphasize the influence of heredity on human behavior, said the letter, "for it has brought psychologists and other scientists under extreme personal and professional abuse at Harvard, Berkeley . . . and elsewhere. . . . Such influences are well documented." The letter recalls the censure, punishment, and suppression of unpopular scientific ideas by Hitler and Stalin, and continues: "Today, a similar suppression, censure, punishment, and defamation are being applied against scientists who emphasize the role of heredity in human behavior. Published positions are often misquoted and misrepresented; emotional appeals replace scientific reasoning; arguments are directed against the man rather than against the evidence."

The letter goes on to assert: "A kind of orthodox environmentalism dominates the liberal academy, and strongly inhibits teachers, researchers, and scholars from turning to biological explanations." Signers of the letter declare: "We deplore the evasion of heredity reasoning in current textbooks, and the failure to give responsible weight to heredity in disciplines such as sociology, social psychology, social anthropology, educational psychology, psychological measurement, and many others.

The letter was signed by 50 psychologists, including eminent members of the profession.

A reader of the older psychology texts (*e.g.*, William James, and William McDougall) finds long lists of instincts that are presumed to guide human behavior. These authors present them not as original or controversial ideas, but rather in the spirit of codifying or systematizing what was then accepted as common knowledge.

5. Why do we now speak of "gender differences" instead of "sex differences," as we did a generation ago? This change in our language was promoted by a 1955 article by John Money, in which he advised that the terms "sex" and "sex differences" be restricted to references to the sex organs and their function, and that all other male-female differences be labelled "gender differences." This change in language was, of course, welcomed by the women's liberation movement, which was advocating the downplaying of male-female differences.

6. Cultural relativists challenge statements about human nature that transcend cultural boundaries, by dramatizing the known exceptions. We live in a world where giants and drawfs are not unknown, yet the world also recognizes height and weight norms for populations at large.

7. John Paulk describes his experience in a residential program for Christian homosexuals, in his 1998 book, *Not Afraid to Change*.

8. Dr. Money was awarded the 1985 American Psychological Association Distinguished Scientific Award for the Application of Psychology, and in 1987 was one of four recipients of a prestigious award from the National Institute for Child Health and Human Development, "In Recognition of Outstanding Research Accomplishments."

9. The Hebrew Bible tells us, by implication as well as by explicit statement, what the ancient Hebrews were like. For example, the ban against "one man lying with another" suggests that this was not an uncommon occurrence. The Bible says, Honor thy father and thy mother, which suggests that this was a problem even in those days. But the Bible does not have to ask parents to love their children, as Rabbi Gunther Plaut observes (page 106), and this tells us something about human instinct.

10. This harem pattern is characteristic of present-day gorillas. Comparing gorillas to humans, three differences stand out. (1) The adult male gorilla is about twice as big as the female. It is a fact that the adult *male* human is much closer to the body size of the adult *female* gorilla. (2) For a harem leader, a ferocity of temperament complements his body size. (3) Gorilla males show little interest in their offspring, unless the infants are unprotected by adult females. Human males of most cultures are protective and nurturant of their offspring. In these three important respects (and in others), human males resemble the female of their species both in physique and temperament.

Is it legitimate to compare humans to gorillas, if humans are more closely related to present-day chimpanzees? Comparing humans to gorillas is useful because the earliest hominid species resembled the present-day gorilla in its sexual dimorphism, or male-female differences (Leakey & Lewin, pages 115-117).

2 The Curve of Variation

Variation is the indispensable prerequisite of evolution, and the study of variation is therefore a most important part of the study of evolution. – Ernst Mayr, page 88.

Darwin observed three basic facts about living things. From these three simple facts, he constructed a theory of evolution, which has become the basic theory of modern biology. First is the fact of *variation*: no two members of the same species are exactly alike, and some of these traits are heritable (or *genetic*), transferred from one generation to the next. It is a common observation that no two siblings are exactly alike, but to a degree all siblings resemble their parents. In a litter of dogs or cats, no two litter mates are exactly alike, either.

Variation is not only true for individuals of the same generation, but every generation is slightly different from previous generations. This happens because heritable changes occur at *random* within individuals. Most of these heritable changes (called mutations) are harmful, and individuals who bear them never survive to reproduce. Most mutations lead to early miscarriage or spontaneous abortion, or result in failure to survive infancy. Once in a while, however, a mutation occurs that makes the individual *better* able to survive, better adapted to its environment.

> Don't think of a successful mutation as one that necessarily makes the individual stronger. A mutation makes the individual better adapted to a particular environment. For example, a species of flies migrates from the mainland to a windy island. There, a mutation created a variety of "insect-flies;" unable to fly because their wings are vestigial and therefore useless. Because of this disability, they never got into the air, where normal flies often get blown into the sea. On a wind-swept island, the crippled flies have just what it takes to win the battle of survival.
>
> Writes Mayr (pages 96-97): "Gene mutations are due to errors of replication during cell division. Even though the replication of the DNA molecule during cell division . . . is remarkably accurate, occasional errors do occur."

Second is the fact of *overproduction*. Living things tend to reproduce far in excess of what is needed to replace the dying population. Of all those that are born, only a few survive to give birth to the new generation.

Darwin's third principle is remembered by the phrase, *"the survival of the fittest."* Those who survive and reproduce are believed to be better adapted to their environment than those who perish. Some survive and reproduce because their development has been shaped by a mutation that gives them a new advantage in adapting to their environment, or in the struggle for survival. These sur-

15

vivors tend to pass on those traits that have helped them adapt to the environment in which they lived, traits that are therefore said to have *survival value*.

Discussions of evolution most often focus on the second or third principle—on the imperious drive to reproduce, or on "the survival of the fittest," but in this chapter, our focus will instead be on *variation*, on what it means for an individual to stand at a particular point on a curve of natural variation.

Observe a tree in full leaf. No two leaves are exactly alike, and yet there is an *underlying order* to their variation. To behold this underlying order, some autumn day, scoop up a large bagful of leaves that have fallen to the ground from a single tree. Patiently, measure the length of each leaf, and record your results on what statisticians call a frequency table. You will discover that a majority of leaves are neither small nor large but are of average length, or close to the average. You will discover that the more a leaf deviates from the average, the scarcer it is. Thus, a frequency graph of your leaf measurements takes on the shape of the familiar curve of normal distribution, the bell curve.

You can also generate a normal distribution curve by tossing 10 coins 100 times, recording how many coins land heads up on any trial. Or try measuring the individual body weights of a normal classroom of school children. As you look over the class, you might observe that children of average weight are the best-dressed, because clothes of average size are easier to find than very small or very large sizes. The average-size children are more comfortably seated; school seats are made for children of average build.

Now shift your attention from the average children to those who stand at the ends of the curve. Boys who are small and thin are likely to be at a disadvantage socially, as well as at sports and games. Children who are overweight (or even obese) are likewise at an athletic and social disadvantage. The plight of the overweight or obese person (child or adult) says something about the cause and cost of substantial variation. The tendency of the body to store surplus calories as body-fat is genetic, to an extent, and has survival value in an environment of scarce and uneven food supply.

In the obese person, we see a trait that *in moderation* once had survival value. In excess, however, it becomes a liability. A moderately overweight person is well-adapted to survive short periods of starvation. In normal times, however, an obese person is vulnerable to various degenerative diseases. Stress on his circulatory and skeletal systems make him vulnerable to hypertension, heart disease, back pain, and joint problems.

It is easy to observe variations in *physique*: height, weight, body build, and facial appearance. Less tangible are differences in *temperament*. Let us consider two traits of temperament that may have a significant genetic component: risk-taking and aggressiveness. Both these traits seem to follow the same principle: that a moderate endowment is adaptive, favoring survival, while an extremely low or high endowment can become a survival disadvantage.

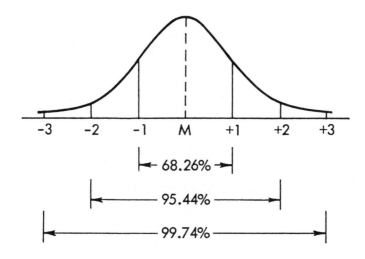

Figure 2.1, The normal distribution curve. The mathematics of the curve allow it to be scaled on the base-line in sigma units (-3, -2...+2, +3) below and above the mean (M). A known portion of the distribution lies within any area of the curve. Thus the area from mean to +1 sigma contains 34.13% of the total population. The six areas marked off above, from left to right or vice-versa!) contain about 2%, 14%, 34%, 34%, 14%, and 2% of the population. The normal distribution curve (the bell curve, the normal curve) is a major concept of statistical theory.

To reproduce, the individual must compete, so an average endowment in daring and aggressiveness has a survival advantage. A person who is very low in either daring or aggressiveness is clearly at a disadvantage as a reproducer. But an extremely high endowment of either of these traits may become a disadvantage for survival, for various reasons: the person becomes a social nuisance, is hard to live with, or engages in activities that endanger his survival.

Persons who are extremely high in either risk-taking or aggressiveness choose dangerous sports. They use safety equipment to take even greater risks than they would otherwise take, so that "safety equipment" actually makes the sport more dangerous, rather than less. The most aggressive players in football, for example, use "safety equipment" as tools of aggression. Safety helmets are used as battering rams, a physical threat to both the aggressor and his opponent. In boxing, too, "safety equipment" has made the sport more dangerous, not less.[1]

In this book, our focus will be on traits of human temperament that *all* persons, male and female, have in common, though females usually have a higher endowment of some traits, and males usually have a higher endowment of others. On the average, males are more aggressive and females are more nurturant. (In Chapter 7, the physical basis for gender differences is studied in detail.)

What is the origin of "typically masculine" and "typically feminine" traits? What happens when a male has a high endowment of traits characteristic not of most males, so that temperamentally he is neither typically male nor typically female? This is the *low-masculinized brain (LMB) male*, [2] who is at the center of this study. What is the genetic basis for this phenomenon, and what are the consequences for personality development and sexual orientation? These are some of the questions that this book explores in detail.

Why do males and females differ, *yet overlap*, in their temperamental endowment? The physical characteristic that most clearly differentiates us from other species is a highly-evolved brain that has an enormous capacity for learning, a brain that has made the human species the dominant creatures of our planet. No other creature is at home in both the arctic and in the tropics. No other creature so radically reshapes (and degrades) the environment, not only covers the earth from pole to pole, but flies through the skies and plunges into the depths of the seas. No other creature learns such complex languages,[3] and conveys a culture from one generation to the next.

The price of this potential is that newborns are born utterly helpless. Children spend their first 16 years as learners, and adults must spend much of their time and energy as *parents*: protecting, nourishing, and teaching their young over a childhood and adolescence so prolonged that it is found nowhere else in nature.

A helpless newborn human can survive only with the close and constant protection of its mother. So encumbered, the mother's survival is enhanced if she has the prolonged protection and support of a mate. Because most of their adult lives will be spent as parents and partners, human males and females have evolved traits especially adaptive to the roles of wife, husband, father, and mother.

The fossil record indicates that the human species evolved from a hominid similar to the present-day gorilla in the physical trait that anthropologists call sexual dimorphism: a difference in physique between males and females. In man's remotest ancestors, males were almost twice as big as females. This degree of *sexual dimorphism* suggests that man's remote ancestors lived in a *harem* society, where one dominant, ferocious male controlled a harem of perhaps six or so females. Very gradually, over hundreds of thousands of years, various hominid groups shifted from harem to other patterns of social organization, leading to the *tribe*: groups of more-or-less permanently bonded male-female pairs and their offspring.

The tribe was an adaptive social organization for a species whose adult females were frequently encumbered with helpless infants, and whose young had a prolonged period of childhood dependency. What kinds of traits would be adaptive in this social organization? No longer adaptive was the ferocious, towering physique of the harem leader, nor his dominant, threatening temperament. As the father of born-helpless, slow-maturing young, it would be adaptive for the mature male to have the temperament of a dependable, protective mate of an encumbered mother: a watchful father, a good provider, a good teacher, a good friend.

How nature shifted the curves of male physique and temperament (very gradually, over hundreds of thousands of years) to fit his changing role as mate and father is discussed in detail in Chapter 7. Here we will note that this transformation narrowed both the physical difference and the temperamental difference between males and females. Now the *average* male was only slightly more dominant and object-oriented, and the *average* female was only slightly more nurturant and people-oriented. Instead of a yawning chasm between male and female temperament, there was now an actual *overlap*.

Variation in male temperament[4], like more visible variation in male physique, ranges from highly masculine to so minimally masculine that, temperamentally, a small minority of males sense that they are *temperamentally* more like females than like other males. Those LMB males who are *also* of delicate physique are easily recognized as the gender-discordant boys of their generation. LMB males are likely to be more artistic than athletic, they prefer the quiet indoor world to the rough-and-tumble outdoor world. Highly gender-discordant boys would rather play with girls than with boys, and are more likely to try on Mother's shoes than Daddy's hat.

A reader may respond: "That's very interesting, but I know several gay men who were *not* gender-discordant boys and the idea that they have 'a female temperament' would be altogether foreign to them." If temperament is the product of a person's *total* makeup, a low-masculine temperament cannot be not the same as a female temperament. Rather, it is a *human* temperament somewhat (or very much) less masculinized than is true of the average male. Just what it means for the brain to be less masculinized will become clearer when the reader studies the already-mentioned Chapter 7.

Homosexuality is a complex phenomenon full of exceptions. The male homosexual population is an extremely diverse one, as Chapters 20 through 25 acknowledge. In this brief chapter, we have tried to describe one general principle that applies to a significant portion of the male homosexual population, and to a minority (but not a tiny minority) of the male population in general.

Tendencies toward male homosexuality (that may either be embraced or rejected by life experience) derive in part from a very high endowment of a trait that, in moderation, has a distinct adaptive value. Like other traits (*e.g.*, the tendency to store surplus calories as body fat, the tendency toward risk-taking and aggressiveness), a moderate endowment is adaptive, but a very high or very low endowment is another story. About half of gender-discordant boys grow up to be homosexual men. Why? And why only half? *What happens to the other half?*

These are some of the questions that will guide our study of male homosexuality.

The ancient Greeks idealized the golden mean, and evolutionists have dryly observed that nature favors mediocrity.[5] For men who are genetically disposed to rank near either end of the normal distribution curve on certain critical traits, life is not so easy as it is for those who occupy the comfortable middle ground.

NOTES TO CHAPTER 2

1. Tenner discusses at some length (pages 214-219) the consequences of extreme risk-taking and aggressiveness in sports.

2. The *low-masculinized brain (LMB) male* is a new expression but not a new concept. Karl Jung referred to the spirit that counterbalanced masculinity in the male, as the anima, W.H. Sheldon referred to *gynandrophenia*. Richard Green entitled his book on gender-atypical boys, *The "Sissy-Boy" Syndrome*.

3. Even a person who has never learned a "foreign language" knows two languages: his native tongue, and the language of mathematics, at least to some extent. (If he can read music, he has learned a third language.)

4. Here we are using the word *temperament* to cover the inner life as a whole, including feeling, motivation, and cognition.

5. The author recalls from a lecture in his beginning psychology course many years ago, that his professor (S. Edson Haven) said, "The normal distribution curve will appear on the flag of the Utopia." In this memorable statement, the professor must have meant that a good society will take full account of the implications of the fact of human variation: that it is unrealistic and therefore unfair to treat all persons alike because *individuals differ* and these differences deserve to be respected, that the average citizen, those who place in "the comfortable majority," enjoys a natural advantage over those who happen to belong to a minority, and that a good society will compensate for nature's unfairness.

The normal distribution curve describes the result of *chance variation*. The natural world is ruled by chance and all its inhabitants are, to an extent, creatures of chance. This truism is expressed in the biblical words, The race is not to the swift . . . nor bread to the wise, nor riches to the intelligent, nor favor to the men of skill; but time and chance happen to them all (Ecclesiastes 9:11).

3 Human Sexuality and Evolution

A theory of homosexuality worth taking seriously must branch off from a general theory of human sexuality. Perhaps homosexuality can then be understood as a variant of human sexuality in general. But why does human homosexuality have to be "explained?" Doesn't homosexual behavior exist throughout the animal world? Isn't it part of "nature's diversity"? Not according to evolutionary psychologist Glenn Weisfeld (page 245), who writes that male homosexuality "is rare in most species in the wild," but common in domestic animals, and in animals raised in captivity. Among humans, on the contrary, male homosexuality seems to be a fairly stable characteristic, appearing in about three per cent of the male populations, generation after generation. Many cultures, ancient and contemporary, traditional and modern, include a sexually discordant male group, as Chapter 10 documents.

Sexual behavior is not as natural as breathing because everyone breathes more or less the same way; breathing is little affected by learning. Sexual attitudes, however, not only vary remarkably from one society to another, but there is also enormous variety within a given society in the sexual attitudes of various individuals. "The most remarkable thing about sex," writes LeVay (1993, page 105), "is its diversity. Probably no two persons on earth have exactly the same ideas about who or what is sexually attractive or what would be the most appropriate way to consummate this attraction." This diversity suggests how much a person's sexual tastes and aversions are shaped by accidents of learning, of individual experience.

Sexual behavior is not as natural as breathing, yet sexual behavior is natural. Nature's plan is to equip every individual with the means—that is, with the equipment, the impulse, and the skills—for both survival and reproduction. Psychologists Frank A. Beach and Harry Harlow have contributed significantly to our understanding of how apes and monkeys, man's primate cousins, develop their reproductive skills.

Infantile sex play

Psychologist Harry Harlow devoted his career to observing the behavior of monkeys, both in free play and under controlled conditions. A major finding of his was that the experience of infantile play was crucial to attaining a normal adulthood in general, and to attaining normal sex skills in particular. Specifically, Harlow established that monkeys who were deprived of physical contact with their peers during their first year of life would spend their adulthood emotionally crippled and unable to perform the sexual responses typical of their species.

Free-ranging infant monkeys are always interacting with each other: play-

21

fighting and play-copulating,[1] grooming and tumbling. To the casual observer, these behaviors look like random expenditures of simian energy, but Harlow and his co-workers saw a clear pattern in this welter of antics: male and female infants showed a distinct difference in their behaviors. In males, rough-and-tumble play predominated, and females were inclined to perform acts of grooming, which Harlow interprets as expressions of the monkeys' "affectional system." Figures 3.1 and 3.2 illustrate this clear gender difference.

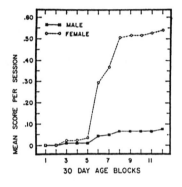

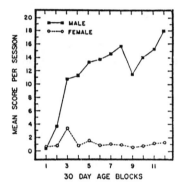

Figure 3.1. Frequency of grooming occurrence responses made by males and females in the playroom. (From Harlow)

Figure 3.2. Frequency of "rough and tumble" play of two males and two females . . . in the (first year of life. (From Harlow)

Field observation convinced Harlow that the free play of little boys and girls showed the same gender difference:

> [Harlow writes:] Several months ago I was present at a school
> picnic attended by 25 second graders and their parents. While the
> parents sat and the girls stood around or skipped about hand in
> hand, 13 boys tackled and wrestled, chased and retreated. No lit-
> tle girl chased any little boy, but some little boys chased some
> little girls."

The question may be asked: Do the gender differences characteristic of American boys and girls prevail in other cultures? The Whitings conducted a study of child life in six different cultures.[2] Their findings are summarized in Figures 3.3 and 3.4, which shows three behaviors in which boys scored higher, and three in which girls scored higher. To summarize:

Boys *(solid lines)*
seek dominance
seek attention
horseplay, assaults, insult

Girls *(broken lines)*
nurturant: offer support
nurturant: offer help
act sociable

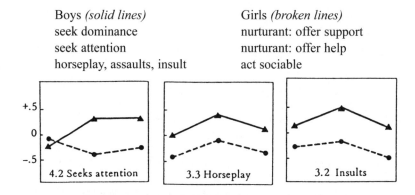

Figure 3.3 .Comparison of boys and girls of six cultures (combined groups, total n=136); behaviors in which boys scored higher. (From Whiting and Whiting)

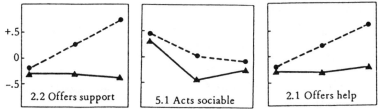

Figure 3.4 .Comparison of boys and girls of six cultures (combined groups, total n=136); behaviors in which girls scored higher. (From Whiting and Whiting)

One of Harlow's experiments yielded especially provocative findings, even though his monkey subjects paid heavily for making this contribution to human knowledge. Harlow took a group of macaque newborns and kept them in individual wire cages during their first year of life. They could see and hear other monkeys, they could even call out to other monkeys, but they could not touch or be touched by others; no play-fighting, no play-mounting. Result: the macaques were psychologically crippled for life.[3] At maturity, these males would not copulate with normal females who were at the peak of estrus.[4] Wire-cage raised females had great difficulty in copulating with normal males, and those that did become pregnant were unable to relate to their offspring in a normal way. Harlow's findings were more recently expanded by the research of Baker and Bellis, reported in 1995. In 1968, Sackett reported that his rhesus monkeys reared in isolation were not so disabled as Harlow's macaque monkeys. Sackett reported that male rhesus monkeys who had been reared in isolation seemed to be sexually aroused by seeing a female but they lacked the skills needed to express it.

From this kind of evidence, Weisfeld concludes (page 169): "Primate sex seems to require a lot of learning. This is especially true of the male. . . . Peer-isolated male rhesus monkey and chimpanzees do very poorly when presented with a receptive female once they are mature. . . [S]ome of the social skills of sex [are] learned in childhood . . . by observation, practice, and instruction. Then at puberty, orgasm provide[s] an opportunity for fine-tuning these motor skills shortly before the onset of fertility."

Masturbatory behavior

This is a common behavior in many species of primates: male and female, immature and adults, captive and free-living.

It begins before puberty in both monkeys and apes. [Gorillas do not masturbate.] Males manipulate the penis with a foot or hand or with his mouth, and females insert their fingers or foreign objects into the vagina, or they may rub against projecting objects in the environment. In adult males masturbation frequently culminates in ejaculation.

. . . [Masturbation] has often been recorded for sexually mature males having free access to receptive females (Beach 1949, page 63).[5]

Courtship behavior; adult sexual curiosity and excitement

Beach describes how male and female adult primates sniff, nibble, lick and touch each other's genital area. The sexually-excited male sometimes bites the female severely.

[T]he male rhesus may insert his fingers in the genital opening of his mate prior to coition and male apes often indulge in extensive manual and lingual exploration of the vaginal orifice (*ibid,*, page 56).

In response to the male's digital and lingual explorations, the clitoris of the female chimpanzee becomes erect and can be seen to move spasmotically. Genital reflexes on the part of the female sometimes occur in response to extra-genital contact with the male (*ibid,*, page 57).

Males quick and impartial, females patient and selective. The female may be much more than merely "receptive" to the male's sexual advances, as she actively seeks copulation. Beach (1949, page 58) describes the sexual initiative of female primates:

Female monkeys often evoke coitus by assuming the mating position in front of the male and exposing their genitalia for his inspection. Sexually desirous female apes behave in similar fash-

ion, bending forward at the hips and exposing the swollen sexual
skin and the genitalia to the gaze of any potential partner. . . .
Females of many primate species sometimes handle the penis
thus inducing complete erection (ibid., page 58).

Tanner & Zihlman report (page 594) that "*in 19 copulations observed among free-ranging, nonprovisioned chimpanzees, 14 were initiated by females.*" This observation suggests that protohuman females chose mates who, in their judgement, showed a good potential as partner and father, a process that selectively favored those males who carried genetic tendencies to be protective but also gentle, friendly, and helpful:

> Mothers chose to copulate most frequently with these compara-
> tively sociable, less disruptive, sharing males—with males more
> like themselves (Tanner & Zihlman, page 606).

> Females preferred to associate and have sex with males exhibit-
> ing friendly behavior, rather than those who were comparatively
> disruptive, a danger to themselves or offspring (*ibid*).

At virtually all levels of animal life, the sexually active male is quick and impartial, the female is patient and selective, and usually favors the biggest, healthiest male available, a tactic that gives her offspring a genetic advantage. The evolutionary implications of this phenomenon of female mate selection, observed throughout the animal world, is discussed by Williams (pages 182-184), by A.J. Batemann, by R.A. Fisher, and by O'Donald. How this tactic helps solve "The Puzzle," is further discussed in Chapter 27.

Copulatory behavior. The male monkey "mounts the stooping female from the rear, grasping her body at the hips and clasping her legs with his feet" (*ibid,*, page 58). The behavior of apes, however, is more variable.

> Adult chimpanzees usually employ the technic of rear entry
> while the female stands bending sharply forward at the hips.
> However individual variations are not uncommon and complete
> copulation has been observed at times when the male is seated
> on the floor and the female lowers herself upon his thighs with
> her back toward him (*ibid,*, pages 58-59).

LeVay (1993, page 47) offers a detailed description of the "reflexes" that constitute the act of coitus in humans:

> The basic components of coitus in humans are (1) erection of the
> penis; (2) engorgement of the walls of the vagina and labia majo-
> ra, lubrication of the vagina by glandular secretions and transu-

dation [sweating], and erection of the clitoris; (3) insertion of the penis into the vagina (intromission); (4) pelvic thrusting by one or both partners; (5) elevation of the uterus, with a consequent forward and upward rotation of the mouth of the cervix; (6) ejaculation of semen into the vagina; and (7) orgasm, the intensely pleasurable sense of climax and release, often accompanied by increases in heart rate, flushing of the skin, muscle spasms, and involuntary vocalizations.

Orgasm triggers the massive release of an opiate-like hormone, oxytocin, from the pituitary gland, LeVay notes (1993, page 51). Does the release of oxytocin deliver that intense feeling of pleasure associated with orgasm? An experiment by Michael Murphy suggests that it does.[6]

Discrimination between strange and familiar partners. Even among the sub-primate mammals, there is much evidence of preference for familiar sexual partners.[7] However, notes Beach (1949, page 70), "the effects of familiarity with a particular partner are most evident in the case of primates." Beach's notes include observations of sexual jealousy and "the Coolidge effect" (see endnote 15), as well as foreplay.

> Pairs of rhesus monkeys which have lived together for long periods of time ordinarily indulge in considerable sexual foreplay prior to coition, but when such animals are given new mates they tend to copulate immediately, dispensing with any preliminaries. Extreme familiarity sometimes is associated with a decrease in the frequency of sexual relations between monkey pairs, but strong emotional bonds often are established during a protracted period of cohabitation. Both males and females show evidence of extreme resentment if the sexual partner engages in relations with a third individual (1949, pages 70-71).

Need for sexual practice. Beach observes (*ibid,*, pages 69-70) that "there is little or no indication that specific sexual practice is essential to effective copulation as far as female monkeys and apes are concerned. On the contrary it appears that, with the advantage of normal play experience, a virgin female is capable of all essential responses in coital patterns the first time that she is placed with a sexually competent male." The case is quite different, however, for male sexual behavior. Not for animals of most lower mammalian species, but for male primates, "there are indications that sexual *experience* is essential to successful coitus." Beach continues (*ibid,*, page 69):

> One immature male rhesus monkey was placed with a mature female and the pair remained together for several years. The male frequently showed erection but all attempts to mount and achieve intromission were awkward and incomplete and only

after a long period of practice did this animal become capable of efficient and normal copulation. Similar observations have been made upon other males of the same species, and the same situation appears to obtain in the case of male apes. Inexperienced chimpanzees, although they exhibit sexual excitement in the presence of the female do not demonstrate the ability to carry through the various elements of the copulatory pattern; and such ability is acquired only after several years of experience.

Evidence at the human level clearly parallels Beach's observation of the dramatic difference between male and female monkeys in their need for practice, to perform the sexual act. Consider the fact that a New York agency that answered telephone questions about sex (Community Sex Information) in 1975 reported clear-cut differences in the questions asked by men and by women. Women asked medical questions about birth control and abortion. Men callers, mostly single and in their early twenties, were often "profoundly misinformed and disturbed," according to founder Ann Welbourne. Male callers showed a perplexity about the mechanics of sex. This generalization was based on over 15,000 telephone calls.

The writings of gay educator and laboratory biologist Simon LeVay erroneously minimize the role of experience in becoming an effective male partner in heterosexual intercourse. Writes LeVay (1993, page 47), heterosexual intercourse is "so simple, one hardly needs a brain to do it." He goes on to explain that "many of the neuronal circuits that mediate coitus lie not in the brain but in the spinal cord. Copulation is a series of reflexes: one thing leads to another."[8]

Behavior of animals raised in captivity. *Homosexual behavior, momentary and enduring, often appears in animals that have been raised in captivity.* Mounting behavior, clasping the partner and showing pelvic thrusts similar to those of the copulating male, has been observed in mammals of all kinds: the rat, guinea pig, rabbit, porcupine, dog, lion, sow, sheep, cow, and horse, as well as in the primates. Males mount males, females mount females. In the excitement of sexual foreplay, the female sometimes mounts the male, and then reverts to her feminine pattern. Unlike these expressions of momentary sexual excitement, some primates express what looks like "mutually satisfactory 'homosexual' relations," observes Beach (1949,, page 65):

> Sexual interaction occurs frequently between male monkeys . . .
> and in at least some cases anal penetration is achieved and all of
> the external signs of ejaculation can be observed. It should be
> noted that these relationships may develop between males that
> have never been isolated from females—that are not in any sense
> of the term sexually deprived. Adult animals with ready access to
> the receptive female will upon occasion ignore her and engage in
> coital behavior with others of their own sex.

> In some pairs either male assumes the feminine position at the slightest indication of desire on the part of the partner and masculine and feminine roles are played interchangeably by both individuals. In other situations the masculine role is played exclusively by one male and the feminine by the other. Such a relationship is most likely to be formed when one male is larger, stronger, or more mature than the other. When this type of partnership arises the dominant male may protect his partner from attack by other monkeys, allow him certain food-sharing privileges and in general treat him as a feminine consort.

Beach adds (*ibid,*, pages 65-66) to his description of habitual primate homosexual behavior that "the evidence . . . tend[s] to favor the belief that exclusively heterosexual or homosexual behavior in human beings is a product of individual experience and learning. It appears probable," he adds, "that in the absence of cultural channelization, many, if not all, men and women would possess the capacity for complete erotic response to members of either sex." That is the thesis of Chapter 5.

Human sexuality an evolutionary emergent

This survey of primate sexual behavior suggests the general shape of the evolutionary heritage of the human species. Given this wide variety of sexual activity in non-human primates, Beach must have wondered: Why is the behavior of the great majority of humans so sharply focused on an exclusively heterosexual adaptation? Twenty-nine years after the publication of his 1949 article, Beach offered a two-factor answer to this question: (1) The human species evolved during a hunting and gathering economy, when gender role differentiation had significant survival value; therefore the species probably evolved a genetically-implanted bias to adopt a gender role for themselves and to foster this path of development in their offspring.

So dominant is this human tendency to adopt a gender role, Beach concluded (1978, page 124) that human sexuality is an evolutionary emergent, quite different from animal mating:[9]

> [H]uman sexuality is about as closely related to mating behavior of other species as human language is related to animal communication, and that relationship is distant indeed.

The second factor favoring adoption of a gender role relates to (2) the "fetal" condition of the human newborn, a condition unique in the primate world. The helplessness of the human newborn made the survival of both infant and the encumbered mother contingent on the support and protection of a close-bound mate.

Human physique and sexual behavior

By happy coincidence, man's upright posture, so functional for the male hunter and the female gatherer, resulted in anatomical changes that favored a permanent sexual partnership. Over hundreds of thousands of years, the gradual assumption of a truly upright posture tilted the human pelvis forward, a change that had significant consequences for sexual behavior. In the female, this anatomical change shifted the vaginal opening forward, to favor frontal vaginal entry. Amply padded buttocks similarly serve to push forward the pelvis of the supine female body, further facilitating frontal entry.

Writes Beach (1978, page 148): "The coital pattern predominant in all human societies is some variant of the face-to-face position."[10] Frontal entry is a radical change from the rear-mounting sexual posture characteristic of the mammalian world, including virtually all[11] other primates. Frontal entry has three important consequences: (1) It brings the partners face-to-face and thus makes sexual insertion a more intimate interaction. The exchange of words[12] as well as feelings, emotions, and facial expressions makes the face-to-face position worthy of the term sexual intercourse rather than copulation. (2) It enables the partners to engage their lips, tongue and teeth in the service of sexual excitement. (3) The face-to-face position makes it possible for male and female pubes to press against each other, putting them "in continuous or rhythmic . . . contact [which] tends to result in secondary or indirect stimulation of the clitoris" (ibid,, page 148). Beach conjectured that the female orgasm is a uniquely human capability,[13] and serves to bind the male-female partnership.

LeVay would probably disagree with the belief that the face-to-face position was so important in redefining coitus from copulation to sexual intimacy. Perhaps LeVay expresses a gay man's indifference to the stimulus-value of a sexually aroused woman's facial expression, her utterances, her heaving breasts and engorged nipples, when he writes (1993, page 53): "From the point of view of the insertive partner, anal intercourse differs in only minor respects from vaginal intercourse."[14]

On the basis of their biological capabilities, we would expect males to seek many brief sexual encounters,[15] and females to want fewer, more selective, and more enduring sexual ties. (A male can impregnate at least one woman every day, but a woman can bear only one child a year.)[16]

Male-female differences in sexual predispositions

This difference probably has a genetic component. Down through the ages, this difference in predispositions probably put a strain on many partnerships; the woman wants both partners to be monogamous, the man expects his woman to be monogamous but he reserves for himself the right to casual sex.

Maccoby reports (page 205): "In a study of community college students, Feldman, Aranujo and Winsler" (1994) found that over half [the young men in a relationship] had 'cheated' on their partners despite an explicit commitment to be monogamous. Although young men value their commitment to their primary partner, they are more open to casual sex with others than are young women. And many young men, although they have had multiple partners themselves, say they want their future wives either to be virgins at marriage or to have slept with only one partner—themselves—before marriage." An Australian study (Moore and Rosenthal, 1993) yields similarly divergent attitudes of boys and girls.

"The passion of sex" is necessary,[17] write Potts and Short (page 130) in their 1998 survey of the evolution of human sexuality, *Ever Since Adam and Eve*, to weld together into an enduring partnership a man and a woman who have strong *but very different* behavioral agendas. Sexual passion and "falling in love" overcome this clash of genetic interests and make possible enduring partnerships that promote the survival of their offspring.

Is the sex drive stronger in males than in females? Males masturbate more frequently. When U.S. college students are asked if sexual arousal frequently interferes with their studying, males are more likely to answer yes (Weisfeld, page 169). When college students were recruited for a study (reported in 1985 by B. Singer) requiring a month of sexual abstinence, men were far less willing to participate than were women. *None* of the 15 male volunteers completed the study, whereas all 300 of the women reportedly did!

The appeal of the female figure

Another important characteristic of the human female physique, note Potts and Short, is the prominence, position and sexual function of the breast. *In no other species is the female breast so conspicuously displayed, and is so well developed in the non-pregnant female.* As in other mammals, the breasts of the female chimpanzee do not develop until the first pregnancy. Write Potts and Short (page 133): "[W]e are probably the only species in which the breasts have an erotic significance. We are the only species in which the breasts develop at the beginning of puberty, long before the first menstrual period or ovulation."

Potts and Short conjecture (page 133) that human breast development is a trade-off for suppression of olfactory and visual signs of ovulation in the perianal area.[18] In other words, just as redness, swelling, and sexually exciting odors around the perianal area once invited rear entry, now the erotically appealing and responsive female face, breasts and pubic hair tuft invite frontal entry.

At adolescence, girls become pleasantly soft to the touch[19] and more shapely, thanks to fatty deposits[20] widely distributed just under their skin and particularly around their breasts, buttocks and thighs. Hormonal changes that induce the menstrual cycle also produce psychological tendencies characteristic of post-menarchial girls: daydreaming, personal adornment, and an interest in boys.[21]

"[C]ross-cultural comparisons identify [the female breast] as a source of sexual arousal and a locus of erotic sensation for females. . . " (Beach 1978, page 146). Potts and Short agree (page 159): "In all cultures, the young female breast appears to have an erotic significance." How did the paired breasts of the human female evolve into such an important secondary sex organ, so prominently positioned and so appealingly contoured by fatty tissue?

The human breast evolved into an organ of erotic significance after it had migrated from the abdomen—the typical mammalian location of the nipples—to the chest. Noting the erotic advantage of this location, Potts and Short comment (page 84): "[A]s the manufacturers of T-shirts appreciate, one of the best places to advertise a message is on the human chest." Now the combined erotic appeal of a receptive female's facial features (head hair, eyes, mouth) and breasts invites face-to-face interaction and makes frontal-entry intercourse as likely for humans as changes (like perianal redness and swelling) favored rear entry in monkeys and apes.

The primary function of the breast is, of course, to nourish the young. By happy coincidence, for a female with upright posture, the nipples are advantageously positioned at chest level, facilitating the nursing of the infant as she cradles it in her arm. The nipples of female monkeys and apes are similarly located at chest level, a location as well adapted to two-legged creatures as the abdominal location suits four-legged mammals.

Male sexual development

In adolescent boys, testosterone activity produces significant changes in physique and power. (See Figures 3.5, 3.6, and 3.7.) Testosterone enlarges the penis, and the erectile response makes it a penetrating organ. Adolescent boys experience seminal emissions through wet dreams and masturbation.

For the great majority of adolescent boys, in the words of Eleanor Maccoby (page 224), "the onset of puberty brings with it a strong increase in interest in the other sex."[22] Whether this curiosity enlarges the boy's social life, or whether his sexual activity is limited to masturbation and same-sex play seems to depend, in part, on peer support. In Chapter 9, we will note that peer group support seems to play an important role in emboldening adolescent boys to interact with girls, socially and sexually.

While parental voices warn the adolescent boy of the dangers and hazards that can result from boy-girl intimacy, his buddies give the boy tips and advice on making sexual contacts. A boy may make his first contact with a prostitute along with a company of buddies. They use the same prostitute and talk over their experience with her in graphic and explicit detail, which gives the total experience both homoerotic and heterosexual dimensions.

Male aggressiveness is clearly evident in the rough-and-tumble tendencies of young boys, and serves to establish a boy's status in his group. In adolescence, aggressiveness reaches new levels, consistent with the adult human male's muscular power and endurance. An American professor recalls that adolescent friendship usually began in athletic competition:

> The unfortunate ones are those without athletic ability or inclina-
> tion. They become the loners, friendless and introspective—if
> they have the gift, artists and scholars. Adolescent friendship is .
> . . confrontation. What matters is who is taller, stronger, more
> agile, more skillful in hitting, throwing, passing, catching, dunk-
> ing. Friends wrestles . . . . When I was fourteen or fifteen I wres-
> tled my best friend to the floor in the hallway of our apartment
> house and we beat each other's head against the floor. We used
> to thump each other's arms to see who could hurt each other
> more. The freedom we had to hit each other was a mark of
> friendship (Goodheart, pages 67-68).

In virtually all cultures and in virtually all periods of history, men are more aggressive, more risk-taking, and competitive. Thus, male aggressiveness[23] that during boyhood expressed itself in rough-and-tumble play, now more directly serves the pursuit of sexual gratification.

The adult human male—broad-shouldered, well muscled, now sexually very well-endowed (compared with his pre-pubescent physique), aggressive and competitive—appeals to the nubile female as protector, defender, provider, and lover.

Unregulated, sexual passions would take a heavy toll on a hominid population, as competition among muscular, lustful males escalates into mortal struggle. In the contest between reproduction and self-destruction, some hominid groups did better than others. Darwinian theory suggests that where individuals bore clearly visible signs of status differences, those groups would enjoy a survival advantage.

The big penis: its evolutionary, social, and psychological significance

Biologist Jared Diamond (1997) notes that the adult male human has a much larger penis than any other primate. The gorilla has a penis about the size of a small boy's, and it serves very well its function of insemination. Diamond conjectures that the human penis evolved as a "display organ," like the mane of the male lion, rather than only to serve its sexual function. We are very familiar with two functions of the penis (excretory and reproductive); perhaps this organ also serves a third function: display.

> Why display? What survival value could have produced a penis so much larger than necessary for its reproductive function? Man evolved as a social animal. Male group bonding is probably an older, more primordial phenomenon than male-female pairing.

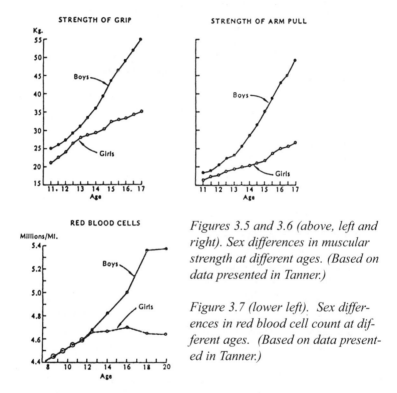

Figures 3.5 and 3.6 (above, left and right). Sex differences in muscular strength at different ages. (Based on data presented in Tanner.)

Figure 3.7 (lower left). Sex differences in red blood cell count at different ages. (Based on data presented in Tanner.)

For a group of males to function effectively, outbreaks of aggression and competitive strife must be minimized. As Chapter 27 emphasizes, a group that has its recognized leaders, a group in which every member has his rank and knows his status, has survival value over a group that is repeatedly disrupted by outbreaks of internal competition and aggression. Hence, the survival value of a prominent display organ, whether it be the mane of a male lion or the hominid penis.

This suggests that the human male's curiosity about his own sexual endowment and how it compares with his peers is not an indication of homosexual tendencies, as many males fear. Rather, this interest is probably a basic human tendency, deeply rooted in man's evolutionary past, when for thousands of years the size of his penis was *one* of the characteristics (like good looks, physique, strength, and cunning) that told a man where he stood in the company of other men.

Aside from its function as a display organ, if a large penis gives the male more sensory stimulation, and it is also more stimulating to his partner, this advantage would make the partnership more cohesive and enduring, favoring the survival of their offspring.

A unique characteristic of human female sexual nature

A unique characteristic of the human female is her unscheduled capacity[24] for sexual activity. In other primates, vaginal lubrication prevails only during the estrous period. Only the human female lubricates in response to sexual excitement at whatever time it occurs, independently of the menstrual cycle. Women sometimes experience an increase in sex drive during pregnancy. Weisfeld comments (page 83) that thus "sex provides a powerful marital adhesive *just when a strong bond is most needed* (emphasis added)."

The social animal

Man evolved as a social animal, ready to relate to other men not only as a competitor for sexual partners but also in a variety of other ways: hunting partner, leader, follower, friend, admirer, adorer and worshipper.[25] These interactions involve a certain amount of bodily contact, which probably occasioned some same-sex stimulation and gratification. Male hunting parties that camped overnight away from their mates might, conjecturally, have engaged in some incidental homosexual sex play, similar to what primate observers see of males that have been separated from females of their species.

Consideration of adult sexual activity necessarily leads up to the subject of pregnancy and parenthood. The human newborn is truly a "fetal" creature, helpless for a longer period of time than other primate infants. This "prolonged infancy" has certain biological advantages,[26] but encumbers the mother with both a nurturant and protective role and makes her, in turn, dependent on the support and protection of her partner. The human mother's need for protection and support, encumbered by one or more helpless infants, calls for a close-bonded partnership, and sets the stage for a family organization, which is a typically human social grouping.

> The capacity for sexual reproduction, taken by itself, cannot assure the survival of the human individual nor the survival of the species, since survival requires the protection, nurturance,

care and training of every offspring for a period of at least twelve years or more. An adult female so encumbered cannot fulfill her maternal task unless she is partnered by an adult male who is biologically and socially programmed to perform the tasks of guarding the mate and offspring, and tending to their needs.

Sex can give birth to offspring, but their survival requires that parents not only be capable of caring for them through the years of infancy and childhood, but that they feel closely bonded and dedicated to the task of raising their family.

The human species has been shaped by the natural selection of those traits that enhance the power of the individual and the group to survive and reproduce. Beach suggests (1978, page 138) that natural selection shapes not only our *physical traits* (hands and feet, eyes and ears) but also our emotional tendencies, behavioral capacities, and intellectual capabilities. The develop-ment of a species whose newborn require so extended a period of nurturance, care and training, required that nature evolve adult males and females whose *temperamental tendencies* form parental partnerships that fulfill the imperatives of reproduction and survival. For males and females to develop gender roles, Beach suggests, is nature's way of preparing individuals for par-ticipating in the survival of the species.

In a species in which offspring are born in a helpless condition, their survival is favored if parents are close-bonded, if not monogamous. Then, a mother's "maternal instinct" to nourish and care, can be complemented with a father's instinct to protect and support. In the interest of family solidarity (and survival), nature *limits* the male's testosterone level and thereby limits his drive to seek fresh opportunities to mate with other available females.

Chapter 27 deals in detail with the fact that for hominids to evolve into human beings, it was necessary, apparently, for nature to make the adult male and female far more alike than were their hominid ancestors. This means that males had to divest themselves, over the millennia, of much of their hominid macho: their towering bulk and a measure of their ferocious aggressiveness and compet-itiveness. This link between monogamy, testosterone level, and fatherhood are nicely symbolized by the following observations of bird behavior, and by an experiment reported by John Wingfield:

If you compare the testosterone levels (T-levels) of monogamous sparrow species with their polygamous counterparts, monoga-mous males tend to be lower in testosterone, and their T-level drops even further as soon as they become parents. When the T-level of sparrow fathers of a monogamous species was experimentally boosted (through implantation of a testosterone pump), they lose their monogamous traits. Instead of staying close to their nest and helping to feed their young, the fathers now spent their time and energy chasing available females. The experimenters reported a precipitous drop in the survival rate of the baby sparrows.

Beach (1978) emphasizes that throughout the evolution from hominid to human, man has subsisted on hunting and gathering. In all likelihood, men hunted in groups, and women divided their time between tending to their children and gathering food. It is believed that vegetation constituted about 75 percent of the diet of prehistoric man.

Women are hypothesized to have been gatherers rather than hunters because successful hunting depended upon masculine strength and endurance, and perhaps even certain emotional tendencies such as less fearfulness and greater willingness to venture far from the safety of the home base. The more sedentary role of females was also directly associated with the restrictive effects of pregnancy, the necessity of remaining with the young during the lactation period, and possibly a stronger tendency toward nurturant behavior in general (Beach 1978, page 140).

Division of labor is seen everywhere in nature, and seems to be well established as a survival tactic. We are supposing that nature assigned the roles of caregiver and gatherer to mature females, not that her status resulted from male intimidation.The feminist movement of our time, and the increasing presence of women on college faculties, has fostered some skepticism about the Man the Hunter image, and has called for a re-examination of the role of the female of the species. (See Tanner & Zihlman).

Reconstructing the life of prehistoric man is not an altogether armchair activity, but is based on evidence, direct and indirect. Where early human remains are found, paleontologists also find what look like permanent human settlements, usually accomodating about 25 families, and in these localities are heaps of bones of large animals, some pierced by flint spear heads. Bones of large and dangerous animals like elephants and rhinoceroses suggest that these animals were killed and retrieved by hunting parties rather than individuals. In hunting parties, men developed the traits of leadership, cooperation, planning, and sharing. (Such are the operation of both genetics and experience that both men and women learn to enjoy such "masculine activities" as hunting and fighting, and such "feminine activities" as child care, gardening and cooking.)

As a hunter, man evolved his predilections for stalking, running, risk-taking, killing, and a team playing. Running was an important skill because primitive weapons typically would not kill the animal but only wound it. Eventually, the quarry would bleed to death while the hunters chased after it.

Tanner & Zihlman (page 59) argued that hunting was probably
not important in the life of protohumans because hunting is not
an important chimpanzee behavior, and "we assume chimpanzees
are like the ancestral population [of humans]." Their argument,
however, is not supported by the evidence of prehistoric large-
animal bone-heaps, or by important *differences* between humans
and chimpanzees, in physique and behavior.

Another testimony to the importance of hunting in the life of prehistoric man is the domestication of dogs, which were bred for
their usefulness as hunting companions, for their ability to locate,
track, bring to bay, and even to kill.

The gender role. To approximate an eye-witness view of the life of pre-historic man, anthropologists of past decades have sought out existing preliterate societies whose lives were still untouched by the outside world, and were sub-sisting on a pre-agricultural, hunting-and-gathering economy believed to resemble that of prehistoric man. In 1959 Sahlins reported on twelve such societies. All twelve were clusters of families. *All twelve were observed to practice division of labor by sex.* The transmission and adoption of gender roles may thus be regarded as a survival trait, an enormously adaptive "design for living." Over hundreds of thousands of years, natural selection favored those individuals who were most predisposed to develop and transmit to their young a gender role and a gender identity.

In 1965 Davenport reported that in Melanesian society, like our own, boys of six years and younger usually display a great deal of rough-and-tumble play, gang fighting, and other forms of vigorous social interaction, while little girls play quietly in small groups or alone. Davenport observed that little boys were allowed to run freely all over the village, forming age-stratified gangs, "fighting amongst themselves and getting into mischief, always under the close but permissive surveillance of adults." Little girls, in contrast, "are virtually never separated from their mothers or older sisters while the latter are engaged in household and garden work before sunup to past sundown" (Davenport, page 195). Beach notes (1978, page 133) that in many societies boys and girls tend to choose games that conform to underlying and unlearned male-female physical differences:

[B]oys throw at targets, run races, catch balls, climb trees, and in
general prefer activities for which most males are physically better suited than most females. . . . Girls in the same societies tend

to choose games that demand less energy expenditure and capitalize upon female superiority in fine muscle coordination and
rapid and precise small movements.

Thus, over hundreds of thousands of years, Beach suggests,
Homo sapiens developed into a species of males and females
who had a genetic tendency to adopt gender roles, to celebrate
them, to teach them to their young, to reward and praise them for
fulfilling their gender roles and punish them (through ridicule,
for example) for transgressing their gender roles.

Natural selection favored boys who were happy to play-hunt and fight off
imaginary enemies, and girls who liked to play with dolls and play house.
Natural selection evolved men who enjoyed fulfilling the gender roles of
provider, protector and lover; and women who felt comfortable as homemaker,
mother, and beloved. There is a hint of "economic determinism" (a rather
Marxian flavor) to this theory that the *struggle for existence* caused Homo sapiens to become a species of males and females programmed for well-differentiat-
ed gender roles, and enduring gender identities. From this point of view, "sex-
ism" comes naturally to most humans and a gender-neutral attitude will perhaps
occur only if it is cultivated.

What are the demonstrable indications that evolution has differentially
equipped boys and girls, men and women for their gender roles? Gender differences in natural talents, differences in strengths, and differences in sensitivities,
are detailed in both in this Chapter and in Chapter 7.

Variation is an important characteristic of all living things, and the human
species is especially diverse. In this diverse human population, there is a small
minority of individuals who never develop the male gender role in all its usual
details, who never adopt a strong and stable masculine identity. What of that
minority of males who are more attracted sexually to other members of their own
gender than to available, receptive and inviting females? What can we conjecture
about their genetic makeup? What are their life histories? What do their sexual
practices tell us about their motivations? That is the content of Chapters 9
through 26. What theory can guide us to reach a better understanding of the phenomenon that Potts and Short describe (page 74) as "a profound puzzle"?[27] That
is the question that will be addressed in the final chapter of this book.

NOTES TO CHAPTER 3

1. We introduce the term play-copulation to describe the fact that infant monkeys
frequently mount each other—not only males on females, but males on males, or
females on males—or assume a posture (lordosis) as if to invite copulation. In
infancy, play-copulation seems to have no sexual significance but rather serves
to establish rank or dominance. By the time monkeys reach seven years of age,

taking the copulatory position is a familiar, well-established habit, and now serves a sexual function.

2. The investigators' report presents a "detailed description of child-rearing and child life" in six cultures: subsistence farmers in communities of Okinawa, the Philippines, northern India, Kenya, Oaxaca, and a New England town of 5000 inhabitants. The total sample included 67 boys and 67 girls.

3. Writes Harlow (pages 6-7):

> As month after month and year after year have passed, these monkeys [raised in individual cages for the first year of their life] have appeared to be less and less normal. We have seen them sitting in their cages strangely mute, staring fixedly into space, relatively indifferent to people and other monkeys. . . .

> Some of these monkeys lived in pairs for several years while growing to sexual maturity . . . [and there were no pregnancies]. Instead these monkeys treat each other like brother and sister, proving [Harlow adds, with a touch of humor] that two can live in complete propinquity with perfect propriety as long as no one cares.

4. Harlow reports (page 7) that attempts to breed wire-cage-raised males with normal females "was frighteningly unsuccessful. When the older wire-cage-raised males were paired with [normal] females at the peak of estrus, the introduction led only to fighting, so violent and vicious that separation was essential to survival. In no case was there any indication of normal sex behavior. Frequently the females were the aggressors. . . ."

5. Actually, Beach's 1949 article deals with the sexual behavior of mammals of all sorts—domestic and wild, large and small—comparing and contrasting their behavior with the primates. In this chapter, however, we will focus on his observations concerning primate behavior.

6. Murphy gave an experimental group of men, prior to sexual arousal and orgasm, an intravenous infusion of the drug naxolone, which is known to oppose the action of opiate-like drugs. (A control group was injected with an inactive substance, a placebo.) Naxolone infusion had no effect on the men's ability to become sexually aroused, experience erection and ejaculation. Heart rate and blood pressure were typical of sexual arousal. But the experimental group reported less pleasurable orgasm than the control group. LeVay (1993, page 52) is not completely convinced that this study describes orgasm as an "oxytocin high," and expresses the belief that "much more research is needed." Oxytocin is also released during nursing and childbirth. "Some women describe episodes of intense pleasure akin to orgasm during nursing" (LeVay 1993, page 67).

7. [Writes Beach (1949, page 70)] "There are a number of mammalian species in which mating between strangers does not occur. Groups of porcupines kept together in captivity tend to pair off and engage in coital relations exclusively with one specific individual of the opposite sex. . . The male fox exhibits definite monogamous tendencies and commercial breeders find it necessary to prevent any permanent bonds between a male and a favored vixen if the male is desired for use as stud. Beach continues;

> . . . Some bulls and stallions refuse to serve estrous cows or
> mares of a particular color. Stallions used to serving dark mares
> sometimes fail to copulate with a white one, and jacks which are
> intended for use in mule breeding are never allowed to serve a
> jennet, for after they have done so their responsiveness to the
> mare may be greatly reduced.

8. LeVay adds (1993, page 47): "Nevertheless the brain, especially the hypothalamus, does control and modulate these reflexes, and the subjective experiences connected with coitus, especially the experience of orgasm, obviously require a brain." Ninety-one pages later, LeVay concedes (page 137): "It is likely that life experiences play a significant role in molding the intimate details of a person's sexual drive. Yet even here the potential for inborn differences should not be ignored."

9. The study of "animal homosexuality" is a popular branch of gay studies. One might infer from Beach's 1978 statement, however, that the study of animal same-sex activity has rather a limited relevance to human homosexuality.

10. Because the prone-supine position has been called "the missionary position," it has been wrongly assumed that it is a peculiarly Western posture. It is true, however, that in many societies sexual union is achieved with the woman sitting above her partner. This enables her to "adjust her position and movement to control the degree and frequency of clitoral excitation" (Beach 1978, page 148).

11. The exception is the pygmie chimpanzee, or bonobo, which regularly engages in face-to-face copulation. It should be noted that the bonobo's physique more closely approximates man's than any other primate. Compared with the full-size chimpanzee, the bonobo's body is more slender and its posture more upright.

12. Too often, language is regarded as mediating the exchange of *information*. The exchange of feelings and emotions is, however, an important function of language, and face-to-face intercourse fosters the development of intimacy through the exchange of feelings, both verbally and non-verbally.

Shared feelings of intimacy result in mutual loyalty and build an enduring relationship between partners who know each other's feelings, habits, and idiosyncracies; lovers who feel comfortable with each other.

Beach notes that in a community of enduring pairs, sexual activity is less likely to be "prevented or interrupted by harassment by other individuals," a frequent occurrence in primate societies that lack pair bonding (Beach 1978, page 149).

13. Writes Beach: "We cannot know whether a female chinchilla . . . experiences orgasm" but "thirty-five years of research on sexual behavior in animals have led me to the tentative conclusion that female orgasm . . . [is] a human invention. . . " (Beach 1978, page 147). Potts and Short report (page 77), however, that "female orgasms *have* been observed in bonobo chimpanzees, but, as far as is known, orgasm is a rare accompaniment of female sex drive in other mammalian species." With or without orgasm, females probably experience sex as pleasurable.

14. LeVay claims (page 53) that anal intercourse, a common practice among gay men, is "also surprisingly common in male-female sex." Even if face-to-face intercourse is intrinsically a more intimate interaction, there are several reasons why some heterosexuals sometimes do practice anal intercourse: 1] to avoid pregnancy, 2] for variety, 3] to express contempt for the partner and deny her the pleasure of clitoral stimulation, 4] to avoid facing the actual partner, and facilitate the fantasy of having a more stimulating partner, and 5] to seek a more voluptuous physical sensation, if the partner's vagina has been stretched from childbearing,

15. Potts and Short (page 130), like other evolutionary writers, emphasize "the strong but differing behavioral agendas of men and women." The genetic tendency of males to impregnate many females, has been named "The Coolidge Effect."

> The Coolidge Effect. The story is told that President Coolidge
> and his wife once visited a model henhouse, and Mrs. Coolidge
> noted that there were hundreds of hens but only a few roosters.
> Her guide told her that just a few roosters were enough because
> one rooster could be sexually active many times a day. "Tell that
> to Mr. Coolidge," she commented. When the guide told the
> President what he had told his wife, Coolidge asked: "Active
> with the same hen?" "No," answered the guide; "Each time, the
> rooster has a different hen." Commented the President: "Tell that
> to Mrs. Coolidge."

It is a fact that after copulation, a bull shows no interest in remounting the same cow. But if the bull is presented with a different cow, the bull will readily mount it. Evolutionists argue, therefore, that it is natural that to human males "the exotic is erotic." But for every American male who marries an exotic woman, a dozen marry the girl next door.

16. George Williams describes the difference between male and female sexual interest as follows: "The difference between male and female in sexual interest and behavior parallels their different roles in reproduction. Over the period of a year, an average male can inseminate hundreds of females. During the same period, a female can give birth to only one offspring. This asymmetry predisposes the male to be quick, aggressive, and competitive, while the female is inclined to be reserved, tempting, and calculating. Why tempting? Because she doesn't want to lose him while she is investing time and energy to size him up. Why calculating? To judge his value as a sire and as a father."

17. Perhaps "falling in love" (or sexual jealousy) is necessary to maintain human partnerships, but in many species (especially birds) long-term bonds occur despite infrequent sex. (Weisfeld, personal correspondence.)

18. Potts and Short assert (page 102) that concealed ovulation promotes family living by *not* advertising the female partner's ovulation, and thus attracting other males (outsiders, pubescent male offspring) to her. This reduces the male's need to guard his female partner, and allows him to spend his time and energy on other activities. Privacy of intercourse and covering the genitals, they suggest, also minimize the disruptive effect of sexual competition within the family.

19. In another series of experiments, Harlow established that, given a choice of surrogate "mothers," monkeys clearly preferred hugging a soft-textured "cloth mother" even though she offered no milk, rather than a "wire mother" on whose chest was mounted a full nursing bottle.

20. Potts and Short pose the question, Why do adult females have such a generous quota of fatty tissue: widely-distributed subcutaneous fat, and patterned fatty concentrations (breast, hips, buttocks) which most males do not have? Their answer: they provide nutritional reserves which might be necessary to the pregnant female in times of food shortage.

Why are these fat reserves patterned, rather than uniformly distributed throughout the body? Probably because *Homo sapiens* evolved in a tropical climate, where a uniformly-distributed blanket of fat would be burdensome. That this patterning of fat deposits gives the female erotic appeal is not the only case in which a physical characteristic serves more than one function.

21. In 1939, Stone and Barker compared the social behavior and interest patterns of pre- and post-menarcheal girls of the same chronological age, and demonstrated these behavior shifts.

22. In her comprehensive and very recent (1998) survey of gender differences

over the lifespan, Eleanor Maccoby makes a passing acknowledgement (page 191) of the fact that homosexuality does indeed exist. But by adolescence, for all but this very small minority, heterosexual activity becomes "a strong . . . interest" (page 224), "an uncharted territory . . . intriguing and exciting . . . infinitely satisfying" (page 300).

23. Note Potts and Short (page 197): "Many men get an almost visceral pleasure out of collecting and handling weapons. Numbers of young boys greatly exceed those of young girls in playing the more violent games in amusement arcades." It is significant, they point out (pages 326-327), that in every country more men than women are in prison.

Blum (page xiv) notes that in a 1995 conference on crime and genetics, scientists acknowledged that the genetic basis for male-female differences in aggression was so well-established "that it really didn't make for interesting research."

24. Beach suggests that the human female can have sex whenever she so desires, not that "she is always available," as some biologists have stated. Writes Beach (1978, page 147), humorously: "No human female is constantly receptive. . . . Any male who entertains this illusion must be a very old man with a short memory, or a very young man due for a bitter disappointment."

25. Religion may thus be regarded as another expression of man's *social* impulses, his tendency to band together with peers and also to worship and adore his perceived (or imagined) superiors. Among the ancient Canaanites temple worship involved some kind of male-male sexual activity, disapprovingly described in the Hebrew Bible as "temple prostitution."

26. The long-term advantages, and evolutionary consequences, of a fetal infancy is discussed in some detail in Chapter 27.

27. To put their characterization of human homosexuality as "a profound puzzle" in context, Potts and Short (page 74) write that although many mammals, especially when young, engage in homosexual play, *only in humans* are some adults "exclusively and consistently oriented toward their own sex. *Biologically, this is a profound puzzle. . . . [H]omosexual behavior is the antithesis of reproductive success*" (emphasis added).

It might be added that although some individual cases of mammals (usually in captivity) have been observed to make permanent and exclusive same-sex pairings, *human* male homosexual pairings occur in a majority of human cultures, and in every generation the percentage of such pairings (probably around three percent) probably does not vary by very much.

4 Twenty-Three Differences Between Male Homosexuals and Lesbians

Socially and politically, gay men and lesbians need each other because people need each other, and people are better off doing things together than people acting alone. In public meetings, fights and shouting are less likely to break out in a mixed crowd than in an all-male crowd. The presence of women makes it easier to maintain civility. In organizational life, the natural traits of men and women complement each other: men are more likely to give big money, and contribute an aggressive, competitive, element; while women contribute nurturance, social cohesion, and attention to detail. Women make effective spokespersons and negotiators for "the gay community." Straight men are often more at ease negotiating with a woman (lesbian or straight) than with a gay man. Finally, there is strength in numbers and for that reason alone, it is advantageous for gay men and lesbians to form a united front.

Conceptualizing homosexual men and lesbians as "a gay community" is a fairly recent phenomenon,[1] and this concept has strategic advantages for advancing the gay agenda. For example, to argue in favor of sanctifying and legalizing gay marriage, it is easy to give examples of long-term, faithful partnerships, and good to describe "gay couples" who are raising children. *Never mind that the examples are drawn largely from lesbian couples*; these couples are showcased as "members of the gay community."

From a behavioral science point of view, male homosexuals and lesbians are too dissimilar to be combined for research or clinical purposes, though it is now the practice in gay-friendly circles to include both lesbians and gay men in research and even in treatment discussions.[2]

The dissimilarities between the two populations, however, argue strongly against attempting to construct a theory that would be equally valid for predicting the behavior of both lesbians and gay men. From a biological point of view, writes LeVay (1993, page 112), the evidence suggests "that the factors influencing sexual orientation in men may be different from those operating in women. This is reasonable enough, given that 'homosexuality' is just a label for two phenomena that are *really different things* in the two sexes" (emphasis added).

Men and women differ in what triggers their sexual interest, regardless of their sexual orientation. Women look for a love object with a woman's sensibilities, men with a man's interests. Bailey and a team of researchers (Bailey *et al.* 1994) assembled four large matched samples of men and women (about 70 in each group), straight and gay, and administered a number of attitude tests relat-

44

ed to what a person finds sexually attractive. Results were consistent with clinical observations and everyday experience: men differ from women regardless of their sexual orientation.[3] Here are six gender differences supported by the findings of this research team; differences that distinguish men from women, *whether straight or gay.*

1] **Men show a greater interest in uncommitted sex.** This attitude was measured by agreement with statements like:

> I do not need to respect or love someone in order to enjoy having sex with him/her.
> Monogamy is not for me.
> I believe in taking sexual opportunities when I find them, as long as no one gets hurt.
> I could easily imagine myself enjoying one night of sex with someone I would never see again.

Consistent with this obtained gender difference is the fact that promiscuity is more frequent among gay men. Men are more likely to seek quick, varied sex; hence gay bars, one-night stands, cruising, and bathhouses catering to promiscuous sex and orgies. Bell and Weinberg's 1978 survey (page 308) compared gay men and lesbians in their likelihood to have sex with a stranger.

Table 4.1 Frequency of Sex with a Stranger

	Gay men* (n=574)	Lesbians* (n =225)
None	1 percent	62 percent
Half or less	20	32
More than half	79	6
Total	100	100

*White respondents only reported here.   Findings for black respondents are similar.

....

> "Girls are more inclined to become sexually involved in the context of a romantic relationship, whereas for boys, initial homosexual contact more often involves brief sexual encounters. . . . Gilligan (1982) . . . has theorized a female orientation toward relationships and ties as opposed to a male orientation toward separation and autonomy." (Zucker and Bradley, page 345)

Also consistent with this difference is the fact that the total number of partners is dramatically greater for gay men than for straights or lesbians. Statistics from the Bell and Weinberg pre-AIDS 1978 survey (page 312) show that a majority of lesbians report only one or two partners in the past year, compared with 20 or more partners reported by gay men.

....

Table 4.2 Number of Homosexual Partners in Past Year

	White gay males (n=572)	White lesbians (n=228)
None	3 percent	8 percent
1-2	8	63
3-5	10	16
6-10	12	7
11-19	12	3
20-50	27	3
51 or more	28	0

....

Surveyed during the AIDS epidemic in 1983, gay men were reducing their frequency of sexual contacts (Martin Weinberg *et al.*, 1983, page 174).

When asked (in 1983) how many sex partners they have had in their life, gay men (n=178) estimate a median of 102; 100 male and two female. Lesbians (n=92) report a total of 20 sex partners—an equal number of males and females. (*ibid,*, page 382).

Donald Symons suggests that gay men *experience* what straight men *fantasize*: frequent and diverse sexual contact. "Many straight men . . . would be delighted to stop off during their lunch hour for an episode of anonymous fellatio. If casual sex were socially acceptable, safe and inexpensive as expresso, we might see sex stations at about the same frequency as coffee shops" (Barash and Lipton, paraphrasing Symons).

Consistent with the fact that uncommitted sex has a greater appeal to men, gay or straight, than to women, is the fact that gay males support homosexual prostitution. Sex-for-pay is a well-established service in the gay community. Lesbian prostitution is virtually unheard of. Sex without love, popular among gay men, is almost nonexistent among lesbians. (Blumstein and Schwartz, pages 70-71)

> For men, it is easier to have sex with another man than to fall in love with him; for women, it is easier to fall in love with another woman than to have sex with her.
> Gay men often find their sexual partners by "cruising" well-known bars. . . or seeking quick, impersonal, anonymous sex in rest

rooms, parks, or other semipublic places.
[Lesbians] frequent a coffeehouse that caters to lesbians . . . to
drink . . . and listen to jazz, not to pick up other women.

Lesbians place a higher value on monogamy; male gay partners can more easily tolerate each other's "infidelities." Lesbian partnerships have a higher rate of breakups because an outside affair more often leads to resentment and conflict (Weinberg et al., page 67).

Monogamy is at the opposite extreme of uncommitted sex, and the research of Blumstein and Schwartz confirms that lesbians and heterosexuals (male and female) show concern for whether their partner is monogamous. Potts and Short (page 8) agree:

Gay women more often put loving relationships ahead of physical experiences, and when two women live together their partnership is more likely to be sexually faithful. . . .

Consistent with attraction to uncommitted sex as a male characteristic is the finding of Blumstein and Schwartz that most gay men have their first homosexual experience with a stranger; most women have their first lesbian experience with a close friend.

2] Women are more likely to have had heterosexual experience before becoming gay. Before becoming lesbian, 85 per cent of women had heterosexual experience; only 20 per cent of gay men had heterosexual experience before same-sex experience (Almost 50 percent of lesbians were married before they became gay (Cotton 1975, Miller et al.); only 6 percent of gay men were previously married (Schaefer).

3] Men show a greater interest in visual sexual stimuli. (Presumably, women are more likely to be stirred by words of endearment, caresses, romantic music, etc.) Interest in visual sexual stimuli was measured by agreement with items like the following:

It would be exciting to watch two people having sex.
When I meet someone I find attractive, I fantasize about what
they would look like without any clothes on.
Seeing my sexual partner undress is a real turn-on.

Barash and Lipton note: "A substantial industry specializes in providing visual stimuli [e.g., magazines, videotapes] for male homosexuals; nothing comparable exists for [lesbians]."

4] **Women attach more importance to their partner's status**. Being "treated," and receiving gifts (whether flowers, chocolates, or a diamond ring) are more than fulfillment of a social custom. These acts are expressions of the lover's *willingness* to give, as well as his capacity to give. In the study by Bailey et al., importance of partner *status* was measured by agreement with statements like these:

> Although I don't necessarily expect it, having the other person pay for the date makes me feel good.
> It can be very romantic to get a very expensive gift.
> I would like my partner to be from a higher social class background than I.
> It would be important to me if my partner were highly respected in the community.

5] **Preference for younger partners** is another way in which men and women differ regardless of their sexual orientation. Bailey *et al.* measured this difference with items like the following:

> Facial wrinkles in a potential romantic partner would be a real turn-off for me.
> I find attractive adolescents (aged 16-18) particularly sexy.
> I am turned off by bodies that show signs of aging (such as sagging skin or varicose veins).

6] **Men attach more importance to their partner's physical attractiveness.** This is another widely-recognized truism affirmed by the study of Bailey *et al.* Items like the following were used to measure this difference:

> In the past, I've usually initially become romantically interested in someone largely due to their physical characteristics.
> I wouldn't consider being romantically involved with someone who was significantly overweight.
> I would be happy if my partner were more sexually attractive than I.

Men, straight or gay, are more likely to be stirred by physical beauty. To women, whether straight or lesbian, more important are emotional compatibility, personality and character.

> Men are more easily aroused by visual stimuli. . . . Women favor warm bonds of human companionship . . . . (Potts and Short, pages 77- 78).

Gay men are often puzzled by what draws heterosexual couples together: how a beautiful woman can fall in love with a man who is less than attractive physically. In addition to the five gender differences studied by Bailey *et al.*, the following difference distinguishes between male and female sexuality:

7] **Women are more likely to rate themselves near the midpoint of a heterosexual-homosexual continuum** (the Kinsey Scale). (See Pillard 1990, pages 88-114.) McCormick *et al.*, (1994 page 526) reports: "We found that a score of 4 [on the Kinsey scale] was more common among women than men." The following 16 differences between gay men and lesbians (7 through 22) likewise argue against studying them as a single psychological group:

8] **More men than women are homosexual.** There is little agreement on estimates of the prevalence of homosexuality in males and in females.

Samples and sampling methods vary,[4] the mode of questioning varies, and the content of the question varies. (For example, one survey taker might ask: "Throughout your adult life, have you been exclusively homosexual?" another asks, "Have you been predominantly homosexual for three years or more of your adult life?" or "Have you ever had genital contact with a person of your own sex within the last five years?") Whatever variations in procedure, the results almost always show a greater prevalence of homosexuality among men than among women. Table 4.3, adapted from pages 61-62 of LeVay 1996, summarizes some reported findings.

9] **In general, gay men are more sexually *active* than lesbians**. Gay men begin their sexual activity at an earlier age, engage in sex more often, more often engage in physically intense sex, sadomasochistic sex, show more initiative in their sexual behavior, and are more likely to commit rape.

> Males typically have their first homosexual experience in middle adolescence; female involvement begins in late adolescence or early adulthood. (Martin Weinberg et al., page 140, Zucker and Bradley, page 340; Garnets and Kimmel make the same observation.)

Frequency of sexual intercourse is greater for gay men than for lesbians, especially in the early part of their relationship (Blumstein and Schwartz). It is not unusual for a devoted lesbian couple to stop having physical sex altogether. When male gay couples get bored with each other's lovemaking, they often remain a devoted couple but begin to seek out other sexual outlets. When a heterosexual couple get bored with each other sexually, usually they begin to dislike each other and their marriage is in trouble. But a lesbian couple might stop their physical lovemaking (a phenomenon known as "lesbian bed death") and still be very much in love.

Table 4.3 Reported percentages of gays and lesbians in the general population

Male	Female	Criterion	Source
4 percent	1 to 3 percent of never married or previously married women.	Exclusively homosexual throughout their lives.	Kinsey
3.6	1.7	Reported having at least one same-sex experience in their life.	British study reported by LeVay.
2.8	1.4	Identified themselves as homosexual or bisexual.	Survey by National Opinion Research Ctr., 1992.
6.2	3.6	Have had sexual contact with same-sex person in previous five years.	Recent study at Harvard School of Public Health.
4.4	3.6	Same as above.	Louis Harris and Associates poll reported in NYT, Apr. 25, '93.
2		Have had male-male sex in last 12 mo.	Rogers & Turner

10] **Masturbation is a more common activity with gay men than with lesbians.** According to Weinberg *et al.* (page 384), 46 percent of gay men (n=181) masturbate four times per week or more frequently. This frequency of masturbation is reported by only 22 percent of lesbians (n=92).

11] **Emphasis on sexual performance that is physically intense ("hot sex") is greater with gay men.** With lesbians, affection and emotional bonding are more important than erotic attraction and sexual performance.

> [With lesbians,] lovemaking is an occasional thing, on a par with attending a good concert: fun, but . . . 'not a big deal' (Barash and Lipton, page 71).

Most gay men probably engage in a greater variety of practices, and are also more likely to use drugs to extend their capabilities for sexual performance.

Gay men probably attach more importance to one's physical resources for sexual performance (like the size of one's penis), and to erotic techniques; lesbians probably attach more importance to the expression of feelings of intimacy and devotion.

12] **Aggressiveness as an aspect of sexuality is probably more prominent in gay than in lesbian experience.** In sadomasochism, each partner either expresses or receives aggression.

13] **Homosexual rape more frequently occurs among gay men than among lesbians.** It is also likely to be more violent, and subjugation of the victim is more extreme.

> Male homosexuality mirrors male sexuality: variety-seeking (including quick, impersonal interactions) easily stimulated, aggressive. Lesbianism mirrors female values of permanent bonding and security (predictability, protection).

14] **Likelihood to initiate sex is greater for gay men than for lesbians.** (Blumstein and Schwartz).

15] **Gay relationships are more likely to begin with sex; with lesbians, sex culminates a relationship.**

> For men, both their first heterosexual and first homosexual experience were very likely to be with strangers . . . whom they would probably never see again. The predominant pattern among women was for sex to occur with a close friend, and this to them

was a natural and logical outgrowth of a strong emotional attachment. (Blumstein and Schwartz 1977, page 44)

Like women in general, lesbians adopt a more moderate, stable, distinctly
feminine style of amorous expression:

16] **Kissing and cuddling is more common a form of sexual
expression among lesbians than with gay men.** Gay males are more
likely to practice "masturbating a partner, masturbating in front of a partner . . .
oral sex . . . finger-anal sex . . . oral-anal sex, plus anal fisting and enema play"
(Weinberg *et al.*, page 171).

17] **Frequency of stable monogamy is much higher for lesbians
(and straights) than for gay men** (Blumstein and Schwartz), and lesbian
couples are more likely to raise children, their own or adopted. "[L]esbians tend
to weave lasting monogamous ties, involving high levels of fidelity." (Barash and
Lipton, page 71)

> *A joke told in the gay community:*
> What does a lesbian bring on her second date?
> A U-Haul.
> And what does a gay man bring on his second date?
> What second date?

18] **Lesbians frequently have a good friend who is a heterosexual woman, but seldom maintain a friendship with a straight man. Gay
men feel isolated from heterosexuals of their own gender, but often
maintain friendships with straight women** (Rubin, pages 170-171). A 41-
year old female beautician,married for 24 years, described to Rubin (pages 171-
172) her work experience with men, straight and gay:

> I worked in an office once and I hated it because the men were
> always so snooty and bossy to the girls there, always ordering
> them around and expecting us to jump when they called. But
> here [at the beauty salon], we're more equal, the men and
> women. Of course, they're all gay, and that makes a big differ-
> ence, but a gay man's different.
>
> . . . It's lots more like having a woman friend. . . . [A gay man]
> treats me . . . like I'm more of an equal. . . . He's interested in
> lots of the same things I am. I mean, when he tells a story, it's
> like listening to a girl friend. With most of the men I know, even
> my husband, it's just like, "Here's the facts; don't bother me with
> anything else." But gay men are different; they talk about things

more like women do, and they like to talk about a lot of the same things too—like clothes, and people, and things like that.

A 37-year old graphic artist explains to Rubin (pages 172-173) why he feels more comfortable with a straight woman than with a straight man:

> I find women have an aesthetic sensibility that's closer to my own. So I can go to a concert or a museum or the theater with a woman friend and it feels wonderfully compatible in a way I can't imagine it being with the straight men I know. Or if I'm having trouble in my love life, I can talk to a woman about it easily. Can you just see me telling some straight guy about that, with all that homophobia they have?

19] **There is more evidence of a biological factor in gay men than in lesbians.** After reviewing a number of twin studies, LeVay (1996, page 178) concludes "that genes do influence men's sexual orientation but play little or no role in the development of sexual orientation in women." Dean Hamer's molecular genetics study linked an X chromosome region with male homosexuality, but not with lesbianism (LeVay 1996, page 184).

Overwhelmingly more gay men (90 percent) claim to have been "born that way" than lesbians (about 50 percent). *Lesbians are more likely to have experienced their sexual orientation as a deliberate choice.* Carla Golden differentiates between "primary" and "elective" lesbians; the latter do not recall feeling different from their peers as children.

> Many of the women in our study decided to experiment with homosexual relationships because they felt encouraged by the tenets of the women's movement to examine their feelings towards other women and to learn to be closer to them. The movement had encouraged them to respect and like other women, and for many this novel feeling was closely akin to the feelings they had felt with those men whom they had eroticized. Sometimes these women instigated sexual encounters for ideological rather than erotic reasons (Blumstein and Schwartz 1977, page 43).

Some women were grossly disappointed by their introduction to heterosexual activity, and opt for lesbianism as a more satisfying way to fulfill their sexual needs.

Women often suffer from what has been called "compulsory heterosexuality," having been forced, cajoled, etc., into sex with men whether they are sexually attracted to them or not (Weinberg *et al.*, page 141).

If male homosexuality is more strongly rooted in biology than is the case with lesbianism, we would expect more gays than lesbians to be exclusively homosexual. Indeed, survey findings show that a higher percentage of lesbians report having experienced heterosexual intercourse: 46 percent gay men, 79 percent lesbians (Saghir and Robins, 1975). Lesbians (n=91) are more likely than gay men (n=174) to recall a person of the opposite sex as the partner in their most enduring relationship; 29 versus 18 percent (Weinberg *et al.*, page 4040.

> Gay men are more likely to have had their first sexual experience with another male; lesbians are more likely to have experienced heterosexual sex before they experienced lesbian sex (Weinberg *et al.*, 1983, page 141).

Blum (page 139) quotes the homosexuality researcher Bailey, expressing the belief that the sexual orientation of men seems to be more strongly rooted in their biology:

> I do think there's a biology to homosexuality. . . . For women, it may be a little more flexible. . . . [M]y impression, among self-identified lesbians, is they often have sexual arousal to men and choose not to act on it. They choose to be with women. Women are more likely than men to have feelings toward both sexes. Men are more channeled one way or the other—there's less choice.

If the sexual orientation of women is influenced more by experience than by innate factors, we would expect sexual identity to be less patterned, less predictable, and less stable for women than for men. "Psychological and sociological research has revealed that sexual orientation identities are more fluid in at least some women than they are in men" (Mondimore, page 175).

> Sixty-six percent of lesbians report that they had at some time experienced a major change in their sexual feelings; only 32 percent of gay men report such a change (n=92 women, 182 men. Weinberg *et al.*, 1983, page 379.

> Right now, I'm a lesbian. . . . Nevertheless, there are distinct questions, that is, I'm not sure that I couldn't under the right circumstances have a serious heterosexual relationship. I mean, if my current relationship ended, I might be open to men again. My fantasies still sometimes involve men. I've never had any very satisfactory sex with men. But now that I've found my sexuality . . . I think, just possibly, I could have good sex with men. (Klaich, page 112)

A member of PFLAG (Parents and Friends of Lesbians and Gays) who was the mother of a lesbian, comments on this difference between lesbians and gay men:

> She had never heard a gay man say, "I've decided to be gay." On the other hand, she stated, lesbians, particularly those active in lesbian organizations, often declared that they had reached a decision to go with their lesbian tendencies (Kahn, page 7).

If we say that a homosexual predisposition is more innately based with men, we are saying that it more likely to be felt as a drive than as a choice. That means that men are more likely to feel that they are not in conscious control of their sexual life. They are more likely to be dissatisfied with their sexual orientation, to feel "trapped" by homosexual compulsions, to seek reorientation therapy, or even even attempt suicide.

20] If a lesbian goes into reorientation therapy, she is likely to make a more complete change, than a male homosexual patient makes. In Spitzer's study of 143 men and 47 women who volunteered for a study of persons who had successfully undergone reorientation therapy, only 11 per cent of the men, but 37 per cent of the women, claimed that after therapy they never have lustful same-sex thoughts (Appendix 1).

21] Homosexual men are more conflicted about their sexual orientation than are lesbians, who can incorporate same-sex activity more easily into their lives.

> Women found initial [sexual] experiences much less traumatic than men, and they were less likely to allow a single experience or a few experiences to lead them to an exclusive homosexual identification. Women often felt that such activities were a natural extension of female affectionate behavior and did not have implications for their sexuality (Blumstein and Schwartz 1977, page 43).

> Males reported much more difficulty coping with homosexual behavior and developing a homosexual identification than women. . . . . Masculinity is a major element in men's sense of self-worth, and homosexuality, in the popular imagination, implies impaired masculinity (*ibid,*, page 40).

22] Gay men are more likely than lesbians to acknowledge suicidal feelings and to attempt suicide (Harry, 1982).

23] **Psychoanalytic workers are in greater agreement on the etiology of male homosexuality than on the origins of lesbianism.** Male homosexuality looks more patterned, more predictable, more understandable.

Summary

These 23 differences suggest that gay men and lesbians are two overlapping psychological groups rather than a single psychological group, and that they would more profitably be studied separately. It might be noted that most of the 23 comparisons favor the lesbians. Their behavior is closer to the norms of the heterosexual majority; their attitude toward sex is more moderate, more reasonable, and more spiritual. Perhaps the key difference is that lesbians are more likely to have arrived at their sexual orientation by deliberate choice. That fact would put their sexual activity more firmly under ego control. Gay men, by comparison, are more likely to sense that they are being driven by a dark and less manageable impulse. What are the wellsprings of this impulse? That is the question that guides this study.

NOTES TO CHAPTER 4

1. A 1990 article in *The New York Times* reported that women are becoming leaders of gay organizations that have historically been run by men. (Dec. 30, 1990, I 12:1.)

2. An outstanding (and troubling) instance in which clinically important gender differences are ignored, and "les-gays" are conceptualized as a single clinical group is Ryan and Futterman's 1998 Columbia University Press publication, *Lesbian and Gay Youth; Care and Counseling.*

3. Bailey *et al.* did not set forth to demonstrate attitude differences between gay men and lesbians, but rather to show that gays (male and female) resemble straights of their own sex, in "evolutionarily related" attitudes toward sex. Their reported findings, however, made it possible to compare gay men and lesbians, and the six attitudes reported here were found to be significant at the .01 level of confidence.

4. People who live in large cities or campus towns where gays congregate, have a hard time accepting low estimates of homosexuality in the general population. A survey cited by LeVay (1996, page 63) indicated that gay men formed nearly 5 per cent of London's male population, but only one-half of one per cent of the population of Wales or Scotland. LeVay goes on to report that in the "gay ghetto" of West Hollywood, "self-identified gays and lesbians form about 30 percent of the population, while rural and small-town America is over 99 percent 'gay-free.'"

5 The Homosexual Tendency as a Species-Typical Trait

One of the most widely-quoted paragraphs of The Kinsey Report (page 369) goes as follows:

> Males do not represent two discrete populations, heterosexual and homosexual. The world is not divided into sheep and goats. Not all things are black nor all things white. It is a fundamental of taxonomy that nature rarely deals with discrete categories. Only the human mind invents categories and tries to force facts into separated pigeonholes. *The living world is a continuum* in each and every one of its aspects. The sooner we learn this concerning human behavior the sooner we shall reach a sound understanding of the realities of sex. *(italics added.)*

One can assert that some sort of "homosexual activity" exists virtually throughout the male population if by "homosexual activity" we include dreams, momentary feelings, idle thoughts and fantasies, as well as the performance of homosexual acts. In that sense, tendencies toward homosexual activity is a species-typical trait. In 1905, Freud wrote (pages 145-146 fn.): "*[A]ll human beings are capable of making a homosexual object-choice* and have in fact made one in their unconscious. Indeed, libidinal attachments . . . range equally over male and female objects. . . ." (Italics added.) Only because of social restrictions, Freud adds, is this tendency not more readily visible. In his 1915 essay on Leonardo da Vinci (page 81), Freud conjectures that everyone is unconsciously capable of "making a homosexual object-choice . . . or else protects himself against it by vigorous counter-attitudes."[1]

Fifteen years earlier, in his 1890 *Principles of Psychology* (vol. 2, page 39), William James had already described homosexuality as "a kind of sexual appetite of which very likely most men possess the germinal possibility." In 1935, psychiatrist Karl A. Menninger noted that "homosexuality is never silent, it always expresses itself in everybody's personality in some way or other. . . ."

For decades before Kinsey issued his 1948 Report, scientific studies were placing homosexual feelings and experience in the context of everyday life. For example, in 1929, *A Research in Marriage* was published, based on detailed interviews with 100 married couples under 40. The investigator was Gilbert Hamilton, a psychiatrist, and his respondents were educated residents of New York City. Hamilton's questions covered childhood and adult sex: foreplay, intercourse, orgasm, oral sex, anal sex, masturbation, homosexuality—all sorts of sexual topics. To standardize the interview, and permit the use of questions not ordinarily asked in person, all questions were presented on printed cards.

57

To some respondents, some of Dr. Hamilton's questions were rather upsetting. Hamilton noted (page 18) that questions concerning homosexuality "appeared to be more upsetting to the men than to the women."

Close to half the men (46 out of 100) recalled "sex organ stimulation in play with other boys (page 500). Typically, for about one-third of these men, homosexual play consisted of mutual masturbation. Lesser numbers reported rubbing (13), anal (12) or oral sex (12) (page 492). Seventeen indicated that they had had homosexual experiences (typically, mutual masturbation) after the age of 18 (page 496). (In a 1983 article, Chilman likewise observed that occasional homosexual experiences are fairly common, especially in early adolescence.)

One out of seven male respondents (14 percent) acknowledged that they were sometimes "tormented by a tendency to construct imaginations of yourself in bed . . . [with another male] with whom, in your imagination, you were doing things to produce sexual satisfaction. . . . (page 494). One out of ten recalled a time when they felt "ashamed to show . . . fondness for a particular boy friend . . . lest people suspect you of having unnatural (sexual) feelings for him, or of engaging in unnatural practices with him. . . ." (pages 490-491). One out of ten acknowledged that homosexual imaginings still come to them either in waking (7 percent) or when asleep (3 percent) (page 495).

Dr. Hamilton (page 498) presented a card to all his male respondents that asked, "If you could throw aside all considerations of conscience, decency, fear of public opinion, and an underlying desire to be normal, do you believe that any other [male] would appeal to you sexually?" Seventy-five percent answered no, three percent answered yes. The remaining one-fifth answered yes with qualifications such as "If there were no women in the world," or "Possibly in the case of a girl-like boy."

In 1938 psychologist Lewis Terman published a study, *Psychological Factors in Marital Happiness*. He asked each respondent 75 questions covering all sorts of marital satisfactions and irritants, assigned a marital happiness score to each of his respondents, and correlated this score with their expressed homosexual tendencies.

Terman asked each respondent (page 341): "Have you ever felt sexually attracted to a person of your own sex? (Check) very strongly, strongly, somewhat, not at all." Here are the results for 742 males (page 343):

	n=	mean happiness score
very strongly	4	32
strongly	4	74
somewhat	35	71
not at all	749	68

According to the above results, only that small minority (one-half of one percent) of married men who said they felt *very strongly* sexually attracted to other men scored low in marital happiness. Note that five percent of Terman's respondents claimed to have 'strong or somewhat' homosexual feelings, but attained an average marital happiness score a little *better* than those men who claimed to be "not at all" attracted to other men. Terman concluded (page 343): "[I]t appears that the presence of homosexual feeling is not so incompatible with happy marriage as is commonly supposed. . . ."

The presence of homosexual feeling in a general male population has also been measured experimentally. Full male arousal, penile erection, is easily felt or observed, but Czech sexologist K.W. Freund devised an instrument[2] for measuring *very slight* or only moderate male sexual arousal. With the "Freund gauge," the experimenter measured heterosexual men's responses to all sorts of pictures. Not surprisingly, Freund found that his experimental group responded most strongly to pictures of a naked woman, less strongly to pictures of a naked teenage girl, and even less strongly to a picture of a naked pre-pubescent girl.

Freund also tested his subjects on photographic close-ups of various body parts: (head, chest, pubic region, buttocks, and legs) of *both* males and females: adult, teenage, and preadolescent.[3] *Subjects showed some degree of erotic arousal to virtually all pictures of both male and female nudity.*[4]

But to gay author Bruce Bawer, homosexual feeling is like pregnancy. (There's no such thing as being a little pregnant.) For example, Bawer, spokesman for conservative gay men, argues that a young husband who appears to be experiencing a homosexual fantasy must have been "frightened into" playing the role of husband and father:

> Any reasonably attractive gay man knows what it is like to be
> stared at with anxious longing by a dubious young daddy push-
> ing a pram. What could that mean, but that the young daddy is a
> repressed homosexual who has been frightened into a life of
> "playing it straight" by a homophobic society?
>
> These homosexuals are living a lie, condemning themselves to
> remorse, frustration, and loneliness, and (in pathetic attempts to
> conform to legal and socially sanctioned notions of "the family")
> creating households that are perched on the edge of disaster
> (1993, page 107).

Perhaps there are other possibilities that Bawer does not recognize. Perhaps the carriage-pushing voyeur is more like the professor walking along the street, who stops to look at carpenters building a house. Yes, there is a tincture of envy in watching men who work outdoors with lumber and carpentry tools, men whose work creates something so tangible, so enduring, so useful as a place to call home; men whose work exercises muscle as well as mind. But to suggest that the professor would be happier as a carpenter misses the complexity of human nature, and the place of fantasy and commitment in the human mind.

It would be fair to say that the professor senses a kinship of feeling with the carpenter, though he would never trade places with him. And the same might be said for the young daddy's feeling about the attractive gay man. What is this feeling of kinship based on? Nothing less than membership in the same species that has been producing men with homosexual inclinations, great or small, for as far back as human records go.

Every male is born with some potential for homosexual fantasy or activity. This potential is a by-product of an evolutionary process that effected an overlap of the temperamental differences between male and female, a theory that is spelled out in detail in Chapter 27. This homosexual potential may be quite slight in the majority of men, and it would require special conditions, like a drinking party, to activate it. Kimmel (1996, page 126) quotes from a 1913 psychoanalytic journal the observation that behavior that might seem abnormal, morbid, or immoral when displayed by sober men "may be observed by anyone who has eyes to see, wherever men are drinking heavily . . . every drinking bout is tinged with homosexuality. The homosexual component-instincts, which education has taught us to repress and sublimate, reappear in no veiled form under the influence of alcohol." Similarly, a 1919 article in a psychology journal notes how alcohol leads men to express open affection toward one another:

> When drinking, men fall on each others necks and kiss one
> another, they feel that they are united by peculiarly intimate ties
> and this moves them to tears and intimate modes of address
> (*ibid,*).[5]

So much for conditions that bring out same-sex affection. What kinds of situations lead to homosexual *activity*? Now we are talking about separation from available women, as in military service, in a lumber camp, or by incarceration. A 1983 article by Aldridge describes homosexuality as a common practice among prisoners. More recently, an anonymous article was written by a prisoner (under the pseudonym of Thomas McGrath) who describes himself as a 25-year-old first-time felon and a devout Christian. He offers a first-hand report of how he has seen homosexual behavior emerge in a prison setting.

Thomas

[In a prison environment where inmates have enough freedom
to develop a friendship, what begins as a congeniality of spirits
may quite gradually metamorphose into a sexual relationship.
Friendship, says McGrath (page 83), brings] some stability to our
lives. We may talk into the wee hours of the night with this per-

son and always "hang out" together, like people do on the street. This person may help you out, either by giving you things (food, coffee, smokes) or by helping you deal with problems on the outside. . . . For me, it is my wife and children. You may not have any real way of returning the kindness that this person has shown you, so in your heart you feel obligated to do something. But what?

. . . You'll do things to try to make his life easier, more comfortable, to show your appreciation for the things he's done for you. Eventually, you may become closer, and you may actually develop a physical attraction toward him. It may be mutual, and then the ice will be broken and the subject of sex will be brought up. He may ask you to masturbate him or give oral sex, whatever. Or you may ask to do it. . . This is not the "punk and . . . daddy" situation; it is *companionship*. I have seen this a few times and respect it to the fullest extent. I've seen short-timers commit . . . felonies [inside the prison] because their companions [are serving a life sentence] and they wish to stay with them. I've also seen others leave and go out into the free world, but take care of their companions still inside (McGrath, pages 83-84).[6]

Money (1988, page 106) describes a very different situation that may lead heterosexual men to become homosexually aroused: when they are watching a gay video. For this reason, perhaps, many heterosexual men can enjoy watching a demonstration of lesbian sex, but feel ambivalent about watching a demonstration of male homosexuality.

Alex Comfort (page 209) describes another situation that may unexpectedly lead to homosexual behavior: When two men share a female sexual partner, the men may also engage in sexual play together. Psychoanalytically considered, if two men want to share a female partner, that in itself is a sign of homosexual attraction. But the men need not worry that they are becoming "queer," adds Comfort (*ibid,*): "There is not much risk of this."

P. Fisher (page 19) notes that "there are various circumstances under which homosexual behavior is tolerated [among straight adults] because it doesn't seem to mean much. . . . Most people are familiar with the 'Christ, was I drunk last night' syndrome. Standard procedure here is to become so drunk that one could not possibly be held responsible for one's acts, or even be expected to remember them. . . . College roommates, fraternity brothers, and old buddies on camping trips have been known to drink themselves into such a state that one thing leads to another and they find themselves in bed together."

Young men who are proud of their heterosexual conquests, mature men who have found their female lovers, migrants and immigrants who are separated from their customary sex partners, and married men whose wives are not available for one reason or another, may find a same-sex experience an acceptable substitute.

Public health workers include in their category of men at risk for HIV infection, not only gay men but also MSM: *men who have sex with other men*. Some men are easily tempted to extend their usual mode of sexual gratification, others can enjoy a same-sex partner only under unusual circumstances. This wide range of behavior shades into that male population that is usually, but not always, homosexual. Those men who *are* exclusively homosexual therefore occupy one end of a broad gradient of habits, rather than stand as a separate category.

Active or potential, homosexuality permeates mankind. It has been there at all times, and it continues to challenge the scientific observer not only to recognize its many direct modes of expression, but also to identify the many ways in which this homosexual impulse *indirectly* influences human behavior. (This latter topic is reserved for Chapter 6, "Coping Mechanisms, Good and Bad.")

Prehistoric images of homosexual activity are pictured and described in a 1973 article by Cottie Burland. American Indian cultures[7] dating from about 100 BC up to 900 AD have left carvings of "male figures in strange postures [suggesting] less normal kinds of sexual excitement. The most common of these shows a man crouching with open mouth, apparently expressing sexual excitement. His anal region is lifted as if in imitation of animal intercourse" (Burland, page 121). Accompanying the article is a color photograph of a stone pipe from the Cherokee Indians of Georgia, on which is carved a pair of figures engaged in fellatio (Plate 70, page 119). More familiar are ancient Greek vases decorated with clearly homoerotic themes, usually hidden away in museum storerooms, so as not to offend the sensibilities of museum goers.

When the ancient Hebrews entered the land of Canaan, they found that homosexual practices were woven into the temple rituals of the Canaanites, and there are indications that some Israelites also adopted these modes of worship.[8] To an agricultural people, erection and ejaculation probably symbolized growth, rain, and reproduction, and fit into their worship of fertility. The *mana* principle, discussed in Chapter 9, suggests that the adoration of gods and their human representatives, could lead to interpersonal touch and penetration. The Hebrews gave this pagan ritual the pejorative label of "temple prostitution" and made it taboo.

The Israelites probably sensed that if all things were the design of a Creator, human sexuality had a more significant function than use in a fertility ritual. This was not how the tribes of Israel could become a holy people, "as numerous as the stars of the heaven and the sands on the seashore" (Genesis 22:17). Laws of holiness forbade that a man "lie with a male as one lies with a woman" (Leviticus 18:22).

The Hippocratic Oath contains two implications about homosexual behavior: (1) that it is a common temptation, and (2) that it was inappropriate for a person in a position of power, to demand sexual favors:

[W]hatever houses I may visit, I will come for the benefit of the sick, remaining free of all intentional injustice, of all mischief

Figure 5.1. Zeus pursuing Ganymede (adapted from plate 200, Keuhls, page 225)

and in particular of sexual relations with both female and male persons, be they free or slave (Translated by Edelstein, page 3).

Neither the ancient Hebrews nor the Greeks had a word for homosexuality, which suggests that it was not considered an unusual phenomenon but rather an everyday possibility. The Bible does not say, "Homosexuals: Stop it!" The Bible addresses the *entire* tribe of Israel, saying: "Do not lie with a man as with a woman."

Mankind owes scientific medicine a debt of thanks not only for sparing humanity from the scourge of physical suffering, untimely death, and the bereavement of survivors, but for relieving mankind from the fear that personal afflictions and social misfortunes were punishments for violating God's laws. Disasters of all kinds evoked anxiety about one's own private life, and suspicion of one's neighbors' hidden vices.[9]

All over the world, at all times, a certain portion of boys are born who are decidedly unmasculine in their interests and talents (and sometimes in their looks and mannerisms). In various American Indian tribes distinguished for their fierce warriors and hunters, there were also the gentle berdaches, men who dressed like women and excelled at the womanly arts of weaving and pottery.[10]

In modern times in some parts of the Western world, men embrace each other, kiss, and may walk together holding hands. Anthropologist Kenneth E. Read (1966 page 19) describes the customary greeting among the Gahuku people of New Guinea: two men[11] may embrace each other with one arm while with the other hand they handle each other's genitals.

> [A] highly demonstrative, extroverted, and aggressive people . . .
> their customary greeting . . . was an unfailing source of snigger-
> ing amusement to Europeans; but even in villages, among people
> who saw one another every day, hands were continually reaching
> out to caress a thigh, [and] arms to encircle a waist. . . .

Playful, active, prankish boys who swim together, bathe together, sleep together and explore their world together, often explore each other's sexual capabilities. If same-sex play has not been part of a boy's experience, most boys do have homosexual dreams or fantasies. This is a "common experience," says Pomeroy (page 72), and need not be the cause of fear or guilt.

> [M]ost of these people will never take part in a homosexual act,
> and these fleeting thoughts will never interfere with their hetero-
> sexual lives unless they carry guilt and fear into them.

The prominent sexologist John Money has theorized that the same-sex play of childhood is a necessary step in sexual development; and that, paradoxical though it may sound, the same-sex play of childhood may *contribute* to the heterosexual skills of adulthood.[12] We have already noted that when Harry Harlow deprived infant monkeys of normal play experience during their first year of life, they could not perform the sexual acts normal for their species when they reached adulthood.

Heterosexuals have homosexual dreams, and homosexuals have heterosexual dreams. Hockenberrry and Lieber interviewed 51 homosexual males in various gay gathering places (e.g., bars, bookstores, gay churches) and reported (page 32) that *51 percent said they had both homosexual and heterosexual dreams*.

If homosexual fantasies drift in and out of a boy's waking and dream life, this can be quite disturbing if at the same time he is trying hard to attain a sense of his own masculinity. As Blumstein and Schwartz put it (1977 page 40), "Masculinity is a major element in men's sense of self-worth, and homosexuality, in the popular imagination, implies impaired masculinity." Psychoanalyst John Munder Ross (page 100) describes this basis for homosexual worry in the lives of adolescent boys:

> All men, in fact, have had doubts from time to time about

being "queer," particularly in their adolescence. In other males, all find the idealized and desirable embodiment of themselves. . . . The prospect of sex with a person of the same gender can also hold out the promise of crossing over the boundaries of gender—in a man's case of playing with the tabooed feminine aspects of his sensuality. *Homosexual wishes are natural, healthy components in all of us* (emphasis added).

Having such passing fantasies makes some boys and men worry that they are not really men; that they are homosexual. They reject the inevitable "bisexuality"[13] in their constitution—and by extension, in others. Often their anxiety is transformed into a defensive posture: a caricature of masculinity, and a hostile "homophobia."

Homosexual worry is not the exclusive experience of naive adolescents. A man who claimed that he was enjoying his married sex life was worried that his sexual attraction to another man meant he was in actuality homosexual:

I was married for four years when I started to have these fantasies about a guy I worked with. I would get these fantasies and I would have to masturbate...I began to think I was homosexual... even though I was still sleeping with my wife and enjoying it. But I felt guilty, and I was worried she would find out what I really was (Blumenstein and Schwartz, pages 39-40).

Fags and trade, wolves and punks

In pre-Kinsey Report days, married men, as well as lonely and sexually-deprived singles, allowed themselves to be fellated by "fags," effeminate boys and men who circulated through bars, cheap restaurants, and other places of public congregation, offering their sexual services. They sometimes wore make-up—rouge, powder, and lipstick—to present themselves as imaginary prostitutes. They referred to their clientele as their "trade."[14] Fags competed not only with female prostitutes, but with boy prostitutes, known as punks, who might offer anal sex as well as oral sex.[15] Men who sought punks were known as wolves. Hoboes were another population that often sought same-sex services. Many hoboes traveled in pairs: an older "jocker" or wolf, with his young punk or "lamb" (Chauncey, page 90), perhaps recruited from a city slum.[16]

Early in the twentieth century, New York and other big cities of the North were teeming with unattached men: immigrants from foreign shores, and migrants from the rural South and depressed farm areas throughout the country.[17] These men welcomed the sexual relief and sociability that fags offered. Customers felt that their macho image was preserved so long as they limited themselves to the role of inserter.

A married man who considered himself straight expressed the trade point of view thus (Blumstein and Schwartz 1977, page 39):

> I'm straight, but I need outlets when I'm away from home and times like that. And *it's easier* to get with men than women. So I go into the park, or at a rest station on the highway, and get a man to blow me.[18] I would never stay the night with one of them, or get to know them. It's just a release. It's not like sex with my wife. It's just a way to get what you need without making it a big deal. And it feels less like cheating.

In 1972, William Aaron (page 37) commented: "[I]f you would accuse one of [the men who have sex with fags] of being gay he would likely punch you in the nose. But they rub shoulders with the lavender set, drifting in and out of the shadowy world of anonymous, impersonal sex, and then retreating to the safety of home and family." Typically, they explain that their wife does not satisfy them enough sexually,[19] and that they therefore look for sexual satisfaction outside of marriage. Accommodating fags is simpler (and cheaper) than looking for prostitutes, or having extramarital affairs with women.

For many years, this was an accepted social convention: a man's masculinity was simply not questioned if he played the role of "trade" so long as he was always the inserter. This distinction, which continues to be respected in various parts of the present-day world, was challenged by Alfred Kinsey,[20] whose famous 1948 *Report* forever tainted customers of fags with the stigma of homosexuality.

Humphreys's Tearoom Trade. In his 1970 survey of *Impersonal Sex in Public Places*, the homosexual scene shifts from bars and restaurants to public places like city parks and public toilets, euphemistically called tearooms.[21] The actors change from fags and unattached immigrants, to "queers" and a more mixed clientele that included youths who were willing to be fellated by older men, and a substantial portion of married men who might explain either that their wives no longer satisfied them, or simply that they "get a kick" out of being fellated.

> [P. Fisher (page 56) observed that] most of the apparently heterosexual individuals who frequent the tea rooms are perfectly ordinary individuals, more often than not married with families. . . . If heterosexual sex were as easily and cheaply available, they would much prefer to find their sexual outlet with women. [Some frequent tearooms because they cannot afford a female prostitute]
>
> [A male respondent of Blumstein and Schwartz expressed the

trade point of view thus (1977, page 43)]: There are four kind of men: men who screw women, men who screw women and men, men who screw men, and then there are queers [i.e., the ones who get screwed].

Bisexual hippies. During the hippie days of the 1960s, in some circles of young people, it was fashionable to defy middle-class conventions of all sorts. This "anything goes" attitude is expressed in the following Blumstein and Schwartz quotation (1977, page 38): "I thought as this guy climbed into my bed. 'What the hell? Why shouldn't I? There's no reason why I should cut off my nose to spite my face. It's going to be fun; it's been fun before, and why can't I have the best of both worlds?' Bisexuality seemed like me."

Robert E. Gould, a New York psychoanalyst who had a close look at these young people, was amazed at how easily they shifted back and forth, from homosexual to heterosexual activity. On the basis of clinical interviews, he concluded that many bisexually active hippies seemed quite "normal and well adjusted" (Gould, page 48). He concluded, in fact, (pages 48-49) that in a free[22] society, most humans "would be functioning bisexuals:"

> I have come to believe that if there were no social restrictions on sexual object choice, most humans would be functioning bisexuals. Accident, personal experiences might predispose an individual to lean more in one direction than another without pathology or disorder being involved. Indeed, if all the taboos were lifted, pathology might very well consist of exclusive interest in one sex, regardless of which sex he chooses.

The above quotation introduces the term "functioning bisexual," which to Gould means a person whose sex life includes a significant amount of both homosexual and heterosexual activity. That is how we will use the term, and that is the definition that guided the 1977 study by Blumstein and Schwartz, who between 1973 and 1975 interviewed about 78 men (and an equal number of women) who claimed to have had "a history of more than incidental sexual experience with both men and women" (page 32). Very few of their respondents indicated an equal attraction to either men or women, but claimed "some ability . . . to eroticize both genders under some circumstances" (page 32).

"Bisexual" has also been used in a variety of other ways: (a) that a man is *capable* of either homosexual or heterosexual activity; from our theoretical point of view, that use is meaningless since it simply says that a man is a man; (b) that a man *doesn't care* about the sex of his partner; what Masters and Johnson (1979) called "opportunistic ambisexuals." At this cynical extreme are those sociopaths who "use people for their own ends, then cast them loose" (Socarides 1995, page 18); unfeeling brutes who are "willing to just stick it into anything" (Karlen page

282, quoting Paul Gebhardt); or (c) that a man believes he has reached a level of sophistication that enables him to transcend the limitations of social convention. These men call themselves bisexual, ("I'm AC/DC, I swing both ways") because they want to say that they are different from ordinary homosexuals, and really better than them. It is mainly for this reason that many gay men don't like the term bisexual.[23]

Freudian thought asserts that the homosexual potential is a species-typical trait, and holds that ordinarily a man outgrows it in favor of a heterosexual orientation. In 1905 Freud said, "*I have never carried through any psychoanalysis of a man or a woman without discovering a very significant homosexual tendency.*"[24]

In his widely-reprinted "Gay Manifesto," Carl Wittman (page 321) argued that homosexuality was *only a step* toward becoming "a complete person"; that a truly *complete* person would be sexually responsive both to men and to women:

> Bisexuality is good; it is the capacity to love people of either sex. The reason so few of us are bisexual is because society made such a big stink about homosexuality that we got forced into seeing ourselves as either straight or non-straight. . . . Gays will begin to turn on to women when 1) it's something that we do because we want to, and not because we should, and 2) when women's liberation changes the nature of heterosexual relationships.
>
> We continue to call ourselves homosexual, not bisexual, even if we do make it with the opposite sex also, because saying, "Oh, I'm Bi" is a cop-out for a gay. We get told it's OK to sleep with guys as long as we sleep with women too, and that's still putting homosexuality down. We'll be gay until everyone has forgotten that it's an issue. Then we'll begin to be complete.

America's first openly homosexual psychoanalyst, Richard Isay, declared (1989) that on the basis of his clinical experience, most men who can *enjoy* heterosexual relations (not merely can perform them) eventually get married and deliberately renounce their homosexual tendencies for the sake of enjoying an uncomplicated life in the straight world. John Money (1988, page 183) agrees that a genuine bisexual, by which he means a man who "gets a good deal of gratification" from straight sex, "usually chooses to suppress his homosexual impulses, and *is able to do so comfortably*" (emphasis added).

There is wide disagreement among the "experts" as to how widespread bisexual practice is. Reinisch (page 143) estimates that 10 to 15 percent of the U.S. population actually has sex with both men and women over a period of years. At the other extreme, Laumann *et al.* give survey figures of *less than 1 percent* of men and women who report they were actively bisexual (pages 293-294 fn.). Perhaps the figure is so low because an active bisexual sometimes finds that he must have two sets of friends, and lives in fear of exposure for "living a double life," and for "cheating on his wife" (Klein, pages 129-130).

Most men may have a *potential* for either homosexual or heterosexual activity, but in practice settle down to one or the other. Why? Religious indoctrination or social pressure move many to the heterosexual side. Might some accident of experience lead one to actualize his homosexual potential?[25] A few men are unhappy unless they can have sexual relations with *both* men and women; "the sexual act seems to be the only way they can feel they can make emotional contact with another person" (Hatterer 1965, page 140).

John Money (1988, page 108) asserts that the minority of men who are practicing bisexuals usually rely on the fantasy that their partner is of their preferred sex. Only a few men, he asserts (1988, page 298), "are indifferent to the gender of their sexual partner and therefore will . . . prefer sex with a good-looking woman to sex with a homely man but sex with a good-looking man to sex with a homely woman."

In the book *House and Home* by Gunderson and Morris, the reader is introduced to Rob Morris, who *was living with a woman and intended to marry her and raise a family*, when he met Steve Gunderson, who became his gay lover. Morris (Gunderson and Morris, page 42) asserts that his experience is "not unusual for many young gay men." He had enjoyed both gay and straight sex, knew that life would be easier if he conformed to the straight majority, and longed to have a family. But "deep inside," he knew that his gay nature was stronger:

Rob

[O]n the one hand, I had been comfortable with my homosexuality for a long time—or, at least, I thought I had. On the other hand, I had enjoyed successful sexual relationships with both a man and a woman, and had figured that when I did find my way to a compatible long-term relationship, it might be with a person of either sex. I always felt that this would just happen—that I would meet somebody, male or female, who would determine for me which way my life would go. But I always suspected that it would be a man. Whether it was one or the other didn't trouble me as much as the crafting of the relationship itself.
Deep inside, I knew that I was rationalizing. I was gay and trying to run away from this fact, and I knew I wouldn't be able to fully acknowledge my sexuality until I actually fell in love with another man. Deep down, I knew that in part I wanted to marry Jamie [the woman he had been living with] because I sought to avoid all the conflicts that you take on when you acknowledge

your homosexuality, to yourself and to others. I also wanted to
do it because I longed to have a family.

[I] knew that [for me, marriage would be like it is for most married gay men] . . . I would have a family and then, whenever my
wife went out of town, I would enjoy a fling with a man before
hurrying back to "normal" life. In my heart I knew that what we
had with each other was a great friendship, but not the stuff that
long-term soul mates were made of.

The thin line between straight and gay is also illustrated by a story told by
Jack Hart (page 31), that a prominent male leader of the gay activist movement
of the 1980s "spent most of the [decade] in a secretive relationship with a
woman—a fact which to this day is known only to a small circle of his friends."

The contemporary novelist, John Updike, wrote a short story, "The Rumor,"
around the theme of how fragile is the barrier between straight and gay sensibility. In Updike's story, Frank is an art dealer, married and a father, who nonethe-
less becomes the object of a mischievous rumor that he has a secret boy lover.
His wife wonders whether the rumor might be true, despite her personal experience that theirs is a solid and satisfying marriage. Frank himself also begins to
wonder:

Frank

The rumor had no factual basis. But might there be, Frank asked
himself, some truth to it after all? Not circumstantial truth, but
some higher, inner truth? As a young man, slight of build, with
artistic interests, had he not been fearful of being mistaken for a
homosexual? Had he not responded to homosexual overtures as
they arose, in bars and locker rooms, with a disproportionate terror and repugnance? Had not his early marriage, and then, ten
years later, his flurry of adulterous womanizing, been an escape
of sorts, into safe, socially approved terrain? When he fantasized,
or saw a pornographic movie, was not the male organ the hero of
the occasion for him, at the center of every scene? Were not
those slavish, lapping, sucking starlets his robotlike delegates,
with glazed eyes and undisturbed coiffures venturing where he
did not dare? Did he not, perhaps, envy women their privilege of
worshipping the phallus? And did not he, when the doctor gave
him his annual prostate exam with a greased finger, have to fight
getting an erection, right there in a passive curled position on the
examining table? (Updike, page 206)

Frank's recollections qualify him as a "worrier," described in Chapter 25 as the
last of over 30 varieties of homosexuals.

The power of environmental influences to activate a man's homosexual potential validates the description of homosexuality as a species-typical trait. Perhaps the situation that most typically elicits homosexual behavior is military service, which both puts large groups of men in close bodily contact, separates them from their usual heterosexual partners, and makes them more receptive to same-sex contact. The "homosexual" behavior of sexually isolated men is described in Chapter 24.

Mary Ann Humphrey's respondents offer the following recollections of gay men's sexual encounters with their straight buddies:

> A Navy veteran, gay, recalls (Humphrey, page 22) his sexual activity with married sailors: "I would always look for mature [married] men . . . [who] would make a play for you and then keep their mouth shut. . . . I knew the safe bets were the married guys who were apparently used to something.

> "[Y]ou'd hardly believe it, but one of the techniques, which I outrageously developed, was merely crawling in [bed] with somebody and engaging them in sex and leaving them as if nothing had ever happened. And so long as you never discussed it, it never happened. . . I'm not talking about forcing anybody. . . . [I]t was constant."

> A veteran recalls (Humphrey, page 64) sex between gay and straight men in the Army: "[N]obody did anything they didn't want to do—trust me. . . . There were . . . straights who would have sex with somebody gay, for convenience . . . that happens."

> An Army veteran, gay, recalls (Humphrey, page 68): "[M]y first . . . conquest . . . was with a marine, who was supposedly straight. . . . [T]hey have a saying in the Marine Corps . . . 'Fuck me, suck me, but don't kiss me, I'm straight.' That's their attitude. . . . [T]here weren't any women around, what was a boy to do?"

> Another Humphrey respondent recalls (page 68): "There were many guys, marines, who used the old story of 'I was so drunk last night, I don't remember what I was doing' . . . [That usually meant] let's not talk about it."

> In Vietnam, recalls another Humphrey respondent (page 85):] "[E]verybody drank a lot. . . I didn't notice much concern about whether one was gay or not. . . . Sex in general was pretty free. In fact, I don't think I ever met a marine I didn't fuck. . . ."

> One of Humphrey's respondents (page 94) observed that in Army life, straight men were more openly sexual—in their talk and

their activities—than gays: "[E]very guy that I went to bed with in the military was straight. [He goes on to recall (page 96):] I had sex, without exaggeration, with 99 percent of the guys in my barracks. They would come to the room as long as nobody knew about it. I got the whole gamut of usual excuses: I was so drunk, I didn't know what happened last night, you must have taken advantage of me . . . every excuse you could imagine."

Another Humphrey respondent recalls (page 251): ""I never approached anybody for sex. It just simply wasn't necessary. . . . All these people would just start traipsing to my door. You know, knocking at my door at all hours of the night. I also figured, basically, if I never asked anyone, they couldn't say I asked them. They were certainly not going to tell my commanding officer they asked me."

Another situation that elicits homosexual behavior is the boarding school that is sex-segregated. A well-funded British survey (Wellings *et al.*) involving nearly eight years' work and over 18,000 respondents, yields some interesting reports from adults who as children attended sex-segregated boarding school. They are *three times more likely* (15 per cent) to report having experienced same-sex genital contact during their school years, compared with adults who had not attended sex-segregated boarding schools (5 per cent). Comparing the two groups, however, there was *no significant difference* (2 per cent to 1.3 per cent) in the incidence of adult homosexuality. The investigators conclusions contain three statements: (1) "[H]omosexual experience is often a relatively isolated or passing event" (page 203). (2) "Homosexual experience occurring for the first time in the early teens is unlikely to lead on to more consistent homosexual behavior" (page 204). (3) "Schooling has an important influence on whether someone has ever had a homosexual partner but has no significant impact on homosexual partnerships in the last five years" (page 209).

John Paulk recalls that during the time he worked as a call boy, some of his clients came from the straight world; either they were "deeply closeted" gay men, or they were straight men who, far from home, yielded to a curiosity about what gay sex was really like.

Often my clients were married men, deep in the closet, away from home on business, and using the opportunity to express a gayness only some professional like me might ever know about. One was a noted political figure. . . . He had me for four hours in the most palatial mansion I'd ever seen, swimming in spotlit Grecian fountains with multicolored cherubs (Paulk, page 60).

My best experiences [as an employee of an escort service] were

with men who'd never had sex with another man. . . . In my
eyes, these were straight men. And there was nothing better than
emasculating a straight man. Somehow it put us on the same
footing and made me feel like I was breaking down part of the
barrier I'd felt between myself and the straight world since childhood. (Paulk, page 61)

Carl Jung intuited the presence of an unconscious female element in every
male psyche, and labeled this unconscious process the *anima*.[26] To a Jungian, the
anima is a man's "unconscious feminine personality," and counterbalances his
logical, masculine persona with feminine intimacy,[27] sensitivity, creativity, and
spirituality. The goal for a man's psychic development, from a Jungian point of
view, is not to become 100 per cent masculine, but to gain access to the ordinarily unconscious feminine side of his personality by learning to meditate with his
feminine self as well as with his masculine self.[28]

The anima is . . . responsible for the fact that man is able to find
the right marriage partner. Another function is at least equally
important: Whenever a man's logical mind is incapable of dis-
cerning facts that are hidden in his unconscious, the anima helps
him to dig them out. Even more vital is the role that the anima
plays in putting a man's mind in tune with the right inner values
and thereby opening the way into more profound inner depths.
(Jung, page 181)

[The anima plays a positive function] when a man takes seriously the feelings, mood, expectations, and fantasies sent by his
[female unconscious] and when he fixes them in some form—for
example, in writing, painting, sculpture, musical compositon, or
dancing. (Jung, page 186)

Jung's conception of the anima was drawn from feminine themes and figures
in the mythology, religions, and literature of the world, as well as from his clinical and personal experience. His intuitions anticipated the laboratory findings of
modern embryology that every human organism begins life as a proto-female. If
an organism is genetically male (has an XY pair of chromosomes), during ordinary prenatal development the sex organs *and the brain* are masculinized, and to
the extent that the brain is less than fully masculinized, for whatever reason, the
individual may be said to have a low-masculined brain. Chapter 7 deals in detail
with the topic of brain masculinization, and in Chapter 9 we offer a theory of how
brain low-masculinization leads to feelings of gender deficit and homosexual
attraction.

How did homosexuality become a species-typical trait—a behavior that
occupies the occasional fantasy or dream life of some men, that describes the

periodic behavior of other men, and that describes the well-established sexual orientation of other men? Chapter 27 offers a theory that man's homosexual potential is a by-product of human evolution.

NOTES TO CHAPTER 5

1. Summarizing Freud's views on homosexuality, Jones (vol. 2. page 281) recalls "an axiom . . . about which [Freud] could never be shaken: namely, the natural bisexuality of not only all human beings, but of all living creatures."

2. Named a plethysmograph, "the Freund Gauge" consists of a tube large enough to contain a penile erection in an airtight chamber. The tube is connected to an apparatus that measures the amount of air forced out of the tube as the subject becomes sexually aroused and his penis, inserted in the tube, grows in volume, even slightly.

3. Throughout the experiment, photographs of human figures, and close-ups of body parts, were interspersed with sexually-neutral photographs: landscapes. This was to insure that subjects were not responding to "the Freund gauge" itself, or to erotic imaginings that had nothing to do with the photographs.

4. The only exception to the subjects' generalized arousability was that they were not aroused by close-ups of the buttocks of teenage males.

5. Kimmel gives as sources of these quotations the following two articles:
Otto Juliusberger, "Psychology and Alcoholism," *Psychoanalytic Review* 1, 1913, page 469; and L. Pierce Clark, "A Psychological Study of Some Alcoholics," *Psychoanalytic Review* 6, 1919, pages 270-271,

6. McGrath makes it clear that he is describing what he has observed, not what he has experienced personally. He confesses (page 84): "I don't have the courage to bring this type of companionship to blossom. I'm too much of a coward. . . . [Writing as a bisexual Christian, he adds:] I'm just not into the sex thing for itself. . . I'm this way with both women and men."

7. Crouched figures are of the Adena and Hopewell cultures located in what are now Ohio and the middle Mississippi. Burland wonders (page 121) whether "the man is a shaman in a characteristically deviationist situation" or "whether this represents a socially acceptable form of erotic enjoyment."

It is reported that images of homosexual intercourse are contained in a 1972 publication (pages 82-84), *Phallos: A Symbol and its History in the Male World*, by Thorkil Vanggaard.

Homosexual themes in ancient Greek art are reproduced in Kenneth Dover's

Greek Homosexuality, pictorial section between pages 118 and 119. A more extensive collection of such illustrations are contained in the more recent book by Keuhls.

8. No Israelite woman shall be a cult prostitute, nor shall any Israelite man be a cult prostitute. Deuteronomy 23:18.

9. In a June 8, 1998 broadcast, evangelist Pat Robertson protested the use of Disney World for a weekend of Gay Days, advising: "I would warn Orlando that you're right in the way of some serious hurricanes, and I don't think I'd be waving those flags in God's face if I were you." With these words, this preacher endorsed and perpetuated in our times the ancient fear that natural disaster is a punishment for sin.

Similarly, Reverend Billy Graham once preached, "If God doesn't destroy The United States, Sodom and Gomorrah deserve an apology."

10. A description of the berdaches, and similar groups in other societies of the world, is taken up in Chapter 10.

11. The same greeting, genital-handling, was customary for male-female encounters (and possibly for female-female encounters).

12. Money writes (1988, page 108) that men who "coerce themselves into heterosexuality" before they have had any homosexual experimentation, may lose interest in marital sex and become homosexually active after divorce or widowhood.

13. Here Ross means by "bisexuality" the *potential* for responding sexually to either a man or a woman. Were we to rewrite Dr. Ross's words, we would say: "Heterosexual men reject the inevitable homosexual aspect of their constitution."

This author will limit his use of the term "bisexual" to describe a person who calls himself (identifies himself as) a bisexual, by which he means that it is customary for him to have sex with both men and women. So defined, bisexual persons are described in Chapters 14 and 15.

14. "Trade" is an old-fashioned word meaning "customers," as in "carriage trade" and "tourist trade."

15. In 1931, a New York City investigator was told by a 16-year old punk, the price of his services: a room in a lodging house in Chatham Square would cost $1. The punk charged 50 cents for oral sex and 75 cents for anal sex (Chauncey, page 90).

16. Appendix A (pages 359-367) of Ellis's *Studies in the Psychology of Sex*, is entitled: "Homosexuality Among Tramps," and describes the recruitment of punks in city slums.

17. A 1928 *New York Times* article described New York as a bachelor's Mecca. The city had 900,000 unmarried men: working-class immigrants, and American-born rural youths making barely enough to rent a furnished room. (Chauncey, page 120)

18. Gay men often employ euphemisms to describe their sexual activities: "do me, go down on me, blow me," as if to avoid the embarrassing reality of penis sucking. One patient recalled that his partner refered to a homosexual act as "an aesthetic experience" (author's clinical notes). Nimmons (page 98) insists that gay sex talk is "charmingly earthy" and free of euphemisms that straights resort to.

19. Sex therapist Charles Silverstein (pages 181-182) writes that for many men, oral sex offers more prolonged stimulation than heterosexual intercourse. According to Silverstein, when they attempt heterosexual intercourse many men chronically suffer from premature ejaculation, probably because of anxiety over impregnating their partner, or because of ambivalent feelings about their partner. But the problem may disappear when he receives oral sex. No doubt this drove many a married man to fags, who routinely did for him what his wife would not do. [Writes Chauncey (page 61): many women considered oral sex dirty or per-verted.]

20. Kinsey argued (page 623) that "by any strict definition," a man who reaches orgasm by physical contact with another male, has engaged in homosexual activity "irrespective of the . . . techniques employed . . . ." As for the claim that the inserter is not really homosexual, Kinsey comments (page 616): "It is amazing to observe how many psychologists and psychiatrists have accepted this sort of propaganda. . . ."

Chauncey (page 22) quotes a homosexual bartender who observed in 1983 that for some years he and his friends had found it "a lot harder to find straight guys to do it with." Was this an influence of Kinsey's redefinition of homosexuality, or had the gay lib movement scared off potential trade from mingling with gay men? Whatever the reason, by 1983 the lines were now more sharply drawn between straight and gay men, writes Chauncey, "so sharply and publicly that men were no longer able to participate in a homosexual encounter without sus-pecting it meant (to the outside world, and to themselves) that they were gay."

21. Humphreys writes that "tea" is a British euphemism for urine, which would account for why a men's room would be called a tearoom. Another speculation is that "tearoom" evolved from T-room, which was short for "toilet room."

22. Gould's comment is quoted as the reflection of a psychoanalyst on the mental health of this group of hippies, rather than as a recommendation for the restructuring of society.

23. Many homosexuals do in fact go through a period in which they attempt to deny or suppress their homosexual impulses, and attempt through marriage or heterosexual affairs to "get rid of homosexual feelings." To these gay men, bisexual activity reminds them of that period of struggle and confusion. (Weinberg *et al.*, pages 143-144)

24. This quotation is taken from Havelock Ellis' *Sexual Inversion*, vol. 1 of his *Studies in the Psychology of Sex*, 3rd rev ed (New York, 1915), page 81. In his essay on Leonardo da Vinci (page 99 fn.), Freud writes, "[E]veryone, even the most normal person is capable of making a homosexual object-choice, and has done so at some time in his life, and either still adheres to it in his unconscious or else protects himself against it by vigorous counter-attitudes."

25. For example, a young man may find himself in a work setting where all his co-workers are gay. A young man gets a job as a theater usher, or is attracted to ballet dancing and finds that all of his co-workers are gay. Broke and homeless, an art student is invited to share the comfortable apartment of his art patron who also happens to be gay.

26. Jung also believed that every female psyche harbored an unconscious male element, the animus, which was the source of a woman's logical, rational, aggressive tendencies.

27. Writes Pedersen (page 26), "If a man cannot gain access to the unconscious, he may remain stuck at the persona level and never move beyond a superficial orientation to life."

Pedersen (page 146) tells of an older patient's recollection of "a three-day golf retreat together [with a group of men from work] and, at the end of the trip, he was amazed to realize that nothing of any emotional or personal nature had been discussed among them. By contrast, one can easily imagine that a group of women on a similar outing for three days would end up knowing each other's life history!"

Another Pedersen clinical observation (page 188) on intimacy as a feminine trait: "A patient once told me that he had finally yielded to his wife's request for some time together. When I asked him how that was for him, he said he had suggested that they watch TV or go to a movie, but she hadn't wanted to do that, in fact she turned down all of his suggestions and finally just stayed home and talked. Although she really enjoyed that, he couldn't understand how 'doing nothing' could be so important to her."

Gaining access to his anima, a man discovers not only his positive feminine resources—sensitivity, creativity, etc.—but also his *negative* feminine side: his tendencies to depression, irritability and malevolence. (Jung, page 178).

Writes Pedersen (page 102): "It is one of man's greatest challenges to achieve union or integration and, thereby, greater consciousness. As inner attributes, masculinity and femininity are dynamic complements which *actively* seek each other for balance and integration. . . ."

28. When he was emotionally troubled, Jung believed that his persona and anima were at war. At such times, writes Jung, "for decades I always turned to the anima . . . [and asked:] 'Now, what are you up to? What do you see? I should like to know" (Jung, page 187).

6   Coping Mechanisms, Good and Bad

In *Tuesdays with Morrie*, Author Mitch Albom (pages 39-40) recalls from his college days, a conversation with his professor and mentor, Morrie:

> *One afternoon, I am complaining about the confusion of my age, what is expected of me versus what I want for myself*
> *"Have I told you about the tension of opposites?" he says.*
> *The tension of opposites?*
> *"Life is a series of pulls back and forth. You want to do one thing, but you are bound to do something else. Something hurts you, yet you know it shouldn't. You take certain things for granted, even when you know you should never take anything for granted.*
> *"A tension of opposites, like a pull on a rubber band. And most of us live somewhere in the middle."*
> *Sounds like a wrestling match, I say.*
> *"A wrestling match," he laughs. "Yes, you could describe life that way."*
> *Which side wins?*[1]

If a homosexual potential is so widely distributed in the general population, wouldn't it be healthier if everyone were free to express this impulse more freely? That's a question more easily posed than answered. Let us suppose that every adult male was exclusively heterosexual. Would a heterosexual society encourage everyone to express the full range of his heterosexual wishes? Of course not!

Most men limit their heterosexual activity to a very small fraction of the full range that even their conscious fantasy permits them to imagine. An individual of enormous social privilege—a nobleman, a rock star, a famous athlete, a billionaire business tycoon—has the privilege of acting out a wide range of sexual fantasies. But an ordinary citizen learns to play by the rules and be a good neighbor. Being a good neighbor means you don't take your neighbor's lawnmower, or his wife, or his daughter, or his son, either. Not ordinarily; not unless some special circumstances allow it.

For a person whose heterosexual needs are reasonably well satisfied, partial or indirect gratification of his homosexual impulses may be all he needs. But for a man who has no social outlet for any of his sexual impulses (a celibate priest, for example), his homosexual impulses may get out of control and may lead to behavior that he himself regards as sinful, and requires confession. The church's dictum, "All men are sinners,"[2] suggests, among many other things, that the homosexual potential is species-typical.

Periodic gratification, or sin-and-repentance, is a workable coping mechanism for some. For others, a stern conscience forbids a truce between one's heterosexual and homosexual impulses. Instead, the homophobe is locked in a chronic struggle between his "good" heterosexual feelings and his "evil" homosexual impulses. He combats his "evil" impulses by externalizing them and attributing them to others.

In some men and boys, fears that they are homosexual trouble their conscious mind, and acute discomfort may lead them to seek professional help. They are reassured that they are *not* homosexual, and may be wrongly diagnosed as cases of "homosexual panic."[3] (For a more detailed discussion of this phenomenon, see the section on "worriers" at the end of Chapter 25.)

In the mental life of most men, however, homosexual themes occur in dreams, in passing fantasies, and in the unconscious struggles that surface in the course of psychoanalysis. Typically, these homosexual dreams and fantasies symbolize struggles over dominance and submission, according to a panel of psychoanalysts who discussed "Homosexual Fantasies in Heterosexuals" in a 1962 issue of the *Journal of the American Medical Association.*

If ordinarily most men express only a portion of their sexual impulses, this means that the remainder must somehow be suppressed. Back in 1976, Wilson and Lawson reported an experiment that disinhibited a portion of the homosexual impulses of a group of heterosexual men. The experimenters demonstrated that heterosexual men can be sexually aroused by watching homosexual movies *if they were given to believe* that they have just had an alcoholic drink. (*Being told* that the drink they were given before watching the movies was alcoholic, was actually a *more* effective disinhibitor than allowing them to unknowingly consume a drink that was genuinely alcoholic.)[4]

How do men manage to ordinarily put into action a mere fraction of their sexual impulses, for the sake of abiding by the rules of society? Civilization exists because man is a social animal; most men want to conform. Civilization is also possible because humans have developed all sorts of coping strategies for deflecting or transforming unwanted behaviors; mechanisms of *defense*, Freud called them. Some work better than others; some create problems bigger than the problems them were intended to solve. Here we will attempt to touch on some of the many ways that ordinary men cope with their homosexual impulses.

Benign coping mechanisms

Male companionship permits the partial expression of all sorts of impulses: competitive, narcissistic, and sexual. At informal social gatherings, especially when singing, men allow themselves to embrace each other. Altschuler makes the following observation on the Cayapans, who live in the Pacific lowlands of Colombia (and adjacent lands): On fiesta nights, when alcohol flows freely and couples are dancing to the music of the drum and marimba, "one may see, in various houses, boys and young men on the floor wrapped in each other's arms or, perhaps, seated in a hammock facing each other and holding hands." Altschuler adds:

> This behavior is not specifically homosexual, but it may be called homoerotic. It is noticed only during fiestas, when alcohol flows freely. I have no evidence of specifically homosexual behavior (Altschuler, page 48).

Sports (from wrestling to spectator events) cover an enormous range of possibilities from close physical contact, to completely vicarious activity. Gay authors David Bianco and Michael Rowe have both commented on homoerotic undertones in football and in boxing. Writes Bianco (page 242) on football:

> The players huddle head-to-head, arms wrapped around each other. At the start of a play, the quarterback grabs the ball from between the center's legs. After a touchdown the players hug and pat each other's behinds.

Rowe (page 105) quotes from Joyce Carol Oates' book *On Boxing*, which he praises for its "stunning" insight into sports:

> No sport . . . appears more homoerotic: the confrontation in the ring—the disrobing—the sweaty heated combat that is part of the dance, courtship, coupling—the frequent urgent pursuit by one boxer of the other in the fight's natural and violent movement toward the 'knockout': surely boxing derives much of its appeal from this mimicry of a species of erotic love in which one man overcomes the other in an exhibition of superior strength and will. The heralded celibacy of the fighter-in-training is very much a part of boxing lore: instead of focusing his energies and fantasies upon a woman the boxer focuses them upon an opponent. Where Woman has been, Opponent must be.

The nudity of the showers and locker room, the horseplay, voyeurism, exhibitionism, and joking of those places, afford partial gratification of homosexual impulses, as well as serving the need for physical exercise and sociability. Michael Rowe (page 31) offers an example of the ribald joking that occurs in an army shower-room: "Be careful you don't drop the soap; you've got such a fine ass. . . ."

David Plummer (page 266) quotes a respondent's observation (note the British idiom) that macho boys freely indulge in same-sex horseplay that gays must restrict to safe and private situations:

"[M]ucking around" in the showers was okay for big burly foot-ball players. Mucking around in the dorms, hopping in other beds, touching, grabbing, holding, wrestling was okay for them. 'Cause . . . it was done in a sort of exertive and physical type of play-act-ing. But if you were demure, pale skinned [and] unmuscled and you did that, that's out—you copped it.

Female companionship can even afford a partial gratification of homosexual impulses. Why are some men attracted to voluptuous ladies, and others to girls who are slim and boyish; even boyish in their hairstyle, makeup and clothes, ath-letic and assertive in their style? Discussing the indirect expression of homosex-ual impulses, Fenichel (page 333) noted that some men fall in love with boyish girls "in whom they see the reincarnation of themselves."

Oral sex allows a man to experience a passive form of sexual pleasure with a partner of either sex, while he can comfort himself that *technically* he is playing the masculine role of "inserter." Alfred C. Kinsey, when gathering data for his famous 1948 Kinsey Report, was outraged that some of his respondents protest-ed that *Yes*, they allowed themselves to be fellated by a "fag," but *No!* they were *not* homosexual.[5] This continues to be a popular rule in various places, that only the fellator is a "fag," but the man he services is not. John Money (1988, page 107) describes neighborhoods "where even among the toughest, heterosexually active males, it was accepted to be given oral sex by a known homosexual, either for fun or for money."

Oral sex not only introduces variety into a couple's sex life, but allows hus-band and wife to *reverse* their usual sex roles; the wife can assume the more active role of choosing exactly how and when to stimulate or withhold stimula-tion, when to tease and when to gratify, while the husband just lies back and enjoys it, an experience that comes fairly close to a homosexual encounter. If a man cannot get oral sex from his wife, he may look for a prostitute who will oblige him.[6]

Jokes about oral sex. If a man cannot permit himself to engage in oral sex, he might be able to joke[7] about it:

1. "I wish I could get rid of this terrible headache."
"I had a lousy headache last night. My wife gave me a blow job and it went away instantly."
"Is she home now?"

2. Little girl to her mother: "Last night I peeked into your bedroom and saw Daddy's penis in your vagina. What do you do that for?"
Mother: "That's the way you get a baby."
A few days later . . . : "Last night I . . . saw Daddy's penis in your mouth. What do you do that for?"

Mother: "That's the way you get jewelry."

Jokes about homosexuality. Joking is a conversational mode that makes it easy to talk about homosexuality.

> 3. Patient: "It's my crazy imagination. I sometimes think I am a horse, the most beautiful horse in the world."
> Therapist: "Are you a female horse or a male horse?"
> Patient: "I'm a male horse, you dope. What do you think, I've got problems with my gender identity?"

> 4. Army examiner: "Are you gay?"
> Recruit: "No, but I've slept with a lot of guys who are."

> 5. Policeman (looking into the back seat of a car): "What do you think you're doing?"
> Voice from the car: "I'm screwing my girlfriend."
> Policeman: "OK; I'm next."
> Voice from the car: "Sounds good to me; I've never screwed a cop before."

> 6. Here's one that goes back to rooming house days: One day, four men asked for a room, and they all gave the same name: John Smith. The landlady said, "This is going to be confusing. Tell me your occupation so I can tell you apart." The first man said, "I work at a winery. I'm a cork soaker." The second man said, "I work at the gas plant. I'm a coke sacker." The third man said, "I work at a knitting mill. I'm a sock tucker." The fourth man said, "I'm the real thing."

Because homosexuality is a touchy subject, jokes are more likely to deal with the topic in an indirect or symbolic way. Sex with another man's wife (*troilism, menage à trois*) can be an indirect form of homosexual contact, and is the subject of many jokes:

> 7. At his wife's funeral, a man notices another man crying intensely. Slowly it dawns on him that this man was his wife's lover. He goes over to him, puts his arm around him and says, "Don't feel so bad. I'll get married again."

> 8. Al walked into his bedroom and saw his wife making love with his good friend Jim. Al said, "Jimmy, I have to, but *you?*"

> 9. A businessman says to his partner: "Last night, I took our cashier out to dinner and then had sex with her. She's terrific! I must say: better than my wife." His partner responds: "I've also

had sex with our cashier. She is very good, but I don't think she's better than your wife."

Offensive to gay men, homosexual jokes serve to deflect and deny the joke-teller's own homosexual impulses. The jokes help ordinary guys distance themselves from homosexual activites by exaggerating and distorting them. Most of the following are adapted from jokes that have appeared on the Internet:

10. Did you hear of the three gay guys in San Francisco who stopped a straight woman on the street? Well, two held the woman while the third did her hair.

11. A gay guy pays a visit to his doctor and confides to him that he has a vibrator stuck up his rectum. "No problem," says the doctor; "I'll have it out shortly."
    "Oh, no; don't remove it."
    The puzzled doctor asks: "Then what do you want me to do?"
    "Just change the batteries."

12. A gay man, finally deciding he could no longer hide his sexuality from his parents, went into the kitchen where he found his mother cooking dinner, sat down at the kitchen table, let out a big sigh, and said: "Mom, I have something to tell you. I'm gay."
    His mother made no reply, continuing to stir the pot on the stove, and the guy was about to repeat his statement to make sure she'd heard him, when she looked up and said: "You're gay; doesn't that mean you put another man's penis in your mouth and swallow his semen?"
    Nervously, he answered: "Uh yeah, Mom; that's right."
    "Well, then, don't you ever complain about my cooking again."

13. An usher handed the preacher the collection plate after it had been passed through the congregation. When the preacher saw a $100 bill in the plate, he announced: "Would whoever put the $100 bill in the plate please stand up."
    A gay man stood up and said, "I did."
    Said the preacher: "Since you put that money in the plate, I would like you to pick out three hymns."
    Excitedly, the gay man looked around and said, "OK, well, I'll take him and him and him."

14. How can you tell that your house has been burglarized by gays?
When you come home and discover that your jewelry is missing,

and all your furniture has been tastefully rearranged.

15. As two gay men are walking down the street, they pass a voluptuously beautiful young woman. One says to the other, "It's at moments like this that I wish I was a lesbian."

Entertainment. TV watching, going to the movies and reading novels allow for the expression of many otherwise unfulfilled wishes, including homosexual impulses. The following verse is by Jack Prelutsky, well-known children's poet. With a touch of undisguised envy, the poet celebrates the uncontrollable virility of youth, and enjoys in fantasy what a boy-lover might actually involve himself in:

> I haven't got the least respect
> For teenage boys who get erect.
> A girl walks by, they think "romance!"
> And there's a stirring in their pants.
>
> They're often seated on the bus,
> And though I do not make a fuss,
> It bothers me to see them rise
> In public, right before my eyes.
>
> Some try to hide it with a coat,
> But all the same, it gets my goat
> And, yes, I feel a quiet rage
> That I can't match them at my age.[8]

Riding the bus, this middle-aged man let his eyes idly roam over his fellow passengers. A "100 percent heterosexual" man might fix his attention on an attractive young lady, mentally undress her and fantasize an erotic "brief encounter." But this gentleman finds an adolescent boy "more interesting," and notices (or imagines) that the teenager has an erection. Isn't there is something homosexual about this humorous verse?

A Vietnamese elder, transplanted to America, identifies with the nascent virility of his grandson by playing with the little boy's genitals. The visiting American social worker makes a note of this incident, and reports it as child abuse.[9] From his field work in Africa, Melvin Konner reports (page 302) that when sitting around a fire, !Kung "infants are passed from hand to hand around a fire . . . [from] one adult or child to another . . . [and] kissed on their faces, bellies, genitals, [and] sung to. . . ." The Cayapans, of the Pacific lowlands, commonly play with an infant boy by by holding the child high overhead, and lowering his body so that his genitals fall into the adult's mouth (page 51). (See page 539 for a further comment on this practice.)

Masturbation may gratify many wishes, including homosexual ones. According to a 1994 University of Chicago sex survey (Laumann *et al.*), about 81 percent of married men masturbate.[10] Is this simply a kind of recreation resorted to when a man's sex partner is unavailable? Does masturbation serve a simple mechanical pleasure of sexual excitement? Masturbation can also serve as a celebration of masculine potency without female participation. Sometimes it is accompanied by the fantasy of a male partner. The masturbator knows that in reality, the erection is his own, this symbol of masculinity. The hand is his own, but in fantasy it could be that of a male companion.

Cultural activities like plays, ballets, operas, and museum visits satisfy artistic interests, as they incidentally gratify sexual impulses (heterosexual and homosexual), at least partially. All forms of entertainment exercise the erotic imagination and permit the partial fulfillment of all sorts of sexual impulses.

Protective coping mechanisms

A woman's female identity traces back to an unbroken identification with her mother, but a man must *acquire* his masculine identity, a task that is never quite finished. Hence, women enjoy the luxury of intimate friendship with another woman, unbothered that the more assertive partner may be assuming what may seem like a male role. A "male identity . . . requires its constant protection," comments psychotherapist Lillian B. Rubin (page 102). She compares and contrasts the adolescent friendships of boys and of girls. In both cases, best friends share fantasies, rehearse romantic relationships that lie ahead. They talk about the etiquette of dating and mating. Girls talk about what to wear, how to style their hair and use make-up, how to walk, how to kiss or refuse to kiss. Boys also talk about the mysteries of girls and sex, and describe the girls of their dreams. They rehearse how to approach her, when to speak, when to keep silent, what to do if she says yes, and how to act if her answer is no.

> There is a considerable difference, however, in "the intensity of the emotional connection, [in] the importance they assume in the life of each. . . . Among girls, such friendships often take on a Siamese twin-like quality, so inseparable do the friends seem, so central to their well-being. Among boys, however, even best friendships are more emotionally contained, less insistently focused on the twosome, less deeply involved in each other's inner life.

> "Girls are satisfied to be together and talk to each other. Boys *do things* together: play games together, watch sporting events together, work together, eat together, share in organized activities or hobbies" (Rubin, page 102).

When Stuart Miller decided to conduct a study on the dynamics of men's friendships, the first person he sought to interview, a philosophy professer, said to him, "Male friendship. You mean you're going to write about homosexuality? . . . Could be dangerous for you." When he tried to interview a science professor, Miller was warned, "You must be careful. You know, of course, that people will think you're writing about homosexuality." Everywhere he found the same misconception; he always had to begin by explaining that his subject was not homosexuality (Miller, page 3).

Rubin (pages 103-105) tells of Fred, a 42-year-old high school teacher who had spent more than three years in a men's group "to learn to be closer and more open with other men." He recalled their sharing of intimate thoughts, but they never got to be "great friends" the same way that members of women's groups did.

Fred

We learned how to share some painful things. . . We even talked about . . . real feelings about sex and what it means and how it can make you anxious sometimes. . . . [But our intimacy] never got beyond the room. . . . [W]e didn't get to be great friends. It's not like Lois, the woman I live with, and the women in her group. . . . [T]hey call each other up and talk for hours; they do things together all the time. We just never got that close, that's all.

[W]hen we were in that room, everything was up. . . We even eventually were able to cry there. . . . Nobody ever got very comfortable with it. It wasn't like when a woman cries and you can put your arm around her.

Rubin asked: "Why couldn't you put your arm around a man who's crying?" Fred squirmed uncomfortably in his seat and responded: "Men just don't do that, that's all; it's too uncomfortable. . . I think there must always be some kind of a fear about getting physically close to a man. We used to hug each other when we got together, but even that . . . was tight and self-conscious. You don't let your body go into the hug and the other guy doesn't either."

Herb Goldberg (page 141) tells of a friend who "vividly recalled to me that . . . his flight was delayed twelve hours due to engine problems. Each passenger was asked to share a room for the night with another passenger. My friend was booked into a room that had only one large bed. He remembers how carefully he and his fellow male passenger were as each slept on the very edge of their own side of the bed, in seeming terror of accidentally touching each other."

In 1914, Sandor Ferenczi (Lewes, page 52) interpreted the tendency of his time for men to engage in disputation, dueling, and alcoholism, to a "disdain and loathing felt for homosexuality." This fear of expressing warm and positive friendship (while sober), this avoidance of getting physically close to another man, is the price men pay for warding off homosexual feelings, Ferenczi implied.

Some (perhaps most) heterosexual men avoid friendship with a man who is known to be gay. Here is the experience of a gay man who was dropped quite suddenly by an old friend, once he learned that his friend was gay:

> We were finishing up law school when I got up the nerve to come out to a guy I'd known since high school. I didn't expect him to say "congratulations," but I didn't expect what I got either. While we were talking he tried to be cool, but after that he managed to be going the other way when he saw me coming. A couple of weeks later he had a graduation party and everyone we knew was invited but me (Rubin, page 103).

Rubin (page 102) tells of another gay man, a 29-year-old publicist, who, with some bitterness, recalled how he was abandoned by a "good friend" once he came out:

> It didn't happen right away because he tried to be civilized about it. But he was uncomfortable with me from then on, kind of nervous. . . . It was like I had a disease that was catching or something. I could feel him freeze up even just to shake my hand. After a while I guess we both decided we didn't need it. I certainly didn't; I was having enough trouble feeling okay about myself without him around.

By contrast, lesbians are more likely to maintain close friendship with a woman friend who happens to be straight. Strain in their friendship is more likely to come from the lesbian, who needs the moral support of her lesbian friends more than what she can get from the straight woman. Rubin (page 101) records the complaint of a straight woman that she feels neglected by her closest friend since she became lesbian:

> Angie was one of my closest friends until she came out, but I don't see her much anymore. It's not my fault either; it's hers. She's so damned preoccupied with being lesbian and her new lesbian friends, there's no time for me. It makes me mad. . . . It really hurts; she's been important to me for so many years.

In the final paragraphs of Chapter 4 we discussed friendship patterns between gay men and straight women. At what point does a heterosexual man's protective avoidance of gay men escalate into a neurotic, even hostile, homophobia? But before we discuss neurotic homophobia, let us consider what might be called "ordinary homophobia."

Ordinary homophobia[11]

A 2002 telephone survey (national sample of 200 respondents) measured attitudes toward various minority groups, including Native Americans, Catholisc, Muslims, Chinese, born-again Christians, and homosexuals. Respondents were asked how familiar they were with homosexuals, and how favorably (or unfavorably) they felt toward homosexuals. Of persons least familiar with homosexuals, 88 per cent expressed *unfavorable* feelings toward them, and only 12 percent expressed favorable feelings toward homosexuals. Of persons who claimed to be familiar with homosexuals, 69 per cent expressed *favorable* feelings toward them. Persons unfamiliar with homosexuals were most likely to harbor unfavorable attitudes toward them, empirical support for the viewpoint that ordinary homophobia is an expression of xenophobia, the fear of strangers. In humans and in other creatures, strangeness commonly evokes a fear response.[11]

Simon LeVay, gifted biological scientist and gay man, confesses that he cannot understand homophobia. From a biological standpoint, a heterosexual should be happy to see homosexuals wasting their seed on each other. "In biological terms," writes LeVay (1996, page 209), "homophobia is deeply incomprehensible." The answer is simple: Homophobia is a psychological phenomenon, not a biological one, and to understand it, one must adopt a psychological point of view.

Comics and novelists, attuned to the human psyche, know how to put their audience in touch with their inner selves. Comedian Jerry Seinfeld asks (pages 54-55), "What causes homophobia? What is it that makes the heterosexual man worry about this? I think it's because deep down, all men know that we have weak sales resistance. We're constantly buying shoes that hurt us, pants that don't feel right. Men think, '. . . I can be talked into anything. What if I accidentally wander into some sort of homosexual store thinking it's a shoe store and the salesman says, "Just hold this guy's hand, walk around a bit, see how it feels. No obligation, no pressure, just try it." ' "

Back in 1968, Martin Hoffman observed (page 190) of heterosexual men who regard themselves as quite liberal and free of homophobia, that they cannot help but feel acutely uncomfortable when they see gay men dancing together and embracing. It becomes clear that such a person's irrational response to witnessing homosexual behavior suggests that he "cannot tolerate his unconscious identification with men who are acting out their homosexual feelings."

Novelist Norman Mailer wrote (page 226), "There is probably no sensitive heterosexual alive who is not preoccupied at one time or another with his latent homosexuality, and while I had no conscious homosexual desires, I had wondered more than once if really there were not something suspicious in my intense dislike of homosexuals." The simple dislike of homosexuals may be labelled "ordinary homophobia" to differentiate this attitude from "disruptive homophobia," "neurotic homophobia," or "malignant homophobia," each of which will be described in the paragraphs that follow.

A University of Georgia study by Henry E. Adams demonstrated experimentally what has always been assumed, that homophobia serves as a defense against homosexual arousal. Adams studied 64 heterosexual male college students, with an average age of 20, and objectively divided them into two groups, homophobic and non-homophobic, on the basis of their responses to a 25-item Index of Homophobia Questionnaire. All 64 were shown videotapes of hard-core gay male pornography. Sexual arousal (measured by penile tumescence) was recorded by 54 percent of the homophobic group, compared with 24 percent of the non-homophobic group.[12]   Twenty years' work in adolescent psychiatry leads psychoanalyst Lynn Ponton to conclude (page 161): "A masculine heterosexual orientation is often achieved at least in part by stigmatizing and devaluing a homosexual orientation."

The sociologist, Michael Kimmel (1996, page 8) argues that in contemporary society, men feel insecure. Why? Because corporate employment does not give a man the feeling of security his ancestors got from the ownership of land, or the mastery of an independent craft and ownership of its tools. One result is an increasing interest in leisure activities such as sports, including spectator sports. Another result, says Kimmel, is *homophobia*, which is *not* just a fear of homosexuals, but a fear that one is not "a real man:"

> *Homophobia is the fear of other men*—that other men will unmask us, emasculate us, reveal to us and the world that we do not measure up, are not real men . . . [that one's claim of manhood is merely a pose. Kimmel quotes the literary critic, David Leverenz, who argues that homophobia] 'has nothing to do with homosexual experience or even with fears of homosexuals. It comes out of the depths of manhood: [it is] a label of ultimate contempt for anyone who seems sissy, untough, uncool' (emphasis added).

Homophobia, Kimmel and Leverenz argue, is an expression of status insecurity. There is a difference between Kimmel's point of view and the position held in this book. The difference is this: Kimmel suggests that felt status is a social construct and that homophobia, therefore, is likewise a social construct. In this book, we recognize sex-role and status-striving behavior as aspects of mammalian behavior pervasive enough to justify the conjecture that a person's regard for his status as a male has biological as well as social roots. If, as Kimmel and Leverenz suggest, ordinary homophobia expresses a male's feeling of threat to his status as a man, this would suggest that ordinary homophobia has biological as well as social roots.

Neurotic coping mechanisms

Sexual inhibition. In 1913, Abraham Brill, pioneer American psychoanalyst, delivered a paper in which he described 12 patients who complained of impotence, which Brill attributed to a lack of homosexual gratification (Katz, pages 149-151).

Men come to therapists complaining of low sexual desire. They fail to experience full sexual arousal when touching a woman. They suffer from chronic erection deficits, and during sexual intercourse may feel an absence of sensation: "numbed out," they may say. Physically, they seem to be perfectly normal, but they are not *enjoying* their sexual opportunities. Typically, masturbation is their one sexual outlet, and the fantasy that accompanies their masturbation provides an important clue as to the nature of their problem.

The sexually inhibited man's masturbatory fantasy may include some heterosexual content, but it is predominantly homosexual, according to psychotherapist Eva Margolies. If masturbation arouses gay imagery, and he has fleeting homosexual thoughts at other times, he is sure that deep down inside, he must be gay. This is a secret that fills him with embarrassment, guilt, and shame, for he shares the straight world's revulsion for homosexuality. As Margolies puts it (pages 235-236), "[H]e is at war with himself. On the one hand, his fantasies turn him on. At the same time, they disgust him. He may also fear that the more he fantasizes about something, the more likely he is to act on it," which he does not want to do.

Alan

These inhibited ones include men who are physically and socially attractive, active professionals, and successful businessmen. They may actively date many different women, but do not get intimately involved with any of them. These men may remain sexually inexperienced at thirty, or even forty. In desperation, one such patient, Alan, enrolled in a sexual surrogate therapy program. For the first time in his life, he experienced sexual intercourse. "I was physically functioning," he recalled with disappointment, "but never really felt turned on" (Margolies, page 124).

These inhibited men show physical characteristics and life experiences of some gay men: asexual appearance and manner, shyness, a hunger for male affection based on a physically or emotionally absentee father, and an avoidance of heterosexual contact based on an intense emotional relationship with his mother. (Margolies, page 121) They cannot function heterosexually, and they dare not cross the line into the gay world because to them it is a world of shame and loathing. The case of Alan is summarized from Margolies, page 124:

Alan was a college-educated, self-employed accountant, sexually inhibited and greatly disturbed by the homosexual fantasies that accompanied his masturbation. Boyhood experience gave him the foundation for a homosexual adulthood, a lifestyle which he totally rejects. Alan had both a sexualizing mother and a rejecting father. A nasty case of acne and a flat-out rejection by the first and only girl he asked out in his teens, made his adolescence a nightmare. His mother's exposure of her body to Alan, stirred his sexual feelings, which he was deeply ashamed of. He also had sexual feelings toward his sister. He was popular with his circle of boys and formed tight bonds with his male friends, but he felt completely unattractive to girls.

In college he became especially close to one of his roommates, and on a trip to Florida over Christmas break, it became obvious to both young men, neither of whom had ever had conscious homosexual feelings, that there were such rumblings between them. Alan never acted on these feelings, but they persist, to this day, in his masturbatory fantasies.

Alan buried his confusion in his career as an accountant for many years. But as he got older, the questions about his sexual preference greatly distressed him. He attempted to gain heterosexual skills and experience through a sex surrogate therapy program. Margolies quotes Alan's comment: "I was physically functioning but never really felt turned on." While in therapy with Margolies, he had a series of brief encounters with women, and then a six-month love affair, marred by strong sexual conflicts and an intense emotional relationship with his mother. When Alan lost his major client, he dropped out of therapy.

In some cases, writes Margolies, the conflict over homosexual or incestuous attraction is so intense, the victim "completely avoids sex with a partner" (Margolies, page 89) and masturbation is his only sexual outlet. When finally they gain heterosexual experience, they find that touching a woman's body fails to evoke a full sexual arousal, and they show a special aversion to touching their partner's vagina. During intercourse, they are apt to "numb out," lack sexual sensation and lose their erection.

Margolies reports some success in teaching these inhibited men to accept their homosexual fantasies, to tolerate them, even enjoy them, and *use them* to enhance sexual pleasure.

Margolies says she helps patients enjoy their fantasy life: "fantasizing about what comes naturally to him. . ." (page 126) "A man who fantasizes about homosexual experiences is not necessarily gay any more than the woman who fantasizes about being raped actually wants to be raped" (page 236).

"Sexual imprints are parts of us," Margolies teaches (page 126). "When you consciously try to shut those imprints out, you shut out your general sexual feelings. The man who comes to understand that his homoerotic impulses do not make him homosexual, and who begins feeling okay about fantasizing about what comes naturally to him when with a woman, starts having some pleasurable heterosexual experiences. The fact that he is fantasizing about a man does not detract from the fact that in reality he is with a woman. So over time what develops is an increasing positive attitude toward sex with a woman. . . . Not surprisingly, while his sex drive toward the opposite sex is on the rise, his homosexual fantasies begin to disappear."

"Once a man becomes comfortable using fantasy with his partner, amazing things begin to happen, [Margolies reports.] I have worked with men who have had little or no sexual desire for years, who begin consistently to enjoy intercourse with their partners when they bring [same-sex] fantasy into their lovemaking." (page 236)

"Low sex drive" is a common complaint heard not only by therapists and marriage counselors in private practice, but also at university and hospital clinics across the land. Ann Landers gets hundreds of letters from everywhere, from unfulfilled wives who complain about their husband's sexual inhibition. Margolies is not the only clinician who has linked low sex drive with homosexual impulses. John Money (1988, page 106) observes that what a sex therapist may label "inhibited sexual desire [may in fact result from an] unfulfilled homosexual desire."[13]

Jack Nichols, author, editor and promoter of sex-role freedom, laments (page 208) that most American men, he believes, flee from the passive and receptive aspects of sexual interaction. Their vigilance against slipping into a passive or receptive role, Nichols argues, robs these men of their ability to give or receive sexual pleasure.

Compulsive Sexual Activity. Since the biological function of coitus is reproduction, and since since the offspring's survival is favored by an enduring partnership between parents, it is not surprising that persons normally feel physically drawn toward a potential sexual partner whom they find attractive, appealing, even loveable. Why, then, do men become sexually involved to females whom they perceive as grossly unattractive? In his recollections of Army life when stationed in Germany, Frank McCourt (1999, page 146) tells of a buddy's advice that Frank go along with a group that was looking for sex with half-starved refugee girls dressed in rags and "ready to do anything" for a few packs of cigarettes. "Don't be a goddam fool, Mac, you're a kid, you need to get laid too *or you'll get strange in the head*." (Emphasis added).

The Homophobic Don Juan. To most men, sexual activity is followed by a sense of fulfillment and a period of relaxation. For a heterosexual Don Juan, however, one sexual episode only whets the appetite for another sexual adventure, so driven are they to prove their ability to excite women. Fenichel conjectures (pages 243-244) that some men behave like Don Juans because they are "unconsciously homosexual . . . [and therefore] aroused by sexual contact with women but not satisfied. . . . [The homophobic Don Juan] vainly seeks satisfaction in more and more [heterosexual] activity."

Socially disruptive and sociopathic homophobia

One important test of a good society is whether it protects the basic human rights of its unpopular members. A democratic society cannot permit individuals to harass and ridicule gays, denounce gays, or torment them. Owens tells of a number of high school boys who were tormented because they came out as gays, or were suspected of being gay:

> When it was rumored in his freshman year that he was gay, Randy, a high school student recalls: 'I was spit on, pushed and ridiculed. My school life was hell' (Owens, page 73).

> Paul, a big, bleached-blond gay teen, was dragged into a bathroom stall by eight boys who called him faggot while bashing his head against the toilet and burning his arm with a lighter. Later, mowed down by a truckload of students while on his bike, he spent months in a body cast *(ibid,* page 73).

> Owens (page 75) tells of Tom, who "was physically abused and verbally harassed all through high school after he accidentally became aroused in the locker room shower. He always kept his eyes down for fear of repeating his indiscretion."

> When Brent, a 16-year-old gay, was confronted by homophobes in the locker room, a black student intervened to protect him: "Hey, dude. Are you gay? . . . That's cool. Kind of like being black." "The rest of the time in the class," Brent notes, his defender "dressed for PE next to me. I really admired that" (*ibid,,* page 72).

Man is a social animal, and ostracism is the cruel price that gay men sometimes pay for identifying themselves as homosexual.

Owens (page 48) reports a 19-year-old gay man, athletic and energetic, who likes to play football but has no friends with whom to play. He laments: "I have no friends that are guys. . . ."

Julian, a young gay suicide survivor recalls: "People used to pee on me in the shower. . . People were slamming me into lockers. . . . I would be standing at a urinal and someone would come up and kick me in the small of my back. . . [I] had to hide in a stall in the bathroom. . . . I used to get punched a lot in the locker room. . . I couldn't learn [at that school]" (Owens, page 97).

Owens (page 106) tells of Grant, who had been having sex regularly with a star on his high school football team. Now they barely acknowledge each other in school. "[S]ince it was rumored that I was gay," Grant explains, "he didn't want to get a close identity with me."

Owens (page 110) documents the case in which homophobic harassment destroyed a good student's will to succeed. This 16-year-old recalls: "I was in the locker room, and this guy who didn't like me starts going, 'Brent sucks dick,' and soon the whole locker room was full of guys shouting this for . . . three minutes. And I had to pretend I didn't give a shit . . . but really I wanted to kill myself. . . . [W]hen I started to cut school . . . I had a 4.0 grade average, and within months I went to Ds and Fs."

That homophobic harassment serves the psychological needs of its perpetrators does not justify this activity, any more than a school must tolerate the destruction of property or the disruption of classroom order because it is for some the preferred way to discharge pent-up rage. Home, school, and society must defend the physical safety, and freedom from harassment, of every law-abiding person regardless of sexual orientation, declared or suspected. This is not a pro-gay rule. This basic rule of civilized behavior must be learned and practiced.

A mechanism of defense may be labeled a failure when it fails to relieve the individual of his psychic tension, when the behavior burdens the individual with additional psychological problems (e.g., social conflicts, personal enemies). Appendix 2 records an interview with Bob, a conservative Christian young man whose homophobic burden caused him much personal discomfort and blocked his professional goal of a career in social work.

Verbal taunts can escalate into physical violence. Too late for remorse. The damage has been done. Owens describes several incidents that culminated in violence about which the perpetrators may later have felt genuinely remorseful.

Owens (page 76) tells of "an article in the Los Angeles Times

[describing] parents 'who battered their own son into insensibili-
ty' after finding homosexual literature in his room."

Owens (page 77) tells of Rob, a high school graduate, who was
at a party with his gay friends when he was discovered there by
his brother and his brother's friend Steve. "Steve disclosed Rob's
sexual orientation to Rob's parents. In a confrontation a week
later in which Rob attempted to force Steve to recant, he shot
Steve ten times at close range, killing him."

Malignant homophobia. In some persons, conflict over their homosexual
impulses becomes a major internal struggle that leads to self-sabotage and physical assault upon others. Money (1988, page 110) labels "malignant bisexuals"
those persons who regard their heterosexuality as pure and righteous, and their
homosexuality as sinister and evil. They may preach and legislate[14] against
homosexuals; spy, trap, assault, and kill them.[15] A malignant bisexual lets himself
be picked up by a gay man, have sex with him, and then attempt to exorcise his
own homosexual guilt by assaulting and maybe killing him. Roger Brown's roving partner encountered such a person in Edinburgh.

Roger Brown recalls (page 44) that his friend told of how he
picked up "a big solid Scotsman with red hair and in kilts. He
turned out to be straight and a faggot-hater. My antennae must
have been thrown off by his Scots accent. . . Anyway, when I had
done my thing—which he gave every sign of enjoying—he hit
me in the face and bellowed: 'This is what I think of fucking
cocksuckers.' Luckily I was fully dressed and got out of the door
[his face badly battered and swollen] and headed back to the
hotel before him."

Money (1988, page 110) accuses persons who persecute homosexuals or tolerate their persecution of harboring "lesser degrees" of the exorcist syndrome. "If
it were not so . . . they would live and let live those who are destined to have a
different way of being human in love and sex. They would tolerate them as they
do the left-handed. Tolerance would remove those very pressures that progressively coerce increasing numbers of our children and grandchildren to grow up
blighted with the curse of malignant bisexuality." Gay men need the protection
of the law against the threat of malignant homophobics, just as every citizen
deserves to be protected against antisocial predations. Gay men must also learn
that "safe sex" means more than using a condom, and that they must vigilantly
avoid entrapment by potential malignant homophobics.[16]

NOTES TO CHAPTER 6

1. One interpretation of this Socratic dialogue is that life is full of conflicting *options*, not that life proceeds by making conscious choices between conflicting goals. The direction in which we move depends on chance events, and also on our values and our loyalties. Sometimes we embrace one option and reject the other; sometimes we work out a compromise between conflicting dualities.
The above comments seem to ask, "Why can't homosexuals control and channel their sexual impulses in a way that enables them to lead an easier, less problem-laden life in a heterosexual society?" The answer is that, while for the ordinary male, the homosexual impulse is a passing fantasy, for the homosexual, that impulse is a driving, imperious force. It's the difference between a man who can pass up a snack because he's not really that hungry, and a man who is ravenously famished.

2. The concept that all men are sinners goes back to Genesis 4:7: Sin lieth at the door, but thou shalt rule over it.

3. The topic of "homosexual worry" is a common psychological phenomenon, but "homosexual panic" is a psychiatric concept: the symptom of a severe mental disorder. Homosexual worry is accompanied by chronic anxiety; homosexual panic is marked by psychotic terror and wild excitement or catatonic paralysis.

According to Glick, the psychiatric concept of homosexual panic was introduced by Kempf in 1920. Although the study of homosexual panic lies outside the scope of this book, a brief description of it would say that homosexual panic describes an onset of schizophrenia marked by homosexual delusions (Glick), like the delusion that one has been threatened with sexual assault, that one has been doped or hypnotized, or that someone has been mixing semen into one's food. Schizophrenic delusions are *wild distortions* of ordinary thought, for homosexual thoughts that lie quietly in the minds of ordinary people.

4. Wilson and Lawson randomly divided a group of heterosexual males into two groups: one was told that they were given an alcoholic drink, and the other told they were given a non-alcoholic drink. In each group, half were in fact given alcoholic drinks, and half were not. All were then shown two pornographic movies, one heterosexual and one homosexual. All subjects were measured for penile arousal. *No real difference in penile arousal could be related to whether the subject had consumed alcohol or not*, but there was a significantly greater tendency for subjects to become sexually aroused if they *had been told* that they had just had an alcoholic drink.

5. Kinsey thought it odd that a married respondent sometimes told him he had "sex relations with his wife in a homosexual way" (page 616). From a technical standpoint, Kinsey believed he could only categorize "mouth-genital contacts between males and females . . . [as] heterosexual" (page 515). But the fantasy of

a man who receives oral sex can easily drift from heterosexuality to homosexuality, as "the inserter" just lies back and enjoys it. Likewise, Kinsey thought it was odd that "some males who are being regularly fellated by other males without, however, ever performing fellation themselves . . . insist that they are exclusively heterosexual and that they have never been involved in a truly homosexual relation." Kinsey regarded this view as a "pretention" and a "fiction" (page 616).

6. Scanzoni and Mollenkott (pages 89-90) describe "one military chaplain with an evangelical affiliation [who] reported to a civilian pastor friend that during overseas service, he had encouraged the men in his charge to visit prostitutes . . . . When the pastor asked why he had given such advice, the chaplain replied simply, 'To prevent perversion.' [Apparently] . . . the chaplain's sole concern was to prevent homosexual acts, and to further this goal . . . sex with a prostitute was considered acceptable, since at least it was heterosexual."

7. Jokes number 1, 2, 3, 5, 7, and 8 are adapted from Strean.

8. "On Youth," from *There'll Be a Slight Delay, and Other Poems for Grown-Ups*, by Jack Prelutsky. William Morrow: New York, 1991.

9. As told to the author by a Vietnamese social work student.

10. Interviewers asked 3,159 married respondents whether they had masturbated during the past year. Response rate varied by age, sex, religion, and educational level. Average for the entire sample was 62 percent for men, 42 percent for women. The average for well educated (advanced degree) married men was 81 percent.

11. The telephone survey, unpublished, was conducted in May 2002 by Leo J. Shapiro Associates, Chicago, Il. The term homophobia was coined by George Weinberg, and appeared in his 1972 book, *Society and the Healthy Homosexual*.

12. Subjects were shown three four-minute clips of hard-core pornography: (a) heterosexual, (b) lesbian, and (c) gay. Each subject attached a gauge to his penis, which measured changes in its circumference, indicative of erection. Both groups, homophobic and non-homophobic, were equally aroused by heterosexual and lesbian clips, but the homophobic group was significantly more responsive to the portrayal of gay sex.

13. No implication is made here that all, or even a majority, of complaints of low sex drive stem from dread of homosexual impulses.

14. Money (page 110) notes the 1986 confessional biography in which a former U.S. Congressman from Maryland, Robert E. Bauman, closeted gay man, docu-

mented an ultraconservative and homophobic career.

15. In *Billy Budd*, a novel by Herman Melville, a blond, young, well mannered, and exceptionally handsome young sailor is wrongly charged with mutiny and murder. Billy Budd is sentenced to death, though the ship captain is not really convinced that the boy is guilty. The captain's conscious rationalization is that this innocent man's execution will serve a good purpose. It will warn the crew of the danger of mutiny, and help maintain law and order. The reader may conjecture that unconsciously the captain was trying to get rid of his sexual attraction to this handsome young man.

16. In November of 1998, Matt Shepard, a physically slight college student, went alone to a gay bar on the edge of town, and left in the company of two strangers who posed as gay men, but were in fact malignant homophobics. The next morning, Shepard was found dead. The nation was outraged at the senseless murder of this gay college student. Newspaper editorials and letters-to-the-editor offered a variety of remedies: (a) enact tougher hate-crime laws, (b) initiate school programs and policies that combat harassment of gay students, (c) initiate programs that honor gay students, (d) silence (or at least muffle) the anti-gay rhetoric of Christian conservatives. Rare, almost absent, was the warning that gay men exercise caution in their choice of sexual partners, and never get into a car with two complete strangers and let them drive you off into the night.

7   Brain Differences and Gender-Discordance

If you show a biologist a human brain, and ask him if it came from a man or a woman, the biologist would be guided by the fact that a woman's brain is usually a little smaller than a man's; otherwise they look identical. To the naked eye, they look identical, but are they really? No, they are not. Psychobiologist James Weinrich states (page 155) that there are "a couple of gross anatomic differences between male and female brains, and lots of differences [are] visible under a microscope." (Weinrich lists five papers, published between 1964 and 1985, on differences between male and female brains.)[1]

Hidden gender differences in brain structure and function undoubtedly correspond to readily observable gender differences in physique and behavior. The adult male physique has about 30 percent more muscle mass than the adult female. A physique capable of more powerful action is probably guided by a more action-oriented brain. Males and females differ in many behavioral tendencies that have little to do with upbringing. Across most cultures, males tend to be more aggressive, competitive, and sexually active; females are apt to be more nurturant, more sensitive, more verbal, and usually more artistic. It seems more than likely that hidden differences in brain structure and function underlie the anatomical and behavioral differences we can easily see. Even though he is highly critical of existing brain-differences studies, neuroanatomist William Byne expresses the belief that the ambiguity of results so far is due to methodological difficulties rather than the absence of gender differences in brain structure:

> Science writer Robert Finn quotes Byne: "[I]t's tremendously difficult to do morphometric studies in the human brain. I would be surprised if there weren't sex differences in the human brain, since there are sex differences in just about every organ system in humans."

Here we will review the evidence for gender differences (and sexual orientation differences) in behavior, and we will look at neurological laboratory evidence of brain differences between males and females, and between straight and gay males. We will also examine clinical findings—facts about gender differences in brain function that can be gleaned from human misfortunes and misadventures.

Learned versus innate gender differences; the nature-nurture question revisited

Do men and women think and act differently because they were raised differently, or are there systematic gender differences in behavior that are not the product of social learning only, differences in behavior that probably correspond to microscopic brain differences? This is a bold question to ask, for those of us who are still living in the shadow of Margaret Mead's world of cultural determinism.

To believe that gender differences are learned roles is not only supported by Margaret Mead's classic anthropological reports, but is also supported by our conception of the human as a marvelously adaptive creature, born in a "fetal" state that allows for about 15 years of learning before a person reaches sexual maturity. Culture patterns the activities that fill the years of childhood and adolescence, but the developmental schedule (the fact that humans mature at around age 15, not at age 5) is genetically implanted in the human species. If the human species is compared with other primates, humans are genetically programmed for an extended developmental schedule. This "design for living" strongly suggests that humans are allowed this generously extended growing-up period to adapt to novel and changing environments, to acquire a behavioral repertory based on experience rather than on innate tendencies.

Our willingness to believe that gender differences are learned rather than innate, also expresses a belief in the psychological equality of the sexes, and rejects a traditionalist ideology that assigns to women a social role now widely condemned as subservient and inferior. But does allegiance to the principle of equal rights for women require a belief in the identity of male and female brain structure and function? Moral issues are important,[2] but they must not becloud our understanding of human nature.

Evolutionists believe that *Homo sapiens* evolved over thousands of years during which men hunted and fought, and women gathered food and nurtured offspring. Survival and reproduction did not come easily, and an evolutionary viewpoint would suggest that hominid father and mother evolved different and complementary roles (as Chapter 3 sets forth) that favored both reproduction and the survival of helpless offspring into adulthood.[3]

Differentiation is a basic evolutionary tactic. It is plain to see that although newborn human males and females are almost identical, except for their genitalia, the average adult man and woman are physically quite different, and their remote ancestors were significantly more so. On the average, boy and girl, man and woman, are probably temperamentally different and innately so, because form and function go together in nature as well as in human artifacts. The human brain has probably not changed in the last 50,000 years. In an information age, we are still equipped with hunting-and-gathering brains.

Behavioral differences between males and females

Do males have a stronger sex drive than females? Males show a remarkable readiness to engage in sexual behavior, a readiness easily triggered by visual stimuli. When male rhesus monkeys watch a companion copulate, their own testosterone levels climb some 400 per cent (Blum page 228). Male birds are sexually stimulated by the sight of a female. (Female birds respond to song, food, and courtship.) There is strong evidence, writes Blum (page 227), that testosterone promotes a rapid visual response.[4]

Throughout the animal kingdom, instances abound in which males are more easily aroused and more quickly complete their reproductive function, while females are more deliberate and discriminating in their mating behavior. To measure the differences in how readily men and women are sexually aroused, researchers compared the sexual arousal of college men and women (measured indirectly by skin temperature and pulse rate) as they listened to a wide range of recorded conversations between men and women. Some men responded more strongly and hotter physiologically to male-female conversations on such innocuous topics as choice of college major or career than women did to explicitly erotic conversation. A smile or a friendly voice may be all it takes to get a man aroused and raise his testosterone level[5] (Blum, page 228).

In Chapters 3 and 4 we examined evidence that men are more readily aroused sexually than women. In Germany, a pair of sexologists, Schmidt and Sigusch, recruited a group of college students to attend a program of sexually explicit episodes on film, in slides, and in story-telling. The following day, participants were asked to fill out a questionnaire (as they had done before attending the program) about what they had done and felt sexually during the last 24 hours. Results showed that 28 percent of the males reported having masturbated after attending the program, twice as high a percentage as reported by female participants. Surveys suggest that the average man thinks about sex three to five times a day, and the average for women is several times a week to several times a month (Blum page 228). Science writer Blum (page 233) comments on how readily males are aroused sexually:

> The same system that revs them up at the sight of a centerfold,
> that causes teenage boys to develop erections from vibrations on
> a school bus, that makes casual conversation a turn-on, tumbles
> them more easily into pleasure.

The nurturant gender role of females

Adult males fulfill their parental role when they wander off, hunt, and return to their home base[6] with food. Females, on the other hand, demonstrate many inborn tendencies that clearly deserve to be categorized as "maternal instincts." These behavioral tendencies relate not only to the protection and feeding of infants, but also include a tendency to comfort, to listen, to communicate, and to bond—to establish interpersonal attachments.

If mother is caring for the young while father is hunting for food, aren't listening and talking as important to the female role as aggressiveness, physical endurance, and spatial orientation are to the male role? Blum argues (page 68) that it makes sense for evolution to have given women an advantage as a talker and listener:

> Mothers have to communicate with children—not just to comfort them, but warn them of danger. This protects the individual child, and may, in an expanded picture, be essential to the overall survival of the species. Researchers regard such communication—nurturing, protective—as so necessary that they suggest it fostered women's verbal advantage over men.

Interpersonal vs. object-attachments.   Little girls play with dolls, and little boys play with trucks. Bigger boys like to get together with other boys to do things: play games, make things, conduct club meetings, complete with rules and status differences. Girls find a best friend with whom they want to talk, and just be together. "Interpersonal attachment[7] is a bigger deal for women than men," Blum argues (page 217), "and that's . . . true in all cultures and times." She continues:

> It has an adaptive significance for the survival of the species. If women didn't attach, babies wouldn't survive.

Sensitivity.   Women are not only more sensitive than men to sound, they are also more sensitive to other stimuli: smell, taste, and touch. Moir (page 179) speculates that these gender differences probably correspond to inborn brain differences:

> Women pick up nuances of voice and music more readily, and girls acquire the skills of language, fluency, and memory earlier than boys. Females are more sensitive to the social and personal context, are more adept at tuning to peripheral information contained in expression and gesture, and process sensory and verbal information faster. They are less rule-bound than men.

Brain differences between men and women

When we talk about "the human brain," frequently we are referring to the cerebral cortex (the cerebral hemispheres, or cerebrum), a paired structure that mushrooms out of the brain stem and covers it with a layer of neural tissue with a bumpy, crunched up surface.[8] The brain stem (or old brain) mediates all the activity that keep the organism and the species alive: breathing, heart-beat, regulation of body temperature, searching for food, avoiding danger, fighting off threats, and satisfying the sex drive. Since the old brain mediates hunger, thirst, fear, aggressiveness, and the sexual appetite, one might conclude that the emotions, as well as life-essential reflexes, spring from the old brain. Neuroscientists have even localized that portion of the old brain in which the emotions are mediated, and have named it the limbic system.

The cerebral hemispheres also mediate some reflexes but, more uniquely, the cerebral hemispheres govern our conscious experience: seeing, hearing, talking, understanding, learning, remembering, planning, thinking, and doing. The brain not only governs action but also governs inhibition: the delay, regulation, control, or deliberate suppression of action. As a result of brain injury to the frontal lobes, a person may become wildly impulsive, lacking in the inner controls that are normal for an adult person.

The effects of disease and injury have taught us that areas of the cerebrum are highly specialized and that, in general, the left half of the brain mediates language (speech, grammar, vocabulary) and the right half mediates visio-spatial perception.

Is the cerebrum also involved in one's emotional life? Yes, since the perception of danger means that one perceives both the dangerous object (or situation) and the emotional meaning of the object. Likewise, the perception of a pleasurable object (or situation) means that one perceives both the object and its emotional meaning. A person's emotional life springs from the limbic system of the old brain, but also involves the cerebral cortex; normally, the area of the brain that perceives objects also perceives the emotional meaning of the objects.

Does the brain of the average man and woman differ in how they respond to emotional information? Here is how Sandra Witleson studied this question. She presented emotionally-charged visual images separately to the left eye and to the right eye, to men and to women, making use of the fact that images received by the right eye are transmitted to the left side of the brain, and those received by the left eye are transmitted to the right side of the brain. Results: men only recognized the emotional content when the image was transmitted to the right side of the brain. Women recognized the emotional content whichever side of the brain the image was transmitted to. *In men, emotional functions seem to be more specific, more specialized, more restricted to one side of the brain..* Women's emotional responses are more likely to spring from both sides of their brain.

Is an emotionally-disturbing event more likely to overwhelm the female brain? Researchers at the National Institute of Mental Health asked ten men and ten women to recall the saddest images of their lives. While participants recalled the scene, they were hooked up to a brain-imaging device (a PET, or positive emission tomography) that produces a picture of their brain activity.[9] "In both sexes, the front of the limbic system glowed. But in women, the active area was eight times larger than in men" (Blum, page 217).[10]

Science writer Anne Moir comments (page 111): "Not for nothing does he 'say it with flowers'—he cannot say it with words. Many men send their loved one a birthday or anniversary card—that's no problem; the trouble arises when it comes to wondering what to write on the darned thing. Men do not have such easy access to the language of love." Perhaps "the language of love" is not unknown to men; they know the words "I love you," but may not consider it macho to express them in writing. (What Moir suggests is a cognitive problem may be, at least in part, a motivational one.)

Just as most people are right-handed, most people hear better with their right ear than with their left. Women are more acute listeners, and hear more effectively with both ears (Blum, page 59). Women's ears are also more sensitive to loud noises.[11] According to Blum (page 68), women who spent their intrauterine beginnings with a twin brother (a fraternal twin, of course), lack this gender advantage.[12] Did the embryonic brother's testosterone "masculinize" his twin sister's inner ears?

"At how young an age are females better listeners than males?" Blum asks (page 67). She points to a classic study by Martin L. Hoffman, who observed the responses of one-day-old infants to various sounds—animal calls, computer-generated language, babies crying. "All babies responded more intensely to another human in distress, but females (one-day old females) responded more intensely than males." Female humans are not only better listeners than males, in some ways they are also better observers. By four months of age, girls show more interest than boys in observing faces (Kagan, 1970). In a 1985 study by Babchuk et al., college students were shown eleven pictures of infants expressing an emotion, and were asked to identify the emotion. Girls surpassed boys for all expressions studied. Child-care experience did not affect performance.

Some clinical findings. Working in a Bethesda, Maryland hospital, a psychologist, Herbert Landsell, observed that men and women are affected differently by similar brain damage, which further suggests differences in brain organization, Moir reports (page 42). Men with right-side brain damage did badly on spatial IQ tests; women with right-side brain damage did not. Men with left-side brain damage were three times as likely to suffer from a language problem than women who suffered exactly the same kind of damage. Landsell concluded that the male brain is much more specialized in brain function. In women, there seems to be more interaction between the right and left hemispheres.

Some scientists believe, says Moir (pages 47-48), that this gender difference in hemispheric specialization leads to an important difference in the emotional life of most men and women:

> [A] man keeps his emotions in their place; and that place is on
> the right side of the brain, while the power to express his feelings
> in speech lies over on the other side. Because the two halves of
> the brain are connected by a smaller number of fibers than a

> woman's, the flow of information between one side of the brain and the other is more restricted. It is then often more difficult for a man to express his emotions because the information is flowing less easily to the verbal, left side of his brain.
>
> A woman may be less able to separate emotion from reason because of the way the female brain is organized. The female brain has emotional capacities on both sides of the brain, plus there is more information exchanged between the two sides of the brain. The emotional side is more integrated with the verbal side of the brain. A woman can [more easily] express her emotions in words because what she feels has been transmitted more effectively to the verbal side of her brain.

Scientists may quarrel about how specific or general or conclusive to make statements about gender differences in brain function, but some of these statements are backed by hard evidence. For example, the statement that for women, the emotional side of the brain is in better contact with the verbal side, is supported by the fact that the anterior commissure (a small band of nerve fibers connecting the right and left lobes of the brain) is noticeably thicker in the female brain than in the male (Allen and Gorski, 1991). In 1992, Allen and Gorski also reported that a cross-sectional area of the anterior commissure is larger in gay men than in heterosexual men (LeVay 1993, page 123). These observations may be the basis for the belief that women, on the average, are more intuitive thinkers; that they can more readily coordinate their thoughts and feelings, and that gay men are more attuned to the way a woman thinks because that's more like how they tend to think.

The principle that the male brain functions in a more compartmentalized way, is demonstrated in a study in which men and women, hooked up to a PET (a brain imaging device described in endnote 9, page 118), were given rhyming tasks (*e.g.*, "What words rhyme with cake?"). As they worked on the task, a particular brain region (the inferior frontal gyrus) was activated. In most men, only the region on the left side of the brain was activated. In most women, both right and left hemispheres were activated.[13]

Taken together, these findings suggest that the brain functions of women are more richly connected and operate more globally. Somewhat by contrast, the brain functions of men are more sharply focused, more concentrated. Does this mean that men have a tendency to be more analytical, more objective, more abstract in their thinking; better able to ignore thoughts that might interfere with what they are doing? Does this mean that women (and men with low-masculinized brains) tend more readily to see relationships between diverse objects, that they are also more intuitive and more artistic? Laboratory findings on sex differences in brain structure and function suggest that the answer may be Yes.

Prenatal brain masculinization

Life begins for male and female alike with a fertilized egg that develops at first into a proto-female embryo.[14] For the first six weeks of life, male and female human embryos look exactly alike. Then, in those embryos equipped with a Y chromosome, are the sex organs and the brain bathed in male hormones, and thus gradually become masculinized. As Figure 7.1 shows, the gradual masculinization of the sex organs can be observed (in autopsy) by the naked eye; masculinization of the brain requires microscopic study.

As the embryo continues to grow beyond the first six weeks of life, each and every embryo would develop into a female unless a Y-chromosome mechanism[15] initiates a process that saturates the embryo in male hormones and thus masculinizes both the brain and sex organs. Masculinization of the sex organs almost always produces typical male genitalia, while brain masculinization seems to vary considerably. There is evidence that some male brains become more masculinized than others. In a few males, perhaps, the brain is hardly masculinized at all. Differences in the degree to which the male brain has been masculinized during the prenatal period very likely sets a predisposition toward the individual's future sexual orientation. This is the thesis of a comprehensive 1987 article by Ellis and Ames, and a 1993 book by Simon LeVay.

There are differences in degree and differences in kind. There is no mistaking a penis for a vagina, and ordinarily (with rare exceptions) there is nothing in-between. In general physique, however, it is obvious to every ordinary observer that humans range over an unbroken continuum from extremely masculine to extremely feminine. It is unusual, but not unknown, to encounter a man whose general body build is boyish rather than mannish, or to encounter a woman whose body build is rather intermediate, something in-between a female figure and a male physique. The evidence is beginning to indicate that the brain of men and women also differ in degree of masculinity.

Variations in brain masculinization

Probably, some women have brains that are extremely feminine, most are typically feminine, and a few are more masculine than feminine. Likewise, some men's brains are probably very highly masculinized, most are moderately masculinized, and there is a small minority of men whose brain is hardly masculinized at all. This condition may validate the naive self-description of an unhappy homosexual man who lamented: "I am a male with a female brain." So acute is the discomfort of some men to live with what they regard as "a female brain," that they willingly undergo an extensive program of hormone treatments, and multiple surgeries including castration and an attempt to rearrange penile tissue to form a vagina and clitoris.[16]

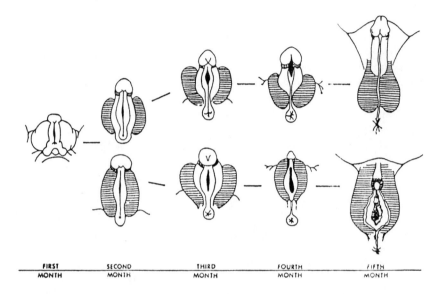

FIRST MONTH   SECOND MONTH   THIRD MONTH   FOURTH MONTH   FIFTH MONTH

Figure 7.1. During the first six weeks of prenatal life, the labioscrotal folds of male and female embryo are identical. Without the influence of sex hormones, the external folds (and internal tubercule) develop into female genitalia. Under the influence of male sex hormones, the same folds and tubercle develop into male sex organs. During the same prenatal period, sex hormones differentiate the brain of the male fetus, sex differences which are visible under a microscope.(Adapted from Silber, page 148).

Three testosterone peaks in the male lifespan

There are three testosterone peaks in the male lifespan: the prenatal, the "rough and tumble" years from about five to eight, and the one that ushers in puberty, with its maturation of the genitals and masculinization of the general male physique. (Does pubertal masculinization also effect brain changes? Very probably they just wait to be discovered.) It should be added that prenatal, fifth year, and pubertal masculization may be quite independent of each other. Some homosexual men may have a low-masculinized brain, but ordinary observation-leaves no doubt but that in general, homosexual men have a normally masculin-ized physique, including fully developed sexual organs.[17]

Animal studies in masculinization

The most direct and dramatic evidence of brain masculinization can be observed in animal laboratories. The process of brain masculinization can be more readily demonstrated in animals than in humans, partly because what is still permissible to do with infant animals would be criminal to do with to human infants. Also, it happens that in humans brain masculinization both begins and ends before birth.

Laboratory rats, however, have a very short prenatal period. They are born just 22 days after conception, at a stage of development similar to the fetus of other mammals. Since the masculinization of the brain of male rat pups continues for a period of time after birth, this process can be closely followed on slides of brain tissue, thanks to high-power electron microscopes.

Biologists have studied the process of brain masculinization in the male rat pups step-by-step by comparing slides of brain tissue taken from rats at various stages of development and comparing changes that occur in the brains and behavior of male rats and female rats. Laboratory workers can actually observe how male and female rat brains become more and more differentiated, week by week. Moir (pages 24-25) summarizes the observations of biologists, noting that they point to "specific differences in the length of some nerve cell connectors, a different pattern of branches, different pathways which chemical messengers of the hormones take to reach different destinations in the brain. The strands of nerve cells are [observed to be] much denser in the male rat, for instance, and some of its brain-cell nuclei [or clusters] are up to *eight times larger*" (emphasis added). As the animals mature, the brain of male and female become more and more different. LeVay (1993, page 26) also describes how the androgens (testosterone and similar steroids) reshape the male brain:

> Androgens "can cause one group of brain cells to become more electrically alive, another less active, and another to form a particular set of synaptic connections or synthesize a particular chemical. Steroids can even control whether brain cells live or die."

There is a portion of the brain known to regulate sexual behavior, an area that is part of the medial preoptic area of the hypothalamus. In the laboratory rat, this brain area is visibly larger in males than in females. When this brain area in a male animal is destroyed, not only does it cease to perform typically male copulatory acts, but it may also begin to show typically female behavior, like female posturing (lordosis) in the presence of a stud male.

When a group of male rats is given access to receptive females, it is clear that some males are much more lively, more active sexually, than others. When the most active males and the least active males are identified and killed (in the name of Science) and their brain areas compared, it is plain to see that the most active males had larger medial preoptic areas (LeVay 1993, page 90).

In animal studies, masculinization of the preoptic area could be increased by giving the rat an extra injection of testosterone while this area of the brain was still developing. A more provocative fact is that the brain masculinization of unborn male rats could be *reduced* by subjecting the mother to environmental stress, a treatment that is known to reduce the amount of testosterone available to her unborn male young.

An effective daily "stress treatment" consists of confining the rat during the last week of pregnancy to a clear plastic tube three times a day, and shining a bright light on it for 45 minutes. Result: the rat's male offspring are born with low-masculinized brains and behaved more like female rats.[18]

A simpler way to demasculinize the brain of male rats in utero, is to inject the pregnant female with an androgen-blocking drug (like flutamide). Male rats born from these pregnancies display the same demasculinized characteristics as castrates.[19]

Rats are not the only animals on which scientists have studied brain masculinization. In monkeys, as in humans, brain masculinization begins and ends before birth. The effect of testosterone on behavior (and, by implication, on brain masculinization) was demonstrated by a series of studies by Goy and his associates at the University of Wisconsin, Madison; first reported in 1967 (Phoenix, Goy, and Young), and continued through the 1970s.

When a group of pregnant monkeys were injected with testosterone, female offspring were found to engage in more rough play and do more play-mounting than untreated females. It was later found (Goy, Bercovitch, and McBriar) that by varying the time of pregnancy at which testosterone was injected, female offspring showed systematically different masculine traits.

> When injections had been given early in pregnancy, the female
> offspring engaged in more male-type play-mounting than did
> untreated females, but their level of rough play was not elevated.
> But when injections were given late in pregancy, the female off-
> spring showed elevated levels of rough-and-tumble play.

It therefore appears that the introduction of extra testosterone affects whatever aspect of brain masculinization is taking place at that time.

When human female fetuses are exposed to testosterone

What would happen if a human female fetus was bathed in male hormones? Such an experiment would of course be grossly unethical, but a rare genetic disorder variously called CAH (congenital adrenal hyperplasia) or AGS (adrenogenital syndrome) causes just that to happen.[20] (The syndrome can be quickly recognized when the girl is born and she can be promptly treated with drugs that restore the normal hormonal balance.) Several scientific papers[21] have documented the fact that as CAH girls grow up, they display more male-typical interests than their unaffected sisters: CAH girls would rather play with trucks than with dolls, and they score better on spatial ability tests in which boys typically outperform girls.

Regardless of whether Dörner's findings can be replicated or not, there is this evidence linking low-masculinization to a shortage of testosterone during a critical prenatal period. A medical misadventure[22] resulted in the fact that a number of male human fetuses were exposed to a below-average amount of male hormone. Psychiatrist I.D. Yalom *et al.* studied a group of boys, ages 6 to 16, who had been so "treated" (or mistakenly mistreated) during their prenatal life. When examined, interviewed and tested, these boys demonstrated a lack of assertiveness and aggressiveness, a lack of athletic ability, a lack of general masculinity, and a female pattern of their skill functions.

Homosexuality and low brain-masculinization

The German biologist, Günther Dörner, attempted to demonstrate the effects of maternal stress on the sexual orientation of human males. He reasoned that the end of World War II was a period of unusual environmental stress, so he accumulated a list of men who were born at the end of World War II. He reports that for this sample of men, homosexuality was found at a higher rate than for men born at other periods of time. So sure was Dörner of the accuracy of his findings, that he recommended testosterone injections for stress-burdened pregnant women who knew their unborn offspring was male, and who wanted to avert the likelihood that their son would be homosexual. [When he suggested this medical practice at an international symposium, Dörner was denounced for proposing "endrocinological euthenasia" (Mondimore, page 131).] LeVay (1996, pages 167-169) reports of a number of careful attempts to replicate Dörner's findings, and that they have failed to demonstrate any correlation between maternal stress and homosexuality.[23]

Homosexuality and bain laterality

Left-handedness. One line of evidence linking brain masculinization to homosexuality, is inferred from the knowledge that left-handedness is connected with a brain that follows a female organizational pattern. Homosexuals are more likely to be left-handed than chance would allow, according to a 1990 report by biologists Cheryl McCormick *et al.*[24]

The tendency toward left-handedness, it seems, is not absolute but is a matter of degree, and gay men show a greater tendency in the direction of left-handedness. Lindsay gave a 14-item questionnaire on hand preference to   two matched groups of men,[25] 94 gay and 100 straight. The results are shown on Figure 7.2. Note that most gay men are right-handed, but the percentage of right-handedness is smaller for gays than for straights. Note also that in this sample of 194 men, three percent are ambidextrous, and *all* are homosexual. Both left-handedness and homosexuality exist in all degrees, and so does left-handedness. Both seem to be related to brain laterality.

Hearing acuity. McCormick *et al.* compared the right and left ear hearing acuity of 32 gay men, 32 heterosexual men, 30 lesbians, and 30 heterosexual women. They then compared the linkage between left-handedness and hearing acuity in male and female gay and heterosexual groups. They reported that in this linkage, gay men resemble lesbians more than they resemble heterosexual men. The investigators conclude (1994, page 525) that this finding suggests that gay men and lesbians share "a neurological characteristic [that is] likely [to have been] present from birth, and . . . suggests that a neurobiological factor is involved in the origin of sexual orientation."

Fingerprint asymmetry. Hall and Kimura have contributed a provocative study linking fingerprints to brain dominance, and demonstrating the similarity in brain dominance of gay men and women. Most people, men and women, have more swirls on the fingers of their right hand than on their left. More women than men show the opposite characteristic: they have more ridges on their left hand than on their right; they are leftward asymetical. Hall and Kimura reported in 1993 and 1994 that gay men are more likely than straight men to be leftward asymetical.

Now Hall and Kimura set out to demonstrate that those gay men who resembled women in fingerprint asymmetry also resembled women in brain dominance. Men in general are left-brain dominant, in most women the brain functions bilaterally. By employing an ingenious test of brain dominance,[26] the investigators were able to demonstrate that those gay men whose fingerprints were leftward asymetrical, were also more likely to show bilateral brain function, rather than left-brain dominance.

Visio-spatial ability

The "Mental Rotations" problem is one in which the subject is presented with the drawing of an object and asked, How will the object look when rotated 90 degrees? On such a test of visio-spatial ability, homosexuals performed significantly more poorly than a matched group of heterosexual men.[27] On tests of verbal ability, however, gay men outperform their straight counterparts.[28]

It can of course be argued that there are gender differences in verbal and spatial ability because boys and girls have different learning opportunities, and that all mental differences between gay and straight men are culturally determined. Even though the groups have been carefully matched for education and athletic experience, obtained group differences never deliver absolute truths. With that qualification, it can be reported that in McCormick *et al.* (1994, page 525) "gay men showed lower spatial ability compared with heterosexual men and [also showed] a different cognitive profile of abilities in spatial perception relative to fluency skills."

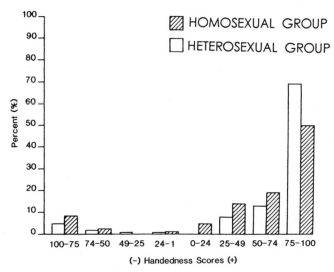

Figure 7.2. Distribution of handedness scores in matched groups of 94 homosexual men, and 100 heterosexual men. (From Lindsay)

Sanders and Ross-Field compared the spatial ability of matched groups of homosexual men, heterosexual men, and heterosexual women, 63 subjects in all. Instruments were a water level test, and a mechanical diagrams test.29 On both tests, homosexual males resembled heterosexual females more than they resembled heterosexual males. The investigators conclude (page 280) that their findings point to "a biological determinant of cognitive ability. . . ."

The LH response

In another study, the response tendencies of gay mens' brains were demonstrated to resemble the female norm. At a certain point of the menstrual cycle, there is a surge in a woman's estrogen output, and this triggers a leutinizing hormone (LH) response, which is believed to be mediated by the hypothalamus. Suppose you gave an estrogen injection to three matched groups of individuals: (1) heterosexual women, (2) heterosexual men, and (3) gay men.

You would of course expect female brains to make the female-typical LH response, and the male brains not to. But would the brain of a gay man respond (perhaps to a lesser degree) in a way that resembled the female norm? Dörner claimed to have demonstrated this in his German laboratory, and in 1984 Brian Gladue *et al.* reported the successful replication of this finding in the United States.30 (See Figure 7.3.) Given an injection of estrogen, 25 heterosexual men showed no LH response, but a majority of gay men showed an LH response that resembled the normal female response. [It should be noted that only nine of the 14 gay male subjects (just 64 per cent) gave a strong LH response, which attests to the heterogeneity of the male homosexual sample.

Gay-straight differences in size of hypothalamus structure INAH3.

It is clear that a gender difference in the size of certain areas of the hypothalamus prevails for laboratory rats. Is it also true for humans? In 1989, Allen and Gorski reported laboratory evidence that this was true. They found two structures buried in the hypothalamus that were larger in men than in women. One structure (code-named INAH3) was between two to three times larger in men than in women, and this difference applied to males and females of all ages.

In 1991 LeVay reported on a comparison of the preoptic areas of the hypothalamus of a sample of gay men who had died of AIDS, and of the same brain area of a sample of unselected men. His findings were not the result of a "fishing expedition;" his research plan was based on a substantial body of laboratory knowledge. LeVay reported, as shown on Figure 7.4, that "INAH3 [the hypothalamic structure researched by Allen and Gorski] was between two and three times larger, on average, in heterosexual men than in the gay men whose brains I examined" (LeVay 1996, page 143).[31]

An update on homosexuality and brain differences is the subject of an article by Robert Finn, science writer, in a 1996 issue of *The Scientist*. Homosexual and straight men seem to differ, on the average, in skills that suggest differences in brain masculinization rather than differences in training or experience. Psychologists Hall and Kimura, for example, gave a "Throw-to Target" task to 20 heterosexual males and 20 homosexual males, matched for age, sports history, and hand strength. Results "provide new evidence suggesting an association between sexual orientation and motor-performance profiles" (page 395).[32]

Concluding questions. What would a male with a low-masculinized brain be like? As an infant, he would be quieter, less vigorous than most males, less interested in objects than in people or dolls (which may be conceptualized as substitute babies). As a boy, he would be more interested in quiet, indoor activities than in rough-and-tumble outdoor activities; more interested in playing less interested in objects than in people or dolls (which may be conceptualized as substitute babies). As a boy, he would be more interested in quiet, indoor activities than in rough-and-tumble outdoor activities; more interested in playing with girls or helping his mother around the house. Favorite activities would be

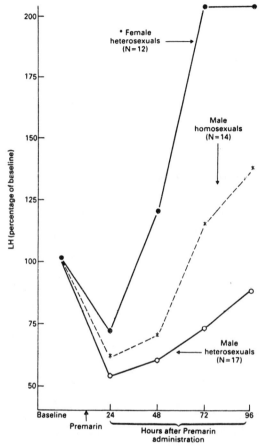

Figure 7.3. How female heterosexuals, male homosexuals, and male heterosexuals differ in LH (leutinizing hormmone) response to a single injection of Premarin, an estrogen. (Adapted from Gladue et al., 1984.)

playing house, or playing school. Perhaps he would like to walk around in his mother's shoes and wear her clothes. As an adult, the chances are a little better than 50-50, according to the longitudinal study by Richard Green, that he will be either homosexual or bisexual.

But what if he does not become a gay man? Is he more likely to be a misfit or a successful person, a good husband [33] and father, a good friend, an artist, musician, teacher or a member of some other helping profession? If Richard Green had studied those of his subjects who did not grow up to be gay men or bisexuals, we might have some answers to those questions, but he did not.

Figure 7.4. In search of INAH-3

In the late 1980s, Roger Gorski and his colleagues at UCLA found a tiny structure (INAH-3) in the human brain that was three times as large in males as in females. This finding paved the way for Simon LeVay's discovery of a similar difference between gay men (who had died of AIDS) and a presumably heterosexual control group.

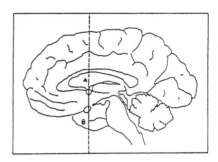

To find cluster number 3 of the Interstital Nuclei of the Anterior Hypothalamus (INAH-3), you would need a human brain and a well-equipped biology laboratory, including a high-power electron microscope. Or you can look at these figures and be guided by the following paragraphs.

Slice away the front end of the brain along the plane indicated by the vertical line in the top figure. The middle figure magnifies a portion of the surface revealed by removing the front end: a small rectangular area as tall as the center portion of line A-B in the top figure.

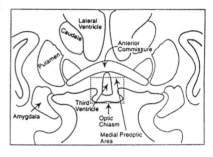

The bottom figure magnifies the small area in the center of the middle figure, enclosed by dotted lines. Four patterns of dots, vaguely resembling shoe prints, represent the interstitial nuclei. The encircled 3 identifies INAH-3.

LeVay (1996, page 131) supplements the bottom figure with the following note: "The drawing is semi-diagrammatic: all four nuclei are not usually seen in the same transverse slide." *Figures adapted from LeVay 1996, page 131.*

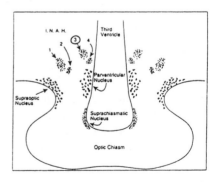

However, we are not altogether in the dark about what happens to men who probably have strong genetic tendencies to become homosexual but, for whatever reason, do not. This evidence comes from studies of gay men who had a straight twin brother. We will examine this evidence in Chapter 19. In Chapter 26 we will propose a program of research that may advance our understanding of gay men, and also of those straight men who share the gay man's homosexual predispositions.

NOTES TO CHAPTER 7

1. Weinrich refers to the 1964 paper of Young, Goy, and Phoenix, papers by MacLusky and Naftolin 1981, McEwen 1981, de Lacoste-Utamsing and Holloway 1982, and Swaab and Fliers 1985.

2. The principle of equal rights for women—economic, educational, legal, and social—rests on moral grounds, not on the premise that men and women are either physically or psychologically equal.

3. Why are human newborns so utterly helpless, compared with other primates? This important topic has been already touched upon and is taken up in further detail in Chapter 27.

4. A Russian proverb goes: "Men fall in love with their eyes, women with their ears."

5. Blum (page 228) cites an article by Goleman on differential responses to conversation.

6. Is male superiority in tests of spatial reasoning the result of learned role differences, and cultural encouragement? Or is this an innate difference evolved to equip the male for his role as a hunter and defender of his home territory?

7. Women pay a high price for this tendency to become so deeply attached to other people. According to Blum (page 218), "Scientists believe that women are more likely to suffer from depression than men because they suffer more deeply from interpersonal loss. Prolonged grieving overtaxes their limbic system to the point that it finally becomes unresponsive and lethargic; the neural circuits have become worn out, and the result is a collapse into numbness." Back in 1947, the reported rate of depression for women was eight times as high as for men. Currently the rate is twice as high.

8. Why does the brain show such a hilly, crunched-up surface? Nature designed the cortex to have a maximal surface exposure, like a home or auto radiator. Perhaps surface exposure favors a richer blood supply, which promotes neural functioning.

9. LeVay (page 35) explains how PET (positive emission tomography) scanning

enables an experimenter to "look inside the brain" of a living person, and see which regions of the brain are most active at a particular moment:

> In this procedure . . . water is labeled with a short-lived radioactive isotope . . . and injected into the bloodstream of a human subject. The subject is then required to do some task—to read, say, or to do mental arithmetic. While this task is going on, the distribution of the radioactive isotope within the brain is determined by an array of detectors ranged around the head.
>
> The reason this technique yields information about neural activity is that there is a [high correlation] between neuronal activity and blood flow. If the neurones in a small region of the brain increase their activity, blood flow to this region is increased to allow for the extra metabolic demands of the active neurons, and so the level of radioactivity in this region increases.

10. Blum's source is *Newsweek*, March 20, 1955, "Gray matters," reported by Sharon Begley.

11. Blum reports (page 67-68) a study in which 24 men and 24 women were asked to turn up a speaker until the volume began to feel uncomfortable. Result: men appear to tolerate sounds twice as loud as women tolerate.

12. Blum gives her source as an article in *Discover*, May 1994, pages 14-15, entitled, "Quiet-eared Women and the Men Born with Them."

13. Shaywitz *et al.* conducted their brain imaging study with 19 males and 19 females, all right-handed. They report (page 607):

> During phonological tasks, brain activation in males lateralized to the left inferior frontal gyrus regions; in females the pattern of activation is very different, engaging more diffuse neural systems that involve both the left and right interior frontal gyrus. Our data provide clear evidence for a sex difference in the functiona organization of the brain for language . . . .

14. Remnants of the human male's proto-female beginnings are certain female physical features that, curiously, are permanent features of the male physique. Hidden from view is a regressed müllerian tube, which in females develops into the internal female sex organs. More obvious are those proto-female organs which lie at the surface of every male chest: the nipples.

15. Biologists describe the process by which the embryo is converted from proto-female to male: A single gene on the Y-chromosome produces TDF (a "testes

determining factor") which causes the embryonic gonads to develop into testes rather than ovaries. The testes then begin producing testosterone, a hormone that flows through the fetal bloodstream and masculinizes the organism. Testosterone shapes the external male sex organs, as it also stimulates the wolffian ducts to develop into the internal male genitalia.

Testosterone can be detected in the fetal bloodstream of a male fetus two months old; its concentration gradually increases until at 14 weeks the testosterone level of a male embryo shows about the same concentration as a boy at puberty. Then it sinks to low levels, and at six months after birth, the baby boy's testosterone level is only one-tenth of the adult level.

A detailed and technical description of this process is contained in an 1987 article by Ellis and Ames, who argue that fetal undermasculinization of the brain is a key factor in the genesis of homosexuality.

16. For reviews of articles on sex reassignment surgery, see 1986 article by Abramowitz, and 1990 article by Green and Fleming. Abramowitz concluded that in seven per cent of the cases, the outcome was tragic.

A 2001 article by Krege et al. offers this state-of-the-art report (not very encouraging) on transsexual surgery: The authors describe a "challenging" surgical procedure for forming a vagina-like pocket from the skin of the penile shaft, and converting the glans into a sensitive "clitoris." From 1995-2000, this procedure was followed on 66 male patients. Minor complications (like narrowing of the urethra) occurred in 36 per cent of the patients, and 14 per cent suffered major complications like necrosis of the glans or urethra. Krege sent out a long-term follow-up questionnaire and 31 of the 66 responded: 90 per cent said they were satisfied with the cosmetic result of the operation and could experience orgasm; 58 reported that they were having sexual intercourse. *Over half of the patients (35 or the 66) did not respond to the questionnaire.*

17. In a pioneering study of San Francisco homosexuals conducted back in the 1930s, E. Lowell Kelly determined by direct observation and by interview that homosexual men are physically quite normal.

18. LeVay, 1993, page 90, credits Ingeborg Ward at Villanova University with discovery of this "maternal stress effect."

19. Neumann *et al.*

20. For a description of the CAH process in biochemical terms, see LeVay 1996, page 121.

21. This research is found in Berenbaum and Hines, Berenbaum and Snyder, and Resnick *et al.* A 1990 paper by Berenbaum summarizes studies in this field.

22. Their mothers had been having difficult pregnancies and doctors had been prescribing a medication that was suggested by animal research. This medication was later found to reduce the amount of male hormones available to their unborn boy. When this became known, use of this medication by mothers-to-be was promptly stopped.

23. LeVay (1993, pages 125-126) reports an interview study that attempted (but failed) to find support for Dörner's hypothesis:

> Michael Bailey and his colleagues . . . interviewed women who
> had had at least one gay and one straight son. The women did
> not report any excess of stressful events during the pregnancies
> that gave rise to gay sons.

24. This report was confirmed by a meta-analysis of 20 studies on handedness, covering a total of 2,400 subjects, male and female. Results showed a significant relationship between handedness and sexual orientation, reported investigators Lalumière and Zucker.

25. The groups were clients at a London (England) STD (sexually transmitted disease) clinic that serves both straights and gays. Clients were asked to fill out the questionnaire for purely research purposes, and this request was rarely refused.

26. For a test of brain dominance, subjects wore a set of earphones through which different words were presented simultaneously to the right and left ears. If the subject hears more clearly the word presented to the right ear, the left hemisphere of his brain dominates (because of the crossover between ear and brain). This is the case for men in general. If neither ear has a consistent advantage, the brain is functioning bilaterally, which is more likely to be the case for women.

27. All subjects were given a 20-item questionnaire to survey their background in mechanical drawing and science courses, familiarity with hand tools and arranging objects. On the basis of their responses, no significant differences were found between the two groups. The investigators (Gladue and Beatty, page 107) concluded: "[O]ur results are more compatible with a biological than with a psycho-social explanation of . . . sexual orientation differences."

28. Wilmot and Bierley compared the performance of 20 heterosexual and 20 homosexual males on verbal and nonverbal IQ. Homosexuals scored significantly higher on verbal IQ, and lower on nonverbal IQ.

29. Two water level tests were used, to test how clearly the subject understood

that no matter at what angle a bottle is held, the water level is always horizontal. One test used simple drawings, and required the subject to draw a line indicating the water level, assuming that the bottle was one-third full. The other test used a mechanical simulation of a bottle which the experimenter tilted at different angles, while the subject turned knobs to show the correct water level.

The Vincent Mechanical Diagrams Test presents various mechanisms composed of levers, cogs, or pulleys, and asks the subject to indicate what movement each mechanism would produce.

30. The experimenters' sample of gay men included only men who "reported a long-term pattern of sexual behavior and fantasies involving male partners" (page 1498).

31. Even though LeVay's findings were predictable on the basis of animal laboratory studies, skeptics asked: Could the small size of gay men's INAH3 be the result of homosexual activity . . . of AIDS infection? LeVay answers (1996, page 145): "It will not be possible to settle this issue definitively until some method [not yet known] becomes available to measure the size of INAH3 in living people. . . ."

32. [The] Throw-to-Target task required subject to lob a Velcro-covered ball underhanded toward the center of a carpet-covered frame mounted on a wall around nine and a third feet away. Each subject was allowed five practice trials with each hand before 10 test trials. Error scores were calculated as the distance from the center square (Wilmot and Bierley, pages 398-399).

33. There are research indications, discussed on page 462, that a wife's satisfaction correlates positively with her rating of her husband's "femininity" (which in this book would be described as his low masculinity): a good husband is described as compassionate, warm, and sensitive to the needs of others.

8   Gender-Discordant Boys
from Biblical Days to Modern Times

The biblical story of the twin sons of Isaac and Rebekah, Jacob and Esau, shows us that in biblical days, attention was already drawn to the difference between the gentle, thoughtful, sedentary man, and his rough, active, outdoorsman brother. Jacob is described as "a mild man who stayed in camp" (Genesis 25:26), and was his mother's favorite.

Their father, Isaac, preferred Esau the hunter (25:28). Jacob is portrayed as a dreamer whose dreams brought him to the presence of God, who promised that Jacob's offspring would be a source of blessing for the whole earth (Genesis 28:10-15).

In rabbinical lore, Jacob is described as smooth and handsome at birth, while his brother was blood-red, hairy, and born with fully-developed teeth. Jacob spent all his life in the pursuit of learning, while Esau became a hunter and a dissipated idolator. To the rabbis, Jacob symbolized the spiritual beauty of Israel, and Esau portrayed "the ugliness of the pagan world—its wars and bloodshed;" Jacob was regarded as "a model of virtue and righteousness," "a great and holy man" (*Encyclopedia Judaica*, "Jacob").

What this Bible story says about masculine variation is that gentleness and brutality can be brothers, even twin brothers, and that both may be the sons of the same noble sire. (And gentle Jacob's twelve sons included two fierce warriors, Simeon and Levi.) The story unequivocally identifies the man of gentleness with spiritual beauty and closeness to God; and his violent brother is identified with the less admirable side of humanity. Gentle and patient Jacob was also a man of substantial virility: father of twelve sons (and one daughter) from whom sprang the twelve tribes of Israel.[1]

The topic of individual differences has always been part of modern psychology. The first major study in this area focused upon individual differences in intelligence. Alfred Binet pioneered this work in France, and Lewis Terman brought it to the United States, where it dominated psychology in the 1920s and 1930s. Sigmund Freud focused upon individual differences in personality and character. His presence in American psychology was established by the Clark University lectures, which Freud was invited to present in 1911. The founder and president of Clark University was psychologist G. Stanley Hall. Clark was the only university in the world to bestow an academic honor on Freud during his lifetime.

Sheldon's Studies in Physique and Temperament

In the 1930s, a large-scale study of individual differences in temperament was begun by William H. Sheldon, Yale University professor who held both an

122

M.D. and a Ph.D. He was interested in how temperament might be related to physique, and he amassed a vast archive of 4,000 photographs of Yale University freshmen. (Rather recently this archive was destroyed; it was regarded as no longer of research value and was believed to include nude photographs of many Yale alumni who went on to become public figures.)

Here we will draw on Sheldon's findings regarding male physique and temperament. It is easy to assume that men can be ranked from a highly masculine extreme to an almost feminine extreme in body type. When Sheldon tried to rate a large group of men by their degree of masculinity, what problems did he run into? What did he discover about the shape of the curve from one end of the distribution to the other?

Working with his population of 4,000 college students, Sheldon found that the majority of men do not stand midway between extremely high masculinity and extremely low masculinity. In their physique, the majority of men are decidedly on the masculine side. Extremely masculine men are common, but "males who most closely resemble women . . . were found to be very rare." (page 283) Sorting a sample of 2,000 photographs into seven ranks, from very unmasculine to very masculine, only two or three cases seemed to belong to ranks one or two, whereas hundreds of cases fell into ranks six and seven.

Sheldon learned that to rate physique accurately, you had to ignore skin and hair texture, because differences in physique were more or less independent of differences in hair and skin texture. Quite commonly, men with rather unmasculine physiques did have very masculine hair and skin texture. Effeminate hair and skin texture was even more of a rarity among men, Sheldon found, than unmasculine physique.

Studying his subjects, Sheldon found that in a general way, behavior followed structure; most men with a very masculine physique also had a very masculine life history, and most men who were extremely effeminate in body build, had a very different life history. Expressed statistically, physique and temperament, according to Sheldon, correlate about +.80 (page 368). Here is a summary of two extreme cases Sheldon describes (on pages 136-144, and 159-173):

Boris

Boris "has an extremely powerful, massive upper body," and his bodily hair has "a sharply masculine distribution." His face is bony and muscular, with powerful jaws. From babyhood he has been extremely active. "During the first six years there were many fights, with Boris usually the winner." At the age of "six, he boxed four rounds with a 9-year-old boy at a a public exhibition."

In high school Boris was an "athletic star of first magnitude, excelling in all of the organized sports, and he was undisputedly the best fighter in the school. He was already fighting as a lightweight in summer boxing tournaments." He was barred from participating in high school athletics, however, because of poor academic performance, and the charge that he had physically attacked a male teacher. He several times was offered university athletic scholarships, but was dropped for poor scholarship.

Girls always found him attractive, and challenged him to demonstrate his sexual capabilities. When he was a young teenager, a girl about three or four years older than him became sexually aggressive and tried to masturbate him. Boris decided "that he could do a better job than she could." When he was around 14, a high school girl "insisted upon investigating as to whether he was yet 'grown up.' They both decided that he was." Girls continued to hound him, Boris said. From age 14 to 21, he "estimates that he had sexual intercourse with possibly 30 or 40 different women who were not prostitutes."

By Sheldon's assessment, Boris is an undisciplined fighter; lacking in senstitive appreciation, insight, lability of mind, compassion, and restraint. For him, "sexual intercourse . . . is a realistic, matter-of-fact business. He cannot remember ever having an erection at the thought of a girl, or as a result of reading, or from looking at pictures. . . . Erection is for the most part the result of physical intimacy and contact. Intercourse itself is an exercise requiring from ten minutes to half an hour, 'depending on how much cooperation I get.'

". . . When no women are available he will masturbate about once a week, almost always when awakened at night by an erection. He is not aware that dreaming ever has anything to do with these noctural erections."

Sheldon contrasts the case of Boris, an obtuse and extremely masculine, active, and aggressive person, pursued by girls all his life, with the case of Christopher, a sensitive, weak, effeminate and reclusive boy. Ignored by his childhood peers , and lonely through adolescence and young manhood, Christopher was finally "discovered" in graduate school by a more mature woman who was looking, we suppose, for a discreet sexual partner.

Christopher

Christoper presents "an extremely weak, fragile physique." His body expresses "softness and relaxation [rather] than strength and energy." His face is marked by a "delicate, thin-lipped mouth . . . shaped almost exquisitely, like that of a pretty girl," and a weak chin. "The skin texture throughout the body is fine, and the skin is strikingly white. The head hair is luxuriant, light brown, fine in texture, and has a long wave. Secondary hair is sparse, showing essentially feminine distribution. The eyelashes are long and silky." But Christopher's general body shape, Sheldon notes, is not effeminate.

"Christopher was an 'angelic child.' He rarely cried, never had a temper tantrum, never got into mischief, and caused no trouble of any sort."

As a child he was always rather awkward "and seems to have been accepted by the boys of his generation as a harmless nonentity who enjoyed a license to be let alone." He never tried to play baseball, football, and never learned to swim. He never played much with girls. "He spent much of his early childhood wandering around alone, or staying home with his mother."
"At age 4 he was fond of sitting in a favorite little chair in the kitchen, where he would apparently daydream for half a day at a time, almost without moving. Another of his favorite occupations was to walk about the yard, apparently aimlessly but actually living out a complete romantic drama in imagination. . ."

An unhappy childhood was followed by a frustrated adolescence, during which time he admired his powerful erections and wasted this "splendid adolescent sexuality with no outlet but the despised masturbation. . . ." His mother assured him that some day sex would bring him great happiness. Meanwhile, he was weak, shy, and friendless. He occupied his time collecting stamps and pennies. His parents tried, unsuccessfully, to encourage him to develop hobbies of a more social nature, to learn to dance, or to take part in school plays.
"Saturdays he generally stayed home all day, sleeping most of the forenoon . . . lying in bed and indulging in a kind of fantasy . . . intermediate between daydreams and night dreams. In the afternoon he usually would read, but never anything touching on school work. . . . [His reading was chosen for sexual stimulation, and he also] read all of Dickens twice."

He then attended a small coeducational college, living in the attic of a rooming house, and living a lonely, passive life. "During the entire four years of college his mind was preoccupied with sex." Movies were his main entertainment. He walked the streets at night "in the forlorn hope of 'picking up' a female." He always carried with him three dollars for a prostitute, which he was told was the going rate, but he never found one.
An indifferent student, Christopher "majored in education, and

after graduation enrolled for graduate work in the School of
Education of a midwestern state university. There he established
a very satisfactory sexual liaison with a sensitive young woman
some two or three years his senior. . . ." He did fairly well in
graduate work, and was working toward a Ph.D. degree.

Of Sheldon's two extreme cases, which one reported a homosexual
encounter? Not Christopher, who was too shy for social contact of any sort, but
Boris, whose splendid physique attracted the interest of boys as well as girls.
When he was about five, Boris engaged in "mutual excitation" with a group of
older boys. "At age seven an older boy tried to practice fellatio on him . . . [but
Boris] 'beat up the guy'" (page 136).

The case of Christoper is interesting because here we see at close range a very
gender-discordant boy who did not become homosexual.[2] In itself, this is not so
unusual; perhaps no more than one out of two gender-discordant boys becomes
homosexual. What does the case of Christopher tell us about how those who do
differ from those who don't?

In the popular imagination, effeminacy has long been associated with homosexual behavior. Nowadays, gay men learn to suppress their effeminacy,[3] since
potential partners are known to be attracted nowadays to "straight-looking" men.
But not long ago, "fairies" painted their faces and wore feminine articles of clothing to signal their availability to men to whom "fairies" were acceptable as pros-
titute-substitutes. But was the use of cosmetics and feminine dress nothing more
than a signal to their trade? Or could it have been an expression of their personalities, as well? When they were small children, had these "fairies" been effeminate boys, or sissy boys, who liked to dress up in mother's clothes, wear mother's shoes, and rouge their cheeks?

Early research in male gender-discordance

In 1973, Saghir and Robins interviewed 90 homosexual men and reported
that two thirds recalled "having been girl-like during childhood." Only three per
cent of a heterosexual control group recalled such a childhood (Saghir and
Robbins, 1973, pages 118-21). In 1974, an Arizona State University sociologist,
Frederick L. Whitam also had the hunch that sissy boys grow up to be gay men.
To test his hypothesis, he visited bars, parties, and recreational places in both
Phoenix and New York, and located 107 young men who claimed to be gay, and
were willing to answer a few questions about their early childhood. Whitam gave
them a questionnaire asking them to recall whether as a child they had certain
gender-atypical interests: playing with dolls, dressing up in women's clothing,
playing with girls and talking to older women. (Their responses were matched
with a control group of 68 men believed to be exclusively heterosexual.)

Whitam's findings showed that gay men recalled such gender-atypical childhood interests significantly more often than straights. For example, almost half (47 out of 107) of the gay men recalled a childhood interest in cross-dressing, and none of 68 exclusively heterosexual men recalled such an interest.

Unsatisfied with the early recollections of adults, behavioral scientists began to study study gender discordant boys directly. In 1983, Richard Green reported a study in which adult raters viewed the tapes of children at play. A group of 27 children ranging in age from 4-10 years included 12 "sissy boys," an age-matched group of 8 ordinary boys, and 7 age-matched girls. All were video-taped walking, running, throwing a ball, and telling a story. (They all wore the same clothing, and swimming caps were worn to conceal differences in their hair.) Adult raters viewed the tapes, presented in random order, and rated each behavior on a five-point scale from "very likely male" to "very likely female." As expected, "sissy boys" were consistently ranked intermediate between the two control groups.

In 1984, Zuger reported on a follow-up study of 55 males brought to a clinic because of "feminine" behaviors. He reported that two thirds eventually became homosexual.

Richard Green's longitudinal study of sissy boys[4]

In 1987 Richard Green published a longitudinal study that paralleled the Zuger study. Green located 66 gender-discordant boys, ages 4 through 12, and matched them by age range with a control group of 56 randomly selected boys. Interrogation of their parents showed that 35 percent of these gender-discordant boys began cross-dressing before their second birthday, and over 90 percent were cross-dressing before their sixth birthday. (Of the control group, only 20 percent ever cross-dressed, and another 20 percent rarely cross-dressed). For 82 percent of the gender-discordant boys, their best friend was a girl. (This was true of only two percent of the controls.)

Green then waited for his subjects to grow up. After 15 years he was able to locate 44 of his original group of 66 "sissy boys." His finding: three-quarters of them were determined now to be homosexual or bisexual.[5] Of those 35 controls who could still be located, only one—less than 10 percent—was homosexual.) It is the conclusion of this and other studies[6] that *childhood gender discordance is the most accurate single predictor of adult homosexuality.*

These studies show that gender-awareness and cross-gender interests begin at a very early age, in some cases by the first year of life. Only a small minority of boys in general are attracted to girl playmates, to dolls, and to girl's clothing. It would not be such a great leap of inference to suppose that "sissy boys" act differently because they feel different: they feel more feminine than most boys; these anatomical boys are, to a significant extent, temperamentally female.

Autobiographical recollections

Recalling his sissy-boy childhood, a young man at a Christian ex-gay conference recalls:

> Nothing would have made my father happier than for me to have been his hunting buddy, but I just wasn't wired that way. My older sister was happy to go along with dad when he went hunting or fishing. One day, I heard my grandmother say to Mother, "Sally should have been born a boy, and Sidney should have been the girl."[7]

This chapter draws heavily on *Farm Boys*, by Will Fellows,[8] a study based on about 50 interviews with homosexual men who grew up on midwestern farms. The interviews are a rich source of recollections about a felt gender-discordance that dates back to their earliest childhood. Additionally, the interviews cover their sexual experience, marital history (25 percent of them had been married), and adult experience.

On the farm, gender roles are very well defined. A man's domain emphasized fieldwork: tending crops in the fields, and taking care of farm machinery and vehicles. The woman's domain centered around housework, but extended to the garden, and to caring for the chickens and milk cows. Women and girls were sometimes expected to help the men, but boys were discouraged from showing any interest in women's work. The *Farm Boys* interviews suggest that the sharp definition of gender roles in farm society makes life especially difficult for the gender-discordant boy.

Appeal of cross-gender role. The following interview excerpts emphasize the boys' attraction to the cross-gender role, and discomfort with their assigned role. Cross-dressing, playing with girls' toys, cooking, baking, sewing, and caring for animals expressed their natural interests, as the following excerpts from Fellows' book indicate:

> [Terry:] When I was real little, playing with my sisters and cousins, I would dress up like Annie Oakley. I'd put on a skirt over my jeans and cowboy boots, and even had socks for boobs.[9] My mom said, "*Your dad doesn't like it when you dress up like that.*" The message was that I was not to be feminine. . . I was to be masculine, butch. On the other hand, there was nothing wrong with a girl being a tomboy and holding her own. . . . I tried to excel at sports, dated girls, and stayed in the closet, playing the butch role. [He later married and became a father.] (Fellows, pages 12-13)
> [When Everett and his brother Andrew played cowboy games, Everett always played the damsel in distress.] I would put my

mother's and sister's discarded nylons on my head for long hair, and wrap a cloth around me for a dress. (Fellows, page 207)

[David recalled that his aunt] would bring all kinds of old dresses and purses and hats—even little bottles of cologne and old lipsticks. My younger brother and I would put this stuff on and parade around.
. . . My parents would laugh and take pictures. (Fellows, page 136)

Playing house and indoor craft activities appealed to Fellows' respondents when they were young boys.

[Doug:] One day I saw a doll house in a toy catalog and I thought, there you have a nice litle house . . . so I asked for a doll house for Christmas. . . . I didn't act embarrassed by it. . . My older brother made a big deal out of that, and *for years I was ridiculed* as the little brother who asked for a doll house for Christmas. (Fellows, page 145)

[When David told his parents what he wanted for Christmas, they would respond, "*Oh, that's for girls*,"] but still I wanted things that other boys wouldn't want, like an Indian bead craft set, a loom to make potholders, a little aluminum tea set, and a Betty Crocker baking set. (Fellows, page 133)

Artistic and musical interests. Fellows' interviews contain an impressive number of references to artistic and aesthetic interests, covering a wide area of activities:

[Cornelius:] Surreptitiously I learned to crochet and embroider from my sisters. I was really quite good at handwork, but I wouldn't allow my brothers to see me doing it. When I was seven or eight, my mother . . . taught me how to work [her new sewing machine]. I loved to work that machine and would sit at it for hours, hemming sheets and pillow cases. (Fellows, page 35)

[Dennis:] I got into embroidery in my early teens. I liked doing things with my hands, and I liked embroidery because you had colored threads, nice pictures of flowers and little animals, and when you got done you had something real prettty. Dad didn't like that I was doing it—it was sissy—so I didn't make a show of it. My mother bought it for me in the first place, so it must have been okay with her. One time I told a kid from school that I would let him see my embroidery if he promised he wouldn't tell. I showed it to him and the next day in school he told everybody, which was disastrous. I didn't do embroidery again. I became very conscious of what male things were, of what one does and doesn't do. *I've always been envious of women* who could pull out their knitting and do that while they're talking or watching television. (Fellows, pages 86-87)

[Norm] *I'd watch Grandma crochet and I wanted to learn how to do that* . . . so I learned how to crochet, and that was my hobby. (Fellows, page 117)

[Henry] Joining choir in my sophomore year got me out of phys. ed. one day a week. I loved music anyway. I loved singing. . . . I also wanted to learn to play piano, and bugged my parents until they finally let me take lessons. For some reason, *my dad hated music and didn't want one of his sons being a musician.* . . . (Fellows, page 66)

[Ken Y. recalls that in 4H club] . . . I wasn't interested in doing any of the farm activities. I wanted to get into drama and speech. . . Each club in the county put on a skit . . . . I designed the whole act and got costumes for everyone. . . . (Fellows, page 286)

[Joe:] *I was always interested in a lot of the traditional queen things*—clothes, cooking, academics, music, theater. . . . From the sixth grade, I was in various choirs—large choir [one of five boys and forty-five girls], madrigal groups, solo ensemble. (Fellows, page 294)

[Doug:] For a while I wanted to play a muscial instrument . . . and in my early teens I started to take voice lessons. I also started geting teased rather mercilessly by my older brother about this sissy activity. [Doug adds that he gave it up after three years because] I really didn't like the discipline of practicing, but deep down a lot of it had to do with being pegged as a sissy. (Fellows, page 145)

[James:] When I was four or five years old, *I knew there was something different about me* because of the things I liked to do.

[James tells of picking bouquets of apple blossoms, of his joy in seeing the first violets of spring, of enjoying the beauty of the wild flowers in the woods and hills around the farm,] and I never heard my brothers talk about them. (Fellows, page 107)

[Flower-arranging was another interest of John's, and at the county fair he competed "with about fifteen elderly ladies and one other young man," and won best-of-show twice.] (Fellows, page 100)

[David:] My older brother went out for football and track, but I just wasn't into that. I liked gardening, and my mom would let me order some gladiolus bulbs or something different. . . . I was good in the garden. (Fellows, page 136)

Mechanically untalented. Fellows' respondents expressed regret that they "didn't fit in" as a member of a culture in which a sharp distinction was made between men's work—outdoor, mechanical, muscular—and women's work. They were embarrassed at how poorly they compared with a skillful older or, worse yet, younger brother. They considered themselves to be mechanically clumsy and ill-adapted to the repair and maintenance of farm machinery and vehicles, which they were introduced to at a very early age.

[Todd:] My brother Tony and I started . . . to drive a tractor [at about age six] . . . We started out doing the things that didn't require a whole lot of brains. . . When you got into junior high . . . hopefully . . . you'd pick up all the mechanical skills. I never did. I was always saying, "Dad, I don't know what's wrong, but it's not working." . . . I wasn't getting it and Tony was. . . It drove me crazy! From then on, my father and I grew further and further apart. (Fellows, page 305)

[Richard:] If you're under ten or so, it's pretty normal for a boy to be doing housework. But if you're over ten, you'd better be out doing men's work, driving a tractor and that kind of thing. I wasn't real thrilled about driving tractors—it was just too over-whelming—but I liked doing the things that I could kind of day-dream while doing. . . . (Fellows, page 173)

[Martin:] I felt like a damn fumbling idiot around farm machin-ery. My older brother was good at that kind of stuff, and that made me worse by comparison. When I would screw up, my dad would say, "*Oh, go up to the kitchen with your mother.*" I think it was his way of saying that I had to decide whether I was going to be a sissy or whether I could really help on the farm. . . . Lots of times, instead of going to the kitchen, I just went off some-where. I had books and magazines—history and adventure sto-ries, mostly—stashed in places around the farm, and I would go off and read. (Fellows, page 162)

[Mark:] It was pretty well-known, maybe even from kinder-garten, that I was going to be an artist. I just exhibited that talent and it took root. God, the number of times I grumbled about being out on that fucking tractor going back and forth over the fields. And the number of times I grumbled about getting dirty with grain dust. (Fellows, page 202)

Close to mother. Distaste for and discomfort with outdoor and mechanical work stood in contrast with their attraction to cooking, baking, serving, and sewing. Domestic skills acquired as young boys were further developed and put to good use as they became older.

Did a feeling of closeness to mother make housework attractive, or did the attractivess of housework foster a feeling of closeness to mother? Did mother feel especially protective of a boy who didn't fit into his gender role? Whatever the dynamics, "A large majority of my subjects," writes Fellows (page 12), "identified more closely with, and generally had richer and more satisfying relationships with their mothers and other females than with their fathers and other males."

> [Henry:] My older brother worked outside with Dad. He was kind of Dad's buddy and *I was Mother's friend.* . . . I played house a lot, and my mother would . . . pretend to help me. She made it fun and often made me laugh. *I liked dolls* when I was four, five, six years old. Nobody seemed to be too upset about that, not even my dad. I remember him saying a few times, kind of as a joke but not a real put-down, "Henry should've been a girl."(pages 60-61)

> [David:] I helped [Mom] with the house-cleaning, gardening, and cooking, while my two older brothers helped my dad with the farm chores. *I preferred to work with Mom.* (Fellows, page 133)

> [James:] *Often I wished I could be at my mother's side* to cook and bake and sew, but in German Catholic farm families only girls did those things. When we would go visiting, I was very interested in how the house was decorated, what type of food was on the table, how well-dressed they were. Needlework, knitting and crocheting fascinated me, and I really wanted to do them. But had I done them, I would have been ridiculed for being such a sissy. My uncle would have started it and it would have spread out from there. Even my grandfather would say, "Oh, you don't want to do that. That's girl stuff" (Fellows, page 98).

> [Jim:] My brother was enough older and stronger that he could help Dad do the outside stuff [on the farm]. When the first of my sisters was born, I was delegated to the house to help mother so that the meals were ready when my father and brother needed to come in and eat. I was glad, because I enjoyed cooking and all of those things that go along with keeping house. I learned to appre-

ciate a lot of the things that farm women do and most farm men take for granted. (Fellows, page 77)

[Jim:] I did a lot of cooking and baking—pies, cakes, cookies, most everything. . . And there was always canning. . . My mother and I would do the canning and freezing. . . . (Fellows, page 77)

[John:]. . . I liked baking and had a knack for it. I made a lot of jelly rolls and cookies. . . . I helped a lot with the house cleaning too. . . . I loved to iron and we ironed everything, even the bed sheets. The stuff I did was considered girlish by my older brothers, but it never bothered me enough to keep me from doing it. (page 107)

[John:] I became the major canner and freezer, and loved helping can peaches. . . I became an excellent pickle maker. . . [When the family butchered hogs,] I would saw pork chops, and wrap them up for the freezer, and help my mom make sausage. (Fellows, pages 107-108)

[Ken:] There was a division of labor in our household: the girls were in the house and I was in the barn. . . I was never encouraged to do any of the household activities, but I liked doing those things. I would bake on occasion, and my mother was very much into canning and freezing and often neeeded help with that. . . . I really liked helping . . . . (Fellows, pages 285-286)

[Harry:] One Sunday we had a family gathering of all the aunts and uncles and cousins. I was flying around there helping serve . . . and one of my uncles said, "He's going to make somebody a good wife someday," and I thought, hmmm. (Fellows, page 70)
[James:] *I had some dolls and a tea set and spent a lot of time playing with one of the neighbor girls.* That was the subject of considerable scorn and teasing from my older brothers, but my mom seemed to think it was all right. (Fellows, page 107)

The farm work that Fellows' respondents were most attracted to included animal care, flower gardening, and record-keeping. In the following recollection, David, in his oral testimony, touches upon some of these interests. (Note that his recollection describes a very talented four-year-old, who composed and sang a different song to each of the family's 30 cows!)

[David:] There were lots of mechanical things on the farm that I was no help with, but I could handle the record keeping and I loved taking care of the animals, which included delivering lots of calves. [To each of over 30 cows he sang a different song, all of which he had made up himself at the age of four. He tells of his distress when he learned, at the age of four, that one of their calves was to be sold.] (Fellows, page 11).

> [Bill:] I never wanted to be a tractor jockey, but I could never get enough of working around livestock as a boy. My dad didn't spend a lot of time with the livestock, but I learned a lot from my grandfather and my uncles. In the springtime, when everybody else was busy doing fieldwork, I was much more at home with the cows. . . . (Fellows, page 154)

Several respondents told Fellows (page 10) that they liked to raise and care for chickens. Some took a special interest in raising exotic breeds.

Distance from father. In a 1975 paper, Richard Green (pages 344, 351) related the adult male homosexual's "male affect starvation" to the fact that many of these men had been deprived of normal contact with a father figure. Green reported that of his clinical sample of 65 gender-discordant boys, almost one-half (40 percent) "had been permanently separated from their biological father by the age of four—a much higher rate than the general population."

Similarly, Fellows (page 19) generalizes that some of his respondents "believed that their attraction to other males was fostered, at least in part, by receiving too little affectionate attention from their fathers and other males. . . . More than one man wondered if his father's distance and lack of affection was the result of discomfort at seeing 'gay' characteristics in his son" (page 19). A number of recollections characterize paternal distance or hostility:[10]

> [When James was four, his older brother was killed getting off the school bus, and since that time] my childhood felt very lonely. . . . *My dad just kind of disappeared.* He went out to work early in the morning, came back for meals, and went back and worked until dark. He was never much for words when things got difficult. [Through the years,] dad was always difficult to reach (Fellows, page 98).

> [Myron:] My dad didn't allow my brothers and me to have opinions on anything. We were told what to do and what to feel, and we were never allowed to be angry. . . . *Dad and I were distant* until I got to be fourteen or fifteen, and then it became hostile. I just got tired of being treated like I wasn't even a person, verbally abused and slapped around, so I got back at Dad by being smart-mouthed. It didn't solve anything, but it gave me some increment of satisfaction to outwit him sometime (Fellows, page 112).

[Norm:] Dad was such a mean bastard, nobody ever wanted to be around him. He was always very demanding, rather brutal, and things had to get done his way. He and Mom fought all the time, and he would often take it out on the kids (Fellows, page 116).

[Everett:] Daddy was only too happy to finally have a son, but I think there was something about *the gentleness of my nature* that *frightened him and he just pushed me away*. . . . [Father was physically abusive, and would also joke with his younger brother about] what a sissy I was. It was communicated to me very strongly that I was somehow inferior as a male. (Fellows, page 206).

[Frank M. had an alcoholic, abusive, hypercritical, and distant father. He never attended any of Frank's high-school football games, track, wrestling, or plays.] He never said, "You've done a good job," or . . . "I'm proud of you." Part of my yearning to be with a man is a yearning for that kind of recognition. I want a man in my life who will give me that (Fellows, page 200-201).

[Frank adds that his father was "very much against" Frank's wishes to go to college, and Frank drove off to college only after having a fistfight with his father and beating "the living shit out of him. . . ."] (Fellows, page 200).

[Myron:] Dad would make cruel remarks about my brothers and me in front of friends or relatives. . . . [Dad and my brothers were slender; I was fat.] Dad would make remarks like, "You got tits just like a woman." I can remember that like it was yesterday, and it's been thirty-five years. I became so self-conscious about my body I almost refused to take phys. ed. in high school, and I would never go swimming or take my shirt off. (Fellows, page 112)

[Myron:] *My dad used to tell me I was a mistake—that I was supposed to be a girl*, but something went wrong. Since I was treated like I was supposed to have been a girl, I was really confused about what I was supposed to be and how I was supposed to act. Dad spent all his time with my older brother, teaching him everything. I just couldn't work with machinery well enough to please Dad, and he was not subtle in letting us know if we didn't do something right. I was relegated to being Mother's helper. . . . We had a big garden and did a lot of canning and freezing. I also took a keen interest in cooking. My mother was very encouraging and supportive of my endeavors, so I was willing to try almost anything. (Fellows, page 112)

[Henry had an older brother, and his strong-willed father "desperately wanted a daughter" when Henry was born.] By the time I was four years old, *I knew that he didn't like me. . . .* I often wanted to sit on his lap, but he would never let me. . . . One time, when I was twelve, we had a houseful of . . . [guests]. There was no place to sit, so I sat on Dad's knee and he flicked his hot cigarette ashes down my back. I left the room crying, hurt and humiliated (Fellows, page 59).

[James:] My uncle Al . . . was extremely handsome and in a lot of ways I really admired him. He had been a naval aviator in World War II and was a nut on sports. . . . I helped him out a lot on his farm, working from morning till night. . . . Al would go on tirades--calling me sissy and yelling at me for not playing sports well enough. I would never amount to a hill of beans because I couldn't play baseball, and I didn't know how to drive a tractor properly (Fellows, page 96).

[Harry:] I always wondered if Dad played both sides of the fence. If my mother and sister and I were gone for some reason, he always got one of his older brothers to sleep with him. This brother was about ten years older, and he and his wife hadn't slept together for years. . . I thought this was a little queer. (page 71)

My [younger] brother Andrew was appropriately macho. He was the hunter and the trapper, so Daddy thought he was wonderful. By the time Andrew was nine, my father got him a real .22 to hunt with. . . . It was appalling to me that Andrew actually took pleasure in killing animals. [Andrew would use his rifle to terrify and tease Everett and his younger sister.] (page 206)

[Joe:] I was involved in high school play production. My parents very much frowned upon my activities because they took me away from farmwork. They didn't attend my concerts or plays, and that hurt. . . . My parents wouldn't even attend my graduation [from college]. (Fellows, page 295)11

Athletically clumsy. Athletic activities were a source of frustration, embarrassment, and dread, according to the recollections of Fellows' respondents:

[Robert:] I dreaded gym class. . . . Not only was I inexperienced at games, but I dreaded showing myself nude to strangers. . . . I could rarely catch a ball, and my balance was terrible—I had never ridden a bicycle. (Fellows, page 58)

[Robert:] When it came time to choose up sides for games, I was always chosen last. [Robert developed a friendship with a varsity basketball player, by helping him with Latin declensions, and in return, they would meet at the gym during free periods and Augie would give him pointers on basketball.] I was soon fairly adept at free throws. (Fellows, page 58)

[Henry:] My worst fear in high school . . . was having to take phys. ed. and be in the locker room with the other boys. I suppose I was afraid I'd get a hard-on, even though other boys did frequently, much to my fascination. But more than that, I think it was the competition—playing football and basketball. I didn't know how. We didn't play those games on the farm. . . . [When the city boys were playing basketball,] we farm kids could go over to a corner and talk and stay out of the game. (Fellows, page 65)

[Henry:] There was something horrifying about phys. ed. and I hated it. . . [Basketball] was the most foreign thing in the world to me. The city boys had no mercy and would chew us farm boys out royally when we did something wrong. Very often, I would get sick and stay home on the day I had phys. ed., especially if we were going to be wrestling, which I hated most of all. (Fellows, page 66)

[Dennis:] [My older brother is] the exact opposite of me—he likes guns and golf, he's a Republican. (Fellows, page 90)

[John:] I went through elementary school being a really good ball player. . . . But adolescence kicked it out of me. Partly because of my brothers, I lost confidence in my athletic ability. Phys. ed. in high school was probably the worst punishment I ever had to endure. I felt self-conscious and uncoordinated, and resented having to take it. (Fellows, page 108)

[Tom recalls that in high school] I was a tall kid, so I was expected to do the basketball thing. . . . We didn't have all that sports stuff in country school, and I hated basketball, so I didn't do it. (Fellows, page 186)

On the basis of his clinical experience, Fitzgibbons concludes that the ability to play sports is second only to acceptance by one's father in developing a positive masculine identity. Poor motor coordination becomes, therefore, a major factor in homosexual attraction:

If by the time you are four or five years old, you cannot catch a ball or kick a soccer ball, you will be excluded, isolated, rejected, and often ridiculed. Such boys are called queer, faggot, and they are beaten up. Victims respond with enormous anger toward their oppressors; they want to kill them. (Lecture, Washington, D.C., 1997)

Feelings of isolation. Some of Fellows' respondents recall feelings of isolation, rejection, and shame over being so different from their peers. A lack of experience with male friends can be aggravated by an avoidance of close male friendships, for fear it would reveal an awakening homosexual desire:

> [Henry:] I was a real good friend of one of the other boys in my [eighth] grade. He kept asking me to stay overnight at his place. Naturally, we would have slept together. I never went, because I was sexually attracted to him and was afraid that once we got to bed I would grab his cock and start playing with it, and that would be unacceptable (Fellows, page 65).

> [Everett:] So much of the time during junior high and high school, the pressure to conform, to be masculine, ate at me a lot. If I'd had an inordinant amount of teasing on any given day, I would get real melancholy, and would sometimes go out in the woods to cry. . . . (Fellows, page 212)

> [Dale:] I always have felt badly that I was never one of the guys. I was never athletic, I never hunted, I never understood the thrill of talking about pussy and tits. (Fellows, page 196)

Emotionally expressive. Ridicule, rejection, and punishment for their gender-discordant traits, came from parents, siblings, and other relatives. Several of Fellows' respondents recall that as boys when they felt hurt they were easily moved to tears. A boy who could not live up to the rule, "Boys don't cry," was in for unhappy times, as the following recollection indicates:

> [Cornelius:] Once I cried because I couldn't ride along when somebody in the family was taking the company back home. My mother said, "So you cry when we say you can't go? I'll give you something to cry about!" and she whipped me with a switch, very hard, on my behind and legs. *Experiences like these deeply affected my ability to be very spontaneous about any expression of feeling.* (Fellows, page 35)

Compensatory efforts. Respondents also recalled how desperately they tried to compensate for their "flaws" by becoming "the best little boy in the world."[12] Exceptional obedience, politeness, earnest commitment to farm and household work responsibilities, and outstanding school performance, were some of the special efforts recalled by pre-homosexual boys. Often their church involvement was greater than that of their parents (page 14). This is how Richard described his effort to be "a wonderful child":

> [Richard:] [G]etting good grades, being polite, not drinking, doing the things I was supposed to, going to church and being the altar boy. I felt it wasn't fair that my mother would be out working on the farm and then she would have to come in and cook the meal while everybody else sat around. So I became her helpmate, setting the table and doing those kinds of things, even as I got older. (Fellows, page 14)

Nearly all of Fellows' respondents "believed that they were essentially born with a homosexual orientation" (page 19). His farm upbringing helped James see his condition as just one more example of nature's diversity:

> [James:] On the farm, I learned to appreciate nature, and for me being gay is a very natural thing. Some cornstalks do not bear ears of corn, some gilts [female pigs] do not have babies. Normally when you raise breeding stock they reproduce, but not everything fits into place perfectly. On a farm, you accept that some things are out of the ordinary. . . . That helped me to accept being gay. One time, a neighbor had paid a lot of money for a bull, but it wouldn't breed any cows. It's a natural thing—it happens in nature. (Fellows, pages 100-101)

NOTES TO CHAPTER 8

1. Rebekah contrived to have Isaac bestow his final blessing upon Jacob (Genesis 27). For this, Jacob earned Esau's murderous enmity (27:41), and Rebekah quickly arranged that Jacob flee to Haran "to find a wife" (27:42-46; 28:1-4). Jacob's infinite patience is demonstrated by his willingness to work for Laban seven years as the bride-price for Rachel (29:21-30), and work another seven years because Laban had substituted his older, less attractive daughter Leah for Rachel.

According to the biblical story, the twelve tribes of Israel sprang from Jacob's twelve sons: four by the unloved Leah (Reuben, Simeon, Levi, and Judah) (29:31-35). Rachel, because she was barren, gave to her husband her maid Bihlah, who bore Dan and Naphtali. Leah's maid Zilpah gave birth to Gad and Asher (30:9-13), Leah herself bore Issachar and Zebulon (30:14-21). Finally, after years of barrenness, Rachel gave birth to Joseph (30:22-24), and then to Benjamin. Two of the sons (Simeon and Levi) are fierce warriors (Genesis 34). Joseph, Jacob's favorite son was, like his father, a dreamer and a thinker.

2. Appendix 2 also describes a case in which a gender-discordant boyhood did not lead to a homosexual adulthood.

3. At a celebration, it may be permissable for a gay man to sometimes "camp it up" and act outrageously feminine. Effeminate mannerisms are an ingredient in in-group homosexual humor. Masquerade parties, and Gay Pride Parades are two occasions when gay men may dress as "drag queens," and to display an exaggerated femininity.

4. Sissy is a diminutive for the word sister. Sissy boy describes the boy who acts more like a sister than a brother. The *Encarta Dictionary* labels sissy boy as an "offensive term." This term is used in the title of Richard Green's book, *The Sissy Boy Syndrome* (1987). Green is a gay advocate as well as a scientific researcher. In this book, chosen term will mainly be used when we refer to his study.

More neutral equivalents to describe these boys, who do not quite conform to the masculine norm, are 'cross-gender,' or 'gender-discordant.' In this book, we will favor the term 'temperamentally androgynous,' which was introduced in Chapter 2, and discussed in end note 2 of that chapter.

5. Green's methods of classifying his subjects' sexual orientation, *a number of whom were sexually inexperienced at the close of his study*, is seriously flawed. For example, Green reports no reliability checks; classification of his subjects was made on the basis of their reported fantasy, dreams, or sexual experience— if any. These biases suggest that the percentage of gender-discordant boys who become gay men, reported at 75 percent, may be closer to 50 percent. (This author is indebted to Zucker and Bradley for alerting him to the methodological shortcomings of Green's study.)

Despite these shortcomings, Green's sissy-boy study is regarded as a classic, and as conclusive evidence that gender-discordant boys develop into gay men. For example, in his 1993 book, LeVay reports (page 113): "Green studied markedly 'sissy' boys as children and then followed them through to adulthood; [Not true; many of Green's respondents were still teenagers at the end of his study.]the great majority of them eventually became gay or bisexual." Not true.

6. In 1981, Bell, Weinberg, and Hammersmith reached the same conclusion after an exhaustive study of 600 homosexual men (with a 300-man control group).

7. Heard at a workshop at the 1997 annual convention of Exodus International, Auburn, Kentucky.

8. In 1992, Will Fellows placed a notice in 26 midwest gay and lesbian publications, announcing his search for gay men who grew up on a farm, and would be willing to be interviewed for a book on this topic. No payment was offered. About 120 men responded by phone or mail. The investigator also recruited a small number of subjects from friends, or friends of friends. From this group, 75

audiorecorded interviews were made in 1992 and 1993.

Subjects ranged in age from 25 to 84. Of the 75 recorded interviews, Fellows selected "the 50 more substantive and representative" to be transcribed, and then chose 26 of the 50 for full-length representation in his book. From the remaining 24 transcribed interviews, Fellows selected quotations for use in discussing various themes. The book, *Farm Boys*, was published by the University of Wisconsin Press, 1995.

The Fellows interviews are an important resource in the study of homosexual men, for several reasons: (1) They are fairly recent. (2) They are a non-clinical group; men who were not recruited in a treatment facility. (3) They grew up on a farm, away from the influence of an urban gay community. (4) They grew up on a farm, where gender roles are sharply defined (what boys and men are expected to do is quite different from what girls and women ar expected to do). This environment seemed to have sharpened their early awareness that they were different from most boys.

9. Here and in all quotations from Fellows, emphasis has been added by this author.

10. There is no shortage of clinical and anecdotal reports of homosexual men who report an excess of mothering and a deficit of fathering. Psychoanalytic theory describes the homosexual's father as typically absent, distant, or hostile. This is not always true, insists Marmor, who writes (1980, page 11): "Over the years I have seen a number of homosexuals who had close relationships with affectionate and caring fathers."

But do research studies support the generalization that homosexuals' fathers are usually absent, distant, or hostile, and mothers close binding? S. Fisher located 58 studies—published between 1936 and 1986-- that attempted to test this Freudian generalization. He summarizes (pages 165-166) the results of these studies as follows: 14 of the studies (24 percent) failed to support the Freudian generalization, and 44 (76 percent) supported the Freudian generalization, either as it concerned father only, mother only, or both parents. Of these 44 studies, forty studies found fathers of homosexuals to be described as cold and distant, and only four studies found mothers described as close-binding and intrusive. These findings would seem to suggest that *male homosexuality is more likely to follow from a deficit of fathering than from an excess of mothering.*

11. This recollection describes parental hostility, not paternal hostility, to the respondent's neglect of his farm-boy role. Here we are assuming that the primary objector was father, and that mother acquiesced to father's outrage.

12. *The Best Little Boy in the World* was the title of a 1973 book by John Reid (pseudonym of the author, Andrew Tobias) on growing up gay. Twenty-five years later, in 1998, Tobias wrote *The Best Little Boy in the World Grows Up.*

9 From Gender Discordance to Homosexuality

Feelings of alienation, the mana fantasy, and the adoption of a homosexual identity

When homosexual men recall the emotional life of their boyhood, certain patterns of experience emerge. As a young child, many pre-homosexual boys preferred quiet indoor activities to outdoor rough-and-tumble games. Helping Mother in the kitchen, playing house or school, dressing up in Mother's clothes, are among recalled activities, so richly documented by Fellows and cited in Chapter 8.

> In 1973, Saghir and Robins asked 90 homosexual men (and a heterosexual control group) about their childhood. Of the homosexuals, 77 per cent reported having no male buddies, having avoided boy's games and having played predominantly with girls. In 1981, Bell, Weinberg and Hammersmith reported (page 85) that 19 percent of 604 adult male homosexuals said that half or more of their friends in grade school were female, compared with one percent of a heterosexual control group.

Nature or nurture?[1] Gender-discordant boys seem to be naturally drawn to the companionship and interests of Mother and female age mates. This suggests a genetic tendency but Hewett (page 596) argues that experience alone can go a long way to implant an effeminate adaptation. Suppose, argues Hewett, the parents really wanted a girl. The child senses this from how he is treated, and wants nothing more than to please his parents. Suppose his golden curls excite the envious admiration of his parents' friends, this impression can "exert its effect long after the curls are gone. There is the need to feel cherished and special . . . safe from a world peopled with frightening creatures who can ridicule and strike and hurt," writes Hewett.

Experience alone can teach a boy, Hewett argues, that the adoption of feminine attitudes is a way to win parental love. In such a case, writes Hewett (page 598): "the child will gradually withdraw from masculine occupations and interests and substitue feminine ones. . . . [This] feminine orientation has as its chief purpose the avoidance and alleviation of anxiety." If he is lucky, says Hewett, before this "false self" becomes firmly established, the boy may encounter "the love of a suitable masculine figure . . . [and] turn the tide so that the child learns to view masculinity as desirable and free of fears." Question: Does clinician

142

Hewett describe the typical gender discordant boy, or is he describing a patient who feels miserable because he was forced, by special circumstances, to adopt a feminine orientation?

The rough-and-tumble activities of all-boy play groups parallel the aggressive all-male play groups of young primates[2] and seem to serve common social functions. Play-fighting partners are often friends, so play-fighting is not usually antagonistic. What looks like the random display of boyish energy, actually serves specific purposes: it provides practice in fighting, demostrates one's strength and fighting ability, and establishes one's status in the dominance hierarchy[3] of the group.

At about age three, children begin to compete—to compare their performance with others. They strive to enhance their pride and avoid shame. A 1976 study of preschool children (Strayer and Strayer) showed a clear, linear rank order based mainly on physical prowess. Through play fighting, participants also learn to collaborate and cooperate. Rivalry, social comparison, dominance striving, success motivation, and social competition appear to be universal activities, characteristic of all but the severely retarded (Weisfeld, pages 53-54).

There is probably something critical in this difference between the early childhood play experience of pre-homosexual boys and boys in general. Pre-homosexual boys are more likely to play quietly with mother, sisters, and girl friends, while boys in general are engaged in rough-and-tumble play with other boys. It is as if through early play experience, a child becomes habituated either to members of his own sex or to the opposite sex, and is thus primed to later eroticize what is less familiar to him. Accordingly, D. Werner and also Bem, trace adult homosexual attraction back to childhood play activity, and use the themes "familiarity breeds contempt" and "the exotic becomes erotic." [4]

Pre-pubescent feeling different

What comes out clearly in the recollections of many homosexual men is that they knew from early childhood that they were different, and more importantly that they lacked certain marks of masculinity, they had trouble acquiring a clear and stable masculine identity.

> I grew up on a farm. . . . I was a sissy right from the start. On a farm, the male and female roles were very clearly defined. Outside, it was hot, and you had to work like a bastard. . .and you're filthy. I didn't want that. . . .The alternative was to make busy work in the house and to relate to your mother. . . .You could read books. So I opted for that. Unconsciously my behavior became what would, back then, have been construed as feminine, effeminate, sissy. It still is to this day, but I love it. I'm really not into physical hard work. . . . (Fellows, page 217)

If you were a guy, you were born to farm. You were born to be a total, typical, straight male—to play sports, to hunt, to do everything a guy was supposed to do. I knew from the beginning that I didn't fit into that. (Fellows, page 307)

My father was a man of many skills: a mechanic, a builder, and a hunter. My two brothers shared his manly interests, but not I. A Christmas family picture shows my two brothers at my sides, one holding a machine-gun, the other a rifle. I am in the center, holding my ventriloquist doll. (Oral testimony at Exodus Conference, 1997.)

From the beginning, it seems I knew that I didn't fit in. I felt unwanted and ashamed. . . . I always felt I was different from other children, especially the boys. I compared myself to them and always felt inferior. . . . [My father] wanted me to play sports. I never felt comfortable to play them. . . . I hated not knowing how to stand or hold a bat or how to throw a ball or shoot a basket .. . . I feared being ridiculed. (Cohen, page 217)

[At age seven,] in second grade the tortures began. I was clumsy and unathletic; I wore glasses; I was not interested in spectator sports; I had my nose forever in a book; I formed friendships most easily with girls. I had an age-inappropriate fondness for opera. I was fascinated by glamour. I was shunned by any of my schoolmates. When I went to sleep-away camp the summer I was ten, I was teased and tormented regularly and called a faggot—a word that bewildered me as I had not formulated sexual desires of any kind to myself (Solomon, page 206).

Bell, Weinberg and Hammersmith (page 86) asked their male homosexual respondents, who recalled that they felt different, "In what ways do you think you were different?" Here are a few answers they received:

I had a keener interest in the arts.
Mentally I was very different. I was forming a basic hate pattern for people in general.
I couldn't stand sports. . . . A ball thrown at me was like a bomb.
I never learned how to fight.
I began to get feelings I was gay. I'd notice other boys bodies in the gym, and masturbated excessively.

A gay man describes a painfully uncomfortable childhood, when he recalls:

I was gay from as far back as I can remember. . . . My way of coping was to attempt to manage a great deception; to pretend that I was just like everyone else; to act like I was having a good time, when I was in fact very uncomfortable; to fake enthusiasm, when in fact there was a great fear. I was in pain and I was confused (Tobias 1998, page 238).

A gay man, interviewed by author George Stambolian (pages 94-95), recalled his pre-homosexual childhood with these words:

As a child I had always been afraid of boys. I didn't play any sports, I couldn't even throw a ball, and if someone threw a ball at me, I would run away. I found it all too rough and in bad taste. So I played with girls, and the boys started calling me sissy. I didn't know what that word meant at first, but I knew by the sound of their voices that it wasn't something very nice. But I did their homework for them, and that was my clever solution to a love-hate relationship.

Monette recalls (pages 69-70) from his high school days, when he was "the possessed voyeur of the locker room, dumbstruck by the Parthenon frieze of heroic male flesh parading to the showers after practice." Comparing himself with these "manly beauties," how he "hated the soft androgyny of my own body:"How small I felt beside them. . . . [Andover's rule that every boy had to take gym] dragged me wincing into the showers, me who hated the soft androgyny of my body, which somehow managed to be both scrawny and plump at once.

In 1995, Johnston and Bell reported an extensive questionnaire study that compared the recollections of two groups of college men: the responses of 49 gay students recruited through a gay student organization were compared with the responses of 84 male volunteers in undergraduate courses in human sexuality and educational psychology.

The best predictor of subgroup membership (r=.55) *was body image.* Gay men recalled that while growing up they regarded their body as relatively feminine, or as equally masculine and feminine. The next best predictor (r=.44) was the likelihood that as boys, gay men felt more similar to their mother than to their father (page 623).

A "powerful predictor of subgroup membership" was "a liking for or dislike of stereotypical boys' activities" like baseball or football. Approximately 84 per cent of the sample could be correctly identified on the basis of their attitude toward sports alone. As boys, gay men "felt different from other boys . . . (69% versus 27%)," and this difference became even greater during high school (94% versus 40%). Predictably, gay respondents recalled having been more accepted by girls, having had more female friends than male friends, and "were less likely to have 'hung out' with an all-male group" (*ibid,*).

Labeling

If the gender-discordant boy tries to hide or downplay his nonconformity, his peers are insistent about reminding him and broadcasting to their world that here's a guy who doesn't fit into the masculine role. H.S. Becker, in his 1973 study of the sociology of deviance, introduced the concept of labeling to underscore the power that adolescent peer groups have, to tell a person what he really is. Blumstein and Schwartz (page 38) find this concept useful in summarizing the recollections of some of their adult homosexual respondents.

> Several male respondents who had been labeled the "class sissy" had felt that surely they must be sexually odd, and that their oddness was recognized by their peers. They had believed that their peers knew more about them than they had known themselves, and this was often self-fulfilling when it came to sex-object choice.

Merle Miller (page 48) recalls the constant reminders of other boys that he was critically different:

[S]ome boys in the third grade took one look at me and said, "Hey, look at the sissy," and they started laughing. It seemed to me now that I heard that word at least once five days a week for the next 13 years, until I skipped town and went to the university. Sissy and all the other words—pansy, fairy, nance, fruit, fruitcake, and less printable epithets. . . . It's not true, that saying about sticks and stones; it's words that [do] break your bones.

Bell, Weinberg and Hammersmith's statistical study leads them to conclude (page 185): "The sociological notion that homosexuality often results from fortuitous labeling by others is not supported all all by our findings." Rather, the investigators suggest that the "different" boy's peers see through whatever attempts the boy makes to hide his differentness.

A homosexual patient recalled that when he was younger he dressed up for Halloween and "everyone thought that he was a girl who had dressed herself like a boy. . . . [T]he experience had a deep meaning for the patient because, psychologically speaking, it illustrated exactly his life's predicament: 'a woman's soul in a man's body'" (Braaten and Darling, pages 277-278).

Hero worship

Pre-pubescent adoration of "real boys." To cope with this felt deficit, the gender-discordant boy is likely to envy, adore, and worship those boys who are perceived as being unambiguously and gloriously masculine. "Having a crush" on such a boy makes the prepubescent gender-discordant boy's heart pound.

> Andrew, a young . . . gay man, remembers noticing at age eight the beauty of his swimming instructor, an older boy of sixteen (Owens, page 19).

> At eight I fell in love with Neal, this guy who rode my bus. . . . I guess he was fourteen. . . . I always wanted to sit with him or be next to him. . . . I spent my childhood fantasizing about men, not sexually . . . . but just being close to them and having them hold me or hug me (*ibid,*, page 20).

> Owens (page 20) cites the recollections of other homosexual men who recall that as boys—as young as second graders—"scanning underwear ads . . . looking for an outline of what lay beneath."

> I knew I was clearly checking out the guys in the shower after soccer practice. This scared the shit out of me (*ibid.*, page 23).

> In every grade, there was at least one boy that I had a certain fondness for. . . . And later on . . . I recognized this as crushes. I wanted to spend as much time as I could with them (*ibid.*, page 20).
> This adoration of masculinity is sometimes mixed with a sense of panic that "something is wrong" with this secret curiosity:

> A 22-year old gay man "recalls the panic at age thirteen or fourteen when I saw a Bloomingdale ad for Calvin Klein underwear that I could not take my eyes off of"" (*ibid.*, page 29).

Similarly, Andrew Sullivan (1995, pages 7-8) recalls his mixed feelings, as a boy of seven or eight, over his feeling of "intense loving" for the bare-chested man he saw on television:

> I remember when I was around seven or eight seeing a bare-chested man on television one night and feeling such an intense loving for him that I determined to become a doctor. That way, I figured, I could render the man unconscious and lie on top of him when no one else was in the room. But then, I quickly realized, I would be found out and get into trouble. I spent most of the night awake, working out this scenario, and ending up as confused and as overcome by desire and when I had begun.

> The first hints of my homosexual inclinations came shortly after puberty. I found that from time to time I would be aroused by

another boy. The excitement was not distinctly sexual: I wasn't certain what it was. But I would feel myself drawn to another boy, want to be around him, want him for a friend. There was a certain fascination with the male body, a particular masculine beauty that affected me more deeply than comparable feminine beauty. It never occurred to me to think of myself as a homosexual—I'm not sure I had any clear idea that there was such a thing. (P. Fisher, pages 15-16)

This same mixture of feelings—adoration and bewilderment—was reported by a patient of Mondimore, as he recalled an adolescence experience that was both thrilling and bewildering. (Our emphasis here is on pre-pubescent antecedents of a homosexual identity, but this clinical testimony is included because of the patient's emphasis on his adoration of masculine beauty):

I was in the dressing room of the high school auditorium getting props ready for the play that we were rehearsing when another boy walked into the room wearing only his briefs. Like a lightning bolt, this thrill went through me that I had never felt before—I couldn't take my eyes off him. . . . I had never seen such a broad-shouldered, muscular good-looking guy—maybe I had never noticed guys in this way before. It was disorienting—I wanted to say, "Wow, look at this!" but I could tell that no one else was noticing what I was noticing. . . . I wasn't really understanding these new feelings—certainly not the intensity of them, not at all. . . (Mondimore 1996, page 166).

"Fooling around"

A New York gay man recalls the sexual "fooling around" that occurred at summer camp when he was about 12 years old. His interviewer (Kahn, page 110) summarizes:

[S]ome of the boys engaged in mutual masturbation. Once a counselor took down [the respondent's] pants and began to fondle him. [He] resisted. 'I felt as though I was being pushed into something I wasn't ready for,' he recalls. The next summer, [he] agreed when another camper suggested mutual masturbation. He was embarrassed, however, when the camper told another boy what they were doing. The other boy exclaimed, '. . . Do you do that?' [He] grudgingly admitted that he did. The boy suggested that they go outside. He pulled down [the boy's] pants, got down on his knees, and approached [the boy's] penis with his mouth. Shocked, [the boy] asked what he was doing. 'A blow job,' he replied. 'You're not really going to do that, are you?' . . . 'Oh no,' he replied,' I just wanted to see what you'd say.'"

A gay man who recalled a rather repressive childhood (his parents taught him not to play with himself or even look at his genitals), was shocked at the sex play that took place at the summer camp he attended at age 12 or 13:

> [H]e was embarrassed when boys played with each other in the showers and when one of his bunk mates insisted upon displaying his erections (Kahn, page 118).

Kaufman and Rafael (page 5) describe the hunger of a prehomosexual boy for same-sex contact—and the ostracism, shame and anxiety that may result from his first, clumsy attempts to gratify this urge:

> You sleep over at your friend's house. . . the one you've been staring at and have even imagined touching. You're . . . fifteen. . . . You're both under the sheets—sleeping in the same bed. You want to reach over and touch, feel, caress—but you're afraid. So you hope your friend reaches for you instead. You pray for it. You lie there listening to your own breathing, listening to your friend's breathing as well. At last you summon up your courage and you do it—you actually reach over, holding your breath, praying that your friend is sound asleep. Hesitantly, your fingers explore. You caress softly, hoping your friend doesn't wake up.
>
> The next day in school, you notice your friend whispering to everyone as you come in. They're all staring at you, pointing, sneering. . . . Then, later that day in gym class, one of those tough kids walks over to you while you're sitting on a bench and looks down at you, sneering, "I know what you want. I know what you are, You're a faggot, a queer!" The words scream in your mind. Everyone is watching, hushed, while you're paralyzed, trapped, exposed to all those watching eyes. All that day, you're followed around, taunted, jeered at. As much as you try to hide, to escape, you can't. Afterward, the watching eyes are inside of you as well, as if you're jeering at yourself.

Monette (page 51) recalls when he participated in "Richie's club," a group of five boys who combined naughty pranks and boyish eroticism:

> The game they played was called "I dare you," each of us taking a turn to dare the boy beside him. *I dare you to go take a leak in the mailbox. To lay a turd on the Dennings' doorstep. To take Richie's dick in your mouth.* By keeping it kinky and slapstick, they somehow avoided perceiving it as sex. We all had boners,

but nobody ever came. It was mostly raunchy talk, all very tough-guy, an indoor sport that only lacked a ball.

Early sexual maturation

Storms offers evidence that male homosexuals reach sexual maturity earlier than heterosexuals. These boys reach sexual maturity while they are still living in a largely all-boy world, before they are encouraged to show an interest in girls. Little wonder, Storms concludes, that early-maturing boys are more likely to pair sexual awakening with other males.

Early onset of masturbation and same-sex play

Masturbation and same-sex play are common experiences of not only pre-homosexual adolescents, but of all teen-age boys. Perhaps a homosexual identity is favored not by early sexual maturation *per se*, but by the early adoption of same-sex play and the practice of masturbation-to-orgasm. For some time before the onset of ejaculation, it is possible for a boy to achieve a "dry orgasm," and this repeated experience, achieved through either masturbation or same-sex play, may be especially characteristic of a pre-homosexual boyhood.

In 1973, Saghir and Robbins compared the childhood recollections of gay and straight men. According to their findings, almost two-thirds of gay men masturbated with another boy before adolescence, at a rate more than double the figure reported by straight men. Survey and clinical data suggest that pre-pubescent sexual experience (not just "sex play," but repeated stimulation to orgasm) may provide the reinforcement that lays the foundation of adult homosexuality.

> Hatterer (1980, pages 103-106) describes a compulsive homo-
> sexual, Tom. When he was 10, his adolescent brother repeatedly
> forced him into fellating him. "The one time [Tom] tried to
> reverse their roles, Robert raged at him, 'What do you think I
> am? Some kind of a fag or something?'" Hatterer adds that Tom
> fellated some of his brother's friends. He also masturbated daily,
> to re-live his erotic excitement as fellator of older boys.(The case
> of Tom is also mentioned in Ch. 17.)

> Similarly, one of Fellows's respondents, Cornelius, recalled
> (pages 38-39) repeated pre-pubescent sexual stimulation. He
> recalled that at the age of four, he was drawn into sex play by the
> grandson of the family laundress. When he was five, a hired man
> on the family farm snuggled Cornelius and played with his penis.
> Cornelius continues: "In one way or another, I had sex-play with
> six of my seven [older] brothers—fondling and masturbating
> each other to orgasm. . . . It usually occurred at night when we

would be sleeping together, like it was happening in our dreams, and we never spoke about it."

Habitual pre-pubescent sexual stimulation to orgasm is different from the occasional expression of sexual curiosity, or adolescent experimentation—a difference that panicky parents often do not understand:

At age fourteen, Paul was placed in a group home for three years and forced to attend a sexual offenders group because he had attempted to touch the penis of a younger boy in his mother's foster care (Owens, page 111).

Late sexual maturation

Late sexual maturation, as well as early maturation is found in the recollections of homosexual men. Life is not easy for boys who do not fit into "the comfortable majority."

Dan was a firefighter, the stereotypical image of a macho man; handsome, muscular, athletic, and educated. However, he felt inferior to other men and attracted to adolescent boys. Dan was a late bloomer. He entered puberty around fifteen ears of age. When he had to shower with the other boys after gym class, he felt ashamed and embarrassed because of his lack of physical maturity. (Cohen, page 42)

Identity confusion

At puberty, the pre-homosexual boy comes to realize that he is emotionally stirred by other boys. At that time, most of his peers are showing a sexual interest in girls, which he does not share. This realization is experienced as an identity confusion,[5] what Mondimore (page 166) describes as a "state of bewilderment and disorientation . . . often accompanied by profound anxiety and fear, uncomfortable feelings that cause the individual to try to resolve the situation quickly."

Richard Troiden interviewed a large number of homosexual men on their boyhood recollections and compared the recollections of 108 informants who said they felt different during their childhood years, with 149 who said they felt different during their high school years. Members of each group were asked, "In what ways did you feel different during . . . [those] years?" Responses show a clear-cut (though less than complete) difference between the two age groups. The younger group recalled a more general sense of alienation or inadequacy, while the older group was occupied with homosexual thoughts or activity. Tables 9.1 and 9.2 report Troiden's specific findings.

While the pre-homosexual boy is engaged in his lonely struggle of identity confusion, his heterosexual peer groups are solidly united in the group enterprise of entering the world of boy-girl relations.

Peer group support

Belonging to an all-boy play group is a typical boyhood social experience and, paradoxically,[6] an important gateway into the heterosexual world of adolescence. Studies of adolescent behavior strongly indicate that full membership in a male peer group is an important preparation for making the transition to a *heterosexual* adulthood.

> Maccoby (page 209) summarizes the findings of the 1962 longitudinal study of Kagan and Moss as follows: The investigators "reported that boys who had been most fully involved in male peer activities during their grade school years had the least difficulty moving into relationships with girls when they reached adolescence: they were comfortable in beginning to interact with girls and in pairing off with a girlfriend. By contrast, boys who had been peripheral to male peer groups in grade school, or who had been loners . . . more often had sexual anxieties."

Before adolescents begin to pair off into boy-girl couples, groups of teen-age boys mingle with groups of teen-age girls—at parties, at dances, at malls, and in other gathering places. Same-sex group members give each other the support, guidance, advice and criticism that eases their transition into the new world of heterosexual interaction.

The moral support of one's male peer group plays an important role in guiding a boy's heterosexual experience (see Feldman, Brown, and Canning): encouraging him to date and become sexually active, discussing details of how to get along with girls, assuring him that it may even be acceptable to get a girl drunk in order to seduce her, assuring him that most women enjoy being coerced into having sex, showing him how to find girls who are sexually accessible, or inviting him to join a group that will have sex with some willing girls. Looking at erotic pictures and telling "dirty jokes" helps correct the over-idealization of womanhood that is part of many boys' upbringing. Joking redefines women as potential partners for the enjoyment of sexual pleasure. The all-boy gang that began with rough-and-tumble play now evolves into a group of teen-age buddies who help each other find their place in the heterosexual world, and assigns status to its members on the basis of their courage to venture into the heterosexual world. Boys who lack this social experience are bound to have a socially difficult adolescence.

For boys, an important motive for having heterosexual experience is that he thus gains status with his peer group. As Maccoby writes (page 208): "Manhood is displayed by having sexual relations with multiple females. It is not enough to be sexually successful; one must be known to be successful. Young men therefore brag about their conquests to other males (and probably exaggerate their prowess)."

Table 9.1 "In what ways did you feel different during your childhood years [prior to 13th birthday]?"

	Responses
A general sense of alienation [interpreted here as insufficient peer-group bonding]	22 percent
A sense of general inadequacy	19
Experiences warmth and excitement in presence of other males	15
Did not share many interests . . . with age-mates	14
Effeminacy	9
Awareness of and fascination with male body	6
A medical or physical disability	6
Was a self-designated homosexual	4
[G]uilt over sexual activity with other males	2
Other	2

Source: Troiden, page 364.

How heterosexually active are U.S. teenage boys? In 1973 Sorenson conducted a detailed survey of the sexual behavior of boys age 13 to 19 and reported that boys could be divided into three groups: (1) the inexperienced (41 percent), (2) the monogamous (15 percent), and (3) the adventurers, defined as boys who had three or more partners in the previous month (24 percent). Sexually active adolescents have their first sexual experience at the median age of 15 and reported having intercourse about once a week. Monogamists have more frequent intercourse than adventurers.

Are Sorenson's "findings" biased by the tendency of boys to exaggerate their sexual conquests? Male bragging sessions are common cross-culturally, according to Freedman.

A 1995 report by anthropologists Palmer and Tilley illustrates how gang membership favors heterosexual experience. In the early 1990s, the city of Colorado Springs faced an epidemic of a sexually-transmitted disease and it became necessary for health authorities to investigate the sexual practices of the young people of that city. It thus became apparent that members of young male gangs "not only achieved a kind of power/money status within their community, they [also] had an unusually high number of female partners, compared to the non-gang members involved in the outbreak" (Blum, page 268).

Table 9.2 "In what ways did you feel different during your high school years?"

Less interested than peers in members of the opposite sex	40 percent
Felt "unduly" interested in . . . [other males]	14
. . .[Because] of sexual activity with other males	11
A sense of gender inadequacy	11
[S]omething seemed to be missing . . . [from opposite-sex relations]	9
Was a self-designated homosexual	4
Alienation	3
Homosexual activity was more satisfying than heterosexual activity	2
Other	5

Source: Troiden, page 365.

The pre-homosexual adolescent boy does not enjoy the emotional support of heterosexual gang membership or the support and guidance it affords. Bawer (1993, page 233) describes the "loneliness and confusion . . . discomfort . . . rage, [and] insecurity" of the pre-homosexual adolescent boy. "He feels incredibly alienated, different, [and] weird" because the straight majority—peers and adults—treat him with "prejudice . . . disdain, and condescension. . . ." This feeling of alienation can be life-threatening, Bawer argues elsewhere (1996, pages 231-232): "Every day gay kids commit suicide because they've been rejected by their parents, or terrified that they will be."

Note that Bawer, a gay advocate, emphasizes the adolescent's feeling of social rejection. But in the testimony collected by Weinberg *et al.*, the emphasis is rather on the adolescent's inner conflict and confusion as to what he really is:

I [also] had heterosexual feelings (page 143).
I [also] had heterosexual fantasies (*ibid,*).
I [also] got turned on by reading about heterosexual sex (*ibid,*).
I felt I hadn't given heterosexuality a chance."

> I felt that it was unnatural. . . . [S]ex with the same sex was
> unthinkable; I got turned off to the same sex through fear. . . . I
> was very angry about my homosexuality (*ibid.*, page 144).

"Peer pressure;" parental vs. peer influences. Environmentalism, learning theory, and psychoanalysis have all supported the pervasive belief that the most powerful influence in shaping personality and character is parental treatment. This widespread belief has been sharply challenged by the writings of Judith Rich Harris, an unaffiliated scholar, summarized in her 1998 book, The Nurture Assumption: Why Children Turn Out the Way They Do. Harris' controversial thesis that childhood development is significantly shaped by peer influences has won strong support from Pinker (pages 392 ff.), who describes Harris' socialization theory as "a major contribution to modern intellectual life." From this perspective, the rough-and-tumble play of childhood is the boys' efforts to establish their rank in their play group. Intending to improve their child's life by moving into "a better neighborhood," parents may instead be delivering to their child the dislocating status loss of becoming "the new kid on the block." Research on the development of male sexual orientation may lead to the finding that peer group experience can actually be a stronger influence than the over-controlling mother or distant father.

The Seduction Question

Do homosexual men seduce teen-age boys? This is a question about which there is much controversy. Distressed homosexual men in treatment often describe being introduced to homosexal play by an older person, and recall a mixture of feelings: abuse, seduction, excitement, and fascination. (See pp. 325-327.) Significantly, the boy may willingly return to the same situation:

> A man who lived in the apartment building had a photographic
> darkroom and when I visited him there, he would pull down my
> pants and masturbate me. I used to wear pants with an elastic
> waistband, so it was easy to pull them down. (Author's clinical
> notes.)

> My first homosexual experience was with my music teacher. I
> had my lesson at his house one evening and he invited me to stay
> at his place overnight. (Author's clinical notes.)

Mac[7], a gay man who participated in the study of Adair and Adair (page 115) recalls that at age 14, he was "going with a girl" who thought it would be fun to take her boyfriend to the gay beach in Santa Monica. There the handsome lad received a welcome that the average adolescent never experiences:

I was, I guess, a fairly hunky little teenager, and I walked out
there, and the chicken hawks descended on me en masse. I got
invited to parties and did things and met people, and people took
me out. And I said, "Fantastic! This is for me!"

"Fantastic! This is for me!" Mac responded to the "chicken hawks," who
probably assumed that Mac knew he was at a gay beach. Mac didn't say: "Leave
me alone . . . Don't bother me," or "Can't you see I'm here with my girl friend?"
Instead, Mac clearly welcomed their attention. This *receptivity* to a homosexual
invitation is evident in many recollections of first-time "seduction" by a man or
older boy.

An awkward transition

Solomon (pages 206-207) recalls an awkward entry into homosexual practice:

As I began to experience piercing sexual desire, I kept it a secret.
When an adorably cute guy made a pass at me during a glee club
trip, I thought he was just trying to get a rise out of me and that
he would betray my ugly news to the world; and to my eternal
sadness, I rebuffed his advances. I chose instead to lose my virginity to a stranger whose name I never learned in an unsavory
public location. I hated myself then. During the years that followed, I was consumed by my terrible secret, and I bifurcated
myself into the helpless person who did revolting things in base-
ment lavatories and the bright student with lots of friends who
was having a great time in college.

Adoption of a homosexual identity

Taking this step lifts the individual out of his bewilderment, confusion, and
disorientation. It now answers all the troubling questions: "Who am I?" "What
sort of person am I?" "Where is my life going?" Finally he can say, "I am gay."
As Mondimore's patient recalled, *"Finally it all made sense."* Here are the concluding words of Mondimore's patient, Frank, who was disturbed by the thrill he
felt at the sight of "a half-naked, broad-shouldered, muscular, good-looking
guy:"

. . . I wasn't really understanding these new feelings—certainly
not the intensity of them, not at all. Then one day, I was on the
subway home from school and some guys were joking around
and one called another a "fag." I had heard that word ten thousand times before, but this time it penetrated to somewhere different in my brain. "That's it," I thought; "that's what this is all

about—I'm gay." *Finally, it all made sense* (Mondimore 1996, pages 166-167, emphasis added).

In an interview with Father Thomas H. Stahel (Sullivan 1995 pages 212-213), Andrew Sullivan, a practicing Catholic, recalled that adopting a homosexual identity and acting it out, brought such a profound sense of relief from shame and confusion that he compared this episode to a religious experience:

> After an enormous spiritual struggle, he "experienced coming out" as a homosexual and now allowed himself to feel "the experience of loving someone or being allowed to love [another man, Sullivan recalls that *he felt] . . . an enormous sense of the presence of God—for the first time in my life*" (emphasis added).

In some ways, being publicly identified as homosexual is a social liability, but it can also bring one recognition for leadership and courage. A gay activist recalls (Kahn, page 26) that his leadership role began unexpectedly when he "ventured into a meeting of the university gay organization during an election of officers and found himself elected president." A summary of the interview continues:

> No one else, he explains, was willing to sign letters and represent the group in public. "Suddenly I was an activist," [he] declares. . . . "I became . . . Mr. Gay Liberation on campus." After two gays were thrown out of a restaurant . . . [he] mounted a boycott. His name appeared in the newspapers. "I was never happier in my life," he recalls. "I had a sense of freedom. I didn't give a shit who knew."

Owens (page 43) notes that many gay men "speak of the exhilaration of attending their first [gay] pride or rights march." P. Fisher (page 240) recalls his feeling of "profound relief" when he finally entered the gay world:

> Many gay people are lonely and unhappy until they enter the gay world. Their lives may change so radically when the do that there is a tendency to feel the millennium has arrived. . . . After years of never daring to speak the truth about oneself . . . there can be a profound relief in encountering the openness of the gay set.

Why does gender confusion lead to same-sex attraction?

The gender-discordant boy feels more sensitive, more emotional, more drawn to the friendship of girls and women, and he also feels less drawn to rough-and-tumble games, less aggressive, and therefore less masculine. Beach (1978) notes that a child is indoctrinated with his sex role from the earliest years of life: what name he is given at birth, how he is dressed, what toys he is given, what play-mates he is encouraged to play with, how much mischief he is allowed to com-mit, all contribute to his awareness that he is a boy, not a girl. Beach insists that this is not merely a cultural fashion that can be turned on or off.

Throughout the evolution of the human species, survival has been favored by the fact that men and women fulfilled complementary roles: man as hunting party member, a protector, and a tool-maker; woman as a food-gatherer and a nurturer and teacher. The fulfillment of complementary sex roles has figured so prominently in human survival, Beach argues, that this tendency to teach and adopt a gender role undoubtedly has a genetic basis.[8]

Man is a social animal, and sensing that one feels different and does not share the interests of others in his age-sex group, is a troubling thought, leading to the questions, "Why am I so different from other boys?" "Am I a boy or a girl?" The growing gender-discordant male feels increasingly separated from kith and kin. Family gatherings such as a wedding, instead of celebrating the joys of kinship, become trials in enduring the pain of estrangement. Michael Rowe (page 182) describes the experience of a gay man at a family wedding:

> [T]oo many family weddings [are] spent fending off intrusive
> questions by relatives who ought to know better, or, in the case
> of friends' weddings, being exiled to the outer perimeter of the
> dining hall, sitting at the 'singles' table surrounded by the bride
> and groom's family criminals, cast-offs, degenerates, and termi-
> nally-single relatives whom everyone else in the family has
> given upon; a . . . valley of the social lepers.

Rowe's observation describes the experience of a person who has already reached adulthood. The observant gender-atypical teenager gets a foretaste of what loss of status feels like. Loss of status generates the chronic anxiety that is imbedded in male gender discordance.

Because the male gender is the dominant gender in virtually all societies, a loss of status as a male is felt as a fall in status. That is why it is much more dis-tressing for a boy to be called a sissy than for a girl to be called a tomboy. (She may, in fact, regard this label as a rise in felt status and as a boost to her self-esteem.)

This feeling that one cannot fit into the masculine role: Is this the origin of a gay man's frequent feeling of alienation? Gay-affirmative ideology is quite insis-tent that gay unhappiness stems directly from *social oppression*, from outer social forces of his contemporary world. It is the ostracism and shame heaped upon the homosexual by an intolerant majority that is the basis of the gay man's pain, which may lead to substance abuse, depression, and suicidal thoughts. Beach (1978) suggests that a gay man's chronic anxiety stems from doubts that go back to his early childhood: Who am I? Am I the equal of other creatures shaped like me? Am I a boy or a girl? What is my place in the world?

Felt status is an important ingredient in a social creature's basic sense of security. At the infrahuman level, felt status has its counterpart in established patterns of dominance or "pecking order." Dominant male animals attain higher testosterone levels than animals of low status.[9]

> Bernstein *et al.* reported that simply by removing the highest-ranking monkey in a group, the others undergo surges in testosterone level, demonstrating that a rise in rank elevates testosterone level.

Among men, a rise in testosterone has been observed to accompany winning a tennis or chess match, and graduation from medical school (Mazur and Lamb).[10]

Low dominance at the animal level corresponds to the human experience of inferiority feelings, labeled by Alfred Adler as the master motivator of human behavior. (The concept of inferiority feelings corresponds with a sense of deficit, and with the popular concept of "low self-esteem.")

How do homosexual feelings emerge from (a) a sense of deficit, and (b) adoration of a stranger who seems to have what one lacks? Martin Hoffman (1968, page 139) recalls a clinical case of a troubled homosexual, in which it became clear that when he saw an attractive young man, the stranger's presence "disturbed, confused, annoyed him in some inexplicable fashion." To a pubescent boy, the emotional experience of adoration leads to sexual arousal (as a result of "high-level non-specific autonomic arousal," in the words of psychologist Daryl Bem). By imagining that he could fellate the handsome stranger, the patient transformed his anxiety into the anticipation of sexual pleasure. Thus, "by sexualizing the problem, our patient transformed a distressing situation into a pleasurable one . . . he was able to transform a minus situation into a plus (*ibid*, page 1968)." The "longing to be close" of his boyhood days, is now experienced and expressed as a desire to physically merge with, to penetrate and to be penetrated by a real man, [11] to relieve his felt deficit, and endow him with those sought-after masculine qualities. It is as if homosexual activity is driven by a pre-programmed, pre-logical belief [12] that certain attributes can be transferred from one person to another through contact and incorporation.

Homosexual behavior as a mana ritual

The prelogical magical thinking of young children has been described by developmental psychologists. Similarly, social anthropologists observe in many cultures, rituals guided by a belief in mana: a magical power that is transferable through contact or penetration. A preliterate tribesman takes special pleasure in eating the flesh of those animals he admires for wanted powers such as speed and endurance, so that these virtues will transfer into his own body. In present-day Venice, a landmark of St. Mark's Square is the Clock Tower, atop of which are two scantily-clad, muscular bronze Moors who lift their mallets to strike each hour. A travel guidebook notes this Venetian belief: "anyone stroking the Moors' exposed nether regions is assured of sexual potency for a year."

Homosexual activity may similarly be interpreted as attempts (guided perhaps by unconscious and prelogical thought processes) to make contact with the perceived (or imagined) masculinity of the partner, and thus overcome a felt deficit. Oral sex, or fellatio, for example, is practiced by both heterosexuals and homosexuals. Masters and Johnson (1982a, page 75) directly observed the oral sex behavior of both homosexual and heterosexual couples. They reported: *"Most homosexual males . . . did swallow the ejaculate, while most women, whether wives or assigned partners, did not."* By the primitive logic of mana, swallowing semen incorporates the partner's masculinity.

> Hoffman (1968, page 295) similarly finds the primitive logic of mana useful in describing homosexual fellatio. He compares fellatio to the ancient religious rite "in which the participant eats the flesh and drinks the blood of the divine animal . . . in order to get the mana or vital power which is present within the animal."

In anal sex, the receptive partner often expresses a special satisfaction from receiving his partner's seminal discharge. Gay men sometimes boast that their physique and good looks are "strictly genetic," rather than the result of gym work and plastic surgery, suggesting that their semen contains a special mana. LeVay notes (1993, page 54) that "some gay men have a strong lifelong preference for receptive anal intercourse . . . [and suggests] a psychological need for bodily penetration. . . ."

> A male respondent says to a Weinberg *et al.* interviewer: "In every article I've read that refers to . . . [the fact that gay men] don't use condoms, I have yet to read anyone who seems to know why. It's because [giving and receiving] ejaculation is part of the satisfaction for many people, men and women" (Weinberg *et al.*, page 248, emphasis added).

> The primitive wish to incorporate the partner's semen collides, tragically, with the rules of safe sex. What leads a gay man to

> incorporate an adored partner's semen, at the risk of contracting
> the HIV virus? Simple carelessness, or an 'unconscious belief' in
> the magical power of *mana?*

For many years, clinicians have sensed the magicalistic aspect of homosexual thought and behavior. In a 1963 psychoanalytic panel discussion, anonymously reported in the *Journal of the American Medical Association*, two of the participants pointed to this aspect of homosexuality. Weiss (Anonymous, page 43) referred to his patients' "life-long search for a partner in whom he can find what he would like to have within himself . . . . a magic mirror symbiosis." Gershman (ibid, page 42) likewise characterized homosexual behavior as "ritualistic and magical. . . . Homosexual strivings are really efforts to achieve completeness through fusion with his distorted conception of a virile male."

A few generations ago, many homosexual young men presented themselves as "female impersonators," painting their faces, adopting the mannerisms and accessories of women, to attract men who were very masculine but not very particular about how they got their sexual release. One of Fellows's farm boy respondents spontaneously recalls the fantasy that accompanied his cross-dressing: that it would help him attract "a real man."

> [James:] Sometimes, when my parents were gone, I would
> admire my mother's clothes and put them on. . . and fantasize
> that if I could dress like this, maybe some of those guys would
> be attracted to me. It really turned me on; I would get an erec-
> tion. (Fellows, page 97.)

The bygone days when fairies offered themselves to trade are well documented by Chauncey and others. Nowadays, gay men are more likely to accentuate, even exaggerate, the appearance of youth, masculinity, and good looks, knowing that this is what attracts a willing male partner today.

Heterosexuals are similarly attracted by physical traits; both men and women respond to signs of youth and good looks. But heterosexual partnerships are more likely also to be based on admiration of the partner's personality and character, on shared background, shared interests, shared values, shared activities, shared friendships, and shared goals. Homosexual partnerships, on the other hand, frequently bring together individuals of grossly different backgrounds and interests: men who are attracted almost exclusively by an opportunity to exchange or acquire (as if by magical infusion) youth, good looks, power, [13] or physical masculinity. [14]

Daryl Bem has offered a much simpler explanation of why the gender-discordant youth is attracted to maleness. Bem uses the axiom "the exotic becomes erotic" as an explanatory axiom. He reasons that just as straight men are attracted toward their gender opposites, men who feel like women, are also attracted toward an opposite, and for them the opposite is another man. (Their partner may also have a chronic gender-discordance problem, but what makes the partner attractive is that he *looks* like a man and *acts* like a man.)

Folk wisdom tells us that "opposites attract," but folk wisdom also says "birds of a feather flock together," and "oil and water don't mix." The exotic can be appealing, but it can also arouse feelings of the uncanny, of disgust, or arouse fear or anxiety. Exotic foods, exotic religions, exotic music, exotic peoples and exotic places all evoke a wide range of responses, ranging from enchantment to disgust. The principle that "the exotic becomes erotic" sometimes applies to human behavior and sometimes it doesn't.

Embrace and ostracism

Self-identification as a gay person is a mixed experience. As he rids himself of his burdensome secret, as he feels a new freedom to love another man, he may also experience the bitterness of ostracism from kith and kin.

> Even though he described an event that took place a year ago, writes Herdt (1997, page 56), this gay teen's voice was full of indignation: "'My parents couldn't deal with it,' a nineteen-year-old youth said recently . . . of his coming out: 'My mother said, "You are dead to me. How can you be queer?" She said there would be no family name (I am her only son) . . . . It cannot be." She kicked me out [of the house]. She refuses to talk to me. I had to go and live with my lover. This was a year ago. She still acts like I don't exist.'"

What is the right age for gay self-identification? The gender-discordant teen ager who feels unhappy and confused about his same-sex attractions—should he be counseled to give himself time to gain experience and emotional maturity, or should he be encouraged to adopt a homosexual identity right away and unburden himself of his chronic self-doubt? A guide for gay men published in 1977 [15] advised the teen ager with same-sex attractions to wait until he reached the age of 25 or so before adopting a homosexual identity. But times have changed, and adolescent boys who are troubled by same-sex attractions are nowadays encouraged to consider adopting a homosexual identity when they are as young as 14.

High school counseling programs, the Internet, gay-advocacy books (like *Queer Kids*, by Robert E. Owens) and programs, and a pro-gay social environment explicitly promote the early adoption of a homosexual identity. Advises Owens (1998, page 41): "No rules exist for coming out, so each individual must improvise."[16] On the contrary, Heidi Kulkin *et al.* (2000, page 9) warn that "coming out" at an early age may deprive an adolescent of important friendships. He may lose the friendship of boys who can help him negotiate the difficult years of adolescence, but who simply cannot cope with having a close buddy who admits to being gay. "Coming out" too early may "intensify feelings of abandonment and isolation" and therefore increase "risk factors pertaining to suicide" (pages 8,9):

> Adolescence, being a time of confusion and identity formation, is difficult for all young people. . . . Some young people confronted by a friend who admits to being gay may not be able to handle the information. . . . The loss of friends during this critical time of development . . . seems to intensify feelings of abandonment and isolation for gay or lesbian young people.

What is the responsibility of parents, schools and society to the chronically unhappy gender-atypical boy? Can he be helped to better adapt himself to his age-gender group, and prepare for a heterosexual adulthood, by counseling, by learning athletic skills, by compensatory or remedial learning of social skills? Can he then get "a fresh start" in a new school environment where he will not be dogged by an old and outworn label? These strategies and others have been developed by Fitzgibbons, by Rekers, and by others. Therapy for sex-discordant boys is a topic of a 1995 textbook by Zucker and Bradley.

With or without compensatory or remedial training, or counseling, about half (or more than half) of androgynous[17] boys eventually adopt a homosexual identity. What happens to the other half? It would be worth knowing but there do not seem to be any research findings in this question.

Gender-discordant boys in other cultures

Anthropologist Frederick Whitam has done field work in Guatamala, the Philippines, and Hawaii. Everywhere he observed cross-gender behavior among some young boys: "playing with toys of the opposite sex, cross-dressing . . . preference for female playmates, and preference for the company of older relatives." They were regarded as sissies, and expected to become homosexual as adults. (Whitam, 1983, page 222) In the next chapter we will take a closer look at what historians, travellers, and anthropologists have observed of gender-discordant boys, and their adult counterparts in other cultures of the world.

NOTES TO CHAPTER 9

1. "Nature or nurture" is an elliptical expression that can have at least two meanings: (1) Is it nature or nurture that shapes this phenomenon? or (2) Does nature or nurture play the dominant role in shaping this phenomenon?

2. Gender-segregated play groups are characteristic of young monkeys and apes as well as humans. While young male monkeys and apes are play-fighting, young females typically stay close to their mothers and to other adult females, and close to infants. Lovejoy and Wallen report that young female rhesus monkeys were three times as likely as their male age-mates to approach and remain near infants.

Maccoby (page 321) conjectures that "girls' greater interest in dolls may reflect the same tendency."

3. This is not to say that play fighting *alone* establishes a boy's status among his friends. In human society, other factors undoubtedly contribute to a member's status, such as: athletic skill, physique, personality, social skills of all sorts, family prestige, intelligence, money, school performance, and special talents.

4. Of course, play opportunities do not fall upon a child randomly. Some boys seek out little girls to play with, and would rather help Mommy around the house than play outdoors with wild little boys.

Now let us try to put the folk sayings of "familiarity breeds contempt" and "the exotic becomes erotic" into learning-theory terms. When the boy whose childhood has been dominated by females (mother, sisters, girl playmates), becomes pubescent, he already has established habits and attitudes (largely non-erotic) toward females. His new feelings attract him toward objects that arouse his curiosity, objects about which he has no well-established habits, objects toward whom he can more freely relate in new ways prompted by his new feelings. Boys in general, whose childhood has been dominated by other boys, are relatively unencumbered by pre-pubescent habits and attitudes toward girls. In adolescence, they are relatively free to "discover" these new creatures and relate to them in new ways prompted by their new feelings.

5. Heterosexual men can also recall adolescent confusion over their sexual identity, but the feeling is not so deep or persistent. One straight man, a Weinberg *et al.* respondent, recalled, "I had homosexual fantasies. . . . I had my first homosexual experience during group sex and liked it." Another respondent recalled, "I was scared of the opposite sex; I wondered if I feared the opposite sex more than being attracted to them" (page 142).

According to Weinberg *et al.*, (page 369) 63 percent of gay men recall a period of adolescent confusion, and 27 percent of heterosexual men also recall a period of adolescent confusion about gender identity.

6. At a very early age, children prefer to play with children of their own sex. In 1974, Michalson *et al.* demonstrated that one-year olds preferred age-mates of their own sex, rather than age-mates of the opposite sex. When two male and two female one-year olds were placed at the four corners of a room and were free to crawl toward any other child, boys usually crawled toward boys, and girls toward girls. Even at 12 months, babies can distinguish the gender of other babies, though adults often find the distinction difficult to make. (Unpublished study reported by Lewis, page 332.)

Consistent with the 1962 findings of Kagan and Moss (see text of this Chapter), a 1995 study by Feldman, Brown, and Canning "reveals that the boys who were best liked by other boys in the sixth grade—and who were presumably centrally involved in male peer-group activites—were the ones who started their sexual activity at an especially young age, and who had had the largest number of sexual partners by the time they reached high school age. They were popular and gregarious in high school" (summary from Maccoby, page 210).

Paradoxically, initiation into adolescent boy-girl interaction seems to depend so much on the support and guidance a boy gets from his male buddies. In other words, *a boy who is strongly bonded to his male buddies, is likely to find it easy to enter into the world of boy-girl interactions.*

7. Mac is the name this author assigns to a respondent called Mark in the Adairs' book, since Mark is the name of another person mentioned in this book.

8. Although civilization has changed drastically since 8,000 years ago, when human societies followed an agricultural, craft or industrial way of life, the human species evolved during hundreds of thousands of years *prior* to the dawn of civilization, when humans subsisted by hunting and food gathering. During this long period human survival hinged in part on the adoption of what we would today call complementary gender roles. (In 1978, Beach still used the term sex role.) The human species, Beach argues, has a genetic tendency toward the adoption of gender roles.

Can we assume that all pre-agricultural human societies adopted complementary gender roles? Fifty years ago, anthropologists searched for those surviving societies that were still practicing a hunting-and-gathering economy. In 1959, Sahlins studied 12 such societies, and reported that *the division of labor by gender prevailed in each and every one of them.*

9. Weisfeld writes (page 53): "A male monkey that rises in dominance rank typically experiences elevated testosterone levels (Rose *et al.*, 1975). This effect occurs even if the monkey rises in rank because its superiors have been removed from the enclosure."

10. Weisfeld notes (page 54) that rise in testosterone follows winning at a tennis or chess match (or graduation from medical school), but "no such change occurred in men whose success was due to chance, as in winning a lottery."

Weisfeld devotes a chapter (pages 48-62) to dominance and status as a basic tendency in animals and humans, part of their evolutionary heritage. Writing from a sociological perspective, however, Kimmel (page 9) regards status-striving as 'a social construct.' Unlike their ancestors, who derived their sense of security from ownership of land, or mastery of an independent craft and ownership of its tools, today's corporate employees become "ambitious and anxious, creatively resourceful and chronically restive. . . ."

11. To the outside observer, the gay man is not having sex with "a real man" if his partner is troubled by the same felt deficit. The fact is, many homosexuals are particularly attracted to masculine-looking men, to men who are actually straight (though perhaps a little drunk) or even married. The erect penis symbolizes masculinity, and masturbation is a celebration of masculinity. When the gay man is fellating an erection, regardless of whose it is, he can fantasize that it belongs to what he regards as "a real man."

12. Magical thinking is common in young children and in preliterate people. This observation suggests that a belief in mana is based on some pre-programmed human tendency to believe in magic, superstition, and the supernatural. Perhaps this brings us close to Jung's belief in innate ideas. Or is an unlearned belief in *mana* not too different from the mental component of unlearned behaviors (what once were called instincts) observed in all animal life? 'An unconscious belief in the magical power of *mana*' is an awkward statement that even seems to smell suspiciously of mysticism. But it is no more mystical than the statement commonly made by evolutionary psychologists, or socio-biologists, that a person is 'driven by his genes' to do this or that. Both statements are *confessions of ignorance*. We simply do not know the details of those internal events that lead to the observed behaviors.

13. The attraction of homosexuals to men of wealth and social prestige can easily be labeled crass opportunism. It is worth bearing in mind, however, that wealth and prestige also symbolize power. Our theory suggests that the homosexual is driven by a feeling of deficit, and therefore seeks to attach himself to a symbol of power.

14. Homosexual prostitutes offer the *mana* of youth or good looks in exchange for money. What is the nature of the exchange by which homosexual partners both 'give' each other something of value? Perhaps one partner has a muscular physique and the other partner has a big penis; perhaps one partner has plenty of money (which symbolizes social power) and the other partner has youth and masculine beauty.

15. Woods, Richard. *Another Kind of Love; Homosexuality and Spirituality*. Chicago: Thomas More, 1977.

16. This author found on the shelves of his village public library the 1998 book, *Queer Kids*, by R.E. Owens, Jr. In this book, the author encourages young teenagers who 'know' they are gay to come out early, and advises their parents (page 126) ". . . to view homosexuality and bisexuality as healthy forms of sexual orientation, not unlike heterosexuality."

17. A dictionary definition of androgyny emphasizes an *appearance* that is indetermediate between male and female. In this book, androgyny refers to an *inner life* (motivation, feeling, cognition) intermediate between male and female.

10 Homosexuality at Other Times and in Other Places

Classical scholars describe the ancient Greek cult of man-boy love, celebrated in poetry, rationalized by philosophers, and very explicitly depicted in the vase paintings of ancient Greece (now in some museum collections, but usually hidden away, in deference to puritanical sensibilities).[1]

Historians note that Spanish missionaries of the seventeenth century tell of American Indians males who dressed and lived like women. World travelers and, more recently, anthropologists have made similar observations in cultures all over the world, in preliterate tribes and in old civilizations, in groups that are in contact with the rest of the world, and in groups that are virtually isolated.[2] An understanding of homosexuality requires some familiarity with the specifics of these diverse observations.

We learn that in some cultures homosexuality was honored, in others it was looked down upon, in some it was tolerated, in some it was punished by death. In the highlands of New Guinea, the Sambia required that for a certain period of their life, boys fellate mature youths and unmarried men, to ingest "the men's milk" necessary for growing into manhood.

Some cultures defined the homosexual as one who lets another man thrust his penis into his mouth or anus, but the inserter is not considered homosexual at all; he was simply using a homosexual as a substitute for a momentarily unavailable female partner.

What is or is not "homosexual" is so thoroughly defined by local conditions, some sociologists have declared that homosexuality is a "social construction" rather than a psychological fact. One could even assert that language is a "social construction" because nothing could be more different, for example, than Greek and Chinese. The language of a hunting culture has a different vocabulary than the language of a fishing culture, a highly stratified society has different language rules than a less stratified society, and so on.

In some ways, language is a "social construction." But language production also depends on structures of the human mouth and throat, and on the human brain. Language acquisition follows certain laws of learning, and linguists claim that all languages have certain common features as well as certain differences. If language is a "social construction," it is also a psychological phenomenon rooted in human anatomy. In some ways, homosexuality may be a "social construction," but in other ways, it is a variety of behavior based on human anatomy and physiology.

FOUR HOMOSEXUALITIES OF ANCIENT GREECE

Gay advocates are fond of pointing out that from ancient Greece, that fountainhead of Western civilization, flowed a high level of development of architecture, sculpture, painting, philosophy, poetry, drama, and man-boy love. Kirk and Madsen (pages 366-372) argue that an understanding of the Greek idea of man-boy love can show us what is wrong with homosexual behavior today, and how to correct it. We can learn about the Greek way from the writings of "Ken Dover," which is how the authors refer to Sir Kenneth Dover, British historian. A study of what other scholars (*e.g.*, Karlen and Keuls) have written suggests that there were in fact four homosexualities in that ancient civilization. We will first describe these four behavioral norms, and then discuss the underlying factors that promoted the emergence of these customs.

1. **The penetrators.** Ancient Greece was dominated by a tiny leisured upper class. In all of Attica (of which Athens was the center), perhaps 10 percent of the population consisted of free citizens, about 85 percent were slaves, and about five percent were free non-citizens.[3] This vast population of slaves included war captives, who were vulnerable to all sorts of exploitation, including sexual. The rape of women, and the anal penetration of men, not only gave the victors erotic gratification, it also served to humiliate the defeated. Some male slaves became homosexual prostitutes. Anal copulation was a common form of heterosexual activity,[4] so there was relatively little difference between the sexual penetration of male or female. It made a vast difference, however, whether one played the role of penetrator (which defined who was the manly partner), or submitted to being penetrated. The man who had "a hospitable rear end" was the object of ridicule and censure. "The comedy of Aristophanes . . . is rich in obscene and scatological invective, [and] abound in abusive terms alluding to anal sex." A common insult was "gaping ass hole" (Keuls, page 291).

It should be stressed, as it has already been implied, that the opprobrium applied only to the person who submitted to anal penetration. The active role of penetrator, on the other hand, demonstrated both status and virility, whether the partner was male or female. The penetrator might well be a married man, and was free to shift from male to female, as opportunity arose.[5]

A slave might be forced to submit to anal penetration but for a free man to do so would label him a prostitute. "From Demosthenes, we learn that persons convicted of male prostitution could not enter the temples, make speeches, or initiate official proceedings." In contrast to this severe censure, no censure was applied to penetrators. (Keuhls, page 297)

2. **The passive homosexuals.** In ancient Greece, as elsewhere, there were adult males (citizens) who invited anal penetration, even though passive homosexuality was explicitly censured and ridiculed, labelled as the behavior of a prostitute or slave. How does one explain that? This oddity did not escape the attention of Aristotle (as presented in Dover, page 170), who speculated that for these men, the rectum must be part of their genital system. Perhaps that is where their seminal fluid is formed and that is where friction creates sexual pleasure.

Anal penetration evokes just a small ejaculation, Aristotle observed, which makes the urge of the passive homosexual insatiable. For those who are predisposed by nature to seek anal penetration, experience strengthens this desire. Dover (page 170) quotes Aristotle's speculations on the genesis of passive homosexuality:

> Those who have been accustomed to be subjected to [anal] sexual intercourse . . . at the time of puberty . . . [take] pleasure with the recollection arising in them when they are so dealt with. . . . [F]or the most part, however, the habit arises in those who are as if naturally so disposed. If a man is lustful and soft, all these developments come about more quickly.

Aristotle regarded passive homosexuality as constitutionally defective, as "constituted contrary to nature" (quoted by Dover, page 170).

3. **Military homosexuality.** Homosexuality was practiced in the armies of ancient Greece. Dover (page 192) tells of a Thebian army "composed entirely of pairs of homosexual lovers; it was the hard core of the Boiotian army, a formidable army at all times, throughout the middle period of the fourth century. . . ." The military commander Pammenes is credited with advocating "this type of pairing as a principle of military organization."

4. **Man-boy love.**[6] This is the most celebrated form of Greek "homosexuality." The word is put between quotation marks to raise the question, Can man-boy love be regarded as homosexuality in its modern connotation? No, not if today homosexuality refers to a sexual orientation that is (a) permanent and (b) based on mutual relationships. In man-boy love, the man (erastes) was usually married (presumed to be having a normal married life), and the man-boy relationship would end when the boy (eronymos) grew into manhood.

Man-boy love is lavishly celebrated in Greek poetry and vase painting. More than half of the surviving elegaic poetry of the classical period consist of a corpus of 164 short verses ascribed to Theognis of Megara, and are "predominantly of homosexual character, addressed to boys or expressing feelings about boys" (Dover, page 10). Poets praised "the beardless and beautiful youth." The following poetic line is attributed to the lawgiver Solon: "Boys in the flower of their youth are loved; the smoothness of their thighs and soft lips are adored" (Karlen, page 79). Perhaps the same line has been alternatively translated, "When in the delightful flower of [his] youth one learns to love a boy, yearning for thighs and sweet mouth" (Keuhls, page 284).

"Poets and philosophers debated over whether a youth was most beautiful before he had a beard, when down started to appear on his face, or a bit later," Karlen comments (1980, page 79). "Hair on the legs and chest usually meant the end of the affair. Now the young man was supposed to have intercourse with women and with males younger than himself," Karlen adds.

Somewhere on the vase, at the bottom or on the side, might be written a tribute to the eronymos: "Hikites is beautiful." Dover (page 122) tells of a vase inscribed: "Give me that promised between-the-thighs." Sometimes the inscription is under the glaze, indicating that the vase was a custom-made luxury item. In other cases, the inscription was added after the vase was fired.

The vase paintings of man-boy love sometimes picture the eronymos as more of a child,[7] sometimes as an adolescent. Typically, the erastes faces his beloved; with one hand he fondles the boy's genitals, with the other hand he strokes the boy's chin: so soft, and hairless, in contrast with the bearded erastes.

Vase paintings of man-boy love often show the erastes bearing gifts: a purse, a chicken, or a small deer. Sometimes an erotic moment is depicted: the erastes bends his knees, bows his head, thrusts his phallus between the boy's thighs. The boy's response seems more affectionate than erotic.[8] The custom of man-boy love required that the erastes do more than bestow gifts, more than adore the boy's youthful charm, more than seek sexual relief. The erastes was also supposed to be teacher, mentor, guide, and counselor to his beloved.

In Greek mythology, abduction of a boy to serve as an eronymos is punished in a most tragic way, as expressed in the Oedipus drama. Laius, king of Thebes, falls in love with the boy Chrysippus, and abducts him. At the time, "an oracle had foretold that Laius, in punishment for this act of rape, would sire a son who would kill him and marry his own mother—Laius' wife, Iocasta" (Keuhls, page 289).[9] Laius vows never to have sex with his wife, to avert this disaster but once, when drunk, he does just that. Thus Oedipus is born, and the grim prophesy is fulfilled.

Plato's Symposium is described by Karlen (1971, page 28) as "a grand, long paean to homosexual love." Plato argued that "the beautiful is good . . . men are better and more beautiful than women; hence love of men is the highest love. Socrates added that . . . the most important beauty is not physical but moral" (as summarized by Karlen 1980, page 79).

Even if The Symposium defends homosexuality, that does not mean that there was "vast social acceptance" of its thesis, Karlen notes (1980, page 80). Many of Plato's contemporaries: "Plutarch, Lucian, Herodotus, Aristotle, and many [others] . . . spoke of homosexuality in tones that ranged from disapproval to scathing" (Karlen 1980, page 80).

Why man-boy love?

Scholars suggest a number of social conditions that may have led to the cult of man-boy love. None of these conditions are unique to the society of that time. Possibly some combination of the following factors led to the emergence of the cult of man-boy love:

1. **Escape from the female.** Women occupied a very inferior position in

Greek society. Segregated, taught how to run a household but otherwise uneducated, dominated by both her husband and her father (even after she married), held in contempt and regarded as a necessary evil, neglected by her husband (who often preferred the company of mistresses or prostitutes), women often developed unpleasant personalities, and became either passive or unpleasantly aggressive.

> So distasteful was marriage, to some men, that in the sixth century B.C, the legislator Solon suggested . . . a law making it compulsory (Karlen 1971, page 16).

> We keep heterai [mistresses] for pleasure, concubines for the daily care of our bodies, and wives for the bearing of legitimate children and to keep faithful watch over our house (Pseudo-Demosthenes, Against Neaera, quoted by Keuhls, page 267).

> You hate women profoundly and therefore you are now turning to boys (from the comedy The Sea Gulls by Cratinus, quoted by Keuls, page 274).

2. Unmarried daughters of citizens were sequestered. If a girl lost her virginity before marriage, her father could sell her into slavery. Girls were taught to run a household, perhaps to write a little, but otherwise they were uneducated and not prepared to share a husband's interests. Since young ladies of their own class did not exist, for all practical purposes, young male citizens looked elsewhere to satisfy their social and erotic needs. Beautiful boys resembled virginal girls. A beautiful eronymos was better than a prostitute—male or female.

> Boys are beautiful . . . for as long a time as they look like women (the hetaera Glycera, as quoted by Athenaeus, from Keuhls, page 274).

3.The erastes were a privileged aristocratracy. Free to spend time away from work or household duties, citizens belonged to the "privileged 10 percent" of ancient Athens and could afford the time and money that courtship of an eronymos entailed.

4. Ancient Greece was a culture of military societies. The culture glorified masculinity, downgraded women, and favored a cult that claimed to prepare a boy for manhood.

5. The gymnasium segregated the sexes and glorified the male physique. Physical training served to prepare boys for military life. The word gymnasium comes from gymnos, which means naked. Boys spent a great part of their day naked or lightly clad, exercising, racing, and wrestling.

6. **The ancient Greek culture glorified beauty of all kinds.** Whether natural or man-made, whether visual, like architecture and art, or verbal, like poetry and epics, Greek culture was devoted to beauty. Both female and male beauty was celebrated in Greek sculpture. In ancient Greece, the oboe was played only by slaves because it made the player's cheeks puff out unattractively (Karlen 1971, page 29). The following story suggests that to the Greek mindset, love of beauty triumphs over logic or justice:

> When the famous courtesan, Phryne, was brought to trial in
> Athens for debauchery in holy places, a crime punishable by
> death, her lawyer tore away her robe, revealing her breasts, and
> the judges acquitted her. They felt that such beauty must be a gift
> of Aphrodite, a sign of divine grace. (Karlen 1971, page 28)

The cult of man-boy love was devoted to the worship of boyhood, which was praised as a uniquely beautiful stage of human development.

ANCIENT CHINA: MAN-BOY LOVE A PRIVILEGE OF THE ELITE

Sexual customs among the elite of ancient China parallel in some ways, the man-boy love customs of the aristocrats of ancient Greece. In a very recent (2000) book by Chou Wah-Shan, the author describes a culture in which beautiful boys of the lower classes were the sexual privilege of the kings and nobles of ancient China, men who also had wives and concubines.

Sometimes a favorite boy, thanks to his looks and graces, grew up and rose to a high position in the imperial courts. This was recognized in ancient political writings as a threat to good government. Wrote the great philosopher Mozi (as quoted by Chou, pages 29-30):

> Rulers employ . . . men who happen to be . . . pleasure-featured
> and attractive. . . [Such a person] will not necessarily turn out to
> be wise and alert when placed in office. If men such as these are
> given the task of ordering the state, then this is simply to entrust
> men who are neither wise nor intelligent, and anyone knows that
> this will lead to ruin.

From ancient days to the modern era, sex with a beautiful boy of the lower classes continued to to symbolize a man's social power. In 1860, a Western writer estimated that in one Chinese city (Tianjin) alone, there were 35 male brothels, with a total of 800 boy prostitutes (*ibid.,* page 26).

Chou reviews the considerable Chinese homoerotic literature, including Dream of the Red Chamber (Hong Lou Meng), said to be the most famous novel in Chinese history. In this novel, the protagonist pursues both young servant boys and girls when unable to have sexual relations with his wife. In Qing Sacrifice, a young man, Wen, wants to marry the daughter of a rich man, who has Wen imprisoned. He escapes and becomes an actor in a theater, where he is admired by a scholar, Han. They become intimate friends. Wen sells himself to a wealthy villain who is sexually attracted to Wen. Wen gives the money to Han to help him pass his examinations, then kills himself to express his fidelity to Han. Wen is reincarnated and resumes his love with Han, who passes his scholar's examination. More recently, a popular novel by Zeng Pu (1872-1935), entitled Flower in a Sinful Sea (Niehai Hua), portrays a loving relationship between a scholar and his fifteen-year-old courtesan. The boy is described as having a beautiful, white face, pretty eyes, a small mouth, a delicate and slim body, smooth skin, and elegant, soft gestures. The appeal of this homoerotic literature to the Chinese public as a whole, is indicated by the fact that this book was reprinted fifteen times within the first two years of its publication, and sold more than 50,000 copies.

THE ALEXANDRIAN KINAIDOI

Montserrat (pages 147-148) cites from the Christian polemicist Clement of Alexandria, whose book, *The Paedagogus*, describes the Alexandrian upper class life of the second and the beginning of the third centuries CE. Clement wrote disparagingly of the *kinaidos* (plural *kinaidoi*), "the passive and unmanly partner in a homosexual relationship":

> [T]hey pay too much attention to their appearance. They shave off their beards or pluck them out with tweezers, and have their bodies entirely depilate . . . *Kinaidoi* arrange their hair in elaborate womanish styles, and perfume themselves with scented oil. . . . They dress in impractical, trailing garments and wear too mch jewelry.. . . . *[K]inaidoi* are recognizable by their voices and deportment . . . [They lisp and] mince around effeminately with head on one side. . . . *Kinaidoi* also have a feminine, languid bearing, and make studiously graceful gestures while trying to preserve the elegant arrangement of their clothes.

> [T]hey go around in packs; they are entertaining, if riotous compay, and consort with rich childless women whom they amuse with their sexual gossip. There is even a characteristic noise kinaidoi make, "a noise in their noses like a frog, just as if they kept their spleen stored up in their nostrils."

BISEXUALITY IN EARLY MODERN JAPAN

During what is called the Tokugawa period of Japanese history (1603-1868) male-male sexual activity was extremely common in towns and cities, "a salient feature of mainstream culture" "formally organized in such institutions as samu-

rai mansions, Buddhist monasteries, and male brothels linked to the kabuki theater," according to historian Gary Leupp's book on this subject (page 1). The
popularity of this activity is indicated not only by erotic prints of that era, but by
written records of many kinds:

> local histories, works of art history, studies of the popular the-
> ater, biographies, diaries, law codes, personal testaments, med-
> ical treatises, popular fiction, travelogues, humorous anecdotes,
> and satirical poetry (*ibid*, page 2). Leupp (page 3) estimates "that
> nearly six hundred literary works of the period dealt with homo-
> erotic topics, and that at least seven of the fifteen Tokugawa
> shoguns (military rulers) had well-documented, sometimes very
> conspicuous homosexual involvements." References to same-sex
> interactions could be translated as "the way of youths," "the way
> of men," "the beautiful way," and "the secret way" (*ibid*, page 1).

"[T]he literature of that period candidly acknowledges men's passion for boys or
female-role actors (*ibid*, page 3)."

Japanese cities and large towns were inhabited largely by men. Women and
children were mainly kept in the countryside. Women were likewise absent from
priestly and martial groups, and male-male sex was the prevailing adjustment to
this virtually all-male environment. Participation in male-male sex did not indicate a lack of interest in women. Leupp notes (pages 3-4): "the sources suggest
that heterosexual relationships, including marrige, were widely viewed as compatible, even complementary, with male-male sexual activity. There is some evidence for exclusive homosexuality, but bisexuality appears to have been the rule.
. . ."

Custom ruled over sexual practices, which were apparently limited to anal sex.
(Oral sex is not mentioned or described in the records of that time.) Custom also
dictated that the older man was always the inserter. According to Leupp (pages
122-123), "the ideal partner for the 'older brother,' or paying customer, seems to
be a boy between fifteen and eighteen."

BERDACHE CUSTOMS OF THE AMERICAN INDIANS

Early travellers and missionaries observed among the American Indians males
who dressed like women and did the work of women. This custom was observed
among the Crow, Hopi, Navajo, Omaha, Seminole, Zuni, Chippewa, the Plains
Indians, and others. By the late nineteenth century, however, "the berdache (pronounced (bur-DASH) role appears to have dwindled drastically or vanished altogether. . . ." (Whitehead, page 502). During the depression of the 1930s, Omer L.
Stewart reported that among the West Coast Indians, male prostitutes offered
their services for 25 cents. Stewart regarded this as a vestige of the berdache custom (Stiller, page 771).

Figure 10.1. Customer with boy prostitute. From a painted scroll by Nishikawa Sukenobu (1671-1751). Source: The Complete Book of Erotic Art, by Phyllis and Eberhard Kronhausen, Bell, 1987)

Missionaries riveted their attention on what they saw as a gross perversity, a violation of God's laws, proof positive that the American Indian was truly a savage creature. They referred to the gender-crossing custom as hermaphrodism or prostitution. Indeed, the word "berdache" comes from a French word (adopted from ancient Persian) for boy prostitute. European observers simply did not see the berdache custom in its cultural context, argues Whitehead. We fail to understand the cultural meaning of the berdache custom, she argues, if we simply regard the berdache as an American Indian form of homosexuality.

Writers on American Indian life also mention male homosexual activity of a spontaneous variety, activity that had nothing to do with the berdache custom. For example, sex play among Mohave boys was not considered "homosexual" (Whitehead, page 525, fn. 6). Homosexual acts between men "of ordinary gender status were known to occur or were recognized as a possibility among a number of tribes on which data are available. In some cases, such behavior seems to have met with no objection . . . More often it was . . . [discouraged] as some sort of evil, inadequacy, or foolishness . . ." but this had nothing to do with the berdache custom (Whitehead, pages 510-511).

Anecdotal records on the sexual behavior of berdaches is mixed and contradictory. Anal intercourse, a widespread homosexual practice in many parts of the world, seems to be absent among the Crow Indians, according to Ford and Beach (page 133). But "oral-genital contacts are fairly frequent." The authors continue:

> A few Crow men adopt women's dress and mannerisms, and live
> alone. Adolescent boys and occasionally older men visit these
> bate, as they are called. The bate stimulates the boy's genitals
> orally. One informant stated that there were four such men in his
> community and that seventeen of his adolescent friends visited
> them occasionally.

Hill (page 276) suggests that among the Navaho, anal intercourse was
believed to cause insanity, but it was believed that this act could be safely be performed with a berdache. There are also indications of berdache heterosexuality.
An 18th century French observer, Pierre Liette, tells of "women and girls who
prostitute themselves" to berdaches (Katz 1976, page 288). One Zuni berdache
claimed to be the grandson of a berdache, and another Zuni berdache "was credited with having fathered several children" (Whitehead, page 512). It seems that
some berdaches were homosexual and some were not. Whitehead (page 514) is
skeptical of the argument that the berdache custom was based primarily on
homoerotic desire. Temperament and occupational interests, rather than erotic
attraction, appear to have been the controlling factors in the recruitment of
berdaches.

How did an American Indian male become a berdache? Sometimes a male
was taken captive in war, and simply assigned the role of "wife" in the household
of his captor. Sometimes "prenatal influence" played a role: if a pregnant woman
dreamt of weaving, it was a sign that she was bearing a girl. Dreams of warfare
were omens that she was bearing a boy. Sometimes the boy himself had dreams
or visions that he was destined to become a berdache. More commonly, however, a boy or adolescent was ushered into the role of berdache because he displayed the behavior or expressed the occupational interests of the opposite sex;
because he showed more interest in weaving, beadwork, gardening, or housework, for example, than in playing boys' games, or with bows and arrows.

> These manifestations were greeted by family and community
> with a range of responses from mild discouragement to active
> encouragement according to prevailing tribal sentiment. . . . They
> were signals that the youth might be destined for the special
> career of the gender-crossed (Whitehead, page 503).

Sometimes a boy was put to a test to decide whether he should be raised as a
berdache. The anthropologist Omer L. Stewart (in Stiller, page 771) describes
this traditional situation-test:

> [The boy] would be placed in a small brush shelter or on some
> dry grass, and on one side would be placed a bone awl, a basket
> or a piece of pottery. . . and on the other [side] a bow and arrows.
> . . . Then the child was frightened, usually by setting the struc-

ture or grass on fire, and [the boy] was judged according to the
implements which were chosen. If a boy under conditions of
fright . . . would pick up women's implements, he was judged to
have tendencies which would probably lead him to become a
berdache in adult life.

Among American Indians, there was a very sharp division of labor along gender lines. Men's work was men's work, and women's work was women's work.
Men and women concentrated on tasks that belonged to their gender alone.
According to Whitehead (page 506), "neither sex ordinarily does what both sexes
do." Men hunted, fished, built canoes, managed political affairs, conducted communal ceremonies, and waged war. Women raised children, made baskets,
weaved, shaped and decorated pottery, prepared food, and tended gardens. It was
almost as if men and women belonged to separate societies, and it is not surprising that in Williams's book on American Indians (page 276), there appears a photograph of a Zuni tribe in which men and boys are all arrayed on one side and
women and girls are on the other side.

Weinrich conjectures (page 344) that if the inhabitants of a small
American town posed for a picture, they would group themselves
by family, not by gender, and that this difference symbolizes the
importance of gender in the American Indian culture.

There were exceptions to the rule that barred berdaches from masculine
activities: "among the Illinois . . . the berdache could go to war but bearing only
a club, not, as in the case of ordinary men, the bow and arrow" (Whitehead, page
506). Berdaches might also participate in warfare by carrying food, or retrieving
the dead.

If a boy showed more interest in women's work than in men's, he was dressed
like a girl and destined to become a berdache. Pierre Liette, the 17th-century
observer of the prairie-dwelling Miami Indians noted (Katz 1976, page 228) that
most boys played with bows and arrows. But if a boy showed more interest in
the spade, the spindle, or the axe, he was dressed like a girl:

[T]hey are girt with a piece of leather or cloth which envelops
them from the belt to the knees, a thing all women wear. Their
hair is allowed to grow and is fastened behind the head. They . . .
are tattooed . . . like women . . . and they imitate their accent. . . .
They omit nothing that can make them like the women.

The berdache-to-be might make it very clear that he rejected male occupations and preferred female occupations, as a Mohave informant explained to
Devereau (page 503):

When there is a desire in a child's heart to become a transvestite, that child will act different. It will let people become aware of that desire. They may insist on giving the child the toys and garments of its true sex, but the child will throw them away and do this every time there is a big [social] gathering.

Preference for female occupations was apparently the main factor in ushering boys into the role of berdache, although effeminate mannerisms, a piping voice, female speech patterns, an interest in female clothing, timidity, or "feminine ways of laughing and walking" (Whitehead, page 505) might also identify a future berdache.

Aside from adopting female dress and work roles, in some tribes, berdaches performed special ritual functions at dances, ceremonies, and feasts.

> Navaho, Cheyenne, and Mohave lore [describe] the berdache's exceptional abilities as a matchmaker, love magician, or curer of venereal disease . . . expresses the logic that the berdache unites in himself both sexes, therefore he is in a position to facilitate the union of the sexes (Whitehead, pages 505-506).

Greenberg (page 180) cites the 17th Century observations of Father Marquette that Illinois and Nadowesi berdaches ". . . are summoned to the councils, and nothing can be decided without their advice . . . Through their profession of leading an Extraordinary life, they pass for . . . persons of consequence."

In some tribes, the berdache was also called upon to perform tasks that were culturally designated for neither men nor women: tasks like handling corpses and tending the ill (Whitehead, page 506).

Though excluded from most masculine activities, like hunting and warfare, berdaches were active participants in tribal life: officiating at certain ceremonial functions, for example. The Navaho prized the berdache, who was capable of doing the work of both sexes. He was often promoted to the head of his natal household, in the belief "that his presence guaranteed them wealth" (Whitehead, page 506).

It has been argued that, because of the white man's prejudice against cross-gender behavior, European observers never got an accurate picture of Indian bedrache customs, either from direct observation or from interrogating Indians. There seems to be evidence that the Indians themselves regarded berdaches with a good deal of ambivalence. Berdaches were accepted and even regarded with awe, honor, and reverence. They were also scorned, disliked, ridiculed, teased, derided, taunted, joked about, and laughed at. To an extent, this belittlement of the berdache may have been a response to the white man's known disapproval of this custom. But Greenberg suggests that the Indian also had his own reasons for belittling the berdache: (1) He did not risk injury or death in tribal warfare. (2) He disregarded the tribe's incest taboos. (3) He aroused a man's own cross-gender impulses. (4) He claimed supernatural powers, and ordinary Indians had mixed feelings toward those who controlled their lives. Indians even joked about their chiefs, which underscores their ambivalence toward those who controlled their lives.

It was a custom of the Santee Dakotas to formally and permanently exile from their village a berdache who flirted with and seduced men of his village. (This was severe treatment, similar to punishment for murder.) The ousted berdache would take up residence in a neighboring village where he was welcomed by the women "who were grateful for his contributions to women's work, and by the men, who were happy to partake of his [sexual] 'hospitality'" (Greenberg, page 183).

Under no necessity to marry, berdaches held a status similar to that of divorced and widowed women who were regarded as "everyman's 'sister-in-law'" There is fragmentary evidence that some berdaches adopted divorced or widowed women as heterosexual partners. There are also records of berdaches marrying ordinary men. These appear to be secondary marriages to men who already had one or more wives. "The data on these marriages are insufficient to permit much generalization," writes Whitehead (page 510), but they were probably guided by economic incentives.

Whitehead suggests that boys were motivated to jump the gender gap because it was plainly evident to them that a talent for "woman's work" could lead to wealth and social prestige. Women produced basketry, textiles, pottery, tipis, fur goods, and garments decorated by painting, quillwork, or beadwork. Intra-tribal gift exchanges and intertribal trade earned wealth and prestige for talented and productive producers, and women controlled the wealth produced by their own labor (Whitehead, page 519).

Although barred from some masculine activities by the "polluting" influence of menstrual blood, Indian women could attain a high level of wealth and social power. Oscar Lewis described the Piegans of the Canadian plains, where wealthy women dominated their husbands and were accorded the title of "a manly hearted woman":

> It takes most women six days to tan a hide which a manly heart-
> ed woman can do in four or five days. A manly hearted woman
> can bead a dress or a man's suit in a week of hard work, while it
> takes most women a month. An average worker makes a pair of
> moccasins in a week, while a manly hearted woman can make it
> in little over a day. These excellent workers were able to produce
> over and above the personal needs of the household. A manly
> hearted woman was therefore an economic asset, which is the
> only justification the Piegan give for a woman dominating her
> husband (Lewis, page 178).

Living examples of productive, prosperous, and prestigious berdaches could have provided an incentive for gender-jumping, to boys who seemed naturally inclined to "women's work." Acccording to Whitehead (page 522), "investigators were frequently told that the berdache performed the tasks of women better than actual women." Simms (page 580) reported that Crow berdaches often had "the largest and best appointed tipis." Hill (page 275) writes of wealthy and productive Navaho berdaches:

> They knit, tan hides, make moccasins, are said to be excellent
> sheep raisers, and excel as weavers, potters, and basket makers.
> The last three pursuits contribute substantially to their wealth, as
> especially are basketry and pottery making . . . and they are able
> to trade these products extensively with their own and other peo-
> ple.
> Attempts have been made to portray the berdache custom as
> "Native American homosexuality." Certainly, there are some sim-
> ilarities between the berdache custom and the activities of gay
> Americans, but there are also glaring differences. Mainly,
> berdache status appears to have been motivated by an interest in
> [or, perhaps, a talent for] occupations that were culturally desig-
> nated as feminine. "Sexual object choice was very much the
> trailing rather than the leading edge of gender identification"
> (Whitehead, page 512).

The berdache custom emerged in a culture where sex-roles were sharply differentiated, where male artistic expression was strongly inhibited, and where the potential rewards for "women's work" (artistic gratification, wealth, power, and prestige) provided incentives for gender-discordant boys to jump the gender gap. Homosexual behavior might *or might not* accompany berdache status.

In a 1986 publication, W.L. Williams writes that berdachism has not become extinct, as some have thought, but lives on as a continuing tradition in many Indian tribes from Alaska to Mexico's Yucatan. He quotes a traditionalist Navaho woman of the Southwest, who spoke of her nadle (the Navaho term for berdache) uncle:

> Nadles are well respected. They are seen as very compassionate
> people who care for their family a lot and help people. That's
> why they are healers. Nadle are also seen as being great with
> children, so parents are pleased if a nadle takes an interest in
> their child. One that I know is now a principal of a school on a
> reservation. Everyone knows that he and the man he lives with
> are lovers, but it is not mentioned. They help their family a lot
> and are considered valuable members of the community. Their
> sexuality is never mentioned; it is just taken for granted. No one
> would ever try to change a nadle. That is just their character, the
> way they are. Missionaries and schools had a bad effect on stig-

matizing homosexuality among more assimilated Indians, so it's not as open as in the past. But among traditionals, nadle never even went underground. It has just continued. They are our relatives, part of our family. (Quoted from Money 1988, pages 99-100)

Through conversation with an art professor at a New Mexico college, Edmund White learned about Arnie, a Native American man in his sixties who "holds a respectable position in the community" and carries on the berdache tradition of his people. White documents (pages 99-100) the professor's story of Arnie:

Arnie

When he was just six years old, his parents told him he would not become an ordinary male but would be a 'substitute woman.' This prediction was offered simply and matter-of-factly to the child, who accepted it in the same spirit. Though he does not strike others as effeminate, he has always played the "female role" in sex. His sexual partners have always been the straight men of his village, those whose wives are absent or ill or ill-disposed toward them; they knock at night on Arnie's door. He likes men who have at least four or five children, a proof of their virility. . . . He is short, thin, smooth-skinned, wonderfully pacific.

[Anglo gay friends] have tried to convince him he should sleep with gay men, but he regards the idea as laughable. He does not frown on gay men . . . but homosexuals he thinks of indulgently as "sisters," nothing more or less. (Or as "bird lovers," since the word in his language for penis is "bird.") His own approach to sex (and his place in the pueblo) is so secure he senses no need to question it.

THE XANITH OF OMAN

In a 1977 report, Wikan described the behavior of the xanith (pronounced ha-neeth) in an Arabic town of Oman. Of 3,000 male adults in that town, there were about 60 xaniths (two percent of the male population) who manifested a distinctly cross-gender role. Clearly recognizable by his dress, grooming, and behavior the xanith wear clothes of solid colors, well-fitted and tight around the waist like a female. In Oman society, men wear white, and women wear patterned cloth in bright colors.

In Oman, men cut their hair short, comb it away from the face and keep their head covered. Women oil their hair, part it in the center, comb it diagonally and keep their heads covered. Xaniths oil their hair, part it on the side, comb it forward, and go bareheaded. Men and women use perfume only on festive occasions and during sexual intercourse. Xaniths are heavily perfumed most of the time, wear makeup, walk with a swaying gait, and speak in a falsetto voice.

A xamith moves freely among women behind the purdah, that part of the house where women are secluded. He shares their social life, their intimate gossip, and their domestic activities. At a wedding, he joins the women singers while the men play musical instruments.

In a culture where female prostitution is outlawed, the xanith is permitted to work as a prostitute. He may work as a house servant, or he may live alone. He may decide to reclaim his status as a man if his family will arrange a marriage for him, and if he produces the postnuptial bloodstained cloth, public evidence that he has deflowered his virgin bride. As a married man, he need not give up his feminine mannerisms. He is also free to later relinquish his male status and again live as a xanith.

THE MAHU OF TAHITI

Men in Tahiti display a wide range of behavior, from extreme masculinity to extreme effeminacy. Heterosexuality comes easily to all males, including the extremely effeminate. Extreme effeminacy "does not disqualify someone from being regarded as a normal man, and there are many such men in Tahiti with wives and children" (Lindholm, 1982).

In every village, one effeminate man—and only one—assumes the highly-privileged role of mahu, which permits him to dress as a woman and engage in casual homosexual relations with men in the village. "He may remain a mahu all his life, or abdicate his role and raise a family" *(ibid.)*.

For centuries, travellers to Tahiti have brought home tales of the mahu. Anthropologist Gilbert Herdt (1997, pages 100-101) describes the traditional life of these persons, "dramatic and fun-loving and full of life," from childhood to adulthood.

> As a young child, a boy may have begun to take on the charac-
> teristics of the women's role and tasks around the house. He may
> have taken a woman's job in later life. Some mahu, however,
> seem to have been more like other men and not so womanly in
> their appearance or practices. As a mahu, the individual took on
> not only the woman's daily role but also her part in traditional
> dances, songs, and festivals. Although the mahu was sometimes
> an object of joking and pranks, he was nevertheless a sexual
> partner of many of the same men who made fun of him in pub-
> lic; and the mahu were fully accepted in Tahitian society. The
> mahu were often known to enjoy same-gender sexual relations as
> adolescents and as adults. The typical form practiced was oral
> sex, in which the mahu would fellate his partner; there did not
> seem to be much, if any stigma, attaced to this practice, particu-

larly if it was clear that the other man did not suck the mahu. But there are also stories told in which the partners might turn around and want to fellate the mahu as well.

It is not clear that all of the individuals who were thought to be mahu in old Polynesia were homosexual in the sense that they generally or exclusively preferred the same gender for romance and sexual relations. Certainly, their male partners were expected to marry and have children. It is possible that some of the mahu were what we might call bisexual—attracted primarily to the other gender but still on occasion desiring their own gender and performing the mahu role. Some authorities believe that the mahu functioned primarily to support the local masculine/feminine gender role dichotomy in social, economic, and political activities. In this view, each traditional village had the customary role of one mahu who served to clarify and define the masculine model [by contrast], a powerful reminder of a negative role model of what not to be for the other men.

In recent years, Western civilization has transformed the mahu into a tourist attraction. According to Herdt (1977), the mahu has adapted his traditional skills in song, storytelling, and dance, to fit into the tourist industry, participating in shows, beauty pageants, nightclub acts, and prostitution. The mahu attract gay and lesbian tour groups from the United States, Australia, and Europe. The Westernized mahu wears the clothes and makeup of women, and may be thinking about having a sex change operation. Herdt concludes his acknowledgement of these Western influences with the hope that in the villages the mahu will continue its distinctive traditional customs.

THE KATHOEY OF THAILAND

Modern Thailand attracts western tourists with its its thriving sex industry: sex clubs, female prostitution, male prostitution, massage parlors, and a variety of erotic and pornographic media. Just as Paris has evolved an elaborate tourist-oriented restaurant industry based on France's traditional devotion to good eating, Thailand has evolved a sex industry from its tradition of open sexuality.

Traditionally, female prostitution was widely practiced in Thailand. This service complemented the custom of arranged marriages, and in Thailand men of all ages regularly visited prostitutes in villages and town. Prostitutes were not stigmatized; they could give up this work, get married and have children. Homosexuality was also visible and tolerated; "generally more accepted than in many other cultures," according to Herdt (1997, page 148).

Herdt (*ibid,*) describes an advice column in a most popular Thai magazine, that publishes many letters from distraught homosexual men who are counseled on their specific problems[10] and generally advised "to accept their same-gender desires and try to be happy with them" (*ibid,*).

The above paragraphs describe Thailand as a sexually open society, and yet "male homosexuals who stand out from the crowd may be stigmatized for it" (Herdt 1997, page 149). In defiance of this popular bias are the kathoey, male homosexuals who dress and act like women in manners that range from moderate to dramatic and exaggerated ways "with loud and abrasive language and aggressive overtures—uncharacteristic of the Thai people in general and women in particular. . ." (*ibid,*). Many kathoey apparently look so feminine that they could easily pass as women, but they take pride in their male genitals. Some kathoey have ordinary jobs, some work in prostitution. Kathoey are the topic of a recent BBC documentary, "Lady Boys." It tells the story of two teen-age kathoey of the 1990s.

Herdt adds that Kathoey have some basis in the mythology and ancient lore of Thailand, mentioned in critical texts that suggest the very old and lasting importance of this figure in Thai culture.

THE SAMBIA OF NEW GUINEA: The Making of a Headhunter

The Sambia headhunters in the highlands of New Guinea, believed that male potency is transferred from older boys to younger boys by means of fellatio. To achieve the fierce manhood of a headhunter, a pre-pubertal boy must leave the society of his mother and sisters and enter the secret society of men. Woman's milk has helped him grow from infancy to boyood, but to become an adult he must now be fed men's milk, the semen of mature youths and unmarried men.

From middle childhood to puberty, boys perform this ritual on older youths on a daily basis. At puberty, they in turn will offer their semen to younger boys. This daily ritual occupies from ten to fifteen years of a boy's life. When he reaches marrying age, his family negotiates the procurement of a wife and arranges his marriage. He then embarks upon the heterosexual phase of his life, made possible, it is believed, by his years of exclusively homosexual experience. In *Guardians of the Flutes* (pages 2-3), Herdt describes this custom:

> Elders teach that semen is absolutely vital; it should be con-
> sumed daily since the creation of biological maleness and the
> maintenance of masculinity depend on it. . . [During the time
> when they perform the daily secret ritual for transferring semen
> from the older to the younger boys,] youths and boys alike must
> absolutely avoid women, on pain of punishment. . . Females are .
> . . believed to be contaminating—their menstrual blood polluting
> and worse, lethal. So all heterosexual relationships, intrigues, and
> even casual conversations between boys and girls are blocked,
> and forbidden.

[T]he final outcome [of this upbringing] is [marriage and] exclusive heterosexuality.

The Arapesh, the Mundugumor, and the Tchambuli

Also in New Guinea, Margaret Mead stumbled upon three neighboring preliterate societies that were strikingly different in their prevailing sex norms.[11] Settled in areas just a few miles apart were the mountain-dwelling Arapesh, where both men and women both expressed "feminine" traits; the river-dwelling Mundugumor, where both men and women behaved in rather aggressive "masculine" ways; and the Tchambuli lake dwellers, where the women seemed rather "masculine" and the men were caricatures of "femininity."

Ranking these three tribes from the poorest to the richest, the Arapesh come first. Living on the sides of barren mountains, cultivating hillside garden patches, life was difficult for the Arapesh. Men and women shared more or less equally the struggle for survival—expressing gentle, loving, cooperative behaviors toward each other, toward their young and toward their neighbors.

The Mundugumor lived in a fertile area near the side of a river. To protect their rich lands, where they grew tobacco and picked coconuts, it helped that they became fierce warriors and headhunters. Unlike the gentle, loving Araphesh, Mundugumor mothers handled children roughly. For example, they left them hanging on the wall in their cradleboards until their crying could be no longer endured.

"Wealth brings strife," and so it was for the Mundugumor. The warrior role seemed to generalize, so that husbands and wives fought with each other and taught their children, both male and female, to be violent and arrogant. Like the Arapesh, there was little difference in the temperament exhibited by men and women, according to Mead.

This is how the Tchambuli were so different: men and women displayed distinctly different temperaments, but to Western eyes, as to Margaret Mead, the women seemed very "masculine," and the men resembled a female caricature. Like the Mundugumor, the Tchambuli occupied a fertile area, and had once been headhunters. When Mead visited them, the women did virtually all the work that kept their society going: raising the children, gardening, fishing, and food-preparation. Men spent their time in ceremonial and artistic activities—in painting, music, drama, in ornamenting their bodies, and in arranging their hair. It was also common for men to gossip and indulge in petty jealousies.

How did it happen that Tchambuli men adopted ways so characteristic of some idle rich women in Western society, while Tchambuli women did most of the practical work? This "design for living" was probably established when headhunting was a full-time job and domestic affairs was left entirely up to the women. The concept of "cultural lag" goes far in describing the Tchambuli way of life as Margaret Mead found it.

What is of special interest here is that Mead (page 293) found no male homosexuality among the Arapesh or Mundugumor, where no sharp boundaries were maintained between "womanly ways" and "manly ways," but she informs her reader, however indirectly,[12] that male homosexuality was to be found among the Tchambuli. Comparing the Tchambuli with their Arapesh and the Mundugumor neighbors, it is clear that in the Tchambuli culture, not only are gender roles more sharply defined, but the culturally-defined role of the Tchambuli male was more inhibiting, more narrowly resticted, and offered fewer choices of lifestyle,[13] than was the Tchambuli female sex role. Mead (page 307) observed that Tchambuli society "contains a larger number of neurotic males than I have seen in any other primitive society."

Margaret Mead's comparison of these three New Guinea societies suggests that male homosexuality is most likely to arise in those societies that make the male gender role restrictive and burdensome, in cultures that sharply specify exactly what is a man's work and what is a woman's work. It seems that men are less likely to seek an escape from male status if male status permits the adoption of a wide range of life roles.

THE AUSTRALIAN BODY-RUBBERS

Greenberg reports (pages 35-36) that among the Australian aborigines, a girl may be engaged at birth, but when her betrothed is sexually mature, the tribal elders may be reluctant to deliver her to him, because they need her for gathering food. Meanwhile, the promised bride's older brother is required to act as a substitute wife, serving the waiting husband's sexual needs by greasing and rubbing his body.

THE LANGO OF EAST AFRICA

Potts and Short (page 76) describe the berdache customs of the Lango, a tall and slender people of northern Uganda. Not only do they permit gender-discordant men "to dress as women and become the wives of other males, but they even go so far as to simulate menstruation" by cutting the skin of their inner thighs.

THE BITESHA AMONG THE BALA: Dropouts in the Congo

Alan P. Merriam studied studied the Basongye, an agricultural people who live in the Democratic Republic of the Congo and maintain a sharp differentiation of gender roles. Only men occupy themselves with war, hunting, fishing, palm nut cutting, and the like. Only women gather firewood, cook, and carry water. These roles are almost never reversed "for it is considered shameful for a person of one sex to assume the tasks and roles of the other." Merriam (page 74) quotes a Bala informant:

Women's work is shameful for a man to do. If a man did women's work before he was married, he would probably get accustomed to it and then he could not change his habits and would never be able to get married. Also, the women would think he was a woman, and no one would marry him. . . . A man can help his wife collect wood or bring water if he does so in secret in the forest. When they get near the village, however, she should take the load and carry it in. Many men do this.

Merriam reports on male transvestites, called bitesha (singular: kitesha), among the Bala. He writes (page 94): "Such individuals play a role which allows escape from normal male responsibilities." Merriam quotes an informant's description of the bitesha:

He doesn't want to work; he doesn't want to be with other men; he doesn't even have a concubine; he eats everywhere except at his own house; he doesn't do things that other men do; he never keeps a job; he . . . acts like a woman, that is, rushes about hither and yon and wiggles his hips when he walks.

Merriam notes that "betisha wears women's clothing. . . . Among male bitesha, there are 'male' amd 'female' types. They pair off and have homosexual relationships, according to my informant. Merriam describes the only kitesha in the village, who lived with his kitesha wife, and visits bitesha in other villages. (He explains: "Bitesha always stay with bitesha because all bitesha are friends.") "In my conversations with him, he emerged as an intelligent man, but with a personality which differed sharply from that of other male villagers."

Merriam's informant (page 95) "says he was a kitesha from the moment he was born but cites no reason for this." Merriam adds (page 97): "His costume consisted only of a wraparound skirt, the ends of which were arranged to open at the front; he did expose himself and seemed to enjoy doing so. The fact that his upper body was left bare was considered to be abnormal and symbolic of his association with women." Merriam quotes his informant (page 95):

Yes, I am a kitesha. I don't like to do anything. I only like to eat. I don't like to work in the fields. . . I don't like to wear a shirt or trousers. I like to stay with women. I like to steal.

Merriam concludes (page 97): "It seems clear that not only is the role of the male kisheta in Bala society firmly patterned but that there are numerous expectations of the individual, recognized both by himself and by other members of the society. It also is evident that the position is one which enables the kitesha to avoid the normal male role. Indeed, this probably is its function."

THE HIDJRA OF INDIA

Potts and Short (page 77) also provide the following description of India's hidjra, a cast that ranks even lower than the untouchables. Groups of hidjras include homosexuals, intersexes, transvestites and male castrates. It is "the custom that any [male] child born with abnormal-looking genitalia will be given to the hidjra, who will rear it as one of their own." These groups "make a living by traveling through the countryside . . . offering entertainment at birthdays, weddings and funerals for a small fee, and subsequently having sex with their guests. . . . If they receive insufficient gifts for a performance, their ultimate sanction is to sweep up their skirts exposing their mutilated genitalia."

RURAL NORTH MEXICO: Jotos and Machos

Anthropologists Alonso and Koreck argue that the label "homosexual" as is understood in the States does not adequately describe northern rural Mexican populations, that this designation (like "heterosexual" or "bisexual") is culturally specific rather than universal.

In contemporary "Anglo" culture, all men who sexually engage other men, whether actively or passively or both, are socially regarded as homosexual, and so regard themselves. A radically different norm prevails in northern rural Mexico where "males who [only] play the active macho role of insertor in homosexual encounters generally are not conceptualized as homosexuals" (page 115).

In the rural areas of northern Mexico, where Alonzo conducted her research, young males were honored for displaying a masculine identity if they demonstrated the qualities of autonomy, mastery, valor, and virility on a day-to-day basis. One way in which a post-pubertal male wins this honored reputation of being macho is to become a chignone: ("a fucker"): the active, penetrating sex partner. Heterosexual anal intercourse is widely practiced both to avoid pregnancy, and to preserve the girl's virginity. This practice blurs the distinction between heterosexual and homosexual intercourse. A boy's anus is not that different from a girl's.

Machos are free to engage in sexual activity with either jotos (passive male partners) or females without being stigmatized. The insertor's masculinity is not diminished if his partner is a pre-pubertal boy or a joto. Alonzo conjectures that for a macho "to emasculate another man may represent *the ultimate validation of masculinity*" (Alonzo, page 119, italics added).

Prior to marriage, some machos have anal sex with pre-pubertal boys, and after marriage continue to seek both male and female sex partners. Some macho males initiate sexual activity with both post-pubertal girls and effeminate boys. "They continue to utilize both sexual outlets prior to marriage, but discontinue or only occasionally use, homosexual outlets following marriage. Still another pattern [allows romantic and sexual involvement with both jotos and women, both before and after marriage]" (Carrier, page 78). A wife has no direct influence over her husband's sexual conduct, and may not even know of his activity with jotos (which also puts the wife at risk of HIV infection).

Stephen O. Murray (page 52) offers a similar report of homosexual attitudes among Latin Americans. He describes "the sexually omnivorous hombre who doesn't have any preferences in 'object choice:' the man for whom 'meat on the hook is meat on the hook, no reason to be choosy; no opportunity would be allowed to slip by and it doesn't matter who or what you fuck as long as you fuck' . . . [a working principle for one who] just can't get it with his girlfriend often enough, or at all, and [a gay man is] there as a temporary substitute or relief." Murray quotes an Argentine writer: "The sexual problem of the young man is acute. They're poor, and love is expensive. They don't have enough money to pay for a girl, [still less to marry and set up a household,] so they turn to homosexuals."

Murray (page 64) agrees with Alonzo and Koreck that the passive role in sexual intercourse "is considered a source of pollution, reduced autonomy, shame and powerlessness."[14] (Alonzo, page 117) The joto is stigmatized because he was born with a male body but allows himself to be "opened and penetrated like a woman" (*ibid*). In macho-joto sexual contact, fellatio is often part of the foreplay, but anal intercourse is considered the culminating act (Carrier, page 79).

Jotos accept their "contradictory gender identity . . . [They] dress as women on festive occasions, wear make-up, adopt female names, and use female pronouns to refer to each other. They often engage in feminized occupations, such as work in restaurants. They never have sexual relations with each other but only with machos. Indeed, when one informant was asked whether jotos had sex with each other, she answered that this would be 'impossible,' since it would be like two women 'going to bed' together. (Lesbianism is not a culturally acknowledged possibility.) She explained that jotos themselves said they were women born in men's bodies (and indeed some take female hormones in order to make their bodies more feminine)" (Alonzo, page 117). Males who play only the passive role in anal intercourse are ridiculed as effeminate and are the butt of social ridicule, but they are not ostracized to the degree and extent that homosexuals are in conservative communities of the States.

Alonzo comments in more detail on the social rank of jotos: ". . . In one community, jotos run a restaurant which is patronized by 'respectable people.' The owner, a joto, is a pillar of the community, who is respected for supporting his mother and siblings, and who is invited to important community functions. . . . While it is not quite 'respectable' for women to be too friendly with jotos, some mentioned lending jotos feminine apparel for wear on festive occasions, and others spoke highly of one joto's home. On the whole, though jotos are stigmatized; they are more objects of pity and amusement than of horror and avoidance." Alonzo goes on to say that "decent" married women prefer that their husband have sexual encounters with jotos than with female prostitutes, or have a concubine. *Jotos are less likely to disrupt a marriage and break up a family* (Alonzo, page 118, italics added).

It is true that in urban parts of Mexico, one can find middle-class men who adopt the role of American gays, and play both active and passive roles in anal intercourse. These "internationals" are unknown in rural Mexico, according to Alonzo (page 119).

Homosexual Life in Europe and in England

In this chapter, our sampling of homosexual life has focused in on ancient, preliterate and non-western cultures, although our sampling could have included more information on homosexual life in the Western world of today and yesterday. Descriptions of 18th century life in London refer to "molly houses," taverns where homosexuals were known to congregate. There "men would sit in one another's laps, kissing in a lewd manner and using their hands indecently" (Ellis, page 46).

There are also references in 19th century writings to homosexual life in the big cities of Europe: Paris, Berlin, and St. Petersburg. Readers interested in historical details on homosexual life in the Western world may wish to consult Havelock Ellis (1915) and Chauncey.

Other Observations of Cross-Gender Groups

According to Money (1988), cross-gender groups have also been observed in Polynesia, in Hawaii, in Samoa (faa fa' fini), in Burma (acault), and in Tonga. Greenberg has made an in-depth study of variations in homosexual practice (to support his thesis that homosexuality is a "social construction"). A culture may enforce arbitrary rules (e.g., a boy may be penetrated only by his sister's husband). Greenberg's observations include man-boy sex intended to transfer magical powers as well as masculine traits and skills. He likewise notes that homosexual behavior is often related to a shortage or unavailability of women, because of polygyny, military or hunting activity, taboos, or prolonged engagement.

How prevalent is homosexual activity? To answer this question, Cleland Ford and Frank Beach in 1951 surveyed 76 human societies on which there was some documentation regarding homosexual practices or prohibitions. Their analysis was based on the Yale Human Relations Area Files, a collection of thousands of anthropological reports, indexed for comparative study. Ford and Beach found that in almost two-thirds of the 76 cultures surveyed (49, or 64 percent) some variety of homosexual activity was considered normal at some specified time and for some specified members of the community. Usually, homosexuality was displayed by a variant of the bedrache, a male who dressed and behaved like a woman. In some societies, this role was chosen, while in others, some boys were raised to assume that role. Homosexual behavior could also be involved in puberty ceremonies, as in the Sambia, or were designated for a particular stage of life.

Ford and Beach found that in no society was homosexuality the dominant form of sexual activity, and in more than one-third (27, or 36 percent) of the cultures studied, homosexual behavior was considered unacceptable, and discouraged by social pressures.[15] There were some indications that even where 'prohibited,' one could find hidden and rare expressions of homosexuality. (page 130).

Discussion

The widespread incidence of gender-discordant adult male groups in traditional societies throughout the world leaves no room for doubt that inherent in the human species is the tendency for a minority of boys to gravitate toward the female role, and that this tendency usually stays with them throughout their adult lives. Most of these traditional societies maintain well-defined, explicit rules and customs governing the dress, economic and social participation of its berdache group. In the contemporary Western world, on the other hand, the goal of homosexual spokesmen is nothing less than full participation throughout the length and breadth of society.[16] This goal is claimed in the name of social justice and civil rights, and is unquestioned by many of those who regard themselves as enlightened people of good will.

NOTES TO CHAPTER 10

1. Vase paintings with erotic themes, both heterosexual and homosexual, are lavishly illustrated in Dover's *Greek Homosexuality*, and in Keuhl's *The Reign of the Phallus*.

2. Freud credits Iwan Bloch (1872-1922), a practicing physician and a historian by avocation, with redefining homosexuality from a medical subject to an anthropological phenomenon. Bloch was perhaps the first person to systematically document the existence of male cross-gender groups—"berdaches"—in various cultures of the world.

3. Karlen (1971, page 32) estimates the population of Attica as 25,000 citizens, 10,000 free non-citizens, and 150,000 to 300,000 slaves.

4. Keuhls (page 276) notes that in Athens anal penetration was the preferred mode of sex, especially with older and lowlier partners. She argues that anal penetration expressed aggression and domination. It gave less sexual gratification to the female partner than vaginal intercourse and expressed the penetrator's disdain for his sex partner.

5. This standard, that sexual penetration is a masculine act regardless of the gender of the partner is, of course, shared with many cultures of all times. See note 14 of this chapter.

6. The original meaning of the word pederasty was man-boy love, but in more recent years, various other meanings have been attached to the word, like homosexuality in general, or anal intercourse. Man-boy love, a translation of the Greek word, seems to better serve our purposes.

7. For example, Ganymede, the legendary boy whose beauty excited the desire of Zeus himself, is pictured on page 63 of this book. As he is conventionally portrayed in Greek art, he too he is shown as a young boy playing with a hoop.

8. Writes John Munder Ross (page 83): "Back in the classical gymnasiums, pubescent boys were required to let older men stick their erect penises between their legs [defined as intercrural sex] and ejaculate while the youths themselves remained detumescent, like forbearing and demure girls doing an older man's bidding. Any other homosexual act was frowned upon and punished in Athenian society."

9. Frightened by the prediction of the oracle, Laius decided never to have intercourse with his wife again, but he was carried away one night when he came home drunk. Oedipus, who was born of this drunken lapse, grows up to marry his mother and kill his father. According to Keuhls (page 289), Laius has sometimes been called "the inventor of pederasty."

10. Correspondents describe "heartbreak stories of men who fall in love with men, are involved with married men, [or] are worried about sex 'through the back door' (a favorite metaphor for anal sex. . .)" (Herdt 1997, page 148). Uncle Go, the advice-giver, "stresses the importance of anal sex" (*ibid,*).

11. When *Sex and Temperament* was first published (1935), what are now termed "gender roles" were still called sex roles: social, expressive, (as well as sex-partner) behaviors designated as appropriate to males or females.

12. Contrast Mead's direct and simple statement (page 293) "There was no homosexuality among either the Arapesh or Mundagumor" with her roundabout statement (page 294) that the Tchambuli man may suffer "the misery of being disturbed in his psycho-sexual life. He not only has the wrong feelings but, far

worse and more confusing, he has the feelings of a woman."

13. A Tchambuli woman had a very wide choice of roles, since women did virtually everything that kept the society going, while the men engaged in ceremonial activities, artistic activities, and personal adornment. The fact that the "coquettish play-acting personality" was characteristic of Tchambuli boys (page 288), and that Tchambuli men characteristically engaged in gossip, quarrels, bickering, misunderstandings, avowals, disclaimers, hurt feelings and petty jealousies (page 257) further suggests that in Tchambuli society, the male role was an uncomfortable one. Writes Mead (page 275): "The men are conspicuous maladjusts, subject to neurasthenia, hysteria, and maniacal outbursts." She compares the neuroticism of Tchambuli men with the happy life of Tchambuli women:

> For fifty quarrels among the men, there is hardly one among the women. . . . They sit in groups and laugh together, or occasionally stage a night dance at which, without a man present, each woman dances vigorously all by herself the dance-step she has found to be most exciting (Mead, page 257).

14. Murray (page 64) relates the story told by a gay man who picked up a muscular adolescent who asked to be penetrated anally: "I fucked him and he enjoyed it. . . . Then, still naked, he asked me, 'And if anybody catches us here, who is the man?' . . . I replied, perhaps a little cruelly, 'Obviously, I am the man since I stuck it into you.' This enraged the young man, who was a judo expert, and he started to throw me against the low ceiling. . . I was getting an awful beating. 'Who is the man here?' he repeated. And I, afraid, to die on this one, replied, 'You, because you are a judo expert.'"

15. Greenberg (pages 74-76) lists about a dozen tribes the world over in which homosexual practices are extremely rare, never recorded, are believed to be a disgusting crime, unnatural and revolting, or are punishable by death.

16. Kirk and Madsen suggest, for example, that in a forthcoming election, the list of candidates for the office of President of the United States should include a qualified gay person, even if he (or she) has no chance of winning. This would force people who believe in equal rights to champion the rule that in principle a gay man or woman should be free to run for any office for which they are qualified.

11 The Worship of Youth

In the argot of the gay world, a man who is attracted to teen-age boys is called a "chicken hawk." Edmund White (page 325) describes a friend as "a convinced but discrete chicken hawk," and who himself looks much younger than his actual age. His friend's "erotic fantasy is to be a youth among youths, not a dirty old man preying upon them. . . His first affair started when he was six; his lover was the neighbor boy, a more plausible twelve. . . He is an artist and he loves beauty with a connoisseur's eye. Who is more beautiful than a young man of sixteen?"

Through 35 years of marriage, Carol's husband had led a closeted gay life. Over the years, Jim had worked as administrator of a large church, partner of a personnel placement firm, husband, father, and pillar of a conservative community. When his gay life finally became a fact that he could no longer hide, the change in Jim's behavior most noticeable to Carol was his obsession with youth. She observed (Grever, page 50):

> *Flashy clothes and expensive toys excite him.* . . . He likes
> movies, I like to read. . . . *[H]e likes city excitement*, I like quiet
> mountain walks. . . . My circle of friends narrows but deepens by
> the year. . . . *Jim seems compelled to surround himself with
> crowds of jazzy kids. He dresses like a twenty-year-old.* . . . *He
> dyes his hair and shaves off his graying beard.* All of his energy
> is directed toward the surface (emphasis added).

Middle-aged homosexuals often try to look like men in their twenties. Many gay men in their twenties try to look like teen-agers, by bleaching their head hair, removing their body hair, cultivating a slim, boyish figure, dressing, talking, and acting like teen-agers. The teen-ager (real or imaginary) is one of about four major types[1] attractive to gay men, types who fulfill the gay man's "search image."

The choice of a boyish lad may be based on any combination of four factors: (1) The boyish lad is "*a narcissistic object choice.*" He is a representation of the searcher himself, who would like to treat the lad with the care and tenderness that he would like his mother or father to have shown toward him. [Hoffman (1968, page 195?) correctly notes that *heterosexuals* also make narcissistic love-object choices.] (2) The boyish lad combines both masculine and feminine features. To the boy lover, the sight of a young boy's body gives the partner *relief from the castration threat*, for here is "a girl with a penis." (3) In Chapter 9, we introduced the conjecture that the homosexual act may be regarded as *performance of a mana ritual.* According to this formula, a young man's penis regarded as a fountain of youth. (4) Finally, let us consider this reality factor: that a young lad may be readily available for sexual exploitation by an older brother, relative, neighbor, caregiver, teacher, or priest.

194

Attraction to the boyish lad, fair-skinned and hairless (except for a head of sandy or blond fine hair), childlike in physique and personality, a search image of this sort betokens a hankering for a male with female qualities. Young boys are males without masculinity, often downright girlish in body form and in hair and skin texture: blond, rosy-cheeked, red-lipped. With his high-pitched voice and playful manner, a young boy arouses, Fenichel conjectures (page 331) a gay man's "latent *heterosexuality*." Most gay men, he conjectures, cannot completely "free themselves from their biological longing for women. . . . This acute longing . . . compels them to choose boys, but the boys must have a maximum of girlish and feminine traits. . . They are actually looking for 'a girl with a penis.' " Fenichel's conjecture suggests why so many gay men hunger for a sexual partner who is both young and boyish.

The psychoanalyst Sandor Rado also stressed that every homosexual man is a "*latent heterosexual.*" Buried in his psyche (and perhaps in his genes) is the desire to mate with a woman. Writes Rado (pages 181-182):

> Fear of the opposite sex may drive this desire underground, but neither this fear nor any other force, save for schizophrenic disorganization, can break its strength. Individuals with mates of their own sex are impelled by this underground desire to generate a vicarious male-female pattern that will achieve for them the illusion of having, or being themselves, a mate of the opposite sex. This potent underground version of the . . . male-female pattern deserves to be recognized as the foremost aim-image . . . of these individuals.

Especially appealing to gay men with the boyish search image are those men who are pedomorphic by nature, who continue to exhibit a distinctly boyish appearance, in face and body build, well into late adolescence and even into adulthood. It is no accident that blond hair is so attractive to gay men. Both males and females are often blond in childhood, and their hair darkens as they mature. Fair hair is therefore a sign of youth, like smooth, hairless skin, which gay men find so attractive. Here and there, hirsute "bears" surface in the gay world, but the great majority of bodies displayed in the gay media are smooth and hairless. Gay newspapers commonly advertise body hair removal services.

British journalist and gay man Michael Davidson (pages 152-153) recalls his intoxication over the "startlingly beautiful" boy he found in the showers of a public swimming pool in pre-Nazi Berlin:

> One day, naked beneath the showers, I found the most startlingly beautiful person I'd ever seen: a living, and lively, Beardsley decoration for 'Salome'--he might have been the original Beardsley prototype, except that he was an improvement on the artist's

invention. He had all the Beardsley sin, but none of the corrup-
tion. . . . Ivory-white skin, parchment-pale, with a fervent scarlet
mouth and huge sable eyes, full of black fire; a mass of romping
black hair, thick and lively as a bear's. . . .

But, I quickly found, it wasn't only his face that was intoxicating;
it was a glittering personality and the incomparable *friendship* he
gave--in his magic company differences of age, culture, language, vanished: he made me his equal and partner. . . . I had
found at last the 'divine friend much desired' . . . .

We must have been an astonishing sight, Werner and I: roistering
round Berlin with our arms round each other's necks; both with
long bare legs and open necks . . . drinking a great deal, embracing and spooning in public places and generally behaving outra-
geously--I skinnily ugly and 30 years old; he dazzling in looks,
with that astonishing head and face in which the angelic and
demonic were tantalizingly blended.

Gay men romanticize the man-boy love of ancient Greece. In their proposal
for stabilizing and strengthening the contemporary gay community, Kirk and
Madsen (pages 366-372) explicitly propose more partnerships between older
men and younger men. Sexual involvement with a boy under the age of 18 risks
arrest and incarceration as a pedophile, so prudent gay men must settle for a
young man who simply *looks and acts* like a boy: shy, playful, laughing, prankish; a young man who has who has a boyish physique and all the other physical
marks of boyhood.

Not unknown is a *heterosexual* search image not unrelated to man-boy
love–the search for a girl with boyish features. This ideal is celebrated in the
1919 novel by the English aristocrat John Buchan, *Mr. Steadfast*. In this robust-
ly masculine adventure story, written with pre-Freudian naivete, the hero falls in
love with a young woman who looks and acts very much like a beautiful boy
(page 22): "I stared after her as she walked across the lawn, and I remember
noticing that she moved with the free grace of an athletic boy." Later in the story
(page 106), he ponders over having fallen in love with this "young girl with a
cloud of gold hair and the strong, slim grace of a boy." Still later (page 208), "I
remember the way she laughed and flung back her head like a gallant boy." The
hero also recalls (page 252): "I loved to watch her . . . with her elbows on the
table like a schoolboy."[2]

Man-Boy Love

Responsible gay spokesmen denounce man-boy love, and try to exclude their
advocates from Gay Pride parades. A 1990 article by Thorstad expresses the ten-

sion that exists between the gay movement and what the author calls "the cross-generational love movement:"

> [Thorstad (page 282) complains that the present-day] gay movement limits its concerns to what consenting adults do in private. . . . [I]t has de-emphasized sex, and seeks to sanitize the image of homosexuality to facilitate its entrance into the social mainstream . . . [concentrating on] the priorities of an upwardly mobile adult gay middle class ('guppies'—gay urban professionals). In short, the gay movement's agenda is being determined increasingly by straight society, rather than by homosexuals themselves.

> In present-day America it is all right to talk or publish books about boy-man love in ancient Greece or the pederasty of great men like Byron. But it is quite another matter to leave the academic ivory tower and acknowledge that boy-love goes on in every neighborhood (Thorstad, page 268)

The more daring gay writers express impatience with social and legal prejudice against pedophilia.[3] Edmund White (page 310) proposes, for example, "to lower the age of consent to twelve for boys and girls, regardless of whether the sex involved is straight or gay and regardless of the age of the older partner," and to permit children as young as twelve to work as prostitutes.

In his Introduction to *The New Gay Liberation Book*, editor Ed Richmond (page 19) likewise asks for a fresh re-examination of the entire issue of man-boy sex. "Personally," he writes, "I am much more horrifed by [an] adult's religious assault on helpless and impressionable children. *Caring for one another should be a right, and the sexual pleasures that are sometimes the result of this affection are not going to wait for the twenty-first birthday* (emphasis added)."

Dirk

Edmund White (pages 312-314) interviewed a boy-lover, whom we will call Dirk. This sad-faced 36-year-old gay man had a 12-year-old lover, a relationship that started when the boy was nine and he was first attracted to Dirk when the boy was at the beach with his mother. "He started coming over to my house," says Dirk, and they have been lovers ever since. White asked: "Does his mother know?" Dirk's answer implies that she doesn't want to know, because the boy seems to be benefiting from the relationship.[4]

> Says Dirk: "She knows as much as she wants to. She knows that he was cranky before and had trouble in school and in his schoolwork and that now he's calmer and getting good grades. She could know more if she asked her son, but I don't think she

wants to know the specifics--she knows we're friends; what she sees is positive."

"Did your friend take the sexual initiative with you?" White asked. Dirk's reply was: "Absolutely. I've been with kids since I was 22, and in every case kids are the aggressors." Dirk admits he is turned on by sissy boys, but "like most pedophiles, I'm scared of them. An effeminate boy blows your cover. People suspect something's going on. . . . [P]arents are worried about him and guard him carefully. So I end up with all-American, butchy little straight boys."

Sad-faced Dirk is burdened by the real possibility of imprisonment,[5] and now tells White he is thinking of finding a job where he can work with kids but will not get sexually involved with them.

> "This stuff scares the shit out of me. I'm not a psychopath. I couldn't take imprisonment. I'd --I'd just die. The guy who got me into this scene [was] in prison for ten years. He was given drug therapy and shock therapy. He's out now, but he's a vegetable."

As they discuss his sexual desires, Dirk admits to White, "I guess I'm screwed up," and confesses that he wishes his tastes were less dangerous. (He has had sex with adult men, but "more as a favor to them than as a pleasure of my own.") "The energy this takes up! Sometimes I've felt I was losing my mind. I could have accomplished so much more if I hadn't been cursed--or if society had been different."

LONDON PEDOPHILES. Wilson and Cox obtained the cooperation of a London all-male pedophile self-help group and in 1978-79, 77 of the members returned a written questionnaire. A large majority (71%) said they were attracted to boys of 12, 13, and 14, "the years immediately preceding puberty" (page 17). Wrote one respondent: "I think I like young boys because they have little or no body hair and their bodies are more effeminate, and more loving" (page 20).

One-third of the participants in the study expressed a willingness to be interviewed. The authors offer a number of case histories, including a lengthy report on Adam, described as a "committed exponent" of pedophilia who "seems to be extremely happy in his present circumstances, [and] expresses no desire to change. . . His enthusiasm for pedophilia is somewhat overwhelming:" [In the following summary of the authors' interview with Adam, paraphrases are enclosed in brackets, like this sentence, and all other statements are direct quotations from pages 78-81.]

Adam

[This "extremely happy" pedophile] thinks that the cause of his pedophilia may lie in the absence of his father, who was involved in military service during these early years. It is his experience among the boys he has been involved with that those who enjoy sex with a man often do not have a strong father, whereas boys who have a good relationship with their father do not appear to derive as much satisfaction from a sexual relationship.

[Adam describes his mother] as a disciplinarian who dominated his life, bossing him and being "very hard" on him. . . His father was described as a "ghost" who just wasn't there. He apparently shared very little with his father as he grew up and their relationship seems to have been quite minimal. Sex was a topic that they never discussed. . .

[Adam says] that as a boy he had been involved with a number of men . . . including anal intercourse with an uncle.

He sees himself as having been pedophilic since he was fourteen or fifteen. He is now thirty-nine. He has had homosexual relationships with adults, although these are described as being the consequence of friendship. He has not derived much satisfaction from sex under these conditions. . . . .

Adam . . . indicated that he was exclusively homosexual in his pedophilic interests. . . The age range that he finds ideal is 10-14 years with 11 being the optimum . . . Eleven is described as "a magical age."

[Adam recalls relationships with 19 boys, five of which he describes as "deep relationships." In two cases, the boy's mother "were aware of the situation and did not object." Adam described a situation in which the mother was especially supportive:]

She allowed him to sleep in the boy's room when he visited and would leave him in the house with the boy until very late at night while she and her husband went out.

[T]here are thousands of kids all over London just waiting for an adult to come along and say, "Hello, hold my hand, let's go for a walk. . . . " Kids want an adult, kids want to have a relationship with an older person. Whether it's sex or anything else they don't really mind as long as they can have an adult they can turn to, somebody they can confess to."

. . . Much of his activity with children would appear to be non-sexual in motivation and intended to make children happy or assist in their development. "If you just want sex with a kid then I don't think you're a pedophile. I like to think of myself as a person who could help kids grow up . . . a teacher, a mentor, someone he can come to for advice. A person who just wants sex with kids I regard them . . . as 'dirty old men.'

[Adam insists that sex with a kid must be consensual.] "If a kid says No, that's it, and they know this." Just what they do is up to the boy: "I have tried everything. I really leave it to the boy to decide what he wants." He recalls a period when he was actively having sex with seven boys. "One wanted anal intercourse with me, several of them were quite happy to have 69, several only wanted mutual masturbation, others were more into kissing and fondling. I left it more to the child to develop his sexual preference. I was quite happy to follow along because anything sexually with a child I'm happy with."

With respect to the psychological qualities of children that he finds attractive Adam says: "It is difficult to explain. With children—with boys—I can talk easily. I can talk to them at their own level. I can boss them. I can be bossed by them. I can be part of them and they can be part of me. But with older people I just can't communicate. . . I've had relationship with gays, but my only topic of conversation has been boys. . ."

Specific features that he finds attractive are two large front teeth, a small nose and short hair. Body hair is disliked and once a boy reaches puberty and starts to grow body hair sex is no longer of great interest. . . Adam says he finds [body hair] "obnoxious and horrible."

An unbroken voice is another important marker of an attractive boy. "Kids whose voices haven't broken and have no body hair, they're terrific." . . . . .

[Adam has had four arrests and convictions, resulting in probation, a fine, a short prison sentence, hospital commitment, medication (Silbestral), and psychiatric treatment. He submitted to psychiatric care not because he wanted to change his behavior, but rather as a back-up when and if, he was brought before the courts for pedophilic activity. He accepts the fact that eventually he will get a ten-year prison sentence.]

He says he is completely happy with his lifestyle and has no desire to change. "I would hate to be anything else; I wouldn't want to be cured."

PROVOCATIVE TEEN-AGE BOYS. What makes Dirk unusual, and his sexual taste so dangerous, is that he started his relationship when his friend was *nine years old.* Typically, a man-boy lover is attracted to an adventurous lad of about 12 or 13, like the eronymos of ancient Greece. For example, Rossman (page 161) describes such an interaction:

> We were clowning around on the tennis courts and I saw this man had an eye on me. I didn't know who he was, but I saw his Mustang and figured it might be my ticket out of that dull neighborhood, so when he smiled I walked over to his car. I was only thirteen, but I knew what I wanted. He asked me if I'd like to go to his place and listen to some records and when we got there I asked if I could take a shower, because I was hot and sweaty. He said he'd take a shower with me and I said O.K. I enjoyed it all and started going over there to listen to records a couple time a week or whenever I got horny.

White recalls an incident from his own boyhood, when he started an affair with an older man. When he was 15, White recalls, he had "a brief affair with a man in his forties." After boldly sitting down next to the man on a park bench and chatting with him, the 15-year-old then followed the man to his car.

> At last he smiled and said, 'What do you want from me?' I was always trying to seduce men [writes White] but they feared me as jail-bait."

Kahn (page 124) interviewed a gay man who recalled that when he was in high school, he "made advances to teachers and slept with three of them. . . . At Brooklyn College he slept with several more. He spent a summer with a professor who directed an opera festival."

One of the Adairs' respondents, George, recalled (Adair and Adair, pages 67-68) how as a young adolescent hitchhiker, he repeatedly tempted older men into having sex with him, and was always lucky enough to get away with it:

George

As an adolescent, I was interested in having sex with men who were older than me. . . . I'd hitchhike to school and hope that some guy would pick me up who I could have sex with, maybe in the car. . . . Imagine a ten- eleven-, or twelve-year-old. . . puts his hand on your leg. . .[or otherwise shows] he is sexually interested. Some guys just absolutely panicked, you know. I would have sex with a guy, and then he would say, "If you ever see me again, don't come near me--and I don't ever want to see you again. Goodbye! Get out of the car!" and off they'd go. They'd be scared to death. I always thought it was strange that I couldn't establish a relationship with anybody. . .I couldn't understand. And it was never explained to me until I was older that these people were afraid of the law, which is very restrictive.

One of Kelly's respondents, a 24-year old homosexual, recalled how at the age of 13 he offered to help dry off a 32-year-old house guest who was taking a bath:

I helped in rubbing his back and I could hardly keep myself from kissing his buttocks. . . . Although knowing he had rubbed himself dry in front, I had to do it all over myself for him; I lingered so long over him . . . that he began to have an erection and tried to put it in my face. I refused to accept it, although I wanted to (Kelly, page 307).

PEDOOPHILE PRIESTS. For many years the policy of the Roman Catholic Church, to protect its reputation, shielded those priests who misbehaved sexually. In 2002, newspapers and other news media carried stories of "child abuse by pedophile priests." This publicity led to a public outcry for a change in Church policy that would keep abusive priests away from children. Pedophile is a euphemism and it is also a legal term, for in criminal law a pedophile is a person who has sex with persons who are legally underage. In this case, the law does not distinguish between children and young teen-agers. When, on rare occasion, reports revealed specific incidents, in the great majority of cases the "children" involved were young teen-age boys.[6]

Nine years before U.S. newspapers "discovered" this story, Burkett and Bruni published a book, *A Gospel of Shame*, that carefully examined this phenomenon. Burkett and Bruni interviewed counselors of clergy with sexual disorders, including the director of the Menninger Clinic, where about 55 pedophile priests had been sent for treatment. This experience indicated that priests do *not* act out their sex drive with young boys simply because young boys are so readily accessible to them. No, the priests' sexual attraction to young boys was present (subconsciously, preconsciously, or consciously) *before* they entered the priesthood, and they chose the priesthood in their hope that "*the mere act of ordination would trigger a mystical transformation that would lift their desires*" (pages 51-52).

Many men who enter the priesthood, partly to control these tendencies, *do* manage to do so through conscious renunciation, to fulfill the priestly life as they idealize it. Those who are able to resist pedophilic opportunities might be said to have a more firmly organized character, and a deeper commitment to leading what they believe is a life of holiness. Some priests find, to their disappointment, that the transformative power of ordination, faith, and prayer does not work for them, and they now rationalize their way into sexual interactions with young boys. They are not monsters or predators, as newspaper headlines suggested. They are better described as persons with a loose or poorly integrated character structure, that permits them to do what they know is wrong. They.are not too different from those doctors who seduce their patients, lawyers who have sex with their clients, teachers who have sex with their students, or bank executives who embezzle millions with the rationalization that "no one will go hungry."

Sexual impulses intrude into the flawed priest's work in unexpected ways. A hypothetical example: 14-year-old Jimmy visits Father Bill for consolation over the death of the boy's grandfather. Father Bill takes Jimmy into his lap, strokes him, caresses him, and whispers words of comfort. Jimmy continues to sob. When Father Bill lays his hand between the child's legs, Jimmy's weeping stops and he giggles with sensual pleasure. Jimmy returns for more sessions on Father Bill's lap and the stroking and fondling continues. "You are special to me," Father Bill whispers, "and you must not tell anyone about these special moments." If the boy enjoyed it and came back for more, why years later did he complain of abuse and emotional damage? Because *in retrospect* he felt it was morally wrong, blamed the experience for his loss of faith and homosexual thoughts, and was tempted by the possibility of a large financial settlement.

The flawed priest tries to undo his wrongdoing through prayer and confession. Writing in the June 17, 2002 issue of *The New Yorker*, Thomas Keneally, who was for six years a seminarian, suggests (page 64) that this was a popular tactic for a priest who had yielded to temptation:

> A commonly heard aphorism during my youth was that God
> never sent a temptation for which he did not also send the grace
> to combat it. . . . If the child molester repented and went on a
> "retreat" where he prayed to Christ, directly or by using the
> Immaculate Virgin as an intercessor, he was considered capable
> of rising above any further temptation.

The errant priest knows how to weave together words to justify unacceptable behavior. His vocation makes him an expert in exploiting the power of words: in prayer, in blessings, in giving words of comfort, in offering words of counsel, in sharing words of wisdom, or in uttering words of warning. For example, Dale comes to Father Frank with a confession of lustful thoughts, which he describes in graphic detail. Father Frank is sexually aroused and rationalizes his impulse to stroke the boy's penis. The priest tells the boy this act is an exercise in "desensitization:" he will stroke the boy's penis and just short of ejaculation, Dale must tell the priest to stop. "No matter how you go to the altar, as a priest or to marry, this will help you," the boy remembers the priest telling him. "You are special.

You are pleasing to God. But you have a corruptible side and you must learn to control it."

The priest's *words* transformed sexual play into an act of loving-kindness, and now *words* intimidate the boy to keep their ceremonies a secret. Each of the partners makes a unique and complementary contribution to this secret activity. The child brings his boyish curiosity about his own body and about the adult world, his boyish mischief and pleasure in watching a priest do something grossly unpriestly. The priest brings a naivete that makes him, in a way, an emotional equal to the boy he is now abusing.

Some priests had entered seminary when they were as young as twelve, and parted ways with ordinary boys who did secret, naughty things together. As adolescents, some seminarians never dated. Now, as adults, their sexual impulses compel them to break their pledge of chastity and it is natural, in a way, that they turn to the very age-group that years ago they separated from, when they first decided to become a priest.

Perhaps the errant priest had renounced the pleasures of the flesh because, as a boy, he had himself been sexually abused, and at that time, for him, sexual pleasure took on a forbidden, bewildering quality. Like Father York, a pedophile priest, who recalled to his psychiatrist that at the age of twelve he had been forced to have oral sex with a priest. Now a street priest, who ministered to the poor and to minorities, a tireless youth worker and sympathetic counselor, Father York was also a pedophile:

Father York[7] and Bill

In 1960 Father York graduated from a Boston seminary, where he had prepared for the Roman Catholic priesthood. Of the 77 men in his graduating class, five (about eight per cent) would be publicly accused of sexually abusing children. Father York was among that group. Barely a year after his ordination, a man reported Father York to the police for sexual abuse of his 11-year old son. (Father York denied the charge, and the case was dropped.) When he was finally arrested in 2002, more than 30 people had accused him of acts of sexual misconduct.

Vilified as "a marauding sociopath," Father York was also a dedicated youth worker, a street priest honored for his work with runaways, with the poor, with blacks, and with young gay people. A Boston woman told newspaper reporters that when she was nine, Father York has helped her recover from sexual abuse at her church by another Roman Catholic priest. She remembered Father York as her hero and protector. She could understand why for years, top officials of the Boston Archdiocese protected him, vouched for his character, and allowed him to continue his work as a street priest.

Newspaper photographs that show Father York in his younger and middle years portray a very handsome man, which may in part explain why, when he was still a seminarian, he was drawn into a sexual affair with a priest faculty member. Father York's sister-in-law recalled to newspaper reporters, "He never showed any signs of stress people might exhibit. He was very solid and well-adjusted," which is another way of saying that Father York had the gift for dissociating his sexual activities from the rest of his life. His story fits the pattern of child abusers who had themselves been abused as a boy. According to the notes of a psychiatrist who interviewed Father York in 1994, at the age of 12 the future street priest had himself been sexually abused: forced by a priest to have oral sex,

Father York's sexual involvement with boys went beyond isolated incidents of abuse. He had a cabin in a nearby forest preserve, and took groups of boys out there for weekend retreats. "They would always be one bed short," recalls the sister of Bill, one of Father York's regular guests, "so Bill would have to sleep with Father York." For a year and a half, between ages 12 and 13, Bill slept with Father York on weekend retreats, and Father York warned Bill that "he would burn in hell" if he told anyone what went on there.

Bill did not have Father York's gift for dissociating his sexual misbehavior from the rest of his personality and character. Bill began having trouble in school, eventually became a drug addict, decided he was gay, moved to San Francisco, and in 1998 died of AIDS.

Professor Eugene Kennedy, former priest and retired professor of psychology, has studied priests with troubled sex lives. He described the story of Father York as classic. "In his mind," said Prof. Kennedy, "he was an angel for saving these boys; that was his rationalization. . . . He got tremendous gratification thinking he was their savior, which kept him from recognizing that he is the predator."

When Homosexuals Were Encouraged to Enter the Priesthood. A few decades ago, the Catholic Church actually encouraged young men who were troubled by homosexual thoughts or practices to enter the priesthood. The 1967 *Catholic Encyclopedia* gave two reasons why a devout homosexual should consider this career choice: (a) to seek "the help of grace" to overcome his homosexual tendencies, through a life of religious devotions, and (b) to dedicate his life to "a vocation of service to God and to men." The 1967 *Encyclopedia* offered this advice in the section on Homosexuality:

> [The homosexual] needs a vocation of service to God and to men
> that the priest[hood] can help him to find. . . . A homosexual is
> just as pleasing to God as a heterosexual, as long as he makes a
> sincere effort to control his deviate bent with the help of grace.

Estimates vary as to how widespread is homosexual activity in the priest-hood. Bess asserts (page 138) that the Catholic priesthood is "heavily gay," and cites the writings of Jeanine Gramick *et al. The Kansas City Star* estimated that between 25 and 45 percent of American priests are active homosexuals.

Currently, the Roman Catholic Church does not uncritically accept seminarians who are known to be struggling with homosexual impulses. Most unlikely to be accepted are men who are known to be *practicing* homosexuals.

BI-SEXUAL PEDOPHILES. What of man-boy lovers who insist that they are not homosexual? Rossman (pages 198-199) quotes a man who makes an argument that nicely interweaves the concepts of bisexuality, the split personality, and pederasty:

> I'm happily married, with fine children. I don't know what to
> call the secret identity I have which is known only to a few inti-
> mate friends. Pederasty is a minor aspect of my life which I
> refuse to let overweigh more important things. I have two friends
> who gamble. One of them deserves the label of gambler because
> he is a compulsive gambler, continually losing his wages. No one
> thinks of the other as a gambler, although he enjoys himself at
> the races. He keeps his life in balance, and his gambling—like
> my pederasty—is not compulsive but is something he enjoys. . . .
> [I am] simply a normal man who happens to enjoy sex horseplay
> with boys of thirteen or so.[8]

In the above paragraph, man-boy love is characterized as an incidental recreation. At the other extreme are "a number of unpublished philosophical papers by pederasts," referred to by Rossman (page 195), in which pederast clergymen and others "describe pederasty as a God-given mystical experience."

Writes Rossman (page 183): "In England a number of [clergymen] have written poetry about boys; for example, the Rev. E.E. Bradford [writes]: 'Our yearning tenderness for boys like these / has more in it of Christ than Socrates'. . . . J.G. Nicholson considered pederast love as a path to God. Another Anglican, Henry Somerset, spoke of sexual delight with a boy as 'both our lives are bathed in love divine.'" Trivialized as a recreation or elevated as a "love divine," pederasty is widespread, writes Thorstad (page 268): "boy-man love goes on in every neighborhood."

Man-boy love may be viewed as an extreme case of a theme that runs through male homosexuality: *the adoration of youth*. Just as men in general feel same-sex attractions to some degree but manage to suppress them, many gay men find boys sexually appealing but consciously renounce the impulse to actually engage boys in sexual activity. Instead, they settle for young men who have a boyish appearance and a boyish manner. Pedophiles are homosexuals who *lack the inner control* of their impulses. [9] Sex advice columnist Dan Savage (Chicago Reader, Sept. 27, 2002) agrees that "the overwhelming majority" of men who are sexually attracted to boys "never, ever act on their desires:"

> [M]ost men and women with a sexual attraction to kids—something they didn't choose—struggle mightily against their desires all their lives and never act on them.

Finally, let us counterbalance an abundance of clinical and anecdotal data with some survey findings. A large-scale survey reported in 1986 that three per cent of males, and seven per cent of females, recalled that before they were thirteen years of age, they had had sexual contacts with men.[10]

NOTES TO CHAPTER 11

1. Other types that fulfill the gay man's search image are The Real Man, the Daddy, and The Exotic Type. The Real Man may be signaled by (a) a well-muscled, masculine physique, (b) a psychologically or physically dominant type, (c) a bearer of masculine symbols: military or police, (d) a laborer or farm worker, or (e) an available heterosexual (and preferably married) man.

A few gay men are attracted to a Daddy, who can offer symbolic and/or economic and social support. Some gay men are attracted to Exotic Types: men of other ethnic backgrounds, other cultures, or other social classes. But the *dominant* theme of gay movies, gay videos, and gay stories suggests that the most popular search image is the beautiful boy.

2. The author, John Buchan (1875-1940), Ist Baron Tweedsmuir, wrote 50 books while pursuing an active career in politics, diplomacy, and publishing. His books include biographies, historical novels, and fast-paced adventure stories that glorify the British upper class, while suggesting that only a thin line separates civilization from barbarism.

3. Pedophilia is basically a legal term describing a sexual interaction with a person who is legally underage. The law does not differentiate between children and persons in early or middle adolescence. Pedophilia is a crime, and many gay spokesmen, understandably, argue that homosexuality has little or nothing to do with the molestation of *children*, noting that children abused by men are statistically more likely to be *girls* than boys.

In this chapter we review the evidence that some homosexual men, known in gay argot as "chicken hawks," *are* sexually attracted to teen-age boys and engage boys in sex when circumstances allow it. In this book, we refer loosely to gay men who are attracted to adolescent boys as pedophiles. Men who favor this practice prefer the terms man-boy love, or intergenerational sex.

More responsible gay men advocate restricting sexual contacts to men of legal age. In this spirit, Kirk and Madsen make a seven-page argument recommending partnerships between mature men and younger men. At the end of their argument they state explicitly: *"we do not advocate adults having sex with minors under any circumstances whatever"* (page 372).

4. It is not unusual for a pedophile to claim that his boy has benefitted from their relationship. Dirk's 12-year-old boy seems to have been a neglected child who was looking for someone who really valued him. It seemed to Dirk that the boy's mother "didn't want to know" what was going on between Dirk and her boy.

A delinquent boy is invited to live with his social worker, who not only shows him affection (that sometimes leads to sex), but gives him much more. He provides for the boy's basic needs, demonstrates good work habits, introduces him to his friends, takes him not only to movies but perhaps to plays and concerts, engages him in serious discussions, encourages him to think and plan for his education.

True, they fondle each other when they sleep together. If the boy had been living in a cruel and nasty world, he would now accept this practice as the price he must pay for enjoying an otherwise decent life. When man-boy love advocates claim that their boy lovers enjoy a net benefit from their relationship, in some cases they are probably correct.

Homosexual pedophiles probably depend significantly on neglected boys, delinquents and runaways. The Dutch lawyer Edward Brongersma wrote an article (see References) sympathetic to man-boy love. He cites (page 160) a report (Rossman, 1976) that "gives several examples of social workers achieving miracles with apparently incorrigible young delinquents--not by preaching to them, but by sleeping with them. Affection demonstrated by sexual arousal upon contact with the boy's body, by obvious pleasure taken in giving pleasure to the boy, did far more good than years in reformatories." Brongersma (page 160) tells of an Amsterdam juvenile judge who in a public speech "openly advocated this form of social therapy." This is a sample of the persuasive case that man-boy lovers make to support their position. The rebuttal is often couched in legal and moral terms rather than on the basis of evidence.

5. Dirk's worry is probably related to the fact that he is attracted to boys of such a young age. Fifteen years of experience interviewing man-boy lovers in the

United States led Rossman to report (page 13) that "only one percent of practicing pederasts interviewed had been arrested. *Less than 3 percent* of men guilty of an indictable pederast offense ever go to prison (italics added)." On the other hand, in 1979 it was reported that at a meeting of a pedophile association in Germany, 54 percent of those attending asserted that they had been convicted in a court of law (Brongersma, page 151).

6. For example, an article in the *Chicago Tribune* of June 20, 2002, describes three cases of "child abuse" by Roman Catholic priests. In one case, a priest was accused of abusing two 15-year-old boys. A man accused another priest of sexually abusing him when he was 14. In another case, the victim was an adolescent boy of 18 when the abuse occurred.

7. Consistent with the style of this entire book, pseudonymns are given to each case. The case of "Father York and Bill" is based on a news item in *The New York Times*, May 19, 2002.

8. Parker Rossman, associate professor of religion in higher education at Yale University, conducted an in-depth field study of "the pederast underground." He concluded (pages 40-41) that the hobby of man-boy love is widely practiced by rings of married men and "solid citizens." The journalistic expose of such a ring was documented in the 1966 book, *The Boys of Boise*. Rossman refers to similar groups in other parts of the country.

9. Is social conformity a good test of psychological health? Not always, but to expose oneself to the moral outrage of society, and to severe punishment by the criminal justice system, raises questions about the person's understanding of the social values of his culture, of the value he places on freedom and independence, and on his ability to control his impulses.

The attraction of gay men to boys is recognized and served by the many videos and stories that feature distinctly boyish-looking gays. The *impulse* to have sex with a boy is not a crime but to *act out* that impulse is a crime. Most gay men who have this impulse resolve it in a way that is neither antisocial nor potentially self-destructive--for example, by finding a partner who is boyish in his looks, talk, dress, and behavior but is of legal age. Homosexuals who are not so prudent are the natural clientele for runaway boys.

10. Findings on child-adult sexual contacts, reported by Cameron *et al.*, are drawn from an extensive questionnaire regarding their sexual experiences, given to a total of 4,340 adults, drawn from random-probability samples of persons in Los Angeles, Denver, Omaha, Louisville, and Washington, DC. The man involved in child-adult sexual contacts was most often identified as a caregiver.

12 Cruising: In Search of the Beautiful Stranger

In the old days, when homosexuality was stigmatized as both illlegal, immoral, and sick, fairies and trade[1] interacted quickly and anonymously in out-of-the way places: public toilets, public parks, and at highway stops at the edge of town. The following reminiscence is taken from the autobiographical essay of a public park cruiser of the 1970s:

> I love having sex in the park. I love the dark. I love the hint of
> city lights and the streetcars moving on the hill like great tin fish.
> I love the quiet, the shrill, invisible birds, the damp grass, the
> thunder of a high wind in the trees. I love getting a hard-on as
> soon as someone gets within 10 feet of me. I love the sudden
> hand and sound of zippers . . . the quick, dissolving cum
> (Anonymous 1976, page 13).

Many people of good will believed that public hostility was driving homosexuals into anonymous sex at such inappropriate places.[2] It seemed obvious that if society would only lift the stigma from homosexuality and grant gay men the right to exercise their sexual orientation without ostracism or fear of arrest, things would be different. Homosexuals would then behave like their beterosexual neighbors.

This is what was hoped for and forecast, but events proved otherwise. The decriminalization of homosexuality, and the de-pathologizing of homosexuality *did* change certain details of homosexual cruising, but the practice of cruising[3] continued. Now gays could command more comfortable--even luxurious--cruising areas, but the search for quick and anonymous sex partners continues, quite contrary to previous hopes and predictions.

"Anonymous sex," "promiscuity," "the one-night stand" *describe* a sexual practice, while at the same time disparaging it. Writers on gay behavior have adopted the term "multiple partnerships" as a more objective, less value-laden term. Martin Duberman, historian and gay advocate, notes (page 19) that the sex-positive term "adventuring" was introduced in the 1970s to replace the word "promiscuity." But in the current gay literature, the term "adventuring" is non-existent.

Before the HIV-AIDS crisis exacted a heavy price on gay promiscuity, gay activists lauded this practice as something better than "the usual coldness and fragmentation of heterosexual community life." In a 1969 article, Goodman hailed sexual promiscuity as a "profoundly democratizing" practice:

210

> [Q]ueer life . . . can be profoundly democratizing, throwing
> together every class and group more than heterosexuality does.
> Its promiscuity can be a beautiful thing (but be prudent about
> VD). I myself have cruised rich, poor, middle class, and petit
> bourgeois; black, white, yellow and brown; scholars, jocks and
> dropouts; farmers, seamen, railroad men, heavy industry, light
> manufacturing, communications, business and finance, civilians,
> soldiers and sailors, and once or twice cops. There is a kind of
> political meaning, I guess, in the fact that there are so many
> types of attractive human beings.

Gay spokesmen of the 1990s expressed a rather different attitude toward gay promiscuity, multiple partnerships, or adventuring. For example, Simon LeVay (1996, page 49) regarded it as a "prejudicial statement" to say that homosexuals tend to seek multiple partnerships. But a *Handbook for Gay Men*[4] published in the year 2000, clearly describes cruising and recreational sex as the prevailing norm in gay life:

> Some people argue that gay men should settle down and behave
> themselves as soon as possible. . . . Others, including me, dis-
> agree. Your . . . first few years as an out gay man . . . are for
> experimenting, exploring, and learning, not for settling down
> (Outland, page 97).

Outland offers some practical advice to the gay novice on how to make quick sexual connections:

> If you are really interested in meeting someone for sex, or maybe
> for a make-out session, it is often easier to do it on your own
> than with friends. . . . [When you're alone, you can make a move
> and fail without the embarrassment of having] your friends . . .
> watching you (Outland, pages 37-38).

> [At a bar you have to make conversation before you have sex,
> but] in most sex club environments . . . you can share an orgasm
> before you've shared names. . . . This ultracasual approach to sex
> indisputably turns it into a less intimate act, which can lead you
> to use sex as anything from a hobby, something to do when
> bored, or as a compulsive pursuit. . . [Not nice,] but most of us
> spend at least some time single, dissatisfied, and horny (*ibid*,
> page 61).

> You are walking down the street and all of a sudden there *he* is—
> everything you've ever wanted. And he's looking back at you the
> same way. . . . You both stop, smile, and introduce yourselves.

Next thing you know . . . . A meeting like this is one of the adventures that is part of life in your new world. Don't expect it on a constant basis, but when it comes along, and it feels right, enjoy it (*ibid*, page 69).

The worship of beauty. Gay men are much more attracted by physical appearance, or by even by a particular kind of look: blond or swarthy, powerful or boyish, working class or sophisticated. A gay man may cruise all night, going from bar to bar, not because he cannot find a willing partner, but because he is looking for a particular *type* of person. Almost everyone is looking for youth[7] and masculine good looks, but a cruiser may be paying extra attention to a particular feature: eyes, teeth, hair. When he meets a willing partner who satisfies his special "search image," he excitement can be overwhelming. Every man bas his own search image or "type":

My type is butch, around 5'8", tall and has dark hair, a fair complexion, trim physique, and a big dick (Levine 1990, page 154).

An American gay man of Italian descent, had a prominent nose and was sometimes approached up by a fellow gay who asked him if he was Jewish. When he answered no, his prospective partner was disappointed, having hoped to have sex with a Jew (Author's clinical notes).

The search image. It seems quite evident that in their search for anonymous sex, many homosexuals were never looking for just anyone, but for a partner who seemed to possess certain alluring qualities: *youth, good looks*, and *masculine power.* To some homosexuals, masculine power was conveyed by tall stature, a muscular physique, and a large penis. Some looked for the image of a manual laborer, for other signs of status,[5] or financial power, or for a military or police uniform. (In times past, the appeal of a uniform even attracted some homosexuals to railroad or streetcar conductors.)

Marks of youth, good looks, and masculine power seemed to have an erotic appeal to homosexuals. Good looks, youth, and power are attractive to heterosexuals, too. But straights are usually interested in the whole person: his or her social background, personality, talents, character, education, attainment, interests.

Among straights, too, strangeness also conveys a certain allure. The exotic is erotic; that is a theme of movies and romantic stories of all times.[6] But most men find a more relaxing comfort in status-equals. Such are some of the similarities and differences in what straight and gay men find attractive.

Variety is not the *spice* of life, it was the food of life to a gay man interviewed by George Stambolian (page 149):

From the age of twelve or thirteen until I was about twenty-two, what I wanted most was to suck cock. I started with my friends in the neighborhood, and by the time I was sixteen, I was riding around the city in my father's car looking for trade . . . [and invited into the car] guys just walking around looking for something to do. They were usually boys my own age, mostly from ethnic working class families like mine, and mostly straight. . .went after the ones who were hot--budding men who knew what they had. I would talk to them about sex, usually about girls or about dick and being horny. And the hottest moment was when they suddenly understood what I wanted without my having to say it. Then they'd let me see what they had. It fascinated me that each body and each cock was different, with different proportions and a different feel. . . . I thought the whole thing was an endless mystery.

In 1968, Hoffman (page 195) commented that compulsive fellatio is so irrational, so dangerous an activity, "it virtually requires a psychodynamic explanation. . . ."

[The compulsive fellator] frequently picks up rough-looking young men, *e.g.*, hitchhikers and servicemen, and tries to persuade them to let him bring them to orgasm by fellatio. He is often a typical client of hustlers. As a result of his efforts, this individual frequently is assaulted and is occasionally murdered. . . .

The search is both reality-oriented and fantasy-driven. Whether straight or gay, a man who is seeking a lover is bound to envision both attainable and unattainable qualities. The straight man is probably looking for someone who will put excitement into his evening; the gay man is more likely to be searching for someone who will *change his life*, an intoxicating hope that is likely to be unfulfilled. Here is how Walt Whitman expressed this homosexual fantasy-wish:

Lover divine and perfect Comrade,
Waiting content, invisible yet, but certain,
Be thou my God

Thou, thou, the Ideal Man,
Fair, able, beautiful, content, and loving,
Complete in body and dilate [expansive] in spirit,
Be thou my God.[8]

Gay men rightly resent the charge that they are seducers of the naive and innocent. But it is undoubtedly true that the receptive newcomer is much more readily recognized and invited if the newcomer also embodies boyish good looks. Boyish good looks lowers the invisible barriers between the gay cruiser and the naive but receptive newcomer. There are barriers on both sides; the cruiser does not want to be accused of making unwanted advances; the newcomer feels tempted but he may also be shy and uncertain. Good looks lower the barrier. Perhaps this explains the very high incidence of good looks in the male gay population.

Posner reasons that because gay men are powerfully attracted to handsome men, and women do not find good looks quite as sexually arousing as men do, *it takes very little effort for a good looking man to find a homosexual partner.* Posner expresses this inference in economic terms when he writes (page 123)

"[T]he costs of homosexual sex to the handsome man will be lower relative to his costs of heterosexual sex than they are to homely men."

Andrew Sullivan reflects (1998, page 189): "I realized one day that many of my friends were actually good-looking, and that, although many of them had other attractive characteristics, I was not exactly indifferent to their physical appearance." Michael Rowe (page 53) notes that in the gay community, the openly-gay photographer's model enjoys an especially high status, for this is "a community that venerates physical perfection at the expense of any other human quality. . . ." Rowe recalls (page 71) saying to a friend: "You cook gourmet meals, you dance like liquid sex, you live on a *boat* for Christ's sake. And you're so handsome it sets everyone's teeth on edge. . . . " What Sullivan and Rowe observed is more than just a contemporary fashion. Almost a century ago, Havelock Ellis noted (page 290) that "a marked characteristic [of homosexuals] is their youthful appearance."

Because physical attractiveness is such a highly valued trait in gay society, a handsome adolescent is free to venture into a same-sex situation without fear that he will be ignored or rejected. A handsome youth gets an enthusiastic reception when he steps into the gay community, deliberately or "by mistake." Seduction by a female before he is ready for sexual intercourse, can be a bewildering experience and demand skills he may not have. Homosexual play with another male is so much simpler. Most boys experience some homosexual play, but does the exceptionally attractive boy encounter earlier, more enticing, more frequent or more flattering invitations to engage in homosexual play?

Is the handsome lad more repeatedly sought after by homosexuals, and is he more likely to realize his homosexual potential? Don Jackson's junior high school experience led him to imagine (page 24) that "all handsome boys are gay":

> Freddy, a beautiful curly-headed boy, invited me to spend the
> evening listening to his records. He seduced me. I was ecstatic

with joy. I've always wondered why nothing like that ever happened to me sooner. When they entered junior high school, gay boys who had felt different and isolated now were constantly together, partly for their own safety. We were afraid to be alone. Other boys teased us and called us sissies and queers. . . . We thought all handsome boys were gay. To our eyes, "het" boys were smaller, uglier and less developed.

Is good looks truly the most important social appeal a gay man can have? In Los Angeles, a team of psychological investigators, Sergios and Cody, decided to put this question to a statistical test. They obtained a group of one hundred gay men in their twenties and thirties, each of whom was rated by a panel of judges for physical attractiveness. The men were paired at random, and sent to a two-hour tea dance. After the dance, each man was asked to rate his partner for over-all desirability and asked whether he wished to see him again.

In a follow-up study, the men were asked whether they had actually tried to see their partner again. Statistical analysis showed that physical attractiveness was the main determinant of whether a gay man liked his partner or tried to see him again. Men who themselves were homely or good looking had the same motivation: both were interested only in whether the date was good-looking.

Note Hatterer's description of Tom (1980, page 80):

[His] extraordinary good looks met a movie ideal; he had ruddy skin, a strong jaw, sandy-blond hair. He was thin-waisted, broad-shouldered, and had a taut, muscular body. An elaborately patterned nylon shirt clung to his torso, and skintight jeans to his small, firm buttocks. . . . His blue-grey eyes darted quickly and stealthily, cruising everything in sight. Sometimes his nostrils flared and his lips pursed as he controlled signs of smoldering anger and sensuality.

A boy whose parents were divorced, once asked his father, who was now a gay man: "Daddy, how come your boy friends are so much better looking than Mommy's boy friends?" Clark (pages 67-69) acknowledges the fact that a disproportionate number of openly gay men are especially handsome. He is inclined to think that they were not born that way, but that their good looks come from "the freedom from tension that comes with an openly gay identity." Besides, gay men spend more time and money on their appearance "so as to be found worthy of desire," and they also watch their diet.

"Freedom from tension" does not seem to explain "movie ideal" features. Physical attractiveness alone does not lead to homosexuality but if a boy's homosexual potential is just strong enough, physical attractiveness may lower the barrier to his entry into the lifestyle. In "The Homogay," first published in *The Christopher Street Reader*, Ethan Mordden describes a gay man of his acquaintance. This muscular but facially unattractive male was very bitter. How can you "hold your beautiful gay lover?" he asks. Not by having a "fabulous carnal technique"; most gays know most techniques. By being well-muscled? By having a big cock? These are important for tricking but not for love, for a lasting partnership. Sad experience led this bitter gay man to conclude: "[T]here is only one way to hold a lover: by having a handsome face . . . I do not" (Quoted by Kirk and Madsen, page 314, emphasis added).

Comment Kirk and Madsen (page 325), "[T]he lurkers in rest rooms . . . [are not all] incapable of a one-on-one relationship . . . they're unable to conduct their hunt via . . . the bar-and-party circuit . . . because they're not good looking. . . . [T]he beauty queens . . . have decreed that the ugly must cease to exist."

The gay journalist Michelangelo Signorile (1997, page 83) also discusses the plight of the gay man who doesn't fit the macho body image. He quotes a short and thin gay man of 41 who says he is looked down upon by other gay men and feels like a second-class citizen:

> "I hate all those guys. . . . They don't look at people as people, just as objects. . . . I'm a talented, knowledgeable person, very successful and financially secure. I have a lot of interests and I think I'm the kind of man who is a good companion. But those fellas don't want anything to do with me because I don't have a body like theirs. . . ." Signorile asks him why he doesn't look for someone just like him? He answers: "I'm just not attracted to that type. . . . I don't like skinny guys. . . . When it comes to sexual attraction, I like the muscled guys. . . . I hate those guys--even though I want to have sex with them."

Signorile worries that because physically unattractive gay men get so desperate, they allow their partners to have unsafe sex with them.

> [Larry is a 27-year-old gay man, a professional nurse who weighs 220 pounds and is five foot nine.] He goes out to bars and often to sex clubs and baths and often does drugs . . . all too often engaging in unsafe sex. "I've allowed men to fuck me without condoms on more occasions than I can count, quite honestly. . . . I meet someone who's really, totally attractive, someone I've always wanted. . . I let him call the shots, tell him we'll do whatever he wants to do." (Signorile 1997, page 24).

Watching an attractive man exercising nearby, an old friend (a well-built 34-year-old) confides to Signorile (1997, page 25): "If I were drunk, I'd probably allow him to fuck me without rubbers. . . . What worries me is that I feel so beneath guys like that, I'd allow them to do *anything*."

As a West Village clone put it:

> All that matters to me is how they look. They could be as dumb
> as shit, or as boring as hell, but if they have a nice face, a big
> dick, or a good body, I'll fuck them (Levine 1990, page 182).

A gay author interviewed by Stambolian (page 49) deplores the gay emphasis on physical beauty. "I've had sex with some extremely beautiful men, including some film porn stars and musclemen. Few of them were as exciting, accomplished, or downright lusty as a Com Ed worker I picked up, quite skinny, but
extremely sensual and sexual, whom I continued seeing for years."

Stambolian's respondent compares this skinny but sensual partner with narcissistic musclemen whose idea of sexual pleasure "is to pose for you while you
kneel in front of them and jerk off." Since the interview was for an article to be
published in the gay journal *The Advocate*, the respondent offers this advice to
gay men who might worry about being ridiculed for choosing a partner who is
less than handsome: "[S]ee whomever you want, and if your friends say anything, just play into their own fantasies and tell them, 'He's got a huge thick
dick.' That *always* shuts them up."

The gay bathhouse is a virtual fantasyland for cruisers:[9] comfortable, secluded, safe, a treat for exhibitionists and voyeurs alike. Gay columnist Brian
McNaught (pages 10-11) recalls his first visit to a gay bathhouse, where he was
recognized (his picture accompanies his newspaper column), but snubbed
because "He has no body."

> On my first and only trip to a gay bathhouse, I was a nervous
> wreck because I so wanted to be accepted--no, *embraced*--into
> what I identified as the gay erotic brotherhood. My mind was
> filled with exciting sexual fantasies. . . . I entered the locker
> room.
>
> Two gay men on benches were reading the local gay newspaper
> in which my syndicated column appeared. One recognized me
> from the picture that accompanied the column. "Hey, it's him!" I
> heard him whisper to his friend. I was exhilarated. Feeling terri-
> bly shy, I hoped they might start a conversation with me.
>
> "He has no body," his friend replied as I finished undressing. . . .
>
> For years to come, I would look at myself in the mirror and hear
> the words, "He has no body."

What about gay men who do not go cruising for sexual partners but search
for partners by placing ads in the classified section of *The Advocate*, Judith
Reisman accumulated 7,407 "In Search Of" (ISO) ads that appeared in that publication between 1988 and 1992, and compared them with 2,885 ISO ads placed

by men during the same time period in a general magazine, the *Washingtonian*, appealing to a similarly affluent and educated readership. Her content analysis brought out clear differences between what *Advocate* and *Washingtonian* readers were looking for, and indicate that gay men who use the *Advocate* classifieds are looking for some of the same characteristics as men who cruise the gay bars are looking for.

> Gay men were likely to be advertising for a teen-ager with exceptional sexual endowment, sexually exciting and interested in sado-masochism. Sex-for-pay was more likely to be offered to gay ISO readers than to the general ISO reader. Absent from the list of significant differences were references to good looks as a sought-for trait.

> By contrast, a content analysis of ISO ads in the *Washingtonian* indicated that men in general were likely to be advertising for a woman with certain personality traits, who shared certain interests, for a possible long-term commitment.[10]

Cruising strategies

Levine[11] describes in considerable detail (1990, pages 146-174) the strategies and conventions of "cruising": searching, signaling, negotiating, and consummating a sexual adventure. Here's a summary: A and B know the likely meeting spots, and what times of day these places are particularly "cruisy." They find a location where they can see and be seen. Moving about, they keep searching until they find their "type." They make eye contact, stare intensely at each other, glancing up and down each other's bodies. Staring, smiling, winking, A strokes his own crotch. B tweaks his own nipple. Now they move toward each other, and engage in small talk, related to drinking, drugs, and finding out if their special erotic interests match up. Closer range enables them to better gauge each other's physiques.

> Clothes often camouflaged a man's actual build. Flannel shirts hide puny arms or a flabby stomach. Jeans may cover a small cock or sagging butt (Levine 1990, page 164).

> If either loses interest, he may leave with an appropriate excuse, like "Sorry, gotta go now." If their interest in each other has survived small talk and close inspection, conversation would lead to the question, "My place or yours?"

More on gay narcissism

While cruising, the gay man must be wary of the gay man who is just "posing" (sometimes called standing, or modeling). In his Glossary, Levine (1990, page 231) describes posing as "to stand alone, with a blank expression, in a conspicuous spot." Chapter 21 describes the gay narcissist, who would rather spend an hour seeing how many men he can attract sexually than to actually have sex with one man. One observer described the poser as one who "believes that it is below his masculine dignity to ever approach anyone else. He will usually stand like the steadfast tin soldier for hours on end, wondering why this isn't his particular night."

The lure of the stranger. A gay man may have sex with a stranger, known as a "trick,"[12] or with a "fuck buddy," "date," "boyfriend" or his "lover." Every clone[13] likes to "trick," to have sex with a variety of handsome young strangers. This goal--"Sex with strangers, the more the better"--was expressed by a popular gay saying, "So many men, so little time," a saying that appeared on t-shirts, greeting cards, and was the theme of a song played constantly during the summer of 1983 in gay bars and discos (Levine 1990, page 149).

It is a psychological truism that strangeness means ambiguity, and ambiguity fosters fantasy. ("The exotic is erotic.") So well-entrenched is this attitude, West Village gays believed there was "something wrong" with having sex with another West Village clone: "group norms forbade sex between men who were friends" (Levine 1990, page 91). Clones therefore "mainly had impersonal sex"[14] (Levine 1990, page 182) This is how one West Villager expressed his feelings:

> Familiarity for me kills desire. Knowing someone is a turn-off because their personality ruins the fantasy I have of them. Besides, sucking the same dick and fucking the same ass is a drag. Variety, after all, is the spice of life (Levine 1990, page 181).

Harvard professor of psychology Roger Brown, offers two observations from his long experience as a gay man,[15] on the erotic power of *strangeness* in same-sex sex. *First*, he recalls (page 77) from his considerable experience with call boys, that "it is on the first date . . . that the sex is best. *It is on this first date, if ever, that the boy gets hard and goes in for deep kissing* (emphasis added)." He continues:

> One wonders why. Perhaps strangeness or anonymity is simply an aphrodisiac. . . . Perhaps . . . the boy, like the client, has a fantasy, a dream . . . which is least disturbed because information is minimal, on the first date.

Secondly, Brown makes this interesting observation on gay porn movies. If you want to know "what gets gay men hot," Brown advises (pages 227-228), look at the dominant themes of gay porn movies: (1) all-male settings like pool halls (no women); (2) shady, secluded (sometimes disgusting) places like alleys; (3) it is *anonymity* that evokes "peak sexual excitement": "performers never recognize one another . . . There is never any sentiment . . . never any suggestion of a continuing relationship"; (4) dominance-submission is a more likely theme than reciprocity; an actor may "perform almost-disgusting personal services on command"; (5) risk of discovery also generates sexual excitement. Comments Brown: a successful porn director "knows what gets gay men hot, as few others do."

Danger an aphrodisiac. "[T]he tussle with fate," writes Browning (page 166) "is . . . an aphrodisiac." Kaufman and Raphael quote a gay man to whom it is clear that for him danger,[16] risk, and excitement are important aspects of sex:

> I really get off on sex in public--the riskier the better. Parks are great, but bathrooms or stairwells are the best because there's so much more chance of someone finding you. Even if I had the shades up and the lights on, a bedroom is a complete turn-off to me. It's just way too ordinary and dull (Kaufman and Raphael, page 25).

> I can't get it off unless I get that adrenaline rush going. I stopped at this rest area and there was a guy in the john, obviously cruising. There were all these people outside the building, and it was so blatant I loved it. I followed him into a stall. My heart was pounding I was so scared. We started jerking each other off right there. And then the outer door opened, there were footsteps--I thought I'd die. What a rush as I came (*ibid*, page 196)!

In his widely-read and reprinted 1972 essay, "A Gay Manifesto," Carl Wittman called upon gay men to "stop mimicking straights" by forming marriage-like partnerships, and enjoy what gay life is all about: recreational sex and erotic experimentation. Variety calls for ever-changing partnerships, which continues to be an enduring difference between gay and straight sexual experience –at least a difference in *degree*, since the "brief encounter" and "one-night stand are not unknown in the heterosexual world.

Wittman characterizes anonymous sex as a rejection of conventional values, but Steve Gundersen (page 35) found that for a time, it was easier for him, a believing Christian, to have one-night-stands than to establish a permanent committed relationship:

> I had been taught to think that it would amount to living in sin. A

one-night sexual encounter was different: I could have such an encounter, and then, in the morning, devastated by an overwhelming sense of guilt, I could pray for forgiveness, and by the time I got back to the office everything would be fine.

In the West Village gay culture of New York City, "tricks" often exchange telephone numbers but very rarely see each other again. If they do, "tricks" become "fuck buddies" (casual friends who profess *no* emotional attachment or commitment, but call on each other for sex play).

> "I try to turn my 'tricks' into 'fuck buddies' whenever I can. 'Fuck buddies' make it so much easier to get laid. 'Cruising' takes too much time and energy, and often you go home alone. 'Fuck buddies' mean instant sexual satisfaction. You can also do things with them, like go out for dinner, see a movie, or watch TV. It's sort of like 'boyfriends' but with no strings attached" (Levine 1990, page 202).

According to Levine (1990, page 203), the lure of anonymity usually wins over the convenience of a familiar partner, and clones "usually tired quickly of their 'fuck buddies' . . . after a few weeks."

The gay man seems to be always on the alert for someone new and different. Over a period of months, Moshe Shokeid, a married Israeli anthropologist, was studying New York City's gay Jewish congregation and observed that the first seats to be taken, before the regular Sabbath service, were those that gave the best view of the entrance. It was important for members to see whether any interesting newcomers might be arriving that evening, so as to be sure to meet them at the social hour (the Oneg Shabbat) following the prayer service. Shokeid admits that he tried to avoid conversation at the synagogue. He sensed that polite conversation was usually an overture to cruising,[17] and he "didn't want to waste anyone's time."

The gay man may be looking for a real-life partner, but he is also wishing for the fulfillment of a fantasy of finding an extraordinary person with whom sex will be a transforming experience. In Holleran's 1978 novel, *Dancer from the Dance*, the author's protagonist ruminates over this unattainable wish:

> The vast majority of homosexuals are looking for a superman to love and find it very difficult to love anyone merely human, which we [all] unfortunately happen to be. . . . [The protagonist speaks of] the great homosexual disease--the sanctity of the face seen and never spoken to [and then compares homosexuals and romantics:] It was the most beautiful illusion of homosexuals and romantics alike: if only I'd loved that one. . . (Quoted in Bawer 1993, page 204).

Holleran contrasts dreamy illusion and harsh reality: "The most insulting moment . . . [when daylight breaks, and one is] still on his knees [and] looks up from the cock he's been sucking to see the light. . ." (*ibid.*).

If, as Holleran says, "the vast majority of homosexuals are looking for a superman," this suggests that they are hoping to find someone *who can transform them* into a more complete person. In a 1914 paper, Freud discusses homosexual love for a person to whom is attributed qualities one wishes for, but doesn't have. This is a form of *self-love*, or narcissism, Freud conjectured when he wrote (page 90) that a man can love himself as he was, he can love someone who was once a part of himself, or he can love *"what he himself would like to be."*

The notion that the homosexual is looking for a sex encounter that can fill his gender deficit, raises two questions: (1) Does it make sense to look for a superman at a homosexual bar? (2) How much experience does it take to discover that magical transfers of power simply don't happen in the real world?

Two homosexual partners may see in each other desirable traits in which they themselves are lacking; one partner may have a great physique, and the other may have a handsome face. To a realist, "Seeing is believing," but to a dreamer, *"Believing is seeing."* As for the harsh truth that magic just doesn't work, this is also a fact of life in preliterate cultures, where magical rituals, usually unfulfilled, continue to be practiced generation after generation. In our culture, believers continue to pray, even though petitionary prayers usually go unanswered.

David I. Gottlieb, a psychiatrist, interviewed several male homosexuals to explore the inner life of gay men. "What is your attitude," he asked one of his respondents (page 39), "if somebody is more attractive than you?" This question evoked an answer that was both sophisticated and introspective:

> Well, I think this is really a primitive idea, but the physical contact somehow makes you feel more powerful, more attractive, more self-centered. There's a tendency to feed your own narcissism. It's a little bit of a cliché, but I think the attractiveness of the other person seems to rub off. . . . During the sex act the attractiveness of the other person becomes part of you and enhances you.

A respondent of George Stambolian (pages 150-151), whom we will call Eduardo, tells how his adoration of blond WASP college boys led him to hunger "to taste them and get inside of them . . . to experience what it would be like to be like them. . . ."

Eduardo

Said Eduardo to his interviewer: "I . . . developed a passion for blonds. I hadn't really known any blonds as a teenager. Everyone in my city was dark, mostly Italian. Then I went to college, and there were blonds everywhere. It was a tremendous sexual shock. I couldn't get over the color of their hair and eyes, the smoothness of their skin, or the whiteness of their asses. I would almost get ill looking at them in the showers. . . . [M]ost of those students were upper-class WASPS, whose gestures, codes of conduct, and social values were very unlike my own. . . . I practically had to learn a new vocabulary, a different way of phrasing things and pausing. They seemed to belong to another order of human life. It was as if the rest of us were made of flesh, while they were made of something else . . . I wanted to taste them and get inside of them. . . . I wanted to experience what it would be like to be like them. . . . [Eduardo fantasized that he could rub a magic ring that would enable him to] be that person in the sense that I would be able to feel his body from the inside. I would know what it was like to have that skin, or those legs, or that cock with its special shape and weight and pressure. I would know how clothes would feel against that ass . . . and knowing what it was like to see the world that other way."

"Getting inside those blond men meant fucking them," the interviewer suggested. Eduardo answered: "Very much so."

To a gay man, a Berkeley Ph.D., a writer and translator who was once a devoted Catholic and Christian Brothers novice, the homosexual episode has the transforming qualities of a religious experience:

The first time you suck dick . . . it really is like Holy Communion. Mystical. Know what I mean? (Browning, page 81)

Holy Communion is literally to eat the flesh of God, and so to be one with God. To eat God is to be liberated from the alienated division of the self, to lose the self. [In this man's spiritual quest] . . . to eat cock was in some profound measure to find the unity that divided the dictates of his spirit with the drives of his flesh, and so to eat cock became a Holy Communion (*ibid*, page 82).

Browning recalls the testimony of the 16th-century Saint Teresa of Avila, "who recorded in her journal how God had entered her with a long golden spear, at its tip 'a point of fire' penetrating to her entrails with a pain so sweet that one can never hope to lose it." Browning asks (page 82): "If spirituality can be a metaphor for orgasm, why cannot orgasm be a metaphor for spirituality?"

It is as if the cruiser is looking for the kind of person he himself would like to be, and plays with the fantasy that contact, or interpenetration, can transfer these wonderful qualities from one partner to the other.

A gay man's recollection of the onset of same-sex attraction expresses the theme of wanting to touch and be touched:

Guy

"When I was thirteen, I started having these new feelings about a beautiful boy I knew, Bobby S. He was handsome, and athletic, and so nice--everybody liked him! He was just what I wanted to be. I didn't understand my feelings, but I knew they were the biggest thing in my life; the whole world looked bright and colorful, and the most beautiful things in it were his smile, and his eyes, and his hands. . . . I daydreamed about Bobby all day, and drew his picture in my notebook, and thought about calling him, but I was scared. I wanted just to be with him, to hang around him. . . . I felt that I wanted him to touch me--maybe hug me. One day, in a friendly way, he put his hand on my shoulder--I almost fainted. That night, in bed, I had fantasies about him, but even then I was shy--even in my thoughts I didn't want to dirty him--my love was so much more important than my sexual feelings" (Kirk and Madsen, page 315).

Trait-fixation.   Several clinical observers (Hoffman 1968, page 168, Gottlieb 1977, Masters and Johnson 1979) have noted that some homosexuals are attracted to some particular trait, one feature, one characteristic, rather than to the whole person, which leads not to love but to erotic arousal. Intimacy requires an interest in the total person. Trait-fixation keeps homosexual relations on a safely impersonal level. To the clinician, trait-fixation resembles object-fixation, paraphilia: an erotic interest in a particular body part or object, like feet or shoes. Nicolosi (1991, page 127) relates this pattern of behavior to promiscuity:

When interest in these traits diminishes through familiarity, there follows a loss of interest in the rest of the person. . . In comparison, heterosexual men seem less trait-fixated.

A client of Nicolosi's reflects on his striving to "connect" with someone who has the masculinity that he feels is lacking in himself (Nicolosi 1991, page 158):

The issue for me is a disconnectedness from my masculine identity. . . . I've always had a tremendous craving for the masculine. . . . I see that I'm trying to bond with [other men sexually] so that I can feel a part of them, connected with them, equal to them, and not to feel that I'm less and the other man's more.

All men, straight and gay alike, take a special interest in their own penis, and in penises they see in locker rooms and in public showers. (See discussion of the penis as a status symbol, pages 32-34.) But gay men have a very special interest in this body part, both because it symbolizes masculinity and because it is the penetrating organ, the means by which they can become connected and effect a magical transfer of power. Semen takes on a magical importance, as it transfers the partner's physical substance. A 15-year-old respondent expresses this fantasy in his interview with Shere Hite:

> "I get very aroused when seeing other guys' dicks, especially in physical education, and I love anal sex. To be penetrated by your partner, and knowing that *something of him has entered your body*, brings much delight and pleasure. I also love fellatio, and swallowing semen is great. . . " (page 292, emphasis added).

Is this the fantasy that can even lead men to ignore sensible precautions that could prevent HIV infection?[18] Author Eric Marcus (page 193) reports that a well-educated, intelligent man of his acquaintance[19] recalled that he had engaged in unprotected anal sex with a stranger:

> I had a conversation not long ago with an acquaintance who is very well-educated, in the heart of middle age, and a real enthusiast about life. He told me a story about how he had unprotected anal intercourse with a young man he had just met. . . "And he ejaculated inside me". . . [he said]. I was astonished--no, horrified. "How," I asked, "could you do that?" This man, who had read all the same articles I have and knows people who have died from AIDS, said, "It felt like the right thing to do. I trusted him. He told me that he'd tested negative."

Andrew Sullivan makes an impressive personal confession (1998, page 41) which suggests how strong and uncontrollable may be a gay man's wish to have unprotected sex with an attractive stranger; stronger than the resolve to avoid contracting HIV:

> I contracted the disease in full knowledge of how it is transmitted, and without any illusions about how debilitating and terrifying a diagnosis it could be. . . . But still I risked getting it. . . . I remember in particular the emotional spasm I felt at the blithe comment of an old and good high school [heterosexual] friend of mine, when I told him I was infected he asked who had infected me; and I told him that, without remembering any particular incident of unsafe sex, I really didn't know. The time between my negative test and my positive test was over a year, I explained. It could have been anyone. "*Anyone?*" he asked incredulously. "How many people did you sleep with, for God's sake?"

> Too many, God knows. Too many for meaning and dignity to be
> given to every one; too many for love to be present at each; too
> many for sex to be very often more than a temporary but power-
> ful release from debilitating fear and loneliness. My heterosexual
> friend, of course, instinctively saw my sexual life as . . . an
> unthinkable lapse into irresponsibility--and I do not wish to deny
> that at some obvious level, it was.

> Sullivan adds (page 54) that after his infection, he did his best
> "to be public about [his] HIV status and to tell most, if not all, of
> [his] sexual partners. "If asked, I never lied," he recalls. "*But it
> was amazing, perhaps, how infrequently I was asked*" (emphasis
> added).

In Chapter 2 we observed that in sports, when new safety equipment becomes available, the accident rate does not drop proportionately because risk takers using the safety equipment now take greater risks than they had taken before.[20] Similarly, new medications (protease inhibitors) have made it possible for a sig-nificant number of HIV-positive men to prolong their years of normal health if they adhere to an endless regimen of pill-taking. (For some there is the risk, according to *The New York Times*, of "debilitating, occasionally fatal, side effects.") But because medical progress in the treatment of HIV has been so sub-stantial, unprotected sex has become more and more common among gay men.

The New York Times (August 19, 2001) reports that from 1994 through 2000, the percentage of San Francisco gay men who reported having multiple partners and unprotected anal sex has *doubled* (23.6 to 47.1 per cent). *The Times* also reports research indicating that factors which increase the likelihood that a man will have unprotected sex and multiple partners include the use of drugs and alcohol, making Internet contacts, and a background of child abuse.[21] Now that gay men were no longer surrounded by death and dying, for some men, at some moments, the pleasures of multiple partnerships, direct bodily contact and the free exchange of bodily fluids make the risk of HIV infection an acceptable risk. Are these gay men unique in choosing an immediate pleasure over the remote risk of suffering and death?

Columnist George Will sees an interesting parallel between unsafe sex and cigarette smoking. It is well known, he notes, that cigarette smoking may lead to the remote likelihood of a painful death from lung cancer. One-fourth of all smokers die prematurely because of smoking and lose on average twenty years of life expectancy. Before the 1964 surgeon general's warning, about half the nation's adults smoked. Today, about one-quarter of adults, predominantly the poor and poorly educated, smoke. Those cigarette smoker's willingness to trade the immediate pleasure of cigarette smoking for the remote risk of lung cancer parallels some gay men's attraction to the immediate thrill of unprotected sex with a stranger, despite the remote risk of HIV/AIDS.

Even before it posed the life-threatening risk of HIV/AIDS, anonymous sex sometimes carried the risks of robbery and physical assault. This is how psychologist John Money (1988, paraphrased) once expressed his worry over the cost of anonymous sex:

> The allure of sex with a stranger makes the homosexual vulnerable of falling into the hands of a person who has a hidden agenda, who will bring their sexual engagement to an unexpected and unwanted ending--brutal, sadistic, possibly murderous. Add to this risk, the risk of falling into the hands of a homophobic exorcist,[22] where sex can lead to punishment and possibly even to death.

In praise of straight men. Like the "fairies" of a few generations ago, some gay men dream of encountering the truly heterosexual man who is open to a brief gay encounter. Perhaps he is a married man whose wife is out of reach. Maybe he is slightly (or very) drunk. Such a contact would truly be a *mana* experience.

> In personal ads, gay men frequently describe themselves as a "straight-looking" male looking for a "straight-looking" partner. ("No nelly-queens, please.")

In a remarkably candid essay, "In Praise of Straight Men," Rowe and Oliver pinpoint the characteristics that make straight men look refreshingly different from homosexuals, and seem especially attractive as sex partners. There is a tincture of envy in their description of men who "couldn't give a damn" about wearing "rumpled khaki Dockers that droop slightly in the butt," men whose "bodies are just right for an active life, gotten through actual sports, played for fun," rather than from scheduled workouts. "Cute fathers with their squalling spawn strapped into backpacks. . ." (Rowe, page 73).

In the old days, recall Rowe and Oliver, "'straight trade'" was the barometer by which our forbears gauged what was hot. If it was gay, it wasn't hot. If it was straight, hubbahubba, it was a 'real' man." Nowadays, sex with a straight man is apt to be a fleeting lapse rather than an ongoing relationship. Ephemeral experiences such as these "haven't dissuaded many of us from our quest; in fact, if anything, they have simply served to whet our appetites for the exotic and usually onetime--embrace of these [heterosexual] creatures" (page 74).

"Those of us who love straight men love them to be different because, to us, different is erotic, exotic, and infinitely worth celebrating. We've been proclaiming virtues of diversity for years, at least in as much as it applies to the validity of our own difference as gay men" (page 79).

NOTES TO CHAPTER 12

1. Trade (meaning "customers") referred to men who claimed to be straight but were willing (perhaps eager) to be fellated.

2. See pages 328-329 For the 1980 prediction of Judd Marmor. More recently, gay-affirmative therapist Walt Odets (1995 page 128) asserted that gay men are not driven to anonymous sex because society restricts the opportunity of homosexual men to fulfill their sexual needs in more normal and wholesome ways. Gay apologists are wrong, Odets insists, when they argue that anonymous gay sex is the result of social oppression.

3. Cruising, searching for impersonal sex with a stranger, is a popular practice in urban centers. Not *all* gay men cruise.

4. Coming Out; *A Handbook for Men*, by Orland Outland, is a 2000 publication of Alyson Books, foremost publisher of gay scholarly and popular publications.

5. Some homosexuals take a special interest in having sex with men who are known to be married, for example. According to Chauncey, "fairies" rouged their cheeks and wore feminine clothes because they believed that "real men" were attracted to signs of femininity.

6. Lovers from different backgrounds are themes of *Romeo and Juliet, John Smith and Pocahontas, Abie's Irish Rose, Sayonara, South Pacific, Two for the Seesaw*, and many other works.

7. According to Levine (1990, page 154), most West Village gays look for youth; a few look for "daddies," very masculine-looking older men.

8. Excerpted from Whitman's "Gods," *Leaves of Grass*.

9. Walt Odets (pages 128-129) observes that the gay bathhouse is the perfect setting for same-sex sex without intimacy, to accomodate those gay men who cannot integrate their sexual feelings with feelings of intimacy:

> The bathhouse environment allows purely sexual interactions disconnected from more whole human interactions, an idea taken to literal expression in the "glory hole," through which you can insert your penis into an adjoining room and have it sucked by you-never-had-to-know-who. This is sex with a mouth--or for the receptive partner, a penis--rather than with a person. Needless to say, such sex is free of the complexities, problems, and anxieties provoked by feelings, which become an inescapable part of more complex human interactions. . . . A psychotherapy patient, very active in the bathhouse scene of the seventies, said that it was his

standard practice on entering a bathhouse "to get an erection immediately, so that I didn't spend too much time talking and risk getting intimate with anyone."

10. Statistical differences (significant at the .005 level) of Reisman's findings may be summarized as follows:

Traits and activities sought by gay men

a] *Explicit sexual references.* Terms like "horny," "hot," "sensual body rub," "plumbing, "male call," "good hands," or "big meat" appeared in 98 percent of A (Advocate) ads, and 14 percent of W (Washingtonian) ads.

b] *Teen-ager sought.* Over half (53%) of A ads sought teens; 1 percent of *W* ads sought teens.

c] *Sadism/masochism offered or sought.* Ads referring to S&M, leather toys, master and slave, and like terms. A ads 25 percent; W ads 0.4 percent.

d] *Partner of certain sexual dimensions sought.* Only A ads (22 percent) specified sexual dimensions of partner sought. (Examples: well hung, giant tool, 8-inches, uncut.) Less than one percent (0.4%) of *W* ads alluded to physique, with words like "buxom" or "Reubenesque."

e] *Prostitution offered.* Though illegal, some ads suggested paid sex. Terms used in the *W* ads: satisfaction guaranteed, $100 in, $150 out. Terms used in the A ads: 24 hrs., VISA or Mastercard. W had 5 percent such ads; A had 63 percent such ads.

Traits and activities sought by men in general (Washingtonian advertisers)

a] *Long-term commitment.* Phrases like "seeking long-term companion," "serious," or "possible lasting union" appeared in 86 percent of W ads, and only 2 percent of A ads.

b] *Partner with shared interests sought.* Expression of non-sexual interests in sports (*e.g.*, skiing, volleyball), travel (*e.g.*, Bahamas, mountains), recreation (*e.g.*, sailing, cycling, beaches, picnics), cultural activities (*e.g.*, music, reading, poetry, gardening) or family (*e.g.*, children) appeared in 49 percent of W ads, and only 3 percent of A ads.

c] *Partner with certain personality traits sought.* Advertiser ISO partner with humor, honesty, sincerity, clean habits, or intelligence; is looking for someone who loves children, is adventurous, romantic, smart, neat, or "can make me laugh." *W* ads: 42 percent; A ads 4 percent.

11. Martin Levine's 1990 dissertation describes the life of gay men, known as "clones," in New York City's West Village. "Clones" were not a uniquely West Village phenomenon. Kimmel (1996, page 279) estimates that this hyper-masculine variant of gay men "constituted roughly one-third of all gay men living in the major urban enclaves of the 1970s." Nor did "clones" disappear after the 1970s. Signorile's 1997 *Report* laments the devotion to muscle-building that dominates gay life.

Martin Levine's unique field study was based on seven years (1977-1984) as a participant-observer. Levine paid dearly for this experience; shortly afterward, he died of AIDS.

12. To a prostitute, "trick" refers to a paying customer. West Village gay men used the word "trick" to mean a one-night stand, sex with a stranger.

13. West Village gay men were known as "clones" because of the uniformity of their "butch" appearance and behavior.

14. In this regard, West Village clones agreed with Bell and Weinberg's 1978 San Francisco sample (page 308). In that group (574 white males) 79 percent reported that more than half their partners were strangers.

15. Why did this distinguished (and well-closeted) American psychologist write a candid memoir of his homosexual life? In "About the Author," Roger Brown explains: "It's a contribution to the anthropologic record."

16. The attraction of some gay men to risk and danger, brings up some very unsettling questions: When is unprotected sex due to a lapse of vigilance, and when does it actually enhance sexual excitement by adding an element of risk and danger? If a gay man has been victimized (robbed, beaten or murdered) by a predatory partner, when was it due to the victim's naivete, lack of judgment, and when to his attraction to risk and danger? Is there an overlap between attraction to risk and danger, and suicidality? This question is raised again in Chapter 21 (*The Adventurers*).

17. Shokeid estimated that 40 percent of the partnered members of the synagogue found their partners at the synagogue.

18. AIDS-prevention advertising stresses "Use a condom every time," but carefully avoids mentioning two significant risks of gay sex: (1) multiple partnerships, and (2) anal sex. Needless to say, this deference of AIDS-prevention advertising to gay sensibilities, irks many public health workers.

19. The gay journalist Signorile also confessed, in a TV interview, that he once had unprotected sex with an attractive stranger.

20. Gay men are not the only people who respond to increased protection with greater risk-taking. Bicyclists' head injuries have actually increased since the widespread adoption of bike helmets. Bicyclist head injuries rose from 66,820 in 1991 to 73,750 in 2000, according to *The New York Times* of July 29, 2001.

Bicycle helmets, comments *The Times*, creates "a sort of daredevil effect, making cyclists feel so safe that they ride faster and take more chances." Similarly as auto brakes have become more effective, thanks to anti-lock design, drivers have tended to drive faster and some accident rates have risen. Comments *The Times*: "Insurance companies have long been familiar with the phenomenon, which they call moral hazard. [*Perhaps better called "the daredevil effect"?*] Once someone is covered by an insurance policy there is a natural tendency for that person to take more risks."

21.*The Times* article reports: "Studies indicate that a variety of circumstances increase people's vulnerability to sexual risk-taking. For example, gay men who were sexually abused as children, a study by Dr. Jay Paul and his colleagues at the [San Francisco] AIDS prevention study center . . . suggests, are more likely to engage in uprotected sex as adults. Drugs and alcohol play a large role.

"And in one study, still unpublished, Dr. Grant Colfax, the director of HIV Prevention Studies at the San Francisco Department of Public Health, and his colleagues found that men who met sexual partners on the Internet were more than four times more likely to have unprotected sex with a partner of unknown or opposite HIV status."

22. As described in Chapter 6, a homophobic exorcist, in John Money's jargon, is a man who is so violently homophobic (because of his inner--perhaps unacknowledged-- conflict over his own homosexual impulses) that he first seeks out a gay partner and, after their sexual episode, attempts to punish him in one way or another.

13 Long-term Relationships In Gay Life:

Something Like Marriage, But Not Quite

Our discussion of cruising and one-night stands must not obscure the fact that some gay men hope to some day find a long-term partner, and some do. Where the penalty is high for identifying yourself as a gay man, there is an incentive to live alone. In an unfriendly environment, two men who live together as a gay couple may suffer. Bawer (1993, page 254) recalls the time he stepped out of the apartment building with his partner, and the building superintendent spat in his face. Bawer reflects:

> Living alone, most gay people can conceal their sexuality; living together, a gay couple advertise theirs every time they step out of the house together. Is it any wonder, then, that so many gay men have historically been promiscuous, shunning long-term relationships in favor of one-night stands?

But as more gay men step out of the closet, and public acceptance of homosexuality increases, as more gay residential centers are established, gay lovers have less need to hesitate to live together.

Three points of view on gay long-term relationships.

The radical camp. Among homosexual men, there are three major points of view regarding long-term sexual partnerships. At one end of the relationships spectrum stands the radical individualist, for whom cruising and one-night stands are a way of life. The radical camp celebrates homosexuality as a freedom from partnerships of *any* kind, homosexual or heterosexual.

While the straight community promotes "family values" and all the virtues that go with them--responsibility, altruism, conservatism--radical gays regard themselves as defenders of individual liberty and honesty. Radical gays are the most visible part of the gay community, and the noisiest. Gay bars serve the custom of cruising, and other gay-oriented consumer services compete to cater to the gay man's hedonistic and individualistic tastes.[1] When the Adairs interviewed George (page 78), he expressed the point of view of the gay man who is satisfied with this individualistic lifestyle:

George
George, who is openly gay for many years, and has worked as a

gay activist, says of his social life, that he has six close personal friends, but that his social life is separate from his sex life. With one exception, and that was long ago, "I've never had a steady lover. My sex life is pretty much occasional pick-ups, you might say." People keep telling him he should have a steady lover, but he answers, "Why should I judge my life on what society expects of me? . . . It's worked all right for me, and I'm not going to go bananas trying to satisfy somebody else."

Novelist Edmund White (according to Bawer 1993, page 170) endorses the viewpoint of those who applaud the practice of promiscuity, rejecting the practice of permanent partnerships. Forget about "love"--it only breeds jealousy and possessiveness. Instead, enjoy the Brave New World of pure and uncomplicated sex. Gays who "pair off" are self-haters who are trying to mimic straights.

In Wittman's "Gay Manifesto," first published in 1972 and widely reprinted, the author deplores gays who complicate their lives by mimicking straight marriage, and warns that "gay marriages will have the same problems as straight ones, except in burlesque:"

> Traditional marriage is a rotten, oppressive institution. Those of us who have been in heterosexual marriages too often have blamed our gayness on the breakup of marriage. No. They broke up because marriage is a contract which smothers both people, denies needs, and places impossible demands on both people.
>
> [T]o accept that happiness comes through finding a groovy spouse and settling down, showing the world that "we're just the same as you" is avoiding the real issues, and is an expression of self-hatred.
>
> We have to define for ourselves a new pluralistic role-free social structure. . . . It must contain both the freedom . . . to live alone, live together for a while, live together for a long time either as couples or in large numbers, and the ability to flow easily from one of these states to another as our needs change (pages 333-334).

Homosexuality may alienate a gay man from his family and from straight society in general. Some gay men have been so ostracized by their birth family that they don't even expect their kinfolk to attend their funerals.[2] Anthropologists see kinship ties in every culture; there seems to be a basic human need for membership in a primary group, and radical individualists, like almost all gay men, surround themselves with circles of friends: close friends, good friends, friends, and acquaintances.[3]

The bachelor cliques. There is also a sizeable middle group in the gay population whose agendas are quite different from either the radicals at one end or the conservatives at the other. These include gay bachelors: gay men, either closeted or open, who follow bachelor lifestyles that revolve around private social cliques rather than public places like gay bars. This option probably requires a higher socioeconomic status, since each member must afford to periodically play host to his whole circle of friends. Also, he must have living quarters large and comfortable enough for private entertaining.

The conservative gay man. At the other end of the spectrum is the truly conservative gay man, whose homosexuality is not an "alternative" lifestyle, but one that adheres to heterosexual norms so closely that perhaps we could call their design for living a *variant* lifestyle, whose adherents do their best to match the ways of the middle-class majority. The gay conservative ideal is to find a life companion, maintain a permanently monogamous partnership, own a home, perhaps in a small town or in the suburbs,[4] raise one or more children (adopted, or from a previous marriage), belong to a church, and play an active role in the larger community."

"The open partnership." Monogamy is not a popular concept in gay writing. McWhirter and Mattison, who researched gay couples, avoid the word monogamy altogether, and instead refer to "sexual exclusivity."

Gay therapist Don Clark (page 173) warns that "monogamy can do as much harm as good if it is used unquestioningly and without regard to its suitability at given periods in the relationship. . . . If one or both partners become restless and want other sexual experiences, new agreements that continue to recognize the primacy of the relationship while permitting some sexual involvement elsewhere and meeting the needs of both partners, must be worked out as quickly as possible."

Unlike the radical individualists and the gay bachelors, there are those gay men who choose to maintain some kind of enduring partnership--a partnership that is, paradoxically, both committed and "open." As Kaufman and Raphael explain (page 244): "Monogamy simply may not be possible or desirable for many gay men[5] . . . who find it impossible and oppressive to remain [monogamous] over the course of life. What is needed is a deliberately conscious approach by each couple to determine how best to deal with inevitable sexual attractions and desires for others, and with potential sexual encounters."

Compared with heterosexual partnerships, gay partners are likely to be much more different from each other: much more diverse in age, ethnicity, educational attainment, and socio-economic background.[6] Younger gay men often choose a partner near their own age. But as gay men grow older, they feel the need for a younger partner.

The gay psychoanalyst Richard Isay argues that differences provide "emotional tension and excitement" in an intimate relationship. With a heterosexual couple, the sex difference provides the 'complementarity factor' that gay couples do not have, and they need to find some other kind of complementarity to make sex exciting. Ethnic difference, socio-economic difference, or age-difference may afford gay couples the excitement of complementarity that straight couples find in sex difference, says Isay.

Older gay men, whose sexual drive is more limited, may especially need the extra excitement that a younger partner can provide. When disease and death has begun to narrow his circle of age-mates, an elderly gay man may discover a fresh experience of sexual passion if he has the money to attract and hold a lover twenty or thirty years his junior. Isay regards this tactic as, paradoxically, both "a denial of reality" and also healthy:

> [Though the pursuit of a lover twenty or thirty years his junior
> may seem frantic or unrealistic, there is something healthy about
> this denial of the reality of the encroaching end of life.] "By
> becoming more affirmingly gay and by seeking out a love that
> nourishes his sense of well-being, an elderly man usually
> improves his physical health and enhances his emotional health,
> and may, thereby, [extend his active] life" (Isay, page 152).

Gay men living in "open partnerships" usually are guided by a set of rules and understandings quite different from those followed by most heterosexual married couples, or by gay-married couples. These rules give the partners both the variety of erotic experience that the gay appetite demands, along with the security and stability that an ongoing partnership affords. Here, for example, is Barash and Lipton's description (page 71) of how Alfonso and Scott have managed their ten-year relationship:

> [This gay couple] consider sexual fidelity out of the question:
> both enjoy quick bouts of intense but impersonal sex with
> strangers. Like other confident male homosexuals, each accepts
> his partner's desire for sexual variety but within certain guide-
> lines.. . . . For Alfonso and Scott, this means that encounters with
> additional lovers may take place only outside the home. (For
> other gay couples, additional lovers may be permissible only if
> brought home and shared, only if talked about, only if not talked
> about, and so forth.)

When asked why they want sex outside the relationship, here are some of the answers gay men gave to McWhirter and Mattison (page 253):

> "All my sexual needs are not met by my partner. Sex together

gets boring at times, and I need new material for my fantasies."
"My partner is not really my sexual type. I still like to have sex
with a certain type of guy."
"It's fun and adventure. The more variety and number of partners,
the more adventure and fun."
"I have some kinky sexual interests that my partner doesn't share."
"We have found that having sex with others often enhances our sex
together afterward."

Published in 1984, the findings of the McWhirter and Mattison study are generally consistent with how gays have for many years been describing enduring
relationships.

In their 1978 interviews, the Adairs (pages 37-39) quote Rick who describes
his partner David as "the person with whom I've loved and lived for the past sixteen years." He describes himself as married to David, but candidly adds that
their relationship is not monogamous. "It doesn't feel comfortable for me; *there
are needs that I have that are not met in the one-to-one relationship*" (emphasis
added).

A gay author recalls a personal experience that illustrates how to homosexual partners, friendship and sexual fidelity can be two very different matters:

When I was in my early twenties, I tricked out with a famous
playwright--my first infidelity to my lover of two years. After I
had sex with the playwright, he told me that I made love exactly
like this kid he'd met a week before--and he named my lover,
whom I promptly telephoned from the playwright's apartment.
We all dissolved into peals of laughter.[7]

Rules and practices concerning outside partners vary. Some partners insist
that outside affairs *not* be discussed; others insist that they *must* be informed, but
not teased. Additional lovers may be permitted only if they be brought home and
shared.[8] Hatterer (1970, pages 397-398) warns that when a man brings a third or
fourth partner into a relationship, he may be consciously or unconsciously seeking "to destroy, humiliate, or devalue his partner:"

His partner may then also introduce other men into the relationship to retaliate. Ultimately, a chaotic round-robin or mutually
destructive interpersonal activity occurs. The anarchy of homosexuality takes over, and the cruelty, hostility, and depersonalized
aspects of the relationship surface.

In his 1977 description of gay life, Loovis (page 130) also admitted that there
is a fidelity problem in gay relationships. He proposed to solve it by *redefining*
fidelity. Wrote Loovis: "[I]n order not to violate fidelity," both lovers might

together have sex with a third person "satisfactory to both lovers." Going to an orgy together is likewise "not considered unfaithfulness. . . . Refreshed and relieved, [they can] link arms and return home."

Loovis adds: "Another method of retaining *a fair facsimile of faithfulness* is the one night a week each gay lover spends away from the other. . . . This is *exactly parallel* [so Loovis argues] to the 'boys' or girls' night out' arrangement between heterosexual couples, and it usually works, for both straight and gay" (emphasis added). These suggestions are in keeping with the 'designs for living' McWhirter and Mattison reported seven years later.

How can a partner who is in an "eminently compatible" long-term love affair be seized by a sudden compulsion to have sex with a stranger? Loovis (pages 130-131) an insider with a gift for literary expression, describes this experience:

> One . . . suddenly sees a stranger in the street, their eyes meet, and they are off to bed at the stranger's place. I would say that the cheating lover has had an irresistible experience of beauty in the person of the stranger, which time and circumstance allow him to indulge. He comes across a perfect exterior "type" and must have union with him. When it happens, a force is loosed in the cheating lover that he feels he must succumb to or perish. My advice to such a lover is to do it and forget it, never mention his lapse to his lover whom he really does love--and try not to let it happen too frequently. That experience of beauty, which is irresistible, by the way, is one of the most mysterious and awe-inspiring in the entire homosexual galaxy of experiences.

Sometimes one partner would opt for monogamy but his mate insists on the freedom to cruise. Such was the experience of Roger Brown, who admits (page 84) that he "hated [his life partner] Al's compulsive cruising." Brown pondered over why Al persisted in the practice of cruising: "I had never thought of raising the question of fidelity because I could not imagine that there would be any temptation. What we had together was incomparably better than anything a stranger could offer. It engaged the whole of the body and spirit. It was a transcendent experience, the best thing in life. Apparently not, though. Al wanted anonymous sex as well." Brown recalls his partner's comment, "I never said I would give up cruising, you know. It's not really the sex that's important. It's the excitement. The danger and the chase."

Kirk and Madsen, in their 1990 study, (page 318) lament the fact that "relationships between gay men don't usually last very long." This is an old lament. Kinsey in 1948 had observed (page 633) that "long-term relationships between two males are notably few." Kinsey continued:

> Without such outside pressures [as social custom and legal restraints] to preserve homosexual relations, and with personal

and social conflicts continually disturbing them, relationships
between two males rarely survive the first disagreements.

Yet most gay men are genuinely preoccupied with their need to find a lover.
In other words, everybody's looking, but nobody's finding. Among 'permanent'
gay partnerships, the 'wayward impulse' is inevitable. Write Kirk and Madsen
(page 330):

> Yes, that wayward impulse is as inevitable in man-to-man affairs
> as in man-to-woman, only, for gays, it starts itching faster. It's a
> disastrous aspect of human nature that, sooner or later, no matter
> how fortunate we may be, the bird that we glimpse in the pubic
> bush starts to look more appealing than the bird that we hold in
> our hand. And no matter how happy a gay man may be with his
> lover, he's likely, eventually, to go dowsing for dick.

> [T]he gay community has never had any tradition of faithfulness
> . . . to serve as the cement that might hold roving lovers together.
> In our experience, unfaithfulness between gay male lovers as
> often as not spells the beginning of the end.

Loovis (page 126) speculates that the popularity of the one-night stand does
not simply mean that gays prefer promiscuity, but that gays "are still looking . .
. [for] that one individual who can heal them, mend their dividedness," for an
enduring love relationship. To Loovis, the long-term love affair fulfills a deep
human need--"for that one person with whom to share the deepest and most significant experiences of life. . . . A gay person can subsist on casual love and sex
relationships, but it is meager fare, as opposed to the wonder and delight of a love
transference that endures." But this is more of a romantic ideal than an observable fact. Gay couples often say, "Most of our friends are gay couples." But sharing a domestic life, and friendship with other couples, clearly does not imply a
monogamous relationship.

Why does a couple dissatisfied with maintaining a monogamous relationship
continue to live together? "As friends of mine have said," writes DuBay, (page
143) *"a good roommate is worth much more than a good lover."* Their sexual
lives are something else; they are still driven by the search for something or
someone new, so long as their health, their energy, and their looks hold out. They
are forever vulnerable to some "mysterious and awe-inspiring force" that one
"must succumb to or perish."

Same-sex unions often incorporate the virtues of friendship more effectively
than traditional marriages; and at times, among gay male relationships, the openness of the contract makes it more likely to survive than many heterosexual
bonds. . . . There is more likely to be a greater understanding of the need for
extramarital outlets between two men than between a man and a woman. . .

Something of the gay relationship's necessary honesty, its flexibility, and its equality could undoubtedly help strengthen and inform many heterosexual bonds.

Gay therapist Don Clark (page 174-175) maintains that an outside affair can actually "enrich us in ways that can deepen the relationship with our primary partner," by making the gay man a more experienced and therefore a better lover:

> Many of us have been taught that love is like a loaf of bread: if someone takes a bite out of my loaf, there will be that much less bread for me. . . . One might instead compare love to a muscle and consider that the more you use it the more it grows. . . If you are going to share sex and loving with people other than your partner, it is your responsibility to provide adequate verbal and physical reassurance to your partner that he or she is not valued any less, or you will suffer the considerable consequences, which can include the loss of the relationship.

Does it work? Can gay couples continue to live together while they continue searching for fresh excitement? No two cases are exactly alike. In some cases, sexual jealousy and rivalry lead to a break-up. In other cases, the sexual aspect of their partnership ceases altogether, but the couple has developed a friendship so strong that it overcomes any differences in sexual habits. A couple may have also developed a web of common interests--an apartment filled with jointly-owned possessions, joint-ownership of a home, a circle of friends, shared hobby and business interests--so enveloping that they continue to live together despite their lack of sexual interest in each other.

Advice to straights: try open marriage. In the heterosexual world, Sullivan notes, monogamy is in trouble; the prevailing divorce rate makes that much clear. Heterosexual couples can learn from their gay neighbors, says Sullivan, how to unburden themselves from the restrictive demands of monogamy, and enjoy a more satisfying life together. Sullivan admits that gay couples can afford to be more experimental since "the lack of children gives gay couples greater freedom. Their failures entail fewer consequences for others. But something of the gay relationship's necessary honesty, its flexibility, and its equality could undoubtedly help strengthen and inform many heterosexual bonds," Sullivan advises (1995, pages 202-203).

Nimmons surveys a number of studies (pages 82-91) on "the gay rescription of monogamy," research that firmly establishes the fact that most long-term gay relationships are non-monogamous, or open. (page 89) This permits gay men to be more honest, less deceptive, than heterosexual marrieds, according to a 159–respondent study[9] cited by Nimmons (page 89). It is easier to be honest with each other when a couple is free to decide whether to practice "sexual exclusivity" (as a minority of perhaps 25 per cent of gay couples do) or not. What's more important, monogamy or honesty? "[T]he cultural norms operating in our social milieu allow committed couples an option that most couples in the dominant culture don't have" (Nimmons, page 90). Nimmons concludes: "[T]his cultural innovation holds huge portent for the larger society" (ibid, page 91).

Survey Data on Gay Partnerships

Bell and Weinberg found that close-coupled partners tended to be happier than open-coupled gay partners. Open-coupled men appeared to be "less happy, self-accepting, and relaxed. These differences seem to suggest that the open-coupled relationship reflects a conflict between the ideal of fulfilled monogamy and dissatisfactions within the partnership" (page 221). "[O]pen-coupleds worried about their cruising, especially about the possibility of being arrested or otherwise publicly exposed—perhaps because of their partner's ignorance of their cruising activities. . . . . [T]he open-coupleds reported more sexual activity than the typical homosexual respondent and broader sexual repertoires, but the men tended to have trouble getting their partner to meet their sexual requests. . ." (page 221). An interviewer reported of an open-coupled: "He said that he could not say whether he was in love with his roommate because he did not know what love really is" (page 222)

Survey Data on Fidelity of Heterosexual Couples

Married heterosexuals are not known to be perfectly faithful, either.[5] In 1992, a University of Chicago survey team personally interviewed a national random sample of 3,432 persons on their sexual life; 1,660 married adults were asked how many sex partners they have had since the age of 18. Here are their findings (Laumann et al., pages 179-180):

Number of Partners	Percentage	
1	37.1	Median=2
2-4	28.0	Mode=1
5-10	19.4	
11-20	8.7	Range=1 to 600
21 or more	6.8	

Though monogamy is upheld as an *ideal* in straight society, "outside affairs" are not unknown. Divorce lawyers, marriage counselors, and readers of "advice columns" get the impression that adultery is a rather common occurrence.

According to Laumann's findings, the average married adult claims to have had only two sex partners since the age of 18, and about one-third claim to have had as many as five sex partners or more since the age of 18.

THE BREAKUP

Clinical records show that the breakup of a partnership is the number-one psychological crisis that leads a gay man to seek psychiatric treatment or counseling (Hatterer 1970, page 395): "Rejection and abandonment by one's partner lead to depression, anxiety, loss of self-esteem, and suicidal preoccupation or attempt." Hatterer's patients bemoan the futility of trying to make a gay partnership last:

> Patient to Hatterer (1970, page 127): "I don't believe that a homosexual marriage can exist for more than a limited number of years because I've tried so many times and failed so often."

> Patient to Hatterer (1970, page 141): "[O]f the hundreds I've known there are a few couples, one living together for twenty years . . . they love each other but not the kind of love I want. Sex is apart from it. They each have their series of young boys. They can afford them. Then there are dozens of others that make it only for one year, or seven, and then whammo . . . the explosion. The suicide gesture or booze--not unlike men and women but worse, more vicious, more brutal. . . ."

> Patient to Hatterer (1970, page 141): "One of the reasons I came for help was that I realized how I couldn't spend my life looking for someone who could never fill the bill. . . . [In all my partnerships] I tried to make them like a heterosexual marriage . . . loyalty . . . fidelity . . . to be the man, not the woman . . . but I always liked another man . . . that's what was wrong. . . . All I know is it just never works, at least not for me!"

Sometimes the breakup occurs because it can no longer be denied that the partners are so different in their intellect, sociability, age, and lifestyle; that their pattern of dominance and submission has changed; or that one is being excessively exploited sexually, interpersonally, or economically. Character flaws may doom a partnership to failure, because of one of the partner's passivity, dependency, or aggressiveness. A shaky relationship usually breaks up when one partner finds "someone else more physically attractive, sexually gratifying, younger, or more psychologically suitable to predetermined fantasies. . . ." (Hatterer 1970, page 395).

Some gay men are attracted to each other because they have so

much in common: age, interests, education, socio-economic
level. Other partnerships come together because each member is
so different: one is older and rich, the other is young and handsome; one is mature and sophisticated, the other is a naive protegé.

Sometimes the benefactor-partner discovers that his handsome young protegé
is too narcissistic, too opportunistic, or too exploitative, and is ready to part company. Or the young protegé matures, becomes more independent and now wants
a very different kind of partner. What may have been a good bargain at the out-
set of the relationship, becomes intolerably lopsided five or ten years later, as the
older partner ages and the younger partner grows into maturity and independence.

Marvin

Hatterer (1970, pages 392-393) tells of Marvin, a 33-year-old
New York advertising man who brought "a beautiful 18-year old
boy" from California, to live with him. Marvin supported him
financially, but became unbearably jealous, hypercritical, and
possessive. Meanwhile, John became a successful art student,
found friends at school, and even found himself a girlfriend.
With the encouragement of a therapist, whom he was now paying for out of his own earnings, he was planning to marry her. In
a violent parting, John told Marvin "he could not stand him and .
. . had come to find his body repulsive."

Factors favoring the durability of a lasting gay relationship

How long will an "enduring relationship" actually last? According to
McWhirter and Mattison (pp. 213-216), the couples who stay together longest
are those who have at least a few years' difference between them. Each partner
brings something unique to the relationship: one brings the glamour of youth, the
other brings the benefits of experience, stability, and perhaps financial worth.
Partners closer in age are likely to be more competitive about finding outside sex
partners (McWhirter and Mattison, page 260).

Former partners: good friends or bitter enemies?

One of the striking differences between gay and straight partnerships is that
when a straight couple breaks up, that usually signals the end of their relationship. When a gay couple cease to be lovers, however, they may remain the best
of friends. An observer of the gay lifestyle recalls:

When a straight man breaks up with his girlfriend, the break is
often decisive; it's very hard to move from the end of their affair
into an ongoing friendship. However . . . many--if not most--gay

men who break up continue to be best friends. And they may
even continue to live together. They may enter into a period of
rivalry during which each of them tries to meet somebody new
first. When that phase wears out, their friendship gets mellower
and better. This is something which seems unthinkable to most
straight people; they don't know how we can do it. . . . The idea
that . . . when love ends, the friendship can continue astonishes
many outsiders.

The same observer recalls: "Again and again I've seen two men who have
stopped being lovers continue to live together; as for myself, I can count on several ex-lovers as close friends." He notes that the ripening of a gay relationship
comes when over the years sexual attraction has faded or become diverted, and
romantic attraction is then transformed into what might be called a feeling of kinship at its best. After they have weathered "the storms of jealousy and the
diminution of lust," the couple settles down to a long-term relationship of best-
friends-who-used-to-be-lovers. [10]

Gay advocates and Establishment mental health workers have given radically different pictures of the break-up of homosexual partnerships. Writing back in
1961, Hewitt (page 601) observed that because homosexual partnerships are
based on unrealistic expectations,[11] they bound to end in painful disappointment:

Every homosexual relationship, however ecstatically entered
into, carries the seeds of its own destruction from the beginning
and when it is terminated as it inevitably will be, there are horrendous repercussions which are peculiarly painful and disruptive. . . . If it is claimed that no rage can compare with that of a
woman scorned, it can be truthfully said it is still mild compared
to that of homosexual rejection.

More recently (1993, page 152), Nicolosi describes gay partnerships as
bedeviled by cheating, teasing, fights, jealousy, rage, suspicion, envy, restlessness, and disappointment:

Homosexual relationships are so characteristically volatile,
because the homosexual hates what he loves. He realizes on
some level that no man can fulfill his unrealistic expectations. . .
. [Nicolosi also notes (*ibid*, page 185):] In all my work with
many couples, both homosexual and heterosexual, the most violent domestic arguments have occured in male relationships.

How much these clinical observations apply to the non-clinical gay world, is of
course, a major question.

Outstanding examples of successful lasting gay partnerships

A lasting partnership requires that each person respect the other's point of view. Freud believed that as a rule, homosexual men are too self-centered, too narcissistic to develop mature partnerships. Psychoanalyst Heinz Kohut (Elson, pages 29-30) questioned Freud's generalization, and testified that experience had acquainted him with "some very [well-] developed homosexual relationships in which the partner is very much recognized as an individual in his own right. There are stable long-term relationsips among homosexuals in which the partner is recognized and loved very much as an independent human being who is permitted a certain degree of being different from oneself." Couples who have lived together for many years are heroes of their community, and are sometimes greeted with applause when they arrive at a party or social gathering.

In their 1978 book of interviews, the Adairs showcased Mac,[12] a gay man who works among the corporate elite. It bothers him, Mac admits, that "people automatically assume that gay people don't form close attachments of any length or duration. And that's just not true." Mac himself has been with his partner 14 years and "virtually all of my friends are in couples. Most of our friends have been together for ten years or more. They are people who live relatively normal kinds of lives, interesting lives too" (Adair and Adair, pages 119-120).

Around the time of Mac's interview, Bell and Weinberg (pages 132, 346) reported that only 10 percent of gay men, in their San Francisco sample, were in long-term relationships, open or committed. Their data were collected during the 1970s in gay bars, where close-coupled gay men were likely to be underrepresented. The AIDS epidemic has undoubtedly increased the number of gay men who are attempting to maintain stable, even monogamous, partnerships.

Move from the San Francisco bars of the 1960s to Bawer's conservative gay world of the 1990s, and the popularity of committed gay partnerships does not change too much. Bawer admits (1993, page 253): "The idea of a committed relationship seems to [many gay men] as absurd as homosexuality itself seems to many straight people."

Personal experience versus survey findings

Now let's supplement personal experience with survey findings. What can statistical studies add to eye-witness experience? In 1984, McWhirter and Mattison reported on a five-year study of 156 male couples (312 individuals) "in loving relationships lasting from one to thirty-seven years" (page ix).

At the beginning of these many partnerships, many individuals spoke about, thought about, or hoped for sexual fidelity. "My parents were faithful to each other, and I expected us to be the same" (page 250). But such hopes, they soon realize, are simply contrary to homosexual tendencies, and, of the 156 couples surveyed, *not a single couple reported sexual fidelity lasting longer than five years* (page 252).

What McWhirter and Mattison found in their five-year survey parallels what Roger Brown (page 32) observed in forty years of everyday observation: that he could recall only *one* "lifelong, productive, happy, and, I think, monogamous male marriage. . . . The cruel paradox of fidelity in male homosexuality is that the couple that stay together for longer than seven months are mostly those that are sexually 'open.'"

A more recent and better-controlled study of gay couples was reported by Kurdek in 1991. This investigator studied the practices and attitudes of 77 gay couples, compared with a control group of 85 heterosexual couples, matched for age and education.[13] Every respondent rated his or her satisfaction with their rela tionship, and the importance they attached to sexual fidelity (1=not important, to 9=very important). Findings were quite consistent with what is generally believed to be the differences between gay and heterosexual couples. With their partner's knowledge, homosexual men often engage in sex outside of the relationship. The investigator (page 186-187) regards this finding as *"the most salient difference between homosexual and heterosexual couples."* The major difference between homosexual and heterosexual couples was that "gay couples placed a lower value on fidelity" (page 190). With heterosexual couples, fidelity was positively related to relationship satisfaction, but this was *not* true of gay men (page 185).

Consistent with Kurdek's 1991 findings is the norm expressed by *A Handbook* for gay men published in 2000 by the number-one publisher of scholarly gay publications: *gay monogamy is a rarity* (Outland, page 145):

> It is rare to find two men who are inherently monogamous and powerfully attracted to one another. It's more likely that one monogamous man will fall for someone who considers sex to be a recreational activity, akin to cheating in his heart and mind as picking money off the sidewalk would be to robbery. If this couple are lucky, the sexual adventurer will find that sex with the monogamist is so good that sex with anybody else suddenly feels like a waste of time. Otherwise, there will need to be some significant give-and-take on both sides to make the relationship work.

The author of the *Handbook* suggests a compromise that has worked for him: the more adventurous partner agrees that in his casual sex habits there would be "no repeat partners that might jeopardize [the committed] relationship." The monogamous partner settles for *"a monogamy of the spirit."* The author also recommends that the monogamist do some soul searching: Does he really value *monogamy*, or is he just jealous, or afraid of losing his partner "to someone better in the sack?" (Outland, page 145, emphasis added)

The reality of the gay world versus the claims of gay marriage advocates

Advocates of legalizing gay marriage build their case on the "fact" that gay couples live in stable, monogamous partnerships not unlike a heterosexual marriage. In *Virtually Normal* (page 183), Sullivan claims that "even in our society as it is, many lesbian and gay male relationships are virtual textbooks of monogamous commitment. . . ." Similarly, Reverend Peter Gomes, chief minister at Harvard University, himself a gay man, pleads on behalf of those gay believers who have embraced "a form of homosexuality in which loving, monogamous, and faithful persons [seek] to live out the implications of the gospel with as much fidelity to it as any heterosexual believer."[14]

In his 1998 book, Andrew Tobias documents the 17-year partnership of Mitchell Adams, commissioner of revenue for the State of Massachusetts, and Kevin Smith, who until recently was chief of staff for the governor of Massachusetts. Writes Tobias: "For many years, they shared a home with Kevin's parents. . . . Mitchell Adams is the godfather of three." Adams spoke to his church congregation about his struggle to come to terms with his homosexuality, and concluded that he now lives with his partner, his partner's widowed mother, and a "house . . . full of kids, infants, and golden retrievers" (Tobias 1998 page 239).

As the need for companionship becomes stronger than the need for sex, older gay men men sometimes develop stable partnerships:

Alphonse

Brechner (page 223) describes a homosexual respondent as a 64-year old man who has been living with his 66-year old partner for 30 years. He is in love with his partner though they have not had sex together for the past ten years. His partner chooses not to have sex because of physical changes that are attributed to his diabetes, hypertension, and medication. The partner still feels happily paired, says he enjoys life, still has a moderately strong interest in sex, and masturbates two or three times a week.

Two different worlds. One of the Adairs' respondents is Mac, a gay man who has risen to the top of the corporate ladder. Like most of his friends, Mark lives with a gay partner. His experience leads him to conclude that the gay and straight worlds are two very different worlds, each with its own special advantages and disadvantages. Comparing heterosexual marriage and living with a gay partner is like comparing apples and oranges. These two "designs for living" are different kinds of relationships for different people. Mac concedes that gay men miss out on some of the gratifications of straight life, but argues that a gay lifestyle has its own rewards. He expresses his thoughts on this trade-off in the following words:

Mac

I think gay people have more fun than your average married guy in a home with two or three kids. You have more time and more money. You don't have to take responsibilities. Like, for example, I can be "Uncle Mac" and lavish presents and things on my nephews and take them to the zoo and give a great old time. When they get tired and cranky, I take them back to mommy and dad . . . dad [who] has just finished paying two hundred bucks for their teeth.

Sometimes the grass does look greener on the other side of the fence. You miss the joy of children. . . I really [would] love to have children. It's the one thing I miss a lot. You miss the respectability, the "country club acceptance" that married life confers. It doesn't happen to be important to me, but to some people that is important. (Adair, page 120.)

The unfulfilled prediction.   For years, gay apologists have claimed that the practice of cruising--homosexual multiple partnerships--was *forced* on gay men by a hostile society, one that denied gay men decent jobs, housing, and freedom from harassment. Gay apologists predicted that as gay men come to be accepted as members of the larger society, they would adopt a more stable way of life, and abandon the makeshift practice of cruising.

Clearly, the documented facts do not fulfill those predictions. Instead, it seems apparent that many, probably most, male homosexuals in long-term relationships attempt to combine the practice of cruising with the practice of open partnerships. Lesbian couples undoubtedly find it much easier to maintain a loving and lasting monogamous relationship. The telescoping of gay men and lesbians into one "gay community" serves social and political goals, but obscures significant differences between the majority of gay and lesbian partnerships.

NOTES TO CHAPTER 13

1. Bawer (1993 page 33-34) offers the following hypothetical sketch of a typical gay radical:

Born into a more or less ordinary family in Wisconsin or Missouri or Georgia, he lives in a small walk-up apartment in a gay ghetto like Greenwich Village or West Hollywood or San Francisco's Castro district. He holds down a job that is marginal and at least vaguely artistic; he socializes almost exclusively

with other homosexuals, he dines in gay restaurants, dances at
gay clubs, and drinks at gay bars; and his reading matter consists
largely of gay-oriented magazines and of novels by and about
gays. . . . His politics [is] uncomfortably left-wing; his manner of
dress would probably draw stares on the main street of the average American town or city. He is active in at least one AIDS-
related organization . . . a social-service group like Gay Men's
Health Crisis or an activist group like Queer Nation. . . .

2. Shokeid documents the life of a gay synagogue community in New York. He
notes (pages 78-79) that when a member dies, his family might participate
grudgingly in the funeral or refuse to attend altogether.

3. [Writes Browning, page 158]: No matter how gay people feel about domestic
partnership and gay marriage, most share a core belief: Our friends are our family. . . . For those gays who felt themselves alienated from their blood relations,
comradely friendship often developed as a substitution. Yet if friendship is to
offer more than escape from solitude, it must carry the . . . genuine power of family . . . .

Casual sex contacts, at one extreme, and lovers, at the other, only describe the
two extremes of commitment and intimacy. The entire gamut runs from trick,
number, fuck-buddy, lover, and husband (White 1980, page 150). Browning conjectures (pages 156-157) that some gay men use recreational sex to keep friendships alive:

> I wonder whether making sex . . . recreational, we [gays] have
> learned to re-form it into a tool for building diverse forms of
> comradeship. By stealing sex away from the restrictive laws of
> marriage, by acknowledging its myriad meanings, gay men have
> shown how lust contributes to the bonds of friendship. By
> devaluing the taboo of sex among friends, they may have begun
> to shine more light on the complex and various ways of intimacy
> that can be arranged in emerging gay families.

Proponents of this point of view argue that marriage is a bankrupt institution, as
divorce statistics show; that the monogamous ideal leads to hypocrisy and frustration; and in a world of overpopulation that there is less need than ever for families that "breed."

4. In his 1997 book, *Life Outside* . . . , Signorile applauds the fact that today's
young gay men enjoy the gains that were fought for in the urban centers, but now
realize that they need not move there to enjoy the benefits that were won there.
"As gay men in small-town, rural, and suburban America are now coming out,
rather than take on the lifestyle of the gay ghettos, many are staying in their

hometowns, and keeping their hometown values while living their lives out of the closet" (page 206).

5. The place of monogamy in gay life is viewed very differently by *observers* of gay life, and by *advocates* of gay marriage. Note the pleadings of Clark page 234, Sullivan page 239, Nimmons page 240, and Oatland page 245. See also Epilogue, Part 2, Question 12.

6. In an attempt to make a virtue of this fact, Clark (page 63) writes: "I like the democracy that permits [gay men] to flow across the usual social barriers of income, education, ethnic identity, nationality, and religion."

7. This author lost the source of this published item, and apologizes to the writer of this observation, and to the reader.

8. Most gay men agree that an open partnership best fits their lifestyle but there is endless discussion, even conferences, on exactly what should be the rules of an open partnership. "Only when we travel?" "It's OK if neither of you knows the person?" "No staying overnight?" "Never in our house?" "No kissing?" "No anal sex?" "How about stable threesomes or even foursomes?" White writes (1980, page 34): "The variations are endless. . . Shall the lovers describe the outside adventures to one another or stay discretely silent? One couple might decide . . . there's one night a week for tricking out."

Nimmons (2002, page 82) applauds this "gay rescription of monogamy." He describes a conference on options for maintaining an open relationship to "a roomful of rabbis . . . [offering] an endless inventive series of interpretations on their erotic Talmud." Nimmons continues (page 86) that thus are gay men evolving "a nuanced emotional erotic etiquette, one that functions to spare feelings, maintain bonds, and respect boundaries."

9. See W.M. Burdon in References.

10. See endnote 7.

11. Hewitt (page 599) describes a gay man's unrealistic attitude toward a new partnership: he feels "an overwhelming urge to merge himself with another. . . . His sense of self and his identity become lost in the personality of another. This longing to surrender oneself often reaches the height of ecstacy that seems at times to have religious overtones and is part of the reason why so many homosexuals experience a new relationship as an integrating force which releases their blocked off energies."

12. In the Adair study, this respondent is named Mark. Here he has been renamed

Mac because the name Mark has been given to another respondent.
13. Most of the respondents lived in the Midwest. Of the 85 heterosexual couples, about half (n=49) were married.

14. Rev. Gomes argues that the Bible's condemnation of homosexuality refers to *the homosexuality of biblical times:* "All they knew of homosexuality was prostitution, pederasty, lasciviousness, and exploitation. These vices, as we know, are not unknown among heterosexuals, and to define contemporary homosexuals only in these terms is cultural slander of the highest order." Rev. Gomes's argument invites two comments: (a) *How does he know just what was the range of homosexual interactions during biblical times?* (b) His characterization of gay men who are "loving, monogamous, and faithful" most likely describes only a small minority of homosexuals of this or any generation.

Rev. Gomes suggests that there are many monogamous gay partnership but that they quietly elude the notice of casual observers or researchers. This is similar to Bawer's argument that there are a many quiet, conservative gay men, but research and public observation continue to focus on the noisy radical minority of the gay population.

14 In and Out:

Straight-to-Gay Shifts and Vice Versa

Inborn, irreversible, natural; like left-handedness. Predictable in its onset and chronic in its duration, like male-pattern baldness or adult diabetes. Surprisingly, this "conventional wisdom" survives, despite the abundance of evidence that in fact homosexual behavior comes and goes in the widest variety of ways. It may emerge at 14, or not until well into middle age,[1] or may exist side-by-side an appetite for heterosexual gratification. When researchers Philip Blumstein and Pepper Schwartz launched their study of bisexuality, they were surprised to discover (pages 36-37) that many men simply could not be sorted into stable categories of homosexual, heterosexual, or bisexual, and that a respondent himself was "often unaware of his . . . ability to change," and had to be interviewed several times to note the discontinuity of his practice.

What test-retest revealed about sexual orientation. *Blumstein and Schwartz's findings suggest that if Kinsey and his co-workers had interrogated 7,500 males twice, after a five-year interval, instead if interviewing 15,000 males only once, he might have uncovered a somewhat different body of "scientific knowledge."*[2] The phenomenon that Blumstein and Schwartz describe in the abstract is contained in this recollection of a gay man in his thirties (Stambolian, page 158):

> [F]inally . . . I had sex with a woman after not having done it or thought about it in more than twenty years . . . She was beautiful and had a lovely boyish body, so that made it easier for me. She also knew I was gay and completely accepted that. And she was as interested in my sexuality as I was in hers. . . . [I] realized that being gay was not some kind of inalterable destiny and that an element of free choice was involved. . . .

All is flux, as the Greek philosopher Heracleitus (6th century BC) put it, and sexual practices are no exception. Exploratory homosexual play is fairly common among adolescents. A pair of boys may form an exclusive and fairly enduring sexual partnership. The partnership breaks up when they grow into adulthood and one or both get married. Havelock Ellis reported (1915, page 24) that among the peasants of Switzerland, homosexual relationships between boys were "not uncommon," and lightly spoken of as "Dummheiten" or "foolishness."

As Blumstein and Schwartz (page 37, italics added) concluded from their 1977 study, "childhood and adolescent experiences are *not* the final determinants of adult sexuality." Yet, *21 years later,* a "comprehensive guide" to care and counseling of lesbian and gay youth declares that "by the time . . . [of] early adolescence . . . social interaction and sexual strivings [lead to] an adult identity. . .

251

. (Ryan and Futterman, page 5). These advisors to health care workers continue (page 27): "A common response among health and mental health providers to an adolescent's concerns that he or she might be lesbian or gay is to deny or minimize such concerns. This response is generally based on the misconception that homosexual behavior is merely a 'phase' or 'stage' that adolescents ultimately grow out of. . . . [Expressing this "misconception"] may undermine the client-provider relationship and result in increased anxiety, secrecy, and failure to share pertinent information." In other words, even though it may be true that his homosexual feelings may be only a phase that he might outgrow, don't tell him that because that may undermine his trust in his counselor. So goes the "logic" of Ryan and Futterman.

Same-sex experimentation during one's teenage years is no bar to a heterosexual adulthood, but some settled heterosexuals may once again act out their homosexual potential. *Circumstances alter cases*. As a result of isolation, alcohol, anxiety, emotional stress, (or for no apparent reason), a man's sexual orientation may shift from straight to gay. In the words of Clark (page 109), "Perhaps a heterosexual man has faced a crisis--death of his spouse, divorce, unemployment or some other financial crisis-- and he regressed to the sexuality of his early teens."[3]

A 24-year-old college student says, "I definitely consider myself straight but I know what gay feelings are, and they are most likely to surface when I am feeling lonely and friendless. In my experience, the most vivid and powerful surge of homosexual feelings occurred when I entered college. Here I was in a totally new and strange environment where I had no male friends at all" (adapted from an Internet testimony).

Alcohol may lead to the expression of hitherto repressed impulses. Alcohol, and the recovery from alcoholism, effect interesting changes in a person's sexual impulses and behavior. Clark describes (page 109) a homosexual alcoholic who recovers, thanks to AA (Alcoholics Anonymous), and "now spontaneously takes a sexual interest in women." Money (page 108) describes the reverse situation: a recovered heterosexual alcoholic who now wants to express his homosexual impulses.

Dr. Howard J. Brown, a gay man who was New York City's Health Services Administrator, notes (page 39) that gay men "discover their sexual nature in a variety of ways and in a wide range of ages. Some have been happily married for years when they find, abruptly or gradually, that their sexual relations with women leave them unsatisfied and that it is men they crave." He recalls (page 44) the case of Larry, who after an adolescence of homosexual play, was at the age of 19 "sleeping regularly with a girl . . . liked having sex with her--but there was something missing." He returned to homosexual activity and found that more satisfying. Also, Brown (page 65) tells of a professor who discovered his homosexuality in his middle fifties, divorced his wife of many years and became "one of the most beloved [gay] figures on campus."

Clark (page 42) offers two examples of heterosexual men who may drift into homosexual practice: (1) "[T]he soldier or sailor who gets drunk, wanders into a gay bar (accidentally on purpose) and swears he remembers nothing the next morning when he awakens in bed with another man. . . . (2) [T]he macho man who goes on extended hunting expeditions, fishing trips or to other places where there are no women and the lets a queer have his way with him because his virility requires a release of sexual tension, and he somehow mysteriously forgets how to masturbate," Clark adds, with a touch of irony. Our discussion of situational homosexuality in Chapters 5 and 23 describe how prison life[4] leads to homosexual practice.

Alex

Clark (page 108) also tells of a colleague who did not adopt a gay lifestyle until after he was a married man and a father. When he was long separated from his wife, and had been living as a gay man for some years, much to his own surprise he began "seeing more and more" of a woman with whom he was having "wonderful sex."

He mused: "I think I am really confusing my children. It's a good thing they're adults now and can take such things more in stride--and even offer Dad some advice now and then. First they had to get used to the idea that I was gay and really did like men. It took a little while but they're comfortable with it. Now, I've been seeing more and more of this woman I met last year--and the sex is wonderful! I don't think any of us were quite prepared for this turn of events. Especially since I continue to feel physically attracted to many more men than women. They're teasing me about whether they're going to get a second mother or a second father."

Walter

A Christian ex-gay offers this oral testimonial at an ex-gay convention: He sensed that he was beginning to recover when he began to notice that a good friend of his, a woman friend, actually had breasts. "I had always thought female breasts were the most ridiculous things God created. One day I noticed that this friend had breasts, that they were rather large, and that I liked them. (Laughter.) It blew my mind. In a few weeks we were engaged, and then we were married." (He learned that he had not been quite ready for marriage, but apparently it worked out well enough that he was now willing to talk about it.)

Klein points out that many of the people on lists of "famous homosexuals" (Klein's list, pages 142-143, lists 26 men) were, in fact, functioning bisexual.[5] Some were, at one point in their lives, married *not* to cover up their homosexuality, but married to a woman with whom they were deeply in love.

For example, Klein (page 147), writes that Oscar Wilde--widely regarded by gay men as "one of us" -- was for the first thirty-two years of his life "a lusty, enthusiastic heterosexual . . . and for the next fourteen years, until his death in Paris in 1900, he operated on an equally lusty and enthusiastic homosexual level." Klein (page 140) quotes from the biographer of Wilde, H. Montgomery Hyde:

> "[W]e know that at the outset of their married life Wilde was
> deeply in love with his wife and that they experienced normal
> sexual intercourse. . . [H]e seems to have been an enthusiastic
> lover. . . . [O]n the occasion of his first separation from his wife .
> . . when he was lecturing in Edinburgh, he wrote to her: 'O exe-
> crable fates that keep our lips from kissing, though our souls are
> one. . . I feel your fingers in my hair and your cheek brushing
> mine. The air is full of the music of your voice, my soul and
> body seem no longer mine, but mingled in some exquisite ecsta-
> sy with yours. I feel incomplete without you.'"

Gay author David Bianco does not agree that Oscar Wilde was ever a "lusty, enthusiastic heterosexual." According to Bianco (page 42), before Wilde married, his effeminate mannerisms and unorthodox clothing labelled him as a "Maryanne," and "to silence gossip Wilde married . . . and quickly fathered two children."

Klein (Chapter 9) offers biographical notes on the heterosexual lives of other men popularly listed as "famous homosexuals." On his list of men who married after living through a homosexual phase are Maynard Keynes, and Lucien Happersberger, whose love affair with James Baldwin inspired his 1956 novel, *Giovanni's Room.*

In addition to sexual deprivation and emotional stress, Money (1988, page 106) lists other experiences that can arouse a heterosexual male's homosexual potential. If he shares a female partner with another man, this may lead to same-sex play.[6] Watching a sexually-explicit videotape (heterosexual or lesbian) may arouse a man's homosexual potential. A heterosexual man may also be capable of same-sex anal intercourse if he fantasies that his partner is a woman.

The ease with which a man can shift from heterosexual to homosexual is illustrated by a story told by Roger Brown (page 77). He tells of a young man who applied for a job at a call boy agency named Dream Boys, mistakenly supposing that his clients would be women. When his assumption was corrected, "he switched orientations without missing an appointment. We have much to lear-from the young," Brown muses.

The term *trade* is gay jargon for heterosexual men who are willing to be fellated. "Let me trade you" is an offer of oral sex without an expectation of mutual lovemaking. There is a gay saying, "Today's trade is tomorrow's competition," which means that a heterosexual man who is willing to be fellated may gradually become a full participant in homosexual activity. This metamorphosis is well-described by a gay writer interviewed by Stambolian (page 49):

I've met straight men who take my phone number and keep seeing me. They show me pictures of their wife and kids. The first
time they'll get blown, the next time they'll jerk you off, the
third time they'll fuck you, and the fourth time they'll blow you,
the fifth time they'll get fucked. So in the end you're totally
involved in mutual homosexual sex with them.

Benjamin

Here is the case of Benjamin, cited by Hamer (pages 64-65). He says he was
"always attracted to women" and finally married "a terrific girl" who, sadly,
began to nag him, and then abandoned him altogether.

> [At first, she] seemed to appreciate me for what I was rather than
> how I looked or money or any of that bull. I fell head over heels
> in love and we were married right after I graduated. . . . I was
> always worried that she married me just to get out of her parents'
> house rather than [for] any real love on her part.
>
> The marriage was okay for a while, but pretty soon it started
> falling apart. First she started nagging me: "Why don't you make
> more money? Why can't we have a decent car?" and so forth.
> Then she started just not being around. It was really lonely to
> come home to an empty house. Finally, she just walked out the
> door, and a week later her lawyer sent me papers claiming "men-
> tal cruelty". . . .

After a divorce, his two gay brothers started taking him to the gay bars, and
during the next two years, Benjamin "slept with three or four different men." (At
the bars, says Benjamin, "I was more the pursued than the pursuer. . . .") He then
started dating a girl he had known for some time through a church group. "[W]e
had a friendship before romance [he adds]. We went out together for almost three
years before we got married. . . Now we have four children, and our thirteenth
wedding anniversary is coming up soon. I'm very satisfied in my marriage both
emotionally and sexually. I don't regret my gay phase, but I certainly have no
interest in returning to it, either. To me it was an important part of finding out
what I really wanted in life."

During the two-year period between his divorce and his remarriage,
Benjamin thought of himself as bisexual, and then as gay, like his two brothers.
The fact that he remarried after two years, and after thirteen years of marriage
says he is "very satisfied . . . both emotionally and sexually . . . [and I] have no
interest in returning to" his gay interlude, argues that Benjamin identifies as heterosexual, and that his homosexual interlude was influenced by (a) the emotional distress of a failed marriage, and (b) the social support of his two homosexual brothers.

The brother-in-law sex partners

After many years of marriage, a wife may lose her interest in sexual activity, and is no longer sexually attractive to her husband. It may be easier for the husband to find a willing male sex partner than an attractive female,[7] and this is what sometimes happens. In the Brechner survey (page 219-220), 30 men reported one or more homosexual experiences after the age of 50. One of these respondents was a 63-year old man married for forty-one years who has not had sex with his wife for six years. After 35 years of marriage, his wife is no longer sexually attractive to him though "we still love each other and get along just fine."

> [After 35 years of] going in the same hole in the same way every time, and my wife's putting on weight and losing her figure, she no longer sexually arouses me.

He now has sex with his brother-in-law who is "in the same boat as I am (that is, no sex with his wife) so we have developed a sexual relationship with each other."

Another Brechner respondent, a 56-year old man who finds sex with his wife of sixteen years unsatisfactory, reports (page 221) that his only extramarital relationship since age 50 was with a 40-year old man. Over a period of two months, they had three sexual encounters. Explaining why he terminated the relationship, he comments: "With family relationships to maintain and protect, it is difficult . . . [here in Alabama to maintain] homosexual relationships."

Officer O'Neill

Howard J. Brown (pages 164-165) tells of a New York City police officer, veteran of the Korean War, a man of 40, married and a devout Catholic. After five years of marriage, he was the father of four children. His wife didn't want to have any more children, and in order to carry out that decision, she told her husband she wanted to give up sexual intercourse.

One evening on duty, he set out to entrap a homosexual and arrest him. Instead, he found that he really liked the young man. The gay man propositioned Officer O'Neill, who "found that sex with the man gave him far more satisfaction than sex with any woman ever had. From that moment on, O'Neill considered himself a homosexual." Officer O'Neill found a lover and moved into an apartment with him.

Hal

A homosexual business owner tells how he "inherited" his business. Since he was 15 years old, he worked for the owner, a coarse fellow who spent all of his time "building up his empire" and avoiding his wife, who was "a shrew who'd all but completely castrated him. . . ."

On a buying trip, the young assistant seduced his 50-year old boss "and it was the first time in his life he'd had any sex with a man, but he took to it like a duck to water. . . . We had an affair for ten years. His wife died and he left me his business, having no children or living relatives in this country" (Hatterer 1970, page 433).

Trevor

Clark (page 243) tells of Trevor, a college student who had been "gay for a year" because his best friends, whose social idealism interested him, happened to also be gay. One of them sensed that Trevor wasn't really gay, and laughingly told him so. Trevor did some soul-searching and had to agree.

> [Trevor] . . . knew that he found several of his male friends attractive and so he reasoned that he, to, must be gay. He had a boyfriend for a short time and then a serious lover relationship for some months. It was one of his gay male friends who helped him to recognize that while he was capable of sharing affection and enjoying sex with a few males, the people who most strongly sparked his erotic attraction and the individuals to whom his heart was drawn most strongly were women. He had gone overboard in his attempt to be accepting of gay identity. He had correctly located some gay feelings of his own but ignored his stronger non-gay feelings. He laughed when he told me about it but also admitted that it was not at all funny at the time. "I had to go through a long period of coming out to my gay friends as being basically straight."

Ike and Elmer

An ongoing University of Minnesota research on twins reared apart, led by Thomas Bouchard, Jr., documented the case of a pair of monozygotic ("identical") twins, whom we shall call Ike and Elmer, whose life histories illustrate the fluctuation of sexual orientation.

Ike identified as bisexual until age 19 when he became exclusively homosexual. Elmer had a homosexual affair between the ages of 15 and 18, but later married and regarded himself as exclusively heterosexual. *(According to Kinsey's definition of "who is homosexual," the fact that Elmer had had a same-sex affair from age 15 to 18 would put him in the "10 percent" category of homosexuals.)*

Tex

Edmund White (pages 147-149) tells the story of a Texas millionaire who had been "married happily for ten years and then met a handsome guy from Oregon and fell for him." The deacon of a Baptist church, like both his father and his father-in-law, "[I]t never occurred to me," Tex confessed, "that two men could love each other."

> My wife and I met at a Baptist college, married young and had a boy and a girl. Although I had fooled around with guys, it never occurred to me that two men could love each other. My wife and I were married happily for ten years and then I met a handsome guy from Oregon and fell for him. I told my wife the next day I wanted a divorce but I never confided that I was gay. . . .

> My lover and I bought an old Victorian house . . . [for $30,000 and spent $60,000] fixing it up. . . . For two years no one [in town] would speak to us, just whisper behind our backs. But we hung in there. . . . Eventually we joined a country club as a couple and were invited to all the parties.

> [Eventually Tex and his handsome lover broke up, Tex admitted.] He wouldn't work. I set him up in several businesses, but they all failed. Finally he blamed me for his failures and left me. I've moved to Dallas and started a whole new life. It's very exciting.

G.I. Joe in Tokyo

We have already noted Hatterer's observation that some men who are too timid to approach a woman of their own social milieu, find that they can respond erotically to an exotic woman in a far-away land. Hatterer recalls the testimony of an Army veteran who thought of himself as homosexual:

> [I]n Japan . . . I found out that it was possible for me to become sexually excited by a woman. Even though I didn't know the language I had the most beautiful time with this eighteen-year old Japanese daughter of a man with whom I was stationed. She completely accepted me. She was so sweet and loving and all she cared about was being with me and making love. Even though we never went all the way,[8] all of my homosexuality seems to have disappeared for that time. . . (Hatterer 1970, page 313).

Lane[9]

Liss and Welner describe a case of spontaneous emergence of heterosexual interest in a 24-year-old who had reported a typical sissy-boy childhood, had engaged in homosexual activities since the age of ten, had worked as a hairdresser, and had been exclusively homosexual for at least eight years prior to coming to a psychiatric clinic for help in overcoming his homosexual habit so that he could get married and have a family.

Six weeks of aversive therapy was prescribed (case reported in 1977) but the patient resisted this type of treatment. After four and a half months, his therapist left the clinic, and the patient's treatment lapsed for three months. When the patient returned with a complaint of anxiety and depression, his new therapist limited treatment to supportive treatment only, no aversive therapy. The therapist gave no attention to Lane's homosexual habit. Four months later, the patient reported spontaneous sexual arousal when he was physically close to women, and began to be heterosexually active. He subsequently married and raised a family[10]

Mark

When Dean Hamer (page 63) was collecting blood samples to explore the genetic basis of homosexuality, he met Mark, a young man who says he knew he was gay by the time he was 10. He came out in college, and was always "more interested in having a steady boyfriend than in one-night stands. I met my lover, Barry, when I was 22 and he was 19, and we were together for almost seven years. I paid his tuition all the way through school. After he graduated he got a good job in another city, and we were only able to see each other on weekends. . . . I remained faithful, but he started seeing other guys and eventually he dumped me for some hot young man. Two years later, Barry got AIDS. By that time, the new boyfriend was long gone, so I ended up taking care of Barry all through his illness. I was heartsick when he died. Despite everything he did to me, I still really loved him.

"Cindy came into my life [Mark continues] just around the time Barry passed away. She was everything I'd ever sought in a lover: intelligent, caring, funny, supportive, you name it. And she was really good looking in a pixyish, perky sort of way. So we started sleeping together. At first that's all we did--sleep--but pretty soon it became a sexual relationship as well. Of course she knew all about my gay past, but she's a firm believer in bisexuality.

"Cindy and I got married seven years ago, and I haven't slept with a man since. I guess you could say I'm a gay man who loves a woman. If we ever broke up, I'm not sure if my next partner would be a man or a woman."

In the case of Mark, as in other cases discussed in this chapter, a shift from homosexual to heterosexual orientation occurred without professional treatment.

Emmett

Mark's story, a change of sexual orientation triggered by the death of his lover, has a certain parallel in the case of Emmett described by Reinisch (page 143): "a 65-year-old man who was happily married for 45 years" when his wife died. Within a year, he "fell in love with [a] man." Until the death of his wife, he insisted, he ". . . had never been attracted to or fantasized about another male."

Money (1988, page 108) expresses his skepticism of reorientation therapy by commenting, "If the individual [who undergoes a spontaneous change of sexual orientation] were in some type of treatment, the transition might be wrongly construed as a therapeutic triumph." Throughout the healing arts, spontaneous remissions are known to occur, and for this reason there is no substitute for scientific research.

Weinberg *et al.*'s bisexual population had no illusions about the permanence of their sexual habits. Interviewers asked 47 male bisexuals: "Is it possible that someday you could behave either exclusively homosexual or exclusively heterosexual?" *Eighty-five percent* answered yes (Weinberg *et al.*, pages 33, 317).

> Five years later, the investigators actually re-interviewed the same respondents to estimate the shifts or stability of their sexual lives. "*[C]lose to 90 percent* of the men reported a change in the direction of their sexual behavior" (*ibid.*, page 219, italics added). Included in the reasons for change were new friendships, and new social opportunities that came with a change in jobs. Some men said they had decided "that the heterosexual label more accurately fit them; [they cited] problems of self-acceptance . . . undergoing therapy, a spiritual transformation, a desire for monogamy, wanting a traditional marriage, and having a baby" (*ibid*, page 222).

Shifts in sexual orientation over the lifespan--spontaneous or situational--are amply documented in both this Chapter and in the next. These facts collide with the claim that homosexuality is a fixed condition. For many individuals, a homosexual orientation may be a stable and lifelong characteristic. But from the standpoint of theory-building, it is necessary to respect the evidence that sexual impulses and habits often change over time, in a way that is quite different from handedness or eye color, or diabetes or pattern baldness.

Martin S. Weinberg, staff member of The Kinsey Institute, after many years of sex research, concluded (Weinberg *et al.*, page 8): "[L]earning plays a significant part in helping people traverse sexual boundaries . . . and that bisexual activity is inseparable from a social environment that provides varied sexual opportunities."

Proponents of the genetic hypothesis use two arguments to defend their viewpoint against erosion by the facts of bisexual activity: (1) Bisexual activity is the sign of a gay man's struggle against accepting his "true" homosexual impulses. (2) Bisexuality, like heterosexuality, is a separate and different sexual orientation. The evidence, however, does not support these arguments. Variation in male sexual activity exists in an unbroken continuum, as the famous Kinsey Scale indicates. This variation results from the interaction of both genetic and environmental factors, and what we call "bisexuality" describes practices characteristic of the middle areas of the Kinsey Scale. Our chosen topic is a complex one, and it does not serve our understanding of it to ignore its complexities. Simon LeVay (1996, page 55) acknowledges that the diversity and fluctuations of sexual orientation indicate that apart from genetic influences, human sexuality is also the product of "non-genetic influences." By "non-genetic influences" could LeVay be referring to *life experience*?

NOTES TO CHAPTER 14

1. Marjorie Garber reports (page 276) that when LeVay, who defends the genetic hypothesis, was challenged to explain how "a 40-year-old guy who's married and with children" can one day come out as gay, LeVay "compares the gayness of such men to other genetic traits, like that of adult diabetes, that do not manifest themselves until later in life. [Said LeVay:] 'Their sexuality is probably just as genetically loaded as are kids who realize they are gay when they are 12 years old.'" A comparison of homosexuality with diabetes is unfortunate because (a) diabetes, unlike homosexuality, does not come and go, and (b) diabetes is a degenerative disease.

2. Test-retest is, of course, a standard practice in psychological research to measure the consistency, or reliability, of one's findings. Practical considerations, unfortunately, often rule out the scientific precision of test-retest.

3. Although he admits that a shift from straight to gay desire may be a regression brought about by an emotional crisis, Clark (page 109) exercises his gay-positive outlook by adding that this shift also betokens a new freedom from social restraint, a new sophistication that recognizes homosexuality as an alternative lifestyle.

4. Patterned and predictable homosexual practices regularly emerge in prison populations. The more aggressive prisoners recruit anyone who is youthful looking, or delicate, to serve their sexual needs. A strict distinction is maintained between men and "girls." Men perform anal penetration; "girls" fellate men.

Heger reports that in the Nazi concentration camps of World War II, there was widespread same-sex practice. Camp guards adopted homosexual inmates to serve their sexual needs in exchange for extra food and special treatment. Ironically, in a place intended to detain men for having committed the "crime" of homosexuality, guards actually recruited young local boys (Polish boys, for example) and seduced them into performing homosexual acts in exchange for extra food and protection from harm.

5. Klein (page 142) expresses indignation that bisexual men have been 'wrongly' labeled homosexual. The distinction is, in fact, arbitrary. Most gay men have had some heterosexual experience, and others shift back and forth in their choice of sexual partners.

6. The fact that a man invites another man to share his sex partner, a convention known as troilism, is psychoanalytically considered an indirect expression of

homosexuality. It is therefore not surprising that this recreation leads to same-sex play.

7. In most cases, no doubt, a man whose wife was no longer interested in sex, looks for an available (and suitable) woman, even though a male partner might be easier to find and engage.

8. Can a couple "make love" without "going all the way?" Of course; in its older meaning, "making love" referred to kissing, embracing, caressing, fondling, and words of endearment.

9. Lane's change in sexual orientation is described by Liss and Welner as a spontaneous change rather than a therapeutic success, even though the patient had originally asked for help in overcoming his homosexual habit. After a lapse of treatment, he had returned with a complaint of anxiety and depression, and was then given supportive therapy only. Here is a more detailed summary of the case, paraphrased from Liss and Welner's report:

> Lane was born in a small Missouri town, the only child of parents who had been childless for 15 years of marriage. As a young child, he spent much time with his mother, playing with dolls and engaging in other "feminine activities" with her (Liss and Welner, page 102). His father showed no interest in helping Lane learn to play baseball or master other masculine skills.
>
> He recalls that at the age of four he played games with both girls and boys and engaged in mutual exploration with boys. At ten he was participating in mutual masturbation with one or two special boy friends. At 12 he believed that he was homosexual. He had progressive erotic interest in males from this time on, developed a preference for a masculine male type, and had homosexual fantasies. At 15 his sexual activity also progressed from mutual masturbation to homosexual oral-genital relations and anal intercourse. He enjoyed being the passive member but could also perform the active part. From the age of 15 on until he was 24 he had relations as often as several times a week with multiple partners, but never a prolonged relationship. Because of the community atmosphere on homosexuality he felt compelled to date girls.
> In the last year of high school and before college he trained and practiced as a hairdresser. On one occasion, at the age of 16, he had intercourse with a girl, at her invitation. Subsequently he had the opportunity to have intercourse with this same girl and also another girl but on both occasions he was impotent because he was not aroused. He continued to actively practice gay sex through college, having relations each week with no long-term

relationship. He came for therapy when he was 24 after at least eight years of exclusively homosexual activity, in order to be helped to overcome this tendency so that he could have a family and a heterosexual future.

Lane's therapist prescribed aversive therapy, and also gave him 100 mg of amitriptyline per day or an equivalent antidepressant drug to relieve mild depressive symptoms. He was also encouraged to seek heterosexual partners. Lane visited a prostitute twice but was impotent on both occasions. He continued his homosexual activity. Therapy was interrupted when his therapist left the clinic after four and a half months of treatment.

Three months later, Lane returned to the clinic and reported that his depression and anxiety had increased. He was seen in a series of weekly sessions, devoted entirely to supportive therapy. Lane was encouraged to discuss his daily activities and feelings. The sessions were not explicitly directed toward overcoming homosexuality, and no aversive treatment was given.

Four months later, Lane began spontaneously to notice evidence of sexual interest in women. He began to have erections if he was physically close to a woman. He had previously had many friendly and brotherly relations with girls but now for the first time described a definite erotic feeling toward some of them. This change in behavior was not directly related to the contents discussed in the sessions, and he was not actively encouraged or reinforced to discuss or explore his sexual feelings. For the following six months Lane's sexual behavior was characterized by intermittent homosexual fantasies followed by masturbation or nocturnal emission stimulated by cruising. His reported arousal by women appeared to fluctuate and at times was minimal, especially following homosexual cruising.

Then, unexpectedly, the patient began spontaneously reporting heavy petting, and eventually had intercourse with a close friend's girl friend. Subsequently, for eight months, he had active heterosexual relations, sometimes choosing partners without considering consequences. An occasional episode of premature ejaculation was compensated for by his being able to have more prolonged sexual activity immediately afterwards. The patient continued to be seen at the clinic to discuss daily problems, as he did before; sex is not the major topic. . . . He is now engaged to be married.

10. Personal communication.

15 Homosexual Men Who Marry

In Chapter 13 we described gay men who maintain a long-term partnership with another gay man. Here we will survey what is known about men who identify themselves as gay (or bisexual) and marry a woman, usually with the serious intention of making the marriage last, perhaps to raise a family and gain status in the straight world. Sometimes the wife knows, while at other times, she doesn't.

In other cases, the marriage is for appearances only: the man has his lovers, and so does his wife. Sometimes a gay man will choose a lesbian for a wife, and both derive some of the benefits of a marriage, while respecting each other's sexual habits.

> The grown daughter of gay and lesbian parents "called their story a 'panegyric of marriage' because 'each found permanent and undiluted happiness in the company of the other. If their marriage is seen as a harbor, their [outside] love affairs were mere ports of call; it was there that both were based" (Maddox, page 211).

Interviewing gay men who are or have been married, yields a most diverse range of comments, from enthusiastic endorsement of this tactic to strong warnings against it.

> An old trade unionist, a closeted gay now widowed, says, "I had my arms around her when she died. She never knew. But it wasn't a strain keeping it from her. I've loved and not lost. I couldn't run off. We were married forty-two years. She was a wonderful wife to me'" (Maddox, page 211).

> A divorced gay man, father of four, says to Maddox (page 56): "I think that any girl who even suspects that her boyfriend is homosexual should run in the opposite direction. *They make terrible husbands*. Nobody has ever abandoned homosexuality because of marriage in my experience. Nobody. They always revert to it. It is stronger" (emphasis added).

Is marriage to a woman a sufficiently widespread practice among gay men to justify our study of it here, or is this a phenomenon so rare that the topic is of little theoretical importance? In the 1950s, when Evelyn Hooker was collecting her heterosexual control group, she dropped four married men because they also had "extensive homosexual experience" (Hooker 1957, page 20). A 1987 (April 27, part 2, page 11) article in *The New York Times* describes a New York City support group for wives of gay men. In a 2001 publication, the director of a San Francisco support group for women married to gay men estimated that 4,300 wives and husbands have contacted her over the past 14 years (Grever, page 9).

In 1983, M.W. Ross estimated, on the basis of a cross-cultural study, that about 15 percent of all gay men either have been or are currently married. Isay (page 105) reports a study of 789 homosexual men, in which 10 percent were married. (Isay notes that at the time of their marriage, 60 percent of the wives were not aware of their husband's homosexuality.)

What makes the phenomenon of gay men who marry relevant to this study? Because here, too, we witness the enormous psychological diversity of men who identify themselves as homosexual, a phenomenon that is central to our thesis: that homosexual behavior does not show the uniformity of an inherited trait but displays a diversity of habit patterns that are more likely to be the interaction of both genetic and environmental factors. One example of this diversity of the married homosexual population is that it includes (a) men who at the time they married wondered whether they were really homosexual, (b) men who knew they were homosexual, and (c) *men who claim that they never experienced homosexual attractions until many years after they were married to a woman.*

Many young men who marry are not very sophisticated or insightful about their sexual needs. They see that friends, whom they used to "fool around with" as teenagers are giving up the same-sex horseplay of their adolescence, and entering the young adult world of courtship and marriage. They say to themselves: "If they can do it, why can't I?"

Perhaps an optimistic minister, or a well-meaning doctor, has advised them that a good wife will put an end to their bothersome homosexual attractions.

> A homosexual, now married, had told a doctor about his problem, "and he said to me, 'Oh, that's nothing! All you need is a girl you like very much. You get married and it's all over.' So I did as he told me, but it was not over." (H.L. Ross, page 388.)

> When George married Lucy, he was not a double-dealer. "I wasn't trying to fool anybody," he says. "I just suppose I successfully fooled myself . . . for a while. I had had contact with other men, but I had written these off as unimportant--as a lot of homosexuals seem to do: they think, It's a temporary thing, but not really me. It never really crossed my mind, growing up, that homosexuality would disqualify me for marriage. When the thoughts got too uncomfortable I just shut them out" (Maddox, pages 28-29).

Why do homosexual men marry? Many men feel free to marry even though they are in the habit of allowing themselves to be serviced by homosexuals in the once-popular tradition of "trade," described by Humphreys, Chauncey, and others. Trade insist that they are heterosexual, and would even deny that they are bisexual. This activity was discussed in Chapter 5.

Some men who regard themselves as homosexual marry because they find the gay world uncomfortable. They would rather live in the mainstream of straight society, become a husband and father, and pursue a clandestine homosexual life. They may enjoy a mutually affectionate relationship with their wife, cuddle with her, perhaps even have sexual intercourse with her. Maybe she learns about his "other life," maybe not.

> I've been gay as far back as I can remember. I haven't had sex with my wife for twenty years. All my sex is with men, and mostly with one man. Still, I sleep with my wife every night, cuddle with her, care about her and lead the life of a pillar of the community. I'm gay but my life isn't (Brownfain, page 179).

> I'm gay on the inside and straight on the outside. But its on the outside that I live my life. The things I value most are my kids, my marriage, my job and social life (*ibid.*, page 179).

> I've always been gay but I was programmed to marry. That program is just as powerful as my sexual desires. Just say I'm a gay man who is able to have sex with one woman (*ibid.*, page 179).

What makes a gay man decide to look for a wife? It has been noted (Grever, page 42) that gay men who are also British aristocrats have special reasons to marry: to make their social position more secure, to perpetuate a prestigious family name, and to secure their inheritance.

An evolutionary point of view would suggest that the desire to raise a family is deeply rooted in human nature. It is an important motivator in the lives of a sizeable majority of men, regardless of social position or sexual orientation. So concludes Brenda Maddox (pages 55-56), investigative journalist who interviewed in depth 47 married homosexuals. "In the closet or out, most [of the 47] homosexuals interviewed . . . declared frankly that one of their reasons for marrying was the desire for children. For some it was the only reason." As Brownfain's respondent put it, he felt "programmed to marry."

> A formerly married homosexual tells Maddox (pages 56-57): "I knew I was bisexual since I was seven. I knew I had a very strong attraction to my own sex. I *always* wanted to marry. I always wanted children." The father of a girl and a boy, he recalls: "I absolutely adored being a father" (Maddox, pages 55-56).

One divorced gay man, totally committed to the gay life style, keeps photographs of his handsome children around to display to the partners whom he brings home. He wants to show off what he's got. *Almost every homosexual father interviewed for this book brought out pictures of his children* (*ibid*, page135, emphasis added).

Most said that if starting out now, they would not marry, but that fatherhood was one of the pleasures they would not have missed. "I can't regret my marriage, because that would mean regretting my children. They are the joy of my life," said a social worker (*ibid*, page 135).

A married homosexual man reflected, "One of the reasons I married is that I wanted [to be] a father for a family. I was very lonely and wanted a nest. Nlow I have a nest, but it is a love nest only when my [homosexual] friend is there" (H.L. Ross, page 388).

Hallam Tennyson, great-grandson of the poet . . . gives talks at homosexual meetings in London [accompanied by] his daughter Ros. He is divorced. "My children are to me the miracle of all time. Ros and Jonny are straight, but, perhaps because I'm gay, they have a natural identification with the handicapped of society. I loved bringing them up. My nostalgia now is not for my own childhood, but for theirs: it was one of the happiest times of my life" (*ibid*, page 135).

There are young men who have experienced both gay and straight sex, are not quite decided about their sexual orientation, and hope that getting married will help them make up their mind. Or they may be in a state of "wavering denial"[1] of their gay tendencies, and hope that getting married with her will activate their "latent heterosexuality." They know they were capable of heterosexual arousal, they marry a woman they find attractive, and after an active sex life with her for a few years, once more begin looking for homosexual experience to supplement or replace their married sex life. Sometimes they continue to feel a strong bond of affection with their wife and children.

Grever's study led her to conclude (page 34) that some homosexual men marry as an expression of denial. "Disturbed or frightened by their feelings, they may believe that marriage will help their same-sex desire disappear. They may want to change this aspect of themselves and believe that a sexual and marital commitment to a woman will achieve this difference."

The fact that a man is gay does not mean he is unmoved by feminine charms. On this subject, a married gay man is quoted by Maddox (pages 29-30) as follows:

> I've never been repulsed by women at all--I've always found
> them very pleasant to be with, and still do. I'm not really sexual-
> ly attracted to them, but I am attracted to their femininity, good
> looks and charm.

Tallying the many reasons why a gay man might marry a woman, Grever (page 44) reminds her reader: "[W]e must not ignore love! Sincere affection and abiding love are often expressed by many gay/straight couples, both before and after disclosure of the man's homosexuality. Obviously, homosexual and hetero-sexual men may marry for many of the same traditional reasons."

At the conclusion of her study, Maddox writes (pages 211-212): "What is clear . . . is that many homosexuals, in or out of the closet . . . feel that the two sexes are needed to make a home, and that marriage is their goal, if only they can find the right person." Her in-depth interviews led her to conjecture that "there may . . . be a complementarity between the sexes that . . . draws them to each other."

M.W. Ross compared 21 married British homosexuals, with 21 who were never married, and found (as expected) that the homosexuals who married were more conservative and had a more negative attitude toward homosexuality. He also surveyed homosexual men in Sweden, Finland, and Australia, and noted what percentage of them were married. As predicted, Ross found that the more tolerant the country, the less likely it was for a homosexual to marry.[2]

Richard Isay (page 107), the gay-affirmative analyst, regards marriage as "a worthwhile compromise for some gay men." They may find a woman they feel a genuine love and affection for, "even though there is no erotic attraction." They may willingly acquiesce to the value that their family members and friends place on marriage. They may have had a bad homosexual partnership, and vaguely feel that there is something unsatisfying about homosexuality, even though it contin-ues to occupy their fantasies. Isay warns, however, that the consequences may be disastrous for a functioning homosexual to marry "simply for the sake of con-forming with the accepted structure of society or in the hope of curing his con-dition . . . ." (Isay, page 108).

Clark (pages 258-259) notes that most gay men who marry women do so "in good faith, having been led to believe that [their] heterosexual feelings combined with love for [their] intended were proof that [their] gay feelings could and should be discounted as being not very important. Most of [them] were taught by books, therapists, counselors and cultural mythology that if one has both hetero-sexual and homosexual feelings and there is real love on the heterosexual side, then the homosexuality is just a phase. It is the experimentation or fooling around reported in novels and biographies detailing boarding school days. It is that harmless childhood infatuation with a friend or older idol that helps one learn one's proper sex role through identification. At worst, we are told we were developmentally delayed or a bit confused, but a good heterosexual marriage should take care of all of that."

"Trapped in a miserable marriage." Brian Miller (Humphreys and Miller, page 151) laments that many homosexual men "enter into marital unions thinking they can repress or overcome their homoerotic desires. Nearly all [says Miller] report that they married beause they perceived that as the only viable means of achieving a stable home life, loyal companionship, and the pleasures of fatherhood. On the other hand, they perceived the gay world as 'transitory,' 'shallow,' and 'ridden wth violence.'" Unable to establish themselves as members of a gay community, they are reduced to seeking homosexual contacts in marginal, dangerous, or grossly inappropriate places, where they risk physical assault or arrest for "lewd and lascivious conduct." For example, Miller tells of a married homosexual who was beaten up for propositioning the best man at his daughter's wedding. The distressed spouse, aware of her husband's homosexuality, "feels she cannot leave him because of a combination of religious and financial reasons."

To tell or not to tell. If a man chooses not to tell his prospective wife, he might be wishfully hoping "to put his past behind him," and get a fresh start as a husband and lover. He may fear that disclosure of his homosexual past would be emotionally disturbing to his wife, and spoil their chances of making the marriage work. He might be engaging in a simple act of denial: "it isn't important, it doesn't matter." He may rationalize: "Does a woman tell her prospective husband everything about her past: her past affair(s)? abortions? childhood illnesses? family illnesses?"

Eichberg advises that if a gay person wants to marry and have children, he must openly discuss his sexual orientation with his prospective wife. Otherwise, when she discovers that her husband has withheld from her an important fact about him, she will justifiably feel that she has been fooled, duped, and manipulated.

> [T]he most loving thing to do is to discuss this openly prior to marriage. This is an act of love and respect for your intended spouse, since it gives that person clear choices in terms of the form of the relationship. . . Not discussing one's sexual orientation before marriage, like withholding any other information that may lead the other person away from a commitment, is a manipulation. . . (Eichberg, page 161).

What do we know about women who marry homosexual men?

Sometimes a woman falls in love with a man whom she knows is gay, and wants to marry him, convinced that her love will change him. Maddox, who interviewed about 25 women who married homosexuals generalizes (pages 64-65): These women "tend to be virgins when they marry, or close to it: no critics of performance, but rather nice plain girls who want a home and children, who are sexually inexperienced and have never wanted sex so much that they could not do without it, and who are prepared to overlook a lot for a nice companionable man who is not trying to jump them."

Myra S. Hatterer, a psychiatrist who interviewed a dozen wives of homosexuals, reports that these 12 women *without exception* were sexually and socially inexperienced prior to marriage, and considered themselves as failures in competing with other women for men. Their mothers had low self-esteem, seemingly victims in their own marriage. Their fathers were tyrannical, seductive and ineffectual as males, sometimes bisexual or homosexual themselves (paraphrased from Maddox, pages 64-65).

Marriage to a gay man may demand so many compromises, and carry such risks, it requires more than a tincture of masochism to play the role of wife to an active homosexual. For example, one of Maddox's respondents (we will call him Zack) spoke proudly of how well his married life was going, how sexually satisfied is his wife, how successfully they are raising their family, and how uncomplaining his wife is about the STDs (sexually transmitted diseases) she has contracted from him. The husband is a journalist who does much traveling and usually practices his active gay life in other cities. His uncomplaining wife is a schoolteacher who devotes herself to school and local youth clubs. Here is Maddox's record of his story (pages 71-72):

Zack

My wife knows [about my gay life], but she is a remarkable woman. . . . a very private person. Her attitude has made it easy for me. I have the best of both worlds. . . . I am faithful to my wife. I sleep with my wife. There are just some things I need that she can't supply. . . She accepts [my habit of cruising] and lives with it because she loves me. I have had every sort of venereal disease. And have passed them all on to my wife. She's never complained. It's a measure of the sort of woman she is. She's had treatment; we've been to the same VD clinic. . . . We never talk about divorce. I've no regrets. I'm very conscious of how fortunate I am. I'm very happy at home and with our relationship.

When the truth is out. Carol Grever, who was married for 35 years before she discovered that her husband was gay, made a study of the phenomenon and estimated (page 9) that in as many as two million couples in this country, the husband is gay. Grever asserts (page 16) that when a woman learns that her husband is gay, either through his admission or when it becomes obvious, in 85 percent of the cases this fact leads to separation, immediately or after a short while. "[T]he remaining 15 percent continue their marriage, usually with some mutually devised alternative strategy."

Deciding to stay together only because of the children "is almost always a bad idea," says Clark (page 261). But the marriage may be a very good one in many other ways, Clark continues, and if the wife is not too homophobic, she should consider staying together. If the couple does stay together, the marriage could be just as sexual and as sharing as it was before. Of course, marriages change from year to year anyway, and "changes are not likely to be the sole result of the disclosure" that the husband is gay (Clark, page 261).

There is an enormous range of a woman's reactions to the knowledge that her husband is homosexual. Some wives of gay men readily accept their husband's homosexual needs, and some are even relieved to know that they are not competing with another woman. Some worry about their husband's health or safety. At the other extreme are wives who reacted with deep emotional suffering. Here are the statements of two of Grever's respondents:

> "The inequity of the whole situation wounded me terribly. I felt lonely and cheated. Worse, I felt utterly inauthentic, pretending to the outer world that our marriage was ideal, knowing that it wasn't even a marriage. Lies and half-truths were a daily necessity. I couldn't even talk honestly with my own mother. There was no security anywhere" (Grever, page 31).

> Said another wife: "I was suffocating in the closet of secrecy" (*ibid.*, page 33).

Suppose the wife knew her husband is gay, but didn't realize how involved--socially, emotionally, and sexually--he must be with other gay people. Or how much personal freedom he needs to conduct his gay life. At this point, the wife "may need to claim the same freedom at this point, or . . . she may find the gay spouse's freedom intolerable" (Clark, page 261).

If the couple decides to stay married, all sorts of questions come up: How much does the wife want to know? With whom (*e.g.*, friends, relatives, children) will they share this information? Clark (page 262) offers the advice: "[R]emember to respect one another and to offer mutual support during this sorting period. It is also a good idea to set aside quiet times of appreciation during which you enjoy your relationship rather than examine it. When it all seems too taxing and complex, and it will, think whether you would change places willingly with bored couples who seem to have nothing left to say to one another."

Some men tell their prospective wife of their homosexual attractions before they marry; others do not. Maddox (page 72) generalizes that if a man tells a woman before marriage that he is gay, she often brushes the information aside and assures him that he will grow out of it, or that she promises to be tolerant. Some wives learn about their husband's bisexuality accidentally. Grever observed (page 58) that "many homosexual husbands leave clues about their true identity, sometimes for years before they come out. It almost seems that they want their orientation to be discovered by their wives, avoiding the pain of putting the truth into words. There is a gradual buildup to disclosure--perhaps a cache of homosexual magazines discovered in the bedroom or the sudden development of new, single friends. "My husband, Jim, [Grever recalls] [suddenly] became passionate about volunteer work with our city's AIDS Project. . . . [H]e volunteered in the office . . . and became a major donor. Why the sudden interest in this particular cause? . . . Perhaps these husbands leave clues because they fear telling the truth, thus inducing even more guilt and anxiety."

A shocking discovery of her husband's secret life sometimes evokes a response that is less than friendly:

> She caught me in the act after we were married one year--walked in when she was supposed to be at work. She never let me forget in spite of all her whoring around. Well, we raised our kids and now [after 24 years] we're stuck with each other. When we fight we threaten to split, but it hasn't happened so far. It could be worse (Brownfain, page 183).

> I told my wife before we married. We were in our last year of college and we both thought we were sophisticated. She said, "It's no big thing, not if you love me." To me trust is part of love. The marriage [after 12 years] is working fine. I get carried away at times. She doesn't say anything, just gets quiet, and I get back on track" (*ibid.*, pages 182-183).

> I'm a Christian. . . so I told her. We were both 19 and she didn't know what the hell it was all about. Neither did I. But she never forgot I told her and she's never learned anything since [in 29 years of marriage]. It was the worst thing I could do. She watches me like a hawk. I put up with it because I know she really loves me. I can't say I love her the same way, but I do care (*ibid.*, pages 182-183).

> I love my wife [of 12 years] but she's a terrible bigot about everything that doesn't fit her narrow concept of life. I just do what I have to do when I'm out of town. It takes nothing away from her and she's got no complaints. . . . This is my hobby (*ibid.*, page 183).

Brownfain, who studied a group of 60 married bisexuals, interviewed eight wives who knew about their husband's homosexual activities. Their awareness began "with a mingling of shock, disbelief, anger, resentment, and rage, moving on to gradual understanding, and finally acceptance in varying degrees" (Brownfain, pages 183-184). Several claimed not to understand homosexuality but "depended on love and their religious beliefs to see them through" (*ibid.*, page 184). Most expressed the hope that he would never fall in love with his gay partner, and were relieved that their husband was not involved with another woman. A married man with a gay lover isn't usually under pressure to choose. "The Other Woman" usually makes her lover choose between his wife and her.

Wives worried about their husbands going to dangerous places in town, staying out too late, or bringing home venereal disease. They hoped their spouse's "outside activities" would not lead to the neglect of his wife and children.

A 1997 article calls upon heterosexual women married to gay men, to use their unique positon "to teach [socicty] the true meaning of full acceptace of all sexual orientations" (Vennard, page 14).

Living in two worlds

With some men in chronic conflict over their homosexual impulses, marriage is a gesture of denial.[3] Some men use out-of-town business trips to conceal occasional homosexual binges. Some of these men "do come out of the closet during middle age, often when they've achieved considerable financial success, and may even have started a family" (Socarides 1995, page 68).

Some men do manage to stop their homosexual activity when they marry. Others get married but venture out to make a homosexual contact from time to time. Some men risk getting married, even though their homosexual habits and impulses are so strong that they are bound to interfere with married life. Sometimes the help of a therapist is sought, and together they face a life problem that in some instances has no easy answers.

> Whether to continue the marriage or get a divorce or continue
> the marriage while the husband is in treatment are among the
> most difficult clinical problems to be faced. These decisions are
> particularly difficult in cases in which there are children. If the
> couple divorces and the man lives as a homosexual, decisions
> about when, if, and how to convey information about the
> patient's lifestyle are issues to be evaluated (Sanders, page 354).

John Paulk (page 60) tells of this encounter when he was the employee of a gay escort service. We will call his client Rex:

Rex
One night I went to the home of a very nice, straight-seeming man, who told me all about his wife and two children. . . . [H]e

showed me pictures of his wife all around the house. I was puzzled; in fact, I asked, "Why am I here?"

He explained that he'd had an intense relationship with a male lover back in college. Then his lover died in a car accident. He'd never gotten over the man's death and had never pursued another such relationship. Eventually he'd gotten married. "But I'm gay," he said. "I've kept it a secret all this time. I don't want to get deeply involved with any other man. My college lover was the only person I ever really cared for or ever will."

Tom

Nicolosi documents the case of Tom, age 40, a successful business owner, who was content to lead a double life of gay man (he was in a relationship with a 24-year-old employee), and a husband and father of two children. He sought Nicolosi's help when his wife learned about his secret life and demanded a separation. This was not the first time he sought the help of a therapist. He had seen several therapists before, and their tactic was to reconcile Tom with his condition, to help him to "learn to live with it:"

[A therapist] told me I must accept my sexual orientation. But where did that advice leave me? Outside affairs with men are incompatible with my marriage. For years I tried to live in two worlds. That therapist left me sitting on a picket fence--with the sharp end up my ass (Nicolosi 1993. page 194).

[The therapist advised me,] "Live with it. Others have lived with it, so can you." I said to him, "But I can't." He said, "You have to accept it, because you cannot change what you feel. This *is you*, and you have to be true to yourself" (Nicolosi 1993, page 195).

Claude

Howard Brown (page 115) tells of a gay man, a physician who had been actively homosexual for nine years before he married. "Claude has been married for fourteen years now and has three children, of whom he is immensely fond and proud. Each time we meet, he tells me that he greatly prefers his heterosexual life to his former gay life but that he still considers himself a homosexual. Why? 'I enjoy sex with my wife,' Claude told me, 'but my dreams and all of my fantasies are gay. And I still have homosexual urges that are just too strong to deny. About once a month I have to make love with a man.'"

A design for living. Maddox (pages 83-84) interviewed a woman, age 45, a New York City advertising executive, who for ten years had been "best friends" with a gay man: holding hands, kissing, cuddling, spending weekends and traveling together. Her constant companion makes no sexual demands, and that seems to suit her so well that she would gladly marry him if only he would ask, and they could "spell out in detail both our roles."

Agnes

We've spent weekends together in his apartment, and we've taken trips together. . . . We hold hands and kiss (he's a "toucher" and so am I) but we've never had sex. He is more fun to be with than any person I've ever known. He sends me flowers and candy and expensive presents. I would drop everything to go wherever and whenever he suggests. . . He lives alone, *but most of his male friends are gay*. He makes good money at his job with a major network, but I know he's lonely--although he puts up a good front. He gets upset if I happen to be busy--even when he calls at the last minute. . . . [W]e see each other constantly, and the subject [of marriage] could very well come up. He always wants me to be with him at company parties and dinners -so much of his life is in the totally "straight" world populated by wives. . . . I'm afraid I wouldn't want our [married] life together shared with gays en masse--although I like most of his gay friends. I would also be a bit afraid that marriage to Hal would make me more possessive of him. . . . [W]e'd have to spell out in detail both our roles, and each partner [would] promise to play his faithfully. That's the only way marriage to Hal could work for me. But if we did make it work, *life would sure be full of fun!* (emphasis added)

Signorile, a journalist who has made a specialty of ferreting out closeted homosexuals, reports (1993, pages 211-212) on two elected officials in Washington, D.C.,[4] who are in fact gay. Elected official #1 is married to a woman who is "completely aware of the circumstances and accepts them. They have several children, who have kept her busy, and her life has always been separate from her husband's." Her husband's senior aide is also his lover, and they are inseparable. Signorile adds: "This official has not only voted anti-gay but has supported the most horrendous homophobes in America."

Official #2 is a closeted Congressman with a good voting record on gay rights. He is married to a woman and denies having married just for cover. "She was someone that I'd been really close to for a very long time. We had a close friendship," he says, admitting "It was not really romantic."

She wanted to get married and it was certainly a good move for her, marrying a congressman, and there were many parts of the marriage that were very good. That is no longer the case. It

became a frustrating situation for her. She did have romantic
interests with others--and so did I.

Even to a divorced gay man, there may be advantages to having once been married. Dan Woog (page 85) reports that a gay teacher who was once married and
is also a parent, believes that "having a daughter helps legitimatize him in the
eyes of some members of the school community."

White (page 4) recalls three gay friends who "married quite successfully, but
. . . never entirely abandoned gay life." Comments White (page 313) on gay men
who marry: "[M]any marriages, especially in highly visible professions such as
the arts, politics and fashion, are fronts for gay men; if they're to be successful
the wife must enter into the arrangement clear-eyed, knowing it's in part a business deal. She should be the sort of woman who prefers money and status to
romance, or who doesn't mind seeking love from an outside lover. . . . [Such marriages can also be very close.] A few years ago a famous conductor shocked
everyone with the sincerity of his grief after his wife's death. Everyone had
assumed the marriage had been cynical, but he was inconsolable and went to bed
for a month."

Duane

Duane is a gay man who very deliberately got married during the 1950s,
when he was 24 and his wife was 20. Their marriage was *not* a social cover but
important to him because he *wanted to raise a family*. In a lengthy interview with
the writer Stambolian (pages 62-72), he tells how he was attracted to a shy, naive
girl of 19, how deeply he enjoyed the role of fatherhood, and how, toward the
end of the marriage, he planned an exit strategy (revealed in the passage below)
that would minimize his wife's emotional pain. His testimony also suggests that
the success of his "design for living" required a certain level of affluence. (For
example, he pursued a gay lifestyle in the city while his wife and children were
living in their country home.) Here are some excerpts from Duane's testimony:

> [T]he great majority of my sexual experiences were with men . .
> . [though I also dated girls.] I can't really say I had a desire for
> them, but seeing women was much more comfortable because
> there were guidelines. . . . I guess I wanted . . . everything. I did-
> n't want to be limited to social situations where only single or
> gay men could be. I thought that dating and eventually marriage
> would allow me a fuller social and personal life as well as a vari-
> ety of other things, high among them children.

> [At age 23,] I had been through six years of gay life and gay sex
> without finding any joy. Also I was not an especially handsome
> young man. I really didn't fit into the pretty young . . . gay scene

of the time. I found what was around me to be silly. . . . *Women found me attractive. . .* Men seemed to be interested only in my youth and my big dick (emphasis added).

[T]hen I met my wife on a blind date. She was nineteen and I was twenty-two. She was malleable clay, and she looked up to me, and that made me feel very good. She was extremely shy and quiet, which forced me to speak a great deal, even though I was also a shy and awkward kid. After our first date, I didn't see her for a couple of months, then one evening at a concert, *she* came to me to say hello. I was being *chased* by this girl, and that made me feel good, too. Within two months I had made the decision that she was going to be my wife. We were married about thirteen months after that.

She also had the kind of wonderful family I had always wanted [Duane's parents divorced after four years of marriage], and they accepted me as a son.

[My first years of marriage] was like walking through a movie. We did all the things typical young marrieds did in that period. We had married friends, dinner parties, went out a lot. And at home we got along very well. I learned how to share life with another person, and I enjoyed learning that and being with her. When our first son was born two years after the marriage, he became the focus of our lives. I can't accurately describe the feeling of pride and love my wife and I shared that first year after his birth. He was a beautiful, alert baby, and I remember clearly thinking of him as a miracle.

[M]y marriage became more real to me, and my warmth and affection for my wife grew even more. . . . I was more than happy to do the early morning feedings, the diaper changes, anything to show my wife how pleased I was, how I appreciated her awkward pregnancy and difficult delivery. . . During that period, I was almost totally content except for one gnawing thing--I could not will away my desire for sex with a man.

[Eventually, Duane went to the baths for gay sex, and for a time felt that he was now living "a fuller life." When Duane suffered a serious heart attack, he decided] that I wanted to lead the rest of my life, whatever life I had left, as a homosexual. But then I discovered that my wife was pregnant with our third child. That put the decision completely aside. The one thing I would not do would be to abandon the baby. I arbitrarily chose to stay married another five years, enough time for the child to get at least a start within a family unit. Given my own experience as a child, this was vital.

[Meanwhile, Duane's wife, who had been a shy 19-year-old when they met, was now] her own person . . . less withdrawn and more socially active. She was a mother, and that meant a great deal to her. . . . [Their third child was "difficult and cranky" and after a year, his wife "broke down and said she had to get out of the house. . . "]

[W]e got someone to take care of the kids, and with my insistence she went back to school. . . [W]e owned a second home where she and the children spent summers, so I was able to have gay sexual activity when I was alone in the city.

I had never experienced lust for my wife, even though I was able to perform sexually with her quite successfully. I was always comfortable with the female body . . . but I knew I preferred fucking men. Men's asses, not just the fucking of them but their visual quality, are far more exciting to me than any part of a woman's body. I can enjoy a woman's body intellectually and emotionally, and I can appreciate its beauty, but a man's ass has the greatest erotic appeal for me. [Duane decided "to keep his sexuality secret" from his wife because he sensed that she wouldn't understand. She would want to set rules about what he could or couldn't do. It would be painful to her, and restrictive to him.]

[When Duane felt it was time to separate, he decided] that she had to ask me to leave . . . I would not be the one to ask. . . . [That] would hurt her even more. If I left because she told me to go, she would have a greater sense of pride. Duane had been staying out a lot, and they were now fighting a lot. Finally she asked, "Don't you think it would be better if you left?" [Relieved, Duane replied: "Yes, I think so." He recalls, "It was very painful, for both of us."]

[They discussed their separation, their plans for their children, and agreed that a formal divorce was unnecessary. It seemed to come as a surprise to her that Duane then said to her "I had been considering trying sex with men (not quite true), and if it was successful, I would probably be living the rest of my life as a homosexual."]

[Duane's wife seemed to have no concept of how gay men lived. "Would I now proceed to walk around town wearing dresses?" She consulted a psychiatrist about what to tell their children about their father.

[At the beginning of their separation, Duane's wife was morose.]
She didn't know where to go or what to do. But she has now
completed her education and found a wonderful job, and within
two months of our separation, she met a man whom she's still
seeing. . . I think she's finally experiencing what I could never
give her--a man who truly desires her, who lusts after her sexually.

[Duane reflects that now that he is separated,] I would be happy
to find a truly adult male homosexual . . . [worthy of being a life
partner. When he tells gay men he's still raising children, they]
often say, "How wonderful. I love children!" But when I tell
them I can't see them this weekend because I have to be with my
children, and that I don't know them well enough yet to incorporate them into the life of my family, there is resentment.

[After describing many years of marriage that began with
warmth and affection and ended with quarreling and separation,
Duane reflects:] I wanted children. I was willing to turn worlds
upside down to have them. I love my sons, and I hope that love
will continue to grow. They are the only people in my life who
have truly never disappointed me. . . . It's been a joy being with
them. I have no regrets.

[Of his three sons, Duane says:] We are very close. I've spent a
lot of time and energy with them because I've wanted to,
because they're wonderful, delightful children. And they seem to
be very fond of me. . . . [Duane hopes his sons will accept their
father's homosexuality when they learn of it, but Duane hopes
they don't think] that if daddy is gay, then it's all right for them
to be gay. *I don't want that . . . for the same reasons that I
wouldn't want my sons to be black. It's a harder life* (emphasis
added).

[Duane's interviewer asked him to talk about how he felt about
his sons. His rambling recollections included the words:] When
they were kids, we always played ball together, and I enjoyed it
and enjoyed watching them enjoy it. We don't play at sports anymore or visit museums. They do that with friends now. There are
no more tears to wipe away, and kissing them is more awkward
now, for them, never for me. I suppose the thing I love about
them now is that I've watched it all happen. . . . I'm proud of
them and pleased with who they are, and they are each very different. In common, they have kind hearts, and that is important
to me. Their mother and I have, together and separately, con-

sciously and unconsciously, molded three young men. Judging by comments from teachers and friends, so far it is a job well done, and the job seems to be about over.

[On a weekend vacation morning, Duane watched his boys asleep. His] oldest son kicked off his blankets and rolled over on his back clutching his hard-on, which had found its way out of the opening in his pajamas. I smiled thinking of myself at his age and of all the places my dick has been since. Where and how would he choose to use his? And his brothers? Would they be happy?

Dr. Fred

Eichberg (page 75) writes of Dr. Fred, a medical doctor who regarded himself as bisexual. The woman he married knew about his sexual orientation. They had three children. At the time she died, Dr. Fred was in practice with his eldest son. Now widowed, Dr. Fred decided that he would now come out as a gay man. In his letter to his three children, he explains that their mother knew about his sexual orientation:

[Y]es, Mother knew [I was bisexual]. *In fact . . . this I really think helped to make our marriage especially close. As you know, we shared a lot of love together* (emphasis added).

But those days with Mom are over. After she passed away, my life has come to have a different meaning for me. I have decided to live the remaining period of my life in a way that will give me most satisfaction.

I have never regretted my marriage, nor the fathering of you children. I consider myself to have been blessed with a rich life surrounded by loving family.

A rich man has many friends (Proverbs 14:20)

In all countries, wealth and the privilege that goes with it favors extramarital adventures of all sorts: heterosexual *or* homosexual. As a man grows older and gains in both wealth and prestige, expression of his homosexual tendencies becomes increasingly easier. Wealth attracts younger men. Where money is no problem, it is easy to arrange clandestine meetings. "High-powered jobs also allow them to travel alone, away from their families" (Grever, page 39).

Among those men who have had no adult homosexual experience before marriage, and had no conscious desire for gay sex until after many years of marriage, the wealth and privilege that may come with middle age leads to a belated activation of their homosexual potential. A man in such a situation may eventually divorce his wife, or quietly supplement his married life with homosexual experience. A British respondent of Maddox, Lionel, illustrates this pattern of experience:

Lionel

Maddox (pages 49-51) documents the case of Lionel, a married man in his late fifties who has been actively homosexual for only the last six years. "Where was homosexuality the first fifty years of my life?" he asks. "Some fantasies, yes, in adolescence, but nothing came of it. *I wasn't fighting back in adult life. I just never thought about it.* I'm not looking for the great homosexual love. . . [either, but] I feel very lucky, I've got a super family and the bonus of having satisfactory sex outlets as well" (emphasis added).

He loves his new life, his interviewer concludes. "He feels healthier, happier, nicer, more relaxed in every way; he is puzzled, in fact that his wife [who knows nothing about Lionel's homosexual life] has not noticed the change in him. 'If I told Jane, it might lessen her respect for me. She's always very caustic when homosexuality is mentioned. . . . It's dishonest, of course, not telling her [or my two daughters] and I am bothered about that.'"

Lionel describes his wife as a woman with a puritanical upbringing and a quick temper. Bright and well-educated, she works as a part-time textbook editor. Lionel comments, "I never felt she got much fun out of life. She derived her satisfaction from books. . . . There was not much sex activity between us ever. She never seemed to enjoy it." This raises an interesting question: Would Lionel have been as likely to seek an outside sex life if his wife were a more gratifying sex partner?

Lionel describes the married side of his life: "At home in the evening, we get out the bourbon and sit out on the patio and talk over the day." When they mingle in public, they are regarded as an interesting couple. Says Lionel: "We complement each other. People are sometimes astonished at us."

In addition to his homosexual social life, Lionel counsels gay men and is active in a gay religious group. He says, "I'm not in constant danger because I'm not wildly promiscuous. I would lose my job if my gayness were found out. . . . I've been active in the homosexual movement because I can make a contribution."

Lionel's job is an important one as jobs go; he is an executive in an electrical-engineering firm, where he manages a big staff and controls a three-million-dollar budget. His position makes it easy for him to find time for homosexuality. "The nature of my job is night committee meetings," he notes. "One or two more aren't noticeable. An afternoon in bed is always possible. My current friend and I go to his place when his wife's away or we go to our beach house. Or hotels. Some of my gay friends have apartments."

Maddox concludes that for six years, Lionel was living "a life finely balanced between security and risk, marriage and homosexuality, fidelity and fun." Any gay man he is in contact with could turn him in and threaten both his economic and social life, he says, but none has ever threatened to do so, and the prospect does not seem to weigh on Lionel's mind. Besides, risk-taking has a special appeal to gay men.

Conservative Christians. Gay men who are also devout and conservative Christians sometimes marry, trusting in the transforming power of faith and prayer to make them a good husband and father. The following two cases fall in this category:

Rolf

"I was leading a homosexual life--cruising, using pornography--but I wanted to get married. I met a woman who found me attractive. She was a 25-year-old school teacher, and wanted to get married. She accepted my proposal; then I lost my nerve and decided to break our engagement. I confessed my problem. We had a long talk, and the result was that our wedding was moved up from December to August. At our wedding, I cried not out of sentiment but out of fear.

"Fortunately, God had given me a woman who loved me and would support me. I learned to be intimate in non-sexual ways, like rubbing her back, or even scratching her back. At first, to become sexually aroused, I had to imagine that I had a male partner. Once my wife said to me, 'You imagine you're having sex with a man.' How did she know?

"I was in therapy for 12 years. I learned that there is a difference between physical attraction and love. One day I looked at my wife and she appealed to me sexually. I knew that my wife was God's gift to me, and He wants me to love her.

"I never really felt bisexual. At first, I had to imagine that my wife was a man, before she appealed to me sexually as a woman. Some homosexuals can perform sexually with a woman, some cannot. There are wide individual differences among homosexuals on this matter" (Oral testimony at an Exodus conference, 1997)

Quincy

Quincy is an American Baptist minister who grew up in a devout Christian home. After high school graduation, he felt called to the ministry, and attended a church-affiliated college and divinity school.

Bright, talented, and good-looking, Quincy enjoyed the company of girls and since high school he did all the right things. While serving in the Army during World War II, he discovered the bisexual side of his nature. After the war, he attended a divinity school. At a dorm prayer meeting, Quincy shared his burdensome secret, and his fellow seminarians responded with fervent prayer and laying on of hands. His same-sex desires seemed to disappear, but they came back. After more prayer meetings, Quincy felt that he was free at last.

In 1949 Quincy met Rose, his future wife, in Greek History 304. "She knew my gay friends," he recalls, and we married in 1953, after four years of friendship, because "we both believed that a good woman could cure gayness in a man." Quincy knew he had been gay but "I thought I was cured--the miracle of transformation," thanks to all the time "I had spent . . . in prayer with my hunky straight friends."

"When we married, sex was like Niagara Falls--exciting and completely satisfying! I loved her and wanted to be with her forever." Hodgkins disease and bad medical treatment destroyed Rose's health. In 1958 she died while pregnant, after only five years of marriage. "Her death was a great loss. I grieved for years; tears always came to my eyes when I visited her mother, who lived to 90."

Quincy never lost touch with his gay and bisexual friends from the Army, college, and seminary. In 1967, nine years after Rose's death, Quincy became sexually active again; he has since had several gay lovers, and in 1998 informed this author that he has been in a relationship that has lasted for eight years (personal communication).

Homosexuality and traditional Jews

To Orthodox Jews, marriage and fatherhood are religious duties, and homosexual tendencies do not exempt a young man from fulfilling these *mitzvoth*. This trait may reduce a man's bargaining power on the marriage market but, as everyday observation very clearly shows (and as gay advocates like to stress), men with homosexual tendencies are often men of intelligence and talent, and have many admirable traits of character and personality. Some women to whom marriage and motherhood are important--and they are very important to an observant Jewish woman--may discover that their best choice is to marry a good man who happens to have homosexual tendencies, but promises to renounce them, just as he renounces eating shellfish or working on the Sabbath.

As the content of this chapter has amply demonstrated, many gay men can be loving husbands, adequate sexual partners, and proud fathers. How they manage their homosexual impulses is another matter. Within an Orthodox context, how a woman responds to being the wife of a man with homosexual tendencies is, likewise, another matter. "Dr. Ruth" Westheimer advises these men to: (1) give marriage a chance, if they can perform sexually with a woman, (2) fantasize having sex with a male partner, if that makes sex more exciting, and (3) *don't* discuss their homosexual tendency with their wife. Orthodox Jewish therapists undoubtedly have extensive clinical experience in dealing with homosexually-prone married Orthodox men, and with their wives, but there is little in the clinical literature on this topic.

> When an Orthodox Jewish man comes into my office and says he is attracted to other men, I ask him, "In your fantasies, can you imagine being with a woman? Can you feel some arousal?" If he says yes but he is also attracted to men, I tell him, "Keep your mouth shut. There is no point in telling that to anyone . . . even if it is a burden on you. When you feel aroused homosexually, try to place the image of a woman in your mind."

> [I]f a traditional Jew with gay fantasies has to be married, and if throughout his life he must place pictures of men into his mind in order to be aroused, difficult or painful as this may be, so be it. . . . [What is important is that he can become aroused with his wife and maintain] a functioning sexual relationship within marriage, as that is a must within the tradition.

> I'm not talking about someone who absolutely cannot achieve an erection with a woman. I'm talking about someone who has never had sex and is attracted to men. If that man desires a cure--and virtually all yeshiva students with this problem do so desire a cure--he can make himself, via his mind, to be sexually functional with a woman. Whether any of this is fair to the women married to these men is another matter (Westheimer, pages 60-62).

Liberal rabbis, on the other hand, now regard homosexuality as an alternative lifestyle, and are increasingly willing to perform "commitment ceremonies" to Jewish gay couples. Orthodox rabbis, and "Dr. Ruth," continue to counsel marriage and parenthood to all young men who are committed to the traditional Jewish life.[5]

Brownfain's married bisexuals

Brownfain interviewed 60 married bisexuals[6] and reports that *one out of five had their first adult homosexual relationship after the age of 40.* One out of ten was 50 years old before experiencing adult gay sex. Several, including those whose initial adult gay sex experience occurred at a somewhat younger age, for years "had not a glimmer of their homosexual potential." Brownfain observes, "This, of course, flies in the face of popular wisdom that our sexual desires are settled once and for all in childhood" (*ibid.*, page 186). Here are some of his abbreviated "clinical notes:"

> [Brownfain (page 184) describes a man of 57 who has had] two marriages and six children. To his consternation and pleasure, at age 55 fell instantly in love with a male graduate student whom he met at a party. The love, obsessive in nature, was unrequited but it did reveal to him *an aspect of his sexuality he had never suspected.* He regards his wife as the great love of his life. She is not opposed to his exploration of the gay world (emphasis added).

> Age 35, happily married for 12 years, two children. One year after marriage, began a sexual relationship with his best friend. They are lovers in an exclusive arrangement, meeting one night a week. Wives know and [the] couples socialize. Stability, regularity, and discretion characterize the marital and extramarital life (*ibid.*, page 184).

> Age 72, married 37 years, three children, seven grandchildren, an elder in the church. Retired at 65. At age 68 took a course at a community college on anthropology of the city. Teacher took class to a gay bar. He was intrigued and returned on his own. Continues to go to gay dance bars and enjoys an active sex life with partners considerably younger that himself. Wife does not comprehend his sudden devotion to dancing and concludes that he is in his second childhood (*ibid.*, page 184).

Over the years 1981-1983, Brownfain studied such a group that held monthly get-togethers in a motel in the metropolitan Detroit area. Its 60 members ranged in age from 30 to 75, and were married for anywhere from 8 to 48 years. All were living in conventional marriages except two who were recently divorced. Members did not limit their gay sex to activities within the group, but engaged in anonymous sex with pickups, or used homosexual prostitutes during out-of-town trips. Why did they resort to casual sex when they were members of a gay sex group? For the same reason that gay men who are in long-term partnerships are also attracted to casual sex: for the thrill, excitement, and variety of risky sex:

> [Brownfain interviewed a 47-year old man who was twice married and the father of two. He was] a frequent visitor of men's

rooms and seeker after glory holes since his adolescence. Highly experienced in homosexual world. His thrill is in the dangers of impersonal sex. Arrested once 15 years ago. Says things are safer now, but dangerous enough to "turn him on" (*ibid.*, page 185).

Brownfain writes (page 185): "The men in this sample were successful in their work, interpersonal relations, and family life. They were comfortable with themselves and did not seriously want to change." All were socially regarded as heterosexual. A few were somewhat effeminate, a few were conspicuously masculine, "but the great majority were in the middle range of unremarkable masculinity" (Brownfain, page 186). The group of 60 included many professional men (physician, dentist, lawyer, professor, clergyman, psychologist, social worker, engineer, teacher), executives, and businessmen, one factory worker, and one farmer.

Although there were many variations in sexual practice, members could be divided into three groups.

(1) Exactly half (n=30) described themselves as bisexuals. They were most likely to have an active marital sex life, and to be content with their marriage.

Some of the men reported having an intense level of sexual interaction with their wives in the early years of marriage, which faded with the years . . . [and] many of the men continued to initiate sex with their wives (Brownfain, page 181).

(2) Almost half (n=25) described themselves as gay. Some were uncomfortable in the gay world, or chose for other reasons to marry and live within the comfortable mainstream of society. Some regret having come of age before the era of gay liberation.

(3) Eight percent of the members (n=5) insisted that they were *heterosexual* and regarded gay sex as a hobby.

I think I'm really heterosexual. I like the gay thing. It's exciting and great for my ego, but I've done without it for long stretches and I could easily give it up if I had good reasons. It's really a sideshow for me. My marriage is the main event (*ibid.*, page 179).

Father of three, a man of 56 who claims to love his wife and have had no such feelings about men, two years ago had his first homosexual experience: "It bowled me over. I've had a number of experiences since then and they all bowl me over. But they don't take anything away from my marriage. I feel about homo-

sexuality the same way I feel about New York City. I love to
visit but I wouldn't want to live there" (*ibid.*, page 185).

These categories are constantly shifting, Brownfain warns. *"[T]here are men
who in the course of their lives wander from one category to another"* (*ibid.*, page
185, emphasis added).

A few men seem to be moving away from their homosexuality to a probable
exclusive heterosexuality. [Many others] are moving from a tenuous heterosexuality to an exclusive homosexuality. Some have moved back and forth. Most
experience both modes with a variety of emphases (*ibid.*, page 185).

"Troubled but stable" marriages

Asked to rate the quality of their marriage, almost half admitted that their
marriage was either "troubled but stable" (n=13, 22 percent) or headed for
divorce (n=13, 21 percent). Members of the "troubled but stable" group were preserving the marriage for the sake of convenience or "for the sake of the kids." A
moderate majority (n=36, 60 percent) rated their marriage OK. A typical remark
was "We have our ups and downs, but isn't that the way marriage is?" Eight percent (n=5) regarded their marriage as ideal. If you combine these two groups
(36+5=41), it becomes evident that a good two-thirds (41=68 percent of 60) of
Brownfain's group rated their marriage as good or ideal. (Unfortunately, the
investigator did not get a control group of heterosexual married men to rate the
quality of their marriage.)

> A woman who can flout conventionality might be able to tolerate
> (or even enjoy) marriage to a gay man. But the woman whose
> moral standards are conservative and conventional finds that
> marriage to a homosexual puts her in a double bind: the very
> attitudes that make the marriage difficult to endure, also make it
> difficult to accept the option of divorce.

Brownfain found many members of the bisexual group "who love their wife
and children and would not choose to be other than married. . . . [W]ife and children satisfy their affectional and psychosocial needs [while] their homosexual
partners satisfy their erotic needs" (*ibid.*, page 185).

> A gay man of Greek heritage says to Maddox (page 40): "My
> mother will find me a wife. No, I won't tell the girl I'm gay.
> Why should I? Greek men have never told their wives what they
> do outside the home. Lots of them have been gay. Anyway, I
> want children. If she's a sympathetic girl, a warm girl, I'm sure
> I'll be able to perform."

Failed marriages

It is by no means unusual for a homosexual to think about dropping out of the gay scene. Twenty-nine percent (105 men) of San Francisco gays in the Bell-Weinberg study indicated that they had tried to discontinue their homosexual activity. About fourteen percent (or 15) of these men said they had tried marriage, close to the estimates of other studies.

Of course it must be presumed that in the Bell-Weinberg San Francisco study, few of the men who fell into the sample could tell of successful marriages, as all these respondents had been recruited in such places as gay bars, and through gay organizations. (Had their marriages succeeded, these men would not have become part of the population surveyed.) Here are some testimonies on these failed marriages:

> I was having more and more homosexual activity, and she assumed that it was frequent. So I decided to go gay and left her for another guy I was having an affair with at the time (Bell and Weinberg, page 163).

> We weren't getting along. . . . My sex life with her wasn't satisfactory (*ibid.*, page 164).

> I wasn't an adequate sexual partner for her. At first it was a novelty for me and I went wild--then I realized it didn't fit the bill for me. I wasn't interested anymore, and she left (*ibid.*).

The husband tried to conceal his homosexuality, and suddenly revealed it, or his wife accidentally discovered it and could not accept it.

> After I told her I was homosexual, we bickered and fought. After all kinds of accusations, it finally came to an end (*ibid.*).

> She caught me having sex with her youngest brother. She didn't want the kids to know, so she just left with them (*ibid.*).

In each of the above cases, the marriage crashed because the husband could not combine married life with homosexual activity, to his wife's satisfaction. According to Isay, homosexual men were more likely to have wives who would tolerate the homosexual side of their husband's life before the AIDS crisis.

Rick

A participant in the Adairs' documentary film on gay lives tells the harrowing story of a gay man who ventured into the married world. Rick optimistically believed he could enter the straight world simply by getting married. After he realized that it wasn't working, his wealthy father-in-law took Rick to a sanatorium where he was subjected to about 25 shock therapy "treatments."

> After about a dozen years of gay activity, Rick met a girl and decided it was time to get married. "I thought, I've finally grown up and become like all the other kids I've grown up with. I was going to be straight." He continues: "Once we were married and began to have intercourse . . . something was missing. . . . I knew what I was having with her differed drastically" from what he had known as "really good, satisfying sex with a man." After almost five years of marriage and several children, he told his wife "I want to get out. This is not going anywhere for anyone." His father-in-law, a wealthy industrialist, engaged the cooperation of Rick's parents, unsophisticated farm people, to convince Rick to be treated in a mental sanatorium, as an alternative being put in the state insane asylum. At the sanatorium, the doctor said to Rick, "Well, we could castrate you, but let's try some treatments and see what we can do there."

Rick went through the "terrifying experience" of about 25 shock treatments. He divorced his wife, and moved to California (Adair and Adair, pages 31-35).

Dominick

When Dominick, a middle-aged divorced man, came out at the age of 53, he addressed a letter to his adult children, describing "the burden of living a double life." (His letter appears in Chapter 22, pages 414-415.)

Bart

Bart, a 60-year-old married man calls a radio talk show host to unburden himself of the "struggle" he has endured because society "forced" him to marry (Prager, pages 14-15). He admits that he had "a very good sexual relationship" with his wife, but felt deprived that for 29 years, he was obliged to inhibit the feelings he had as "a gay male." Marriage gave him four children "whom I adore. They're wonderful children and they're very successful. I think I gave them some values about life, and they did well in school; they're honorable people."

The talk show host observes that there are "many men . . . who want to have sex with other women and therefore have pain because of monogamy." He doesn't think Bart's case is any different. The radio host commented, with a touch of irony, "Well, society didn't really do too badly with you, did it? You didn't have your ultimate sexual desire, which was another male. All you had was a 29-year partner whom you loved and enjoyed, and four children whom you love" (Prager, pages 15-16).

The talk show host might have said, "I feel your pain" or something to that effect. But can a straight male really feel the pain of a gay man who lives through an adult lifetime without freely experiencing the homosexual contact for which he so passionately longs? Is the "lust" that a married man may feel for another woman the same as the hunger a gay man feels for another man, or is it like comparing a wistful hankering with a wild passion?

The fact that gay men continually take very sizeable risks for sex suggests that the drive for gay sex is much stronger than the romantic longing (or erotic itch) a married man may feel for another woman. Speaking from many years of clinical experience, Socarides (1995, page 19) describes the powerful inner compulsion that drives some homosexuals to have sex with other men: "They can't help themselves. Some of them need [same-sex intimacy] as much as the average human needs air or water--to breathe and survive." Perhaps Dr. Socarides exaggerates a bit for the sake of emphasizing the difference between a passing wish and a driving compulsion.

There are those who try to experience the best of both worlds, gay and straight. For some, it seems to work, while for many it doesn't. Bawer (1993 pages 115-116) tells of a distinguished literary critic who tried, not very happily, to lead a double life: "[A]fter attending a Manhattan literary party or poetry reading and behaving like a perfect gentleman, [he] would sneak off to the Hudson River docks and pick up sailors. The critic, a melancholy man and heavy drinker, never brought the two halves of his life together."

Harry

Harry, one of the Adairs' interviewees (pages 231-232), got married reluctantly. It seemed for him like the lesser of two evils. He so disliked "gay society" and its "screaming queens," that when he was in his twenties, he got married. Finally, after 27 years of marriage, he decided to come out.

In an understated way, Harry concedes that his twenty-odd years of marriage "weren't bad years. . . . *I enjoyed a very nice relationship with the woman I married. . .* She was a person of sturdy independence, was rather boyish in her manner, and was a good companion. And *we had a satisfactory, although unexiting, sexual experience7*

"[T]hen as I came into my forties, I began to despair. This was false to my nature. . . I decided to face the fork in the road. And I took the fork toward my own true nature" (Adair, page 232, emphasis added).

Gordon

Sanderson (pages 17-18) writes of Gordon, a senior citizen whose homosexuality went back to World War I. His lover was killed in the Somme, and Gordon held his homosexuality "in abeyance" while he married, became a father, and "lived a conventional family life." In the late 1970s, his wife died, and Gordon decided to once again give expression to his homosexual feelings after well over

60 years of marriage. He told his 68-year-old son of his decision.

Some Jewish husbands and fathers, after a conventional marriage has been dissolved by divorce or widowhood, marry a gentile woman. Black men are similarly likely to first marry a black woman, and after divorce or widowhood, a white woman. [This is true of the obscure as well as the famous, among whom are numbered Frederick Douglass (1817?-1895), Henry Kissinger, and O.J. Simpson.] No, that's not quite the same thing, and yet a similarity is there. A person's needs can be so manifold, and one can accomodate only a few at a time. After one has shared the marriage experience with the majority of his kith and kin, after one has enjoyed raising a family, one may then yield to impulses he has too long renounced, or satisfied too infrequently and too hurriedly.

Tastes of success

Gay men who married and then divorced sometimes claim that in some ways, their marriage was successful. For example, Maddox (pages 56-57) interviewed a formerly married gay man who believed that his marriage, though it ended in divorce, was successful in two important ways: he "absolutely adored being [the] father" of his two children, and his wife said he had given her "the most perfectly satisfying sex life she could have imagined.:"

Ken

[Ken] knew from experience that he could be sexually aroused by a woman. Then he met a woman who was vivacious, attractive, "gutsy," and she fell in love with him. He told her he was bisexual. Together they went to a psychiatrist who assured them the young man's bisexuality was "just an adolescent phase."

"My wife had to take an awful lot, but we had a perfectly satisfactory sex relationship. It was never from my gut; it was something I did because I was fond of her, because she had a normal sexual appetite. At the end of our marriage . . . she said I had given her the most perfectly satisfying sex life she could have wanted. . . . [But sexual intercourse was performed out of tenderness, plus a strong desire to please, and duty] (Maddox, page 57).

Another case of change in sexual orientation made without therapeutic help is described in *Straight; A Heterosexual Talks About His Homosexual Past*, by William Aaron. He writes that he was an active gay for years, and simply decided to go straight. Several years after he made this move he was both a husband and a father, and reported, "I am functioning heterosexually and enjoying it." In the next paragraph, he admits: "Let me be brutally honest: I'm sure if I let myself, I would still enjoy sex with men, although as time passes, I find it more and more difficult to imagine" (page 15).

Reorienting homosexual husbands

Masters and Johnson (1970, pages 377-380) tell of a 33-year-old man who worked for his father-in-law, a successful industrialist, and was married to his boss's daughter who was "sincerely in love with him."

Edgar and Myra

For all five years of their marriage, Edgar had been an impotent husband. He admitted to the therapist that he had been homosexual since the age of 12, and as an adult, has limited his homosexual life to out-of-town trips and vacations. He had never told his wife that although he was impotent with her, this was not the case with his male partners.

The therapists believed that the husband could not be helped unless he was honest with his wife, but should they expose the husband to the risk that his wife would respond by cruelly hurting and punishing her husband? What if she sued for divorce, threw her husband out of his job (he worked for his father-in-law) and her husband's secret became public knowledge in their small town?

The therapists reasoned that if you decide *not* to make a decision, that in itself is a decision. The therapists decided to take the risk, and advised Edgar tell his wife. A "highly anxious husband" reluctantly agreed to let his wife know about his homosexual past. Myra "acccepted the situation with equanimity . . . and her cooperation while in the rapid-treatment program was total. Edgar developed real interest in heterosexual functioning and the marriage was consummated during the acute phase of therapy. There are now children in the home and the husband is functioning most effectively in a heterosexual manner without return of homosexual demand." Masters and Johnson express the worry that when the couple's son grows into adolescence, this fact may reawaken the husband's appetite for homosexual activity.

The case cited above is taken from the authors' 1970 book, *Human Sexual Inadequacy*, where they report on the treatment of 213 married men referred to them for impotence problems. Of this number, they determined that in ten percent of impotence cases the problem stemmed from the husband's homosexuality.

As therapists, their strategy was to enable the gay husband to also enjoy sexual relations with his wife, not to extinguish his homosexual interests (although in the case reported above, the husband discontinued his homosexual activity). They claim (page 212) to have succeeded in effecting this change in two-thirds of this group.[8] From their 21 cases, there emerges the following composite portrait:

Composite portrait of a Masters and Johnson patient

Typical of background of Masters and Johnson's homosexual marital impotents were the following reports: They were in their middle teens when they were recruited by a young adult male for homosexual activity, which was subsequently ended at the initiative of the elder partner. (pages 179-180). In most cases, that ended the patients' sexual activity until they decided to get married. Masters and Johnson note (page 181): "In most instances marriages were contracted purely as a matter of financial, social, or professional gain with no real identification with, interest in, or for that matter, attitudinal concern for the girls they married."

During courtship, the man may have told his fiancée he did not make sexual demands upon her because he is "protecting the wife-to-be until marriage" (*ibid,* page 181). *Immediately after marriage, the husband may find "little if any difficulty in heterosexual functioning. . .* [but his] basic homosexual orientation surfaces at a later date" (*ibid,* page 181, emphasis added).

Perhaps five to 20 years after marriage, the patient becomes impotent with his wife and reports that he finds marital sex "objectionable, repulsive, or impossible" (*ibid,* page 179). "An overwhelming drive develops to return to homosexual functioning. *This reorientation usually is occasioned by exposure to . . . [a sexually appealing teenage boy].* The revived demand for homosexual functioning, once acknowledged, is consuming. Usually the drive is released initially by turning to the gay-bar society. However, many of these men, after years of repressed homosexual demand, are much more interested in teenage boys than in the occasional pickups of the bar society" (*ibid,* pages 181-182, emphasis added).

Efforts to pursue their homosexual life and also preserve their marriage may fail for a variety of reasons: difficulties with the law, betrayal by male friends or relatives, or discovery by the wife of her husband's homosexual life. Or the husband may lose interest in his wife, their sex life may become coldly impersonal or the husband cannot maintain an erection good enough for sexual functioning. The husband may at first insist that is not aroused because he is "not feeling well, [because of] pressures of work, or [gives] any other excuse that immediately comes to mind" (*Ibid.,* page 182).

The husband may then seek marriage counseling, not because he has any interest in his wife as a sexual partner but because he values her warmth and affection, and to protect his socioeconomic position. Knowing that she is competing with her husband's homosexual attractions, *the wife usually is supportive of her husband's wish to preserve their marriage,* say Masters and Johnson, and the wife therefore plays "a restrained, conservative waiting game in the hope of reconstituting the heterosexual component of their marriage" (*ibid,* page 183).

Why are Masters and Johnson's wives so much more accepting of their husband's homosexuality than wives of homosexuals reported by Grever, Maddox, and Clark? The answer is probably that Masters and Johnson's clientele were a highly selected group: couples who sought the help of therapists because both husband and wife wanted to save their marriage.

Reed

In their 1979 book, Masters and Johnson describe the case of Reed, whose history of homosexuality began at age 15, and continued through college. At age 26 he was cruising the local bars and public toilets. When he decided to go to graduate school and study clinical psychology, Reed tried to conceal his homosexuality. To avoid suspicion, he occasionally took women to dinner or to other social events and, to avoid intimacy, he rarely had more than two dates with the same woman. At age 28, he met a young woman, 23, a talented pianist with whom he had much in common, and they fell in love. To paraphrase Master and Johnson's report (1979, pages 350-353):

> She pushed for sexual involvement, and when he retreated, it was clear to her that he was homosexual. She begged him to seek help because she loved him and wanted to marry him. Reed was overwhelmed by this burst of warmth and offer of commitment.

> They got married but in 18 months he could not achieve or maintain an erection of sufficient quality to consummate his marriage. Finally, they applied at the Masters and Johnson clinic for couple treatment. On the tenth day of therapy at Masters and Johnson's clinic, he began functioning successfully in intercourse, and they subsequently established themselves as a married couple and parents. Reed maintained a successful career as a clinical psychologist, and both partners considered their marriage as effective. Masters and Johnson (page 353) admit that "this storybook type of history is the exception, not the rule. . . ."[9]

This chapter has touched upon the lives of over 25 gay men who married, dramatizing the fact that diversity and change in human adaptations follows from the diversity and flux of life experience. The richness, diversity and complexity of feelings that gay men express toward their spouses, contrasts boldly with the oversimplification of those who say that "gay men who marry are living a lie."

Brenda Maddox asks (page 40): "Now that it is easier for a man to be openly gay, will gay men no longer want to marry? That, she answers, "ignores the enormous variety and shadings of homosexual behavior, which can manifest itself virtually at any time of life and with every degree of intensity, from total commitment to casual indifference. To say that homosexuals will stop marrying is like saying that all homosexuals have limp wrists. Some will, some do; but others will not and do not."

NOTES TO CHAPTER 15

1. An article in *Commentary* magazine by Pattullo suggesting that some young men are "waverers" in their sexual orientation, drew a number of angry Letters to the Editor from readers who expressed certitude that homosexuality is a fixed, perhaps altogether genetic, condition.

2. M.W. Ross found that only 7.5 percent of 176 Swedish homosexuals sampled were married; 12.7 percent of 149 Finnish homosexuals sampled were married; and 13.5 percent of 149 Australian homosexuals sampled were married--a rate almost double in the least acceptant country, than in the most acceptant country. (Anti-homosexuality laws were repealed in Sweden in 1944.)

3. *Denial* is an effective mechanism of defense, a powerful mind game. A man may regularly have sex relations with both men and women and refuse to believe he is anything but straight--not homosexual and not bisexual. He may adopt the Mexican *macho* standard, and only play the role of inserter. A man may insist that he is straight because he engages in same-sex play only with his straight buddies. A newspaper personal ad for "Men Seeking Men" specified: "No gays."

4. For a participant-observer's description of the rather unguarded and easygoing homosexual scene in Washington, D.C. of the 1980s, see the autobiography of Baumann.

5. Rabbi Nicholas De Lange writes (2000, page 113): "Orthodox authorities tend to insist that homosexuals are subject to the requirement to 'be fruitful and multiply', and in current debates about homosexuality and Judaism, one often has the impression that the sin of willfull childlessness is a more cogent objection than the Torah's prohibition on sexual relations between men."

Reform Jewish leaders, on the other hand, have rendered obsolete, null and void the responsa of their revered Rabbi Solomon Freehof, published in 1973. Rabbi Freehof then reported that he was convinced that homosexual practice was contrary to Jewish values. In 2002, Rabbi Peter S. Knobel declared, "I am proud that the Reform movement has sought to fully include gays and lesbians in the [Jewish] community as members, leaders, and Jewish professionals (rabbis, cantors, educators, etc.) . . . ." Nullifying the Freehof responsa was not a spur-of-the-moment decision, Rabbi Knobel noted: "Over the last decade I have spent considerable time on a variety of national Central Conference of American Rabbis' committees dealing with human sexuality, especially the place of gay and lesbian Jews in the Jewish community" (*Chicago Jewish News*, April 12-18, 2002).

At their 1995 annual convention, the CCAR voted overwhelmingly [500 to 3] to advocate *civil* marriage for homosexual couples. In a 1996 issue, *Reform Judaism* published an article by Beth Gilbert, celebrating the synagogue commitment ceremony of a lesbian rabbi and her life-partner. In 1999, the CCAR declared that a rabbi may feel free to conduct a commitment ceremony for a same-sex couple.

6. Brownfain not only describes but also *defends* his group of bisexual marrieds. The group includes "heterosexual men who need to express their homosexual impulses . . . [and] homosexual men who have a capacity to sustain a satisfactory heterosexual relationship," he writes (*ibid.*, page 188).

They are the beneficiaries of the Kinsey Report and the gay liberation movement who are now living in a culture that "allowed them to discover their true sexual natures." If they had reached maturity at a time when homosexuality was still regarded as a sin, a neurosis or a perversion, they would have been forced to live a life of shame, conflict, suppression, denial, or become patients in extended psychotherapy (*ibid.*, pages 186-187).

Brownfain also defends the fact that they kept their bisexuality secret: These men were not hiding from themselves. Rather, they were hiding from others for pragmatic reasons. Through their "self-support groups," and by participating in his research study, they showed a willingness to reveal themselves, "to share their secret and in some measure to be relieved of it" (*ibid.*, page 187).

7. A gay man's description of heterosexual sex as "satisfactory, although unexciting" is consistent with the comparison of straight and gay sex, in Chapter 16.

8. Homosexuality was not the most difficult-to-treat cause of marital impotence, according to Masters and Johnson. More resistant to treatment were cases of impotence in which a significant factor was religious orthodoxy. (Comparative success rates reported by Masters and Johnson (page 212) are: General success rate of all 213 impotence cases: 74 percent, alcoholism (n=35): 77 percent, homosexual influence (n=21): 67 percent, religious orthodoxy (n=26): 50 percent.

9. In their *Homosexuality in Perspective*, Masters and Johnson claim to have altered homosexual preferences in 74 percent of cases. The reported success rate was based on treatment of 67 dissatisfied homosexual men and women, two-thirds of whom (about 45) were married men--some had left their wives and were living as homosexuals, while the rest were still at home, either sexually inactive or leading double lives. *It has been claimed that the authors obtained their high rate of success by accepting only cases that had a very favorable prognosis for change* (Maddox, page 169).

16   Straight Versus Gay Sex

As the last two chapters indicate, some men who can enjoy either gay or straight sex, frequently are drawn to male partners and willingly accept the greater risks and penalties of the homosexual lifestyle. Just what is there about gay sex that makes it uniquely gratifying to some men? An appreciation of basic male-female differences helps one understand why some men prefer a male sex partner.

Female dancers typically are coy and graceful, while male dancers (adults, at least) usually are quick and vigorous. This gender difference also characterizes the sexual behavior of not only the human species but also of man's near and distant relatives.[1] This genetic difference in sexual behavior makes good evolutionary sense: the human female, who at most can bear about one offspring per year, does well to be slow and selective[2] about whom she lets impregnate her. The male, who can (if he's lucky) impregnate one or more females every day, can afford to be quick and bold.

Evolution has endowed each gender with both a physique and temperament to match their courtship style; differences that show up beautifully in the dance styles of men and women throughout the world. Heterosexual lovemaking, like heterosexual dancing, is sometimes an interplay of these two tendencies, and sometimes a *compromise* between the quick, direct and vigorous tendencies of the male, and the slow, coy, teasing, romantic style of the female partner. When we reflect on the fact that a good lover tries to please his partner, we mean that a good lover does his best to strike a balance between his own imperious drive, and his partner's wish for a dreamy, romantic experience.

This genetic difference in sexual behavior is remarkably consistent with known differences in the sexual habits of lesbians and gay men. Cruising is not a lesbian practice. Lesbians usually first get to know each other, and gradually move toward a warm and quiet intimacy, often characterized by kissing and cuddling. But when a gay man sights an attractive and willing stranger, he moves quickly toward an intense and energetic sexual union. Writes Edmund White (page 165): "All men want a sexual adventure that is quick, physical, and uncomplicated. That is what homosexuals offer each other, and that is also what prostitutes (male or female) offer men." White (page 109) quotes the conviction of William Burroughs that all exotic homosexual couplings are quick and explosive but never romantic:

> I think that what we call love is a fraud perpetuated by the
> female sex, and that the point of sexual relations between
> men is nothing that we could call love. . . .

Paul
The difference between gay and lesbian behavior illustrates the difference

297

between what men and women want to get out of sex: women for the most part desire love and intimacy, while men want physical pleasure.[3] Listen to Socarides's patient, Paul, who had had both gay and straight sex experience. To Paul, gay sex met his ideal of pure, endlessly varied and easy-to-get sex, uncomplicated by questions such as: "Do I have to tell this woman I love her? How long can I hold on to her without promising to marry her?" Paul also dwelt on the lack of available women, as compared to the vast number of easily available homosexual contacts of every description (Socarides 1978, pages 199-200). Paul enjoyed the wild freedom of gay sex:

> Paul says that in gay sex "he is 'truly free' as he cannot be with a woman. Fucked him and he did everything I wanted him to do. I had temptations to hit him and I was very rough. I don't like talking about this aggressive side. . . . But I do get a wild feeling from subjugating other men and making them love me and think highly of me the way my father did not" (Socarides 1978, page 227).

In their 1978 San Francisco study, Bell and Weinberg were informed that some 15 percent of his 660 respondents had engaged in heterosexual coitus during the year prior to the interview. Approximately one-fifth of these experienced respondents "volunteered that they felt more competent in their sexual relationships with males. By far, the largest numbers mentioned feeling more at ease or less fearful, nervous, or inhibited with males than with females" (Bell and Weinberg, page 55):

> I feel more relaxed, more earthy, more comfortable with males. There's always a fear with women, a fear that I am not my own.

> It is more exciting with men.

> There was always more of an emotional rapport with a male partner.

> My homosexual experiences have been far and away more satisfactory, enjoyable, interesting, and fulfilling. My heterosexual experiences were primarily a sexual release for me. I felt indifferent about my female partner.

Other interview studies have yielded similar testimony:

Owens (page 31) quotes a high-school student who discovered in a homosexual experience that: "I felt everything that I hadn't felt with a woman."

Freddy, a gay musician says: "Though I still do sleep with women, I haven't for a long while. I prefer sleeping with men. . . . There are different things that you do with a man because of anatomical differences. Sometimes I think it's the abstraction of it--that we're not making babies, just relating" (Adair and Adair, page 169).

Nick recalls a seventh-grade party: "I liked dancing with boys more than dancing with girls--probably because . . . girls were so crinoline covered. . . The thing about dancing with guys is that it immediately became erotic. . . The feelings at that time were: the guys wanted it; [and] the gals [resisted] it" (*ibid*, page 196).

Roger recalls that when he was ready for sexual experimentation, "the male body . . . was more readily available to me. The Catholic upbringing makes it impossible even to think about touching a female body. I was terrifically interested in females when I was, like, in the beginning of sex's manifestation. I was omnisexual. . . But it's easier to relate to males, because I happen to be a male . . . That's why I'm gay" (*ibid*, page 219, emphasis added).

A participant-observer of the gay lifestyle writes that a gay man may appreciate the sensuous pleasure of intimacy with a woman, but feels a wild craving for contact with another man:

. . . There are some gay men who prefer the feel of women's bodies to men's, who are even more comfortable sexually with women, but whose emotions crave contact with other men. They have an *unfinished business with other men*--scary, promising, troubling, absorbing business--whereas their sentiments toward women . . . are much simpler, more stable, and less fraught.[4]

Laboratory observations of Masters and Johnson

Systematic observation of the differences between gay and straight sexual intercourse was conducted in the 1960s by Masters and Johnson. They recruited 42 homosexual long-term couples (84 persons) and directly observed their sexual behavior. The behavior of members of this group was then compared to the sex acts of ten gays who were reportedly not in committed relationships, as well as to a number of heterosexual couples.

Masters and Johnson found that there was indeed a great difference between the sexual intercourse of gays and straights. Gay couples engaged in longer periods of sexual play before reaching a climax. It was as if straight couples seemed

to be in a hurry to "get the job done" (page 65). Straight men gave some attention to their partners' breasts, but women seldom touched their partners' nipples.
Gay couples stimulated each other over a greater part of their bodies, and seemed
to know that they could stimulate sexual arousal by playing with their partners'
nipples (pages 71-72).

In fact, the male nipple is not an altogether "vestigial organ," since it can
induce sexual arousal in heterosexual as well as in gay men. Gay men seem to
know this but, according to Masters and Johnson's observations, heterosexual
women do not usually take advantage of this fact. In the view of medical sex
counselor Theresa Crenshaw (page 111), the male nipple is an important erogenous organ:

> [N]ipple stimulation releases oxytocin in males as well [as in
> females]. . . . [T]he male nipple is much like the woman's cli-
> toris. Its only reason for existence is sexual stimulation.

> [Crenshaw notes that] many men feel ashamed of their desire for
> nipple stimulation as though it makes them effeminate. [She tells
> of a man who wanted to suppress his impulse to rub his nipples,
> who was told] to go ahead and enjoy it.

Oral sex (fellatio) is a standard gay sex act, almost as common as coitus is in
heterosexual union. A comparison of coitus and fellatio may therefore shed some
light on differences between straight and gay sex. Inexperienced males often feel
awkward and insecure about heterosexual lovemaking, and feel that they lack the
skills for being a good lover. Offering a fellator one's penis, erect or flaccid,[5] is
very simple, by comparison.

> As the moment came when he was going to have his first homo-
> sexual experience, David was worried that he would be impotent.
> "The spirit was willing, but the body [he feared] was a dumb and
> stubborn coward." His experience proved otherwise:

> "I can only suggest my surprise when I felt those familiar sensa-
> tions that lead to orgasm. . . . I felt that tingling which culminat-
> ed in a release into Tom's eager mouth. . . . *It seemed so easy*
> finally to be a sexual being, *so deliciously simple* (emphasis
> added), that I let out a strangled laugh of pleasure and self-affir-
> mation, a comic eureka. *Look*, I wanted to tell my body, *Look
> how well we have come through!* . . . It was a long time before I
> stopped laughing, and . . . I told Tom I was not laughing at him
> but at myself. . . (Bergman, page 152).

The fellator, although hypothetically the "passive partner," can play a very
active role indeed, in giving the "inserter" a voluptuous physical experience--

employing his mouth and tongue in various ways, as both partners use their hands in ways that heighten the sensuous experience.

Laud Humphreys' Tearoom Observations

Laud Humphreys, who observed many acts of fellatio performed in public restrooms, reports (1970, pages 71-74): "[H]ands are a very important part of [oral] sex. . . . because you can do fantastic things . . . with your hands to another person's body." Humphreys describes how a fellator handles his partner's penis, testicles, buttocks, legs, and reaches under "the active partner's" shirt, to stroke his chest.

> Humphreys describes the hand play of both partners: the fella-
> tor's "caresses, friendly pats, relaxed salutes, [and] support with
> the hands. . . . Normally, the man who takes the insertor role will
> sustain the action of the fellator by clasping the back of his neck
> or by placing his hands on the partner's shoulders."

The above description may seem unnecessarily detailed, but the details are offered to support Humphreys' comment (1970, page 74) that "a number of my respondents claim that the physical sensation of oral-genital copulation, while not unlike that of coitus is actually more stimulating--or 'exciting,' as they generally word it. . . . [S]ome married men among the cooperating participants say they actually prefer the sensations of fellatio to those of coitus. . . ."

Some women refuse to engage in oral sex, (it is reported that even prostitutes, in certain times and places, have refused to fellate their clients) and some men are even disinclined to ask their wife to fellate them. To some extent, however, fellatio is an accepted part of heterosexual foreplay. Masters and Johnson observed and compared gay and straight couples engaged in fellatio, and reported (pages 72-73) that gay men were more patient, exploratory, teasing and voluptuous in their tactics.

> When either men or women fellated their partner, they made
> similar use of their tongue and lips. But gay males took more
> time, and ranged over a wider area of their partner's body:
> fondling and caressing his abdomen, inner thighs and scrotum as
> well as his penis. There were more pauses, allowing sexual
> excitement to diminish, before recommencing; "teasing," as this
> practice is known.

Another observation about fellatio, made by Masters and Johnson, is that when the fellated partner ejaculated, *male fellators more often swallowed the semen*, women did not (page 75). This observation supports the mana hypothesis of homosexuality, as set forth in Chapter 9.

Masters and Johnson observed (page 139) a higher level of sexual excitement among committed gay partners than among assigned gay partners. Similarly, a higher level of sexual excitement was observed among gays in committed-couple sex than in masturbation.

In Chapter 3, we detailed how beautifully adapted the adult female is, to sexually excite and gratify her male partner. Yet it is now clear that to some men, a male partner is more stimulating and more gratifying sexually. Here it may be noted that many gay men are attracted to young men with boyish personalities and boyish physical features: blond hair, slim, hairless body, *boyish* good looks. Why? *Boyish feature are also wholesomely feminine features,*[6] which would appeal to what Rado, a psychoanalytic observer, would call the gay man's "latent *heterosexuality*" (see page 205). Psychoanalytically considered, to the gay man, a boyish partner is a female with a penis, a female who does not arouse his castration anxiety.

Sexual intercourse might be compared to eating, to the extent that both acts satisfy biological drives. Using this analogy, it is as if Masters and Johnson observed that the gay sex practiced by committed couples was more like gourmet dining, and straight sex was often more like everyday eating. In general, there are no doubt wide individual variations within each population, straight and gay.

There are of course straight couples who practice lovemaking in the most voluptuous and leisurely ways, and gay sex is sometimes inhibited, hasty, and furtive.[7] But Masters and Johnson did observe a distinct difference in the average gay and straight sexual encounter of committed couples. The advantage of gays in making sex play reach higher levels of excitement may be ascribed to what Masters and Johnson call "same-sex empathy"--a gay stimulates his partner the way he himself would like to be stimulated (page 73). Tripp (pages 100-101) described this advantage thusly:

> "The sex techniques of homosexual males are quite effective. . . .
> As a result of their common physiology, partners of the same sex
> know . . . how particular actions feel and how these are likely to
> be interpreted by each other. Thus, male homosexuals, too, are
> often able to make simple techniques exceptionally effective.

Communication. Sharing a common anatomy, physiology and emotional life, men also share a common language, and are more likely to talk to each other[8] about their responses to their partner's actions, Masters and Johnson report (page 73). Heterosexual couples, on the other hand, often will not come out and say whether they like or dislike what their partner is doing. Masters and Johnson (page 68) comment on this finding:

Close observation has suggested that there were many times when women were made physically uncomfortable by their husbands' approaches to the breast.

Although frequently admitting later in private that the observer's impression of . . . breast tenderness [during part of the menstrual cycle] had been correct, the women simply did not inform their husband at the time. The usual stated reason was because "he likes to play with my breasts so much I didn't want to distract him." When the husbands were queried separately, they expressed surprise at their wives' cyclical distress, and the unanimous reaction was, "Why didn't she tell me. . . ."

The authors continue (page 74): "When husbands were interviewed, their most frequent complaint was that their wife did not grasp the shaft of their penis tightly enough. Yet not one man with this complaint had ever taken the initiative and suggested this specific technical improvement to his wife."

Accordingly, Weinrich (page 279) offers the following caricature of a conventional marriage: "Marriage . . . is that state of bliss in which the man is supposed to know everything about sex, hasn't been taught anything about it, never asks his wife what she wants, but wishes that she would tell him. The wife is supposed to know nothing about sex, is blissfully ignorant about it, never tells her husband what she wants, but wishes he would ask."

To gay men, good sex is "hot sex"

Recall the reflection of Socarides's patient Paul that in gay sex, he was "truly free" as he could never be with a woman.

> I don't like talking about this aggressive side [Paul confessed to his therapist]. . . . But I do get a wild feeling from subjugating other men and making them love me and think highly of me. . . (Socarides 1978, page 227).

The combined expression of sex and aggression is in low repute (if not taboo) in heterosexual life, and labelled with pejorative terms like force, coercion and rape. In gay sex, by contrast, the combination of sex and aggression is glorified as "hot sex."

The fact that gay sex allows for fuller expression of the male potential for *both* sex and aggression may have important implications. It may help us understand why homosexual experience can be more satisfying physically, and therefore significantly more reinforcing, than heterosexual experience. It may tell us why homosexuality is such a hard habit to break, once the habit is well established, and why therapeutic intervention is therefore so difficult. Suppose a homosexual habit was born of a fear of women. That fear may disappear but the homosexuality may continue because it is enjoyable in itself.

Laboratory observations of Masters and Johnson parallel the survey results, the clinical and autobiographical testimony of gays who have experienced both gay and straight sex: that gay sex is, on the average, the more intense physical experience. Tripp has noted that this is a claim that straights (homophobes in particular) find hard to accept. In his second edition to *The Homosexual Matrix*, he comments (page 276): "No other sentence in [the first edition] stirred as much hateful reaction as did this:"

> *When two men are excited and unrestrained in their sexual inter-*
> *action, the fire that is fed from both sides often does whip up lev-*
> *els of eroticism that are very rarely reached elsewhere.*

For both men and women, sex may serve as an escape from anxiety or depression.[9] But because gay sex is a more powerful experience, *for gay men, sex may be a more effective strategy to mask emotional distress*. A gay man admits (Kaufman and Rafael page 217): "I'd rather have sex than deal with my feelings. If I get angry or feel bummed out, well, I just look for some guy to get off with. I've got to do it then. There's no other way for me to blank everything out. The craving's so strong that almost anybody will do. I can't afford to be choosy."

Gay sex practices[10]

The topic of gay sex brings up the questions: *What do gay men do, sexually? What do they tend most often to do?* This book is not a sex manual, but these questions are important here because they may throw some light on homosexual motivations, and also because they bear on significant health issues. Here we will survey both older findings and refer to the very recent Handbook for gay men, authored by Orland Outland and published in 2000 by Alyson Publications, the dominant publisher of gay scholarly and popular publications.

An attempt to put gay sex practices into objective words, already begun in the foregoing sections of this chapter, tends to demean homosexual lovemaking. Gay men themselves avoid the direct description of their activities. The most common sexual activity, fellatio,[11] or oral sex, is popularly termed "a blow job." In older times, a fag might say, "Let me trade you." Today, a gay man is likely to use ambiguous language like "Give me head" or "Do me," rather than "Suck my cock." Andrew Tobias admits his reluctance to describe 'what gay men do':

> Straight people sometimes ask, or think of asking, "What exactly
> do gay men do?" . . . I will make a deal with you. I promise not
> to tell you in detail what gay men do if you promise not to tell
> me in detail what straight men do. *I don't want to know.* The
> truth is, when the porn film goes into close-up, I'm not eager to
> look at the gay details either. To me, this stuff is best left private,
> intimate, and in relative darkness. Moonlight. Or candlelight"
> (Tobias 1998, page 91).

The British journalist and gay man Michael Davidson (page 170) points to the paradox that gay sex seems so impellingly right to do but so silly to describe:

> I've always considered that most of the sexual actions one's
> nature drives one unreasonably to perform are too silly for
> words. Why, I ask, does one want to do such pointless things?
> Yet, at the moment, nothing in life seems so important.
> [Listening to a courtroom description of such a sexual act makes]
> one feel not only an imbecile but also a monster; in [the prosecu-
> tor's] mouth things which seemed to one perfectly natural
> become horribly deformed.

Another example of the reluctance of gay men to describe their sex practices: when a gay man was interviewed on a radio talk show, a "little old lady" called in to ask, "I've been listening to all this talk about homosexuality and I just want to know what is it you people do in bed?" The talk show guest replied, "It being National Library Week, I referred her to her local library" (Baumann, page 270).

Older survey data on homosexual practices indicate a difference between what gay men most *frequently* do, and what they *like* to do. Here, for example, are Bell and Weinberg's (page 300) 1978 findings:

*Table 16.1.Favorite Sexual Activity
Of 660 Homosexual Men (552 white, 108 black)*

	White men (n=552)	Black men (n=108)
Performing oral-genital	2%**	3%**
Receiving oral-genital	27%*	18%
Performing anal intercourse	26%	44%*
Receiving anal intercourse	5%	11%
Other (mutual masturbation, sado-masochism, etc.)	40%	24%

(*most favored activity, **least favored activity)

Here, all respondents (white and black) agreed that their favorite sexual activities were receiving oral-genital stimulation, and performing anal intercourse. In other words, in both oral and anal sex the favored position is that of the inserter.

What this means is that the sexual partner with more bargaining power (the younger one,[12] the more desirable one, the handsomer one, the stronger one, the more experienced or dominant or narcissistic one) is more likely to perform anal intercourse and to receive oral sex; and the acquiescent partner is more likely to perform oral sex and receive anal intercourse. (Of course, partners may play "First me, then you.")[13]

Unlike heterosexual intercourse, where each partner brings a unique and complementary physique to the experience, homosexual play is more likely to be influenced by status difference or narcissistic character, which can make sexual intercourse the expression of one partner's demands and the other partner's compliance.

> Micah, living with a lover he described as "a wonderful man," complained that "during sex, Micah played the role of satisfying Bill. Sometimes this was satisfying for Micah, but more often it left him feeling vaguely frustrated and longing for some reciprocity within the relationship" (Cornett, page 66).[14]

The long history of male homosexuality consistently assigns a greater prestige to the acts of receiving oral stimulation and performing anal penetration, and assigns an inferior role to giving oral stimulation and submitting to anal penetration.

> Andrew Sullivan (1995 page 52) notes that before the middle of the twentieth century, men regarded themselves as active or passive, not as straight or gay: "A man, especially in working-class cultures, was not disgraced by having sex with another man, so long as he was the dominant partner. In many cultures in the United States--particularly those of Mediterranean and Latin American immigrants--this is still the case."

> In Army talk, "Suck my cock" is a familiar insult. If one soldier is seen polishing his boots, and another jokingly calls out, "Hey, polish my boots too!" a likely retort is "Suck my cock." To suggest that one would welcome having his penis sucked is no disgrace, but in Army talk, it is unambiguously insulting to be called "a cocksucker."

Masters and Johnson observe (page 264) that aging gays, impotent gays, and gays who are physically unattractive are relegated to "a role of sexual service"-- serving the less favored roles in oral and anal intercourse:

With the loss or absence of physical attractiveness, these men must concentrate on providing pleasure for their casual partners, if they are to continue to attract sexual opportunities.

The Outland *Handbook* contains an interesting statement (pages 33-34):

"You will be hard-pressed to find any man, gay or straight, who does not enjoy receiving a blow job. Why so many gay men also enjoy *giving* blow jobs is a mystery." (Not a mystery if homosexual behavior is regarded as an attempt to overcome a felt deficit in masculinity.)

Although Bell and Weinberg's 1978 survey data identify anal intercourse as a highly *preferred* activity, the 1983 survey data of Weinberg *et al.* (published in 1994, pages 384-392), indicate that oral sex was about three times more frequently practiced than anal sex. Table 16.2 lists the most-popular and least- popular sex activities among a sample of 180 gay men, listed in descending order of popularity, summarized from the findings of Weinbeg *et al.*

Anal sex. In earlier days, when gay sex was often performed in places such as public rest rooms and parks, oral sex was the predominant sexual activity because it can be relatively quick and easy to perform. As gay men gained access to more leisurely settings, the practice of anal sex has become more widespread. It is popularly described as "fucking," which suggests that anal sex is popularly regarded as the gay equivalent of heterosexual intercourse. When public health workers suggested that gay men refrain from practicing anal sex because it is a prime source of HIV infection, a gay advocate protested that this would be like advising heterosexual couples to refrain from vaginal intercourse. This attitude is also reflected in the statement by Simon LeVay, gay biological scientist and educator, (1993, page 53) that "from the point of view of the insertive partner, anal intercourse differs in only minor respects from vaginal intercourse."

Table 16.2. Summary of the most popular and least popular homosexual activities of 190 gay men, surveyed by Weinberg et al. in 1983

1.   Percent performing act a great deal or at least once per week:

Self-masturbation	84
Kissing, hugging, and other non-genital activity	75
Performing oral-genital sex	39
Receiving oral-genital sex	37
Masturbating partner	29
Masturbated by partner	25
Self-masturbation in front of partner	21

(2. Acts less-frequently performed

Perform finger-anal sex	15 percent

(Table 16.2 continued on next page.)

Receive finger-anal sex	13
Receive anal intercourse	13
Perform anal intercourse	11
Perform oral-anal sex	8
Receive oral-anal sex	5

3. Acts least often performed

In contrast to acts performed "a great deal" or at least once a week, are those which only a small percentage of gay men acknowledge engaging in *anytime during the past year* (Weinberg *et al.*, page 393):[15]

Sadomasochism	17 percent
Urination play	13
Anal fisting	12
Enema play	11
Feces play	3

.

In the same spirit, The Outland *Handbook* (page 35) strongly endorses the practice of anal sex:

.

> [M]uch as the far right may say about anal sex being "unnatural," it's hard for anyone who's had really good anal sex to believe that nature didn't design our insides with this experience in mind. . . . Men have a button on the inside called a prostate, which gives them orgasms [just like the clitoris gives a woman orgasms]. Anyone who can push those buttons the right way will never be lonely for long.

As LeVay advises, anal intercourse may differ "in only minor respects" from vaginal intercourse *from the point of view of the insertive partner*, but from the point of view of the receptive partner, the difference is significant, given the differences, anatomical and physiological, between the anus and rectum, and the vagina.

The vagina (even virginally) is an enfolded, thick-walled tube that, with sexual excitement, becomes generously lubricated and readily accomodates an erect penis. By contrast, the rectum is a thin-walled tube lined with tissue that is specialized to absorb water from the fecal mass, which gives it a natural tendency to absorb liquid carrying viruses. The rectum wall is easily ruptured, in which case the body cavity is open to further infection.

The anal sphincters are muscles that resist the intrusion of outside objects. These muscles do not always adapt well to the use of the rectum as a sex organ. Goldstone (page 21) reports a medical study of men who practiced receptive anal sex; 25 per cent reported at least isolated episodes of fecal incontinence. An age-similar group of heterosexual men reported a three per cent rate of fecal incontinence.

Gay sex manuals offer careful instructions on adapting one's anus to sex activity, before attempting to practice receptive anal sex:

> Insert a finger (with nails short and very smooth) or small dildo [into your anus] and try moving it in and out. Gradually move up to several fingers or a larger dildo, until you can accommodate something the size of a cock. You'll learn to relax as you're being entered. . . . You'll also learn the angle at which your body can best accept a dildo. If you later experience pain with a partner, it may be that he's thrusting in at the wrong angle for you (Hart, page 18).

Anal sex requires that the rectum be well-lubricated,[16] and illegal drugs are sometimes used to further relax the rectal muscles of the receptive partner. Oral sex is frequently practiced by strangers, but Hart's sex manual advises that anal sex be practiced by *men who know and trust each other:*

> Getting fucked often hurts the first few times, but eventually your body will learn to relax and enjoy the new sensation. . . . Having the right partner will make all the difference in whether or not you enjoy this new experience. Ideally, do it with someone you already know and trust. . . . Should a new partner want to fuck you, let him know that this is your first time. [Don't let him do it] if he doesn't seem to care. . . . Avoid someone who announces that he never gets fucked. Mister Macho might be fun for some purposes, but he's unlikely to show the sensitivity you'll want for this occasion (Hart, page 17).

Anal sex is an inherently complicated and risky activity. Goldstone's 1999 sex manual, which is written not as scare literature but as a friendly medical guide for gay men, devotes 22 pages of the first chapter to the do's, don'ts, complications, and risks of anal sex: pain, perforation, incontinence, and HIV infection.

Anal sex and HIV risk. Public health workers regard anal sex (like multiple partnerships) as a significant risk factor in the spread of all sexually transmitted diseases (STDs) including HIV. Although remarkable progress is being made in keeping HIV-positive men in good health, HIV-positive men are still at risk of contracting AIDS, still an incurable illness. Public health workers wish they could advise gays to give up anal sex (as well as multiple partners). But gay advisers veto this recommendation, and "safe sex" advertising limits its counsel to using the protection of a condom.

Gay men's attitudes toward safe sex

Is the condom really effective in preventing the spread of HIV? Journalist Mark Schoofs offers the following testimony: "[S]afe sex education saved my life. . . I was in a relationship with an HIV-positive man for three and a half years, and I remain uninfected to this day. It saved my life, knowing what to do." But a recent study showed that more than one-third of young gay men admitted to having unprotected anal intercourse in the last year, "and that many of them believe AIDS is an older man's disease, confined to big cities; that it won't touch them" (60 Minutes, July 9. 1995).

In the larger cities, gay men are already infected up to 50 percent, and yet unsafe sex is a rising phenomenon, according to 60 Minutes reporter Ed Bradley. He interviewed an AIDS educator who admitted that he himself is now infected. "I was in love," he explained. "When I have sex, I'm not an AIDS educator . . . I'm a human being." Reporter Mark Schoofs commented: "The number-one reason that gay men are having unsafe sex is [that] they're in love, and they want to have that kind of physical intimacy that people who are in love have." The simple truth, however, is that anal sex is commonly practiced by men who cannot be in love with each other because they don't even know each other. Perhaps anal sex gives some men an imaginary heterosexual experience, and also tests their erotic skills.

The *Handbook* goes beyond the more familiar sex practices--kissing, fondling, masturbation, oral and anal sex--and discusses a wide range of homosexual foreplay and alternative activities: nipple stimulation (licking, squeezing, pinching), armpit licking, rectal fingering (pages 32-33), toe sucking, phone sex and computer sex (pages 62-63).

While the Outland *Handbook* strongly endorses anal sex, discouraged by public health workers, the *Handbook* also gives detailed advice and cautions on avoiding HIV infection. The *Handbook* reader is advised, however, that for the gay man, some risk is inevitable:

> [Y]ou cannot spend your entire sex life in a plastic bag. . . .
> [T]he only way to make oral sex completely safe is to do it with
> a condom, but anyone who's ever had a dick with a rubber on it
> in his mouth can tell you there is not a whole lot of enjoyment in
> it. Negotiated risk [an idea that has gained currency in the gay
> community] accepts that life is never completely safe, but it also
> realizes that you don't do stupid things like walk in front of a
> speeding truck or get fucked without a rubber and pretend that
> nothing is going to happen to you as a result (pages 27-28, italics
> added).

The Handbook advises gay readers that becoming HIV posititve "is not the death sentence it was a few years ago," but not to be lulled into the belief that nowadays "HIV is no big deal:"

> Today . . . there are medications that can not only prolong your life but also provide a quality of life equivalent to that of an HIV-negative person. [But there are risks and exceptions, the Handbook adds.] Do not let anyone convince you that just because there are now effective treatments the HIV is no big deal. Anyone who tells you that is lying (pages 92-93).

Bisexual perspectives

Some men who have experienced both gay and straight sex express a clear preference for gay sex, or for straight sex. For example, Stambolian (page 81) asked a gay man who had been married twice and was the father of two children, "How do you compare . . . [gay and] straight sex?" His respondent replied:

> There is no comparison. . . . I like the look of [gay sex], the feel of it, the way it smells. It's absolutely basic, an animal experi- ence. That's what we are before anything else--animals. I see myself that way. And there are animals who exist for one reason, and animals who exist for other reasons. I am an animal made for sex with other men.

The physical intensity of gay sex was also valued by those male respondents of Wineberg *et al.* who were regularly having sex relations with both men and women. Here are some of their comments on what they liked about male-male sex:

> With men, there is very little emotion involved. But I find I can go to the limits with [a male partner] physically. Men can endure much heavier physical activity than women can. Sex with men is harder, stronger, and longer than with women. There is more physical than emotional excitement (Weinberg *et al.*, pages 50- 51).

> In terms of physical pleasure, men are much more [attuned to] what turns me on in a way a woman never could. I guess because she does not have the same anatomy (*ibid*, page 51).

> Weinberg *et al.* conclude (pages 51-52): Both bisexual "men and women noted that sex with a man tended to be hotter, more intense, exciting, and passionate. . . . [M]en 'turn [me] on' more, have more sexual energy, provide more sexual sparks and more passion."

Gay sex for passion, straight sex for intimacy. Bisexual men seek a woman partner when they are in the mood for kissing, cuddling, being close, touching, caressing, and intimate conversation. The reflections of Weinberg *et al.*'s bisexual respondents touch on the special qualities of heterosexual love-making:

> Women are described (page 53) as "more affectionate, personal, tender, caring, nurturing, comforting, giving, emotionally involved, loving, genuine, and mutual." This atmosphere of intimacy is expressed by one male in the words: "With women I feel more able to talk about things that trouble me, to reveal weaknesses."

> Bisexual men observe (page 52) that the anatomical fit was better or more natural with a woman partner: "[I]t's physically more comfortable to have sex with a woman. My feeling is that the bodies fit better together." Another respondent says, "With a woman, I subconsciously feel that the act is somehow more 'normal.' . . . Physically, vaginal sex is more satisfactory than anal sex, in that it self-lubricates. . . [With male partners, the sexual act is] more impersonal and less sensitive . . . women are more person-centered and caring during sex."

Weinberg *et al.* (pages 54-56) asked their bisexual respondents when would they look for a male partner, and when would they search for a female partner? Several situational factors were mentioned: Were they in gay or heterosexual company? Were male or female partners available? Touching on internal factors ('What kind of a mood were you in?'), respondents reflected, "If my need is for emotional involvement, I would want to relate to a woman." Another said, "If I'm feeling good about myself, if I'm feeling attractive, I probably would go toward the woman."

One bisexual man's reflections (*ibid*, page 91) point to the fact that gay sex is often anonymous sex, and straight sex is more often an act of intimacy:

> When I have anonymous sex [with a man], I often feel very compulsive and at times it feels dirty. This can make me appreciate the intimate and rich feelings I have with my [female] partner and thus brings us closer together. It sometimes makes me aware of how needy I am. And my neediness is better fulfilled within a primary relationship. But I also sometimes feel that anonymous sex can be very liberating when I'm feeling stifled by my partner.

What makes straight sex different?

What is it about straight sex that bisexual men find "intimate and rich," "personal, tender, caring, nurturing, comforting, giving, emotionally involved, loving, genuine, and mutual?" There is perhaps a touch of envy in the comment of a gay writer, that the man who can satisfy a woman's feminine needs has much to gain in return:

> More than men, women need intimacy, tenderness, constancy, to bring out their full potential as sex partners. They have much to give, and a heterosexual partner can be richly rewarded for meeting his mate's feminine needs.[17]

Moreover, physical intimacy with a woman can activate many fantasies, including the fantasy of making a baby. Even if the couple is doing everything to avoid pregnancy, they can (and perhaps often do) enjoy the rich fantasy that they are engaged in the act that can actually create a new life, even though this time it's only a rehearsal for something within their power to do *for real*.

The evidence is indirect that heterosexual lovers enjoy the fantasy of making a baby. First, evolution would favor persons who found this fantasy pleasurable, for it would foster reproduction. Demonstrating one's potency by becoming a father--intentionally, legitimately, or otherwise--is a most powerful ego boost, and even the fantasy of giving a girl a baby can be pleasurable. Clinical experience indicates that some married women lose their interest in sex after they already have all the children they want. Even though they may go on using a contraceptive, it seems that for some women, the fantasy of becoming pregnant is one of the things that makes sex enjoyable. Finally, how else to explain the fact there are so many "unintended" pregnancies; that reliable methods of contraception are readily available but simply not used? Maccoby (page 203) cites a 1994 study by Larson and Richardson "that the elation of being in love leads adolescents to underestimate the risks [or should we say *to disregard the consequences*] of unprotected sex."

Another difference between straight and gay sex, according to Tripp, is that a gay male sex relationship usually starts out at a high level of excitement, and quickly burns itself out. A straight sex relationship is more likely to begin hesitantly, clumsily, and gradually achieve a sustainable high level of compatibility and mutual pleasure. This is why straight partnerships, he concludes, are more enduring, and why sexual fidelity is more easily maintained. There is even a hint of envy in Tripp's comment (page 153) on this difference:

It is not unusual for a man and wife to retain a workable if not very intense interest in each other for twenty years or longer, but such time-spans are rare in male relationships.

A bisexual patient of Klein's, once reflected (page 48): "[M]en don't excite me as much as women do. Or I should say they don't excite me in the same way. I can become one with a woman if it's good between us. *I have never been one with a man.* It's hard to imagine, as a matter of fact. Sex with a woman is special to me. Sex with a man is wonderful, but somehow it's not special. . . . I'm a man with a man's body and there's no mystery there. Women are very mysterious to me and I find that special" (emphasis added).

Let us say that gay sex celebrates male eroticism. It is synergistic; it amplifies one's capacity for erotic pleasure far beyond what he himself could experience. Perhaps the difference between masturbation and gay sex is like the difference between listening to music on a small player and listening to the same music at high volume on a powerful stereo set with a state-of-the-art speaker system.

But what did Klein's bisexual patient mean when he referred to the feeling of '*being one* with a woman'? Surely, many men experience a merging of identities in gay sex. Perhaps the difference is this: In gay sex, the merging of identities makes one feel like more of a *man*; more handsome, more powerful, more erotic, etc. In heterosexual love-making, the male partner feels like more *than* a man; for the moment he is neither man nor woman but part of a *man-woman union*. At its best, heterosexual love-making becomes a transcendental experience.

Tom

Nicolosi wrote of a patient, Tom, one of those rare persons who was actively involved with a gay lover and also claimed to be deeply in love with his wife of 15 years. (He had been a faithful husband for the first five years of marriage, until the birth of their first child.) Tom's experience gave him an insight into both heterosexual and homosexual love. His therapist asked him, "Do you think the depth of intimacy between two men can ever go as deeply as that between a man and a woman?" In his response, Tom commented on differences between homosexual and heterosexual love, based on 15 years of direct experience:

> I don't think so. Because women bring something complementary to the relationship. They balance out the qualities the man brings to it. . . The sexual experience with men is more . . . more sexual. This sounds strange to say, but sex with a woman is more tame, more inhibited. There is more animal turn-on with a man, while with a woman, it's more emotional, more of a total experience. . . There's another big difference. In many, if not most, gay experiences, the sex starts right at the beginning . . . [and] in most cases the relationship fizzles out quickly (Nicolosi 1993, page 29).

What does a woman want? A 1983 study in marital happiness suggests that what women want from their marriage partner is something quite different from what gay men give each other. Antill interviewed and tested 108 married couples, and concluded (page 153) that women value a husband who is "sensitive to the needs of others, compassionate, and warm." Surprisingly, perhaps, Antill reports a correlation of .61 (p<.001) between wife's rating of her marital happiness with her husband's measured *"femininity."* While gay men give each other vigorous, erotically powerful "hot sex," good husbands give their wives lovemaking that is ardent but also sensitive, warm, and compassionate.

A pro-heterosexual perspective

In gay sex, "simple techniques [can be] exceptionally effective," as Tripp has noted. Males are quick to respond to sexual stimulation, and gay sex is "so easy," a novice is pleased to discover. If a gay man can stimulate his partner just like he himself would like to be stimulated, there is rather little new to learn about how to be a good lover. Heterosexual lovemaking, by contrast, challenges the male to discover a secret world of female sexuality, to penetrate his partner not only physically, but to penetrate an emotional world quite different from his own, to coordinate his capacity for quick erotic arousal with his partner's more deep-seated and slow-moving arousal. The gay man's success as a lover depends more on his physical endowment (the attractiveness of his face, his body, his penis), the heterosexual man's success depends more on skills he has mastered, and on his ability to establish an *intimate relationship*. This suggests that venturing into the world of heterosexual relations requires a relative freedom from sexual anxiety, a readiness to tolerate the risk of coming off as a clumsy novice, a willingness to share one's inner thoughts and feelings, and an interest in his partner not only as a sexual object but also as a person.

Maddox (page 177) records a therapist's observation that gay sex is not so different from masturbation, but heterosexual lovemaking challenges a male to master an entirely new set of skills:

> If the other person is like one's self, one is in effect doing it with one's self. It's the not knowing, the *vive le difference*, that takes it beyond mutual masturbation and into an adventure and sharing.

NOTES TO CHAPTER 16

1. Recognition of this gender difference was noted by Charles Darwin, whose 1871 *Descent of Man* contains the following observation:

> In the most distant classes of the animal kingdom, with mammals, birds, reptiles, fishes, insects, and even crustaceans, the differences between the sexes follow almost exactly the same rules; the males are almost always the wooers. . . . .

2. A reminder that here, as elsewhere, we are describing *norms* that do not cover every individual occurrence. For example, Masters *et al.* (1982, page 335) offer the following recollection of a thirty-one-year-old woman:

> I'd been married for almost ten years and had always been faith-
> ful, but I kept wondering what it would be like to have sex with
> someone else. One night I was out with some friends, and we
> met a few guys who bought us drinks and talked with us awhile.
> One of them was real good-looking and flirting with me, and I
> sort of flirted back. We went off to a motel for three or four
> hours, and it was beautiful sex, fantastic sex, just like a novel.
> That was the end of it, and it just felt good to know that I'd had
> the experience. I never told my husband and I don't plan to.

3. Cupach and Metts (page 215) report: "When asked to describe their sexual relationships, men are more likely to mention frequency of intercourse and activities that are sexually arousing, while women are more likely to mention themes of comfort, responsiveness, specialness, and communication." A long-time investigator of the gender differences of children, Eleanor Maccoby (pages 216-217)) comments, "[In adulthood,] each sex's orientation to sexuality . . . resembles the qualites of interaction that were experienced in same-sex playgroups, insofar as females seek emotional interchange and males more often seek physical stimulation."

4. This author has mislaid the source of this item, and apologizes to both the reader, and to the writer of a good observation.

5. Humphreys (1970) observed that "inserters" sometimes offered the fellator a flaccid penis.

6. Women are more pedomorphic than men; they retain more childlike features: overall size is smaller, eyes are more prominent, "brow ridges and mandible smaller. A woman's skin is soft, smooth, thin and [generally more] hairless . . . and her hair is soft like a baby's. Her cheeks are chubby, her forehead large and rounded, her mouth and teeth small, her voice soft and high-pitched (Weisfeld, page 198). From an evolutionary standpoint, pedomorphic features serve women well: they evoke the male's protective, paternal tendencies.

7. Gay sexual performance is not always as impressive as what Masters and Johnson are reported to have observed. Prudishness and inhibition are also to be found among gays (Tripp, page 95). One gets the impression that Masters and Johnson somehow got a sample of committed gay couples who enjoyed the exhibitionistic aspect of this research. Being the more conventional group, the heterosexual couples may have felt more embarrassed by the presence of the "scientific observers," even though Masters and Johnson probably did what they could to make them feel comfortable.

8. Wells compared the lovemaking language habits of 120 Midwestern university students, 30 in each gender and sexual orientation category. Gay males and lesbians used erotic language significantly more often with a spouse or lover. Gay males more often used slang than did heterosexual males.

9. Baron (page 614) describes a case in which compulsive, ego-alien homosexual activity was "precipitated by feelings of depression and anxiety."

10. LeVay and Nonas maintain that the popularity of various homosexual practices rises and falls from time to time. The 1970s seems to have been a period of intensified and wide-ranging homosexual activity. During that decade, "many men were . . . busy leading lives of furious self-indulgence" (LeVay and Nonas, page 67). Also, "anonymous group sex, rimming (oral-anal contact), fist-fucking, S/M scenes, and drug abuse became the order of the day at scores of bathhouses and sex clubs in New York, San Francisco, and other large cities" (*ibid.*, page 62).

11. Fellatio, the clinical Latin term for oral sex, can actually be traced back to Roman slang.

12. Humphreys tallied the estimated ages of 53 fellatio partnerships, and found that in 40 (75 per cent) cases, the insertee was judged to be the older. One of his "cooperative respondents" had this to say (pages 108-109): "Well, I started off as the straight young thing. Everyone wanted to suck my cock. I wouldn't have been caught dead with one of those things in my mouth! . . . So, here I am at forty-- with two grown kids--and the biggest cocksucker in [this town]!"

13. Sanders notes (page 352) that "many homosexual men easily change positions and roles during or between sexual encounters."

14. Intimacy is, of course, a reciprocal relationship in which each partner is attentive to the moods and feelings of the other. If physical release is all a person wants, an intimate involvement with his partner may seem like an unnecessary burden, "a pain in the ass," as one of Weinberg *et al.*'s respondents put it (page 54).

15. These figures serve as a corrective to reports describing a range of homosexual practices, but giving no indication of the relative popularity or rarity of the various practices. For example, on page 18 of Weinberg *et al.* the reader is told that in San Francisco are to to be found gay bars, tearooms, adult bookstores, "a urine club (for those interested in urine play), an enema club, a 'scat' club (for feces play), [and] a fisting club (where one partner inserts his or her fist in another partner's anus and/or vagina)." These seem to be quite infrequently practiced in the gay male population as a whole.

16. So important is lubrication to anal sex that a popular gay bathhouse adopted the name "Crisco."

17. See endnote 4.

17　Pain and Suffering

Chapter 16 compared the sex life of gay and heterosexual men, and suggested that many gay men experience prolonged peaks of sexual arousal ("hot sex") that surpass the sexual experience of many heterosexual men. Alas, it is also a fact that in the course of their lifetime, from boyhood to old age, many homosexual men endure pain and suffering—both inner and social, both emotional and physical—that is outside the experience of many members of the comfortable majority.

A study of homosexual experience cannot avoid recognizing that pain and suffering is intrinsic to homosexual life as we observe it today. A market-research study released in 1995[1] reported that gay men (and lesbians) are more self-centered, feel increasingly under stress, are more cynical and distrustful of others:

> [According to a Yankelovich Partners market survey reported by LeVay and Nonas, (page 112)] gays and lesbians are significantly more focused on themselves than are heterosexuals. They are more concerned with physical appearance, physical fitness, and keeping up with fashion.

> [The same market survey] reported that gays and lesbians] are more likely to feel under stress, and to believe the stress in their lives is increasing. This increase in stress is felt equally in money matters, employment, in their relationships with their parents, and in their personal lives. They are more likely than heterosexuals to be seeking ways to reduce stress, for example by taking leisure vacations, by taking tranquilizers and sleeping pills, by taking measures to secure their homes and possessions . . . [and by expressing] more cynicism and distrust [toward government, corporations, and individuals] (*ibid.*, pages 112-113).

Feeling under stress underlies substance abuse and, according to LeVay and Nonas (page 208), "numerous studies have reported that substance abuse is more prevalent among lesbians and gay men than among heterosexuals."

> [D]rinking does not decline with age in the homosexual population as it does among heterosexuals. . . . [The 1989 study by McKirman and Peterson also] concluded that marijuana and cocaine use is elevated among gay men and lesbians (*ibid.*, page 208).

It would not be necessary to devote a separate chapter to this topic except that this phenomenon raises several questions, both practical and theoretical.　The most urgent question raised by homosexual suffering is: How can it be reduced, or even eliminated? This practical question raises a number of theoretical questions about the *sources* of homosexual suffering. After examining the theoretical questions, we will return to the practical questions, benefitting (we hope) from a fuller understanding of what brings about homosexual suffering.

The homophobia problem revisited

In a clinical manual edited by James Cassese, *Gay Men and Childhood Sexual Trauma*, gay-affirmative therapists seem to agree that the two major sources of homosexual pain and suffering are childhood sexual abuse and homophobia. Addressing the homophobia question first, why do gay men sense that most straight men don't like them, fear them, or hate them? We have discussed homophobia in Chapter 6, and distinguished between several types of homophobia: normal, neurotic, and socially disruptive or even dangerous.

Most evolutionary psychologists would probably disagree with gay advocates as to what homophobia is all about. Most would probably regard homophobia as a variety of *xenophobia*: the fear of something strange, a gut reaction observed not only in humans but elsewhere in the animal world. Among humans, as we pointed out in Chapter 6, homophobia is also a coping mechanism, a strategy for warding off one's *own* homosexual feelings, a strategy for asserting one's masculinity in a social world where so much importance is placed on developing a clear and stable gender role. Motivation to develop a clear and stable gender role may be genetic, since this has had a distinct survival value in human history.

Then there are what John Money has labeled the malignant homophobes, violence-prone men who react to homosexuals with murderous rage. Police, courts of law, and prisons must protect all members of society against men who commit acts of violence, whether their victims are gay or straight. And gay men must take care not to let themselves be entrapped by a malignant homophobe.[2]

To a gay advocate, homophobia is a much simpler matter. It has nothing to do with instinctive reactions to strangeness. It has nothing to do with defensive strategies to ward off one's own homosexual feelings. Cassese declares that "homophobia is a disguised extension of misogyny directed at the gay male" (page 3). What he seems to be saying is that homophobia is simply an expression of "male chauvinism." Cassese accepts the feminist belief that male chauvinists advocate the oppression of women so that men can continue to dominate society. Male chauvinists hate gays because gays are not "real men," because there is something woman-like about gay men.

How does the day-to-day experience of gay men, from early childhood to adulthood, lead to the feeling that they are an oppressed minority? Even before he becomes of school age, the pre-homosexual boy often discovers that his interests, aptitudes, and talents set him apart from the majority of his peers. The recollections of Will Fellows's farm boys (see Ch. 9) are consistent with the boyhood experiences of many gay men with a distinctly urban upbringing.

The pre-homosexual boy's gender-atypical interests lead him to spend more time indoors, sometimes as mother's helper, while his peers engage in rough-and-tumble outdoor play. The pre-homosexual boy enjoys playing house or school, with little girls. He gains some social skills from this experience but he also misses what rough-and-tumble games, and play-fighting would teach him: how to compete, how to win and how to lose graciously, how to participate in the social and secret world of boys. As an equal among other boys, he would experience *male bonding*,[3] which will teach him how to relate to male peers, knowledge he will draw upon throughout his life.

Human gregariousness and homophobia

Naturalists recognize *gregarious* animals, those that live and hunt in groups. By contrast, many of the cat family, though they pair off to reproduce, are in many ways *solitary* creatures. Wolves, dogs, sheep, and primates of all kinds (except orangtans) are social species. A dog is faithful to its owner because, as a pet, the owner is its closest social tie. In the wild, it is faithful to its pack. Humans are primates, after all, and most primates are gregarious creatures. Status, knowing one's position in its group, is an important determinant of one's sense of well-being. As Campbell (page 133) has put it, "*[F]or humans, for chimpanzees, and for baboons—the problem of life has been, and still is, largely the problem of getting along in a group.*"

The human species evolved in the grasslands of Africa where they were prey to ferocious killers; big, strong, fast and therefore *dangerous*. Primates survived because of group cohesiveness. A single individual didn't stand a chance against a hungry predator, but a *group* of primates could scare the predator off.[4]

For ordinary persons, identifying one's self as a homosexual results in a significant loss of status. The fact that *man is a social animal* means that a major disturbance of his status—with family, with friends, with his work group—will be psychologically unsettling. (He can overcome this disturbance at least in part by gaining status inside a *gay* community.) If this is at the basis of "internalized homophobia," it will take more than a public relations campaign, more than friendly legislation, to dispel it.

To get back to the psychological problem of the gender atypical boy: he senses that he is out of step with the majority. Perhaps this awareness, *by itself*, engenders anxiety in this social animal. Often, the non-conformist suffers ridicule and rejection not only from his peers, but from parental figures as well. Father may reject the boy who fails to fulfill father's hopes. Mother may respond to father's rejection by over-protecting the boy. (Perhaps she wanted a little girl anyway, and is pleased that the child lets her curl his hair and dress him in fancy clothes.)

During his school years, the pre-homosexual boy continues to face isolation and rejection, which may escalate into cruelty and physical torment, depending on what his school environment permits. To some extent, this expression of hostility is generated by his school mates' inner struggle to establish their own gender identities. Tormenting a pre-homosexual boy is one way of asserting one's own masculinity, a tactic that must be discouraged in a civilized society.

Rejected by the cohesive majority, the gender-atypical boy seeks out the companionship of other boys who have been rejected because of their gender-atypical or deviant traits of whatever kind. This further isolates the gender-atypical boy from the majority, and may also foster the transition from homosexual fantasy to homosexual play.

In Chapter 21, we will meet Dr. Jeff, a gay man who recalls that academic and artistic talent earned him the respect of his peers *despite* his gender-atypical traits. This good fortune has undoubtedly been shared by other gender-atypical boys who exhibited socially valuable skills of various kinds: jokesters, entertainers, artists, singers, musicians, or writers. Teachers of the arts should give these boys the moral support they do not find at home or among their peers.

At adolescence, the gender atypical boy is drawn to that social milieu in which he seems to fit: a world in which he finds status and satisfactions that he cannot find elsewhere, a world in which he is "among friends." If he is exceptionally goodlooking, his status in the homosexual world may be very high indeed. Good looks win higher status in the gay world than good looks alone would accord him in the heterosexual world. He enjoys more immediate and more varied access to sexual gratification, and a feeling of liberation from social conventions that restrict the lives of most adolescents. But the conventional majority—family, peers, and work group--look down upon the gay young man's separation from their more restrictive rules of sexual behavior.

Cassese (page 3) describes how homophobia unleashes "the forces of oppression" that damage a gay man's life:

> [H]e cannot legally marry; he can rarely be open about himself
> in the workforce; he can seldom hold a lover's hand in public
> without the fear of assault. He is vulnerable to discrimination in
> employment, housing, medical care. He is belittled as "girlish,"
> "less than a man" by a dominant misogynist culture that demands
> that he behave according to oppressive standards. He is teased
> and tormented in school and consequently often performs below
> his potential academically.

In the U.S., gay spokesmen cry out for legal protection. Let us look at what is happening in the Netherlands, where anti-discrimination laws go back to 1973. *More than 25 years later*, published reports (Solomon, page 203) tell us that gay men suffer from a high rate of depression, and "the rate of depression is higher for closeted people than for uncloseted people." Writes Dutch investigator

Sandfort (*ibid.*), "[I]n the Netherlands . . . we are more open to gayness than almost anywhere else in the world." Why should a gay man hide his sexual orientation in that society? Sandfort's words (*ibid.*) give the answer: "[I]n the Netherlands . . . the world is still straight, and the *strain of being gay in a straight world* is substantial" (emphasis added).

Richard Posner was similarly surprised to learn how in 1990 a Dutch military attaché in Washington responded to a question about homosexuals in the Dutch military. Homosexuality is not a problem in the military, the diplomat asserted, adding that "it has to be considered that *most homosexuals make a secret of their sexual orientation out of fear for reactions*" (emphasis added). Posner reflects (page 307): "[I]f decades of official tolerance have not eliminated social intolerance, one may wonder whether the expectation of eventual complete social tolerance may not be utopian."

Sandfort reports (Solomon page 203) that gay people, even those who are out of the closet with their colleagues seem to feel more isolated from their coworkers and are "less likely to share information about their personal lives with others in the workplace. . . " Why? Because their personal problems are *different*, their family problems are *different*, their health problems are *different*.

The strain of being gay in a traditional family means that the gay man knows he will not fulfill his parents' wish to see their circle of kinship enlarged, as it has already begun to shrink by the death of its older members. When their son chooses a bride, not only does the bride enlarge the family circle, but—if all goes well –her family merges with the bridegroom's family circle.[5] Grandchildren further enlarge and enrich the family circle.

If all goes well, kinship ties and grandchildren are a significant source of emotional security and gratification to aging parents. These are facts that may be only dimly understood but deeply felt by both the gay man, who senses that somehow he has let his parents down, and by his parents themselves. The anxiety a gay man feels about his parents' disappointment is not well described as "social oppression" or "internalized homophobia."

The strain of being gay in a straight world may continue to burden homosexual men long after they win every protection of the law. Why? Because man is a social animal, and those who do not share what is at the center of the lives of the majority—marriage and child rearing—are apt to experience less than full acceptance from their peers. If this is a fact, laws and education cannot eliminate everything that gay advocates call "internalized homophobia."

Gay men as victims of childhood sexual abuse

Kahn (page 239) interviewed the clinical director of a New York City counseling and drop-in center for gay youth. The clinician, himself a gay man, was *"astonished at the percentage of young gays and lesbians who have suffered sex-*

ual molestation as children. He finds this a difficult problem to deal with, as dis-cussion often evokes a traumatic response." For over 35 years this fact has been reported in the mental health literature. In 2002 Nicolosi and Byrd reported eight articles (Finch 1967, Finkelhor 1981, Johnson and Shrier 1985 and 1987, Shrier and Johnson 1988, Dimock 1988, Rekers 1995, and Dickson 1996) indicating that *the recollection of childhood sexual abuse* is characteristic of homosexual men. For example, in 1981 Finkelhor (page 81) reported that he had asked 266 college men the following questions (paraphrased): (1) When you were a child, did you ever have sexual contact with an adult? (2) Have you had a sexual experience with another male during the past year? Results: "Those who had been sexually victimized prior to age 13 by an older person were *four times more like-ly* to be currently homosexually active than those who had had no childhood homosexual experience at all" (emphasis added). In the Summary of their 2002 paper (page 931) Nicolosi and Byrd describe homosexuality as the "reparation of (i.e, an attempt to cope with) early boyhood trauma."

In their 2000 manual on gay-affirmative therapy, Cassese and his co-authors struggle with the fact that *memory of childhood sexual abuse* figures prominent-ly in the minds of many unhappy homosexual men. What complicates gay-affir-mative therapy, writes King (page 26), is that some gay patients (wrongly, King is sure) believe that the abuse experience caused them to be gay. The gay male trauma survivor may suppose that "the abuse caused me to be gay," and may therefore be justified in feeling, "I hate my homosexuality" [6] . . . "I deserved to be abused because I'm gay." It "requires great clinical skill," says gay-affirmative therapist King (page 26), to distinguish between "what belongs to the [patient's homosexual] orientation" and what has resulted from the sexual abuse. King con-cludes (page 34) that treatment succeeds when the patient understands that the abuse was caused by the pathology of the abuser, and when the patient is able "to deeply prize [his homosexuality] as a positive aspect of self":

> Successful treatment of the gay male sexual abuse survivor
> necessitates the careful separation of the client's abuse experi-
> ence from his sexual orientation. The survivor must be able to
> deeply prize [his homosexuality] as a positive aspect of self
> while appropriately externalizing blame for [his abuse] as result-
> ing from the pathology of [the abuser].

King's paper affords an inside look at what sometimes goes on inside a gay-affirmative therapist's office. Here is a patient who says, "I hate my homosexu-ality." The therapist uses "great clinical skill" to bring the patient "to deeply prize [his homosexuality] as a positive aspect of self." Isn't it just possible, Dr. King, that the patient *meant what he said*, and would gladly leave the gay lifestyle if his therapist helped him make the change?

Gay-affirmative therapist Cassese (page 10) considers it a complication that a gay patient who suffered from sexual trauma in childhood, may *defensively*, Cassese believes, recall the abuse experience as a fond or sexually exciting memory. What Cassese apparently does not consider is that perhaps the experience was *both* traumatic *and at the same time* sexually exciting. According to the viewpoint of Alfred Adler,[6] a person's early recollections are colored by his *present* state of mind. This suggests that when the person is in a good mood, he recalls the positive aspect of a childhood experience, and when he is distressed, he recalls the distressing aspect of the same experience. Here are three cases in which the individual recalls *both* the disturbing and thrilling aspects of an abuse experience:

A homosexual patient recalls that at summer camp, when he was a puny child, he idolized a tall, well-developed camper who was also a bully. One night his "idol" forced him to masturbate him twice:

> "Now you know what a real prick should look like," he said. . . .
> What bothers me up to this day is I couldn't say that I resisted
> too much and remember some of the excitement and pleasure I
> got. . . ." (Hatterer 1970, pages 51-52).

Baumann recalls that when he was a very young child, his father, in a fit of drunken anger, had told him that he was not his real son, only an adopted child. Then his mother died of cancer, and his father married a woman who was a stern discipilinarian. When he was five or six, this vulnerable boy had an unexpected experience of sexual pleasure:

> Tommy was a well-built young lad of about twelve or thirteen,
> who, with little warning, coaxed me out of my play suit and pro-
> vided . . . "a blow job." What he did felt good. I was at a total
> loss to understand [my stepmother's alarm] when I innocently
> informed [her] about this wonderful adventure (Baumann, page
> 161).

Hatterer (1980, page 103) tells of a homosexual patient's mixed feelings as he describes an experience of sexual abuse when he was ten years old and "punished" by his 15-year-old brother (for the fact that the older brother had to stay home as a "baby sitter" when he could have been out with his friends, having fun):

> Tom was shocked almost senseless when he and Robert got into
> bed. Robert . . . stretched out on his back, and hissed, "You . . .
> ruined my night, and now you're going to make up for it.
> Here—take my cock in your mouth!" Tom was shaking from

> head to foot, as he'd just been shoved into an alien, freezing
> world; at the same time he was in a state of exquisite excitement.
> . . Robert gazed at the ceiling in a trance of self-gratification
> while he unemotionally but authoritatively instructed Tom in per-
> forming his new duties. Tom was transfixed by his brother's
> large, throbbing erection and by this incredible new activity.

Gay-affirmative therapists attribute the dysfunctional habits (but *not* the sexual orientation) of homosexual men to the effects of childhood sexual abuse.
King (page 24) asserts that sexual abuse survivors may "continue to be eroticized
by stimulation and circumstances that overtly or covertly resemble the abuse circumstances." He continues:

> This is a type of learned behavior that is imprinted as a traumatic
> effect of the abuse. It is repeated in an often excruciatingly dys-
> tonic cycle[7] which is ultimately in the service of the person
> attempting to recover from the trauma.

King seems to be saying that a gay man who is eroticized by dangerous, risky,
or disgusting circumstances, may be seeking to reinstate the circumstances of his
sexual abuse. Why? In his 1920 essay, "Beyond the Pleasure Principle," Freud
(page 22) ponders over this tendency of patients to compulsively repeat "painful
emotions . . . and revive them with the greatest ingenuity." Freud asks, in effect,
What pleasure can there be in reliving painful experiences? In 1945, Fenichel
(page 45) suggests that through the compulsive repetition of painful events the
individual strives "to achieve a belated mastery." Fenichel suggests that this
defensive mechanism of "belated mastery" also accounts for nightmares that re-
enact a traumatic experience, and for the "bad dreams" of little children.

A distressed homosexual patient looks back at his childhood experience of
sexual abuse *as if* that that event caused him to become homosexual. Wrong!
says his gay-affirmative therapist. All right, why is childhood sexual trauma a
special problem with homosexual patients? Is it possible that pre-homosexual
boys are more likely to be molested than boys who will grow up straight? Suppose the gender-atypical boy is an easier target for the child abuser. His rough-
and-tumble brother is more likely to kick and scream, to refuse to submit to the
abuser's wishes. Faced by a child abuser, the pre-homosexual boy has two strikes
against him: he is less aggressive, and he is also hungry for close contact with a
father figure. This is what may make him so vulnerable to adult exploitation. If
this is true, *the abuser and the pre-homosexual boy are attracted to each other.*
This may account for the statistically significant power of a history of child
abuse, in predicting adult homosexuality. At an ex-gay conference, a formerly
homosexual testified:

> When I was a small boy, I was molested by my older brother. By

the time I was 16, I had been molested by a school teacher and by three strangers. *I guess molesters can look into a needy child's eyes and see that he is a candidate for molestation.* I sometimes feel that it was like I had a sign on my back, "Molest me."

Confirmatory survey findings on child molestation. In 1983 a large-scale study of sexual behavior was conducted by Cameron *et al.*, and the findings included recollections of childhood molestations. Of 1,348 adult men, approximately 6 per cent claimed to be bisexual or homosexual. Only *two per cent* of heterosexual men recalled an experience of child abuse (defined as sexual relations with an adult man when the respondent was not yet 13), compared with *fifteen per cent* of the bisexual-or-homosexual group. Typically, the abuser was an older brother or other relative.

Health risks

Gay men must cope with a third source of pain and suffering, not mentioned in Cassese's book but a significant part of the gay man's physical and psychological burden: the health risks associated with the gay lifestyle.

(1) Multiple sex partners greatly increases the likelihood of contracting an STD (sexually transmitted disease). Even prior to the AIDS epidemic, STDs—gonorrhea and syphilis were known to spread like wildfire through gay communities.

(2) Anal sex, highly valued by many gay men, poses health hazards because the rectal wall is easily punctured, and has been evolved to absorb moisture, which is why the HIV virus is so readily absorbed in anal sex. Rotello asserts that the combination of multiple partners and anal sex made the AIDS epidemic "a crisis waiting to happen." If this combination of practices continues, Rotello predicts, another medical crisis is likely to befall gay men.

(3) Goldstone's medical handbook for gay men devotes its first chapter, 22 pages long, to anal sex: its anatomy, hygiene, foreplay, toys, sex technique, pain, and complications. He tells the reader that in "a medical study of men who practiced anoreceptive intercourse . . . *25 percent reported at least isolated episodes of fecal incontinence*" (page 21). An age-similar group of heterosexuals had an only three percent incontinence rate" (italics added).

(4) The combination of oral and anal sex poses special health hazards. When a person gives oral sex to someone who had been

the inserter in the act of anal sex with a different partner, the person who gives oral sex risks absorbing germs from someone else's digestive tract . Washing one's penis after anal sex may remove all visible traces of rectal entry, but may fail to to make the penis germ-free. Although everyone's digestive tract contains a microbial colony, the introduction of another person's microbial colony may cause a digestive disturbance that physicians term the "gay bowel syndrome."

(5) According to The Wall Street Journal (July 8, 2002), AIDS researchers "estimate that there are 40,000 new [HIV] infections nationally each year," and 42 per cent (or 16,800) of these cases result from gay sex.

Apart from the direct health hazard of AIDS, this epidemic darkens the lives of gay men in these two ways: (a) making the untimely death of friends a greater likelihood, and (b) burdening with guilt the gay man who is still HIV-negative. (Gay-affirmative therapist Odets' book focuses on this very topic.)

Extent of emotional pain and suffering

Homosexuals show a high rate of emotional pain and suffering (as reported in Chapter 24): an overuse of alcohol and drugs, a somewhat higher rate of emotional trouble, depression and suicidal tendencies. If all this results from social ostracism and abuse, then it is important to stop the social oppression that is so damaging to homosexual men. Accordingly, believers in social justice,[8] and the more assertive homosexual men themselves, have fought to improve the legal and social status of homosexuals, and have worked to win them a more sympathetic, understanding, and permissive social environment.

Educational efforts and cultural change

From kindergarten to graduate school, many teachers at all levels have dedicated themselves to educate pupils and students to regard homosexuality not as a disability or shame, but as a *lifestyle*. If homosexual men sometimes behave in dangerous and bizarre ways (*e.g.*, sex with strangers in public places), mental health experts predicted that as the social status of homosexuals improves, their rash and risky practices will disappear. For example, in 1980 (page 20) psychiatrist Judd Marmor expressed the belief that homosexual bizarre behaviors are "defensive excesses" triggered by the fears and prejudices of a homophobic majority. Homosexual excesses will disappear, he argued, when homophobia disappears:

The vast majority of homosexual men and women ask only to be accepted as human beings and allowed to live their own lives free of persecution or discrimination. To the extent that they are permitted to do so, we can anticipate that many of the defensive excesses and bizarre "acting out" behaviors that characterize some of the more extreme gay liberationists will disappear from our cultural scene[9] (italics added).

This prediction was made over 20 years ago. Since that time, much has changed to improve the status of gay men. Homosexual acts between consenting adults have been widely decriminalized. Gay men have been sympathetically portrayed in serious literature, on stage, in the movies, and on TV. Openly gay men have been elected to public office, appointed to university faculties, have been accepted into the ministry, the rabbinate, police departments, and in many other trades and professions. Support groups have emerged to help parents cope with distress over their child's sexual orientation and to reunite gays with their families.

Summary and Discussion

Mental health experts wrongly predicted that as the social status of homosexuals improved, dangerous and bizarre sex practices would disappear. Since the 1950s, much has changed to improve the status of gay men, as we have already noted. Today, sex between strangers (with all the hazards intrinsic to this practice) is still commonplace, though now it usually takes place not in public parks and rest rooms, but in comfortable bathhouses, hotels, and other places. Hazardous sex practices of other kinds, and substance abuse, are not unique to the gay lifestyle, but are more common in homosexual life. Considering all the evidence, it is doubtful whether the protection of pre-homosexual boys from sexual abuse alone, and the banishment of social oppression alone, will eliminate homosexual pain and suffering.

A man who feels distressed about his homosexual life needs help to resolve his dilemma or overcome a painful ambivalence. What is at stake is not only his sexual orientation but also his social orientation, his spiritual orientation, his life orientation. Where should he turn for help? A gay-affirmative therapist will assure him that his distress is just "an acute dystonic phase," and that he needs help in reclaiming his gay identity as "a deeply prized aspect of his self."

If he has been in touch with gay thinking, either through reading gay literature or word-of-mouth, he has been warned to stay away from mainstream therapists, who express contempt for the gay lifestyle, and whose tactics for inducing sexual reorientation include aversive therapy, electric shock, and pushing patients into premature heterosexual efforts. To some extent, this may be true, but it is *also* true that there are therapists who keep alive the flame of hope that shines so brightly in the *1970* book by Lawrence J. Hatterer:

The therapist must not project his own values nor should he be unrealistic, hostile, or punitive, and he cannot moralize with or reject the [homosexual] patient. He must be careful not to patronize him or behave in a superior fashion and not resent the patient's values or make him feel that his life-style makes him totally alien to the establishment (Hatterer 1970, page 409).

The patient's ego should be supported by indicating to him the value of his sociability and nonerotic warmth toward homosexual and heterosexual males. Similarly, any ability to give of himself and be altruistic should be encouraged because these traits represent valuable aspects of his nature about which he should be aware. A therapist should show his appropriate belief in and support of the patient's productive work and positive emotionality that is valuable to society and to himself (*ibid*, page 411).

Anthropologists tell us of many cultures with berdaches, homosexual subcultures, reviewed in Chapter 10. What can we learn from these reports? What seems to stand out is that berdaches tend to occupy a distinct status with clearly prescribed roles designating what they may do, what they must do, and what they must not do. They constitute a clearly recognized social group of their own. In our society, on the other hand, gay men have fought for full participation in the life of the majority. Increasingly, our laws, and people of good will, support this goal. How to more fully realize this goal is the task that lies ahead, and how much further improvement of the status of gay men will reduce their pain and suffering remains to be seen.

NOTES TO CHAPTER 17

1. This author tried to obtain the actual report of the Yankolevich Partners study, summerized by LeVay and Nonas) but the organization refused to release it, on the basis that a 1994 study was already 'out of date.' It was therefore necessary to quote from the LeVay and Nonas book.

2. Chapter 6, endnote 16, discusses the tragic experience of Matt Shepard, a physically slight, gay college freshman who met two strangers in a bar at the edge of Laramie, Wyoming. These malignant homophobes posed as gay men, and Matt accepted their invitation to drive off into the night with them in a pickup truck.

3. Male bonding probably begins in the all-male rough-and-tumble play groups of early childhood. Boys learn to enjoy all-boy company, respect each other's status, trust each other, help each other, express loyalty toward their leader and toward the group. Lionel Tiger discusses the male bond as if it emerges at adulthood to favor effective group hunting. Tiger seems to imply that since hunting of

large prey required close coordination of efforts of the hunting party, nature favored individuals who were predisposed to feel strong bonds of loyalty toward other members of their group.

Hunting parties were all-male groups for the same reason that rough-and-tumble play groups usually consist entirely of males: because males are better adapted physically for these activities. Boys are, generally, stronger and more energetic than girls. Adult men can run faster, and have more stamina, than women. Besides, pregnancy and the need to care for infants limited an adult female's usefulness in a hunting party. See "The Male Bond and Human Evolution," Chapter 3 in *Men in Groups*, by Lionel Tiger.

4. The danger of predators was not the only incentive for social living. Campbell (pages 131-132) lists three more evolutionary advantages of social cohesion: 1. "Food finding and food exploitation and handling. . ." 2. "[R]egular access to the opposite sex. . ." and 3. A greater "opportunity for learning" from peers and elders.

5. In the Jewish culture described in *Life Is With People*, (as in other traditional cultures) this aspect of marriage is explicitly recognized and celebrated. If all goes well, parents of the bride and groom (*makhetonim*) may eventually relate to each other like brother and sister. The wedding celebration includes a song and a dance of the trials and joys of makhetoneshaft ("in-law-hood").

6. The topic of this author's 1957 doctoral dissertation, *The Projective Interpretation of Early Recollections*, was a validation study of this Adlerian theory.

7. The statement that the patient describes his homosexuality as "excruciatingly dystonic" means, in plain language, that he tells his gay-affirmative therapist: "I hate being homosexual." To be true to his gay-affirmative commitment, the therapist must assure the patient that with some work the patient will again prize his lifestyle as a positive aspect of his self.

8. As Goethe said, "Two souls lie within my breast." We humans are animals (social animals, to be sure) and therefore have the animal impulse uncritically to affirm our membership in our group, and to reject those who do not belong. But we are also *self-critical human beings*. Most of us strive to fulfill the standards that make us human, like following The Golden Rule, that says "Do unto others as you would have them do unto you." Or obeying the biblical commandments: "You shall not wrong a stranger nor oppress him" (Exodus 22:20), "Love your fellow as yourself" (Leviticus 19:18), and "You shall not insult the deaf or place a stumbling block before the blind" (Leviticus 19:14). It is the mark of a good society that it fosters such pro-social behavior and rewards those citizens who strive to realize their *human* potential.

9. In another context (1980, pages 269-270) Marmor concedes that for some homosexuals, *promiscuity* expresses a basic sexual need:

> The promiscuity of some male homosexuals may rest in some of
> their common underlying psychodynamic patterns. For example,
> in many of them, there are fears of interpersonal commitment,
> intimacy, or responsibility that may play a part not only in their
> avoidance of heterosexual involvement but may also operate
> with regard to homosexual relationships. For such homosexuals
> part of the safety of brief homosexual liaisons rests precisely on
> the fact that such liaisons do not entail expectations of commit-
> ment, intimacy, or responsibility.

18 Two Models
of Human Learning

Chapters 10 through 15 describe homosexuality as such a varied and changing behavior, it seems more than likely that homosexual behavior must have a significant learning component. Thus we bypass the "Nature versus nurture" question, in favor of recognizing that the homosexual habit undoubtedly results from an *interaction* between learning and congenital factors.[1]

Perhaps you noted that the term *congenital* appears in the above paragraph, not hereditary. Why? Congenital describes a trait that appears at birth, whether caused by hereditary factors or by the prenatal environment. For example, a prenatal shortage of testosterone, results in low-masculinization of the brain, and may be caused by some accidental condition. The German biologist Dörner claims to have demonstrated that if the mother is under unusual stress during pregnancy, the result is a shortage of testosterone available to her unborn son,[2] but results of subsequent investigations have been mixed.

For many generations, naturalists have pondered over why the human infant is born so much more helpless than other creatures, so utterly unable to protect itself against harm, pre-programmed only with those reflexes necessary to keep it alive: breathing, sucking, crying, defecating, and regurgitating. The biological advantage of this "premature birth" is that at birth, the infant's head is still small enough to pass through the mother's birth canal.[3] At birth, the brain is still growing rapidly, "unfinished," not quite ready to cope with the outside world. The newborn comes into the outside world as a "postnatal fetus," with a brain-in-the-making, about half a year behind its closest primate relatives in its readiness to cope with the outside world.

When it is a few months old, the infant begins to demonstrate its impressive capability of *learning*. Unlike animals born with ready-made skills, beautifully adapted to a particular environment, the human neonate is born with few inborn skills but with the capacity to learn to adapt to the outside world, and to adopt a culture.[4] It is no accident that humans are distributed over a far wider variety of environments--tropical, arctic, and everything in-between--than any other species.

Most animal brains are more like *machines*, built to perform in a more-or-less specific way; the human brain is more like a *computer*, built to handle a wide range of tasks, depending on how it is programmed or reprogrammed. You cannot change a typewriter into an adding machine, but a computer can be programmed to function as either a typewriter, a calculator, a drafting machine, a type composing machine, a telephone, a game board, or an infinite variety of other machines.

A big difference between the human brain and the computer consists in how easily it can be reprogrammed. Take a computer that has served an English language user, and must be reprogrammed to serve a Spanish language user. Simply delete the English word-processing program, the English dictionary, the English spell-check, and install Spanish-language counterparts. It is not so easy to reprogram the human brain. Once English has become the person's native language, for example, there is no way completely to extinguish it psychologically. One can adopt Spanish as a foreign language, or as a second language, but the person will forever be programmed to think (and perhaps even to dream) in his native language. The human brain is plastic but not infinitely plastic.

Our learning capacity is built into the nature of the human brain. A basic difference between humans and most other animals is that for most animals, only childhood is a time of flexibility, play, and learning. Adulthood follows a more rigidly programmed pattern of behavior. Stephen Jay Gould comments that "we are preeminently learning animals, and our extended childhood permits the transference of culture by education" (1980, page 106). Gould quotes Lorenz's observation that throughout adulthood, humans remain "in a state of development:"

> The characteristic which is so vital for the human peculiarity of
> the true man (that of always remaining in a state of development)
> is quite certainly a gift which we owe to the *neotenous nature of*
> *mankind.* (italics added)"

Experimental studies, everyday and clinical observations lead us to not one but two models of learning: reinforcement theory, the reinforcement model of academic psychology, and the imprinting model introduced by Konrad Lorenz and popularized by John Money. According to reinforcement theory, a habit can be strengthened, modified, extinguished, and replaced, depending on the number of practice trials, and the schedule of reinforcements (pleasant or unpleasant events, *e.g.*, rewards, frustrations, deprivations, punishments). According to the imprinting model, the person is by nature ready at a certain critical time of development, to learn a certain habit. Once it is learned, it is locked into the brain and becomes "part of the person," so to speak. In this chapter, we will consider whether homosexuality can be conceptualized as *an acquired habit*, first according to the imprinting model, and then according to reinforcement learning theory.

Imprinting Theory

The imprinting model is also called the developmental learning process. It emphasizes that what is learned depends on (a) the strength of an inborn tendency, and (b) the precise *timing* of the learning experience (the individual is ready at a particular moment of development to acquire a given habit). If the opportunity presents itself at the moment of readiness, the habit is learned and permanently adopted.

According to reinforcement theory, a habit is acquired through the accumulation of many practice trials, and unless it continues to be practiced, the habit fades away or is lost through disuse. In *developmental learning*, however, a habit is suddenly acquired at a critical moment of development--through a "one-trial learning experience"--and once acquired, the habit becomes part of the person's behavioral repertory: never forgotten, never given up. For example, there is a propitious moment for learning to ice-skate, William James once observed. Similarly, when his child was learning a particular keyboard technique, the father was once told by his child's piano teacher: "This is something a child can learn to do in one day, and it would take a grown-up a week to learn."

The imprinting theory was adopted by John Money from Konrad Lorenz's famous experiment in which ducklings were fooled into following the naturalist around as if he was their mother. Apparently, a duckling (like a baby goat or other baby animal) has an inborn tendency to follow its mother around, and this tendency shows up at a definite period in its life. Whatever creature happens to be close to the baby at that period will be followed around as if it were its mother. At this critical period, most ducklings are close to their own mother, so this "instinctive tendency" serves it well; it has obvious survival value. This habit is highly resistant to change; it is as if a visual impression (a search image) were permanently imprinted in its brain.

John Money argues that this is a good model for describing the *interaction* of nature and nurture, inborn tendencies and social learning, in producing a homosexual orientation. Homosexuality results when "nature and nurture interact at a *critical period* of development and produce an effect that is immutable, or at least, long-lasting" (Money 1988, pages 122-123, italics added). He does not suggest at what point the propitious moment occurs, or exactly what is the critical learning experience.

Money (1988, pages 11-12) describes language learning as another good example of irreversible learning:

> You assimilate [your native language] into a brain prenatally
> made ready to receive a native language from those who consti-
> tute your primate troop and who speak it to you and listen to you
> when you speak it. Once assimilated through the ears into the
> brain, a native language becomes securely locked in--as securely
> as if it had been phylogenetically preordained to be locked in
> prenatally by a process of genetic determinism, or by the deter-
> minism of fetal hormone or other brain chemistries. So also with
> sexual status or orientation, which--whatever its genesis--may
> also become assimilated and locked into the brain as monosexu-

ally homosexual or heterosexual or as bisexually a mixture of both.

Money emphasizes a kind of learning that is "locked into the brain" and cannot be unlearned. He even suggests (1988, page 50) that learning which does not become "locked into the brain" is *not worth studying*:

> . . . [T]here is a biology of learning and remembering. That which is not biological is occult, mystical, or, to coin a term, spookological. Homosexology, the science of orientation or status as homosexual or bisexual rather than heterosexual, is not a science of spooks.

Homosexuality becomes so firmly rooted into the nervous system, says Money, that "it is analogous to left-handedness," and to suppose that a program of "therapy" can alter sexual orientation is as farfetched (and probably as needless) as to try to "correct" the habit of a left-handed person. Money's formu-lation rules out the practice of reorientation therapy, and if this implication is not clear to his reader, Money makes this implication unambiguously explicit:

> Most if not all claimed cures of homosexuality prove, on more detailed investigation, to have been cases in which there was, initially, some degree of bisexuality on which to capitalize. It is in just such a case that the individual may experience a sense of the self divided and in conflict,[5] for the resolution of which he or she seeks treatment to be monosexually one or the other, but not bisexually both together (1988, pages 87-88).

Sometimes a man may spontaneously shift from homosexuality to heterosexuality, Money observes. "If the individual were at the time in some type of treatment, the transition might be wrongly construed as a therapeutic triumph" (1988, page 108). But what does the spontaneous shift from homosexuality to heterosexuality say about Money's imprinting model? It may fit certain cases of lifelong homosexuality, highly resistant to change, but it certainly does not cover the variety of life histories observed by clinicians and researchers. If homosexuality can "spontaneously" (Money's word) come and go, within the lifetime of an individual, that makes the homosexual habit significantly different from imprinting, from language acquisition, and from left-handedness. LeVay expresses the opinion (1996, page 99) that Money's imprinting model "is not a good analogy" for describing how homosexuality is learned.

An example of stereotyped, irreversible animal learning is the inhibition of sexual arousal that occurs as a result of frustration or pain. Frank Beach observed (1949, page 68): *"If rams are repeatedly led to a ewe in full heat but separated from her by a gate they may upon later occasions refuse to approach the female even though the gate is open."* Here, taken from the experience of animal husbandry, is a striking metaphor of sexual inhibition, paralysis or impotence, resulting from a "locked-in" feeling of frustration.

Reinforcement Learning Theory[6]

In most college psychology textbooks, the chapter on learning emphasizes the docility, malleability, teachability, adaptability of the human person. Reinforce his efforts, reward him, guide him, give him feedback, disclose knowledge of results, and you can shape and reshape his habits. Change the reward schedule, punish unwanted behaviors, withhold reinforcements, deprive him of satisfactions, and you can eventually extinguish some old habits, inhibit others, and replace them with new ones. Reinforcement theory emphasizes malleability. The human mind is like Plasticine, the kind of clay that never hardens; it is forever workable. To the developmental learning theorist, the imprinting theorist, the human mind is more like ordinary clay that dries out and becomes brittle. A habit is like a clay vessel: if it has been fired you can shatter it but you cannot reshape it. Everyday life provides examples of both varieties of learning.

Habits become second nature. To people who speak and think in English, this feels like "the most natural way" to think and speak. Similarly, it is the honest, personal conviction of many gay men that their homosexual habits must be truly inborn: "In my very first experience with gay sex, it felt so natural; it felt so right. It felt like I had been doing this all my life." In many cases, this is a fact of inner conviction. Is this personal experience evidence of either the inborn or congenital basis of homosexual tendencies? Knowing what we do about the human mind, we would have to say No. *It is an illusion.*

The human mind's vulnerability to illusions is a topic of endless interest to psychologists, who have catalogued, demonstrated, and experimented with hundreds and hundreds of illusions: visual, auditory, kinesthetic, etc. Perhaps the most familiar illusion, one which we use every day, is the mirror-image illusion. Watch a baby crawl toward a floor-length mirror, and observe his naive response to what he sees before him. Eventually, he learns that what he sees so clearly in every detail, just isn't really there.[7]

But what is the basis of the gay man's illusion that this is *not* his first same-sex experience, that he has done this many times before? The psychological fact is that he has done this hundreds of times before: *in fantasy, in his imagination.* Let us suppose that Gay Guy is 22 years old at the time of his first same-sex encounter. He has been masturbating about three times a week since age 12, always accompanied by some sort of masculine fantasy: himself, a friend, a Hollywood actor, a sports champion, or the handsome stranger pictured in a "body-building" magazine. Physically he was alone, but in fantasy he was interacting with an attractive male partner, and that's what made masturbation, for him, a *rehearsal* for gay sex.[8]

Practice. The first rule of learning, whether you want to learn to play the piano or to play tennis, is *practice*. Another principle of learning (and a very important one) determines how much habit-strength each practice trial builds: How strongly and how *immediately* does the practice trial lead to a *reward*? How strongly does it lead to feeling of gratification?

Piano-playing habits are strengthened by many practice trials, and also by the praise of a respected teacher, by the applause of an audience, and by the pleasure of hearing one's own fingers produce beautiful music. Tennis-playing habits are strengthened by many practice sessions, and also by the praise of one's coach, by visible improvement in one's skill, and by the thrill of winning the game. Sexual habits are strengthened by the number of practice trials, and also by sexual gratification, by the physical thrill of orgasm.

Reinforcement. Learning theories suggest that there is an enormous difference between the habit-forming power of empty, ungratified fantasies or daydreams, and the habit-forming power of a fantasy that lead to immediate *sexual gratification*. This suggests that sexual habits may be rather well-established not by social experience, but by masturbation-to-orgasm accompanied by fantasy.

Masturbation as a learning experience. Generally, puberty begins at about the age of 12.5 years, and ejaculation begins about a year later. But for many months before this, a boy has the capacity for dry orgasms (Weisfeld, page 167). Masturbation-to-orgasm delivers a powerful physical thrill, and therefore makes the fantasy that accompanies such a repeated experience a well-learned habit. The more you practice, *the more satisfaction you derive from each practice session*, the more enduring is the habit. Habit becomes second nature.

Masturbation is a common boyhood practice, and this activity need not be accompanied by the fantasy of a partner of any kind, but is merely the celebration of one's physical powers, as in scratching one's back, or singing in the shower. But fantasy enriches the experience of masturbation. A shy boy may fantasize a sexual encounter with an exotic or faceless female partner, a bolder boy may fantasize a sexual tryst with the his buddy's sister. Quite probably the quality of masturbation fantasies helps shape the person's adult sexual orientation.

Since some homosexual potential exists throughout the human species, the fantasy accompanying masturbation is likely to include *some* same-sex content. Is it possible that adolescents who develop a strong homosexual orientation have developed this habit from a *consistent* program of same-sex fantasies accompanying masturbation-to-orgasm?

One of Kinsey's findings (pages 238-239) was the enormous range of the reported frequency of male masturbation-to-orgasm. Some boys masturbate several times a day, some once a day, some several times a week, some rarely, and a few say they do not masturbate at all. Homosexuals are believed to masturbate more frequently than heterosexuals.[9] According to Weinberg *et al.* (pages 348-349) self-masturbation is the most frequently employed sexual activity of homosexual adult males.

Written for a *straight* readership, advice on how to have a good sex life is very unlikely to discuss solitary masturbation, except for persons who are widowed or otherwise isolated. Quite the contrary, *gay* sex manuals elaborate on techniques of solitary masturbation as an erotic art.[10]

Let us go back to the case of Gay Guy, who since the age of 12 or so has been masturbating to orgasm three times a week, each time accompanying it with a same-sex fantasy. By age 22, he has had over a thousand practice sessions. Without realizing it, he is well rehearsed, he has been powerfully gratified, and has therefore acquired a well-established habit even *before* his first actual same-sex interaction. No wonder it feels as if he has done it before. The habit-building power of masturbation-to-orgasm is probably related to the fact that orgasm is accompanied by a release of the hormone oxytocin from the pituitary gland, which is probably responsible for the feeling of pleasure that accompanies orgasm (LeVay 1996, pages 51-52).

According to Crenshaw (page 96), oxytocin sensitizes the skin in general and the penis in particular, and thus promotes touching, affectionate behavior, and bonding. Crensaw suggests that oxytocin may also *reduce judgement* ("decreases cognition and impairs memory") during moments of sexual excitation. Does this suggest why some men and women—heterosexual and homosexual—fail to exercise good judgment during moments of sexual excitation? The author credits Newton's 1978 landmark article, based on 15 years of research. Crenshaw's book contains a 45-item bibliography (pages 323-324) on oxytocin.

Pillard (1997, page 62) dismisses a learning-theory interpretation of homosexuality by recalling the Sambia report of anthropologist Herdt:

> Herdt studied the Sambia tribe in New Guinea and their mythology of sexual development. A Sambia boy must imbibe quantities of semen in order to become virile and able to ejaculate semen himself. Thus, the pre-adolescent boys fellate older adolescents and young adult men to fill their bodies with the masculinizing fluid. . . . [Since] Sambian youth are having homosexual orgasms year after year . . . and having a perfectly enjoyable time, why don't they become "conditioned" to same-sex arousal and continue to seek it after their time comes to leave the men's hut, to court and marry? [With rare exceptions,] they just don't.

Pillard makes a good point. Similar to Herdt's Sambia observations, it might be noted that army draftees are trained to be combat killers, and are in many ways rewarded for their skills. But when they return to civilian life, they usually become peaceful, law-abiding citizens. The Sambian and army observations probably mean that an individual uses "learning opportunities" to become the kind of a person his society expects him to become.[11]

Generalization. A research psychiatrist's assistant called her director's attention to the fact that in her interviews with men on their emotional life, she noticed that those who had recalled a strong erotic attachment to their mother or sister *tended to be heterosexually inhibited*, and directed their sexual thoughts to masturbation or homosexuality (Hamilton, page 499). To a learning theorist, this observation illustrates the link between *avoidance* and *generalization*. Incestuous thoughts are both stimulating and painful; painful because they threaten the child with the severest punishments. (Not castration, but ostracism.) Avoidance of sexual *thoughts* (forget about sexual activity!) about mother or sister, *if the avoidance is severe enough*, tends to fan out or generalize into an avoidance of sexual thoughts concerning all females, particularly those who resemble mother or sister. Here learning theory interprets the classical psychoanalytical association between homosexuality and the close-binding mother.

The man who has been chastised by his boss, goes home and punishes his son, who then kicks the dog. Why doesn't the employee and his son strike back at their attacker? Because it is dangerous, or *forbidden* by society, and man is a social animal. That's how avoidance leads to *displacement*.

Displacement. Incestuous acts are taboo, and the learning environment of some boys leads them to believe that incestuous *thoughts and fantasies* are also forbidden. When this attitude of avoidance generalizes even further, *any* sexual contact with *any* girl is bad, evil, dirty, dangerous, naughty, and sinful; even thoughts about sexual contact with a girl seem dangerous. Now the boy may deflect his sexual thoughts to less guilt-laden, less dangerous objects: boys and men.

Michael Davidson, British journalist and gay man, recalls such a repressive childhood. He also reflects upon the more open, permissive culture of Southern Italy, where masturbation is no shame, and it is considered natural for a boy to seek opportunities to copulate with available girls or boys. In this social atmosphere, observes Davidson (page 172), "boys grow into excellent husbands and devoted fathers. . . ." In this milieu, Davidson notes (page 172), there is little sexual pathology or adult homosexuality.

Habit-modification. One never stops learning. An experience may be satisfying in its own right, for its own sake, but it may also be regarded as still another learning experience that will shape, change, modify and strengthen a habit. Experience teaches us what works and what doesn't. Knowledge of results shapes our habits accordingly, and makes it possible for one to improve one's performance, to build one's skills, so that the next performance is more skillful and more satisfying than the last.

Habit and choice. As experience shapes behavior, a habit can gradually become firmly established *without* the experience of deliberately choosing to do this or that. For example, as John E. Mayer pointed out,[12] some young men find themselves engaged to be married without ever having *chosen* to do so:

> "[W]e went steady and we liked each other a lot . . . but I didn't think it would ever become serious. . . . I didn't know this would happen." "I never had any thoughts about marriage. . . . I felt that it was best just not to bother pondering about things like this. . . . One day I just found myself trapped." "Everybody says we're going to get married, so we might as well go ahead and do it."

'It seemed like the natural thing to do.' 'I guess we were just meant for each other.' 'Fate.' 'Destiny.' Thus are established lasting behavior patterns without requiring that the individual *ever* make a choice. Habit becomes second nature. But in all honesty to say, 'I never made a choice; it seemed like the natural thing to do' does not put the phenomenon outside the range of learned behaviors.

The family as a learning environment. Most people assume the identity of their same-sex parent, but a person who says: "I am a gay man" is typically expressing an identity that is *different* from his father's. Surely, one's identity as a Georgia Baptist is a learned habit. With a different life history, the same person could feel just as strongly that he is a Mexican Catholic. Could it be that one's gender role identity is also learned, and if so, *how* is it learned? What kind of experience motivates a boy to want to become like his father?

During World War II, for millions of children, father was in the Army and therefore absent from home during the child's growing-up years. Observers of child behavior report that boys raised in father-absent households were more likely to act like girls, both in fantasy and in play.[13] These boys tended to model their behavior after their mother, who was present, rather than their father, who was absent; why?

A normal child is almost always *motivated* to do something: he's hungry, he's thirsty, he wants to go out, he wants to come in, he wants this, and he wants that. He sees that his parents have *independence*: a wonderful power to satisfy all their own wants. A little boy has to cry and beg and plead and wait before his wants are satisfied; while he sees his parents help themselves to whatever they want, come and go as they please, do whatever they want, or so it seems. This kind of everyday experience, feeling chronically *dependent* upon a dispenser of power, leads the child to yearn for the power his parents seem to possess: to satisfy all their wants as they arise (or so it seems) and to possess the power of independent action.[14]

Usually, a girl chooses her mother as a role model because mother is more likely to do the kinds of things that little girls want to do: dress up, take care of baby, work around the kitchen, have friends over, and go shopping. Boys usually want to do just the kinds of things they see father doing: going places, fixing things, getting things, doing things that require muscular strength, and sometimes saying *no* to Mother. If Father is not present to serve as a role model, if Mother is the only model of adult power and competence, *Mother* serves as the role model, and her son displays habits that are more girlish than boyish.

The psychological cost of father-absence is supported by field observation as well as clinical evidence. In a 1975 article, Green described a sample of 65 gender-discordant boys, and found that *40 percent* "had been permanently separated from their biological father by the age of four--a much higher rate than the general population." In 1981, Lamb reported that father-absent children do not get *al*ong as well, with their peers. According to the observations of Kulka and Weingarten, reported in 1979, father-absent children are prone to anxiety and illness. The observations of Adams and Gullotta, 1989, and Santrock, 1996, link father-absence to dependency, impulsivity, aggressiveness, depression, suicide, running away, and drug abuse (Weisfeld, page 304).

Weisfeld concludes (page 322): "father absence is associated with various cognitive, social, health, and emotional problems. . . ." Translated into learning theory, this suggests that father figures guide the growth of the individual from childhood to adulthood, and the absence of this influence leads to personality and character disruptions of various kinds.

Boys and girls are congenitally different in brain organization and in physique, and these differences explain, in part, why boys are more apt to run and to fight, and girls are more apt to sit and play with dolls. Inborn factors may also explain why some boys prefer quiet play rather than rough-and-tumble activities. Whatever the pattern of inborn and acquired determinants, cross-gender childhood habits (like playing with dolls, playing house, or dressing up in Mother's clothes) are often in the life histories of homosexual men.[15] To this extent, learning theory throws light on the classic Freudian observation that homosexual men often remember their father as absent, or distant, or weak, or unappealing--not an available role model or not an attractive role model. There are exceptions to this "rule;" Marmor (1980 page 11) writes: "Over the years I have seen a number of homosexuals who had close relationships with affectionate and caring fathers." This fact may testify to the power of strong constitutional factors, when they are present.

The absent (or weak) father and the over-controlling (perhaps seductive) mother are prominent figures in the psychoanalytic interpretation of male homosexuality. But the psychoanalytic attitude is that homosexuality has a constitutional basis, and when something goes seriously wrong with a boy's upbringing or character development, a homosexual orientation may be the result. Appendix 3 lists dozens of life factors, drawn mainly from the psychoanalytic writings of Fenichel and Hatterer, that may lead to a homosexual orientation.

Most gay-friendly writers repudiate Freud. (LeVay condemns Freud's influence as *criminal*. See end note 20, this chapter.) A striking exception to this tendency is Andrew Sullivan (1998, page 111), who senses in Freud's writings "a calm curiosity" about homosexuality, not the hostility expressed by recent American psychoanalysts. Writes Sullivan (*ibid.*, page 105): "I defy any honest homosexual to read Freud's work in this area and not find something worth pondering about his own development or the associations of his desire. . . . [T]he adult longings . . . [of heterosexuals] echo equally with the sounds of their earliest feelings." Sullivan makes it clear that he does not endorse psychoanalytic treatment for homosexuals, but pays tribute (*ibid.*, pages 120-121) to Freud's insights into 'the family drama' underlying the homosexual:

> I doubt whether any male homosexual will read [Freud's] case studies without glimpsing something of himself in them, without identifying some shards of truth in their otherwise lurid accounts of extreme pain. The range of homosexual experience is truly vast, but it is still undeniable that certain patterns seem common, in particular an often deep and powerful bond with a mother, an estranged relationship with a father, and often dysfunctional sexual and emotional relationships. . . . [A]nyone who has lived for long and kept his eyes and ears open, among male homosexuals, will recognize that some of these patterns are real, although their meaning is obviously open to interpretation. . . . To say this is not, I think, a function of self-hatred. It is a function of honesty.

Attitudes in conflict. In the best of all worlds, skills and tastes and attitudes *go together*, they are synergistic, like a person who loves music, plays the guitar well, and enjoys entertaining people. But Dr. Pangloss to the contrary, for many this is not the best of all worlds, and many therefore find themselves with attitudes in conflict. Like the man who was brought up on a farm and now lives in the city. He has a chronic nostalgia for the farm, but when he is on the farm, he can't wait to get back to the city. Like the rich man who grew up in poverty, and can't fully enjoy his wealth, because he has never shaken off the habits of scrimping, saving, and self-denial. Or like the person whose homosexual attitudes are in chronic conflict with his hopes and dreams of becoming a husband and father, fulfilling the wishes of his parents, and sharing the lives of his heterosexual friends and relatives.

Social oppression vs. inner conflict. Because the "social oppression argument" figures so prominently in the discourse of gay advocates, we will examine this issue once more, this time from the standpoint of the learning process. To understand the emotional life of the alienated person we must make a distinction between one's *feelings* of rejection and oppression, and the *facts* of social rejection and social oppression. Which is more emotionally disabling?

> Joseph Beam, a Black gay poet, writes: "I cannot go home as who I am and that hurts me deeply."

> Write LeVay and Nonas (page 166): "Some degree of pain and suffering is probably [a] universal [part of coming out], because even the teenager who welcomes homosexuality must still grieve *the loss of heterosexuality* and the privileged life expected to go with it" (emphasis added).

Gay advocates probably overuse the label "social oppression"[16] to account for the unhappiness that gay men experience. Social oppression is more accurately represented by persecution, by insults, by police harassment, and by an oppressive laws, than by *loss of felt status*. Normal responses to social oppression include self-protective avoidance, escape or camouflage. The homosexual adolescent develops socially-valued skills; the gay man moves out of his bigoted hometown and resettles in a big city, where he can make friends and enjoy more secure surroundings and the cloak of urban anonymity. Or he outwits the bigots by adopting a facade that he can readily shed when he is among friends.[17]

Gay advocates are probably wrong when they claim that promiscuity, depression, anxiety, alcoholism, drug addiction, and suicide are the result of social oppression. Usually these behaviors are symptoms of deeply *internalized* conflicts, *felt* as oppression and rejection, and do not result from *acts of oppression*.

James

When he was a 25-year-old graduate student, James had his first homosexual experience with "a guy [who] approached me in the library rest room. . . . I loved it but I was so scared I was shaking. . . . I went to a priest immediately afterwards and cried uncontrollably. 'Don't worry about that, it will pass,' he told me. It happens to a lot of guys. You'll meet a fine girl and you'll have some kids.'"

Two years later, James married "a fine woman." He fantasied that she was "more of a sister-in-law," and that he was playing the role of his older brother, who had died in childhood. "I looked at her as being more of a sister-in-law than a wife. And because my brother would have had children, I had children. . . . I thought of my own children as my brother's children."

"In our early years of marriage, sex was okay. I could do it as long as we were having children. But when my wife had a hysterectomy, sex became impossible for me."

James tells of his despondency over his inability to have sex with his wife after her hysterectomy. He tried to suppress his homosexual feelings by becoming very homophobic. "I knew all the dirty jokes about fags and queers. . . ." When he met an attractive gay man and "fell head-over-heels in love" with him, James decided to kill himself:

"I couldn't handle it anymore. . . . I drove my car into [my] barn, and made a serious suicide attempt. There was no reason why it failed, except maybe the grace of God. The vent came loose from the tailpipe. I kind of lost consciousness, rolled out of the car, and found myself on the ground when I came to. . . . My wife took me to the hospital. . . I'm not sure I would have pulled through, had it not been for the way [my wife accepted my confession that I was homosexual]. . . "

James and his wife separated, he "was involved in a relationship for six or seven years," and volunteered his interview when he was living in rural Wisconsin, in retirement.[18]

Internalized attitudes are social rules that have become part of one's *character*. We play by some rules simply because we want to play the game. If we continue to ignore traffic rules, eventually our driver's license gets revoked, or worse. The army promotes attitudes toward dress, like polished boots and short haircuts, but as soon as we re-enter civilian life, army rules are gladly forgotten.

Some rules of good behavior begin as "shoulds" and eventually become "musts;" they become part of our character. Honesty, compassion, loyalty, generosity, sociability, pride in workmanship, love of learning, enjoyment of beauty, love of country, religious faith--all of these attitudes begin partly as "shoulds" taught by parents and teachers and peers, and partly as attitudes we eagerly learn because they were expressed by people we love and admire. In this way, social norms become *interiorized*, as psychologists say; they become part of *who we are*.[19]

It's easy to belittle another person's expression of his values by saying, "Oh, now you're being judgmental!" "Oh, that's a value judgment." "That's just one way of looking at it." One might reply, "Yes, that happens to be *my* way of looking at it," When two parts of one's character are in deep and chronic conflict, a person really needs help. Alcohol, recreational drugs, work, or strenuous play may offer some distraction, but the conflict remains unresolved. Better that a man in deep and chronic conflict look for some kind of relearning experience: a support group, a good friend who is also a good listener, or a professional therapist.

This item appeared in the psychological literature back in 1965: A student came to a college mental health clinic and said to his counselor, "I'm a homosexual and I don't want to be. It's not that simple to give up because I am satisfied with homosexual relations, but I know this is not normal and would like someday to be able to get married and live a normal life" (Braaten and Darling, page 276).

Put into learning-theory terms, an attitude might be regarded as a habit of thought, and a conflict of attitudes is a conflict of habits. Habits are learned; can they also be unlearned? That is the task of psychotherapy: to extinguish unwanted habits and enable the patient to establish more satisfying (more appropriate, more functional, more adaptive) habits.

Learning and unlearning. Put in learning-theory terms, the unlearning of homosexual habits is a major task of reorientation therapy. *Unlearning* can be much, much more difficult than learning. In practice, virtually never are homosexual attitudes *completely* unlearned. Even when therapy is "successful," even if the former patient is in a good marriage, he remembers his homosexual days, and may occasionally feel some degree of same-sex attraction. The difference is that now the appeal is a *distraction* he can easily (perhaps humorously) resist; in the words of an ex-gay, "It's just a pain in the butt." Before therapy, he felt a compelling urge he was powerless to resist. A life crisis, like loss of his job, may make him feel vulnerable again, and he may want to see his therapist again. Although there are many former homosexuals who are now in good marriages and enjoying their role as a loving husband and father, there is a certain truth in the gay advocate's challenge: "You cannot show me one former homosexual who has been *completely* cured."[20]

> The joke is told of a Jewish couple who made the unlikely decision to convert to Catholicism. They became very strict Catholics, and sent their daughter to parochial school. When their daughter grew up, she was attracted to Judaism, told her parents that she was taking instructions for conversion to Judaism, and was even going to the mikvah. Her father was so outraged, he sat shiva for a whole week.[21]

Psychotherapist Steven Richfield recalls how a patient who had moved from a homosexual to a heterosexual lifestyle, acknowledged the limitations of his 'cure:'

> I have come to accept that there is a homosexual part inside of me that I may never be able to get rid of. But maybe I can learn

to live with it. The other day I was at the swim club with my
wife and sons. A man in a very tight bathing suit walked by and I
caught myslf staring and beginning to have fantasies.. But just as
quickly, I stopped myself, told myself it was not such a big deal,
and dove in the water. And it didn't ruin my day. (Cited by
Sullivan 1998, page 165.)

Richfield comments that "even in the most ideal outcomes, it is my belief that
residual homosexual fantasies will emerge from time to time throughout the lives
of these men." Therapy may be considered successful if the patient achieves "a
strong [enough] self-image that provides for a satisfying heterosexual adaptation
which is not *jeopardized* by periodic intrusion of homosexual fantasies" (*ibid.*,
pages 165-166, emphasis added).

Can an adult ever *unlearn* his native language? Suppose an adult Jew escaped
from persecution in Nazi Germany, and resettled in Palestine. He now vows to
learn Hebrew and to erase the German language from his mind completely.[22] Can
this be done? Or will he continue to silently count, to think and dream in German,
even though he has made a deliberate effort never to speak or read or write
German again? Are there lessons we have learned so well, we can never forget
them completely, no matter how hard we try, no matter what kind of professional help we get? Are there habits so well established, we can never[23] unlearn them
completely?

Formerly gay men who join an ex-gay support group, or a Christian ministry
for ex-gays, after years of dialogue, fellowship, supplementary counseling or
therapy, Bible study, and prayer[24] claim that they have gradually reshaped their
identity into that of a member of their church: free to express their "latent heterosexuality" with the woman they believe God has given them to be his help-
meet, to "be fruitful and multiply," and thereby fulfill a command of the Bible.
Some ex-gays[25] eventually do feel free enough from homosexual attractions to
marry and raise a family, and enjoy their status as husband, father, and member
of a Christian community.

An observer at ex-gay gatherings notices that ex-gays do a lot of open
embracing.[26] Many ex-gays continue year after year to attend annual reunions for
prayer, lectures, and workshops. Many also feel a need to actively minister to
struggling homosexuals, just as some recovered alcoholics feel impelled to help
men who are still struggling with alcoholism. The testimony of an ex-gay workshop leader is that he does continue to feel occasional homosexual attractions. He
accepts that as normal for him, and has learned to regard these passing attractions
as nothing more than "a pain in the butt."[27]

Perhaps the greatest disservice therapists ever did to their homosexual clients
was to employ aversive conditioning, a treatment in which a homosexual feeling
is systematically paired with a noxious stimulus, like a 'mild' electric shock, or

a foul odor. Aversive conditioning was initially developed to shape the behavior of animals. This technique has also been used successfully with retarded children, to stop them from behaving in ways that were so disruptive of family life that the retarded children would have to be institutionalized unless their behavior could be made more bearable to other members of the family. What worked with animals and retarded children proved to be disastrous when employed with intelligent young adults. In 2002, Byrd and Nicolosi conducted a computerized search of all published articles on reorientation therapy, which included eight articles on aversive (or avoidance) therapy. *All had been published between 1969 and 1975*. By contrast, their search also produced six articles on group therapy, four of which had been published during the 1990s.[28]

Therapy aimed at sexual reorientation (conversion therapy or reparative therapy) is now variously denounced as ineffective, unprofessional, unethical, damaging, or dangerous.[29] To an extent, therapists have invited this negative attitude because of their past misuse of aversive therapy, and because in the not-so-distant past, prominent psychoanalysts have broadcast an uncritical hostility toward homosexuals.[30] Partly for these reasons, mainstream psychologists are still suspect in the gay world, and have been replaced by practitioners of "gay-affirmative therapy."[31]

Learning straight sex skills vs. learning gay sex skills. One's first attempt at gay sex is more likely to be successful and satisfying than one's first attempt at straight sex.[32] Why? Because there is less to learn; gay sex is more like masturbation, a familiar act, than heterosexual intercourse, which is a very unfamiliar act to the uninitiated male. Gay men also feel freer to *talk to each other* more than heterosexual couples do. Gay men tell each other more often and more explicitly what they want, what pleases them, and what doesn't. This generous flow of information enables a gay man to become an expert lover more quickly, with fewer learning trials than are usually required by his heterosexual brother.

Gay men are also "in more familiar territory;" their partner's anatomy and responses are more similar to their own. They therefore have less to learn about their partner's makeup and wishes. (Straight sex is more of a mystery to the novice, an adventure with what, at first, must seem like an unfamiliar creature who has a partially-hidden anatomy of her own and may have secret wishes and sensibilities of her own.)

Modesty, shyness, and inhibition are more likely to interfere with inexperienced heterosexual love making. Partners exchange less information. Messages are more ambiguous. The encounter is therefore a more fragmentary, more ambiguous, learning experience. Partners don't profit from experience as readily as they would if they communicated more openly, more freely and directly. This is probably the difference between gay and heterosexual love-making, experienced by the majority of men who have had a taste of both and feel that, for *them*, gay sex is better. Differences between straight and gay sex were discussed at length in Chapter 16.

A first homosexual experience is more likely to deliver stronger physical gratification than a first heterosexual experience, which is more likely to be fumbling, awkward, and to an extent disappointing. The first homosexual experience is therefore more powerfully reinforced and motivates the person to seek another same-sex experience. Andrew Sullivan (1995 pages 191-192) recalls the powerful gratification of his first homosexual love affair:

> I remember my first kiss with another man, the first embrace, the first love affair. . . . I was twenty-three. . . . [T]o me, it was like being in a black-and-white movie that suddenly converted to color. . . . [T]he abstractions of dogma, of morality, of society, dissolved into the sheer, mysterious pleasure of being human. Perhaps this is a homosexual privilege: for many heterosexuals, the pleasures of intimacy and sexuality are stumbled upon gradually when young; for many homosexuals, the entire experience can come at once . . . eclipsing everything . . . infantilizing and liberating at the same time.

Gay men have something important to teach their heterosexual friends: talk to your partner about what feels good and what doesn't. Use everyday language. These are practices that make gay sex enjoyable. Information shapes habit-change, and fosters the growth of love-making skills. This basic law of learning operates equally well in the gay world and in the straight world.[33]

Acquired habits vs. the unfolding of gentic predispositions. Given the same amount of free time and money to plan and carry out a vacation, why does one person want to visit crowded cities (like London, New York, Paris, and Mexico City), while another heads for quiet and remote places (like the glens of Scotland, Alpine villages, or the Galapagos islands)? Why does one person go sailing, while another goes hiking, and another visits museums and churches? Some do what circumstances lead them to do, while others do what they've "always wanted to do." For some, it's hard to choose among equally attractive possibilities. In each case, the individual has probably been guided by a variety of learning experiences: people one has known, daydreams one has had, stories one has heard, books one has read, movies one has seen. Learning shapes our attitudes in ways that are complex and subtle; often too complex to be completely unravelled. But that doesn't justify labelling an attitude "inborn" because it defies easy explanation on the basis of experience.

Both Kinsey and his colleague and co-author Pomeroy seemed to have believed that homosexuality was the result of *experience*, not inheritance. Kinsey's biographer, James H. Jones (page 383) quotes from Kinsey's correspondence: "There is absolutely no evidence of inheritance being involved [in homosexuality]." In another letter (page 386), Kinsey more positively describes homosexuality as an acquired habit: "Whether one builds a heterosexual pattern or a homosexual pattern depends . . . very largely upon the satisfactory or unsatisfactory nature of his first experiences."

In 1968, Pomeroy, who by then had succeeded Kinsey as Director of the Kinsey Institute, took time out to write a sexual guide for boys, *Boys & Sex*. After a lifetime of research on sex, psychologist Pomeroy (pages 67-68) voiced a clearly learning-theory attitude toward homosexuality: "When an individual is born, he has the ability to do anything sexually. *What* he does depends on what experiences he has, so it is safe to say that if he is not born homosexual, he is not born heterosexual either. He is simply born a sexual person."

Another veteran of the Kinsey Institute, Martin S. Weinberg[34] likewise concludes (Weinberg *et al.*, page 5) that "sexual attraction is far more complex than biology allows . . . [and is the result of] what people think and do. . . . [S]ociety shapes the choices people make about sex. . . ." Weinberg and his co-authors reject the term "'sexual orientation,' which suggests that sexual preference is established at birth and fixed thereafter," and favor the term sexual preference, to emphasize that "people take an active part in constructing their sexuality" (*ibid.*). "Our study shows that *learning plays a significant part in helping people traverse sexual boundaries . . .* " (*ibid.*, page 8, emphasis added).

NOTES TO CHAPTER 18

1. Cheryl McCormick, and her associates, who have devoted years to successfully identifying genetic factors in homosexuality, thus concludes one of their articles (1994, page 529) with the warning that "the operation of hormonal factors does not preclude the operation of genetic or environmental factors in the origin of sexual orientation."

2. At an international conference, Herr Doktor Dörner caused a near-riot by suggesting that if a pregnant woman who has suffered unusual stress would submit to testosterone injections, she could prevent her unborn son from becoming homosexual.

3. Why didn't nature widen the female's pelvic opening to accommodate a newborn with a larger head? To an extent, this anatomical change was achieved by increasing the average size of the female proto-human, compared with her hominid ancestors. For the female pelvis to become even wider would reduce her aptitude as a runner. Running is an important survival skill, and is favored by narrow hips.

4. The individual "adopts a culture" largely through his ability to learn and use a language. A large portion of the human brain is dedicated to the uses of language: learning, remembering, thinking, talk, and self-talk.

5. Money's acknowledgement that a homosexual "may experience a sense of self divided and in conflict" describes the anxiety that leads a homosexual to seek reorientation therapy. Note that Money does not ascribe the anxiety to "social oppresssion," but to the person's inner conflict between his homosexual and his heterosexual impulses.

Money (page 152) justifies the gay activists' distrust of the medical model for its "historical roots in the diagnostic classification of homosexuality as a *forensic* and psychiatric disease, a perversion and a deviation. *No one relishes being stigmatized as a pervert or a deviate, disqualified from being a human being* (emphasis added)."

In the above quotation, Money suggests that psychiatrists as a group labeled homosexuality as an unlawful [forensic] condition, which is simply a historical untruth. Perversion has an uncomplimentary ring all right, perhaps the result of popular misuse of the term. But the fact is that before psychiatry labeled homosexuality an arrest of normal development, homosexuals were widely regarded as the outcome of moral or biological degeneration, which is far worse.

No one with any familiarity with Freud's thought or writing would conclude that Freud regarded homosexuals as less than human. In the italicized statement above, Money seems to be uncritically parroting gay advocacy propaganda.

6. Reinforcement theory represents concepts of learning that have emerged many years after the "classical conditioning" work of Pavlov and Watson. Writers unfamiliar with the more recent trends in learning theory tend to greatly oversimplify how the learning process is conceptualized in contemporary psychology. For example, the philosopher Michael Ruse naively advises his reader (page 225): "The whole point of the learning theory approach is that human beings start as blank books waiting to be written in. It is not claimed that one kind of writing is better or happier than any other."

Another example of a poorly-informed critic of learning theory: the historian David Greenberg (page 430) wrongly equates learning theory with behaviorism, and suggests that learning theory follows Watson's "refusal to consider biological explanations for differences in persons behavior. . . ." (Watson's left academia in 1920, after a divorce scandal. He worked in the advertising business from 1921 until his retirement in 1946. His last two books on behaviorism, published in 1925 and 1928, were addressed to a general audience.)

Greenberg also incorrectly implies that learning theory ignores the constructs of Freudian theory. On the contrary, much work has been done by learning theorists to test psychoanalytic concepts, and to apply learning-theory principles to psychotherapy.

7. We learn not to ignore the mirror image as "a mere illusion," but to put it to use, to give us useful information (though in reversed position) about ourselves and the world around us, at home and on the road.

8. This concept first appeared in the literature of psychology in a 1965 article by McGuire *et al.*

9. Nicolosi 1993, page 6. Kinsey noted (page 630) that homosexuals reach adolescence at an earlier age than boys in general, and that boys who reach adolescence at an early age have a higher rate of masturbation.

10. Comparison of a popular straight sex manual, with a popular gay sex manual, reveals the following difference: Comfort's *Joy of Sex* deals with masturbation (pages 117-118) as something sex partners can do to each other, with only passing references to "private self-exploration" (page 223) and "adolescent masturbation" (page 165). Hart's *Gay Sex*, on the other hand, deals at length and in detail with an illustrated guide to 'going solo,' advising the reader (page 106) to "look on masturbation as a date with yourself. . . . Schedule an evening alone. . . . Plan for it: some music, candlelight . . . a video with your favorite actor. . . . [T]ake the phone off the hook, and allow yourself to relax and get into the mood."

Similarly, in *The New Joy of Gay Sex* (by Silverstein and Picano, HarperCollins, 1992), the authors devote about three pages and a full-page illustration to self-masturbation. *The New Joy* suggests the use of various visual aids: photographs, drawings, videotapes. Or one may choose to recall a stimulating event from his recent experience:

> Perhaps [one] saw some really sexy guy walking up the street
> this morning, or had a really hot sex scene with someone last
> week, or even just liked looking at the beautiful body of a friend
> at the beach. It's not unusual for vigorous and horny men to
> vividly recall and jerk off less than an hour following a particu-
> larly exciting sexual encounter (page 122).

Similarly, for its Valentine's Day issue, a gay weekly (Chicago *Windy City Times*, Feb. 12, 1998, page 12) advises its readers with a feature story on "how to have fun by yourself on Valentine's Day," describing "wild new sex toys [that] will make you the best lover you've ever had."

11. One person seeks the approval of the majority, and wants more than anything else to be socially accepted by them; another person wants to be embraced by a society of rebels, and strives mightily to conform to the standards of that society. Group conformity is characteristic of *both* "conformists" and "rebels;" it is a question of what group (present or past, immediate or imaginary) does one strive to conform with? What kind of person does one want to become?

12. Indented quotations are from pages 90-93 of John E. Mayer's 1962 study, *Jewish-Gentile Courtship, an Exploratory Study of a Social Process*. Both intermarriage (in the 1950s) and homosexuality were socially unpopular behaviors. The reflections of Mayer's respondents illustrate how a habit may be adopted without ever having to make a conscious choice.

13. See "Doll play aggression in normal young children: influence of sex, age, sibling status, father's absence," by Pauline S. Sears," *Psychological Monographs.*, 1951, 65, No.. 6 (Whole No. 323).

See also *Father Relations of War-born Children*, by Lois M. Stolz, Palo Alto: Stanford University Press, 1954.

These observations relate to boys raised in middle-class homes and middle-class neighborhoods. What of boys raised in subcultures of "single parents," in ghettos where fatherlessness is truly the norm? Here the *street gang* and its leaders seem to fulfill the boys' hunger for a masculine role model. The street gang and its leaders enable the small and powerless to identify with the big and powerful. Thus do street gangs command a loyalty that makes its members willing to risk arrest, incarceration, injury and even risk death. (Note that street-gangs offer a cruel and violent caricature of adult masculinity.)

Marmor (1980, page 11) comments: "[P]eer relationships . . . may present compensating models for masculine identification that make up for the absence of such models within the family. In addition, the mores of ghetto life do not usually reflect the sexual puritanism and anti-heterosexual bias that so often characterizes the background of middle-class homosexuals, both male and female."

Many dwellers of the black ghetto spend some time in prison, where they are likely to be introduced to homosexuality. This establishes habits that are sometimes carried over to life on the outside, and makes the black community more tolerant of homosexual practice. Paradoxically, the black community tends also to be more homophobic.

14. Why a child adopts the ways of his same-sex parent is a classic problem in psychology. Over the years, answers have included (1) the instinct to imitate, (2) the Oedipus complex, and (3) the role model. But *why* does the child usually use his same-sex parent as a role model? A step toward answering this question is offered by Burton and Whiting, whose 1961 article, "The absent father and cross-sex identity" is listed in References.

15. See Whitam, in References. The cross-gender traits of homosexual men is the focus of Chapters 8 and 9.

16. Gay advocates characteristically attribute homosexual unhappiness to social

oppression. If society would only adopt a more benign attitude toward homosexuals, they plead, homosexuals would live in peace and happiness. However well-intended, these commentators fail to distinguish between outside social oppression and deeply-held *personal convictions, or moral standards* that shape the individual's conscience. Perhaps these secularist apologists, however well-meaning, simply do not understand that a sense of morality, what Freud called the ego ideal, is an important part of the human psyche.

17. For many years, some homosexual men have successfully led a "closeted" life, making their homosexual life known only to certain friends and family members. Alfred C. Kinsey is an example, according to biographer James H. Jones. Some homosexual writers have argued that leading a closeted life is intrinsically degrading and shameful; others have said this lifestyle suits them just fine; "It's like belonging to a secret club."

Nowadays, some gay activists consider the closeted life immoral because the gay community needs every gay man's support. Although it served his interest as a journalist to disclose the identity of public figures who were closeted homosexuals, Signorile said he felt morally compelled to "out" homosexual men who have tried to keep their sexual life private. "Outing" is still a controversial issue in the gay community.

18. See Fellows, Will. *Farm Boys; Lives of Gay Men from the Rural Midwest*, pages 99-100.

19. Greenberg (page 431) assumes that patients seeking sexual reorientation are "seeking to escape the social and legal penalties attached to homosexuality in a repressive society." Greenberg argues that these patients are "coerced by society's punitive attitudes and sanctions," and that their desire to reorient their sexual life is therefore "not truly voluntary." Greenberg's conception of the problem apparently does not include the concept of *character*, or a recognition that a person's homosexual actions may be in deep conflict with his character. As a psychoanalyst would say of a person seeking reorientation therapy: his homosexual impulses are ego-alien. Or as John Money has put it (page 88), that the person feels "a sense of the self divided and in conflict."

20. Partly because psychoanalysis cannot "completely cure" a homosexual, many gay scholars show an undisguised contempt for Sigmund Freud. For example, Simon LeVay, who moved from neuroanatomist to educator (co-founder of the Institute of Gay and Lesbian Education) labels psychoanalysis as a "serious crime" and lists it as one of the many damaging and fruitless attempts to cure homosexuality. His list (1993, pages 110-111) throws into one heap: "psychoanalysis, castration, testicle grafts, hormone treatments, electric shock therapy, and brain surgery." LeVay adds: "As far as I can determine, not one of these treatments ever produced the desired result, but the physical and psychological dam-

age done by them must be counted among the most serious crimes ever committed by the medical profession."

21. Hebrew glossary: The *mikvah* is a ritual bath, employed in the ceremony of conversion (and at other times). *Shiva* refers to the Jewish mourning custom. Traditionally, Jews regarded the apostasy of a child as if he or she had died.

22. This is a hypothetical situation; in fact, most German Jews who resettled in Palestine (which is now Israel) continued to speak German, and many learned very little Hebrew. One such person was asked by a visitor from abroad, "Aren't you ashamed of yourself, that after 40 years, you haven't really learned Hebrew?" He answered (in German, of course): "It's easier to be ashamed of yourself than to learn Hebrew."

23. Yes, *never*, from a *practical* standpoint. Since the complete elimination of the homosexual habit is virtually impossible, ex-gays are willing to settle for a significant reduction of the power of the homosexual habit, from a controlling passion to "a pain in the butt."

24. Prayer, Bible study, and preaching are *not* the only methods practiced by ex-gay workers. Books by Consiglio and Dallas (see References) give a closer look at ex-gay counseling methods. For the description of a year-long residential treatment center for "ex-gay strugglers," see John Paulk's book, *Not Afraid to Change*.

25. The term "ex-gay" has been adopted by Christian ministers and counselors to describe the Christian "homosexual strugglers" who come to them seeking relief from unwanted homosexual impulses. This movement is coordinated by Exodus International, P.O. Box 2121, San Rafael, California.

26. At an ex-gay workshop (Washington, D.C., 1997), a participant asked, "When is it OK to embrace another man, and how tight can you hug him?"

27. There are all kinds of attractions, comments a therapist at an ex-gay workshop. Does the attraction have a compelling, irresistible quality, or is the attraction little more than an unwelcome reminder of one's homosexual past?

28. Aversive therapy, a largely discarded psychological treatment, is quite different from shock therapy, a medical treatment for depression that is quite effective though little understood. (Parenthetically, it may be added that modern clinical methods have greatly reduced the physical discomfort of shock therapy.)

Greenberg (page 431) gives the impression that aversive conditioning is a representative mode of the prevailing psychological treatment of homosexual patients. It is not. Oblivious to the facts, it is easy for him and other gay activists to denounce 'those aversive-therapy-happy' psychologists.

29. The 1998 Columbia University Press "guidebook" by Ryan and Futtterman, *Lesbian & Gay Youth; Care & Counseling* is a model of political correctness. In this "guidebook," the reader is warned (page 30) that reorientation therapy is ineffective, unethical, and dangerous:

> Generally unsuccessful over time, attempts to change sexual orientation raise many ethical concerns and often contribute to negative self-esteem and mental health problems. Nevertheless, providers may be asked by parents or *even by youth* (italics added) to assist in changing their sexual orientation. Experts in adolescent medicine recommend against such attempts, which are further cautioned against by the American Academy of Pediatrics:

> Therapy directed specifically at changing sexual orientation is contraindicated, since it can provoke guilt and anxiety while having little or no potential for achieving changes in sexual orientation.

Again and again, authors of the "guidebook" ask mental health workers to accept the gay adolescent's sexual orientation as an integral aspect of his/her persnality:

> Like heterosexual youth who suffer from major psychiatric disorders that require in-patient treatment, some lesbian, gay, and bisexual adolescents may be hospitalized for severe mental health disorders. . . . [C]oming out percipitates an emotional crisis that may resemble severe psychiatric disorders. . . . Adolescents who are hospitalized because of symptoms related to their sexual orientation may encounter psychiatric providers who view such conflict as pathological (*ibid.*, page 64).

> [S]taff may tolerate or even support prejudice and abuse of lesbian and gay teens (*ibid.*). [The "guidebook" repeatedly warns counselors to beware of mental health workers who are unfriendly to gay and lesbian youth.]

> The National Center for Lesbian Rights . . . has documented dozens of cases of adolescents who have been hospitalized and forced to undergo involuntary treatment, which includes intense behavior modification that punishes same-sex feelings. . . attempted conditioning through hypnosis, "desensitization" treatment that associates same-sex arousal with repugnant images, use of a plethysmograph to deliver electric shocks through penile

electrodes . . . isolation and excessive medication (*ibid*, page 64.).

Adolescents who have been exposed to aversive therapies may be mistrustful of further counseling; however, follow-up mental health services are generally indicated, to undo psychological damage caused by such ill-advised attempts (*ibid*, pages 92-93).

Attempts to change sexual orientation from homosexual to heterosexual are rooted in the belief that homosexuality is pathologic or maladaptive. However, homosexuality was declassified as a mental illness more than 20 years ago by the American Psychiatric Association (APA), and no professional mental health associations support "reparative" therapy. In fact, the APA clearly states that "there is no published scientific evidence supporting the efficacy of 'reparative therapy' . . . . There is no evidence that any treatment can change a homosexual person's deep seated sexual feelings for others of the same sex" (*ibid*, page 97).

30. For example, In 1954, the highly respected psychoanalytic scholar Abraham Kardiner wrote of the homosexual's "compensatory vindictiveness and hatred of all people," and went on to compare the homosexual's hatred of women with Nazi hatred of the Jews. He reinforced this ugly comparison by calling attention to the "predilection of the Nazi hierarchy for homosexuality. . . ." (Summary from Kardiner's *Sex and Morality*, by Lewes, page 149.) Psychoanalyst Edmund Bergler was another defamer of homosexuals. His 1956, insult is quoted on page 366.

31. "Gay-affirmative therapy" is the topic of *Affirmative Dynamic Psychotherapy* with Gay Men, edited by Carlton Cornett (Aronson, 1993).

32. Newspaper "experience columns" often share stories of disappointing sexual initiations. Here is a sample from Ann Landers:

I am a 24-year old female. My first time was horrible--a real nightmare. I was 18 and "in love." My partner was 20, also a virgin, and he didn't know what he was doing either. "Instinct" was supposed to take over (or so we were told), but somehow instinct failed. The experience was a total disaster. We both ended up embarrassed, frustrated and unfulfilled.

There has always been a market for books on how to improve one's sexual performance. Now this demand for "how to" guidance is being filled by instructional videotapes and by the Internet. Clearly, many young people (especially men) cannot rely on inborn skills to guide their sexual performance.

33. A therapist tells the author of the experience of one patient: after ten years of

occasional gay sex with pickups, this married man found a gay man to whom he became so strongly attached that they eventually shared an apartment together. What made love-making so incredibly pleasurable, he told his therapist, is that they talked to each other about their feelings so much more intimately than this man had ever spoken with his wife. What led this man to seek reorientation therapy was that he decided that his family meant more to him, after all, than his pleasure with this gay partner.

This same therapist tells of another patient, who was attracted to anonymous sex in bathhouses. If his partner spoke up, this spoiled the experience for him, decreased his sexual arousal. The voice defined his partner as the person he really was; he wanted to have sex with a phantom, so that his imagination could give his partner whatever image fit his desire.

34. Professor of Sociology at Indiana University, Weinberg was formerly a Senior Research Sociologist at the Kinsey Institute for Sex Research, He has directed and analyzed the interviews of hundreds of homosexuals, and is the author or co-author of ten books related to homosexuality.

19 The Genetic Factor Revisited

Throughout this book, we have explicitly recognized the importance of the genetic component of homosexuality. Two pioneers in the scientific study of homosexuality, Karl Ulrichs (1825-1895) and Magnus Hirschfeld (1868-1935), both argued that homosexuality was basically genetic. Gay advocates honor Ulrichs and Hirschfeld for advancing this argument. Freud also sensed that homosexuality had a constitutional component. He probably felt this way because homosexual habits were so resistant to treatment, and because many gay men conformed to a recognizable gender-discordant type.

In more recent years, psychoanalysts have stressed the significance of early experience: the close-binding mother and distant father. Homosexuality is learned, they argue, and can be unlearned. Charles Socarides probably represents an extreme position among reorientation therapists in general. He examines the evidence of Hamer, LeVay, Bailey and Pillard, etc. (Socarides 1995, pages 92-99) and concludes (*ibid*, page 100) with the flat statement: "Homosexuals aren't born that way." Similarly, Christian conservatives, ex-gay ministers and counselors argue that homosexuality is not genetic but acquired through unfortunate environmental influences, or perhaps through prenatal influences.[1]

Therapists focus their attention on the *acquired* aspect of homosexuality because this, after all, is all they have to work with. They cannot alter the patient's heredity. But they cannot ignore the constitutional factor that seems to be present, to a large or small extent. Some clinicians, and some observers, have sensed that there are two basic kinds of homosexuals: those whose homosexuality seemed to be an essential part of their psychological makeup, and "secondary homosexuals," who might or might not be homosexual, depending upon their life experience.

Havelock Ellis (pages 82-83) names a number of writers (including Kraft-Ebbing and Iwan Bloch) who made this distinction. Freud (1905, pages 136-137) likewise distinguished between "absolute" and "contingent" homosexuals. Among contemporaries, Socarides (1995, pages 16-19) distinguishes between "obligatory" and "optional" homosexuals. On Figure 20.4 of Chapter 20 Bert, Bill, Don, and Ed could probably be called "absolute," "obligatory" or "constitutional" homosexuals.

Those who divide all homosexuals into two groups, constitutional and optional, probably oversimplify a complex phenomenon. We probably come closer to the truth if we think of a continuum ranging from totally constitutional to totally optional homosexuals. Most gay men probably fall somewhere in the middle of the curve, where genetic and acquired determinants interact to shape their sexual orientation.

359

Public attitudes toward homosexuality appear to hinge on whether this orientation is indeed inherited. More than one survey has shown that persons with the most friendly attitudes toward homosexuals are most likely to believe that this orientation is inherited. This finding gives gay advocates a strong incentive to popularize and justify the belief that homosexuality is to a substantial degree inherited. Biological laboratory workers who themselves are gay or gay advocates, devote much time and energy to verifying this belief. Some of the results of their research (such as LeVay's brain studies) were reported here in chapter 7.

Dean Hamer looked for "a genetic marker" in the chromosomes of a sample of gay men, and collected blood samples from gay men who willingly let Hamer slip a hypodermic needle into their vein. Hamer's laboratory work yielded suggestive but ambiguous results, leading him to conclude that "gay genes" are more likely to be transmitted by the mother than by the father.

Simon LeVay, scientific investigator, teacher and writer on homosexual research, states without qualification (1993, page 111) that "homosexuality runs in families." But genetic tendencies interact with environmental influences that may obscure, mask or even mimic genetic factors. Congenital factors, lifelong but not genetic, may also mimic genetic factors. For all these reasons, and because homosexual tendencies are based not on one gene but on the cumulative effect of many genes, patterns of inheritance are not as evident as the color of the sweet-pea that grew in Gregor Mendel's garden.

Surveying genetic factors related to homosexuality, LeVay points to the fact that males with Klinefelter's syndrome are more likely to be homosexual than men in general.[2] Klinefelter's syndrome males have an XXY chromosome instead of the normal XY male chromosome, a genetic anomaly that occurs in one out of 1000 (perhaps one in 500) births. XXY males are sometimes mentally retarded, may show behavioral difficulties, are often very tall and rounded in body build, show occasional breast enlargement, have a late puberty, and reduced signs of masculinization (such as little or no body hair). Penis growth is normal but testes never reach adult size. XXY males are infertile, though able to perform sexually. It has been established that XXY males are significantly more likely to be homosexual, *but the majority of them are not*. Some XXY men marry and help raise a family of adopted children. It is believed that many XXY men are never diagnosed, and go through life without ever discovering that they are genetically different.[3]

Why are XXY men disproportionately homosexual? Is it a "genetic factor" at work, as LeVay suggests? Or is their homosexuality triggered by the *social* (and self-image) effects of their symptoms: a delicate, rounded body type, little or no body hair, undeveloped testicles, reduced secondary sex characteristics, sometimes breast enlargement, and sometimes mental retardation?

Would discovery of the genetic markers of homosexuality be a triumph for homosexuals, or a disaster? What if science can predict the likelihood that a male fetus will become a homosexual adult? Many parents cherish the hope that some-day they will become grandparents. Given the information that their unborn child is likely to become homosexual, will they opt for abortion, with the idea of par-enting a child who is more likely to fulfill their wishes for eventual grandparent-hood? Some scientists argue that it would be unethical to dispense such infor-mation about the genetic makeup of a fetus. Others argue that the scientist's business is the discovery and dissemination of information, rather than its man-agement.

A similar argument touches on the question of whether reorientation therapy is "professionally ethical"--or whether it is ethical to help gender-discordant boys acquire masculine skills and get rid of "sissy boy" mannerisms.[4] These are open questions for a society that is being persuaded to define homosexuality as an alternative lifestyle, and to agree that there is no moral difference between one sexual orientation and another.

One of the most definitive studies on the genetic basis of homosexuality was not a laboratory study by biologists, but a field study by a psychologist, J. Michael Bailey, and a psychiatrist, Richard C. Pillard. In 1991, Bailey and Pillard published the results of studying a large sample of homosexuals who volunteered the information that they had a twin brother (56 who had monozygotic--identi-cal--twin brothers, and 54 who had fraternal twin brothers). The Bailey-Pillard hypothesis was that the likelihood that the twin brother would also be homosex-ual would depend on whether they were monozygotic (and were therefore genet-ically identical at conception) or fraternal twins. Their hypothesis was fulfilled: only 22 percent of fraternal twins were both homosexual, while 52 percent of identical twins were both homosexual (or bisexual).[5] Bailey and Pillard also reported a decreasing rate of concordance for fraternal brothers of homosexuals, and for adopted brothers of homosexuals.

If the researchers observed the identical twins' eye color, they might have found that every pair (not just 52 percent) was identical in eye color. If the genet-ic factor were so powerful a determinant of sexual orientation, if identical twins have exactly the same genetic makeup,[6] why were only 52 percent of the identi-cal twins both homosexual (or bisexual)? The finding that only *about half* of monozygotic twins were both homosexual suggests that (1) *homosexuality is multifactorial, and* (2) *it is most probably influenced by environmental factors.*

What kind of *environmental* factors are critical in determining whether a twin becomes homosexual or heterosexual? This question was apparently probed in a limited way, by studying differences in experience between the homosexual 52 percent, and the heterosexual 48 percent of the twin brothers of gay men. Reported Pillard (1997, page 64), "To our surprise . . . the most powerful envi-ronmental influences were not those that the twins shared but those they did *not* share . . . different experiences twins might have (*e.g.*, one takes piano lessons, the other becomes a Boy Scout)--although what those different experiences might be, this research design could not identify." Why didn't Bailey and Pillard make a more intensive effort to study the experiential diferences between the gay twin and his heterosexual brother? When asked, Bailey answered that they couldn't get that project funded.[7]

Bailey and Pillard recruited subjects for their twin study by advertising in gay publications, issuing a call for gay men who had a twin brother. Critics of the Bailey-Pillard study have raised the question of "ascertainment bias:" Wouldn't a gay man be more likely to volunteer if indeed his co-twin was also gay? If this were true, critics argue, Bailey and Pillard's "convenience sample" would *not* be representative of gay-men-with-twin-brothers in general.

To avoid this source of bias, Bailey found an Australian colleague, N.G. Martin, and together they conducted a new study based on a truly random sample of twins, taken from an Australian registry of twin births. *The results of this study showed that only 20 percent (not 52 percent) of male monozygotic twins were concordant for homosexuality, and none of the dizygotic twins (not 22 percent) were concordant for homosexuality.*

The 1991 Bailey-Pillard study has something in common with the 1987 "sissy boy" study by Richard Green, described in Chapter 8. (Green had followed up a group of gender-discordant boys and found that something more than half of them[8] were "homosexual or bisexual" at adulthood.) Both the Green and Bailey-Pillard study uncovered a group of men who were *not* homosexual, even though they resembled a homosexual population in a known way (i.e., in having a gay twin brother, or in having had a gender-discordant childhood). What was different about the large minority of Richard Green's young men who were *not* homosexual (or bisexual)? What was different about the Bailey-Pillard (or the Bailey-Martin) monozygotic twins who did not become homosexual?

To the researcher interested only in the predictability of homosexuality, those subjects who fail to fulfill his hypothesis are of no special interest. Here, however, is a group of men who were not homosexual *despite* the fact that they showed important "predictors" of a homosexual adulthood (a gender-discordant boyhood, a homosexual twin brother). What kind of men were they? Was there anything systematically different about their life experience, compared with those who *did* fulfill the researchers' prediction? Is this population worth studying? Indeed it would be *in a society that valued heterosexuality.*

Stephen Jay Gould (1977a page 245) points to "a confusion between vernacular and technical meanings of the same word." To a geneticist, "inherited" does not mean "fixed," "inexorable," or "unchangeable," but rather that certain individuals hold a varying amount of something genetic in common:

> To a geneticist, "inherited" refers to an estimate of similarity
> between related individuals based on genes held in common. It
> carries no implications of inevitability or of immutable entities

beyond the reach of environmental influence. Eyeglasses correct a variety of inherited problems in vision; insulin can check diabetes.

Developmental vs. obligate pathways

Some genetic endowments follow a single pathway. For example, a human infant will develop into a human adult --not a bird, not a horse--or perish on the way. Geneticists refer to single-pathway development as an *obligate* pathway. Some developmental pathways branch off, however, according to environmental influences, leading to two or more options. For example, a plant grows broad leaves when placed in a swampy environment. The same plant grows narrow leaves in arid soil. Its genetic makeup allows for contingent, conditional, or *facultative* developmental options. This is how a geneticist may conceptualize human sexual development. Every person grows up in an environment of *some* kind. The nature of the environment determines just how his sexual development branches off.

Study of the lives of homosexual men--the variety, the shifts, and the fluctuations evinced--strongly suggests that the "heredity or environment" argument must give way to a realization that *both* genetic and environmental factors are at work here. LeVay accepts this fact when he writes (1993, page 138): "The ultimate challenge will be to establish how the genetic differences among individuals interact with environmental factors to produce the diversity that exists among us." LeVay predicted (1993 page 127) that "it is not unrealistic to expect a gene or genes influencing sexual orientation to be identified within the next few years, since there are at least three laboratories in the United States alone that are working on the topic."[9] But if we do more than pay lip service to the principle that personality (of which homosexuality is one aspect) results from the interaction of hereditary and environmental forces, then we must ask that researchers do more than look for the genetic basis of homosexuality.

NOTES TO CHAPTER 19

1. At a Christian ex-gay conference, a scheduled workshop was devoted to *prenatal influences*. Participants discussed at length the possibility that homosexual tendencies might be implanted through the thoughts or experiences of a pregnant woman that are somehow transferred to her unborn boy.

A self-help book, published in 2000, for homosexuals who want to change (Cohen, pages 50-51) advises the reader that if a pregnant woman has a difficult relationship with her husband, "or if she felt rejected, unloved, or unwanted by him . . . *the unborn child . . . may have experienced these thoughts and feelings* as though they were directed at him or her." This "advice," totally unsupported by biological knowledge of the fetal brain's capacity for "thoughts and feelings," is documented by reference to a book on prenatal influences witten by an author who claims the title of Doctor *(italics added)*.

2. LeVay (1993, page 114) refers to a recent U.S.-Danish population study that found "a highly significant excess of homosexuality among XXY men compared with . . . control men."

This trend was not visible in a 1971 report by Theilgart, an intensive study of 34 Klinefelter's syndrome men, median age=25, range=15 to 54. Two-thirds were single, 10 were married, and one was separated. *Virtually every protocol* indicated problems in sexual identity: severe, marked, or likely. Only one member of this sample of 34 (=3 per cent) was homosexual. The indication is that in this group, "problems concerning the sexual role," "conflicts in relations with the opposite sex," "deep anxiety" or ambivalence over the masculine role, did not result in a significant incidence of homosexuality.

3. Because many men with this chromosomal anomaly do not develop all the clinical signs of the Klinefelter syndrome, some would rather call them XXY men rather than Klinefelter syndrome men.

4. Zucker and Bradley, Fitzgibbons, and Rekers describe treatment programs for children with gender-identity disorders.

5. One criticism of Bailey and Pillard concerns their assertion that 52 per cent of gay twins have identical brothers who are "homosexual or bisexual." What is the authors' definition of bisexuality? Does it describe men who habitually, over the years, have sex with both men and women, or does "bisexual" cover what Kinsey would call a "scale 2 or 3 heterosexual" who has had incidental homosexual experience? The category "homosexual or bisexual" could refer to a population that was 75 percent homosexual and 25 percent bisexual, or a population that was 25 percent homosexual and 75 percent bisexual, a very different sort of group. Is this a statistic (also used by Green) an umbrella term that tends to obscure the facts?

6. Because of prenatal mutations, not all identical twins are genetically identical. (To complicate matters, identical twins may also show congenital differences due to differences in their intrauterine environment. For example, one may have enjoyed a richer blood supply than the other.) Therefore, we would not expect 100 percent concordance, even if homosexuality were completely genetic. Identical twins could be 100 percent concordant for blue eyes because blue eye color is determined by a single gene. The genetic component of homosexuality, on the other hand, is undoubtedly multifactorial.

7. The author had a telephone conversation with Prof. Bailey (Oct. 10, 1995),

two years before Pillard published the fact that they did have some preliminary findings along these lines. This phone call was initiated by Prof. Bailey in response to a letter the author had addressed to him. In that phone conversation, Bailey said something like this: "Why didn't we study the 48 percent of the identical twins who were heterosexual? You pose a good question. I wanted to pursue it but I couldn't get it funded. Now, I think it's too late. Some of those discordant twins are no longer living, and I'm not sure I could locate enough of those who might still be alive."

It is interesting to note that a more recent twin study (Herrell *et al.*) did make a close comparison of *both* members of discordant (gay and straight) twin pairs. The investigators did not look for differences in the men's experience, but gave their attention to differences in suicidality rate. (Results showed that gay twins were significantly more likely to have a history of suicidal symptoms: thought about death, wanted to die, reported suicidal ideation, or had made suicidal attempts).

8. Green's study is vulnerable to the same criticism that has already been directed at the Bailey and Pillard study: how rigorously did he define bisexuality? Not very rigorously, since at the conclusion of Green's study one member of his experimental group was only 14 years old, and about *one-third were still sexually inexperienced*. Green obviously could not classify them as homosexual, heterosexual or bisexual on the basis of their experience, but categorized them only on the basis of their reported fantasy and dream life. Nothing in Green's 1987 book indicates that he tested the reliability of his ratings, as Blumstein and Schwartz's 1977 findings suggest he should have.

This author is indebted to Zucker and Bradley (pages 283-284) for calling attention to this serious shortcoming of Green's widely-cited study, published by the Yale University Press.

9. Identification of genetic factors will require the study of a "pure group" of constitutional homosexuals. Looking for genetic factors in a random group of homosexual men may be compared with looking for the genetic component of male baldnesss in a random group of bald men.
Bald men in general include some with hereditary baldness, intermixed with others who are bald because of an infectious disease, some who are undergoing radiation treatment, and others who shave their heads. Researchers might pick up some of these "false positives," while overlooking men who do carry the gene for hereditary baldness but have had surgical hair transplants. These are not problems for baldness research, but contemporary researchers of "gay genes" probably do not try to distinguish between constitutional and optional homosexuals. At this time the distinction is a clinical and not a research concept.

20   Pattern and Diversity

A population has a central tendency (an average) and a dispersion [measurable by a simple statistic like the range, H-L (highest score minus lowest score), or a complex statistic like the standard deviation]. Does a population of gay men likewise have a central tendency as well as a diversity?

The Pattern

What is the typical homosexual man like? One might reply, The sheer diversity of the homosexual population makes this an impossible question to answer. In 1980, psychoanalyst Judd Marmor said, "The notion that all homosexuals are alike is as absurd as the assumption that heterosexuals are all alike" (Marmor 1980, page 267). Marmor, who had championed the unruly activists who fought for deletion of homosexuality from the APA list of mental disorders, was not typical of his profession. American psychoanalysts after World War II popularized the idea that homosexuals were decidedly unpleasant people. For example, in 1956 Edmund Bergler, prominent psychoanalytic writer on homosexuality, indulged himself in this piece of defamation:

> Homosexuals are essentially disagreeable people . . . [displaying] a mixture of superciliousness, false aggression, and whimpering . . . subservience when confronted with a stronger person, merciless when in power, unscrupulous about trampling on a weaker person. (Quoted by Lewes, page 15.)

Perhaps this characterization, however nasty, accurately described Dr. Bergler's Manhattan clientele, but it was irresponsible (and unscientific) to suggest that his clinical impression described homosexual men in general. Not surprisingly, researchers and students of the homosexual phenomenon have carefully avoided the topic of "the homosexual personality." Unexpectedly, this topic resurfaces in a gay studies book of 2002: *The Soul Beneath the Skin; the Unseen Hearts and Habits of Gay Men*, by cultural anthropologist David Nimmons.[1]

Nimmons' thesis is that there is emerging in the gay community "profound, spontaneous social experiments . . . radical cultural transformations . . . a striking range of cultural innovations in social practice" (pages 4, 5). Before we study the nature of these "cultural transformations," let us consider the fact that a community can spontaneously adopt profound cultural changes *only* if those practices already fit the modal character and personality of members of that culture.

"National character" is a recognized topic of cultural anthropology; Margaret Mead was following that line of thought when she described how the Arapesh, Mundugumor, and Tschambuli tended to be psychologically different from each other. Similarly, Nimmons is actually describing how men inside the gay com-

366

munity tend to differ in character and personality from those outside of it.

What kind of differences does Nimmons see? Briefly, he argues that gay men are a *gentler* people: more compassionate, more nurturing, more altruistic, more intuitive, more sensitive, and less violent[2] than heterosexual males in general. The message of Nimmons' book is that the general reader should appreciate this positive side of the gay culture, and also that more gay men should become aware of what is happening inside their own community, and become active participants in this "cultural transformation."

Nimmons offers detailed evidence to support his generalizations. For example, (on page 42) he cites a University of California research report that more than half of men sampled in gay neighborhoods—54 per cent—"had cared for other men ill with AIDS . . . caregiving rates far above typical gender norms." Gay men volunteer more than twice as much time as their straight counterparts, according to an economics professor's large scale, systematic study cited by Nimmons (page 45). The caregiving propensities of gay men is strongly evidenced by their choice of occupations. Table 20.1 lists occupations in which gay men are over-represented (and, for contrast, lists a few in which gay men are under-represented).

Table 20.1. Ratio of gay to straight men in various occupations

Private home care	27:1	Registered nurse	5:1
Hairdresser	20:1	Therapist (respiratory,	
Kindergarten teacher	14:1	Occupational, speech,	
Librarian	13:1	Psychological, physical)	4:1
Food preparation	12:1	Wallpaper hanger	2:1
Designer	7:1	Mine worker	0:1
Writer	7:1	Construction worker	0:1
Personal service	7:1	Farm worker	0:1
Theology teacher	7:1	Auto repairman	0:1
Special education teacher	5:1		

Data from an unpublished study by John Blandford
(Adapted from Nimmons, pages 50-51).

Volunteerism, like occupational choice, testifies to the caregiving propensities of gay men. According to a large-scale, systematic study (Mallen, 1983), gay men volunteer more than twice as much time as their straight counterparts. These acts of altruism go beyond "taking care of our own," covering anti-violence patrols, sports coaches, education, legal advocacy, and foster parenting, as well as bedside care for AIDS patients (Nimmons, page 45).

Susan Folkman has documented the profound ways that men in gay worlds serve each other's support through sickness and hardship. She has interviewed couples, friends, and life partners who are helping others through periods of need, and reports, "The levels and richness of male caregiving we have documented in [the gay] community are simply unprecedented" (ibid, page 41).

The gentle and caring nature of men of the gay community is evidenced in police records of large cities in which there are gay neighborhoods and gay bars. Nimmons notes (pages 13-14): "It is an open secret known to every cop who walks a beat in America. . . . The level of violence committed by gay men is astonishingly low." Table 20.2 summarizes police statistics given by Nimmons

Table 20.2. Police Calls for Assaults
at Public Bars in Greenwich Village

	Number of Assault Calls	
Year	Straight Bars	Gay Bars
2000	11	1
1999	33	3
1998	6	2
	----	-----
Total	50	6

(page 15). Similar police records exist in Chicago, Denver, Tulsa, and elsewhere. A gay man observed: "Ever notice how when you see drinks served in plastic cups, ten to one you're in a straight bar? The owners know to serve on tap, not bottles, because put a bunch of drunk straight guys together with sharp glass objects, one guy gets smashed and some other guy gets slashed. It's only in gay bars they trust us enough to serve drinks in glasses and beer in bottles" (*ibid, page 18*).

Friendship patterns is another clear-cut difference between gay and straight behavior. Straight men bond around things they *do* together: participate in active or spectator sports, shared hobbies and work tasks. Straight men talk about work, politics, sports, and other practical matters. Gay men are more likely to have close friends, and are more likely to talk about intimate, emotional matters. Gay men are more likely to hold long telephone conversations, not to report an event, but to share each other's feelings. The book *Gay Men's Friendships: Invincible Communities* summarizes Peter Nardi's intensive, in-depth studies of this phenomenon.

It is no surprise that straight women find the companionsip of gay men very agreeable. Writes Nimmons (page 143): "They are our pals, neither lovers nor spouses nor conquests. . . . . We meet women on a turf of greater gender, emotional, and erotic parity." Edmund White's essay, "Straight women and gay men," describes such friendships as "straightforward, amiable, and totally disinterested. . . . . Neither person stands to gain anything except companionship, support, and simple fun." A woman doctor of social work reflects, "The thing I am most turned on by in my relations with gay men is the freshness and directness, the honesty and sense of humor" (*ibid., page 143*).

Another woman who values the friendship of gay males reflects, "There's no such thing as a platonic straight friendship. Straight men friends are hard as friends because they always hit on you. My entire life I have always gravitated to male friends . . . as people, as thinking machines. My closest friends have always been gay men. . . ."(*ibid, page 144*).

Nimmons quotes (page 145) another woman who values the friendship of gay men: "With my gay friends I can discuss anything, like I am talking to my girl-friend. . . . . Nothing's out of bounds, we can talk about anything. . . About sex, about what's going on, his boyfriend or mine, and there's never the feeling that they are talking about something taboo."

To further characterize the loving spirit that hovers over the gay community, Nimmons notes (page 41) the wording of a sign posted at New York's Lesbian, Gay, Bisexual, and Transgender Community Center

Within these walls, we expect to be treated with consideration and kindness. We expect our persons, our property, and our opinions to be respected. We expect our disagree-ments to be resolved with sensitivity and goodwill.

Nimmons cannot help but note (page 43) that what gay men are now doing resembles "the helping roles women have taken for millennia," He acknowledges (page 52) that altruistic behavior may be rooted in genetic tendencies, that gay men may be "hard-wired to help the herd," but the author's distinct and repeated emphasis is on the thesis that gay communities are now developing of a *culture of caring*. "We don't need to resort to biology" to account for gay altruism, Nimmons advises (page 53).

As a cultural anthropologist, Nimmons may feel free to say, "We don't need . . . biology," but an evolutionary psychologist sees in the observations of Nimmons evidence that gay men are indeed showing signs of low brain-mas-culinization, and that this genetic condition is influencing the modal character and personality of gay men.[3]

The Diversity

Reference to "the *modal* character and personality of gay men" are not weasel words but honestly acknowledges that homosexuality is a complex and multi-faceted phenomenon. To say that a person is homosexual does not, as we have learned, mean that he is *exclusively* homosexual; some are but most are not, and that further diversifies the homosexual population. Just as most homosexuals (about 50 per cent) have had some heterosexual experience, many heterosexuals have had some homosexual experience.

Homosexuality is not a pure category; neither is it always a stable character-istic, as Chapter 14 indicated. A very recent (2000) study (Allyn page 332, fn. 19) lists about 30 articles on "the limits of 'identity' as a framework for conceptual-izing sexual desires." Writes the author (*ibid*, page 218):

> [P]erhaps it is not appropriate to characterize one's sexual orien-tation until the end of one's life.

To say that everyone has a homosexual potential, large or small, is like say-ing that "everyone has money." One man might have a stock portfolio worth five million dollars, while another has a piggy bank with a dozen coins in it. There are an infinite number of steps in between affluence and poverty, and the same is true of the homosexual potential. At one extreme are men whose physique, life history, character, personality, interests, and social milieu all lead to a homosex-ual outcome. They are sure that homosexuality describes their "true nature."

> Bawer (1996, page 45) pleads with heterosexuals to "understand that what's natural to one individual isn't necessarily natural to another and to affirm one's homosexual identity is not to defy nature but to embrace one's true nature."

At the other extreme are men whose homosexual potential is so slight as to be almost nonexistent. In-between is a range inside which a person might show consistent or occasional homosexual behavior if prevailing circumstances favored his internal predispositions. In-between the gay and straight populations there is also to be found a population that identifies itself as bisexual, for they have found a place for both straight and gay sex in their sex life.[4] More about them later in this chapter.

Kinsey summarized his findings with a seven-point continuum--showing exclusive heterosexuality at one end, and exclusive homosexuality at the other end. In the middle of Kinsey's gradient (reproduced in Figure 20.3) are persons with equal tendencies toward heterosexuality and homosexuality.

Kinsey not only *surveyed* male sexual behavior, more significantly, he *rede-fined* sexual behavior. At the time when Kinsey was conducting his study (1938-1947), men who allowed themselves to be fellated by fags, did not consider themselves homosexual. The "fag"[5] was homosexual, all right, but (by prevailing standards) the "trade" was not. Kinsey dismissed this claim as a pretension,[6] commenting (page 616) : "It is amazing to observe how many psychiatrists have accepted this sort of propaganda."

The Kinsey rating scale (Figure 20.3) was devised for a 1948 survey of male homosexual *behavior*. After more than 50 years, it is time to modify the scale in a way that points to differences in homosexual feelings as well as homosexual behaviors.[7] Such a rating scale might look like Figure 20.4.

Both Kinsey's original scale, and our modification of it, assumes that the entire population is sexually active, which is not true. Male celibates (discussed further at the end of Chapter 25) include both the inhibited or repressed persons, and those who have consciously renounced sexual activity for whatever reason. These sexually inactive persons include some men who experience "fantasies of intense sexual longing for members of the same sex, yet are prohibited by fears or moral considerations from actually indulging in overt homosexual activity" (Hatterer 1980, page 5).

Turning our attention to the majority of adult males who are sexually active, if everyone's tendency toward homosexual *behavior* corresponded exactly to the strength of his homosexual *feelings*, everyone would fall into one of the shaded cells of Figure 20.4 (running diagonally up the scale). Reality is not so simple,

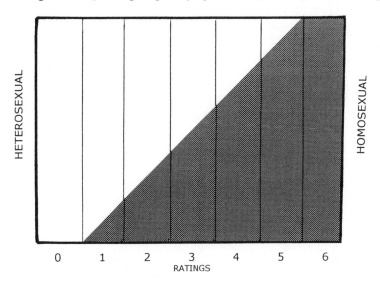

Based on both psychologic reactions and overt experience,
individuals rate as follows:

0. Exclusively heterosexual
1. Predominantly heterosexual, only incidentally homosexual
2. Predominantly heterosexual, but more than incidentally homosexual
3. Equally heterosexual and homosexual
4. Predomiantly homosexual, but more than incidentally heterosexual
5. Predominantly homosexual, but incidentally heterosexual
6. Exclusively homosexual

Figure 20.3. Heterosexual-homosexual rating scale,
adapted from Kinsey et al. 1948, page 638.

however, and there are many men whose homosexual feelings are stronger (or weaker) than their practice. Men who are leading heterosexual lives probably fall into all the vertically-striped cells, and men leading homosexual lives probably fall into all the horizontally-striped cells.

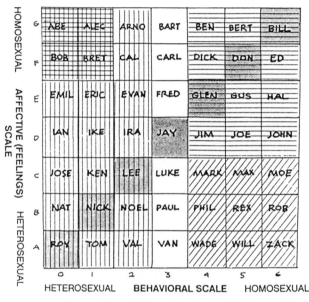

0 and A. Exclusively heterosexual.
1 and B. Predominantly heterosexual, only incidentally homosexual.
2 and C. Predominantly heterosexual, but more than incidentally homosexual.
3 and D. Equally heterosexual and homosexual.
4 and E. Predominantly homosexual, but more than incidentally heterosexual.
5 and F. Predominantly homosexual, but incidentally heterosexual.
6 and G. Exclusively homosexual.

Figure 20.4. This author's modification of the Kinsey Scale, differentiating between behavior and feeling.

*At lower left-hand corner, **Roy**, is exclusively heterosexual, both in behavior and in feeling. **Nat** and **Tom** are predominantly heterosexual, and only incidentally homosexual. **Val** and **Jose** are predominantly heterosexual, but more than incidentally homosexual. Jay is equally homosexual and heterosexual. **Glen** is predominantly homosexual but more than incidentally heterosexual. **Don** is predominantly homosexual but incidentally heterosexual. **Bill** is exclusively homosexual both in behavior and in feeling.*

The unstriped cells might seem to be a "no man's land" that separates the straight from the gay population. But this area is not entirely unoccupied. Unlike gays who regard an occasional heterosexual adventure as a lapse from their usual conduct, or straight men who fall into a homosexual experience as a result of some odd circumstance (*e.g.* inebriation, isolation, etc.), there is a population of men (and women) who identify as bisexual. They claim that it is part of their sexual nature to seek sexual intimacy with both men and women. Some (perhaps a majority) marry and conduct their sex activity in secrecy, a "design for living" that was detailed in Chapter 15.

Bisexual men are not only somewhat estranged from the straight world, they are often scorned by gay men, if the comments of some of Weinberg *et al's* respondents (pages 19-20) are representative. One bisexual spoke up at a conference of gays, lesbians and bisexuals, saying: "I'm frankly appalled and disgusted at the prejudice against bisexuality that I'm aware of within the gay male community." Gay men recall how they resisted the coercion of family and friends to date girls, the speaker continued, and they imagine that bisexuals are gay males who yielded to this social pressure and never outgrew it. Gay men further complain that the very presence of bisexuals obscures the uniqueness of homosexuals and impedes the academic study of homosexuals as a unique group.

Weinberg *et al*. (pages 20, 21) document other complaints by bisexuals that they are misunderstood by their gay brothers: "[T]here's a subtle message in the gay community not to talk about my heterosexual relationships." Another bisexual male says that gays hate bisexuals because gays "can't compete against a real woman. . . . [They] hate bi men because they might give me up for a woman."

How large is this group of men who identify themselves as bisexuals? Estimates vary considerably. Reinisch (page 43) estimated that 10 to 15 percent of the population have sex with both men and women over a period of years. But the 1994 survey of Laumann *et al*. (pages 293-294 fn.) reported that less than one percent of men and women said they were actively bisexual in the sense that they have sex with both men and women. Weinberg et al. report (page 13) that a Bisexual Center existed in San Francisco, and their 1983 study (published in 1994) is based on interviews with 49 men and 44 women members, matching their responses with gay and straight samples.

Returning to our discussion of Figure 20.4, the cell labelled "Rex" represents a person who has predominantly heterosexual feelings, but is in fact homosexually active. Why? "Rex" is a ballet dancer; his director is homosexual and most of his friends and colleagues are also homosexual. He lives in a homosexual world.[8]

Men who would fall in a shaded cell or fairly close to a shaded cell probably feel most comfortable about their sexual orientation; there is a good match between their feelings and their behavior. Men who fall in a cell remote from a shaded cell are burdened by a chronic dissonance between how they feel and what kind of life they are leading. They are probably most vulnerable to alcohol or drug abuse, and also most likely to seek therapeutic help.

The most deviant populations probably fall in the upper left and lower right corners of the grid, farthest from the shaded areas. At the upper left area, cross-hatched, is a group that includes the homophobic: straight men whose homosexual feelings are so strong, they must continually fight them at a high risk to themselves and to others. Future research may tell us who else occupies these cells.

At the lower-right corner, diagonally-striped, are homosexual prostitutes and sociopaths. They engage in homosexual activity not because it expresses their feelings, but either because it has become their way of earning a living, or because it is a tactic for conducting antisocial or criminal activity. Then, there are those men who are so isolated socially, because of personality or physical disorder, for them homosexual activity serves as a vehicle for making social contact with another human being.

Because we live in a world that includes some people who face nothing more than the ordinary miseries of life, as well as some who are clearly psychologically disturbed, a detailed study of the lives of gay men must include a look at those who are mildly or even severely disturbed. This does not mean that most gay men are disturbed, nor does it say anything about what portion of gay men are disturbed. It simply means that gays, like straights, have their share of emotionally troubled persons.

There are many ways of expressing the distinction between those who are psychologically able and those who are mentally or emotionally disabled. There are, to be sure, marginal cases, but most people fit the description of OK or not OK, normal or deviant, healthy or disturbed. Everyday observation makes it clear that human differences range along some sort of continuum rather than fit into two separate categories. So it is somewhat arbitrary where we draw the lines that separates the good, the mediocre, and the poor; just as arbitrary as where we would draw the lines separating the tall, the average, and the short.

What's more, the assessment of psychological functioning is more elusive than the measurement of height. There is, therefore, an ambiguity as well as an arbitrariness about how and where we draw the line between the psychologically fortunate and the unfortunate; about who we label as mediocre, and who we shrug off as ambiguous. In the next five chapters, we will examine the broad range of mental functioning in the male homosexual population, including the most fortunate, the least fortunate, and those who do not quite fit into the category of homosexuals although they often are so grouped.

It would be tempting to think of these 34 categories as "34 types" of homosexuals, but our psychological world is not so simple; most gay men can best be described as a mixture of several categories--one major component and one or more minor components-- rather than as one "pure type."

NOTES TO CHAPTER 20

1. Blanchard *et al.* tested a population of 197 men, and reported that male homo-sexuals scored lower on a scale of violence than heterosexual controls.

2. Since this author has reinterpreted Nimmons' data, perhaps it serves a good purpose to again summarize what seems to be the main intent of the Nimmons book. I believe the intent of the book is twofold: (1) to tell the general reader about the positive side of gay life, and (2) to make sure that gay men know that there's more to the gay lifestyle than cruising and one-night stands, that gay men who "feel isolated, inadequate, and cynical" (Nimmons, page 189), who feel "lonely, alienated [and] disappointed" (ibid., page 191), become part of the "cul-tural experiment" the book describes.

3. As a gay advocate, Nimmons is free to celebrate what he is sure are "profound, spontaneous social experiments . . . a striking range of cultural innovations in social practice" in the gay community, and he can ignore the genetic aspect of the phenomenon. But as a scholar, can he say "We don't need to resort to biology . . . "? If a significant aspect of what look like "profound, spontaneous social exper-iments" can be accounted for by a stable genetic process, then the logic of sci-ence (Occam's Razor) would favor the simpler explanation.

As a cultural anthropologist, Nimmons might reflect on the fact that the desig-nated role of American Indian berdaches included tending to men wounded in battle, and tending to the sick and dying. Significantly, much of the nurturant, pro-social behavior Nimmons refers to occurs in large gay communities that are facing the AIDS epidemic. Three factors that deserve more explicit recognition in accounting for the pro-social behavior of gay men in places like San Francisco are (1) the political solidarity of gay men and lesbians, (2) the AIDS health cri-sis, and (3) the *size* of the gay community. In all likelihood, minority people show more group solidarity when they live large groups: In union there is strength.

4. How stable or well-integrated is their bisexual habit? Weinberg et al. asked their bisexual respondents: "Is it possible. . . that someday you could define your-self as either. . . gay or heterosexual?" About 40 percent answered yes. Typically, the respondent felt it could happen "if I fell insanely in love with some person." One reflected: "If I should meet a woman and want to get married, and if she was not open to my relating to men, I might become heterosexual again" (Weinberg *et al.*, page 33) .

Are the heterosexual, bisexual, and homosexual populations equally stable? To what extent do individuals move back and forth from one group to another? This question was explored in Chapter 14.

5. In our time, many gay men openly acknowledge their sexual orientation and generally engage in both active and passive roles. In Kinsey's day, only fags openly acknowledged their homosexuality. Chauncey describes an era in which fags visited bars, restaurants, and other public places, offering oral sex to the trade: "masculine men" who accepted sexual favors from fags, incidental to their "heterosexual" life. Additionally, there was a closeted homosexual population, some permanently partnered, who were called queers.

6. Kinsey's denunciation of men who seek out the services of fags but deny that they themselves have homosexual cravings, perhaps stemmed from the fact that Prof. Kinsey, though a husband and father, was also engaged in homosexual activities, according to a recent biography of Kinsey by James Jones. [Jones claims to have interviewed men who had been Kinsey's sexual partners. (Personal communication.)]

7. Behavior and feelings are only two dimensions of sexual orientation. Identity is a third dimension. Does the person openly define himself as a gay man, and regard his heterosexual activity as incidental or situational? Or, with the same pattern of activity, does the person define himself as a bisexual, or as a straight who happens to lose control when he gets drunk, or is easily tempted to take advantage of homosexual opportunities? A moving three dimensional block of cells (which might better be displayed on a video screen than on the page of a book) would assign each individual a place that describes his behavior, his feelings, and also his identity.

8. All male ballet dancers are not gay. It is believed that about 30 per cent are straight.

21 "Normal for Me"

A gay man explains: "Homosexuality is as normal for me as heterosexuality is for you." As Bruce Bawer (1996, page 45) expressed it, "[W]hat's natural to one individual isn't necessarily natural to another and to affirm one's homosexual identity is not to defy nature but to embrace one's true identity."

Psychologist Evelyn Hooker became famous for authoring a 1956 research study[1] that showcased a group of nonclinical gay men whose projective test protocols could not be distinguished, by Rorschach experts, from a control group of heterosexuals. Hooker's statistical evidence confirmed what Sigmund Freud and Havelock Ellis had both concluded *half a century earlier*. Freud, on the basis of his clinical observations, wrote in 1905 (page 139 fn.) that to *think of homosexuality as a pathology was already an antiquated idea:*

> The pathological approach to the study of inversion has been displaced by the anthropological. The merit for bringing this change is due to [Iwan] Bloch (1902-3) who has also laid stress on the occurrence of inversion among the civilizations of antiquity.

Freud wrote (pages 138-139) that homosexuality is "found in people whose efficiency is unimpaired, and who are indeed distinguished by especially high intellectual development and ethical culture." Freud was not satisfied merely to set forth his point of view in his scientific writings. He also had addressed the general public in a letter to the Vienna newspaper *Die Zeit* (October 27, 1903) arguing that homosexuals are not sick, nor should they be treated as law-breakers.

> "I am of the firm conviction that homosexuals must not be treated as sick people, for a perverse[2] orientation is far from being a sickness. Homosexual persons are not sick . . . [and] they also do not belong in a court of law!"

In the Preface to the 1910 first edition of *Sexual Inversion*, Havelock Ellis admitted (page v) that he wrote the book to protest "the heavy penal burden and . . . severe social stigma" suffered by men he knew "for whom [he] felt respect and admiration:"

> I was inclined to slur . . . over [the subject of homosexuality] as an unpleasant subject, and one that it was wise not to enlarge on. But I found in time that several persons for whom I felt respect and admiration were congenital subjects of this abnormality. At the same time, I realized that in England . . . the law and public opinion combine to place a heavy penal burden and a severe social stigma on the manifestation of an instinct which to those

persons who possess it frequently appears natural and normal. It was clear, therefore, that the matter was in special need of eluci-dation and discussion.

To support his point of view, Ellis included in his study the case histories of 33 educated and professionally productive homosexual men.

In his 1926 book, *The Doctor Looks at Love and Life*, the physician popular-izer Joseph Collins (page 65) rejects the widespread notion "that homosexual love is pathological in nature." European psychiatrists who espouse this view reach their conclusion on the basis of "asylum experience." On the basis of Collins's private-practice experience, he recalls, "*I have known many well-bal-anced homosexuals of both sexes. Some of them have made distinctive positions for themselves in various field of activity from arms to the pulpit . . . teaching and writing. As a rule, they are persons of taste, refinement and sensibility*" (emphasis added). Why then do they sometimes consult with a physician for sex-ual reorientation? Because, Collins suggests, of society's rejection and the law's punishment of their ways. Twenty-three years before Kinsey "scientifically" measured the incidence of homosexuality, Collins (*ibid*) shrewdly estimated that about "three human beings . . . out of every hundred are born that way."

Students of Laud Humphreys, pioneer researcher of homosexual behavior, noted that the professor displayed in his office a list of 100 famous homosexual notables. (1979, page 143). Potts and Short (pages 60-61) offer brief biographies of notable gay men. Their comments on some of them are summarized (and sup-plemented) in the paragraphs below:

> *Alexander the Great.* When his lover and general Hephastion died, Alexander designed a vast monument to be built in his lover's honor.

> *King Richard the Lionhearted* regarded it as a penance when ordered to sleep with his queen.

> *Frederick the Great*, on the orders of his father, was forced to witness the beheading of his homosexual lover Hans von Katte.

> *Erasmus*, the founder of modern Biblical criticism: homosexual.

> *Christopher Marlowe* quipped: "All they that loved not tobacco and boys were fools."

> *Leonardo da Vinci*, at age 24, was imprisoned for having sex with a [male] youth. When he died, he left his papers to his clos-est male companion, Francesco Melzi.

Michelangelo celebrated male beauty in his statues and in his poetry. Potts and Short quote from a poem in which he exhalts homosexual love:

> The love of which I speak aspires on high;
> Woman is too unlike and little does it agree
>   with a wise and manly heart to burn for her.
> The one, [a same-sex love,] draws up to heaven,
>   the other, [a woman, draws one] down to earth.
> The one inhabits the soul, the other the senses.

Herman Melville "wrote the macho parts of Moby Dick while in love with Nathaniel Hawthorne. . ." (*ibid*).

Henry David Thoreau was attracted to young men, and (according to gay history researcher Ned Katz) fell intensely in love with an 11-year-old boy, Edmund Sewall.

Oscar Wilde. Gay advocates dwell on his gay years, and suggest that he was a lifelong homosexual who married and quickly had children to hide his secret life. In Chapter 14, however, we have noted that a Wilde biographer claims that Wilde's letters to his wife were written by a passionate heterosexual lover.

Written during the first year of their marriage, when Wilde was temporarily separated from his new wife, here is a love letter addressed to his wife Constantine:

> The air is full of the music of your voice, my soul and
> body seem no longer mine, but mingled in some exquisite
> ecstasy with yours. I feel incomplete without you.

Wilde wrote "The Importance of Being Earnest" during his homosexual phase. In this play, he wrote: "Beautiful sins, like beautiful people, are the privilege of the rich. The only way to get rid of a temptation is to yield to it."

Lord Alfred ("Bosie") Douglas, Oscar Wilde's lover, wrote the poem with the line: "I am the love that dare not speak its name." [3]

Somerset Maugham wote of his homosexuality: "I tried to persuade myself that I was three-quarters normal and only a quarter queer, whereas it was really the other way round."

E.M. Forster wrote: "I want to love a strong man of the lower classes and be loved by him, and even hurt by him." Before he wrote *Passage to India*, he had written an explicitly homosexual novel, *Maurice*, but it was not published until after his death.

Alan Turing, "the brilliant mathematician, who broke the code used by the Nazis to transmit messages in World War II, may have contributed more than perhaps any other person to the Allied victory." He was arrested as a homosexual in 1952. An attempted hormonal "cure" led to obesity and breast development and, two years later, he committed suicide (*ibid.*, page 61).

John Maynard Keynes, who revolutionized modern economic theory, married at 42. "[H]is private diaries record his conquest of little boys and male street prostitutes" during his Cambridge days (*ibid.*, page 61) .

T.E. Lawrence, Lawrence of Arabia, "once said of his leadership in the Near East Campaigns of World War I, 'I liked a particular Arab, and I thought the freedom for his race could be an acceptable present'" (*ibid.*).

Rock Hudson "came out of closet as he was dying" (*ibid.*) .The death of his friend of Hollywood days finally moved President Reagan to grant Federal support for a program in AIDS research.

THE ELITE

First, we will list the gay men who most fully meet the standards of good mental health, who make the strongest case that their kind of homosexuality falls well within the range of normal behavior. In 1905 (page 139) Freud noted that homosexuality is "found in people whose efficiency is unimpaired, and who are indeed distinguished by especially high intellectual development and ethical culture."

Here are men who deserve to be called **THE ELITE**.[4] They would be a credit to whatever community they belonged to, and if they are members of the gay community, they give real meaning to the phrase "Gay Pride." Lucky to have both good genes and a good upbringing, they are active, productive members of the business world, they are in politics, in the arts, and in all the professions. Wherever they work, they mingle freely with their colleagues, and may keep their sexual orientation private where it would interfere with their work. Voeller (pages 234-235) describes how a group of successfully closeted homosexual psychiatrists were able to a fool a colleague who boasted of his knack for recognizing gays.

[At] a social event during a professional psychiatric meeting, one of the best known leaders of the opposition to the removal of the "sickness" designation of homosexuality in the American Psychiatric Association's nomenclature expanded on his perceptiveness and boasted of his ability to recognize gays across a crowded room, unaware that the clinic director with whom he was speaking was gay. To add to the tragicomedy, he then introduced three of the senior residents in his training program in psychiatry, and left to talk with other psychiatrists. During the conversation between the residents and the clinic director, two of the three residents acknowledged their own homosexuality and expressed grave fear that their professor might discover their secret (Voeller, pages 234-235).

The inability of "experts" to tell whether a well-adjusted person was straight or gay was dramatized in the famous Hooker study, already mentioned. Here are the comments of a psychological assessment expert, "Judge A," on one homosexual respondent who got high marks in psychological adjustment:

Judge A wrote: "Looks like a well-integrated person. Impulse control really smooth, because he permits all impulses to express themselves in context--both dependent and aggressive. Of all the cases, the best balance of aggression and dependency we have seen. No problem, clinical or otherwise. Relations with others skillful and comfortable" (Hooker 1957, page 28) .

The helping professions have a special appeal to gay men, who sometimes choose to become male nurses, teachers, social workers, and mental health workers. Here is a gay psychiatrist who has earned a place of honor in his profession:

Dr. Jeff

At a social gathering in California, this author was approached by an acquaintance, a staff psychiatrist at a state mental hospital, who said, "Louis, I hear you're writing a book about homosexual men. Let me tell you about a man I work with. We are both staff psychiatrists at a 25-bed acute state psychiatric unit in Los Angeles. We deal with a wide range of mental patients, including homeless street people, criminals, drug addicts and alcoholics. We stabilize acute problems and discharge or maintain others who need continuous hospitalization until they can be transferred to a longer term unit." He proceeded to tell me about Dr. Jeff (not his real name), a colleague of his for the past year and a half. Dr. Jeff is a gay man and also an admirable human being: "In my twenty-three years of practice in institutional settings, I've never had a co-worker I've been so satisfied to work with day in and day out." My acquaintance continued his story:

Typically, when psychiatrists have a conference (this is probably true of other professionals), of course they want to learn from each other and to solve problems together. But there's always an undercurrent of competitiveness. (Who knows more? Make the slightest mistake and your colleague is sure to put you down for it.) With Jeff, there's absolutely none of that. Our professional conversations are free of hidden agendas. Jeff offers his professional insights as well as his personal feelings and very private associations. He fosters an atmosphere of openness and trust, which makes our conferences both intellectually and emotionally satisfying.

We've worked together for a year and a half now, and have faced all kinds of crises. We both have the same rank: staff psychiatrist. We have no Chief (thanks to a budget cut), so we have to work everything out together. I'm a fighter, but I've never had a fight with Jeff. Whatever the problem, with Jeff there's always an amicable resolution. When there's a conflict between us, Jeff usually smiles and says, "You're the Alpha."

Controlling patients who are aggressive and potentially violent is part of our job. It's obvious that Jeff doesn't enjoy physical confrontation, though I'd say that over the last year and a half he's adapted to our needs pretty well. Sure, we've talked this over, and I get the impression that Jeff's mild manner goes back to his early childhood.

When he was a boy, what saved Jeff from being tormented as a sissy was the fact that he always commanded the respect of his peers for his sheer brilliance. He was always at the top of every class, and at graduation from both high school and college he was class valedictorian. Plus he has always been artistically talented: he always acted in school plays, he plays the piano, and is a gifted artist.

Jeff's interest in classical music is so strong, he was continuing piano lessons while in medical school, where he made Alpha Omega Alpha, the medical school honor society. Jeff is an opera lover, an accomplished classical pianist, and enjoys music of all kinds. Jeff has written three novels (unpublished), and likes to write science-fiction short stories. His office is tastefully arranged (mine looks like the battalion headquarters) and is decorated by an original piece of sculpture and several framed prints.

Jeff expresses his artistic talent in quirky and original ways. For example, he once showed me a sketch book in which he had drawn imaginative symbolizations of people we both knew, depicting their personality and mental life. These were not caricatures but stylized abstractions and yet I knew exactly who he was depicting.

Physically, Jeff is good-looking man of 37, slim but beautifully muscled in a way that shows he follows a regular schedule of physical workouts. There's no sign of middle-age bulge. At office parties, nurses bring all kinds of calorie-laden goodies, but I've noticed that Jeff is very sparing about what he eats. At home, he makes regular use of a stair-climber and a set of weights. He dresses conservatively, his shoes are always carefully shined, but occasionally he shows up for work wearing a bright-colored or Hawaiian shirt.

When we have lunch in the hospital canteen, we are often joined by two women who are members of the clinical staff at the hospital. Jeff takes a spontaneous and natural interest in what the ladies are wearing, even their accessories. When the conversation turned to hairdressers, Jeff mentioned that a lady hair stylist does his hair. He can chitchat with the ladies for hours. When we're together alone, our conversation is refreshingly open, honest and candid. At times, our talk shifts from professional to personal matters, and this includes talk about sexuality--straight and gay, tame and wild--with a frankness that is unbelievable. If a few days go by when I've been too busy to chat with Jeff, he'll come up to me and ask: "How are things going, Jim? Is everything OK?"

Jeff was raised in a comfortable suburban home, and offers comments that show he was very close to his mother, and still is. He says he always felt *different,* and had secret boyhood crushes on boys who were handsome and well-built. When he entered puberty, he hated gym class because he was afraid that the sight of naked boys in the shower and locker rooms might give him an erection. Jeff recalls one episode of boyhood sexual play with a male cousin, but kept his same-sex attraction to himself and only when he turned 21 did he become sexually active. When his parents first learned of his sexual orientation, Jeff says "They were devastated." But his parents (especially his mother) have come to accept the fact that their son is gay. Now when Jeff attends family reunions, he brings his partner along.

For his first few years as a gay man, before settling down with a long-term partner, Jeff was a cruiser, with some moderation, testing a wide range of sexual possibilities. His lover for the past few years, is vice-president of a major corporation in the Los Angeles area. They have an ample circle of friends, straight and gay, and have an active social life. Jeff and his partner share a comfortable apartment on the oceanfront, and together they own a vacation home in ski country.

In my discussions with Jeff, I have sensed a maturity rare in a person who has not yet reached the age of 40. When I asked him, "What has been the most maturing experience of your life?" he answered, "The AIDS epidemic. For a few years in the 80s, I was losing half my friends every year. It forced me to answer questions like, 'What is really important?' 'What do I want to get out of life?'" Maybe that's why he left private practice to work with the poor and dispossessed.

A board-certified psychiatrist, Jeff is a valuable member of our team. There is no indication that his sexual orientation interferes with his work. To the average observer, his manner gives no clue to the fact that he is a gay man, and patients do not seem to be influenced by his sexual orientation. (It's not unusual for an abusive patient to call the psychiatrist "a goddam faggot." I think that I--a married man-- have been called that more often than Jeff has.) Perhaps it is easy for a gay man like Jeff to be so nurturant, empathic and supportive; in which case it might be argued that Dr. Jeff has learned to put his homosexuality to good use as a psychiatrist.

(Author's note: A year after writing the above report, and just before putting this book to press, I chanced to meet Dr. Jeff's colleague. "How's Dr. Jeff?" I asked, and learned that he was no longer my friend's work partner. "He left a couple of months ago, said he was frustrated with administrative restrictions, and asked to be transferred to an administrative job, where he thought he could make things at the hospital run smoother. Well, that didn't work out, so he's leaving the hospital altogether. Now he tells me he's taking a job at the student health service of a local university. I believe Dr. Jeff does have a history of frequent job changes."

Though I still regard Dr. Jeff as a remarkable person, this latest report diminishes somewhat the admiration I had for him for dedicating his professional life "to work with the poor and dispossessed." I also wonder about the psychological meaning of his history of frequent job changes. L.A.B.)

Close-coupled gay men best adjusted. It should come as no surprise that Dr. Jeff has a life partner. Back in 1978 Bell and Weinberg published a large-scale psychological study of homosexual men, and grouped them into eight levels of adjustment, from the happiest to the most miserable. They placed in the top category men who were living with a long-term partner, close-coupled.

On the basis of detailed interviews, the investigators concluded that the happiest men in their study—the least troubled, least regretful, least worried, least tense, least lonely—were men in "close-coupled" partnerships. (Second in rank were those men who were in "open-coupled" partnerships, men who lived with a partner but one or both of them regularly sought sexual contacts with others.) Close-coupled partners had the smallest amount of sexual problems, and seem to enjoy a high degree of psychological intimacy:

> They tended to spend more evenings at home and less leisure time by themselves. . . . . Their sexual lives were [more] gratifying to them. They were likely to have engaged in a wide variety of sexual techniques and tended not to report the kinds of problems that might rise from a lack of communication between partners.

> . . . They were less tense or paranoid and more exuberant than the average respondent. [An interviewer describes a close-coupled partnership as follows:] "The apartment which he shares with his lover is very clearly 'their' home. A lot of love went in fixing it up. Interestingly, when I asked him questions about his own siblings, he called in his roommate to help him out with the answers" (pages 219-220).

To persons who know about homosexuals only through stories, jokes, and bad examples, it can come as quite a shock to meet a very decent human being who happens to also be gay. Suppose you grew up in a small town in South Dakota. You had never met a Jew, but had been taught that Jews were crafty, clannish, and defensive. Then you go off to college, and your roommate is Samuel Bernstein. You find him an altogether likeable person, unlike all the stereotypes you were taught belonged to Jews. That was like the experience of Bob, a Christian conservative and admitted homophobe, whose college roommate was Kevin, a very decent and honorable person. What astounded Bob beyond belief (Appendix 2) was that Kevin was also homosexual.

Making the acquaintance of a person--a neighbor, a teacher, a colleague, a teammate--finding him honest, interesting and *simpatico*, and then learning that he is gay, can be an enriching experience that replaces one's stereotypes with direct experience. Recalling his own struggle with homosexuality, which he eventually overcame, psychotherapist Richard Cohen remembers (page 6) one of his homosexual partners, Tim, an art student, as "an exceptional man:"

> We were the best of friends. I learned many things by seeing life
> through Tim's eyes. He had an affinity for nature, and I learned
> to see things I had never seen before. He was and still remains an
> exceptional man.

Bawer (1993, 1996) insists that the majority of gay men--quiet, conservative,
and undistinguished--are in fact invisible to the general public. He blames a
noisy minority of boisterous, radical hedonists for giving the general public a
rather biased   impression of what gay men are like.

> [M]ost gay people are in most ways pretty much like most
> straight people. The main difference is that they're virtually
> invisible. They're essentially silent about being gay; so that the
> basically mainstream-oriented majority of gay people don't con-
> tribute very much to the public image of--or the public dialogue
> about--what it means to be gay. The image is formed, rather, and
> the 'gay' end of the dialogue largely carried out, by that very vis-
> ible and extreme segment of the gay population. (Bawer 1996,
> page 228).

THE NONCONFORMISTS. Contrasting with "The Elite," gay men who
occupy positions of leadership and trust in the general community, is a group of
"contrarians" who make homosexuality synonymous with nonconformity not
only in sexual orientation but in dress, in manners, and in a host of other ways.
If man is truly a social animal (as we have insisted), if conformity is a survival
trait, how do we account *for nonconformity*? Variations of life experience do
make some individuals noncomformists, contrarians, adventurers, risk-takers.
"Birds of a feather flock together," so noncomformists lose no time in finding
kindred spirits, with whom they ever-so-strongly band together (see "the clones,"
described at the end of this chapter) to satisfy *their* social conformity needs. Two
factors that may push an individual in the direction of nonconformity are (a) *birth
order*: the later-borns, and (b) *personality type*: the adventurer.

The later-borns. A number of studies have linked homosexuality with birth
order (Slater 1962, Blanchard and Sheridan 1992, Zucker and Blanchard 1994,
Blanchard *et al.* 1995, Blanchard and Bogaert 1996). *The evidence is overwhelming that male homosexuals are likely to be later-born.*[5] Sulloway has collected evidence on later-borns, and his book *Born To Rebel* attempts to describe
the significance of birth order in shaping personality. Later-borns have many reasons to become the nonconformists that they often are.

Sulloway's book presents a wide range evidence, contrasting conservative first-borns with risk-taking laterborns. For example (page 112), he relates birth order to choice of sports. First-borns favor non-contact sports such as swimming, tennis and golf. Later-borns choose sports that are more physically daring, such as rugby, football, boxing, and parachute jumping.

First-borns tend to be more similar in personality to other first-borns than they are to their own younger siblings (Sulloway, page 21). They tend to be conservative; they respect the status-quo. They have grown up enjoying the security of having been their parents' "first love." He returns his love by identifying strongly with parental authority, by a disinclination to "rock the boat." Later-borns may be "born into the same family" as their older brother(s), but parent-child bonds of affection have already been established. To compete for attention and affection, the later-born learns to act up, to be more adventurous. He *dares to be different.* Does he become a nonconformist to get attention, to win admiration, to reject domination by his older siblings and parents, or because he does not identify so strongly with his parents? Does he underrate his masculinity because it is evident that his brothers are bigger, stronger, and better developed than he is?

The adventurers. Some nonconformists are *not* later-borns, but their interaction of genetic endowment and life experience (tall, strong, intelligent, courageous, curious, defiant) push them in the direction of challenging the status-quo. In a culture of poverty, young adventurers may become juvenile delinquents. In the 1940s, Sheldon and Eleanor Glueck researched the question: What makes a juvenile delinquent? In a culture of poverty, only a minority of boys become delinquents. How do they differ from the majority of their brothers and neighbors who do not? The Gluecks compared the personalities of delinquent and non-delinquent boys. They found that, from early childhood, future delinquents were seen to be assertive, self-centered, adventure-seeking, easily bored, explosive, suspicious of authority, and eager to test the limits of prevailing rules and standards. (By contrast, non-delinquents, drawn from the same population, showed a sense of concern about others' appraisal of their conduct, a capacity for guilt, and a tendency to worry over consequences, *not just to be afraid of the law.*)

Similarly, homosexuality is more likely to be adopted by adolescents who are more assertive, more adventurous, less controlled by conscience or worry over consequences; willing to actually adopt behaviors that their conservative cohorts just daydream about, or joke or worry about. Are we suggesting that homosexuals are juvenile delinquents? *No!* Only that both groups defy social norms, and that both share certain character traits.

A World War II veteran who had worked in Army intelligence recalled that "a lot of the spies he worked with were gay. . . " (Outland, page 7). Espionage is a life of such high adventure that it makes for gripping movies and novels, but it takes a person who is strongly attracted to a life of danger, and has a high degree of intelligence, defiance, and curiosity, to enter this field of work. If it is true that espionage has a special appeal to homosexual men, that fact strengthens the link between homosexuality and adventure-seeking behavior.[6]

THE RADICAL HOMOSEXUALS. Where does nonconformity end and *radicalism* begin? In the 1940s, Eli Segal built a theory and program of therapy around the proposition that the homosexual's main problem was a contempt for society. In his 1965 book (page 166) Hatterer agreed that sometimes homosexuality expresses "contempt for society. Such patients usually have a history of disturbed family relationships and project the conflict into other associations." Herbert Marcuse, the philosopher of radicalism, saw homosexuality as a conscious rebellion against society's emphasis on procreation.

Life experiences predispose some men to take special pleasure in challenging the status quo. Born at another time, they might have become Socialists, Communists, or wobblies. Undoubtedly, there are those who are drawn to the gay lifestyle partly because it made them brothers-in-arms with other oppressed groups: blacks,[7] Hispanics, and women.

Merle Miller (page 57) senses that his "secret problem" was tied up with his feeling of kinship with the underdog: a polio victim, a clubfoot, blacks. Even before he was ready to affiliate with homosexuals, he identified with all kinds of social rejects. He recalls: "I once belonged to 22 organizations devoted to improving the lot of the world's outcasts."

Bawer recalls (1993 page 24) that "a kind, soft-spoken member of the radical direct-action group Queer Nation said to me over dinner: *'I wish I could burn down every church in America'*" (emphasis added). Christopher Hobson (page 153) recalls "several gay liberationists who 'came out' as homosexuals for the first time *after several years of well-adjusted heterosexual life.* They made this step "by the winds of social protest. As Trotsky said of a comrade who had been in analysis for several years, and later became an outstanding Bolshevik diplomat: 'The revolution healed Yoffe better than psychoanalysis of all his complexes.'" If there are those who are "born to rebel," as Sulloway has argued, some are likely to find their way into the gay community. This category may include men whose homosexual potential is just strong enough to tip the balance, when combined with the appeal of radical activism.

In the autobiography as a formerly gay man, Aaron recalls that during his homosexual years, he was always attracted to black men, and recalls that he first permitted himself to be penetrated anally by a black partner. Aaron reflects (pages 124-125), "It may be . . . that submitting to a black lover satisfied me in some other ways than sexual. There was a kind of poetic justice in turning the tables on society symbolically; making myself prostrate before people who had been so ruthlessly put down for no good reason."

As Hart reveals (page 31), one of the best-kept secrets of the 1980s is that "one prominent gay male activist [of that decade] spent most of the 1980s in a secretive relationship with a woman--a fact which to this day [1991] is known to only a small circle of his friends."

A masochistic gay man recalls (told to Stambolian, pages 9-10) that he "grew up in an atmosphere of prejudice directed at others. I saw people abused [by Jews, like himself, as his own father abused his Puerto Rican garment workers.] . . . I've had tremendous feelings of guilt because of it." He reflects: "*My former lovers and all my important affairs have been Puerto Ricans*" (emphasis added).

The Stonewall revolt of 1969 ushered in the glory days of radical homosexuals when, as Bayer documents, annual conventions of the American Psychiatric Association were successfully assaulted through "zapping," "direct action" and "guerilla theater." Writes Levine (1990, page 64): "Activists altered the meaning, value, and social position of homosexuality through . . . militant chauvinism."

Radical homosexuals oppose the gay community's push for gay marriage rights. Michael Rowe (page 124) quotes the hecklers of gay marriage advocates:

> We don't *need* gay marriage! . . . We have better things to think about than being just like straights! How about polygamy? . . . What about threesomes? What if you wanted to marry your *brother*? Or an *animal*? . . . We need to *remake* society! Our work is to *overthrow* marriage! Marriage is a *bourgeois, patriarchist institution!*

Similarly, Andrew Sullivan (1998, page 87) role-plays the gay radical's view (not his) of marriage:

> Marriage of all institutions is to the liberationists a form of imprisonment; it reeks of a discourse that has bought and sold property, that has denigrated and subjected women, that has constructed human relationships into a crude and suffocating form. Why on earth should it be supported by homosexuals?

THE HEDONIST HOMOSEXUALS. What is important to these men is not just the difference between same-sex and opposite-sex activity, but the difference between gratification that is both delayed and measured or limited, and gratification that can be instant, powerful, and virtually unlimited. It is a difference between the Dionysian and the Apollonian way of life, as Ruth Benedict put it in her 1959 book, *Patterns of Culture*.

In conservative married life, sexual union is often a fairly predictable act that comes after a prolonged courtship. In "the gay lifestyle," sexual union can occur minutes after sighting an attractive stranger, and can involve a vast range of erotic practices.

To the hedonistic gay man, the human body is not a temple. It is, rather, a playground. He seeks frequent, casual, recreational, and "hot sex,"-- "cruising" bars, baths, and restrooms to find "one-night stands." He may seek variety not only in partners, but in practices that are both exotic, erotic and sometimes dangerous: group sex, analingus, fisting, and sadomasochism. He may also be receptive to the use of drugs and alcohol, to loosen inhibitions, to extend sexual pleasure to new durations, and to raise sexual thrills to new heights. In the straight world, lovemaking may be a romantic, dream-like, and gentle experience, but to a gay hedonist sex must be vigorous and energetic. [8]

ARTISTIC HOMOSEXUALS. In his book *The Artist in Society*, Hatterer made a psychological study of 300 creative people. He reported (1965, pages 14-15) : "I found a prevalence of homosexuality in a number of discrete occupational clusterings--among interior decorators, [designers of] clothes, hair, and window-displays . . . ballet dancers; concert pianists, organists, people connected with the theatre, and so forth--which suggested that a relationship between homosexuality and specific work identities in our culture does exist."

A basic theoretical issue is raised by the question: Why are homosexuals so likely to be artistic, musical, or literary? Three competing answers are (1) social rejection pushes the pre-homosexual boy in that direction (artistic activity is regarded as a substitute for social interaction), (2) artistic interests are part of the gay man's identification with mother, and (3) an artistic sensitivity is one aspect of the pre-homosexual boy's androgynous temperament.

The testimony of a number of Fellows's farm boys indicates how spontaneously their artistic interests emerged in an environment that did not especially encourage artistic expression:

> Joining a choir . . . got me out of phys. ed. one day a week. I loved music anyway. I loved singing. . . . I also wanted to play the piano, and bugged my parents until they finally let me take lessons. . . . My dad hated music and didn't want one of his sons being a musician. . . . (Fellows, page 66).

> I really got into [flower-arranging, and at a county fair] . . . won best-of-show twice. . . . I was competing with about fifteen elderly ladies and one other young man. The old ladies there thought I was a darling (Fellows, page 108).

> I'd watch Grandma crochet and I wanted to learn how to do that . . . so I learned how to crochet, and that was my hobby. (Fellows, page 117).

> I got into embroidery in my early teens. I liked doing things with my hands, and I liked embroidery because you had colored threads, nice pictures of flowers and little animals, and when you got done you had something real pretty. Dad didn't like that I

was doing it--it was sissy--so I didn't make a show of it. My
mother bought [embroidery supplies] for me in the first place, so
it must have been okay with her. One time I told a kid from
school that I would let him see my embroidery if he promised he
wouldn't tell. I showed it to him and the next day in school, he
told everybody, which was disastrous. I didn't do embroidery
again. I became very conscious of what male things were, of
what one does and doesn't do. I've always been envious of
women who could pull out their knitting and do that while
they're talking or watching television. (Fellows, pages 86-87)

The theory that pre-homosexual boys develop artistic sensitivity and a reflective nature because they are made to feel distant from their peers, is argued by
Andrew Sullivan (1995, pages 198-199):

The experience of growing up profoundly different in emotional
and psychological makeup inevitably alters a person's self-per-
ception, tends to make him or her more wary and distant, more
attuned to appearance and its foibles, more self-conscious and
perhaps more reflective. . . . Many homosexual children, feeling
distant from their peers, become experts at trying to figure out
how to disguise their inner feelings, to "pass." They notice the
signs and signals of social interaction, because they do not come
instinctively. They develop skills early on that help them notice
the inflection of a voice, the quirks of a particular movement, the
ways in which meaning can be conveyed in code. They have an
inner ear for irony and double meanings. Sometimes, by virtue of
having to suppress their natural emotions, they find formal outlets to express themselves: music, theater, art.

Hatterer (1965, page 146) describes artists who "consciously or unconsciously decided to use homosexuality to meet the challenge of big-city life with
its extreme competitiveness." Writes Hatterer (1965, pages 146-147) : "[S]ome
male artists develop a pattern of living whereby they can do creative work only
if they are supported by older, wealthier homosexual men. Often, they also have
homosexual teachers. . . . Some of these artists had been introduced to their field
through homosexual contacts, and if young and insecure, [feel the] need to maintain these associations, particularly because of fears that abandonment of homosexuality would threaten their very survival." If they eventually achieve economic independence, they may lose their homosexual feelings which were, after
all, an expression of their feelings of dependence (Hatterer 1965, page 142).

In his therapeutic work with homosexuals, Hatterer found (1970, page 65)
that change in sexual identity was especially difficult for "the man whose work
identity is inexorably woven into his homosexuality is in daily contact with overt

homosexuals--ballet dancers, clothes designers, hairdressers, and interior designers, to mention just a few. Such contact usually extends to the patient's social life,
and it can become the raison d'etre for living totally within a discrete homosexual subculture."

Often the choice of career was closely associated with the development of a
homosexual lifestyle. Inquiring about their occupational adjustment, Bell and
Weinberg (page 145) found that a number of gay men claimed that their homosexuality was an occupational asset:

> [I benefit from] the floral company's acceptance and understand-
> ing of homosexuality--they prefer to hire gays. . . .

> There [are] a number of gays in . . . [interior decorating], and
> this makes things easier in terms of the rest of society. They kind
> of expect it.

> My homosexuality has assisted my creativity. . . .

> The people I work with are homosexual. Women [customers]
> usually expect a hairdresser to be homosexual. They are not
> threatened by it.

> I'm myself in my business and have a large homosexual clien-
> tele. It has freed me from having to do business in a conventional
> way.

> Most people in display are queer. It's been easier at times to get
> ahead, because I am homosexual.

> I think it has helped me to advance on my present job because of
> the association with my supervisors and co-workers, who are
> also homosexual.

"Treatability and prognosis for change are poorest for persons so enmeshed,"
Hatterer commented (page 65).

THE EFFEMINATE HOMOSEXUALS. Even the most sympathetic
observers of homosexual life have noted the effeminate manners of some homosexuals, described in the argot of gay society as "swish." Such manners include
the willowy, limp-wristed posture, falsetto voice, sarcastic and gossipy humor,
celebrity worship, devotion to theater, opera, and old movies.

In present-day gay society, effeminacy is unwanted; personal ads of "Male
Seeking Male" often read: "Straight-looking, straight-acting male seeks similar
partner. No nelly-queens, please." In gay argot, "drag" described the adoption of

feminine garments and make-up, ranging from subtle (*e.g.*, the slight use of make-up) to the extreme: feminine hat, high heels, gloves, wig, and jewelry. "Camp" describes the most outrageous forms of feminine display. Levine refers to a very ample literature on homosexual effeminacy: Achilles 1967; Altman 1982; Cory and LeRoy 1963; Cory 1951; Helmer 1963; Henry 1955; Hoffman 1968; Hooker 1965; Humphreys 1970; Karlen 1971; Lenzoff and Westley 1965; Newton 1972; Read 1980; Stearn 1962; Tripp 1987; and West 1977. Henry (page 291) describes the extravagant conversational language of effeminate homosexuals:

> Such expressions as "Oh, my word!" "Good heavens!" and "Oh, my dear!" are [common]. In describing ordinary experiences [he] is likely to use such words as "terrific," "amazing" . . . "horrible," "tremendous," "sublimely," "charming," "appalling," "vicious," "loathed," and "madly." Exaggerations are made more conspicuous by placing undue or erroneous emphasis on certain syllables and intonations which leave little doubt of the effeminacy of the speaker.

Many observers (as summarized by Levine 1990, page 57) have noted that "swish" is not an uncontrollable habit among homosexuals, but is a manner that can be turned on and off according to the situation. In a heterosexual environment, and when "cruising" (looking for a homosexual partner), there may be no hint of "swish" in a gay man's manner. But when he is in safe and comfortable surroundings (*e.g.*, at a gay bar or among homosexual friends), his effeminate mannerisms emerge. Stearn (page 29) describes this transformation:

> Many times I saw these changes occur after I had gained a homosexual's confidence and he could safely risk my disapproval. Once as I watched a luncheon companion become an effeminate caricature of himself, he apologized: "*It is hard to always remember that one is a man*" (emphasis added).

This suggests that when a gay man wants to make a good impression, he can suppress any mannerism that is less than masculine, but when he relaxes, he expresses himself in a way that is really comfortable for him. The most outrageous and wild displays of effeminacy are known as "camping it up," and occur at homosexual social gatherings. But in 1979, Humphreys interpreted effeminate behavior as "minstrelization," indicating the gay man's capitulation to society's harsh judgment that gays were not men at all. Once gay men muster the courage to challenge this stigma, went the argument, gay men will then be free to express their masculinity. Ten years later, Levine (and his gay-friendly advisers) endorse this interpretation, that effeminate behavior implies an "internalized homophobia" (1990, page 73) .

For an understanding of adult gay effeminacy, a sociological analysis is simply not enough. A psychological approach would study the development of the *individual*, and note that from earliest childhood, the pre-homosexual child spontaneously displayed the manners and interests that labelled him as a "sissy boy." His cross-gender manners and interests are therefore not to be regarded simply as a defense, as a capitulation to social stigma, but an expression of his lifelong temperament, partly, at least, a genetic endowment. As he grows up, he discovers that women share his temperament, women are more likely to be sympathetic and understanding and supportive, and it is no wonder that he is drawn to women as friends, with whom he can share everyday interests, and continues exhibit some of the manners of women. Hewett (page 595) conjectures that the gay man's "gaydar"—his uncanny ability to sense whether a stranger is homosexual—is based on a sensitivity to subtle signs of effeminate interests and sensibilities in others:

> [Gay men] produce an aura of effeminacy so subtle that it is very difficult to describe. It can be in the way they hold their heads. It may lie in the tone of voice or the inflection. It may reveal itself . . . in his intonation, in his attitudes in general, in his interests, and in his particular value system. . . . The average homosexual is horrified at observing anything in himself which appears feminine and will go to great lengths to hide it from others.

> This author was privileged to observe a workshop for Christian homosexual "strugglers" (men who were trying to reorient their sexual life). A participant told of his embarrassment over a conversation with a young woman he was dating. They were talking about skin care regimens, and the young man told of the various products he used every morning and night. "My goodness," responded his date, "You take better care of your skin than I do of mine."

"To camp it up" is to act outrageously effeminate. A "drag queen" is a homosexual who both dresses and acts like a woman. A person, object, or subject is labeled "fluff" or "swish" to describe him or it as effeminate. Gay men may refer to each other as "girls" and "sisters." They often use the pronouns "she" "her" to describe one another The open effeminacy of homosexual men recalls the days when homosexuals presented themselves as "prostitute substitutes" to men in general (called "trade"), at bars, restaurants, and other public places. In this context, makeup and feminine attire contributed to the illusion that "trade" were enjoying the sexual favors of women.

Is "feminine play-acting . . . an expression of guilt and self-hatred," as Levine (1990, page 66) indicates? If so, homosexual effeminacy would have disappeared as gay liberation replaced guilt and self-hatred with gay pride. That has not happened. Effeminacy--here subtle, there blatant--continues to show up in gay life. Men who as "sissy boys" liked to dress up in Mother's clothes and wear Mother's shoes, as adults love to masquerade as "drag queens," and in everyday life adopt various effeminate touches.

Effeminacy is largely shunned and rejected in gay society[9] but continues to exist, and the female impersonator is a popular figure in gay society. Perhaps the appeal of the female impersonator resonates with the viewer's 'latent heterosexuality,' fulfilling his fantasy of finding 'a woman who has not been castrated.'

Homosexual gossip. One effeminate speech norm has persisted from pre-liberation days: a nasty-tongued, gossipy conversational style known as "dishing." Also called "fag talk" or "chitchat," dishing was widely regarded as a mark of feminine identification (Leznoff and Westley, 1956; Hooker, 1956; Hoffman, 1968; Read, 1980). It is of psychological interest that at a time when gay manners and interests were radically de-feminized, "dishing" has survived.[10]

Spreading damaging information, what Levine calls "dirt," is one form of gossip. In the following example of "dirt," (Levine, 1990, page 112) note that Warren, a gay man, is referred to as a "queen," "she" and "her."

> "Give me all the dirt on Warren's latest fuck up," Jim pleaded.

> "You should have seen her last night," David answered. "That 'queen' is such a mess! She did so many 'ludes' that she kept passing out, right on the dance floor. Then she started to puke, and got so sick we had to carry her home."

In an example of "dishing," two gay men ridicule a dentist acquaintance for his small penis:

> "You tricked with her, the tooth fairy!" Tom snorted, "It's a good thing the Lord made her a dentist, because he certainly didn't give her a dick."

> "I know," Sam chirped in. "She's so ashamed of its size, that she doesn't shower or undress at the gym."

There is, of course, something incongruous about super-masculine gays gossiping about their acquaintances and referring to them as "she" and "her." As one man very candidly put it (Levine 1990, page 135) : *"Darling, beneath all this butch drag, we are still girls."*

Female identity and resistance to change. To Hatterer (1970, page 64), a psychoanalyst who has worked extensively with homosexual men who wanted to change, signs of female identity predict a strong resistance to change. Poorest prognosis occurs when the patient reports that he always had a sense of himself as a female and has never desired to be male, or when the patient feels envious of females and desirous of being in their role in a sexual situation. Young and effeminate homosexuals amuse their friends by "camping it up," by adopting outrageously girlish manners. When they grow into middle age and take on the appearance of an "old nelly queen," and they must accept a position on a lower rung of the gay status ladder.

THE SUPER-MASCULINE HOMOSEXUALS. The above description of homosexual gossip is drawn, incongruously, from Levine's study, described in some detail in Chapter 12, of a community of "clones." The everyday appearance of clones is the super-masculine "butch look." When they are cruising, they usually look for "gym bodies." They are likely to add to their personal ads "no nellies, please." But in an intimate moment, the clone may refer to his friends as "she" and "her."

Top status in gay society is granted to the young and masculine, and Levine's clones are typical of men who claim this position. "Clones" earn their name by their conformity as a group, both in dress and behavior. Typically they wear a white top, dark pants, with close-cropped hair, and are plain-talking and aggressive in manner. Levine reports (1990, page 127) that this style emerged in the early seventies among "trendy New York homosexuals [employed in] fashion and the arts." This "butch look" continues to glorify the masculine image in gay society.

White top and dark pants may be the most common super-masculine attire, but Levine (1990, page 131) describes a variety of other costumes adopted by gay men who want to convey a masculine image: the 'hood look, the urban blue-collar look, cowboy look, and the leather-man look, favored by sado-masochists. Some gay men who strive for a super-masculine appearance adopt the dress and manner of a motorcyclist, military man, woodsman, policeman, fireman, or highway patrol man.

A gay man may subtly modify his masculine uniform, and thus reveal his gay sensibility. He will be more neatly groomed, his clothing more carefully color-matched, and more elegantly tailored than his heterosexual model. His clothes are more form-fitting, to better delineate the contours of his body. (Straights, by comparison, look a bit disheveled, as they wear their clothing loose enough for comfort.) Levine (page 132) suggests this ambivalence over the kind of impression a gay man wants to give, in his description of Frank:

> Frank looked like a well-groomed lumberjack. Everything he
> wore was tailored and matched. His jeans and plaid Pendelton
> shirt fit perfectly. His black wool watchman's cap matched his

black Levis and the black in his shirt. His red thermal undershirt matched the red in his shirt. The brown in his leather belt matched the brown in his hiking boots.

Figure 21.1   A clone partnership crisis. -- Reproduced with permission.

On the job, a gay man might wear clothes no different from the straight majority, and for his social life, change into "butch" garb:

> I look at clone drag as play clothes, just like when I would come home from school as a boy, have cookies and milk, change and go out to play. Now I come home from work, change into clone "drag," and go out to play on the circuit (Levine 1990, pages 143-144) .

Masculine attire calls for appropriate surroundings. Gay entertainment establishments offer a "butch" environment: gray industrial carpeting, white walls, track lighting, black metal pipe railing. Some gay men furnish their apartments in similar style. Walls are gray, and floors covered with industrial carpeting. Furnishings include steel shelving, factory lamps, and wire storage baskets (Levine 1990, page 137).

The most hard-won super-masculine trait is not his haircut or attire, or home furnishings, but his "gym body": beautifully-developed musculature, based on a grueling exercise regimen, sometimes supplemented by steroids or even plastic surgery. But developing a gym body, adopting masculine garb, and inhabiting masculine surroundings does *not* indicate whether the man prefers a "top" or "bottom" role, whether he would rather be the inserter or insertee. Levine's gossiping respondent expresses his ambivalence with the words: *"Darling, beneath all this butch drag, we are still girls."*

Solomon confesses (page 207) that he, like many gay men, cultivated a supermasculine appearance to hide his "homophobic feelings of unmasculinity. [He confesses:] I go skydiving, own a gun, did Outward Bound—all that helps to make up for the time I spend on my clothes, in the so-called feminine pursuit of art, and in the erotic and emotional embrace of men."

In his 1990 dissertation, Levine predicted that the era of "the clone" was coming to an end, but in his 1997 book, Signorile was still worried about the persistence of the cult of body-building, hoping for a gay community that truly celebrates diversity.

NOTES FOR CHAPTER 21

1. In 1956, psychologist Evelyn Hooker published a study that demonstrated that a panel of famous clinical experts could not distinguish between a sample of non-clinical gay men, and a matched sample of heterosexuals. This study supported the movement to depathologize homosexuality; a campaign that led to the 1973 elimination of homosexuality from the Diagnostic Manual of the American Psychiatric Association.

2. The English language is a blend from many sources ("a conglomerate language") and assimilates words from many sources. To an American, *pizza* sounds like an English word, but to a German it sounds like an Italian word. German is a homogeneously *Germanic* language, in which foreign words (Greek, Italian, French, etc.) *sound* like foreign words. In English, *perverse* sounds like a put-down, but in German, as Freud used it, *perverse* was a technical word meaning "contrary, difficult, deviating from the norm."

3. Some years ago (April 3, 1964), a *Time* magazine book reviewer, commenting negatively on a novel about gay life, wrote: "The love that dare not speak its name has become the neurosis that does not know when to shut up."

4. Here begins a list, extending from this chapter through the next three chapters, of 33 homosexual types. These 33 types are indicated by capital letters in **THIS STYLE (CENTURY GOTHIC BOLD)** . These types are presented as descriptive only (phenotypes, as Lewin would say).

5. In a 1936 publication (page 167), W.H. Sheldon noted, though he was not sure why, that later-born children "are frequently more sensitive, fragile, and apparently more imaginative than the older children. These younger ones are likely to be more shy, more introverted, and more tender-minded than the older ones . . . and . . . they tend toward intellectual and artistic careers. . . ."

Researchers have demonstrated quite convincingly that *family position* can predict sexual orientation, not perfectly but to a statistically significant extent. For example, Blanchard & Bogaert compared 302 homosexual men with a matched group of 302 heterosexual men, and demonstrated that homosexuality was positively correlated with the number of older brothers but not with the number of older sisters. Their findings also demonstrated that each additional older brother increased the odds of homosexuality by 33 per cent.

So strong is the evidence linking homosexuality to birth order that biological determinists are unable to ignore it, but are reluctant to concede that the tendency is based on family dynamics—an environmental influence.LeVay, and his fellow biological determinists, has speculated that each male birth leaves some sort of residue in the mother's uterus, and that this residue might somehow incline the laterborn to homosexuality. He admits that his speculation is *impossible to prove.* A rule of the logic of science, called Occam's Razor or the principle of parsimony, is that the simpler and more observable explanation is always preferable.

6. Not to be overlooked is another appeal of espionage to a man highly skilled in homosexual sex, and erotically attracted to military men. The operative can use his skills to win the favor of a military man separated from his usual partner(s) and willing to be sexually serviced by this friendly stranger.

7. According to the Bell and Weinberg study (page 108), black homosexuals are significantly more likely to *perform* anal intercourse than their white counterparts.

8. In his Glossary, Levine (1990, page 230) expresses a gay man's perspective when he equates "hot sex" and "good sex." A heterosexual might insist that quiet, voluptuous, dreamy sex can be more satisfying than vigorous, energetic, and physically exhausting "hot sex."

9. In exceptional situations--parties, gay pride parades, beauty contests, etc.-- gays permit or even encourage "camping it up," flaunting feminine affectations. This custom parallels those customs in the straight world in which behaviors forbidden in everyday life, are permitted on designated holidays (*e.g.*, getting drunk on New Years, begging for treats on Hallowe'en, kissing a neighbor under the Christmas mistletoe, etc.).

10. Ever an apologist, Levine (1990, page 120) interprets the survival of "dish-

ing," at a time when all other effeminacies have been erased from gay behavior, as "an example of culture lag: The masculinization of 'closet' culture was still running its course . . . [and] this practice might conceivably disappear." Hatterer (1965, pages 162-163) interprets the use of cruel humor and sarcasm as an attempt to mitigate and conceal one's own feeling of inadequacy. The chronic anxiety that he is "living a lie" by trying to keep up a pose of masculinity, keeps him on the defensive:

> Many homosexuals are engaged in a continuing power struggle, perhaps unconsciously, to emasculate others or to invite emasculation by means of distorted social and sexual activities. . . . This is often grossly destructive of their intimates. The targets of their humor may return the attacks, with the result that enduring relationships are almost impossible.

Thus, Hatterer sees "dishing" not as an effeminate affectation, but rather as a way of coping with a chronic feeling of inadequacy.

22   The More Ambiguous Ones

Now let us look at several homosexual types whose adaptations raise doubts about their emotional maturity. Psychologically, some are better off than others.

THE CLOSETED HOMOSEXUALS. Not all gay men flaunt their homosexuality. Some choose to remain "closeted," acknowledging their homosexuality to close friends only. The closeted homosexual may wish to maintain a prominent social position that would be threatened by public exposure. He conceals his homosexuality from all but his closest friends, and denounces the hedonistic lifestyle of gay men as "whorish."

Some maintain long-term living relationships. To avoid detection, partners maintain separate apartments. Some avoid a long-term partnership for fear of exposure. They may marry a woman and raise a family mainly as a "cover," or because of their genuine fondness for the woman, and the desire to raise a family. The wife may or may not know of her husband's homosexual orientation. (Gay men who marry was the topic of Chapter 15.)

Before the days of political activism, Marmor wrote (as quoted by Hatterer 1970, page 13) : "I believe . . . that [the visible homosexual] community is a very small part of the whole and that understanding of the submerged or hidden part –the secret and private activities of the world of friendship cliques--is fundamental to an understanding of the whole. In this world are to be found men . . . who rarely, if ever, go to bars or other public establishments, because of their sexually predatory and competititve character. They may have had periods of bar-going but have come either to dislike the bar activities or to fear them because of their threat to the stability of established relationships. Others, especially those of high occupational or socioeconomic status, may restrict their community life to private social cliques out of fear of exposure or arrest. Others may not enjoy drinking or may find sufficient sexual and social companionship in homosexual groups, whether they are living alone or with other homsexuals."

Is the closeted adaptation a sign of good or poor mental health? Does the closeted adaptation protect the individual from psychological stresses, or does it impose a psychological burden upon the individual? Hatterer (1970, page 164) warns that "leading a double life" is risky and can generate self-contempt and anxiety:

> [A homosexual writer-patient] told his family that he had a
> steady girl friend; he told his homosexual mate that he was visit-
> ing his family when he was actually seeking homosexual adven-
> tures. He had given up survival jobs. When his partner came
> home from work each day, the patient was critical and abusive of
> him. At times, his partner turned on him, called him names, told

him he was nothing but a whore. The weight of the accusations proved crushing to the patient who stayed in bed and vegetated. Pressures accumulated and the patient developed great self-contempt, acute anxiety, and became completely unproductive.[1]

Kirk and Madsen (pages 280-285) have also opposed the closeted adaptation, arguing that when gay men become experts at hiding their real identity, this "skill" can have unintended and demoralizing consequences. They can become such adept liars that this "skill" undermines their character.[2] Andrew Sullivan (1995 page 199) recalls that to him becoming more open about his homosexuality, to himself and to others, was a psychologically liberating experience:

When I suppressed the natural [homosexual] emotions . . . I turned in on myself. . . . I developed mannerisms, small ways in which I could express myself, tiny revolts of personal space--a speech affectation, a ridiculous piece of clothing--that were, in retrospect, attempts to communicate something in code which could not be communicated in language. . . . And it came as no surprise that once I had been more open about my homosexuality, these mannerisms declined. Once I found the strength to be myself, I had no need to act myself. So my clothes became progressively more regular and slovenly; I lost interest in drama; my writing moved from fiction to journalism; my speech actually became less affected.

Offering empirical evidence to support Hatterer's clinical judgement, a Dutch researcher, Sandfort, has reported that "the rate of depression is higher for closeted people than for uncloseted people" (Solomon, page 203). In earlier generations, homosexual men might have remained in hiding for self-protection. Today, even conservatives openly identify themselves as gay men, and affiliate with such groups as the Log Cabin Republicans, and the gay branches of various Christian denominations. Colleges and universities have gay student organizations and openly homosexual faculty members, churches are led by homosexual pastors, and major newspapers have writers who openly identify themselves as gay men.

Hidden homosexuals have not escaped sociological scrutiny or criticism. The tactic has been labeled an evasive form of "stigma management" (Levine 1990, pages 60-61). A number of sociologists have identified the closeted or "covering" homosexual (Cotton 1972, Cory and LeRoy 1963, Helmer 1963, Humphreys 1972, Way 1977).

Michelangelo Signorile, a gay journalist, has achieved prominence for exposing public figures who have tried to conceal their homosexuality. Signorile justifies embarrassing the closeted homosexual, saying that a homosexual has no moral right to closet himself.[3]

The closeted adaptation has become increasingly difficult as gay men are urged to become active members of the gay community, to press for civil rights legislation, support for AIDS research, and other projects that require gay solidarity.

The closeted life still appeals to some conservative gay men, according to Bawer. An eloquent presentation of this point of view is Bawer's 1993 book, *A Place at the Table*, in which he argues that many conservative gay men prefer to be closeted for various reasons. No statistical survey, says Bawer, can reveal the true number of homosexuals. But homosexual men have "antennae" that enable them to sense the presence of other gay men, Bawer continues. On the basis of this sensitivity, he estimates that a ten percent figure is about right.

THE FUN LOVERS. Some homosexual men place a much higher priority on *pleasure-seeking* than do most adult men. Masturbation is the most immediately available kind of sexual fun there is. Homosexual publications glorify this sexual activity, and self-masturbation ranks high among sexual activities performed by gay men. Doings typical of homosexual life (going to gay bars, cruising, and having sex with strangers) make it easier and cheaper to find many sexual partners who will do many different things.

Homosexual sexual fun-seekers often place a high priority on other kinds of fun seeking: drinking, recreational drug use, partying, dining, theater-going, and frequent vacationing. They really earn the label "gay." Is this behavior just hedonism or is it such an *extreme* form of hedonism that is deserves a closer look?

If we regard clinical disorders as extreme cases of common personality types, could some of these gay fun lovers be sub-clinical bipolar types: manicky persons whose hyperactive, non-stop fun-seeking is their way of chasing away the blues? This is a question we take up in detail in the next chapter.

THE HYPERCRITICAL ONES. Biting remarks, undeservedly cruel, are frequently heard in homosexual circles, the contributions of those gay men who have a talent for spotting weaknesses in others, and the knack for expressing themselves in brutal language. This talent enables the hypercritical one to assuage his own feelings of inferiority by devaluing others. Privately, he compares every aspect of his own physical and erotic appearance, status, and work identity with all other men, and he regards others as more adequate. Outwardly, he displays arrogance and contempt for others, his defense against a painful and hypercritical awareness of his own inadequacies.

> The consequence of feeling devalued is a ceaseless search for
> new conquests to resupply an impoverished ego and to compen-
> sate for what was not obtained in each earlier unfulfilled con-
> quest (Hatterer 1970, page 197).

Levine (1990, page 112) regards the hypercritical remark, the "put down," as belonging to the homosexual tradition of "dishing," gossiping.

THE "WEAK CONSCIENCE"-SOCIOPATH CONTINUUM. In everyday thinking, people fit into two categories: those who *do* have a strong conscience, and those who *don't*, which includes people who have no conscience at all. An understanding of human nature tells us that there is a broad, unbroken continuum from a tyrannically strict conscience to the virtual absence of conscience that describes the sociopath, for whom it's easy to do the most inhuman deeds "because he has no conscience."

> Too strict a conscience: A Catholic patient recalled that as a young boy he offered the confession: "Father, I left my tricycle out on the sidewalk." Said the priest: "But that's not a sin." "Oh yes it is," said the boy. "I was tempting somebody to steal it." Advised the priest, "My boy, you are being overscrupulous." (Author's clinical notes)

Does a man who is HIV-positive tell a potential sex partner of his condition? Yes if he his a person of good conscience (or has "a well-developed superego," to use the words of psychoanalysis), even though this disclosure would cancel some sexual opportunities.

> *The Chicago Free Press* (Nov. 14, 2001) reported a study conducted in New Orleans by researchers at Tulane University's School of Public Health, in which 269 HIV-positive adults were asked if they told their partners about their HIV status. Twenty-five per cent said they had not told their primary partners, and 75 per cent seldom or never mentioned it to tricks or casual partners.

To an HIV-positive man with a weak conscience, whether or not to disclose is *not* an issue: "Don't ask, don't tell." When a weak conscience evaporates into "no conscience at all," the result is a sociopath, described in the next chapter.

THE SHORT-CUT STATUS SEEKERS. The attainment of high social status usually carries a very high price tag: many years of education, self-development, professional training, work, achievement, social experience. Martin Hoffman has conjectured that there are "certain factors in the modern urban world which lead young men into a homosexual way of life in the relative absence of a strong sexual desire for other men . . . for a period of at least a few years." Lost in a big city, an alienated and confused adolescent is "a nobody" if he is heterosexual. But if he is handsome and willing to act out his homosexual potential, life can be beautiful, if in a rather shallow way. Writes Hoffman (1968, pages 203-204):

> [T]here is a very seductive quality about gay life in the large
> cities which is extremely attractive to the kind of young man
> who wants to be admired and sought after by other individuals.
> For in that gay community he can find a kind of attention, from a
> large number of individuals, which he simply cannot get from a
> large number of women—certainly not without great effort on
> his part. Among the individuals who will actively court him, take
> him out to dinner, buy him presents, and otherwise indicate that
> to them he is (at least temporarily) a very special person, are
> people of prominence and wealth. There is no question that, to a
> number of young men, *homosexuality is a way of rising in the
> socio-economic scale.* The social mobility which is offered to a
> young man by the homosexual world is much greater than he
> would find in the heterosexual world, unless he was very lucky
> indeed. The garage attendant or laundry man will find himself
> attending elegant cocktail parties in San Francisco's Nob Hill or
> Pacific Heights. If he is lucky, he will find himself living there,
> perhaps driving a new sports car or having his way paid through
> college. These are very powerful inducements, and there are
> plenty of boys who find themselves caught up in the gay world
> and engaging in frequent homosexual acts who would otherwise
> not have a compelling interest in sexual relations with other
> males.

P. Fisher, a gay advocate, agrees (page 240) that "for the especially good-looking young homosexual," the gay life brings him in intimate contact with "wealthy and important people:"

> [T]he gay world is characterized by a degree of social mobility
> among different races and social classes not common elsewhere.
> One has a chance to meet and have sexual relations with wealthy
> and important people. A certain glamour and prestige derives
> from being courted by those whom one would not be likely to
> meet in everyday life. . . . A whole new world opens up for the
> especially good-looking young homosexual.

Both Hatterer and Hooker have noted that boys who are separated from their own social or family milieu, and who are attracted to easy money, social status and refinement, may use their homosexual potential to place themselves in refined homosexual circles:

> My family are bores and vulgar people and so are their friends,

and where I've lived all my life, no one really has been very sensitive except a few gay people I knew. When I saw this other world and when I met Frank and saw how beautifully he lived, and his manners and his ways all very different, and then what we had together with each other . . . it was different, too. I don't know whether you know, but sex, beer, and baseball, that's all I heard around my house. When I entered this other world, it was different. Very beautiful things. . . . Frank . . . was a wonderful person. I still have a lot of feeling for him because he showed me a side of life I never knew existed, but the rest of it . . . that's why I left. I couldn't take it. . . . I feel alone, as if I don't have something and someone I once had.

I called him last night and we spent the evening together, and as you would guess, we ended up in bed. He was very sympathetic to what I'm trying to do [overcome homosexual ways][4] and he said that 'if I'm going to get in your way, don't call me.' I left feeling very sad, knowing that he was right (Hatterer 1970, pages 288-289)

No one suspected me [of homosexuality] at school; I was too athletic, too good at sports. . . . I hadn't had any sexual experience until I went to this Ivy League college. . . . Somehow I really felt inferior despite my scholarship, since I had no money. That was until I met this rich boy who lived in the dorm . . . and he ran after me . . . pursued me, you might say. . . . (Hatterer 1970, pages 44-45).

[In the Army] I met a lot of older gay men who took me to theaters and movies, and bought me clothes, and helped me learn what kind of colors go together and what knife and fork to use. A lot of socialization that normally occurs in the home took place for me as older gay fellows did these things for me (Adair and Adair, pages 31-32).

In Chapter 12, Eduardo (page 234) relates his sexual attraction to blond upper-class college students, to his wish to be *like them*, driven by the prelogical thinking of *mana* that this might happen through sexual penetration.

Everyone in my city was dark, mostly Italian. Then I went to college, and there were blonds everywhere. It was a tremendous sexual shock. . . . I would almost get ill looking at them in the showers. . . . upper-class WASPS, whose gestures, codes of conduct, and social values were very unlike my own. . . . I practically had to learn a new vocabulary, a different way of phrasing things and pausing. . . . I wanted to taste them and get inside of

them. . . . I wanted to experience what it would be like to be like
them . . . . and [know] what it was like to see the world that
other way (Stambolian, page 150-151).

THE SPLIT PERSONALITY. Carol Grever was married to a closeted gay
husband for 35 years. After their divorce, she reflected (pages 24-25) that it had
taken her so long to acknowledge her husband's secret life (hidden not only from
others, but to an extent *from himself*) because he was "an expert at leading two
separate lives, one as a husband, father, and church professional, and the other as
an anonymous gay men." She continued:

> "His two identities could be carefully stored in their respective
> compartments and skillfully retrieved as circumstances dictated.
> I'm convinced that his ability to put a lid on his other self saved
> his sanity. When his homosexual actions were put away, out of
> sight in his mental box, he actually could forget them and avoid
> the old guilt that had been instilled in him since the cradle. This
> was his key to survival."

When finally he was forced to discuss his secret life, he said to his wife (page
29), *"It was as if someone else were speaking through [me]."* This statement is
another indication of how thoroughly dissociated his homosexual "secondary
personality" or "alter" was from his everyday personality.

Here is a mental anomaly that has fascinated popularizers of all sorts (novelists, Hollywood, Oprah watchers, and checkout-counter magazine readers) and
has appealed to criminal lawyers as a sure-fire way to explain away their client's
misbehavior. The "split personality" gets a bad name because a split-off fragment
is sometimes psychotic (like the mental patient who hands his doctor a "check"
for a million dollars, and then begs for a cigarette) or dangerous (like Dr. Jekyll-
Mr. Hyde). But if a split personality enables the person to lead a productive life
in a cruel and punitive society, *is dissociation itself a mental disorder?* That is
something of an open question, even among psychiatrists.

Too easily labeled "shameless hypocrisy," here is a condition that can make
it possible for a person to live two (or more) productive lives quite independent
of each other.[5] Is this condition a disorder or is it a *defense* against the psychological threat of social ostracism (divorce, estrangement from one's children,
friends, and relatives, professional ruination)? No doubt, maintaining such a
strategy exacts a high psychological price, requiring a vigilant, defensive posture
that restricts and impoverishes the person's mental and social life.

A personality encompasses many social roles. In a well-integrated personality, all these roles are in contact with one another. (The nine-to-five lawyer may
be a weekend hiker, and during his working hours he can enjoy reminiscing
about a previous weekend or planning his next weekend.) In a well-developed
personality, one's various roles are prioritized, and one has the ability to

renounce or delay the satisfaction of one role, in order to attend to his more dominant role. (The artist is also a lusty male animal. But he celebrates his lust with his wife, not with his model.)

With some individuals, however, their roles are so loosely, so poorly organized that the person does things that he himself disapproves of. This probably comes close to describing the behavior of those doctors who are alcoholic, lawyers who take sexual advantage of their clients, professors who have affairs with their students, or priests who engage in sexual play with boys from their own parish.

The split personality (to use an old-fashioned but very descriptive term) can be a defense against a homophobic and punitive society, and its psychological cost is a powerful argument in favor of a society that not only accepts but also respects its homosexual citizens.

What is now termed Dissociative Identity Disorder (DID) is intended to displace older names for this phenomenon: split personality and multiple personality. Most psychiatrists believe the condition is extremely rare. A few "fervent believers" are convinced that the DID diagnosis has been often missed by clinicians (Frances and First, page 288).

Split-personality priests? What of the Roman Catholic priest who, contrary to his vows of chastity, pursues a secret sexual life? Probably there are a few who would fit the concept of the split personality, cases of DID. An investigative report by the *Kansas City Star*[6] found death certificates of 300 Roman Catholic priests, gathered from 14 states, in which death was attributed to AIDS. This statistic suggests that some of these priests had been living "double lives," seeking anonymous sex, perhaps out-of-town, wearing ordinary clothes. Men do not become HIV-positive from fondling teen-age boys.

THE NARCISSISTIC HOMOSEXUALS. This term is not part of the gay argot, but certain types of gay men clearly show a narcissistic personality.

> [Homosexuals] often want mirrors while they have sex. They're looking at themselves being caressed by another person. They're not looking at the other person. . . . They are in love with their own bodies. (Gottlieb, pages 48-49)

Handsome Man

Author George Stambolian interviewed a gay man who claimed to have worked for "the foreign service" and had travelled extensively. When the interviewer entered the apartment of Handsome Man, he remarked, "There are mirrors everywhere!" His respondent replied: "I didn't put them there, but I love them. I've always had at least one big mirror, and I've spent a lot of time in front of it. . . . I like my body, and I like to look at it. . . . I think it's a beautiful thing to do. It's natural and it's hot."

The interviewer noted a number of photographs of H.M. (Handome Man) in the apartment. H.M.'s reply expresses his narcissistic orientation:

I took some of the photographs myself. I want to study the male body in all its different aspects and to understand what male beauty is. I guess I'm a classicist because I think that the physical form of the human body is really a form of perfection. I use myself most often because I'm the handiest person around, but I also think there's something strange and fascinating about capturing one's own image in a photo or a painting. After all, that's about all that's left when you die. With myself it's also incestuous in a way. It's self-adoration and self-scrutiny, catching the surfaces but also trying to go underneath them, penetrating the inside. Actually, if I had my way, we'd expose our bodies all the time.

[T]hat's why I seek out nudist beaches wherever I go, and I've been to a lot of places. . . . [E]ven when I'm in the apartment, I like to take off all my clothes. Sometimes it's the first thing I do when I walk in. That's how I feel that I'm really at home.

The interviewer asked H.M. what was his favorite sexual activity and, predictably, H.M. answered: masturbation. He described a club he attends that meets once a week to enjoy "touching, smelling, looking, hearing, [and] all the uses of the imagination," but engages in no oral or anal penetration:

[W]hat I enjoy doing most is jerking off, and I think I'm very good at it. After all, it's probably the longest standing sexual activity we have experienced and have done more often than any other. It's also a wonderful form of relaxation and a way to make your mind work not just on sexual fantasies but on all kinds of mental images. . . . I've been fortunate to find men who like to do it together. My lover and I have been involved with a club in the city that meets once a week. . . . I'm also putting together my own group, and the men in it understand that a lot more is involved than just jerking off to come. There's touching, smelling, looking, hearing, all the uses of the imagination. It's not only the dick that's important but the movement of the arm, the way the muscles work, where they go and what they do, the way sensations develop and how they concentrate themselves. We create an environment, a theater with costumes, music, props, videotapes, photos, talk, whatever seems hot or interesting. [H.M. would consider games that include touching, but rules out insertion.] (Stambolian, pages 82-85) [7]

Masturbation has a strong appeal to the narcissistic personality. Like H.M., many homosexuals express an enormous interest in masturbation, and often practice it as a solitary rather than a social activity. In a poem entitled "What Every Boy Knows," a gay poet who calls himself Antler celebrates the place of masturbation in the private life of "Every Boy" from the age of 12 to 20. Here are three excerpts from that poem:

> Every boy knows what it's like
>   when he's really alone,
> When it's safe to jack off with a passion,
> When it's safe to take off his clothes
>   and prance around
> And parade his lubricating cock
>   before every mirror in the house.
>   . . . .
> At the country picnic the 12-year-old boy
>   wanders off by himself in the woods,
>   he knows the perfect spot.
>   . . . .
> The 20 year old mountain climber still digs the thrill
>   of doing it on top of a mountain alone,
> He never tells anyone about it, it's a secret
>   he keeps to himself,
> He still smiles remembering the first time
>   he jacked off from a cliff,[8]
> Ecstatic boyhood semen spurting and spurting,
>   tumbling thousands of feet
>   into the wild valley below. . . .

A homosexual orientation is sometimes preceded by an interest in body-building. An interest in bodybuilding may itself be a sign of narcissism, predisposing the boy to homosexuality.

> [T]hey compare their bodies with those of other boys, and they
> both admire and envy those with better bodies than their own.
> This admiration can take the form of being sexually aroused by
> others, and out of this comes the desire to have sex with the body
> of another person (Pomeroy, page 67).

Clearly narcissistic, for example, is the gay man who makes a habit of "posing" (sometimes called standing, or modeling) in public places. In his Glossary, Levine (1990, page 231) describes "posing" as "to stand alone, with a blank expression, in a conspicuous spot." Levine observed (page 134):

While I was in the Ramrod one Sunday afternoon, I noticed a

man standing by himself, leaning against the pool table in the
middle of the bar. He was tall and good looking, and clutched his
jacket in one hand and a Bud in the other. He stood there for
over an hour, alone, aloof, and expressionless, and ignored all
"cruises." I asked one of the men I was with about his behavior.
He told me that this man was "posing," which meant that he was
acting "butch," and [was] waiting to be "admired."

Some gay men earn a reputation as "cock teasers"; they would rather spend
an hour seeing how many men they can attract sexually than actually having sex
with one man. While most men "cruised" in search of "tricks," some men cruised
more for personal validation, for affirmation of their erotic appeal. Agreeing to a
"trick" might be just a by-product. Levine reports (1990, pages 149-150):

While Tony and I were eating breakfast at Tiffany's, a handsome
man sat down in a booth across from us and began to read the
paper. Tony looked at him, looked at me, and then licked his lips.
He then looked at this man again, who caught his glance, smiled
and returned to reading the paper. Tony then looked at him again.
. . . I asked Tony if he was trying to pick him up. He said that he
"cruised" him not because he wanted to pick him up, but because
he wanted to see if he was interested, and to let him know he
was "hot."

If nature has endowed him with a large penis, the narcissist makes the most
of this advantage, to draw attention to himself. There are several ways he can
dramatize the prominence of his penis. He can wear tight pants that have a "basket," i.e., a bulge at the crotch. He can wear no underpants, to give the outline of
his penis more prominence. He can wear a "cock ring," a leather band that fits
tightly under his scrotum and over the base of his penis. (Installed when the penis
is erect, a "cock ring" retards the flow of blood away from the penis after sexual excitement passes, keeping the penis engorged and larger than its normal flaccid state. In his standing, seated, or walking posture, a gay man can thrust his
pelvis forward to dramatize the prominence of his "basket." A large penis is
praised as "a dick of death." "A size queen" is a homosexual who has a special
devotion to the large penis (Levine 1990, page 231).

Micah describes his lover Bill ("a great guy, [but] just isn't as thoughtful as
I'd like him to be") as a consummate narcissist (Cornett, page 67). How Bill's
beguiling narcissism brought Micah into therapy is described in Cornett's case
notes (pages 64-67):

Micah and Bill
Micah is a 26-year-old gay man who has a well-paying job as an

engineer, lives with his lover, Bill, who is younger than him by two years, and not so well employed. "I have a good relationship and a good job. I'm not living out on the street. I have a lot of friends. It seems like I ought to be happy with my life and not bitching about it." Yet, Micah has bouts of depression and anger. "I slam doors, I hit things, I've even wanted to hit Bill." To Micah, it seemed 'really dumb, crazy, and wrong' to harbor these feelings and 'not know why.' After several sessions, "Micah detailed a relationship with his lover, Bill, which was very con-flictual. Although he maintained that this relationship was 'very good,' he often described instances in which his needs went unmet in the relationship. He found himself unsatisfied sexually and often experienced Bill as financially taking advantage of him. . . . [Bill] would expect him to pay for all of the couple's expenses and activities. During sex, Micah played the role of sat-isfying Bill. Sometimes this was satisfying for Micah, but more often it left him feeling vaguely frustrated and longing for some reciprocity within the relationship."

Eventually, Micah admitted that his anger toward Bill was justi-fied, though he had difficulty "accepting the idea that it's OK to be angry with Bill because he is so wonderful in other ways."

Edmund White (page 148) describes a widespread gay narcissism that is expressed in a relentless self-indulgence and consumerism

Gays not only consume expensive vacations, memberships in gyms and discos, cars, elegant furnishings, clothes, haircuts, the-ater tickets and records, they also consume each other. . . . This rampant and ubiquitous consumerism not only characterizes gay spending habits but also infects attitudes toward sexuality: gays rate each other quantitatively according to age, physical dimen-sions and income; and all too many gays consume and dispose of each other, as though the very act of possession brought about instant obsolescence.

So clearly has the homosexual lifestyle become associated with "self-indul-gence and consumerism," that a 1984 *Time* magazine article on Yuppie couples noted that these childless, two-income couples share many interests with gay men, including: health, fitness, and food. "Yuppies are in a sense heterosexual gays," the *Time* writer mused.[9]

THE LONELY ONES. Homosexuality can be a relief from loneliness. A gay man recalls: "I think the first time in my life that I ever really felt accepted was when I developed a friendship with a boy down the block who was about three years older than me. He was a loner, too . . . had an alcoholic mother and a father who used to beat him because he wouldn't go out and be like the other kids. We began to develop a very close friendship. He seemed to like me and no one had ever liked me before. I wasn't aware of my growing sexual interest in him until one day alone in his house he took out this book and said I'd enjoy reading it. I think I was only about fourteen at the time and I didn't know anything about homosexuality. While reading, he began to fondle me and I immediately became excited and that was the beginning of my homosexuality. For many years afterwards, when things would get very bad, I'd find myself calling him or asking him to come over to my place when no one was home. In a way he was a life-saver, but I realize now that after a while, any kind of rejection or failure made me turn to him . . . and ultimately for sex to get rid of the pain involved in a lot of my relationships and what I was doing in life that I didn't feel were working for me." (Hatterer 1970, page 223)

Richard Troiden studied 150 male gays, and found that they were more likely to recall from their preadolescent years the social experience *of alienation*, than an experience of homosexual excitement (Troiden, 1979, page 363) as Table 9.1, page 153, illustrates. Similarly, Bell, Weinberg and Hammersmith studied 600 San Francisco gays, and reported (page 84) findings consistent with those of other investigators: "that pre-homosexual boys are more likely to have been loners and to have been rejected by other boys."

Why were these boys rejected by their peers? Timidity was one factor ("afraid to venture out beyond the safety of their households"). Others were regarded as sissy-boys ("played mostly with girls"), others were physically frail, or had developed artistic interests that set them apart from other boys (Bell, *et al.*, 1981, page 84). One of the Adairs' respondents recalls (pages 29-31):

Ian

I was very much overweight, not at all a part of the community. I didn't belong. . . almost wanting to be rejected. . . . I met Joe, with whom I fell in love. I was ten. . . and Joe was twelve. . . . He was everything that I wanted to be physically and felt that I wasn't: dark and handsome, with great athletic ability. . . . There was an incredibly strong attraction. He was really a Greek god for me. [The relationship continued for 10 years, with a lot of daily oral sex. When Joe was about 15, he started to date a girl. After each date, they would meet and have sex. When his girlfriend became pregnant, he married her. Rick reflects: I think he was genuinely attracted to this girl.] I don't think he ever stopped to realize that what we were doing was gay. We were just doing what felt good and natural. . . . Had he not been going with a girl who became pregnant, probably we would have lived out life together as a gay life. (Adair and Adair, pages 29-31)

A clumsy or delicate physique (a boy described as uncoordinated, clumsy, frail, fragile, slight, slender, or poorly developed) may be the basis for this perceived lack of masculinity. It may be constitutional, it may be the result of poor nutrition, inactivity, or illness. However it was acquired, the boy's physique leads others to regard him as unmasculine, less than "a real boy." [10]

> In summer camp, there was always at least one boy who got tagged with that faggot label. It was usually someone who couldn't throw a ball and always struck out at baseball—a total wimp, despised by the other boys and shunned by the girls. One summer, I was that boy. I knew there was some truth in what they were calling me.

Dominick, a 53-year-old divorced man announces his coming out, in a letter to his adult children (Eichberg, pages 48-49). With undisguised bitterness, he recalls that his gay identity began with the ridicule his father heaped on little Dominick for not knowing how to throw a ball.

Dominick

I have always been gay, but the sense of shame that accompanied this knowledge was so great that I have never been able to deal with it. It has been like a giant cancer eating its way through my body for forty-five or so of my fifty-three years. . . I have always felt that the reason my father hated me so much, as he was a reasonable man to others, was because he knew, even before I knew, what I was going to be. His way of dealing with it was to mock me in front of my brothers and sisters for being a sissy, imitating the way I spoke, the way I threw a ball, the way I gestured, filling me with shame for my very being. . . .I started at a very early age the masterful cover-up that has ruled my life. . . . I even managed to convince myself that I was not what I was, that I was really like everybody else. . . . After a few years of college, when all my friends were getting married, that's what I knew I had to do. . . . Your mother [Dominick writes to his children] . . . was so beautiful and so much fun and so glamorous. . . . I fell in love with her. . . and we became engaged. My family was ecstatic and so was I because here was proof positive that I was not what I was. And we got married, and you kids came, and I got successful and life was going to be happy ever after, but that's not the way it worked out. The guilt I feel toward your wonderful mother is too painful for me to write about except to say that I love her still and will always love her, but it's a different kind of love now than it once was. The burden of living a double life finally became too great. First came impotence, then the development of a secret life that became dangerous and furtive, then the divorce that so devastated all of us. . . . I can't go on with that cover-up any longer. I want you to know me as I am. However you decide to think about me, it's OK. I love you all.

Dad

THE SHY ONES. The gay community includes just enough radicals and psychopaths to obscure the fact that many (perhaps most) gay men are distinctly shy and quite unaggressive. This is what impressed Rita Mae Brown, a lesbian author who persuaded a gay male friend to help her sneak into a gay bathhouse. She walked around wearing a false moustache, and garbed in a bathrobe instead of a. towel. Of course, she was sexually approached several times. What surprised her was that *it was so easy to say, No.*[11]

> The easiness of refusal is incredible. In heterosexual life . . . a first refusal never sinks in. Men . . . are geared to pursue you. . . . In the bath . . . if you say "No" it means "No," that's all, and that simple "No" also protects fragile egos (Brown, page 15).

Shyness may be the social manifestation of a deep-seated feeling of inferiority, a sensed loss of maleness that leads to a deification of the male organ, a longing for incorporating an idealized male:

> I had all kinds of diseases, one right after another. Being smaller than the rest of the kids in town and underweight, I'd always be tagging along. . . . [At summer camp] one of the guys began to pick on me and I just couldn't fight back . . . it was a mixture of admiring him secretly and even wanting to be like him and wanting to look at him in the nude. He was tall and well-built and . . . well-developed for his age. (Hatterer 1970, pages 51-52).

NOTES ON CHAPTER 22

1. Here, the richness of the clinical observation also makes it ambiguous. Did the patient's demoralization result from: lying to his family? lying to his partner? quitting his job? his partner's abusiveness?

2. Lying can also have a corrosive effect on a person who feels that he must conceal an outside affair from a jealous lover. Said a bisexual patient of Klein's (page 129) "I have sex with other people . . . and I feel guilty because it makes my lover jealous. . . . . In order to survive, I've become a really creative liar."

Comments Klein (page 130) : "Having to lie, to conceal and not be completely what one is--even with close friends-- is a black cloud hanging over the heads of many bisexuals." Again, Klein quotes his patient: "I'm constantly aware no matter where I am or who I'm with that I must be careful with my secret. . . . I long sometimes just to blow it. . . . But I never do and the tension builds. I want to be respected at work and with friends, but my bisexual secret increases my fear of being rejected."

Unique in the psychological literature is Brownfain's characterization of his closeted bisexual group (described in Chapter 15) as men who "are comfortable with themselves . . ." (page 185) that their bisexuality is "life-enhancing" (page 188), that they are not hiding from themselves, but have claimed a sexual identity that they are not ready to freely share with others. "Most [of the bisexual men in Brownfain's research group] . . . did not regard bisexuality as anything other than a necessary way to be themselves" (page 186).

3. Signorile's argument goes something like this: Closet homosexuals include many politicians and other leaders of our country. By hiding their sexual orientation, they give the impression that the gay population is smaller and less successful than it actually is. It would be more courageous for them to stand up and speak out in support of AIDS research and treatment, and to advance the civil rights of all gay men.

4. Gay ideology opposes reorientation therapy. But there are homosexual men who feel miserable about their sexual orientation, and there are therapists—psychiatrists and psychologists—who have had a measure of success in treating them. In Chapter 17, psychotherapy is conceptualized as a program of unlearning and relearning, and Epilogue, Part 1 addresses in depth the topic of reorientation therapy.

5. The psychologically oriented reader asks, Why are some closeted gay men able to "wall-off" their homosexual life, while others wallow in chronic anxiety, depression, guilt and shame? Why is DID an available defense for some and not for others?

An economical response is that individuals differ; some have a natural talent for dissociation, while others do not. A recent (1998) guidebook on mental health conjectures, "[T]he capacity for dissociation exists in us because it provides adaptive advantages that were favored by natural selection. Our ancient ancestors lived in a remarkably dangerous and painful world. Developing the capacity to tune out the most unpleasant parts of their lives helped to keep them going. Certainly, it can be no accident that dissociation is so universally and readily available to human beings or that so many people seek it out through meditation or drug use" (Frances and First, pages 281-282). For those authors' full discussion of "Dissociative Experiences," and suggested additional readings, see their pages 281-293.

A more clinical view of dissociation notes that most DID patients have a history of child abuse, mental trauma, or neglect. That is a significant clue, which leads to the conjecture that when a young child faces a painful life circumstance, he or she learns to minimize the pain by pretending "it's not happening to me. It's happening to someone else." When this skill has been learned and successfully adopted at an age when "make-believe" is an important part of mental life, later in life this skill is available to cope with other emotional conflicts.

6. Reported on the TV program 20-20 of January 5, 2001.

7. The rules and practices H.M. describes are characteristic of j.o. [jerk off] clubs in general, which existed even before the HIV crises, but are now even more popular in gay communities. Avoidance of insertion is of course a safety factor, but j.o.club fans glorify this taboo by "explaining" that erection and ejaculation are such beautiful sights, it's a shame to hide them inside another person's mouth or anus.

8. In the story of his Irish boyhood, *Angela's Ashes*, Frank McCourt (1996, page 299) recall very similar incident, but laced with heterosexual imagery:

> Sometimes I'm up there alone on the heights of [the ruins of a Norman castle] and there are voices of Norman girls from olden times laughing and singing in French and when I see them in my mind . . . I climb to the very top of the castle where once there was a tower and there in full view of Ireland I interfere with myself and spurt all over Carrigogunnell and the fields below.
> . . . [T]he thought of someone watching me brings on the excitement again. . . [I]f there was a milkmaid gawking up she'd surely get excited and go at herself though I don't know if girls can go at themselves when they don't have anything to go at.

9. Alas, in matters sociopsychological, nothing is simple. What Yuppies and gay men have in common are (a) a relatively high educational level, (b) higher-than-average earning power, and (c) ample discretionary income. These three interrelated factors alone could account for similarities in spending habits between these two groups.

What the *Time* writer may be alluding to is that both groups have opted (generally) not to encumber themselves with all the direct and indirect costs of raising a family (including housing, medical bills, insurance, and college funds), but to have more free time, more free (discretionary) money, and more free energy for themselves. This tendency to resist a powerful evolutionary drive to raise a family, may give Yuppies and gay men something in common.

10. Here we are not discussing the gender-discordant boy (described in chapter 8) who establishes a cross-sex orientation in his early childhood—who wants to play with dolls, wants to dress up like a girl, wants to play house. Here we are talking about the boy wants to do all the things other boys do, but lacks the coordination, lacks the strength to compete, and is teased and tormented for his inadequacies.

11. Ms. Brown may be correct in concluding that gay men are unusually unaggressive, but that is only part of the story. The other factors are that bathhouse sex is often rather impersonal. It is also known that some men come to the bathhouse for sex and others come to be viewed and admired. Why waste your time coaxing a "poser" when you could find someone as eager for sex as you are?

23 Gay Men with Bipolar Illness

Homosexuality is *not* a mental disorder. That principle is beyond dispute, as gay advocates insist, and as many mental health professionals agree. But if homosexuals are "like the rest of us," they are also vulnerable to the minor and major ills—physical illnesses and mental illnesses—that may beset any person.

GAY MEN WITH BIPOLAR ILLNESS. The vast majority of men who suffer from bipolar (or manic-depressive) illness are heterosexual, but there are some gay men who suffer from the bipolar (or manic-depressive) disorder. In March, 2000, a Website entitled Coming Out Twice" (comingouttwice.com), dedicated to "lesgay person[s] with a mood disorder, listed a hotline for persons who "are seriously thinking about committing suicide. Also listed were dozens of Internet resources relating to mood disorders in general, as well as to mood disorders within the gay, lesbian and bisexual community.

Additionally, the Website listed Internet articles on religion and recovery, and depression and AIDS/HIV. Four online communities were listed (including a Yahoo! club, *Gay men with bipolar disorder*, and 24 homepages of personal stories of depression, suicidality, and coping with bipolar disorder. Several hours of Web surfing have yielded the following three autobiographical comments posted on the Internet by gay men:

> Being gay and bipolar just screws you . . . but good. . . . There's
> so much around you that constantly beats down . . . trying to
> break you, make you decide to go against everything you believe
> in . . . but I guess it hasn't beat me yet.

An older gay man posts the following autobiographical story on a suicide web-site:

Peter

Sometimes those who love life the most, who experience it with ultimate passion and joy, are the ones who try suicide. Anyone who doesn't at least *think* about it is not evolving.

It was in 1937. I was 17. I was quite serious. I looked down the double barrels of a shotgun but stopped. I put a razor to my testicles but stopped. I took the Mercury out on a country road in the middle of the night at 70+ mph but took my foot off the pedal.

I lost myself in college, coming out, devouring men. Always being a little different, holding the grief and torment inside me.
Am I proud of the fact that I tried it? No. Most of the time I walk around feeling like a loser. When I get close to someone who I am

419

deeply attracted to, my psyche is paralyzed with anxiety and grief. So I hang out by myself rather than be with someone less than what I want.

But I cope. I function. I had been reasonably successful at what I first set out to be. Followed a standard, safe career path until it came to a slow, burning, grinding halt. My mind, my heart was not in that profession. Part of me was suppressed with the whole suicide event.

Back in therapy. I remembered a detail from twenty years ago. It had flashed through my consciousness only once or twice. Pushed back each time because people could not deal with the fact that I attempted it.

The memory: I went to a counselor. I don't remember why. I choked out that I had strong homosexual feelings for my best friend. Patently underevaluating my frame of mind, he told me "many boys feel this way" and "just start dating girls." Was he telling me: Just deny that your feelings are real? Don't trust your heart?

After that, the delusions became stronger, more real. I couldn't tell anyone. . . . [I dreamt I was] in school burning to death. . . [then woke] up in the morning like nothing happened, yet remembering it.

I don't blame the counselor. I don't blame society. Not that I don't want to change it. I accept the fact that life sometimes deals some hefty blows. Since my mother died when I was seven, I have never expected life to be easy. I guess that helped to make me a survivor. In the meantime, out of my tortured soul have come some beautiful works of art. At work, I focus on expressing what is in my subconscious in ways that only the subconscious mind can produce. Beats going to a therapist and it might even earn me a living.

Ryan

A bipolar gay man who had taken a year's sick leave from his job as a university library executive, sends an open letter to his friends and colleagues. Ryan explains that he left work because he was "completely burned out of his job," and has been "treated for severe depression, including four weeks in the hospital. . . . And finally," he added, "[I] came out of the closet as a gay man after twenty years of denial. . . . Ryan continues:

The truth is, I'd . . . spent my whole career, indeed my whole

life, twisting myself completely out of shape to please other people and to keep the peace. The truth is, I savagely repressed the
self-knowledge that I was gay because I was terrified that other
people would reject me once they found out. And the truth is, I
have struggled with depression for many years because I could-
n't be honest with myself about these and other serious problems
in my life.

[M]y life was . . . [a] mess. But, as I have taken the supreme risk
to be honest with other people in my life, I have found (so far)
that my family, friends and associates have not rejected me.
Quite the contrary, my relationships with many people have
improved because, in some cases for the very first time, they are
dealing with the authentic [me].

Familiarity with both male homosexuality and with bipolar (or manic-depressive) *illness and its behaviors* (moods, cognitions, and activity) *reveals a
remarkable overlap.* To an extent, this is true because manic and depressive
symptoms are in fact exaggerations—ranging from subtle to wild—of normal
happiness and sadness. Homosexuals like everyone else, have their cheery and
downcast moods. Whatever its origin, the choice of the label *gay*, once argot and
now a common synonym for homosexual, says something significant about the
euphoric mood so characteristic of gay social interactions. A fondness for partying—for fun and flamboyancy, for *reckless* behavior, for doing outrageous
things, spectacular things—gives a gay social gathering its distinctive ambience.

When "camping it up" escalates into doing strange and reckless things,
bizarre things, homosexual partying takes on some of the characteristic of manic
behavior. When lack of judgment and disregard for the consequences lead to
unprotected gay sex (casually risking HIV infection). and anal fisting (known to
be dangerous and sometimes fatal), gay behavior shades into mania.

Sadness, regret, guilt, and anxiety are likewise moods that pass in and out of
everyday experience, and people commonly reach for a drink (a shot of whiskey,
a cocktail, a beer or two) to lift their spirits. Alcoholic drinks are even more widely used by homosexual men, who are also more likely to be abusers of other sub-
stances, than men in general.[1] In this regard, homosexual behavior merges with
the behavior of men suffering from depression. Solomon (page 202) lists nine
studies that link homosexuality to depression and suicide:

[1] In a recent study, researchers looked at middle-aged twins
one of whom was gay and the other straight. Among the straight
people, about 4 percent had attempted suicide. Among the gay
people, 15 percent had attempted suicide. [2] In another study, a
random population sampling of almost four thousand men
between the ages of seventeen and thirty-nine, 3.5 percent of het-

erosexuals had attempted suicide while almost 20 percent of those who had same-sex partners had attempted suicide. [3] In yet another randomized study of about ten thousand men and women, those who had sex with members of their own gender during the previous year had a significantly elevated rate of depression and panic disorder. [4] A 21-year longitudinal study conducted in New Zealand of some 1200 people showed that those who identified as gay, lesbian, or bisexual were at increased risk for major depression, generalized anxiety disorder, conduct disorder, nicotine dependence, suicidal ideation, and suicide attempts. [5] A Dutch study conducted on 6,000 people showed that homosexual men and women were likely to have substantially higher rates of major depression than heterosexuals. [6] A study of 40,000 youth conducted in Minnesota indicates that gay males were seven times as likely as their counterparts to experience suicidal ideation. [7] Yet another study of about 3,500 students showed that homosexual males were almost seven times as likely to make a suicide attempt as heterosexual males. [8] Another study showed that in a sample of about 1500 gay people (of either gender) were more than seven times as likely to have made four or more suicide attempts as straight students. [9] One study based in San Diego found, among male suicides, 10 percent are committed by gay men.

As depression deepens, the individual is overwhelmed with feelings of pessimism, hopelessness, worthlessness. Thoughts of death or suicide may lead to suicide attempts, or actual suicide. It is a well-established fact that, like bipolars, homosexual men have a higher rate of suicide than men in general.

How do you interpret a suicidal act? If a bipolar patient kills himself, the blame is laid on genetic factors[2] that burdened him with bipolar illness. (Better medical management and more supportive counseling might have prevented the suicidal act.) But if a male homosexual kills himself, he is believed to have been driven to suicide by interiorized *social oppression*.That is the gay-affirmative interpretation.

How deep, or how superficial, are the similarities between homosexual behavior and manic-depressive behavior?[3] How might these two behavioral tendencies, both heritable in part, interact in the life of the individual, and in the life of the gay community? Most of this book describes the behavior of homosexual men. A good portion of this chapter will describe the manic-depressive disorder and its management.

Manic-depressive (or bipolar) illness

At all times of history,[4] doctors of the mind have encountered patients subject to *mood swings* ranging from a mind-racing sense of omnipotence, to a black fog of depression—a disorder that depletes them of energy, crushes their self-esteem, and makes them feel helpless and hopeless. But these are the *extremes* of mania and depression. Milder forms of mania shade into those happy moments that everybody cherishes, and a moderate depression may inspire sentimental, or even poetic, reflections on the "sweet sadness of life," rather than on thoughts of suicide.

Manic behavior that shades into normal high spirits is sometimes labeled borderline, or *hypomanic*, less-than-truly-manic. These persons are said to occupy "the soft bipolar spectrum." The individual is unusually optimistic, extremely self-confident, and very energetic. A bipolar researcher (Hochman,[5] page 33) notes: "Their minds work faster, they may be sharper, even sharper-tongued. . . . They can accomplish a lot, and even though they . . . sometimes act impulsively, they are charming and intense. They generate a sense of excitement, people catch their highs and tend to like them." They may include successful salesmen. What makes hypomania different from normal high spirits? Hypomania is more volatile and irritable. What further links hypomanic behavior to bipolar illness is that the individual also has recurrent depressions.

Jimmy

Jimmy, a 37-year-old musician knew he needed treatment for the manias that kept interrupting his life. But he was reluctant to give up his engaging personality: "I liked my personality when I felt high. I was fun and outrageous, and that's what people expected of me. What's more, it's what I expected from myself. I wasn't sure I wanted to let go. I was afraid I would become a stranger to myself. Psychotherapy helped me grieve for the part of me I had to give up to stay healthy." (Hochman, page 150)

Creative workers sometimes worry that treatment for bipolar illness will reduce their creativity, but Mondimore (page 215) reports that treatment actually increases productivity of artists with mood disorders.

Hypomanics are fun to be with: quick-witted, creative, punning. More extreme signs of *mania* (bipolar I) are expressions of restlessness, rapid speech, grandiosity, feelings of omnipotence, and racing thoughts. He seems to think nothing of doing and saying strange and even outrageous things. In its most extreme forms, mania expresses itself in racing thoughts, disorganized and scattered thinking, fault-finding, angry irritability, intolerance, intrusive behavior, outbursts of rage, spending money with abandon, unrealistic belief in one's abilities and powers, insomnia, uncharacteristically poor judgement, provocative, frenzied and aimless behavior, denial that anything is wrong, seeing no consequences for one's behavior, and abuse of drugs—particularly cocaine, alcohol, and sleeping medications.[6]

During the manic phase, bipolars frequently experience an increased sex drive.[7] Normally heterosexual persons may have homosexual encounters during their manic phase. Powerful sexual urges may lead to nonstop fantasies about sex with strangers, graphic sexual references in their conversation, and a heightened felt need to masturbate (Hochman, page 136).

The depressive phase of bipolar illness manifests itself as a loss of interest or pleasure in ordinary activities, including sex. Sadness, anxiety, decreased energy, feeling of fatigue, difficulty in concentrating and remembering, difficulty in making decisions, restlessness, irritability, sleep disturbances, loss of appetite and weight (or weight gain), chronic pain or other persistent bodily symptoms that are not caused by physical disease are other manifestations of depression. Hochman (pages 32-33) describes a woman artist whose first depression came when she was sixteen:

> [F]or no reason she could understand, she cried all day and most
> of every night. She couldn't eat, broke into heavy sweats, and
> had heart palpitations.

In severe depression, the patient is burdened with feelings of pessimism and hopelessness, feelings of guilt,[8] shame, regret, and worthlessness, thoughts of death or suicide,[9] which may lead to suicide attempts. It is estimated that "one out of every four or five *untreated* manic-depressives actually does commit suicide" (Goodwin and Jamison, page 6). From his clinical experience, Mondimore (pages 18-19) describes a major depression:

> [A] relentless, pervasive gloom . . . continues from one day to
> the next . . . from which the individual cannot rouse himself or
> herself. . . . [T]hinking is dominated by thoughts of sadness and
> loss, regret and hopelessness. . . . The individual . . . feels to
> blame for his or her troubles, and sometimes for other peoples'
> troubles as well. . . . Feelings of inadequacy and worthlessness . .
> . loss of interest in usually pleasurable activities . . . listening to
> music, going to a movie, engaging in the sports or hobbies that
> usually provide enjoyment. . . [F]ood [loses] its taste . . . flowers
> [lose] their textures and perfumes—everything [becomes] bland,
> dull, and lifeless.

Kraeplin (page 25) has described the slow (though nonpsychotic) nature of depressive thought:

> [T]he patient . . . cannot collect his thoughts or pull himself
> together. . . . He is no longer able to perceive, or to follow the
> train of thought of a book or a conversation, he feels . . . inward-
> ly empty; he has no memory, he has no longer command of

knowledge formerly familiar to him, he must consider a long time about simple things, he calculates wrongly, makes contradictory statements, does not find words, cannot construct sentences correctly.

Goodwin and Jamison (page 38) quote J.D. Campbell's description of the *appearance* of a depressed individual:

He appears to [slowly] push himself along, as if he were being held back, rather than propelling himself with normal agility. . . The shoulders sag, the head is lowered and the entire body seems to droop. . . . The angles of the mouth . . . turn down . . . a smile, when it occurs, must be forced, and even then there is something sickly or distorted in its expression. The facial musculature . . . lacks tone, giving the face an inert . . . appearance. . .

The eyes, which normally portray the spark, vitality and curiosity of the personality, are dull and lusterless. In some individuals the eyes have a faraway, unnatural stare, which even the layman recognizes as the mark of extreme preoccupation or mental illness.

Bipolars do not always experience a *purely* manic or *purely* depressive mood. It is not at all uncommon for patients to experience *mixed states*:

various mixtures of mood, thought, and activity components . . . the simultaneous presence of depressive and manic symtoms. . . . The existence of mixed states . . . has been observed for centuries . . . (Goodwin and Jamison, page 44).

Various studies (Goodwin and Jamison, page 44) show that about half of bipolar patients experience mixed states. Similar to mixed states are "rapid cycles." Rapid cyclers are persons who have mood changes that collide with each other from day to day or sometimes within the same day. This is how Dr. Hagop Akiskal, senior science adviser of affective and related disorders, National Institute of Mental Health, describes the life of rapid cyclers:

These men and women zigzag between highs and lows so rapidly they often feel as though they are about to die. They might bounce from euphoria to despair and back again within hours. They are in exquisite pain, out of control, like a race car gone berserk, and sometimes say that they are afraid of being alone with their episodes because they don't know what they will be doing next.

Rapid cyclers can't make plans because they can't predict their mood even a day ahead. They are like yo-yos and feel as though they are being helplessly manipulated by some force outside themselves (Hochman, pages 35-36).

There are two differences between a clinical depression and normal depression. Normal depression is *a response to loss*, like a romantic disappointment, loss of a loved one, loss of a job, or separation from home. Secondly, Mondimore explains (1999 pages 18-19) that a normally depressed person "retains normal reactivity of mood;" that is, he can be cheered up by the company of friends, and he can find some relief in reading, listening to music, or watching a good movie:

> Mourners who might have been grief-stricken during the funeral service . . . can afterward often relax, reminisce about good times with the person who has died, and enjoy catching up with friends and relatives perhaps not seen for a long time. The reactivity of mood is also retained in the lonely or homesick person who goes to the movies and loses himself or herself in a good film. We are able to dispel the feelings of bereavement, isolation, or disappointment—even if it's only for a few hours—if the depressed mood is a "normal" one.

Twin studies[10], family studies, and many years of clinical experience leave no room for doubt but that manic-depressive (or bipolar) illness is *to a significant extent* an inherited trait. As Goodwin and Jamison put it (page 17), bipolar illness is "genetically based, environmentally influenced, and psychologically expressed." The authors (page 729) emphasize that bipolar illness is "fundamentally a medical disorder" because they believe that understanding this fact can "decrease stigma, provide effective and specific treatment, and minimize family and individual responsibility for the origin of the illness." Bipolars show a predictable pattern of anomalous brain activity, but unlike many other medical conditions, however, bipolar illness *cannot* be detected by a laboratory test, as Mondimore (1999 page 149) points out:

> Unfortunately at the present time we don't have any blood tests, scans, or other laboratory tests to make the treatment approach to bipolar disorder as informed and logical an approach can be in other illnesses. . . . There is unfortunately a lot of 'trial and error' and 'wait and see' when it comes to prescribing medications for a specific patient. This can be tremendously frustrating for all involved—for the patient, of course, and for the family members, and, yes, for the physician too.

Bipolars often benefit significantly from drug therapy accompanied by supportive counseling. Adopting such a program of therapy, many bipolars lead normal, productive, fulfilling lives.[11] Closely monitored medication (often lithium or Depakote) is essential, and electroconvulsive therapy (ECT) is often "rapidly effective" (Mondimore 1999, page 129). Psychotherapy also has its role to play.[12] A patient reflects on the importance of psychotherapy to her sense of well-being:I cannot imagine leading a normal life without both taking lithium and being in psychotherapy. Lithium prevents my seductive but disastrous highs, diminishes my depressions . . . slows me down, gentles me out, keeps me from ruining my career and relationships, keeps me out of the hospital, alive, and makes psychotherapy possible. But, ineffably, psychotherapy *heals*. . . . Pills cannot, do not, ease one back into reality; they only bring one back headlong, careening, and faster than can be endured at times. Psychotherapy is a sanctuary, it is a battleground, it is a place where I have been psychotic, neurotic, elated, confused and despairing beyond belief. But always, it is where I have . . . learned to believe . . . that I might someday be able to contend with all this.

> No amount of analysis can prevent my manias and depressions, but no pill can help me deal with the problem of not wanting to take pills. I need both. (Goodwin and Jamison, page 725 adapted.)

Before looking for professional help, many bipolars spend years denying that there is anything wrong with them that they cannot handle themselves, and burden themselves with debilitating and dangerous mood swings. It is estimated that about nine percent of the general population suffers from mood disorders at some time in their life, and that in the United States fewer than one-third receive treatment (Goodwin and Jamison, pages ix-x). In other words, *a sizeable majority of mood disorders are never treated.*

The bipolar-homosexual overlap

Hypomanic, and sometimes behavior that is frankly manic, is popular at some times in some gay circles: "furious self-indulgence" (LeVay and Nonas, page 67), promiscuity, frequent and frenetic partying, drug abuse, poor judgement, and self-destructive recklessness. How else could one describe that sizeable portion of homosexual men who, to the consternation of public health workers, refuse to take precautions against HIV infection? (In the gay world, these men are called "bug chasers.") Recent well-controlled research has indicated that there is a higher incidence of depression and suicidality in the homosexual population.[13]

Is a life of "furious self-indulgence" the predictable consequence of freedom from responsibilities of maintaining a family? Many heterosexual men feel drawn to activities that lay outside their work, marital or parental roles, but are more likely to spend their free time in active or spectator sports, in civic, charitable, fraternal, or church activities, or in any of a wide range of hobbies, rather than spending much of their free time in bars, restaurants, and in partying.

Another overlap between bipolars and male homosexuals is their attraction to creative work. Not every homosexual or bipolar is a creative worker, but there is a significant amount of research evidence[14] that bipolars are over-represented in the creative professions. The attraction of gay men to art, architecture, writing, music, dance, hair-dressing, window display, etc. is well known.

Another overlap between bipolar illness and male homosexuality: they often emerge in the late teen years or early adulthood. It is believed that the first occurrence of both bipolar illness[15] and homosexual activity is triggered by some event, and that the reappearance of the behavior (mania, depression, or a homosexual craving) no longer requires an outside event.

Comment: It seems more than likely that the incidence of bipolar illness is higher in the gay world than in society in general. Paradoxically, however, bipolar treatment and research, and homosexual treatment and research occupy separate worlds with virtually no communication with each other. A search of electronic data bases of the psychiatric and psychological literature, for articles or books dealing with bipolar (or manic-depressive) illness and homosexuality, yielded the following results: Of many thousands of entries, this author located only one article linking bipolar illness to homosexuality:

> A psychiatrist (Kubacki), stationed in a remote semi-rural area in Canada, treated 3,742 outpatients over a nine-year period, between 1971 and 1980.[16] Of this total, he diagnosed 31 patients (13 males and 18 females) as manic or hypomanic. Of the 13 males, all but one reported a sexual or marital dysfunction, 70 percent showed a history of alcohol abuse, a majority (61.5) were unmarried, and over half (7 out of 13) were either homosexual or showed homosexual tendencies. Of these seven, one was married but "confessed to homosexual longings," two were in their early twenties and were "strikingly feminine in their appearance and demeanor" (page 71), and four were active homosexuals. It is interesting that these 13 complaining males were living in a semi-rural area of Canada, remote from any urban center of gay life, where hypomanic and/or homosexual behavior goes unnoticed.

Bipolar illness is the domain of biological psychiatry; its clinicians and researchers have established that bipolar is a medical problem, largely heritable, managed by medication, supportive counseling, and sometimes electro-convulsive therapy. In the treatment of bipolars, it is unthinkable to rely upon psychotherapy as a *major* treatment strategy. In the words of Dr. Jay Amsterdam,[17] (Hochman, page 53) that would be "like getting someone to talk himself out of diabetes."

To the reorientation therapist, whether psychoanalytic or not, homosexuality is an *acquired* habit, and the emotional highs and lows of homosexual life are expressions of the patient's distress over his ego-alien compulsions. Nothing could be more foreign to the therapist's mind-set than that his patient might also be suffering from a heritable mood disorder that can be managed by a program of carefully monitored medication, with supportive counseling. Perhaps the therapist does not think of medical factors because he or she is, in many cases, not a medical practitioner and unqualified to prescribe or monitor medication.

To the gay-affirmative therapist, a clinically depressed gay man is suffering from the result of *social oppression*, "an internalized homophobia," and the depression will be lifted when, with the help of his gay-affirmative therapist, the patient interiorizes a real sense of gay pride.

There is no doubt but that there are some homosexuals who are also bipolar. But there is at present much doubt as to how these two tendencies, both significantly heritable, are triggered, and how they may actually interact. Understandably, bipolar researchers are reluctant to deal with a population that is so highly politicized.[18] If this reluctance can somehow be overcome, life may be better for future generations of men who carry tendencies toward both homosexuality and bipolar illness.

It is believed that a majority of men with bipolar illness never seek treatment. Is the gay community, with its tolerance for odd, even extravagant, and hypersexual behavior, a magnet and haven for some of these persons? *Homosexual men who are also hypomanic; is their hypomania actually a social advantage in certain parts of the gay world* (like "the circuit set")?

> Writes Hoffman (1968, page 204): "One of the most attractive
> features of the gay world, especially in large cities, is that it pro-
> vides a constant round of activities. There are always bars to visit
> and parties to go to; there are always new people to meet and go
> to bed with." Following a promiscuous sexual life promises a
> steady diet of excitement and glamour, unlike the routine and
> settled life with one permanent partner.

Might bipolar illness also account for a gay man's lapses of judgement, acts of recklessness, abuse of alcohol and drugs, and suicidal behaviors?

What of those men who are unhappy, even miserable[19] about their homosexual compulsions? Ordinarily, they are treated by therapists who are committed to the view that homosexuality is acquired through early experience of some sort, and can be overcome through talk therapy alone. Of any portion of these distressed gays, can it be said that their homosexual compulsions spring from a hypersexuality that is part of their bipolar illness? Would their homosexual compulsions be more manageable if they were treated for their bipolar illness? If these questions have been clinically explored, the literature does not record it. If these questions have not been explored, their importance certainly argues against further delay.

Because this chapter addresses a controversial topic, it may easily be misread or misinterpreted. It is well, therefore, to state explicitly what this chapter does not say. It does not suggest that homosexuality is itself an illness, though we must recognize the fact (spelled out in the next chapter) that *some* homosexuals (like some heterosexuals) are also sick. This chapter does not suggest that gay men look for a doctor who will prescribe medication to rid them of emotional problems. Nor does this chapter suggest that because some symptoms resemble some aspect of bipolar illness, a person showing these symptoms should be treated as a bipolar patient.

This chapter does *raise questions*, like Does living in a gay milieu tend to mask the bipolar syndrome? Might living in a community where bipolar symptoms are accepted as part of "the gay lifestyle" prevent men who are suffering from bipolar disorder from being correctly diagnosed and treated? If a distressed homosexual does, in fact, display the bipolar syndrome, is he likely to be correctly diagnosed if he goes to a non-medical therapist, or to a psychoanalyst? The guiding intent here is to raise these serious questions for consideration.

NOTES TO CHAPTER 23

1. See Fergussen study, summarized in Chapter 24.

2. Does a genetic factor lead to suicide? Not necessarily, but when a person faces a severe emotional crisis, whether he attempts suicide depends, in part, on those genetic factors that result in the *full syndrome of bipolar illness*.

The estimate of a person's measurement of suicidality, according to DIS-III-R, is based on responses to the following four questions: (1) Has there ever been a period of two weeks or more when you thought a lot about death—your own, someone else's, or death in general? (2) Has there ever been a period of two weeks or more when you felt like you wanted to die? (3) Have you ever felt so low you thought about committing suicide? (4) Have you ever attempted suicide?

3. A psychiatric advisor notes that mood swings and impulsivity alone may lead to a diagnosis of a character disorder, not bipolar illness. Only evidence of *the full syndrome* of bipolar illness justifies a bipolar diagnosis.

4. Around 400 BC, Hippocrates wrote the following commentary on mood disorders: "Men ought to know that from nothing else but the brain come joys, delights, laughter and sports, and sorrows, griefs, despondency, and lamentations. . . . And by the same organ we become mad." (Goodwin and Jamison, p. 369.)

5. Although Patty Duke is listed as senior author of Duke and Hoffman, quotations from that book are from chapters written by Gloria Hoffman.

6. Goodwin and Jamison (page 214) list 12 studies of bipolar patients' abuse of alcohol, with percentages ranging from 18 to 75 percent.

7. Goodwin and Jamison (pages 36-37) summarize 12 studies (covering a total of 1284 patients) listing a total of 13 symptoms of mania. *Hypersexuality is listed as the fifth most common symptom*, exceeded in frequency only by rapid or pressured speech, excessive speech, hyperactivity, and decreased sleep.

(Eight less common symptoms, in decreasing order, are extravagance, violence, religiosity, nudity or sexual exposure, regression, catatonia, and fecal incontinence or smearing.)

8. A Japanese psychiatrist (B. Kimura, 1965) noted the following cultural difference in what a depressed patient says about his guilt feelings: Japanese directed their guilt toward their parents, ancestors, and fellow workers. Germans, however, were more likely to feel guilt toward their children and toward God. (Goodwin and Jamison, page 180.)

It has become a firmly-established belief among gay advocates that *"society"* is an important risk factor in gay suicidality. Kulkin *et al.* (page 9) lists five articles that support their view that internalized homophobia is "one of the greatest risk factors contributing to the suicide rates of young homosexual people."

9. See Herrell *et al.* study, summarized in Chapter 21.

10. Twin studies point to the genetic loading of manic-depressive disorder. Where one identical twin has the disorder the other twin developes it in about 60 percent of the cases. The figure is only 18 to 20 percent for fraternal twins (Hochman, page 71). Why is the concordance rate only 60 percent for monozygotic twins, not 100 percent? Does this not suggest that the disorder results from the *interaction* of hereditary factors and life experience?

11. A 1999 guide for bipolar patients and families, readable and comprehensive, is *Bipolar Disorders*, authored by psychiatrist Francis Mark Mondimore.

12. Goodwin and Jamison (page 726) admit that "no one type of psychotherapy [individual, group, self-help group, or family] has been demonstrated to be uniquely effective in this patient population," they insist that "formal psychotherapy is extremely beneficial to many manic-depressive patients and unquestionably essential for many others, especially those who are suicidal or unwilling to take medication in the manner prescribed."

13. Two well-controlled studies were reported in the October 1999 *Archives of General Psychiatry*, along with commentaries by gay-friendly researchers. Fergusson *et al.* studied a large sample of young people in New Zealand. Their gay group did not differentiate between gay men, bisexuals, and lesbians, and interviews were conducted by telephone. The report by Herrell *et al.* is based on a population-based registry of young male twins. It was determined that if a twin was gay, he was more likely to show evidence of suicidal behavior than his straight twin brother. (Separate tallies were not made for identical and fraternal twins.)

14. A 15-year study of faculty members of the University of Iowa Writer's Workshop was conducted by Nancy J.C. Andreasen psychiatrist at the University of Iowa College of Medicine. She studied the incidence of episodes of mania or depression reported by creative writers, compared with a control group of hospital administrators, lawyers, and social workers, matched for age, education, and sex.

Andreasen reported that 80 percent of the writers had had at least one episode of mania or depression at some time in their lives. Four had suffered from severe manic disorder that required prolonged and repeated hospitalization. In contrast, only 30 percent of a control group not in the creative arts reported a history of mood disorders.

These group differences are impressive, but the findings must be weighed against the likelihood that creative artists would be more willing to report mood swings, than would hospital administrators, lawyers, and social workers.
Andreasen's study group included eminent writers like John Cheever, Robert Lowell, John Irving, Philip Roth, and Kurt Vonnegut. She reports that families of the manic-depressive writers (siblings, parents) also were more creative than the controls, and had more psychiatric disorders; 41 percent of the writers' siblings showed creativity, as did 20 percent of their parents.

15. Goodwin and Jamison write of bipolar illness (page 6): "One of the most promising lines of inquiry grew out of longitudinal observations: external stress appeared to activate or precipitate some initial episodes of illness, but eventually the illness seemed to take on a life of its own, since later episodes began without obvious precipitating stress. . . . [It is hypothesized that] the limbic system of the brain . . . shows an escalating response to a repetitive stimulus, reaching a point where the stimulus is no longer needed for the disturbance to continue." Similarly, an initial homosexual experience may be triggered by an external stress, and afterward "takes on a life of its own."

16. For one psychiatrist to treat 3,742 patients over a nine-year period, means he treated about eight patients per week. If, during the nine-year period, he diagnosed 31 patients as manic or depressed, and 13 were males, that means he made this diagnosis about three or four times per year, and encountered what seemed

like a bipolar male about once or twice a year.

17. Dr. Jay Amsterdam is director of the depression research unit, University of Pennsylvania School of Medicine.

18. Research on the overlap between homosexuality and bipolar illness cannot be conducted with routine walk-ins at a psychiatric clinic because many homosexuals have been warned to stay away from the psychiatric establishment. Homosexual subjects would probably have to be advertised for, recruited, and paid.

19. For example, a patient pleads to a therapist: "I love my wife and children, but I am usually only able to have sex with my wife when I fantasize about having sex with a man. I have considered finding a gay partner, but I prefer to keep my commitment to my family. The homosexual feelings never felt like who I really am. Can you help me diminish those feelings and increase my sexual feelings for my wife?"

Traditional Jews who are homosexual are chronically distressed over compulsions to engage in acts that the Bible labels "an abomination," feel poorly adapted to give a wife "her portion in marriage" and fulfill the commandment to "be fruitful and multiply." A discussion of this issue is an article by Naomi Grossman, in the April 2001 issue of *Moment* magazine. Many conservative Christians likewise find it difficult to accept homosexuality as a lifestyle.

24 The Emotionally Troubled

"If I were a marriage counselor and saw only marriage partners who were making each other nervous and sick, I would believe that marriage was psychologically and physically damaging."[1] There are therapists who hear homosexual patients plead, "Doctor, you must help me. This is a miserable way to live." And when these patients unfold their stories, it becomes clear that their upbringing was miserable, their growing up was miserable, and their present situation is miserable. It is easy for the doctors to conclude (although Freud cautioned otherwise) that all homosexuals are sick. Doctors were led to this conclusion not only by uncritical "common sense," but by a cultural setting that labeled homosexualiy as sinful, immoral, and illegal. It was an easy mistake for mental health workers to make, and this attitude won mental health workers status and applause in a homophobic society. The plain truth, alas, is that some homosexuals *are* sick.

The emotionally troubled include persons burdened with chronic anxiety, depression, obsessive thoughts, and compulsions. Not long ago, in many quarters it was believed that all homosexuals were sick. It would be just as dogmatic to assert today that all homosexuals are emotionally healthy. The sad truth is that a number of men, gays and straights, are burdened with mental problems. What can we learn about the relative proportion of gay and straight men who are emotionally troubled?

In a 1995 book, not too long after the American Psychiatric Association dropped homosexuality from its list of mental disorders, a leading therapist with a gay clientele, himself a gay man, boldly expressed his clinical judgment that homosexuals are indeed more likely to be emotionally troubled than men in general.

In making this statement, Walt Odets, dared to challenge the prevailing gay ideology that homosexual men are, from a mental health standpoint, no different from men in general. No, wrote Odets, clinical experience indicates that homosexual men are especially likely to be emotionally troubled. Fifteen years of clinical experience inside the gay community led Odets (pages 51-52) to conclude:

> It is my impression that compared to the general population, gay
> men as a group suffer inordinate problems with guilt, beginning
> very early in life. . . . . Developmental description is often
> shunned as a reductionistic effort with the explicit or covert aim
> of pathologizing homosexuality—and, indeed, that has often
> been the case. . . . It is precisely the fear of unearthing pathology
> that caused us to neglect full developmental descriptions of gay
> lives.

By "developmental description," Odets refers to what in ordinary language is called *upbringing*. Something happened in their infancy or childhood that led them to become troubled homosexuals. What about social oppression? Many of

Dr. Odets' patients live in a gay neighborhood, have a gay employer, gay colleagues, gay customers, and gay friends, go to a gay church, and their parents are loyal members of PFLAG (Parents and Friends of Lesbians and Gays). Are these gay men bothered by the thought that the likes of Senator Helms and Reverend Falwell look down on them?

> [Lee, a troubled gay teen-ager, raises the question of social oppression versus inner conflict, when he reflects:] "Not only does society shout at me that I am evil, but an inner voice whispers it as well" (Owens, page 109).

Hedonistic, radical, or narcissistic habits, wealth or good looks may mask an emotionally troubled inner life. But many emotionally troubled homosexuals cannot hide their psychic burden, and live at the margins of the gay community. They may express regret over their sexual orientation, and have no sexual partner (Bell and Weinberg, page 134). Homosexual respondents who never had a lover were also most likely to be unhappy about their sexual orientation, according to the findings of Joseph Harry (page 102).

Recent research findings support Odets' clinical judgment. In October 1999, the *Archives of General Psychiatry* published two large-scale research articles, followed by three commentaries, on the subject of mental health and homosexuality. Both studies drew on general population samples—not clinical samples, not "convenience samples," not volunteers. *Both studies indicated that gays are at risk for a variety of emotional disorders.*

The Herrell study. Herrell and his colleagues obtained access to a U.S. Defense Department registry of of 4,774 male twin pairs who served in the military between the years 1965-1975. From that pool, they isolated three groups: (1) 16 pairs *concordant* for homosexuality: *both* twins homosexual. (Homosexual was defined as having male sex partners after the age of 18.) (2) 103 pairs discordant for homosexuality; one twin who was homosexual, and the other who was not. (3) 4,634 pairs concordant for heterosexuality. This study is therefore based on interviews with 9,506 individuals [2x(16+103+4634)] Each respondent was rated[2] on four symptoms of suicidality: (1) thoughts about death, (2) wanting to die, (3) thoughts about committing suicide, and (4) attempted suicide. The homosexual twin brother scored significantly higher on each of these measures. Table 23.1 presents the findings in tabular form.

The Fergusson study. In New Zealand, Fergusson and his colleagues interviewed by telephone a population sample of 1007 21-year olds living in the city of Christchurch, about various psychiatric disorders (experienced since age 14), and about their sexual orientation (gay, lesbian, or bisexual was defined as having same-sex partners after the age of 18). A total of 28 individuals could be classified as gay, lesbian, or bisexual (GLB)--about 3 percent of the sample.

Table 24.1. Summary of Herrell findings, comparing suicidality of three groups of twins

	Both twins homosexual (n=16 pairs)	One twin homosexual (n=103 pairs)		Both twins heterosexual (n=4634 pairs)
		Gay twin	Hetero' twin	
Thought about death	50 %	48 %	30 %	22 %
Wanted to die	25	26	10	7
Suicidal ideation	56	55	25	15
Suicidal attempt	19	15	4	3

These 28 GLBs were compared as a group[3] with the remaining 979 members of the sample on the percentage who asserted that they had experienced any of eight psychiatric disorders. Obtained results are summarized in Table 24.2. Differences between the two groups attained a level of statistical significance (at the .001 probability level) on seven of the eight categories.

The investigators concluded (page 880) that their "study shows that young people who disclose same-sex sexual contact are at clearly increased risks of psychiatric disorders and suicidal behaviors." They note that their findings are consistent with a large and well-conducted Dutch study by Sandfort et al.

In his commentary on the above two research studies, Remafedi (page 885) notes that the Fergusson findings are also consistent with "10 peer-reviewed studies [that] have found unusually high rates of attempted suicide . . . among young bisexual and homosexual volunteers." In his commentary, Bailey considered various competing explanations of the link between mental illness and homosexuality,[4] noting that societal oppression is only one possibility, an eminently reasonable hypotheses, but it "remains to be demonstrated."

THE COMPULSIVE HOMOSEXUAL. On page 247 of this book, Loovis describes a behavior so compulsive that the individual seems to be incapable of exercising normal judgement:

> One . . . suddenly sees a stranger in the street, their eyes meet, and they are off to bed at the stranger's place. I would say that the cheating lover has had an irresistible experience of beauty in the   person of the stranger, which time and circumstance allow him to indulge. He comes across a perfect exterior "type" and

must have union with him. When it happens, a force is loosed in the cheating lover that he feels he must succumb to or perish.

Martin Hoffman (page 27) tells of David, a bright young man who drops out of college because "he thinks that he would not have the ability to stay home and study, which would be required if he went back to school." He has given up the idea of going to college because he "likes to go out at least several times a week

Table 24.2. Summary of Fergusson study, on the incidence of various psychiatric disorders among gays, lesbians, and bisexuals, compared with remainder of a sample of 1007 21-year-olds

Disorder	GLB Group (n=28)	Remainder of poulation (n=979)
1. Suicidal ideation	68%	28%
2. Sucidal attempt*	32	7
3. Major depression	71	38
4. Generalized anxiety	29	13
5. Conduct disorder	32	11
6. Nicotine dependence	64	27
7. (Other substance abuse/ dependence)	61	44
8. Multiple disorders	79	38

All differences (except number 7) significant at the .001 level of probability.   **Greatest difference.*

to participate in the round of parties and bar-going which his friends like to do. . . ." When homosexual activity takes priority over concern for one's future well-being, and concern for one's health and safety, the gay lifestyle has taken on a compulsive quality.

THE SOCIOPATH is a well-recognized variety of the troubled individual, and might be conceptualized as a pathological extreme of narcissism; *the sociopath is not concerned about anybody's well-being but his own.* There is a tincture of the sociopath in the man who takes pleasure in verbally attacking the most defenseless of his neighbors, for his own amusement and for the for the amusement of his fellows. According to Kirk and Madsen, (page 313) the worst displays of homosexual verbal cruelty emerge at gay bars, "the arena of sexual competition:"

The gay bar is the arena of sexual competition, and it brings out all that is most loathsome in human nature. Here, stripped of the facade of wit and cheer, gays stand nakedly revealed as single-minded, selfish sexual predators . . . and enact vignettes of contempt and cruelty that make the Comte de Sade look like a Red Cross nurse (Kirk and Madsen, page 313).

Sociopathic homosexuals are the bane of the gay community. He may emerge as a con man or pathological liar. Kirk and Madsen (pages 283-284) describe the attractive and personable gay con man who attaches himself like a parasite to a lonely old gay man. The con artist "breathes life into the cliche of the aging interior decorator who takes in the 'young hustler with a heart of gold,' and awakens one day to find his American Express Platinum Card, Rolex, cashmere sweaters, and five hundred in cash all gone with the wind." According to Kirk and Madsen (page 283), students of the sociopathic personality assert that "a surprisingly high percentage of pathological liars are, in fact, gay."

In today's environment, online services and phone sex are among the places where gay psychopaths are to be found. Writes Outland (page 65): "Compulsive liars are inordinately attracted to online services because the anonymity of such environments offers them such a wide berth." He also advises that phone sex attracts more "liars, game players, dissemblers, [people] messed up on drugs to the point of severe malfunction than anywhere else in the gay community. I would actively encourage anyone looking for sex to use phone lines only as a last option," Outland advises (page 62).

Outland's *Handbook* contains two more warnings to gay men not to fall victim to a gay sociopath:

> Boys who run away from home and sell sex "to get enough money for food" will discover that "many of the men who prey on homeless boys insist on having unsafe sex because they are in the position to pay extra for it and don't really give a shit about their partner" (page 117).

> Many gay men "have gone years without knowing they were positive, only finding out when they discovered their lover's HIV medication hidden in the back of the linen closet" (page 91).

THE BOY-LOVERS. Advocates of man-boy love (a topic discussed at length in Chapter 11) have been barred from some Gay Pride parades and from other gay organizations because their practices are frowned upon by many members of the gay community (particularly lesbians).

Because they are attracted to young teen-age boys, not children, boy lovers object to being called pedophiles. Pedophilia is, however, a legal term that does not distinguish between children and young teen-agers, but refers to *sex with a person who is underage*, and (gay or straight) pedophiles are guilty of criminal conduct in the eyes of the law. Because they expose themselves to social ostracism and lengthy prison terms, men who willingly risk such severe punishment for the sake of satisfying their sexual urges, pedophiles mark themselves as psychologically disturbed.

THE SCHIZOID HOMOSEXUAL. A person who has never related well to parents, siblings, or friends on any level, may use homosexuality as a way of maintaining a minimal human contact. Hatterer (1970, page 72) quotes a patient who fits this description:

> Since grammar school I've really been a loner and never liked other kids very much. . . . I never really had any strong feelings for people until I met this group down in the Village who hung out at this bar. When I started doing things with some of them, I felt something I'd never felt before, and I wanted more of that, but I didn't want anyone to start slobbering over me. If they got too close and too emotional, I clear out.

Writes Hatterer (1970, page 63) : "Often the least treatable is one who from his earliest recollections has been totally isolated. Evidence of schizoid behavior forecasts poor treatability and a poor prognosis. . . . [H]omosexuality has become his way of making minimal human contact in a life that is emotionally impoverished."

GAY MEN WHO FEAR WOMEN. Every boy experiences the thought—a passing thought or a persistent anxiety—that he could lose his penis, by accident or as punishment. Perhaps the risk of loss has been implanted by a threatening woman, or he has come to believe that sexual contact with a female will lead to castration. If females are regarded as "human beings without a penis," contact with females is feared because it arouses unconsciously felt threats of castration.

> [Castration shock is a common boyhood experience and in most cases does *not* lead to homosexuality. Castration shock is a common reaction to the first sight of female genitalia. Normally this leads to a determination to master this childish reaction, and to a curiosity to gain some direct experience with this anatomical mystery. On the other hand,] "homosexual men react by refusing to have anything to do with such frightening sights thereafter" (Fenichel, page 331).

Paradoxically, gay men who fear women as sexual partners nevertheless make good friends of women and relate to them with mutual respect. Temperamental androgyny means that gay men feel a temperamental kinship with women, which leads to common interests and values, and to real friendships.

THE WOMAN-HATER. Least amenable to reorientation therapy, writes Hatterer (1970, page 65) is "the patient who has felt a long-standing contempt for women or who has a total identification with them. . . . [He does] not want to alter his homosexuality in any way."

> I've never been attracted to women for as long as I can remember. In fact, I'm repulsed by the thought of having to spend much time with one. . . . [T]hey're all bitches in one way or another. Their bodies are so flabby and sloppy. They just turn me off in every way (Hatterer 1970, page 73).

> In Braaten's study, a homosexual college man remarks: "Women look like cows."

THE HOMOSEXUAL MISFITS. There are men who all their life have been convinced that they are ugly or worthless and will never find a female partner. To connect with another person, they may draw upon their homosexual potential:

> From high school on I've had an extremely negative body image. I feel okay about my face, but I think my body is very ugly, almost grotesque. . . .

> The locker room was the only exposure I had to boys' bodies, when I cowered in a corner, quickly changed for gym, and always avoided taking a shower (Fellows, page 197) .

When Bell and Weinberg combed the gay world of San Francisco for participants in their large-scale interview study, they turned up some odd characters whose homosexuality was probably related to their difficulty in finding a place in the heterosexual world.

> Interviewer notes: "He lives in an ugly, bleak two-room apartment, where he seems to devote most of his time to watching TV. He has no close friends, and those he has he seldom sees. All relationships seem casual and unimportant to him" (Bell and Weinberg, page 226) .

> Interviewer notes: "I felt a horrible sense of resignation about him, of surrender to a dead-end fate" (*ibid*) .

> Interviewer notes: "He says he enjoys drinking more than sex. He kept referring to his drinking when I asked a question about sex" (*ibid*.).

Interviewer notes: "Quite subdued and reticent, he lives alone in his apartment with five cats. There are five different cat food bowls on the floor in the kitchen. One for each cat" (*ibid.*, page 227).

Interviewer notes: "When the interview came to an end, he asked me why he had difficulty relating to people and why people didn't like him, exclaiming, 'I'm always neat, clean, polite, proper.' He seems very lonely to me" (*ibid*).

Interviewer notes: "He seemed like a totally ineffectual, frightened, withdrawn sort of person. He was desperately shy and seemed very afraid of me for the first part of the interview. The house was a fantastic state of rubble, full of boxes of junk, files, and furniture. He explained them by saying, simply, 'I collect things' " (*ibid*).

Interviewer notes: "He has to be one of the saddest, most forlorn human beings I've ever met. He said to me, 'Here I've made it financially and professionally. I could travel anywhere or do anything, but why bother? I'm more lonesome away than I am at home, and I'm desperately lonesome at home'" (*ibid*).

Interviewer notes: "He lives alone in a run-down Nob Hill apartment. He's over fifty years old and engages only in solitary masturbation with male fantasies. This has been the case for over four years" (*ibid*).

Undoubtedly, the lonely ones, the schizoid, and the misfits are overlapping categories. A gay-affirmative therapist, Clark elaborates on a topic that suggests that some of his patients have real difficulty in finding a sex partner, male or female. Clark goes to unusual lengths to justify the roles of the prostitute and erotic masseur, which suggests that he is well experienced in encouraging his patients to make use of these social resources:

[T]here is a cadre of trained fee-for-service erotic masseurs. . . . Erotic massage . . . [simply means] that they offer a sexual release with or without massage. ...[T]he more professional the person, the more willing he or she is to answer questions" (Clark, page 162).

Many cities have professional escorts or consorts working through agencies or freelance who, while possibly prevented by law from advertising sex for a fee, are professionals who are paid for their time. They advertise in gay newspapers, ordinary newspapers, gay guides and the advertising pages of the telephone directory. The more professional they are, the more willing they should be to be interviewed by phone or in person. . . . (*ibid*).

NOTES TO CHAPTER 24

1. Paraphrase of comment attributed to Dr. Wardell Pomeroy, who left the Kinsey Institute to become a marriage counselor, in a 1969 article on homosexuality.

2. Ratings were based on the four-question interview specified by the Diagnostic Interview Schedule, Version III. Revised: (1) Has there ever been a period of two weeks or more when you thought a lot about death—your own, someone else's, or death in general? (2) Has there ever been a period of two weeks or more when you felt like you wanted to die? (3) Have you ever felt so low you thought about committing suicide? (4) Have you ever attempted suicide?

3. The GLB group was too small (n=28) to permit separate tallies of gay men, lesbians, bisexual males, and bisexual females.

4. In addition to social oppression, Bailey suggests (page 884) three other factors as possible causes of emotional disturbance in gay men. (1) There is a "possibility . . . that homosexuality represents a deviation from normal development and is asssociated with other deviations that may lead to mental illness." (2) Prenatal brain development my "make gay men more susceptible to types of psychopathology more commonly found in women. . . ." (3) Perhaps homosexual practices and standards are significant stressors, like the disease risks associated with receptive anal sex and promiscuity, or the emphasis on youth and physical attractiveness.

25   The Not-Quite-Homosexual

and the Pseudo-Homosexual

Typically, a gay man is homosexual in his feelings, in his behavior, and in his identity. What about men and boys who are homosexual in their behavior but not in their feelings, or vice-versa? What about those who are preoccupied with the worry that they *might* be homosexual? Let us examine a few of these categories individually.

TEEN-AGE "HOMOSEXUALS." Teen-age boys who are full of sexual energy, may also be well-indoctrinated to avoid *sexual contact with girls*. For example, the *Boy Scout Handbook* (1990 edition) says nothing about sexual life but devotes two pages to the topic of "Sexual Responsibility." Here is a sampling of the *Handbook's* stern advice to adolescent boys:

> As a young man, you are capable of becoming a father. . . .
> However, the difficulties created by a pregnancy can be enor-
> mous. Don't burden yourself and someone you care for with a
> child neither of you is ready to bear. (Birkby, page 527)

> Irresponsibility or ignorance . . . can cause a lifetime of regret.
> AIDS and venereal diseases spread by sexual contact may under-
> mine your health and that of others. Having a baby before you
> are ready may drastically limit your future chances for education,
> occupations, and travel. (*Ibid.*, page 528)

A respondent of the Adairs recalls a Boy Scout jamboree activity that their *Handbook* says nothing about:

> "I remember around fifth grade. . . during a Boy Scout. . . jam-
> boree, we would try to seduce other boys who were camping out.
> This is still pre-pubic. . . . We'd take off our pants, and. . . rub
> our crotches together and stuff. . . . Everyone was sort of into it. .
> . . There weren't any stigmas yet" (Adair and Adair, pages 195-
> 196) .

Adolescent boys have plenty of opportunity for privacy and direct body contact with other boys: playing together, camping together and sleeping together.
Just as lying in bed alone with a spontaneous tingling erection leads to masturbation, sharing a bed with another boy leads to physical contact, to sexual exploration and experimentation unless this activity is blocked by internalized prohibitions. A boy's first social investigations of his sexual capabilities are likely to
engage other boys rather than girls. As Pomeroy (page 66) put it, "it is the easiest thing to do and boys are much more available."

443

Pomeroy asks: "If a boy comes home and asks his mother if
Jimmy can come over and spend the night, she will most likely
be pleased that he has company and make no trouble about it.
But imagine what she would say if he came home and made the
same request for his friend Mary! In gymnasium classes, on
hikes, at the club-house, or in swimming, boys are often alone
with other boys, undressed, and that is an opportunity they just
don't have with girls. Other boys are therefore much more easily
available for sex experiences."

"During [junior] high school years, it wasn't that unusual for
guys to have some sort of sex or another with one another. But
starting around the ninth, tenth grade, it first started to become
frowned on. It's more like, 'We're over this sort of discovery
period; we're more like boys, and we're generally interested in
gals'" (Adair and Adair, page 198) .

Hatterer argues that such incidental same-sex activity may be motivated not
so much by homosexual desire as by boredom, curiosity, exploratory or adventurous expressions of sexual interest among adolescents and preadolescents in a
society that places obstacles in the way of heterosexual explorations that most of
them would prefer. The diagnostic insignificance of occasional same-sex exploration was likewise noted in the 1940s, by psychoanalyst Otto M. Fenichel (page
112):

Occasional homosexual experiences between adolescents should
not be looked upon as pathological, so long as they appear as
temporary phenomena of adaptation and do not result in definite
fixations.

Narrowly interpreted, learning theory would indicate that since homosexual
play is pleasurable, it would surely result in a homosexual habit. However, boys
who are well-oriented toward fulfillment of their gender role, will intermix same-
sex play with *heterosexual* fantasy, and go on to realize their heterosexual potential. William Pollak (pages 220-223) describes a teen-age boy's transition from
homosexual play to adult heterosexuality.

Scott
Scott's mother discovered that her 17-year-old son "had been
getting together afternoons [with his friend Benson], drinking
beer, and then masturbating each other." Alarmed at their son's
"inappropriate behavior," Scott's parents prevailed upon him to
talk to a psychotherapist. Scott told the therapist that although his
mother is "all freaked out" about having caught him and his
friend "fooling around," to Scott it was "no big deal."

Scott elaborated: "[T]he first time we got together and fooled around, I thought I might be gay. I felt really weird about it. But the truth is, when I hang with Benson and we do stuff together, it's fun and everything, but I'm definitely into girls. I mean, I'm thinking about girls when he and I are together."

From a couple of weeks' therapy sessions, it seemed clear to the therapist "that Scott primarily felt attracted to girls. While he had explored touching Benson's body and had let Benson touch him, the experimentation had more to do with a general need Scott felt to let out his 'sexual energy' than with a true physical attraction to Benson. All of Scott's fantasies were about women. When the junior prom came along, Scott unequivocally decided to take Sharon, a classmate he had 'had his eye on' for several months. Scott's encounters with Benson stopped prior to the end of his junior year and, the last I heard, Scott was living happily with a woman he'd been dating for several years. Scott, as far as I can tell," his therapist concludes, "is heterosexual."

One legitimate criticism of the 1948 Kinsey study is that the investigators' interest in "the human male" did not distinguish clearly enough between adolescent exploration and adult habit. In his 1971 book, Karlen records (page 282) an interview with Paul Gebhardt, who at that time held the late Dr. Kinsey's position as Director of the Kinsey Institute. Karlen posed the question:

"I'd like to ask you about the famous 37 percent in *Sexual Behavior in the Human Male*. That figure, the number of men who've had "homosexual contact to orgasm" at some time in their lives, is used to show the prevalence and alleged normality of homosexuality. But isn't it misleading? Does an act of mutual masturbation at thirteen or one homosexual experience at eighteen have anything to do with what we usually mean when we talk about [adult] homosexuality?"

The Director of the Kinsey Institute candidly responded:

"God, sometimes I wish we'd never published that statistic! When people are young, they can have fairly extended homosexual episodes and then maintain a heterosexual pattern for the rest of their lives."

LOW FRUSTRATION-TOLERANCE "HOMOSEXUALS." Attraction to a quick-and-easy mode of sexual gratification may result from "some impairment of an individual's inner controls—a malfunction of what psychoanalysts call the superego," writes Marmor (1980, page 4):

> When such inner controls are weak or absent, an individual may
> indulge in homosexual behavior for a wide variety of motives
> which have nothing to do with erotic preference.

The gay porno film "The Idol" (Tom De Simone, 1979) dramatizes a young man's frustrating, prolonged struggle to coax an attractive but reluctant young lady to have sex with him. He then gets immediate sexual gratification from a like-minded male. The virtually instant availability of low-cost sex gives homosexuality an appeal that, coming "at the right time, at the right place" to a high-testosterone, low-superego lad, may have a lasting influence on lifelong habits.

Probably most observers would agree that low frustration-tolerance *contributes to* adoption of the homosexual option. [Gallup and Suarez (page 318) take the extreme position that low frustration tolerance "constitute[s] the primary etiology of homosexuality."] Comments Humphreys (1971, page 359) on this appeal of the homosexual option: "In spite of the pill, willing girls are not as easy for the single man to find in our society as are willing seekers of impersonal sex."

A gay New Yorker recalls his first attempt to pick up a sexual partner. His interviewer (Kahn, page 36) summarizes the experience, which was both effortless and gratifying:

> On Eighth Avenue he saw "a tall, good-looking . . . AWOL
> marine about 21. I went up to him and said, 'Are you interest-
> ed?' He was, and five minutes later we were in a hotel room.
> The first time he kissed me, Bam! If I was to have a first experi-
> ence, this kid was the one to initiate me. He was the aggressive
> one, but I learned fast. It was the bursting of a dam!'"

Similarly, Kahn tells (page 104) tells of a respondent who, right after an unsuccessful attempt to get a girl to go to bed with him, quickly found himself a willing male sex partner:

> He drove around until he picked up a man. "At his apartment, I
> decided to go with the flow. . . . We smoked a little pot. We went
> to bed. Whatever he did, I did." [But] when he saw that his part-
> ner wanted merely to use him, [he] felt cheated. "I wanted mutu-
> al feelings of tenderness and love and enjoyable sex," he
> recalled, "making my partner enjoy it as much as I enjoyed it."

A patient confided to Hatterer (1970, page 291): "There's no question about it, it's easier to find a man—and cheaper. Maybe that's what I am, cheap. I know I have a problem in not being able to put myself out. Whatever comes easily to me is what I like." To Humphreys (1971, page 359) a man who frequented tearooms confided: "I want the quick thing . . . and there's always some place to get it. . . . I'm just too damned busy and involved to look for anything else."

Undoubtedly there are a few men who drift toward the homosexual option *primarily* because it is a quicker, simpler tactic for finding a sex partner. For these men, homosexuality results not so much from the interaction of genetic and environmental factors, as from the interaction of low superego and low frustration-tolerance. The popularity of gay masturbation is one indication that low frustration-tolerance is a prominent factor in homosexual life. Compare a sex manual intended for heterosexuals with one written for gay men. The former says little or nothing about lone masturbation. Sex manuals for gay men devote pages, well illustrated, on "going solo." Survey findings also point to the popularity of masturbation among gay men. According to the findings of Weinberg *et al.*, it was practiced at least once a week by 84 percent of their 1983 sample.

SEXUALLY-ISOLATED ADULT MEN. Homosexual behavior is observed in prisons, on warships, and in other all-male societies. Kinsey noted (page 631) that "in most remote rural areas there is considerable homosexual activity among lumbermen, cattlemen, prospectors, miners, hunters, and others engaged in out-of-door occupations. . . . Quite without argot, physical manifestations, and other affectations so often found in urban groups. There is a minimum of personal disturbance or social conflict over such activity."

Inside many prisons, inmates may be either "punks" or "daddies." At some prisons, an unwritten law says that if an inmate is not sexually dominant he must be sexually passive. To make sure that he will not be coerced into playing the passive role himself, an inmate looks for someone who can be coerced into being his passive partner.

> "As one [ghetto dweller] told me, when he had been in the reformatory, 'You needed to show how tough you were right off or you'd be surprised how many cocks you'd have up your ass in one night'" (Meers, page 429).

What of the inmate who is young, boyish looking, or too slight of build to defend himself against a bully who craves sexual relief? Survival favors that he find himself a "daddy" who is husky enough to protect him, and decent enough to become a tolerable and perhaps even a congenial companion. An occasional sexual favor is a fair price to pay for protection against rape at knife-point, assault, abuse, and risk of murder.

Money (1988, page 107) describes the case of Walt, who, before conviction on a charge of street fighting, had been was involved in an intense and sexually active love affair. In prison, he had this "homosexual" experience:

Walt
While taking a shower, Walt caught sight of the smooth, well-formed buttocks of a young, new prisoner, and at this sight his

> penis immediately became erect, as if the sight became a mirage of his girlfriend's body. Since the code among prisoners forbade uninvited sexual contact, Walt faced the corner of the shower room and, under a shower head, masturbated to lose his erection (*ibid.*, paraphrased).

> For the remainder of his months in prison. . . [Walt synchronized his] heterosexual fantasies with fellatio, which he coerced his cellmate, more timid than himself, into performing on him. . . . In the years since his release, he has resumed an exclusively heterosexual sex life (*ibid.*).

Walt "resumed an exclusively heterosexual sex life" after he was released from prison. But according to Sagarin, situational homosexuality may lead to habit-formation. Sagarin reports that ex-prisoners who had been introduced to homosexual activity while in prison continued to seek homosexual contacts after their release. It may also be conjectured that all-male societies—such as the navy and the seminary—give rise to situational homosexuality partly because they attract homosexually-inclined males.[1] The same may be true of lumbermen, cattlemen, and other isolated all-male work groups.

What of a society in which women are present but unavailable? In a 1942 anthropological study, *The Stone Men of Malekula*, Layard reported that the largest island of the New Hebredes, Malekula, was dominated by powerful chiefs who monopolized the women. *There, male homosexuality was universal.* But in other islands, where there were no chiefs, and women were available, homosexuality was virtually absent (Greenberg, page 31).

THE PHYSICALLY DISABLED. Social and physical restrictions make the plight of physically disabled men not altogether different from the life of a male prisoner, whose direct contact, outside the family, may be limited in general, and also limited to members of his own sex. This makes it likely that he will activate his homosexual potential. A boy who is born with a physical handicap also suffers from psychological and social handicaps that begin in infancy. A disappointed father often distances himself from a boy who is born deaf (Zakarewsky), as fathers also distance themselves from the gender-discordant boy. The handicapped boy is not only at risk of being rejected by his father, but is also deprived of normal play interactions with other children.

Children who are placed in residential schools are often sexually segregated, and do not learn to feel comfortable with girls. Growing up in an all-male environment does not prepare them to find their place in a heterosexual world. Disabled boys grow up burdened by their physical deficit. Segregated living—including the use of communal toilet, bathing, and sleeping facilities—stimulate sexual fantasies. These conditions can actuate an even moderate homosexual potential. "[R]esearch shows the deaf population seems to exhibit more homosexual behavior than the public at large" (Phaneuf, page 53, citing interview data of Grossman). On the Internet since 1995, the Deaf Queer Resource Center (http://www.deafqueer.org) claims to have more than 10,000 unique visits per month.

As a child, a blind boy is less aware of the physical differences between males and females at different stages of development. Susan Hicks (page 169) quotes a congenitally blind boy: "I think I know *what* a girl's breasts are, but I'm not sure *where* they are."

Hicks describes some of the difficulties a blind young man has in making social connections in general, including friendships that may lead to marriage or intimacy. He is often burdened by bizarre mannerisms: rocking, swinging movements, finger-twiddling. Unable to make eye contact, he cannot give or receive nonverbal expressions of interest, indicating an interest in getting to know each other better. In a social situation, he does not know what is socially acceptable because he does not know much of what other people are doing.

Swartz compared the sexual sophistication of hearing and deaf college freshmen,[2] finding that the deaf group scored significantly lower on a test knowledge about sexual matters. Rainer *et al.* interviewed a group of males who attended a school for the deaf, with regard to their sexual knowledge and experience. About 20 percent said they knew that there was homosexual activity at their school. More respondents claimed homosexual than heterosexual experience. A study of students' sexual experience was conducted at a school for the deaf whose population included residential students, commuters, and students who lived in the school dormitories but went home on week-ends. Homosexual experience was highest for the residential group, lowest for the commuters, and in-between for those who went home on weekends.[3]

McCabe *et al.* studied 33 men and 27 women (mean age 28) with congenital physical disabilities. Six percent said they were having same-sex experience "often or very often," and 10 percent reported a same-sex experience "once or a couple of times."

For ten years (1985-1994), a quarterly newsletter was published in San Francisco, for "abled and disabled gay and bisexual men." *Able Together* consisted mainly of personal ads.

> A college student saw a blind young man on the street, who
> seemed to need help, and offered to accompany him home. When
> they reached the door of his apartment, the blind man thanked
> his benefactor and stroked his benefactor's crotch, as if to invite
> him inside for sexual play. (Author's clinical notes.)

Canadian writer William Thompson tells how a traumatic experience[4] made him suddenly feel that because he was blind, he was also worthless as a sexual partner. He writes (page 91) about "trying to reconcile my want for the erotic with the immovable fact of my blindness, [which seemed] to negate any kind of claim I have to an erotic life." He continues (page 93): "I felt neutered, repulsive to women in a way I had never felt before. I imagined any woman would turn away in disgust if I were to show any sexual interest in her. Lust was body, and my body was flawed. I felt ashamed every time I lusted after someone and told myself that I didn't deserve to have an erotic life."

David, a gay man, tells of his unexpected encounter with a blind man at a bathhouse (paraphrased from an interview with Stambolian, pages 160-162):

David

Lying prone on a cot in a bathhouse cubicle, awaiting an encounter with some appealing partner, David was approached by a handsome visitor, who then asked if he could introduce him to a friend, and did he mind if his friend was blind? "Go get him. I'll be waiting," David answered.

As he waited, David ruminated: "Now why did I say that? Why was I so certain it would work? Normally, if someone proposes a threesome, I ask to see the person first or at least ask for a description. But I hadn't done any of that, which was all the more surprising since I had never had sex with a blind man and had no idea how I would react. Suppose his blindness disturbed me and suppose I embarrassed him? I thought of locking my door or leaving the room. I even thought of inviting someone else in, to give me an excuse.

"[But] I waited, and when they came back, I was overwhelmed. The friend was younger than the man and beautiful, magnificent really. . . . I noticed immediately how much they resembled each other. I decided they were lovers, two men who instead of seeking out opposites had found and fallen in love with different versions of themselves. It was clear, in any case, that the man deeply loved his friend. It was evident in every gesture he made, in just the way he stood next to him. There was no conversation. Only an exchange of names. The man knelt down on the floor again, and the younger one, the blind one, took off his towel and sat on the bed next to me. He had a beautiful cock, as beautiful as the rest of him, and I found myself wondering if he had ever seen it. I almost asked the man if his friend knew how beautiful he was. But then the young man began touching my face, gently and methodically going over each of my features. And the man talked while his friend did this. . . . He supplied the details that his friend couldn't see like the color of my hair and eyes. Then the man asked me if I would like to know the world the way his friend knew it. He took one of my towels, tore off a strip, and tied it across my eyes so that I was blind too. Now, as his friend continued touching every part of my body, it was as if the sensations had doubled, as if I were more intensely myself than ever before and at the same time someone else. . . .

"[A]fter we devoured each other, kissing, sucking, eating each other, guided only by our hands . . . at last he started fucking me, and so well! And through all of it at different intervals the other man said things, told us things. It was like a verbal counterpoint to what we were doing. . . . I felt the sensation of his voice as strongly as I felt that young man's body inside mine. . . . And when the young man came, and I came, he moaned and cried out with us.

". . . When it was over, we joked about the torn towel, we thanked each other and they left. They could have been lovers or possibly close friends. They could have been brothers, too . . . which would explain the resemblance. I've even thought that the man was straight and had decided to guide his [gay] brother and act as his eyes. But . . . it was certain that he loved that young man very much. . . That night I was his gift to his friend, but it was a gift I had a share in giving, just as I shared the young man's world by being blindfolded."

The interviewer asked, "Did you see them again?" David answered, "No. Experiences like that can seldom be repeated. But I can't tell you how many times I've repeated it in my mind."

THE MENTALLY RETARDED. David Thompson, a British graduate student, reports[5] on those mentally retarded men who engage in homosexual acts in public places—in public toilets and in parks, for example. Interviews with 19 retarded men who were homosexually active, four of whom also had ongoing sexual relationships with a woman (page 231). Some of these men went to public toilets to find sex partners, and others said they were "approached by a man when they were walking around by themselves. . . (page 226)." There were many indications that their partners were not retarded: many drove cars, they were employed, some took their pick-ups to their homes.

Thompson reports (page 227) "a disturbing lack of mutuality" in their sexual activity. Of 19 men interviewed, "all but one of them reported themselves as having been [anally] penetrated, compared with only five saying that they had on occasion penetrated." "[R]eceptive anal sex was never described in positive terms and was *overwhelmingly recounted as painful*," which suggested to the investigator that the that the penetrator did not bother to use lubricant, or worry about the feelings of his pick-up (page 227).

Though the sex experience was usually painful, these men continued to visit public toilets and otherwise make themselves available for sex. Why? "For some, the sex was an exchange they made for getting attention from 'normal' men. . . . Offering sex was essentially one of the only ways they could effectively gain some attention from another person in a world which largely rejects people with learning disabilities. (page 231)." In addition to the four who claimed to be having an ongoing sexual relationship with a woman, eight of the remaining sixteen expressed the wish that they could have a female sex partner (page 233). A group of homosexually active men who yearn for female partners, may validly be categorized as pseudo-homosexuals.

THE HOMOSEXUAL PROSTITUTE. Teenagers may run away from home because they have been accused of (and tormented for) being gay, or have announced that they were gay, and then ostracized. (Although some teen agers become runaways for reasons that have nothing to do with sexuality.) Gay or straight, runaway boys may drift into homosexual prostitution because hunger, loneliness, and good looks move them in that direction. Outland (page 117) characterizes the plight of the teenage runaway:

> Most cities are cold at night, and when you do not have the
> money for a place to live, you quickly find that taking drugs
> numbs the cold as well as the emotional pain you are feeling
> over having been cast out of your home and consequently need-
> ing to fuck old trolls just to get enough money for food.

Merle Miller (page 49) recalls that his first homosexual encounter was with a 17-year old boy who claimed he hadn't eaten in two days. Miller recalls the case of another boy prostitute:

> He was the next-to-youngest child in a very poor family of nine,
> and once ran away from home for two days and two nights. . . .
> [W]hen he got back, nobody knew that he had been gone. Then,
> at 19, he discovered The Street, and he said, "All of a sudden
> here were all these men, and they were looking at me."

Some homosexual prostitutes begin their "career" as gay teen agers who were forced to leave home. They migrate to an urban center where the gay lifestyle is more openly practiced, and there they discover that their youth and willingness to engage in homosexual acts have a much greater market value than their services as an unskilled worker. Some gay teenagers crave the companionship of mature gay men, but they are too young to visit gay bars, and man-boy sex is legally regarded as "criminal conduct." This state of affairs pushes homeless gay teenagers into prostitution. According to one study, the only adult gay men some young male prostitutes knew were their 'tricks' (Boyer, 1989).

Homelessness, bereavement[6] from family, friends, and school, interaction with the marginal, friendless pathological types who seek out teen-age prostitutes—all this is demoralizing. Easy money gives the teen-ager ready access to drugs and alcohol. All this can lead to a premature coming out.

A Christian ex-gay recalls that when he first worked as a homosexual prostitute, he comforted himself with the thought that he did it because he needed the money to live on. After he had found a good job, and didn't need the extra money any more, he continued to feel drawn to the streets. Now he realized that prostitution gave him a gratification beyond the financial gain. Now he had to admit to himself how much he enjoyed being wanted, being worshipped, being adored. "One man paid me just to hug my body. Another man knelt at my feet and wept" (ex-gay conference testimony).

Bradley (pages 113-114) describes the tactic of a 1965 Los Angeles male prostitute who would pose as a hitchhiker but would be careful not to signal to what might be an unmarked police car. (In his area, prostitution itself was not illegal, but *soliciting* for prostitution was.) He signals the well-dressed driver of a Lincoln, who invites the hitchhiker in, and the following conversation ensues:

> "Going far?" the driver asked.
> "Far as I can," the young man answered.
> "That could be a long way. How will I know where to let you off?"
> "You'll know, I guess," the hiker shrugged. . . .
> The driver . . . slowed down the car. "I'll be turning at the next light. Do you want to go that way?"
> "If you want me to."
> To the last answer, the driver smiled and swung around the corner with a flourish. As soon as the wheels of the Lincoln were straight, he leaned over and placed his hand on the inside of the young man's thigh. At the touch, the hiker eased back into the cushions and relaxed.
> What's your name?" the driver asked.
> "Jerry."
> "You're very nice, Jerry, very nice. I think I'm going to like you. How much is it going to cost for me to like you, Jerry?"
> "Whatever you think is right," Jerry replied.
> "I have twenty dollars," the man said. "And enough for a motel room. I, ah, can't take you to my home; we'll have to go to a motel. Is that all right with you?"
> "Yeah," Jerry said, turning to the man and smiling for the first time. "Yeah, that's just fine with me. Let's go!"

THE CELIBATE "HOMOSEXUAL." A certain portion of the adult male population has no sexual contact with persons of either sex. A large national survey by Binson *et al.* reports that 24 percent of men who describe themselves as gay also say they are celibate, and about 12 percent of men who say they are straight are also celibate. This category of celibates includes not only Roman Catholic priests and brothers, but celibate bachelors and also some married men who for whatever reason are not sexually active. Bell and Weinberg found among men who frequent gay bars an "inactive" category: men who virtually never have a sexual partner and whose sexual life consists entirely of lone masturbation.

Some priests say they are "psychically homosexual," but maintain their vow of celibacy. Whether they are priests, bachelors, or sexually inactive married men, are those men who say they are "psychically homosexual," any more homosexual than men who say they are imaginary astronauts really astronauts?[7]

THE WORRIER.[8] In Chapter 5 (page 69) we introduced the topic of "homosexual worry," the anxiety experienced by those teenagers and men who are troubled by the homosexual aspects of their dream life and idle thoughts. They may worry about crushes or close friendships with other boys, or about spontaneous sexual arousals that occurred while they were in male company. A person may feel anxious about the same-sex explorations of his early adolescence, or about homosexual dreams or fantasies. He may hurry into marriage, or seek the help of a therapist to get rid of his "homosexuality."

In his essay on Leonardo da Vinci, Freud conjectured that a man may have a homosexual imagination[9] which is not acted out in his social life, and that homosexual impulses can be sublimated[10] and expressed as creative or artistic work.

Psychoanalyst Socarides (1995, page 104) writes that he and his colleagues help many 'worriers' "understand their confused . . . feelings, [so that they can] go on functioning in happier, more-well-adjusted ways." A significant portion of men who seek help from ex-gay Christian ministries have never engaged in same-sex activity but are troubled by homosexual thoughts and attractions. *These worriers inflate the "cure rate" claimed by ex-gay Christian ministers (and reorientation therapists) because these clients were not practicing homosexuals to begin with.*

Daniel Cappon (pages 45-46) offers the case history of a medical student, whom we will call Austin. His psychiatrist was able to assure Austin that he was only a "worrier." "A decade later he was happily married, the father of three children. He had a thriving practice but was still introverted, muscularly tense, young-looking, and preoccupied with the idea (though not the fact) of insufficient masculinity."

Austin

A medical student, who wanted to become a psychiatrist but later chose another specialty, came with the complaint that he had the idea he was homosexual although he had never had sexual con-

tact with a member of his own sex and had enjoyed heterosexual
intercourse. His image, while masturbating, was always of a
woman. . . . His sleep dreams [like his waking fantasies] were
directed to the opposite sex, though his neurotic preoccupation
with homosexuality had broken through into his dreams . . .
being chased by men with threatening phallic symbols. The reasons for his fear of homosexuality were his lack of aggression,
his avoidance of competitive sports and violent physical contact.
. . his shyness, his looking much younger than his age, his
always being considered to be a pretty boy and a bit of a sissy,
and the impulsive ruminations . . . of wanting to kiss and
embrace men . . . [a] symptom quite common in immature men
who seek better masculine identification and social security and
who have obsessive tendencies. It is usually quite unrelated to
homosexuality.

In a 1981 article, "Teenagers' Fears That They are Homosexual," professor of
psychiatry Gordon D. Jensen (page 48) advised physicians on how to deal with
teenagers who worry about their "latent homosexuality:"

(1) [I]t is all right to let the youngster know your personal preference [regarding sexual orientation]. But it is not all right to be
judgmental or moralistic and to imply that they should be like
you.

(2) Give them a complete physical examination and if they are
physically normal, assure them of that. "The doctor's assurances
often relieves enormous burdens."

(3) Let the patient tell you precisely what their worry is: "affectionate feelings . . erotic feelings, sexual excitement . . . what
kind of activities they engage in, whether touching, sleeping
together, oral sex, intercourse, etc. . . . [I]ndicate that none of
these necessarily are indicative of homosexuality."

(4) [P]atients need to know that a) many teenagers worry about
their sexual identity; b) about 25 percent will have some homosexual experience during their teenage years; c) homosexual
experience or thoughts do not mean that the person is homosexual; d) attraction to a person of the same sex is normal and healthy
and does not mean homosexuality. . . .

 (5) Let patients know that there is nothing wrong with not being
sure about themselves at this age and assure them that they will
become certain with time—perhaps months or even years. . . .

(6) [E]ncourage them to come and talk with you again if they continue to be concerned. . . .

(7) If anxiety persists after a second visit . . . the distress may be of the type that deserves referral to a mental health professional.

Why are some young men so preoccupied by homosexual thoughts, so worried about their homosexual tendencies, that they seek professional help in dealing with this problem? There is some research evidence, noted in the next chapter, that these "worriers" do in fact have some of the temperamental characteristics of homosexuals but that their character structure holds them to a more conventional sexual orientation.

According to psychiatrist Lionel Ovesey, a significant failure experience can trigger fantasy and dreams that become a cause of homosexual worry. These persons suffer from what Ovesey labelled "pseudo-homosexuality." Karlen (page 435) quotes Ovesey's distinction between homosexuality and "pseudo-homosexuality."

> Suppose a guy feels he's a failure as a man—maybe he can't get a job—and he has a fantasy of sucking some great big man's penis. But he doesn't have an erection, feels no arousal, and has no history of homosexuality. Well, how do you explain it? I've found over and over from the patient's own associations that he's trying to repair[11] his failure as a man by sucking masculine strength out of the bigger man's penis. It's a magical solution,[12] so it won't work, and causes further anxiety. But it's a very common mechanism. Psychoanalysts call it introjection.

A youth who is preoccupied with his "homosexual tendencies" may have a talent for poetry, dance or art, as the Braaten and Darling study suggests. *"Many a talented and sensitive man was frightened away from creative occupations,"* Hatterer laments (1965, page 141), *"because of their public and common association with homosexuality."* A better understanding of the difference between homosexuality and pseudo-homosexuality, and between homosexuality and homosexual worry, should have practical consequences. It should encourage creative boys and men to value and pursue their artistic interests.

NOTES TO CHAPTER 25

1. For example, an army veteran, gay, recalls (Humphrey, page 3) that as a young man he read about the "easy sexuality" of army life. "[T]hat's why I went in the military: I thought maybe I could get a part of that action. I just knew there had to be some 'boys' in there that would like to partake of gay sex!"

2. Swartz compared the scores of 203 normal college freshmen with the scores of 38 freshmen attending a college for the deaf (Gaullaudet University).

3. Information obtained from a lecture at an ex-gay conference.

4. Thompson had been blinded in an automobile accident at the age of ten. He continued to have an active, competitive adolescence. He was married and the father of two children when, after nine years of marriage he suffered an accident that caused no physical harm, but left him disoriented and emotionally shaken. As he recalled this traumatic event, his feeling of utter helplessness was intermixed with the sound of his wife screaming for help. The episode left him feeling helpless and worthless ("I couldn't stop crying."), and hastened the end of his marriage, which had long been deteriorating.

5. A significant part of this article deals with the problem of HIV/AIDS prevention among retarded men who are homosexually active.

6. A vocabulary lesson. "Separation anxiety" connotes the emotional suffering that accompanies the experience of being cut off from one's primary social ties. Bereavement, in its older meaning, conveys exactly this meaning, though today the word usually refers to mourning for death of a loved one.

7. The author intended to pose this as an "open question," and let the reader answer it himself. A reader of the manuscript argued that the author owed the reader his opinion, which would go as follows:

In this book (Chapter 5), an entire chapter is devoted to the position that homosexual activity—if we regard dreams and fantasy as mental activity—is a species-wide trait. All men are homosexual in the same sense that "all men are sinners," as some preachers say. However it may be true in a sense that all men are homosexual to a degree, it is none the less useful to distinguish between a professional bank robber and an ordinary citizen who has dreams or fantasies about robbing a bank. The world regards people not by what they fanasize but by how they live.

8. The phenomenon involving "worriers" about homosexual tendencies have been variously labelled. Ovesey refers to these persons as pseudo-homosexuals. "Homosexual panic" has sometimes *wrongly* been used to describe this phenomenon. (See end note 3, Chapter 6.) Braaten and Darling used the label "covert homosexuals" to describe patients who were beset by such worries. This usage is also quite misleading, as a "covert homosexual" can also refer to a *closeted* homosexual.

Nor can "worriers" be called "latent homosexuals," because their preoccupation is disturbingly *conscious*. Hatterer (1970, page 18) rejects the concept of "latent homosexuality" as "ambiguous, essentially meaningless, and nonoperational. . . ."

9. The Strachey translation (page 81) of Freud's Leonardo essay refers to "what is called ideal [sublimated] homosexuality," which in the original German (*Gesammelte Werke*, v. 8, page 148) is described as "sogenannte ideelle Homosexualitat." Strachey apparently confused the German word "idealle" (which does indeed mean ideal) with the German word "ideelle" which means imaginary.

(In his mature years, perhaps Leonardo was an "imaginary homosexual." But at age 24, according to Potts and Short and as noted in Chapter 20, Leonardo was imprisoned for having sex with a youth.)

10. Freud used the term sublimation to describe the transformation of compulsive and unwanted (ego-alien) impulses into aims that are ego-syntonic: consciously satisfying, adaptive, and flexible. Critics have questioned the concept of sublimation on two bases: (1) Just how is an instinctual drive transformed from its original aim to something else? ("Sublimation smacks more of alchemy than of science," said Freud's critics.) (2) Implied in the concept of sublimation is the transformation of an amoral (or socially undesirable) instinct into socially valuable behavior. But "socially valuable" is not an objective standard and is therefore unworthy of a scientific formulation, the anti-sublimation argument goes.

From the standpoint of evolutionary psychology, however, it is quite likely that the human mind has evolved ways of modifying behavioral tendencies in ways that favor human survival. Psychological research into "pro-social" and altruistic behavior represents an interest in this aspect of the human mind.

11. Note the special meaning of the word *repair* as Ovesey and other therapists use it. Popularly, *repair* means to mend or fix, but the word also means "to make whole." Used this way, Ovesey's comment might be restated to say, "He's trying to make whole his fragmented image as a man. . . ."

12. This magical aspect of homosexual motivation is what the discussion of mana in chapters 9 and 12 is all about.

26 Males with a Low-Masculinized Brain (LMB)

A Population Worth Studying

There is a growing body of evidence that male homosexuality is in many cases to *an extent* genetic, and that this condition seems to be based in part on the brain's resistance to the masculinizing influence of testosterone during the pre-natal period, when the male brain is ordinarily masculinized.

Life begins not with birth but with conception. To review the theme of Chapter 7, the lesson of embryology is that humans, like all mammals, are at the beginning of life sexually undifferentiated and proto-female. At about six weeks of age, embryos that are genetically programmed to become male begin to produce the hormone testosterone, which masculinizes the creature, mainly its brain and sex organs (internal and external). No testosterone, no masculinization, and the embryo develops into a baby girl.

If you compare human adults with their hominid ancestors, there is a spectacular difference in the degree to which males and females differ. Nine million years ago or so, male hominids were almost twice as big as females. The two genders gradually merged in body size until, today, human males are only slightly bigger than females *on the average*, and some females are actually bigger than some males. That is to say, size differences between males and females in the earliest ancestors of man were like what we see today in gorillas. In this regard, humans are more like chimpanzees.

If we compare male gorillas and chimpanzees, we are impressed not only by their differences in size, compared to females of their species, but by differences in their temperament. Male gorillas are spectacularly more violent and protective of their territory. Over the course of millions of years of evolution, tendencies toward male violence and territoriality have very gradually but consistenly diminished, so that human males today are *team-players* as much as (or more than) they are competitors, and that they tend to partner with females (as few as one female) rather than defend a harem of about six females.

This transformation didn't "just happen." It occurred because it greatly favored the survival of the species: it transformed groups from territory-defending harems into roving herds of bonded (rather than rival) males, and male-female partners. And this evolving social environment—sheltering, nurturing, protective--made possible the survival of infants born "unfinished," helpless but with an enormous potential for brain growth and development.

Prenatally, testosterone shapes the unborn brain that will some day guide the behavior of a violent, territorial adult male hominid. Young males show this potential by their rough-and-tumble play, virtually absent from the behavior of young females. The fact is that males and females, on the average, differ not only in their temperament, their emotional life, but also in their motivational and cognitive life. That is to say, males and females tend to differ not only in their feelings, but also in what they want, and in how they perceive, remember and think about their environment.

There is growing evidence that differences in brain structure underlie these psychological differences between males and females. We conjecture that for male-female brain differences to gradually diminish, prenatal brain tissue had to become increasingly resistant to masculinization, and developed in ways that more closely resembled the brain (and therefore the mental and behavioral life) of females. This is the process that humanized humans, that shaped us into a species less like gorillas and more like chimpanzees.

Variation is a basic characteristic of living things. *Variation* makes evolution possible. Individual humans probably tend to vary more than most creatures. We conjecture that *variation* in prenatal testosterone-resistance makes some male brains less masculinized than others.[1] These low-masculinized brains (LMBs) give a predictable, relatively stable, minority of males an inner life—the thinking, the feeling, and the motivation—that gives them much in common with females, and predisposes *some* males to homosexual behavior and identity.

In early childhood, low-masculinized brain (LMB) boys regard their mother's activities as more interesting than their father's. They see their mother or grandmother embroidering, and they want to embroider too. You may argue: "That's because they see her doing it, and it looks interesting. *It's all a matter of experience.*" Then why don't his brothers want to embroider? They also see their mother or grandma doing it, but to them it doesn't look interesting at all. They wouldn't think of asking their mother to teach them how to embroider. Is it "all a matter of experience," or is there something *inborn* about some boys' attraction to activities more typical of girls than boys, more typical of women than of men?

"Something inborn" is what Bailey and Pillard were looking for when they looked for evidence that if a gay man had a twin brother, it was more likely that both were gay if they were monozygotic twins than if they were fraternal twins. They had in common more of that "something inborn" than do fraternal twins, or siblings, or adopted brothers.

Will Fellows' farm boys, expressed a dislike for field work, for getting dirty, for driving a tractor, or fixing machinery. These boys, who grew up to be homosexual, recalled how they liked to help Mother cook and can foods. They liked to raise chickens, tend farm animals, and grow flowers. They also liked to read, and sing, and make music.

Laboratory neuroscientists study the behavior of rats, and kill them at various stages of development, because they hope to learn more about humans. As we pointed out in Chapter 7, there is compelling evidence that male brains are masculinized prenatally, some more than others. Probably some male brain tissue to a significant extent *resists* masculinization. This individual goes though life with an inborn tendency to be more spontaneously interested in things that girls and women like. LMB boys are more strongly moved by appeals to their compassion than by their taste for competition. They are more likely to enjoy dancing more than debating. They like to use their imagination more than their mechanical ability. They would rather cooperate than compete.

As boys, some LMB males worry about what seems like this inborn difference, and may sense that they suffer from a *deficit* of masculinity. They admire, adore, and worship the outward signs of masculinity. They crave physical contact with "real boys." As their bodies develop, sometimes their craving develops into a wish to penetrate and be penetrated by other males. Some LMB males become homosexual men. About one-half do not. Available   evidence suggests that many grow up to be good husbands and fathers, and that some work as artists, writers, musicians, mental health workers, and ministers.

All boys take an interest in their bodies and in the new powers and feelings that accompany puberty. Most boys experience some same-sex play and fantasy. If we include dreams and fantasies as activities of the mind, then, as Chapter 5 argues, homosexual activity is a trait shared by the human species as a whole.

In 1938, Lewis Terman published a study focused on psychological factors in marital happiness. He gave each of 792 respondents a marital happiness score based on their anwers to 75 questions covering all sorts of marital satisfactions and irritants. Then he asked them various questions, and checked to see how (if at all) their answers correlated with their marital happiness scores.

Terman asked each respondent (page 341): "Have you ever felt sexually attracted to a person of your own sex?" (They were asked to check *very strongly, strongly, somewhat, or   not at all.*)   Table 26.1 presents the results. According to Terman's findings, only that small minority (one-half of one percent) of married men who said they had sometime felt *very strongly* sexually attracted to other men scored *low* in marital happiness. Note that five per cent (4+35 divided by 792) of Terman's respondents claimed to have had *strong* or *somewhat* homosexual feelings. This five per cent attained an average marital happiness score somewhat higher than the majority who claimed not at all to ever having been attracted to other men. Terman concluded (page 343): "[I]t appears that the presence of homosexual feeling is not so incompatible with happy marriage as is commonly supposed. . . ."

A more recent study of marital happiness was published in 1983 by John Antill. He rated each of 108 married couples, through individual interviews and testing, on the happiness of each partner. Then he tried to determine what were the psychological characteristics that made for a happy marriage. Antill found that the "masculine" traits of assertiveness, forcefulness, dominance, individual

*Table 26.1. How Terman's 792 married respondents answered the question,
"Have you ever felt sexually attracted to a person of your own sex?"*

	n=	mean marital happiness score
very strongly	4	32
strongly	4	74
somewhat	35	71
not at all	749	68
total =	792	

ism, and ambition (whether manifested by husband or wife) were most prevalent in the *least* happy marriages.

The happiest marriages, according to Antill, were those in which husbands *and* wives could be described as cheerful, affectionate, sympathetic, sensitive to the needs of others, understanding, compassionate, warm, tender, gentle, and fond of children. (The obtained correlation between a wife's rating of her marital happiness and her husband's rated *femininity* was +.61, which is significant at the .001 level of probability.) These findings suggest that the LMB man is a better marriage partner than the super-masculine male ("better," in the sense that both spouses express a higher level of satisfaction with the marriage). The LMB husband is, we suppose, more willing to help take care of the kids, and enjoys doing things with wife and children. Perhaps the super-masculine husband would rather go hunting or fishing with his buddies, or when at home sit and drink beer while he watches football on TV.[2]

A low-masculinized brain may actually be an asset as husband and father, but it is not uncommon for boys and men to worry about having unwanted homosexual tendencies. These "worriers" were described as "pseudo-homosexuals" at the end of Chapter 25. Some "worriers" go to mental health workers or ministers to overcome these bothersome tendencies. *They inflate the cure rate because they were not practicing homosexuals to begin with.*

The emotional discomfort of some "worriers" is strong enough to bring them to mental health clinics. Back in 1950, Renaud reported on a study of 31 men who came to a clinic with strong fears of homosexuality. These men, were compared with a random sampling of 93 patients at the same clinic, on their scores on the masculinity-femininity scale of the MMPI (Minnesota Multiphasic Personality Inventory). *Mean score of the "worriers" was closer to the known mean for homosexuals than to the mean of the control group.*

In 1965, Braaten and Darling reported a study that compared three groups of clients at a college counseling service: (1) 34 "worriers" who wanted help in overcoming homosexual thoughts and fears, (2) 42 homosexually active men,[3] and (3) a control group of 50 male patients, randomly selected, being seen at the same clinic for a variety of other reasons. As shown on Table 26.2, compared with controls, *"worriers" consistently resembled homosexuals in temperament, interests, relationship to parents, and resistance to treatent.*

However, "worriers" seemed to differ from homosexuals in *character structure*, as measured by the MMPI. Homosexuals appeared to be bolder, more self-centered, more rebellious and socially outgoing though emotionally shallow. "Worriers" were more likely to be shy, withdrawn, and to have a stronger conscience and a greater commitment to social values.[4]

Terman's M-F Scale. It is an everyday observation that some little boys prefer to play with girls, and some girls earn the label of "tomboy." But it was quite by accident that the same Lewis Terman, already mentioned for his study of marital happiness, became aware of this overlap between the everyday interests of boys and girls. The developer of Alfred Binet's IQ test, Terman wanted to prove that a child's IQ was not only a measure of his present intelligence, but was also a good predictor of his *future* development. In the 1920s, he collected a sample of high-IQ boys and girls, to study them thoroughly and follow them up until they reached adulthood.

Terman wanted to learn everything about how gifted children differed from ordinary kids. Were they interested in different childhood activities, for example? Accordingly, he made up a list of 90 activities and asked his group of gifted children (303 boys and 251 girls, age 6 to 14) to check off those activities they liked. He gave the same list and the same instructions to a control group of the same age range: 8-17; a random group of 225 boys and 249 girls. Much to Terman's surprise, there was little difference between the preferred activities of gifted and average boys and girls. But he found an unexpected and surprising difference between what boys liked to do, and what girls liked to do.

In all fairness to Prof. Terman, let us concede that he did more than discover the obvious. It is common knowledge that every generation has its quotas of "sissy boys" and tomboys. What Terman demonstrated is that there is also a *continous gradation* from the most obviously "sissy boy" to the most macho bully. He established that it is also true of girls: that they range from in a *continuous gradation* from the fairy princess to the rough-and-tumble tomboy. (The curve of variation revisits us.) Of the 90 activities, Table 25.3 shows three groups of 10, each indexed to show its relative popularity with boys. Test scores of Terman's gifted children did not look different from those of his controls: boys averaged 15, with a range of 11-20. Girls averaged 11.4, range 7-17.

Scoring the papers, Terman's assistant found one gifted boy who scored five, a few points *lower* than any of 500 girls. The score was obtained by nine year old Tommy, whose mother, it turned out, was quite worried about her gender-atypical boy:

Table 26.2.Braaten and Darling's three clinical groups compared on attitudes expressed during counseling: percentage of clinical "Yes" ratings[5]

Trait	Homosexuals	"Worriers"	Controls
1. Effeminate expression, voice, gestures, dress, or walk*	29%	26%	02%
2. Strongly self-assertive, hostile and domineering*	20	38	08
3. Narcissism or grandiosity*	24	32	08
4. Liking for and/or participation in the fine arts, dramatics, and literature*	45	50	10
5. Masochistic, physical or psychic*	33	29	06
6. Fear and/or disgust about sexual relations with women*	79	91	51
7. Desire to be a woman*	20	19	0
8. Mother close-binding-intimate*	56	54	20
9. Patient was mother's favorite*	66	71	26
10. Patient did not feel accepted and respected by father*	90	84	43
11. Spent little time with father*	100	78	46
12. Expressed hatred for father	50	36	19
13. Avoided competitive group games*	100	83	20
14. Avoided physical fights*	91	82	19
15. Excessive fear of physical injury*	100	78	19
16. Profited from psychotherapy*	10	12	41

Asterisk (*) means that obtained difference exceeds the probability of .001

*Table 26.3. Relative popularity of 30 play activities,
as voted by 303 boys and 251 girls, age 6 to 14*

Activities most popular with boys	Activities equally popular with boys and with girls	Activities most popular with girls
24 use tools	14 horseback riding	9 jump rope
20 bicycle riding	13 cards	8 dancing
20 football	13 dominos	8 sewing
20 marbles	13 follow the leader	8 playing store
20 kites	13 fox and geese	7 knit or crochet
20 wrestling	13 geography cards	6 play school
19 work with machinery	13 history cards	5 cook a meal
19 baseball	13 tiddley-winks	4 hop scotch
19 tops	13 word-building	3 "dress up" play
18 fish	12 authors	2 play with dolls

Tommy

Besides showing a distinct preference for feminine play and games, [Tommy] frequently dressed himself up in girl's clothes and "dolled" his face with rouge, lipstick, and other cosmetics. When he found that his feminine behavior was beginning to attract the attention and disapproval of his parents and playmates he cleverly found a way to continue it without criticism by writing little plays for neighborhood performances, each carefully provided with a feminine role for himself. A follow-up study six years later showed that the feminine inclinations of [Tommy] had become more rather than less marked. For now, at age 15, one of his favorite amusements was to dress himself as a stylish young woman, apply cosmetics liberally, and walk down the street to see how many men he could lure into flirtation. [Naively perhaps, Terman adds:] It is practically certain that at this time [Tommy] had no knowledge whatsoever about the existence of such a thing as homosexuality (1936, page 14).

Terman, who had developed the IQ test, must have thought he had another great testing idea, for he spent a number of years, with Catherine Cox Miles, developing a 7-part, 500-item M-F Test, also called the Attitude and Interest Analysis Test (with two equivalent forms), introduced in 1936. Nothing much came of it[6] (compared with the spectacular success of the IQ test), but it gave an idea to another Stanford University psychologist, E.K. Strong, who, since 1927 had been developing a vocational interest test. After many revisions, Strong's test (now called the Strong-Campbell Test) continues to be used for vocational counseling.

Strong's basic idea was that people who chose and stayed in a given vocation not only shared certain talent and training, but also shared certain everyday interests, likes and dislikes. The 400-item SVIB (*Strong Vocational Interest Blank*) was given to a sizeable sample of many occupational groups, male and female, to determine what these common interests were. When a client in vocational counseling answered the 400 questions, his pattern of likes and dislikes could be matched with about 40 occupational and professional groups.

Strong borrowed Terman's idea (with modifications of his own) by building

Table 26.4. Mean M-F Scores of 34 Occupational Groups

M-F score	Occupation	M-F score	Occupation
59	Production Manager	47	YMCA Physical
59	Carpenter		Director
58	Aviator	49	Mathematician
57	Purchasing Agent	48	Psychologist
57	Chemist	47 ·	Printer
56	Physicist	47	Lawyer
53	Dentist	46	physician
53	Forest Service	45	City School
52	Engineer		Superintendent
52	Office Worker	43	Social Science
52	Sales Manager		Teacher
51	Math, Science Teacher	44	Architect
51	Policeman	42	Life Insurance
51	Personnel Manager		Salesman
51	Farmer	40	YMCA Secretary
50	Accountant	39	Advertising Man
49	Banker	32	Author-Journalist
47	CPA	35	Minister
47	Real Estate Salesman	33	Artist

an M-F scale into the SVIB. As Strong suspected, the everyday interests of men in some occupational groups were very much limited to the everyday interests of *men* in general. In other occupational groups, men had everyday interests that they shared with women, or which were actually more popular among women than among men. Here is how various occupational groups differed in their average M-F score, ranging from the most to the least "macho." Note that these are *average* M-F scores for these occupational groups. Within each group there is of course a certain amount of variation.

How did Strong intend this information to be used in vocational counseling? That's a good question, but what is important here is that Strong's findings indicate that LMB males are more readily found in some occupations than others. His findings give us a clue as to how LMB males are distributed throughout society.

Research leads. Not all LMB males are homosexual. Experience seems to make the difference; but exactly *what kind of experience?* The test development of Lewis Terman and E.K. Strong suggest that it would not be difficult to obtain control groups for any number of studies comparing the life experiences of homosexual and heterosexual men of matched "brain masculinity."

Table 26.5. Reported behavioral differences between known groups (male-female or heterosexual-gay)

Indicator	Documentation
1. Left-handedness	Lindsay, 1987, McCormick et al., 1990, Lalumiére and Zucker, 2000.
2. Visio-spatial ability (Mental rotations task)	Gladue and Beatty, 1990. McCormick et al., 1994.
3. Hearing acuity dominance	McCormick and Witelson, 1994
4. Verbal ability	Gladue and Beatty, 1990 or McCormick et al., 1994
5. Motor performance	Hall and Kimura, 1995. (Throw-to-target task)
6. LH response	Gladue et al., 1984.
7. Recognition of an infant's emotional expression	Babchuck et al., 1985.
8. Loudness comfort level	(See Blum, pp. 67-68).
9. Verbal IQ	Wilmot and Bierley, 1984.
10. Low physical aggressiveness	Blanchard et al., 1983.

How would you obtain the required number of homosexual subjects? Not by limiting the sample to homosexual men in treatment. In the current political climate, in our more liberal communities and college campuses, it is now possible to openly recruit homosexuals for a research study, as Hall and Kimura (and other investigators) have done. They should be reasonably well compensated for their time, which is customary for human research in the behavioral and medical sciences. Good compensation would make recruitment easier, obtain a more representative sample, minimize dropouts in longitudinal studies,[7] and give subjects an incentive for notifying experimenters of changes of address.

Here is another approach to studying the interaction of genetic and environmental factors in sexual orientation, using not only paper-and-pencil tests, but behavioral measures of known power. The study would begin by collecting four matched groups of men who differ in their *genetic predisposition* to homosexuality, as shown by various tests of brain masculinization. These groups would include: (1) homosexual men believed to have a low-masculinized brain, (2) homosexual men believed to have a highly masculinized brain (3) heterosexual men believed to have a low-masculinized brain, and (4) heterosexual men believed to have a highly masculinized brain.

An ample number of published findings show measurable *psychological* differences between gay and straight men, or differences between males and females, differences that most likely have a strong genetic component. Table 26.5 lists ten such differences. Taken together, these ten findings (and others) can provide a powerful step forward in research on gay-straight differences.

In addition to these ten psychological factors, several *physical* characteristics seem to be linked with homosexuality: outstandingly good looks, and pedomorphism. Hall and Kimura's 1993 finding on the leftward-symmetrical fingerprints of gay men represents another such physical sign. Back in 1966, Schlegel, a German investigator, claimed that homosexual men had an average pelvic opening that was larger than was typical for heterosexual men. (See Figure 26.6.) Perhaps this anatomical difference is characteristic of the pedomorphic physique.

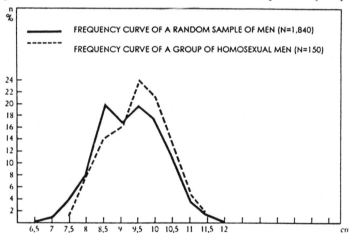

Figure 26.6. Pelvic opening measurements of 150 homosexual men compared with measurements obtained from a random group of 1840 adult males. (Data from Schlegel, 1966)

Information can be collected about each respondent's birth order, his age at puberty, and facts related to gender discordance (*e.g.*, body image, father-absence, attachment to mother, play preferences and aversions, childhood fantasies, etc.). Respondents could be asked to recall facts about his earliest friendships, his earliest sexual experiences: same-sex play, masturbation experience, sexual indoctrination by parents and peers, seduction experience, fears, taboos, etc.

On the basis of his ten scores, and other measures, each respondent can be assigned a total score.[8] Results of this study may answer a number of questions: (1) How reliable are the ten measures? (2) How different are the two groups in their average total score? (3) How much overlap is there in the scores of the two groups? (4) How variable is each group? (5) Are there demonstrable differences (in early childhood, or in present characteristics) between high- and low-scorers in each group? (5) Do any of the scores (or total score) predict which members of the gay group will "spontaneously" change their sexual orientation? (6) . . . which members of the heterosexual group will remain unmarried, have an unstable married life, eventually become gay or bisexual?

Answering these questions calls for a *longitudinal study* of a geographically stable group,[9] with scheduled follow-ups over the lifespan of the respondents. The original population would be large enough to yield four sufficiently large sub-groups (low-scoring gays, high-scoring gays, low-scoring straights, and high-scoring straights), and also large enough to tolerate some attrition over the years. Follow-up findings might replace conjecture and ambiguity with reliable information on the sexual development of American men, and how it affects their long-term well-being. It is not very likely that this kind of research would be undertaken in the present political climate, but fads come and go and a future generation of researchers may enjoy the freedom to conduct scientific research in this area.

When researchers are ready to study the *interaction* of genes and experience, then they will also take an interest in studying those many heterosexual men whose monozygotic ("identical") twin brother is homosexual, and in studying *heterosexual* men who were gender-atypical boys and are now married men of compassion, intuition, and aesthetic sensibility. An understanding of the genesis of sexual orientation (hetero- and homo-) will be advanced more by studying the lives of men of similar brain-masculinization but different sexual orientation, than by the laboratory search for "gay genes."

NOTES ON CHAPTER 26

1. It seems that fetal *brain* tissue is resistant, to varying degrees, to masculinization, but gonadal (sexual) tissue is not. All indications are that homosexual men are fully developed sexually.

2. Lefkowitz (pages 278-279) offers an additional indication that high masculinity is correlated with the violent abuse of women: A psychologist who studied 24 documented cases of reported gang rape on college campuses from 1981 to 1991 found that groups of football and basketball players were more likely to be involved. Does this tendency derive from their genetically-endowed hypermasculinity, or does their aggressiveness result from their group solidarity?

Additional studies relating low-masculinity to marital happiness may be found in Bradbury, Peterson et al., and Gravitz; see References for complete citations.

3. Most of the "worriers" were self-referred, but 42 percent of the homosexuals were sent to the university clinic by dormitory proctors or by the university police for "disorderly behavior." (Please note: this study was reported back in 1965.)

4. This summary interprets, in non-clinical language, group differences in performance on the MMPI (Minnesota Multiphasic Psychological Inventory) : homosexuals scored higher on the Psychopathic Deviate Scale, and worriers scored higher on the Social Introversion Scale.

5. Ratings based on an examination of clinical records. A limited check showed "a high degree of interjudge reliability" (Bratten and Darling, page 283).

6. Kimmel (1996) gives the misleading impression that Terman's 1936 M-F Test was an important instrument for conveying a "social construction" of masculinity. In fact, this test–60 years old at the time of Kimmel's publication-- is of so little interest to the present generation of psychologists, it has not been listed in the standard index of mental tests, *Buros Mental Measurements Yearbook*, since 1953, and is not even mentioned in recent textbooks on mental measurement.

7. The author envisions research *programs*, rather than a single research program. Let different groups compete and collaborate, and replicate each other's findings.

8. Each raw score would be *weighted* by its known power to distinguish between gay and straight groups, to give the total score a maximum of predictive power.

9. An ideal setting for this study would be a municipal college that draws upon students living in their home town, in which a substantial number will continue to reside after graduation.
Here we are calling for a *longitudinal study*: following up of college students, studying their development into adulthood and maturity, a plan that fulfills

Terman's advice that "the proper unit of psychological study is the human life-span." But this research strategy sharply conflicts with the typical doctoral research strategy, which is to design a research project that will not delay awarding the coveted Ph.D. Back in 1936, Sheldon lamented this harsh reality:

> [Sheldon called for] carefully and systematically [collected] observations through a long period of years. . . . [He decried] the sort of research in which you set up an apparatus in October, make observations in November, crank a Monroe calculating machine [the computer of his day] from December until April, write it up as a thesis in May, and either graduate or publish in June. This is not psychology. . . . It is a sort of transitional mongrel offspring of science, born of a questionable three-cornered marriage between physiology, physics, and statistics." (1936, page 167 fn.)

Marquis addressed this problem in his 1948 APA presidential address (page 432), suggesting that more doctoral research be part of a long-term, "integrated series of research activities."

27 From Harem Chief Family Man

Homosexuality as a By-Product of the De-Dimorphism of the Species

We have now reached the end of our examination of a wide range of evidence—clinical, experimental, anthropological, survey, journalistic, and autobiographical. Twenty-six chapters have been dedicated to building a broad acquaintance with what is known about male homosexuals: who they are, what they do, what they want, what they fantasize, what they have in common, and how they differ among themselves. Our subject is complex and multifaceted. We have examined its proudest manifestations, and have also looked at its tawdry underside. It has not been an easy task to present a survey that is both comprehensive and balanced, but this is neither the first nor last book on this subject. If some important aspect of male homosexuality has been either overlooked or overemphasized, fair-minded investigators, scholars, observers, and homosexual men themselves can correct or enrich the record.

Our discussion has not been limited to ordinary observation of homosexual men. We have also examined laboratory findings and other scientific knowledge that can contribute to a theory that can help us understand the origin and dynamics of male homosexuality. The test of a good theory is that it is consistent with most (if not all) of the evidence, both natural and experimental, and that it points the way to learning more about the phenomenon. Additionally, a good theory of male homosexuality will fit in with the dominant theory of the life sciences, *evolutionary theory*,[1] rather than stand out as an exception to it.

A good theory will solve the puzzle of how male homosexuality evolved in a biological world that favored those creatures that were most likely to succeed in reproducing their kind. In this final chapter, we will spell out our by-product theory as clearly as we can, and review the evidence that supports it.

Homosexual behavior is stamped into the historical records of ancient cultures, and has been observed by travelers and anthropologists in many societies, both traditional and modern. Among the many controlled studies we have reported, those of Richard Green, and Bailey and Pillard most clearly suggest the presence of a significant genetic component underlying the male homosexual habit. But to fully account for homosexual behavior, we will have to understand the interaction between both hereditary and environmental forces upon the individual.

> Both environment and genetic endowment make a contribution
> to nearly every trait.—*Ernst Mayr*

In this chapter, we will offer a theory that accounts for the genetic component.

Clinicians have identified a number of environmental influences that may facilitate or interfere with development of the homosexual option. Appendix 3 summarizes how Fenichel, Hatterer and others would catalogue various environmental factors that promote a homosexual orientation.

E.O. Wilson's altruism theory

In 1975 (*The New York Times Magazine* of October 12), sociobiologist E.O. Wilson offered a theory that homosexuality has survived because it is linked with genes that promote altruistic behavior. While homosexuals do not themselves reproduce, Wilson reasoned, *if* they are genetically predisposed to be especially helpful to their kin, homosexuals would thus contribute to the survival of their group. *If* "homosexuality genes" are truly linked with "altruism genes," homosexuality might indeed have survival value for the species as a whole. During the 25-plus years since the article appeared, Wilson's altruism theory has gained no empirical support, and has drawn a number of skeptical and even jocular commentaries from his scientific peers.[2]

A by-product theory of male homosexuality

In our search for a genetic component of homosexuality, we too begin by asking: How did "gay genes" get into the chromosomes of *Homo sapiens?* Our answer to this question takes us back about eight million years, when a gradual climate change cooled down and began to dry out some of Africa's tropical rain forests. Eventually, the shrunken forests were surrounded by grasslands dotted with trees (tree savannas) and stocked with a variety of animals including carnivores as well as small and large grass-eating creatures. Apes had become well-adapted to moving from tree to tree in unbroken tropical forests. Now, an environmental change was creating tree-dotted grasslands. Here was an environment in which ape-like creatures could break out of the forest if they could acquire a taste for animal protein, and thus free themselves from complete dependence on forest foods (leaves, fruits, roots, tubers, etc.).

It is a principle of biology that wherever there exists a potential source of food, nature will evolve some creature who can eat it. Natural selection gradually evolved several new species of apes that were both tree-dwellers and ground walkers, not herbivores but omnivores. Apes that made this shift from an herbivorous to an omnivorous diet had an enormous advantage over those that didn't. Herbivores are tied to the ecological niche that provides their sustenance. Omnivores are free to roam, in search of animal protein of whatever kind. They probably first developed a taste for little things such as bugs and worms and grubs, eggs and hatchlings, lizards and small mammals. Chasing, trapping, wounding and killing large herbivores would probably come a few million years later, as hunting became the group activity of weapons-makers. Free to travel, the omnivorous hominid was destined to eventually cover the earth as no other creature does.

The emergence of bipedalism. About eight million years ago, man's ancestors made a gradual transition from knuckle-walking, like present-day gorillas, to true bipedalism.[3] The fossil evidence indicates that these earliest upright creatures, like other apes, had long arms (and small brains) which made them well-adapted to climbing trees, to escape from carnivores—wild dogs, hyenas, tigers, lions—that also inhabited the grasslands. It sems likely that these early hominids also slept in tree nests for the same reason.

Stephen Jay Gould (1980, page 132) regards bipedalism as an even more spectacular change in human anatomy than brain enlargement, which was to come about two million years later. Bipedalism "requires a fundamental reconstruction of our anatomy, particularly of the foot and pelvis. . . . [I]t represents an anatomical reconstruction outside the general pattern of human evolution." Anatomically, says Gould, the enlargement of the brain was a much easier change in hominid anatomy.

What survival advantages did this "fundamental reconstruction of our anatomy" offer? Did it free the hands for tool-making? No, the earliest upright hominid had too small a brain to suggest that it was a tool-maker, and no stone tools have been found that date as far back as the earliest hominids. The spurt of brain growth (and infantile helplessness) did not come until about two million years later. Meanwhile, paleoanthropologists can only speculate[4] on just what were the survival advantages of bipedalism to the earliest hominids.

Perhaps upright posture made it easy to pick ripe fruits hanging from trees. Creatures that live in the open grasslands are more exposed to the rays of the sun, which would burden them with a greater need for the intake of water. Upright posture (and a head insulated from the sun by a mass of hair) makes the body less exposed to the sun, and also removes the body from heat radiated from the earth. Upright posture makes a creature *look* bigger and therefore less attractive to predators. Upright posture frees the forearms for carrying an infant, or provisions. Upright posture, good vision, and a rotating head give a creature more information about his surroundings than one whose head is in the leaves or high grasses.

Outwitting predators. For whatever reasons, bipedalism emerged and survived for about two million years. Then, five great developments gave a remarkable survival advantage to an upright creature. These five important and interrelated developments are (1) the proliferation of the brain, (2) premature birth, (3) the growth of language, (4) the use of tools, and (5) big-game hunting.

The growth of the brain. Most central of these five developments was the gradual but steady growth of the brain, until it doubled in size as it vastly increased the hominid's intelligence. Brain enlargement could be achieved in part by reducing the thickness of the skull. A gorilla needs a massive skull to anchor its powerful jaw muscles, adapted to tearing, pounding, and grinding rough food. As hands and stone hammers took over these functions, as cooked meat partially replaced rough vegetation, hominids no longer needed large, sharp teeth, massive jaws and powerful jaw muscles. Jaws and teeth could now become smaller, and the cranium needed to be only thick enough to protect a massive brain.

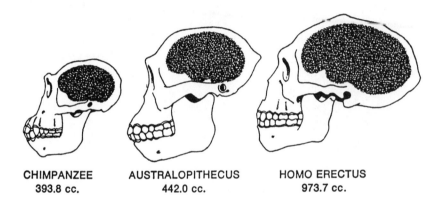

CHIMPANZEE	AUSTRALOPITHECUS	HOMO ERECTUS
393.8 cc.	442.0 cc.	973.7 cc.

Figure 27.1. Average cranial capacities, indicating more than doubling of brain size from Australopithecus to Homo erectus; chimpanzee cranial capacity included for comparison (From Pfeiffer)

Head size could be increased, and the thickness of the skull reduced if the adult head could approximate the proportions of the head at infancy, as Figure 27.2 illustrates. That's just what happened. Compared with other primates, humans are markedly neotenous, not only in head shape, but in other ways as well. As Stephen Jay Gould comments, "[W]e change enough [from birth to adulthood] to produce a notable difference . . . but our alteration is far smaller than that experienced by chimps and other primates" (1980, page 106).

The adult human brain, according to Stephen Jay Gould, weighs, on average, 2.8 pounds, and "to accommodate such a large brain, we have bulbous, balloon-shaped heads unlike those of any other large mammal" (1977a, page 181). Large animals, like elephants and whales, have larger brains than humans, but these creatures need large brains to coordinate their bodily movements. Gould estimates what would be the expected brain size for an average mammal of our body weight, concluding that man is indeed "the brainiest mammal by far." According to Gould, "No other species lies as far above the expected brain size for average mammals as we do" (*ibid.*, page 183).

The logic of evolution raises the question, What was happening in the hominids' environment that now gave intelligence such survival value? A surprisingly simple answer, supported by geological evidence, is that as the climate continued to get drier, trees virtually disappeared and were replaced by bush.

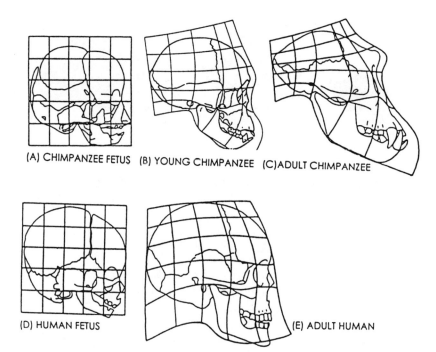

Figure 27.2. Human neoteny, defined as "the existence of juvenile features in an adult animal."
The fetal skull of a chimpanzee (A) and human (D) are rather alike. As it grows into adulthood (C), the chimpanzee skull develops a massive jaw, large teeth, and a thicker skull, to anchor its powerful jaw muscles. Compared with the adult chimpanzee, the adult human (E) is much more like the skull of a very young chimpanzee (B). Human neoteny is marked by a smaller lower jaw, which allows for a thinner skull, permitting a greater brain capacity without increasing head size. (From Starck and Kummer, 1962.)

When hominids could no longer climb into a nearby tree to escape predators, they became meat for the meat-eaters of the grasslands, except for those who were clever enough to stay alive and pass on this trait to a new generation.

With no trees to climb into when danger threatened, hominids now had to *outwit* predators, who were superior to them in size, speed, strength, and ferocity. How did they outwit them? Perhaps by banding together, by stationing lookouts, by issuing warnings, by throwing stones, by making noise, by building shelters and hiding in them, or by using fire[5] to scare predators away.

Without trees to climb into, hominids had to *live by their wits*. Adaptation to a dangerous environment gave a survival advantage to those who were best equipped, genetically, to live by their wits. Every tiny increment of brain power helped their survival and reproductive success. Thanks to the challenge of survival in a treeless, predator-filled environment, the human brain has developed into an organ that has been described as "the most marvelous and mysterious object in the whole universe."[6]

Brain power, so useful for outwitting one's enemies and staying alive, could be put to other important uses that led to still further increases in brain power. As hominids banded together for defense, they tended more and more to live in groups, to become social animals. Combined with close vision and good eye-hand coordination, inherited from their arboreal past, intelligence now expressed itself in curiosity and close observation, in making and using the tools that made early man a hunter and a builder. Intelligence and group living gave rise to communication: the expression of feelings, commands, and sharing information, and fostered the further development of the brain power that is the basis for the ability to learn and use language. By these steps, the hominid brain got bigger and bigger until it became *too big*.

Too big for what? Eventually the hominid brain became too big for the fetus safely to pass through its mother's birth canal. Childbirth became so dangerous, it threatened the life of both mother and child.[7] Nature evolved two strategies for dealing with this crises.

The big momma. According to Richard Leackey,[8] the fossil remains of *A. afarensis*, an early upright hominid, indicate that adult males were twice as large as females. To attain a wider birth canal, hominid females gradually became bigger in general, until at adulthood they were almost as big as males. A taller, bigger female now had a somewhat more ample birth canal, which enabled her to give birth to offspring with a larger head. A larger head at birth gives the infant a head start at becoming the large-brained creature that would, for better or for worse, eventually dominate the planet. "Big momma" could carry more stored fat, to nourish a helpless "fetal" creature born with enormous nutritional demands.

Physiologically, the growing infant's brain is a fantastic consumer of nutrition because it must be built so rapidly. Both before and after birth, the infant depends on its mother for nutrition, and the larger her body, the greater the reserves to draw upon (Krantz, page 103).

Figure 27.3. "Big Momma"

A limestone figure about 25,000 years old, found in Austria. Similarly rotund female figures from 22,000 to 30,000 years old- carved in ivory or limestone, or modelled in clay and fired—have been found in various parts of Europe.

Reproduced from Caird, page 156.

Fatty tissue (which most males are not so generously endowed with) not only serves as a nutritional reserve for her infant. Strategically localized fat also gives the adult female full breasts and wide hips, "advertising" her maternal potential.[9]

"Premature birth" reshapes hominid society

Birth occurs nine months after conception not because after nine months of development the fetus is ready to survive outside the womb, but rather because at that stage of growth, though its brain is still undeveloped, its head is still small enough to barely pass through its mother's birth canal.[10] Humans at birth are "extrauterine embryos," (Gould 1977b, page 369), uttterly helpless, compared with other newborn simians. The human brain is programmed for rapid growth and development after birth, to fulfill its vast potential for learning.

Weisfeld (page 81) contrasts the competence of simian infants, which can grasp their mother's fur with hands and feet, with human infants, which must be "be carried for many months by the mother. . . . Simian mothers can forage even in trees in relative freedom [but] hominid women's difficulty in foraging may have increased the advantage of establishing pair bonds with males who furnished meat and protection."

What kind of an infant is a creature born with only enough reflexes to keep it alive—sucking, coughing, smiling, crying, regurgitating, and defecating—but with this enormous potential for learning a language and adopting a culture? A human newborn born *prematurely*, compared with other apes, is still *truly fetal.* Its finger bones are still cartilaginous. It continues to grow at a fetal rate. It is literally helpless and completely dependent on its mother. (It has been wrongly believed that infantile helplessness was an "effect of civilization." Evolutionary theory suggests that infantile helplessness is an intrinsic part of the process that humanized the hominid.) *If they were to survive their premature birth, a fetal hominid infant needed the constant care of its mother, who in turn needed a close-bonded mate.* That was nature's bargain for evolving a species with a brain so big that its infants *had* to be born prematurely.

The bigger brain also becomes a somewhat different kind of brain—a brain shaped less by instinct and more by a greatly enlarged capacity for learning in general, and for learning a language[11] in particular. Through this gift for maniplating words and symbols, humans could develop and adopt a culture, a body of experience that could be passed on from generation to generation. Learning a language and adopting a culture takes many years. Individuals whose growth rate was systematically *retarded* therefore had a survival advantage. A protracted childhood, followed by *adolescence* (a biological fact, not a cultural invention), further favored parents predisposed to be close-bonded and nurturing.

As members of a family, a society, and a culture, humans could now manipulate the environment as no other creature ever had, and live under a wide range of environmental conditions—from arctic to tropical, from deserts to rainforests—a degree of adaptation attained by no other creature.

A brain wired for learning

Throughout the animal kingdom, creatures are born with ready-made habits: instincts. Their brains are pre-programmed in ways that enable an inexperienced creature to grasp hold of its mother, to distinguish between friend and foe, to feed themselves, to mate, and to care for offspring. A brain pre-programmed to survive and reproduce *in a specific environment* is a marvel of nature. Now nature was evolving a brain that also had an enormous capacity for learning from direct experience and thus adapting to a wide range of environments. Through language, humans could be adopted into a *culture*, and thus profit from the experience of earlier generations. This potential has a powerful survival advantage over a mainly pre-programmed brain, however beautifully it might be adapted to a particular environment.

The human brain is organized for language learning. Language is important for generating, conveying and preserving information, but that is not its only social function. Competition and solitary activity require no use of language. Cooperation and group activity, however, are mediated through language: commands, instructions, threats, censure, entreaty, discussion, negotiation, decision and so on. Language also mediates emotional expression: affection, praise, lust, jealousy, anger and the like. There are of course nonverbal ways to communicate these feelings and attitudes, but language certainly amplifies and sharpens these messages, either fostering social cohesiveness or maintaining social distance. Language enables the individual to deal not only with the present, but also with past, future, and even with imaginary or hypothetical events, which gives birth to mythology, ethics, and religion.

A "premature" infant needs close-bonded parents

A female encumbered with a "premature" infant is more likely to survive if, in turn, it is the member of a close-bonded[12] pair than if it lived on the fringe of a band of males. A helpless infant is more likely to survive if its two parents are closely bonded, if they are creatures that were adapted to fulfill complementary gender roles, if they are creatures that need each other, nurture each other, protect each other, identify with each other, perhaps love each other.

To shape the family into an enduring, cohesive social unit, the sex drive became relatively continuous rather than occasional.[13] Adult hominids were increasingly programmed to prefer a permanent mate rather than copulate with any available receptive female who happens to be ovulating at that time. Signs of ovulation, so prominent in the females of other species of primates, became virtually invisible in the human female, so that ovulation does not make females more attractive to other males. (This topic, introduced in chapter 3, is worth recalling here, in this context.)

Male and female become more alike

Fossils tell us about the *physical* difference between males and females, but give us no direct information about such important facts as the *temperamental* differences between the sexes, or about the *social organization* of the species. Our conjectures about these important facts are guided by what we can observe of prehistoric camp sites, of the life of isolated human cultures that seem to be not too different from what we conjecture was the life of prehistoric man, and of the behavior of chimpanzees, our closest primate relatives, whose gender dimophism is similar to our own.

The average male *A. afarenesis* was almost *twice as heavy* as the female of the species, and a similar difference obtains for the present-day gorilla. In both species, males are not only larger but their teeth are also more menacing: projecting canines and disproportionately large incisors describe the dentition of male afarensis fossils (Krantz, page 92), as well as present-day gorillas.

This degree of gender difference in physique fits a species for which sexual activity is fiercely competitive. We can observe that mature male gorillas fight over the possession of a harem of females, and the same was probably true of A. afarenesis. The meanest, biggest, most ferocious fighter wins, and deposits his genetic advantage into a receptive female. Gender dimorphism made evolutionary sense, writes Krantz (page 102), "when males [were] selected for fighting strength and females [were] selected for reproductive efficiency on limited food resources."

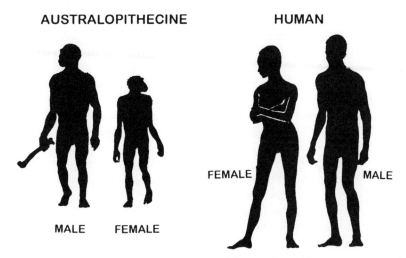

AUSTRALOPITHECINE   **HUMAN**

MALE   FEMALE

FEMALE   MALE

Figure 27.4. Gender differences in size of hominids and humans compared.

In Caird (page 101), this figure is accompanied by the following paragraph: "The difference in size between males and females is much greater in early hominids than in modern humans. . . . For the australopithecines, the [social] system may have been like that of chimpanzees, with a core of related males defending a territory, and sexually mature females migrating in from other groups. The males compete with each other for access, but do not form long-term bonds with them. Human social systems vary enormously, but they are characterized by long-term bonding between males and females, and less overt sexual competition between males."

"The harem was ruled by one dominant chief and surrounded by idle male losers." As dominance gave way to leadership and teamwork, competition gave way to cooperation, and the harem very gradually metamorphosed into a society of paired adults. *A. afarensis* had paid a price for his size and ferocity, and when these traits were no longer a biological advantage, male hominids very gradually became not much bigger than females, and also *more similar to females in temperament.*

In very dimorphic modern species, such as the gorilla and baboon, males, at maturity are twice as big as females, though there may be rather little size difference between males and females while they are growing up. Females reach sexual maturity and stop growing at an earlier age, as males *continue* to grow for several years. When males finally do reach maturity, after their "prolonged adolescence," they are significantly larger, stronger and more ferocious than the females. To males, the cost of this dimorphism is a longer adolescence, a shorter adult life, and the sizeable energy needs of a creature who must always be ready to fight for his troop of females. When this cost no longer served an evolutionary advantage, it was gradually phased out.

How is a male hominid—ferocious, competitive, towering—transformed into a "team player," only moderately bigger than his close-bonded partner? Natural selection takes advantage of those *chance genetic variations,* as a species adopts into its gene pool those irregularites or "errors" (what geneticists call mutations) that just happen to have survival-value. (It takes millennia for this process to work. Most mutations result in physical defects that never survive gestation.) The theory presented here proposes that ferocious, competitive males were transformed both in physique and temperament as many, many small mutations (genetic factors regulating physique-and-brain-masculinization) gradually narrowed the physical and temperamental differences between males and females. Very gradually, male and female overlapped more and more in both physique and temperament. As hominid became human, we could say that males became more like their female partners, significantly less masculinized.

We are now considering the gradual reduction of male-female differences both in body weight and temperament. This process would seem to have been accomplished by both a gradual decrease in adult male size and a gradual increase in adult female size, until the average male was only slightly bigger than his mate.

> By all evidence, size dimorphism began its reduction with the larger-brained pithecanthropines where infant head sizes caused selection for larger females (Krantz, page 102). [In other words, larger females had proportionately larger birth canals, and could therefore give birth to bigger-brained infants. This evolutionary advantage of larger females reduced hominid sexual dimorphism.]

Male and female gorillas are probably as different in temperament as they are in physique, and the same was likely true for male and female *A. afarensis.* When it was no longer adaptive for the hominid to have an overpowering physique, it no longer needed the ferocious temperament of a male twice as large as the female of the species. Now it would be adaptive for nature to evolve a far less ferocious male temperament, a low-masculine temperament that could even *overlap* the modal female temperament, as Figure 27.6 symbolizes.[14]

Many thousands of years elapsed in the transition from harem to tribe and, in all likelihood, intermediate forms of social organization emerged. We see a possible intermediate form in the social behavior of present-day chimpanzees, a species in which gender dimorphism is about the same as in humans. [15] *What is characteristic of chimpanzee society is that male group bonding is much more evident and durable than male-female pairing.* Adult males work and play and defend their tribe together, and sometimes compete for receptive females who wander into the tribe.

Status minimizes social conflict

Unbridled fighting over sexual privilege would reduce the group's potential for reproduction and survival. Nature's way of reducing internal strife, making more energy available for productive group activities (such as hunting and protecting the tribe), and thus promoting survival, is to evolve in each member of the group a sense of its *status* (its position of power and privilege inside the group), and a tendency for each individual to act accordingly. Group productivity and survival are favored when each member seems to "know where it belongs" in a hierarchy of privilege. Then, each member of the group exhibits the *role behavior* matching his status, acts according to his rank. Thus, physical conflict is minimized. Higher status is probably won by members who are stronger, taller, more able, and more intelligent. (In chapter 3, we considered Diamond's conjecture that the large penis was evolved as a display organ, which also contributed to its owner's status.)

Now members of the adult male group could copulate with available females, with a minimum of fighting. (When a group of young men cooperatively share the same available women they re-enact, in a sense, the behavior of their hominid ancestors.) Together, mature males formed hunting parties and also protected their colony, directed by their leader: the member of their group with top status.

Man the social animal

Man's ancestors were genetically predisposed to act as a group. And they also learned from direct experience that "their instincts were right," that group action was far more effective than individual action, both in hunting and in the protection of their colony. Before cooperation became a moral value, cooperation was adopted for its survival value.

As competition became less important, physical prowess and ferocity of temperament also became less important. Whereas the more ferocious male hominids had once monopolized mature females, now all males were "team players" who hunted together, defended their territory together, played together (no doubt), and increasingly tended to pair off into more-or-less permanent male-and-female partnerships. Now mothers more effectively kept helpless infants alive while they also gathered edibles, and while fathers protected and supported their encumbered mates.

Figure 27.5. The knuckle-walker versus the runner: a comparison of ape and human locomotion. Note that only a human can carry something (e.g., a weapon, provisions) while walking or running.
(From Ape Into Man, by Washburn and Moore)

Man the hunter[16]

Leadership, teamwork, strategizing, physical endurance, tool-making skills, and fulfillment of one's role as a provider; all are put into practice in the hunt. Man the hunter often only wounded his prey, and had to outrun it until his prey was exhausted or bled to death. Unlike the knuckle-walking ape, *man is a runner*, whose legs are 10 to 12 inches longer than the ape's. *And man's upright posture frees his arms to carry his weapons or provisions as he runs.*

Big game hunting was necessarily a group activity, and communication became a survival skill. Each member of the group played a specialized role: strategist, mediator, scout, advance runner, spear maker, spear thrower, butcher. Washburn, leading proponent of the "man the hunter" theme, argued (page ??):

It is difficult to imagine the killing of creatures such as cave

bears, mastodons [and] mammoths . . . without highly coordinated, cooperative action among males. . . . From a biological point
of view, the development of [big game hunting] would have
been paralleled by selection for an ability to plan and cooperate
(or reduction of rage).

Prehistoric boneyards show that hominids killed game far too big to carry to
the home base unless the carcass was cut up into pieces individuals could carry
as they ran to the tribal base; ran, to avoid predators attracted to the sight and
odor of flesh and blood. Big-game hunting required that hominids be skilled in
making and using stone tools: not only spears for killing, but knives and cleavers
for butchering.

Nature evolves the caring husband and father

The maternal instinct is well implanted throughout the animal kingdom, but
a sense of paternity is a comparative rarity. Adult male humans, however, seem
to be genetically programmed to invest time and energy in children, "although
the amount of time and energy they spend varies greatly between cultures and
families," as Potts and Short note (page 102). If the survival of a truly helpless
infant is favored by a close-bonded mother and father, natural selection would
make the parenting couple increasingly alike, temperamentally as well as physically, as Figure 27.6 illustrates. Mates who regard each other as equals are more
likely to empathize with each other and identify with each other, stay together
and successfully raise a new generation of hominids.

If males could become temperamentally as well as physically low-masculinized to a degree, empathy and identification would be more easily achieved. To
the extent that temperament is genetically influenced (and there is some evidence
that it is),[17] natural selection would endow males with genetic predispositions that
sharply reduced the masculinization of their temperament as well as their
physique. A less masculinized temperament would make the male more nurturant, more altruistic (as E.O. Wilson correctly intuited), more sensitive to the
needs of others.

Infantile helplessness and female mate selection

Tanner and Zihlman (page 594) report that *"in 19 copulations observed
among free-ranging, nonprovisioned chimpanzees, 14 were initiated by females."*
The authors conjecture that the females favored mates who showed a good
potential as close-bound mates and fathers:

Mothers chose to copulate most frequently with these compara-
tively sociable, less disruptive, [more] sharing males—with

males more like themselves. . . . Females preferred to associate and have sex with [friendly] males . . . rather than with those who were . . . a danger to themselves or offspring (*ibid*, page 606).

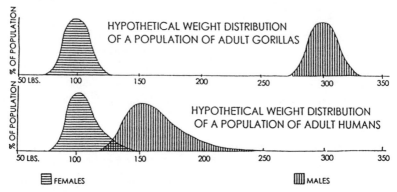

Figure 27.6. Weight norms (hypothetical) of modern adult gorillas and humans compared

Humans are not descended from gorillas, but the two species are compared here to dramatize the difference between a species that is highly dimorphic with one that is not. Anthropologist Michael A. Little advises that on a worldwide basis, adult human males average about 130 lbs. in weight, while females average about 105 lbs.

The phenomenon of *female mate selection*, was introduced in Chapter 3. Female mate selection does not seem to be guided entirely by intelligence or conscious choice. (For example, naturalists report that during the mating season, female crabs are attracted to *younger* males, recognizable by the fact that their shells have a glossier texture.)

Throughout the animal world, females tend to select those mates which will give their offspring a genetic advantage, and protect the mother and her offspring. At an evolutionary stage in which the primary problem of survival is protection of the nesting site and its occupants, the female would be attracted to a mate who was big and menacing, and these would be the genetic characteristics he transmitted to his offspring. But at a later stage of evolution, when mothers were encumbered by "postnatal embryos," it seems more than likely that females would now recognize and be attracted to males who exhibited a *low-masculinized temperament*. We conjecture that, guided by both instinct and intelligence, the receptive female hominid would seek a mate who exhibited the traits of a devoted partner and father: one who exhibited *proto-human traits*, a male who was intelligent, gentle, patient, and caring.

Perhaps the more intelligent females favored males who were not only socia-ble and intelligent but were also *interesting*, males who were playful, humorous, warm, and imaginative. Human courtship must have had its prehistoric antecedents, and those antecedents gave a reproductive advantage to males who were the best entertainers: singers, dancers, storytellers. This is a scenario that would justify the phrase of the anthropology professor who said:

"Nice guys finish *first*"

The scenario presented here offers a radical correction to the image of "cave-man courtship" popularized by cartoons like the one shown here, and suggests that female mate selection was a powerful factor in humanizing our hominid ancestors.

Mutations gentle the male temperament

What is the genetic mechanism by which new traits, like male gentleness, are introduced into the DNA? Mutations are the deus ex machina of evolution. Among nature's "fortunate mistakes" are those genetic flaws that reduced the dimorphism of the male physique, and gentled the male temperament, predis-posing the male to be less ferocious and more nurturing, more sociable and intu-itive, "kinder and gentler," to use a phrase popularized by a former U.S. presi-dent.

Masculinization, like height and weight, is probably governed by a large number of genes rather than by a single gene. Embryological knowledge makes it clear that without the intervention of Y-chromosome genes, *every fertilized egg would develop into a female.* That is to say, every male begins life as a proto-female. The fact that every male goes through life with a pair of nipples (and other vestigial female organs, hidden inside the body[18]) that serve no biological function,[19] is a reminder of the fact that *the human body plan is basically female.* Embryologists describe in considerable detail how genes that reside in the Y-chromosome convert a proto-female embryo into a male, a process that was briefly sketched out in chapter 7.

Why did nature tone down those "masculinization genes" that once made male hominids almost twice as big as the female of the species, and that also gave males a ferocious temperament to match their huge physique? Our theory proposes that this occurred to *reshape the species*[20] from societies of harems and harem chiefs to tribes and families of (at least semi-permanently) close-bonded couples, from fiercely competitive troops to more cooperative (and hence more productive) societies. This radical transformation proceeded over the millennia, by tiny and gradual steps. The evolutionary process does not "plan ahead," does not orient the species toward fulfillment of some remote goal. Evolution requires that each tiny increment of change make its own contribution to survival.

The low-masculinized male brain

The production of testosterone, which is triggered by Y-chromosome genes, bathes the fetus as a whole and normally masculinizes both brain and sex organs. What kind of mutations would selectively moderate masculinization of the brain, but would *not* reduce masculinization of the sex organs of the male fetus? Genetic mutations might make *only brain tissue* resistant to the influence of testosterone, while the sex organs do become fully masculinized. This genetic trait would be based on not one but many genes that render only brain tissue resistant to masculinization to a variable degree, spanning a broad gradient from very moderately resistant to highly resistant to masculinization.

Is a low-masculinized male brain the result of unpredictable factors like chance mutations, or special conditions of the prenatal environment? Or is occasional low masculinization the expression of well-established genetic factors? Weisfeld (page 245) argues that because male homosexuality is a relatively stable and widespread trait in most human societies, traditional and modern, it seems to be tied to some "evolutionarily stable [factor] . . . with some adaptive value . . . . . "

Perhaps moderate low-masculinization makes the mature male a better husband and father than a highly masculinized male, who might be inclined to react to an annoying mate by crippling her, or react to an annoying infant by shaking it to death. A low-masculinized male may share a larger portion of his mate's "maternal instincts," bonding more closely with her, thanks to shared temperamental characteristics.

The curve of variation

In every population, there is for most traits a *curve of variation*. Human males vary in all sorts of traits—height, weight, body build, temperament, and intelligence—not just the degree to which their brains are masculinized. At one end of the curve are those males whose brains are scarcely masculinized at all. They therefore share much of the temperament, feelings and interests of females. Their low-masculinized brain make them the berdaches, homosexual males, "worriers " and other gentle but hetrosexual males of the world.[21]

This genetic tendency for brain tissue to resist full masculinization therefore significantly favors the survival of the species, even though this tendency occasionally produces a male who, because his is an unusually low-masculinized brain, may develop personality traits that lead him not to reproduce at all. This theory—that a genetic tendency toward low masculinization actually favors survival, though it occasionally predisposes to either gender-discordance or homosexuality—is offered here as an alternative to the theory that there are "gay genes."[22]

Low-masculinization as the by-product of a moderated male norm

Did nature want to create populations of berdaches, gender-discordant boys, and gay men? No: brain low-masculinization is a *by-product* of reduced dimorphism, just as there are chance by-products of other evolutionary processes. For example, by-products of man's upright posture are back, hip, and knee problems. Sickle-cell anemia is the by-product of a genetic resistance to malaria.

A few gender-discordant boys may also *look* more girlish than boyish. Low-masculinization of the physique probably does not predispose to homosexuality as much as low-masculinization of the brain. It is this *invisible low masculinization* that predisposes the androgynous male to experience the temperament, feelings, and other innate predispositions of females. So strongly may this bias be felt that he identifies more easily, more naturally, with females than with males.

Our theory holds that the gender-discordant boy has a low-masculinized brain, which accounts for his gender-atypical temperament and interests. He likes to help mother, and plays with girls because he is predisposed to like to do the things that mother and little girls do. Many an adult homosexual does *not* recall having had an outwardly effeminate manner or appearance, but *does* recall that, as a child, his *feelings* were more sensitive and emotional most boys, and his interests were more domestic and artistic. While most boys were engaging in rough-and-tumble play, physical combat, team activity, and competitive sports, what came naturally to pre-homosexual boys was indoor play, reading, writing, conversation, musical or other artistic[23] activities.

A radical[24] reduction of gender dimorphism makes the human male a better-adapted parent of big-brained infants that must be born "premature" to pass through its mother's birth canal. A pair-bonding male does not need the ferocity to defend a harem, and a reduction in masculinization also enables him to reach adulthood earlier.

A prediction that comes close to the truth

Paradoxically, de-dimorphism has a survival advantage for the *species* despite the fact that it occasionally produces a male whose brain is so low-masculinized that he is unlikely to reproduce at all.[25] The fact that low-masculinization, the genetic basis for homosexuality, is so closely associated with a genetic factor that humanizes the human male, makes a 1977 statement by Pillard (page 67) come close to the truth:

> I'm confident that biological knowledge will prove . . . [that same-sex desire is] [26] a valuable trait, selected by evolution precisely because it contributes some quality that was useful, perhaps even essential, to the sudden ascendancy of human beings among all primates.

The best evidence of a genetic component also indicates that homosexuality is *only partially genetic*, that there must also be environmental factors at play here. Exactly what are the environmental factors that trigger homosexual predispositions? John Money (1988, page 207) conjectures that "something happens" in late infancy or early childhood that triggers a behavioral tendency "phyletically programmed into the nervous system," and effects a kind of developmental learning that, like imprinting,[27] becomes a lifelong character trait (i.e., is highly resistant to extinction).

The widest array of evidence on environmental influences on sexual orientation points to that portion of the social environment we could call *family life*: interaction with parents and siblings. Clinical evidence, survey findings, and experimental studies all point to the significance of the family as a learning environment that shapes attitudes of all sorts, including sexual orientation. Many studies (covering thousands of cases) indicate that homosexuality is more likely to occur in males who are later-born. These studies, summarized by Sulloway and discussed in chapter 21 (in the paragraph headed *The Later-borns*), call attention to the importance of the individual's *position* in his social environment, a basic concept of gestalt psychology. The birth-order emphasis on sibling relations complements the psychoanalytic emphasis on parent-child relations. Together, these two approaches to the study of human development emphasize the importance of the family setting.

[Based on his study of discordant monozygotic twins, Pillard (1979, page 64) suggests, however, that *something beyond* parent-child relations (*e.g.*, "one takes piano lessons, the other becomes a Boy Scout") leads one twin to trigger his homosexual potential, while the other does not.]

The LMB puzzle

The psychoanalytic literature has stressed the pre-homosexual boy's identification with his mother, fostered by mother's close-binding (perhaps seductive) behavior. But in her 1983 publication, the British psychoanalyst Elizabeth R. Moberly argued that homosexual behavior stems not from attachment to the boy's mother, but from an alienation from his father: "disidentification with the father," to use Moberly's language (page 43). Homosexuality is not the problem, says Moberly. *It is the striving for a solution*, an attempt to overcome a *felt* masculine deficit. That is the problem. The longing for masculine love is the longing to become fully masculine" (Moberly, page 39).

Like other therapists, Moberly seemed to assume that homosexuality is based *entirely* on experience. Moberly insisted that a deficit in masculine identification stems from a defect or disturbance of the father-son relationship: that father was distant, cold, detached, neglectful, or altogether absent. "[I]t is not the mother-son bond that is the problem, but the absence of the father-son bond" (Moberly, page 47). What looks to a therapist like the patient's mother-fixation may result from his mother's attempt to fill the gap created by the absence of a normal father-son bond (*ibid*, page 45).

If there is a genetic factor (brain low-masculinzation) at work here, the androgynous boy will identify more readily, more naturally, with mother, and have an inherent difficulty in identifying with his father. This may in fact be the basis for what Moberly calls the boy's "disidentification." The gender-discordant boy likes to do the things that mother does, and dislikes doing the things that father does. Father reacts with alarm, distancing himself from a son who fails so utterly to fulfill the father's hopes for a son who will embody and perpetuate what the father regards as manly virtues. In his 1989 book, Dr. Richard Isay, America's first openly gay psychoanalyst, advanced this argument (without acknowledging Moberly's 1983 publication) that maternal over-protection may be secondary to the paternal rejection of a gender-discordant boy.

Although psychoanalytic treatment focuses on *experience*, Freud, in his early papers, conjectured that there were some sort of constitutional factors at work in the making of a homosexual, and that this probably accounted for the very limited success psychoanalysts were achieving in working with homosexual patients who expressed the strong desire to change. The tone of Freud's now-famous letter to an American mother reflects his recognition of this stubborn reality.

The fate of gender-discordant boys does not seem to be fixed by genetic factors *entirely*. What about that substantial minority of "sissy boys" in Richard Green's 1987 study, and the monozygotic twin brothers of gay men in the 1991 Bailey-Pillard and the 1995 Bailey-Martin studies, who did not become homosexual adults?

For both theoretical and practical reasons, it is important to know why some men grow up to be heterosexual despite the fact that statistically, they would be as likely to become homosexual. These heterosexual adult men—the one-time "sissy-boys" and discordant twins—might be called "the forgotten men" of psychological research. Do those temperamentally low-masculine men whose experience does *not* trigger their homosexual tendencies lead miserable, marginal, unfulfilled existences? Or do some of them experience fully heterosexual lives like men in general? Perhaps their low-masculinized brain predisposes them to live even more creative, spiritually richer, more compassionate, *more fully human* lives than the more typical "average male." From both a theoretical and practical standpoint, these questions are eminently worth answering.

A new generation of research workers and gender-discordant boys will replicate and extend both Green's and the Bailey-Pillard findings. A new generation of researchers will master and advance a growing body of clinical and research knowledge, to disentangle fact from fiction, and identify the critical factors that, at specified moments, interact with constitutional factors to determine whether a temperamentally androgynous male does or does not become a gay man. And if he does not, what happens to him? A new generation of therapists and therapy researchers will rise to the challenge of developing research-based programs for helping the gender-atypical boy realize his full potential, and for evolving humane and effective modes of reorientation therapy.

NOTES TO CHAPTER 27

1. Ernst Mayr might rewrite this sentence to read: "A good theory of male homosexuality will fit in with the dominant *principle* of the life sciences, the *evolutionary process*, rather than stand out as an exception to it." According to Mayr (page 275), "Evolution is not merely an idea, a theory, or a concept, but the name of a process in nature, the occurrence of which can be documented by mountains of evidence that nobody has been able to refute. . . . It is now actually misleading to refer to evolution as a theory, considering the massive evidence that has been discovered over the last 140 years documenting its existence. Evolution is no longer a theory, it is simply a fact."

Harvard University professor emeritus and author of over a dozen scholarly books, Ernst Mayr is described by Stephen Jay Gould as "the world's greatest living evolutionary biologist."

2. Wilson presented his theory in his 1975 book, *Sociobiology*, and again in his 1978 book, *On Human Nature*, where he wrote (page 149) : "There is, I wish to suggest, a strong possibility that homosexuality is normal in a biological sense, that it is a distinctive beneficent behavior that evolved as an important element of early human social organization. Homosexuals may be the genetic carriers of some of mankind's rare altruistic impulses." As proof of the "distinct beneficent behavior" of homosexual men, Wilson (page 152) notes that "in western industrial societies, homosexual men score higher than heterosexuals on intelligence tests and are upwardly mobile to an exceptional degree. They select white collar professions disproportionately and regardless of their original socioeconomic status are prone to enter specialties in which they deal directly with other people.

They are more successful on the average within their chosen professions. Finally, apart from the difficulties created by the disapproval of their sexual preferences, homosexuals are considered by others to be generally well adapted in social relationships."

Stephen Jay Gould has commented (1977a, pages 266-267), "There is nothing illogical in [Wilson's] proposal, but it has no facts going for it either. . . ." Gould continued:

> Wilson's intent is admirable; he attempts to affirm the intrinsic
> dignity of a common and much maligned sexual behavior by
> arguing that it is natural for some people. . . . But the strategy is
> a dangerous one, for it backfires if the genetic speculation is
> wrong. . . . Better to stick resolutely to a philosophical position
> on human liberty: what free adults do with each other in their
> own private lives is their business alone. It need not be vindicat-
> ed—and it must not be condemned—by genetic speculation.

In LeVay's 1993 book (page 129), the author makes the skeptical comment on Wilson's theory: "To put it crudely, why do gay men waste so much time cruising each other, time that according to this theory would be better spent baby-sitting their nephews and nieces?"

In his 1994 book, Robert Wright (page 384) asks: "[H]ow many homosexuals spend an inordinate amount of time helping siblings, nephews, and nieces? . . [L]ook at what many of them do spend their time doing: pursuing homosexual union about as ardently as heterosexuals seek heterosexual union. What's the evolutionary logic in that?" Other critics of E.O. Wilson's altruism theory (e.g., Small, page 187) point out that even in societies untouched by modernism, homosexual men are *not* noticeably more altruistic than others.

Probably the most devastating critic of Wilson's "kin-selection hypothesis" is his Harvard University colleague Richard C. Lewontin, evolutionary geneticist and professor of biology and zoology. Lewontin *et al*. point out (page 261) that Wilson offers "no evidence. . . that homosexuals really do (or did in the human evolutionary past) increase the reproductive rates of their sisters and brothers. . . . The story has been manufactured out of whole cloth."

There is a basic truth in Wilson's association of altruism with homosexuality, one that does not at all require his "kin-selection theory." Altruism may be regarded as an aspect of the nurturant, "maternal," feminine temperament, and male homosexuals tend to be temperamentally gender-discordant. The roles of berdaches (as described in chapter 10) do include behaviors that could be labeled altruistic: healing, matchmaking, caring for the sick, and burying the dead. But these "altruistic" roles also flow from two unrelated kinds of cultural influences: (1) berdaches are believed to possess supernatural powers, and (2) berdaches are assigned "leftover" roles—duties that are *unwanted* by other members of society.

3. *Afarensis* is believed to be "the ancestral stock from which all hominid species

evolved. . . ." (Leakey and Lewin, page 115). Recent field research suggests that a terrestrial hominid was evolved a few million years before a portion of the rain-forests were replaced by grasslands. Recent archaeological findings suggest that at the time of *Afarensis*, and since then, there were several species of hominids, and which branch evolved into the human species is not clear.

4. Much of this chapter is necessarily conjectural. We can't be sure about many things concerning man's remote past. We study the direct and indirect evidence, however scanty. We consider the reports of observers of preliterate peoples of modern times (*e.g.*, Sahlins 1959) and study the behavior of man's closest pres-ent-day relatives. Then we fill in the gaps in a way that is consistent with the known facts.

5. Fires are sometimes caused by lightning, and hominids very probably became fire *users* long before they became fire makers. Similarly, they became tool *users* before they became tool makers, adopting rocks as tools for pounding vegetation and breaking open bones and nuts.

6. These words are from a 1929 lecture by Henry Fairfield Osborne, then direc-tor of the American Museum of Natural History (as cited by Caird, page 58). In 1929, Fairfield described the human brain as "marvelous and mysterious." In lan-guage more measured than Fairfield's, Stephen Jay Gould (1977, page 75) describes the human brain as *"our most important evolutionary specialization."*

Present-day evolutionists are not altogether agreed on how a brain evolved by hunters and gatherers has produced a William Shakespeare, an Albert Einstein, and unnumbered persons of genius. Presumably, there were males and females of talent and genius even in prehistoric times—singers, dancers, story-tellers, poets, philosophers, and scientists of prehistory. Perhaps their talents attracted prehistoric "groupies," who were eager to interact and mate with them. Hominid males were also attracted to talented females, like modern men are often attract-ed to women of talent.

7. Thanks to modern medicine, in the last 75 years childbirth has become signif-icantly less painful and dangerous—at least in advanced, industrialized coun-tries. The December 2000 issue of the journal *Pediatrics* notes that maternal mortality in the U.S. has dropped from 582 per 100,000 live births in 1935 to 7.1 in 1998. (Restated: in 1935, for every 172 live births, one mother died; in 1998, one mother died in every *14,000* live births. Imagine a maternity ward in which five babies are born every day. In 1935 ten mothers died at childbirth *during that year alone*; in 1998, one mother was expected to die at childbirth *every four years*.)

The first book of the Bible offers an explanation of why childbirth is painful: to punish Eve for tempting Adam to eat of the tree of knowledge.

> And to the woman he said, "I will make most severe your pangs
> in childbearing; In pain shall you bear children, yet your urge
> shall be for your husband. . . ." (Genesis 3:16, JPS translation)

Through the gift of modern medicine, a product of the human brain, one might say that God has lessened the pain of childbirth. Evolutionary theory offers an alternative interpretation of why childbirth, without medical intervention, is so painful.

8. Write Leakey and Lewin (pages 89-90): "[O]ne of the things we can infer from proto-human fossils [ancestors of the human species] is that there was considerable body-size dimorphism: males were almost twice the size as females, a difference we see in modern gorillas. The body-size dimorphism in primates is always associated with competition among males for access to females . . . with one male controlling access to several females. [Body-size dimorphism] never occurs in monogamous species, where one male has access to only one female."

Elsewhere in their book (pages 116-117), the authors comment: "[I]n the early hominid species—the *Australopithecus* species—the males are as much as twice the size of the females. In Homo erectus, just as in modern humans, there is not much difference between males and females, males being some 10 to 20 percent bigger. Clearly, an important change occurred between *Australopthecus* and *Homo*, one that probably reflects a dramatic change in human social biology."

"Extensive body-size dimorphism, like that in baboons, is usually associated with intense competition among the males for access to the females. . . . A reduction in body-size dimorphism, like that in chimpanzees, is usually associated with reduced competition among males for access to females. . . ." (*ibid*, page 163). Freedman (page 276) notes that "less dimorphic animals tend to share more tasks, including nest-building, care of young, hunting, and the like."

9. As noted in Chapter 2, rounded breasts give the impression that a virginal young woman already has an ample supply of nourishment for her offspring, though what gives female breasts their shape is actually fatty tissue, not mammary glands. Nature "pads the truth" with fatty tissue, to enhance a woman's femininity just as hairiness exaggerates masculinity. A hairy male body looks somewhat bigger (and therefore more ferocious) than a hairless one, a frontal ridge and leonine eyebrows likewise give the appearance of an able protector. Nature similarly endows other creatures with physical signs (such as colorful plumage) that attract mates, or (like camouflage) otherwise favor survival.

10. In his essay, "Human babies as embryos," Stephen Jay Gould notes (1977a, page 72): "Human babies are born as embryos, and embryos they remain for the first nine months of life." He also notes (page 74) that at birth "the brain of a brain of a human baby is only one-fourth its final size. . . . "

11. Developing a language calls for a special vocal apparatus as well as a special brain capacity. There is evidence that apes have a considerable capacity for *understanding* human speech, but lack the vocal apparatus for producing human speech. Diamond 1992 (page 56) speculates that the development of "a vocal tract . . . [capable of] finer control and permitting formation of a much greater variety of sounds." was, in fact, the "leap forward" that gave proto-humans an evolutionary advantage over other hominids, an advantage in communication between individuals and across generations.

The wonder of the human brain is its capacity to have evolved a capacity for not only verbal languages, but also for abstract logic, from which have evolved mathematical languages, the essential tools of science and engineering, and the basis for radical environmental manipulations.

12. Not perfectly monogamous, anthropologists insist, but more closely bonded than most other apes. Gould notes (1977b, page 403): "Many authors have seen in delayed development a primary impetus for the origin of the human family." Gould quotes from a 1939 German source, Versluys and Lorenz: "Protracted development must have greatly strengthened the bond between parents and children. . . . *[Deveopmental] retardation is the biological basis for social life"* (Italics added).

13. Diamond points out that a female gorilla is receptive for only a couple days of the month until she becomes pregnant, and does not resume sexual activity until three or four years after giving birth. He estimates (1992 page 73) that a dominant male gorilla "if he is lucky, [has sex] a few times a year."

14. Male violence is a salient hominid characteristic, Wrangham and Peterson document, in *Demonic Males*. This temperamental sex difference has probably been reduced, but has by no means been erased from the genetic makeup of the human species. Wrangham and Peterson document the fact that in virtually all cultures, males are far more likely than females to commit acts of violence.

15. Chimpanzee males are only about 20 per cent larger than females, about the same ratio as for humans. Robert Foley, Cambridge University anthropologist, notes that comparing different species of primates, reduction in dimorphism "is usually associated with reduction in competition between males and possibly even a significant degree of cooperation." Foley observes that chimpanzees often "cooperate assiduously with each other, in obtaining mates and in defense against other groups" (as quoted by Leakey and Lewin, page 117)

16. A 1976 article by Tanner and Zihlman appears to express a feminist protest of the emphasis on "man the hunter" as shaper of the human species. Tanner and Zihlman argue that man's closest relative is the chimpanzee, and since chimpanzees do not hunt big game, they question the importance of big game hunting in human evolution. [Never mind the heaps of bones of huge animals that are found at prehistoric settlements. Never mind that it is hard to account for the

domestication of the dog except that it was selectively bred for its suitability as a hunting companion. Never mind that chimpanzees are knuckle walkers and that man is a runner.] Humans have a potential for the development of physical endurance that far exceeds the chimpanzee, a genetic trait that strongly suggests that proto-humans were selected for hunting-related skills.

Tanner and Zihlman argue that proto-humans were primarily eaters of grubs and eggs, nestlings and lizards, and that females provided a large part of the family's sustenance. In his 2001 book on "the quest for human nature," evolutionary biologist Stanford acknowledges Tanner and Zihlman's article but does not address its limitations. (Political correctness?) Similarly, in the 1992 *Third Chimpanzee* (page 39), biologist Jared Diamond condedes that the "man the hunter" theme may be an exaggeration of the facts, and suggests that hominids more often contented themselves with smaller prey such as birds and frogs. But he also points out (page 356) that numerous species of big animals probably became extinct after the last Ice Age because they were exterminated by human hunters. The mammoths of North America, the wooly rhino and giant deer of Europe, the giant buffalo and giant Cape horse of southern Africa were probably all exterminated by human hunters.

17. Chapter 7, on brain-differences, presents evidence of the genetic basis for gender differences in temperament.

18. Like the nipples at the surface of his body, every male carries through life the remains of his proto-female embryonic organs. Hidden inside his body are vestigial remains of the Muellerian ducts that, had the fetus not been bathed in testicular hormones, would have developed into fallopian tubes, uterus, and vagina.

19. Gay men remind us that male nipples are erogenously sensitive, which elevate the status of these organs from vestigial to "functional." Males are so easily aroused sexually, many (most?) males enjoy a high level of sex drive without ever discovering the erogenous value of male nipple stimulation.

20. In about a dozen pages, the reader has been rushed through a presentation of how evolutionary forces "reshaped the species" from harems of gorilla-like creatures with brains the size of a baseball, to human communities that have produced the likes of Moses, Jesus, Shakespeare, Rembrandt, Darwin, and Einstein (as well as more than a few tyrants and scoundrels). And all this comes about by "happy accidents" you call mutations? Let the reader who responds, "Hard to believe!" ponder what George Williams (page 26) writes about the power of natural selection:

> Between us and the *australopithecine*, which walked upright but had an ape-size brain, stand a few million years: 100,000, maybe 200,000 generations. That may not sound like much. But it has taken around 5,000 generations [*five percent* of 100,000] to turn

a wolf into a chihuahua—and, at the same time, along a different line, into a Saint Bernard.

21. A young boy who feels temperamentally female—who dislikes rough-and-tumble play, and who would rather play with girls or help mother—is likely (though not certain) to become a homosexual adult. This topic was discussed in some detail in Chapter 9. Chapter 10 summarizes our knowledge of berdache and similar gender-discordant social groups.

22. A number of laboratory scientists have recently been looking for microscopic signs of "gay genes." Simon LeVay (1991), Laura A. Allen and Roger A. Gorski (1992), Dean H. Hamer (1993) and others have contributed to this provocative and controversial fund of studies. The evidence is neatly, if optimistically, summed up in the recent book by Chandler Burr, a science reporter, tantalizingly entitled, *A Separate Creation*.

23. Is the female temperament more artistic? Is the female brain pre-programmed in a way that favors artistic activity? Certain observations about the brain, discussed in Chapter 7, have some bearing on these questions. The left hemisphere of the brain is believed to mediate more analytical and verbal thought, while the right hemisphere mediates more emotional, artistic, musical thought. In the typical female brain, right and left hemispheres are more richly interconnected. Does this enable women to be "more in touch with their feelings"? Does this enable the average woman to better integrate thought and feeling? Perhaps the male artist is typically a person whose cerebral endowment combines female sensitivity with the typical male advantages for sustained work and achievement motivation.

24. The difference between 100 percent and 20 percent sexual dimorphism is a radical difference. According to evolutionary principles, this stature-difference between male and female was closed by the smallest of increments, over a period of millions of years.

25. If their sexual apparatus is altogether normal, how does temperamental low-masculinity sometimes lead to a homosexual orientation? That was the topic of chapter 9.

26. To render Pillard's prophesy completely consistent with the thesis of this book, one need only insert the phrase *"the by-product of"* a valuable trait. . . .

27. Developmental learning is discussed in some detail in chapter 17.

Epilogue, Part 1.

Some Practical Questions

The purpose of this two-part Epilogue is to discuss issues *not* addressed directly in the book but likely to come up during a question-and-answer period (conducted by the author or a reviewer) following the presentation of a talk about the book. While the author's approach has been largely theoretical, members of an audience (like many readers of this book) are likely to be concerned with *practical* questions relating to the topic of male homosexuality. This Epilogue tries to answer some of the practical questions that may occur to the listener to such a talk (or the reader of this book): questions about treatment, gay ideology, homosexuality and artistic talent, genetic tendencies, childhood experience, man-boy sex, worriers, Boy Scouts policy, gay marriage, gay rights, gay pride, and homosexuality and public policy.

Part 1. Treatment Questions

The main focus of this book has been on male homosexuality as a theoretical and research problem. But the subject also raises some practical problems on which conflicting opinions have been strongly expressed. This section, and the one that follows, examine some of these practical concerns.

Some gay men express pride with regard to their sexual orientation, asserting that theirs is a higher form of human experience, or that they are nature's answer to the world population problem. But some homosexual men say, "I am homosexual but I am definitely not gay; I am forever worried, anxious, nervous and sometimes downright miserable about my same-sex compulsions." The dissatisfaction expressed by a patient of Hatterer's (1970, page 418), published 30 years ago, expresses the feelings of *some* homosexuals today:

> Frankly, I can't take this whoring around and getting masturbated by a part of somebody's body who I don't even know. All these years I've been looking for somebody, but no one ever seems right for me, so I've never really lived with one person. The few couples I know who've been living together for years are always playing on the side. The older they get, the younger the men they want. Frankly, I'm wearying of the whole God damn rat-race.

Are *all* homosexuals psychologically disturbed? There was a time, around 150 years ago, when it was daringly progressive to define homosexuality as *merely* an illness. This was a time when it was popularly believed that homosexuals were both morally and physically degenerate. For hundreds of years, homosexuals had been branded as witches and heretics. By 1850, it seemed more civilized, more humane and enlightened, to regard homosexuality as *only an ill-ness*—a medical problem, not a moral problem. After little more than half a century, the illness model was already old-fashioned. In a 1905 essay (page 39, fn. 2), Freud noted that "the pathological approach" had already been displaced. It took about 70 years, and considerable prodding by gay advocacy groups[1] to bring the American Psychiatric Association up to date. After it was forced to renounce the view that homosexuality was a mental disorder, it also condemned reorientation therapy as unethical, ineffectual, and dangerous.[2]

It is true that over the years many homosexual men have been *seriously harmed*, their time and money wasted, and their hopes destroyed by misguided doctors of the mind. For example, Edmund White's best-received book, *A Boy's Own Story*, chronicled 12 years of failed therapy, emphasizing the harm it wrought and the self-hatred it engendered. (White's autobiographical sequel is entitled *The Beautiful Room Is Empty.*)

Should that historical record, dismal as it is, bar distressed homosexuals from seeking help in overcoming unwanted homosexual compulsions? In the jargon of psychiatry, the homosexuality of men whose homosexual compulsion is unwanted, is called ego-dystonic or ego-alien. Their same-sex cravings do not fit in with the rest of their character. They regard their homosexual attractions as a personal embarrassment: "The homosexual feelings never felt like who I really am."

The dispute over whether reorientation therapy works is in part a dispute over facts. The plain fact is that sometimes, not perfectly but to a practical degree, *reorientation therapy* works. So testified Judd Marmor,[3] a prominent, gay-friendly psychoanalyst, in 1980 (page 277), on the basis of his "own clinical experience, and that of other therapists, both behavioral and psychodynamic:"

> [T]here is little doubt . . . that a genuine shift from a state in
> which heterosexual relations are avoided or feared to one in
> which they are sought and enjoyed can be achieved in a fraction
> (somewhere between 20 and 50 percent) of highly motivated
> male and female homosexuals.

Maddox devotes a chapter to summarizing the experience of gay husbands who sought sexual orientation through psychotherapy.

Appendix I documents a very recent, well-designed research study by Dr. Robert Spitzer, who interviewed 200 men and women who claimed that they had moved from homosexuality to heterosexuality with the help of a minister, a therapist, a mentor, or through a religious or secular self-help program. (Dr. Spitzer's name is familiar to persons who know the history of the fight to get the APA to drop homosexuality from its list of mental disorders. At that time, Dr. Spitzer joined forces with gay advocates to make this change.)

The American Psychiatric Association and the American Psychological

Association have both asserted that because male homosexuality is not an illness, sexual reorientation therapy is unethical. Is it ethical, then, to conduct research on, or even *discuss*, the effectiveness of reorientation therapy?

The medical profession very routinely serves distressed patients whose condition is *not* an illness. Is a mole at the end of one's nose an illness? Are small breasts an illness? There is something rather faulty in the logic of a rule that because a condition is technically not an illness, it is therefore unethical to help a patient overcome the condition about which he is distressed.

This cloud of ethical legitimacy seriously hampers research into how to make reorientation therapy more effective. Does this suggest that all homosexuals should undergo psychotherapy? There may be some who think so but, as we have already shown, almost a century ago, Freud (and other enlightened thinkers of his time)[4] said no. Charles Socarides is one of the most highly regarded psychoanalysts of our times specializing in the treatment of troubled homosexuals who do want to change. When asked, "Do all homosexuals need psychotherapy?" he answered (1995, page 116) as follows:

> There are a good many homosexuals who are content with the
> way they are. They function quite well. I don't know why they'd
> want to go into psychotherapy. They wouldn't get much out of it.

Cornelius

Here is the story of a homosexual man who, through psychotherapy, was able to enjoy marriage and fatherhood. What is typical about the story is that therapy did not *completely* extinguish his homosexual impulses. What is most unusual about the story is that it is documented in the pro-gay book, Farm Boys, by Will Fellows, a collection of oral histories of gay men who grew up on Midwest farms.

Cornelius was an 84-year-old retired social worker when he told his story to Fellows. Cornelius recalled that since the age of four, during his school years and in college, he had engaged in sex play with his seven brothers and with other children, as well as with adults. Cornelius had always been reluctant to give oral sex (he said it made him gag). As a college student, he continued his homosexual life. He also dated women, engaged in some "petting" with them but says he avoided intercourse because he didn't want to risk getting a woman pregnant.

While enrolled in a graduate program in social work, he began to feel uncomfortable about being homosexual, motivating him to begin five years of psychoanalytic treatment, five or six days a week. After ending treatment, Cornelius continued to see his analyst "from time to time, to talk about things that were troubling me. . . . [My analyst] gave me a great deal of confidence in myself, and my skill as a social worker grew by leaps and bounds as a result of my analysis. I feel incredibly grateful for my treatment because it enabled me to have sex with a woman and enjoy it, and as a result of that I have two lovely children and four beautiful grandchildren. I feel that having children contributed inordinately to my growth and development as a person," Cornelius testified (Fellows, page 42).

Five years of analysis enabled Cornelius to enjoy marriage and fatherhood, though it did not completely extinguish his homosexual cravings. When he would go out of town, he would get half-drunk and find a male partner for a one-night stand. After 35 years of marriage, his wife died and Cornelius resumed his homosexual life. Analysis was less than a complete success, but the therapy experience did help Cornelius shift from homosexuality to bisexuality, enabled him to enjoy marriage and fatherhood and, he asserts, contributed to his professional skill as a social worker.

John Money, whose writings express a deep skepticism with regard to reorientation therapy, says (1988, pages 87-88) that most if not all claims of therapeutic success are based on patients who went into treatment with "some degree of bisexuality on which to capitalize. It is in just such a case that the individual may experience a sense of the self divided and in conflict, for the resolution of which he or she seeks treatment to be monosexually one or the other, but not bisexually both together." A belief of reorientation therapists, that Money apparently does not share, is that virtually everybody has "a degree of bisexuality," and that *all* homosexuals may in fact be correctly regarded as "latent heterosexuals." This optimism in the person's capacity to change is what fuels the therapeutic enterprise.

There is, to be sure, an element of truth in the gay advocate's skepticism about reorientation therapy. Marmor admits (1980, pages 276-277) that therapy does not *totally* obliterate homosexual feelings:

> The fact that most homosexual preferences are probably learned and not inborn means that, in the presence of strong motivation to change, they are open to modification, and clinical experience confirms this. The kernel of truth in the gay point of view, however, is that once a major pathway to sexual gratification has been established and reinforced by repeated experiences, the tracks of that pathway can never be totally obliterated. Thus although it is possible for successfully treated homosexuals to change their overt behavior from homosexual to heterosexual, the tendency toward erotic arousal by the same sex is probably never totally lost. . . . [T]he fact that between 25 and 50 percent of homosexuals who seek to change their main sexual orientation are able to do so is more a tribute to the strength of their motivation than it is to the specific therapeutic approach involved.

Like men in general, some homosexuals are beset with emotional problems, and there is some indication that homosexual men are more likely to have emotional problems than men in general.[5] Gay advocates worry about homosexual men who seek help with an emotional problem—anxiety, depression, compulsion, etc., but are *not* appropriate candidates for sexual reorientation; they don't want it and they don't need it. Go to a gay-affirmative therapist who is a gay man himself, they are advised, or else you will fall into the hands of a mind doctor who is sure that if a gay man has psychological problems, they are all rooted in the fact that he is homosexual.

True to the spirit of Sigmund Freud, but contrary to the then prevailing climate of American psychiatry, Lawrence Hatterer, in his 1970 psychotherapy textbook (pages 410-411), pleaded against the maltreatment of homosexuals. Do not moralize or patronize the homosexual patient, or treat him with hostility, Hatterer begged. Instead, he urges therapists to help the patient who does *not* want to change his sexual orientation, or *cannot* change it, adapt more constructively to the homosexual lifestyle:

> . . . If he chooses a partner whose socio-economic and intellectual background is not too vastly removed from his own, one who has stable values and compatible sexual appetites, the chances are greater for him to establish and possibly sustain a long-standing viable homosexual living arrangement. . . .

> Sometimes he has to be helped to learn to live with his kind of homosexual adjustment because no other is possible. In such a case, the therapist must not devalue what works for the patient if it does not cause destructive living. . . .

> An analysis of some [homosexual] character problems—passivity, dependency, resorts to power plays, sado-masochism, deceptiveness, defensiveness, grandiosity, arrogance, and habitual denigration—can sometimes help the committed homosexual arrive at a point where he can enter a more stable relationship or group. Even when they are long-standing, these traits can sometimes be modified. A therapist should not give up helping the patient with his character problems just because he knows that his sexual life must remain fixed.

Hatterer's advice,[6] published in 1970, narrows the difference between the "gay-affirmative therapy" of our own day, and what many experienced therapists have been quietly practicing for many years.

Predicting success in reorientation therapy

On what basis does a therapist decide whether the patient is a candidate for sexual reorientation? One patient may plead with him, "Doctor, you've got to help me get this monkey off my back." "Doctor, this is no life for me." "Do you think I'll ever be able to be a good husband?" "I've always wanted to have kids."

On the other hand, no person is capable of making so fundamental a change in his lifestyle simply for the purpose of accommodating someone else, unhappy parents or anyone else. Marmor (1980, page 275) notes that when parents try to push a son into therapy, it is probably the parents who need help, more than the son.

> It is not at all uncommon for a psychiatrist to be importuned by distraught parents to treat a teenage son or daughter whose homosexual propensities have come to light, but in my experience, unless the adolescent is strongly motivated to change, not much will be accomplished so far as changing his or her erotic preference. [Marmor advises the therapist to help the parents maintain their parental ties to their child, and] to help the adolescents . . . accept themselves without guilt or shame. . . .

William Consiglio, a Christian counselor, says that in fifteen years' experience working homosexuals, he has had some success with men who have come to him of their own initiative, but he has *never* had a successful outcome with a patient referred to him by his mother.[7]

Not every gay man is equally likely to benefit from psychotherapy of any kind. Here are some guidelines as to who is most likely to benefit from psychotherapy, and who is least likely to benefit. Whether a patient is a candidate for sexual reorientation depends, first of all, on whether he wants to change, and more importantly, on how badly he wants to change. There is a significant difference between the wistful thought, "Yes, it would be lovely to have a nice wife and happy children," and the discomfort that leads a man to plead, "Doctor, I'll do anything to get rid of this miserable habit."

How badly he wants to change will become clear not only by what he says, but even more forcibly by what he does. Does he want to start treatment as soon as possible? Does he willingly give time, effort, and money to treatment? Does he keep appointments and make good use of them?

What kind of a person he is before treatment will forecast how likely it is that therapy will help him change. Prognosis is best if he is honest and loyal, if he is competitive and achievement-oriented—doesn't want homosexuality to stand in his way—if he is sociable, has one or more close heterosexual friends, if he plays sports, likes family life and children. And it helps a great deal if he is still young, say between 20 and 25.

What kind of a homosexual he is also indicates how accessible he is to change. Would he rather associate with straight people and live in a straight-world? Since adolescence, has he tried dating girls, tried kissing or petting or attempted intercourse? Was he introduced to homosexual play by a sibling or good friend? Have his homosexual acts been limited mostly to mutual masturbation, and have they been isolated from the rest of his life? Has he usually been solicited, rather than having solicited? Does he dislike the passivity of receptive fellatio and anal sex? Does he feel out-of-place among homosexuals and in homosexual settings—bars, baths, etc.? Does he feel anxious, depressed, or suicidal before, during, or after homosexual acts?

The best-prognosis patient also has had the advantage of a strong family background. Mother may have been overprotective and possessive, but she was not seductive or psychotic. Father was assertive and affectionate, and did spend some leisure time with his son. In addition to his father, a grandfather or uncle has served as a healthy role model. He is not an only child, and his siblings respect his masculinity.

By contrast, the homosexual who is *least* likely to benefit from reorientation therapy, has already reached the age of 35 or 40, and regards homosexuality as a private and untroubled area of his life. He has had homosexual fantasies since age five or six, and as a child was seduced by an adult stranger. As a child, he always played with girls, but has avoided female c ontacts since adolescence. He is now settled in a more-or-less homosexual occupation—hairdresser, dancer, interior decorator, etc. He moves in homosexual circles, has daily or weekly orgasms with many partners, likes to be penetrated anally or orally, and has already attempted homosexual "marriage." To his mother, he has been a substitute husband. His parents are detatched physically, and father is narcissistic, unassertive, and indifferent to his son. There are no signs of family unity. The patient is isolated, and feels like an oppressed outsider. He is dishonest and disloyal, detatched, uncompetititive, unemotional, and expresses himself with cruel humor and biting sarcasm. Life crises have led to depression, hysteria, withdrawal, and substance abuse.

The foregoing contrast between high- and low-prognosis patients is condensation of comments by Hatterer (1970, pages 445-464).

Marmor (1980, pages 277-278) summarized the differences between high- and low-prognosis patients as follows: Treatment is most likely to be beneficial to patients who are (1) strongly motivated to change, (2) young (under 35), (3) relative newcomers to homosexual practice, (4) masculine in appearance and behavior, and (5) not without some heterosexual experience.

On the other hand, Marmor continued, the prospects are poor for the patient who has been dragged into therapy by an alarmed parent, for the patient who is over 35, for the patient who has always shunned women, for the patient who has practiced homosexuality for many years, for the patient who is effeminate in appearance and has been effeminate in manner since early childhood.

Feldman and McCulloch concluded a book-length assessment of homosexuals in therapy with the statement that the best single predictor of response to reorientation therapy is the amount of heterosexual experience prior to treatment.

What Therapy May or May Not Accomplish

How often do such practitioners succeed in completely "curing" such a patient, in making a gay man 100 percent heterosexual? *Possibly never*. More reasonable goals, often attained, are: (1) helping him to attract and enjoy a friendship circle of straight males, to understand non-erotic affection, (2) relieving the patient of an unrealistic fear or hatred of women, (3) preparing him to enjoy a romantic, physical, and marital relationship with a woman, (4) enabling him to tolerate occasional, mild, and passing homosexual attractions, and to accept the fact that these feelings are, for him, part of his normal fantasy life, and (5) reconciling him to the possibility that life crises may make him more vulnerable to homosexual attractions, and may call for additional therapy contacts.

Therapeutic success is not limited to the easiest cases, but much depends on how strongly the patient is determined to change. A successful outcome does not mean that homosexuality has been totally erased from the person's psyche, but rather that he can enjoy heterosexual living with only incidental interference by passing homosexual thoughts and fantasies, and that these passing thoughts and fantasies have replaced compulsions which, before therapy, the person once felt powerless to resist.

Recovery from homosexuality is something like recovery from alcoholism. The former alcoholic may still have pleasant thoughts about the comradship and good times of his drinking days, and of the enjoyment of the relief from tension and worry that drinking afforded. But, on balance, he is glad he has said goodbye to his drinking days, and sees less of his old drinking buddies. He acknowledges that they have their good qualities, and he is sorry that some of them may consider him a disappointment or even a traitor. But he has chosen to take a different path in life, and *he is now cultivating a different circle of friends*. Having put drinking behind him, he now feels that his everyday life is richer, he is more in touch with himself and with his world. He also feels that he is enjoying a more wholesome lifestyle.

At the cutting edge of reorientation therapy are those therapists (*e.g.*, Rekers and Zucker) who are working with boys with "gender-identity disorders," to prevent adult homosexuality.[8]

Stages and details of the therapeutic process are described by various therapists (Hatterer 1970, Socarides, Nicolosi, and others). No attempt will be made here to describe, compare, and contrast various therapeutic methods. Instead, we have chosen to summarize the reparative therapy of Joseph Nicolosi because (a) it combines both individual and group methods, (b) it incorporates much psychoanalytic thinking and at the same time, (c) it differs from conventional psychoanalysis, (d) it also differs from nondirective therapy, and (e) Nicolosi's approach is described in detail in his two recent books.

Reparative Therapy

Homosexuals who want to change their sexual orientation are not well-served by a therapist who is distant and nondirective[9] in style, says Nicolosi. These patients need a therapist who will point the way: teach them, guide them, help them, encourage them, and at the same time serve as a role model of male competence. Nicolosi's 1991 presentation of his approach, *Reparative Therapy of Male Homosexuality*, and his 1993 book of case histories, *Healing Homosexuality*, describe a treatment program that combines individual and group therapy aimed at the establishment of a sense of masculine integrity that diminishes homosexual feelings. He promises no cure, no quick fix, but some patients reach the point where they are ready for marriage and fatherhood. Treatment, he says, is "probably a lifetime process."

In working with homosexuals, one tactical error of psychoanalytically oriented therapists has been their distance and detachment. Another error has been to prematurely encourage heterosexual relations.[10] This tactic was supposed to undo a discomfort with women that stemmed from "the over-possessive mother." The reason that this approach is not effective, however, is that it is the homosexual's discomfort with *men* that must be diminished, says Nicolosi, who uses group therapy to achieve this goal. After this is accomplished, the patient will feel comfortable approaching a woman sexually (Nicolosi 1991, page 202).

The principle that "every homosexual is a latent heterosexual" informs Nicolosi's therapy program. Thus, one of Nicolosi's patients, a married man, said, "For many years I thought I was gay. I finally realized I was not a homosexual, but really a heterosexual man with a homosexual problem." Another Nicolosi client reflected, "A problem that used to have a capital 'H' now has a small 'h.'"

Charlie

At 32, Charlie was head of a large university biomedical library. His therapist called him "one of the most intelligent and insightful men I have ever had the privilege to know" (Nicolosi 1993, page 65). After ten years of homosexual living, he felt increasingly that he was missing something, and at his first therapy session said, "I have been part of the gay lifestyle long enough to tell you that when a man craves masculinity so badly that he has to try to suck it out of another guy, then there is—undeniably—a big problem" (*ibid.*, page 66). After two and one-half years of therapy, he jotted down and handed his therapist the reflections of a person whose "sense of satisfaction with my masculinity is now alive and growing." Undoubtedly these notes summarize what he had learned in reparative therapy:

1. I don't crave masculinity any more. Instead, I have claimed it.
2. I no longer overvalue (sexually desire) or undervalue (defensively detach from) the men in my life. Instead, I stand with them as an equal.
3. I have lost my antagonism toward my father and find myself identifying more and more with him.
4. I speak up more often and am far more assertive.
5. In spirit, I am less repressed.
6. In action, I'm more in control. I'm more willing to take risks.
7. Through exercise, I have less hatred toward my own body. I may never be completely free of the limp I've had since I was a boy, but I've been making the most I can of my body.
8. I am better able to appreciate the feminine in women friends because their contrast to myself is now more apparent.
9. I look for the masculine energy in all things and find ways to express it genuinely from within because to do so is to live, and to heal.
10. I have forgiven the men who have failed me, as I have forgiven myself for years of running away. . . . My homosexual tendencies were not a cry to have another man—but a cry to have a manly me (Nicolosi, 1993, pages 86-87, adapted).

An important part of reparative group therapy is learning how to make lasting male friendships. Patients learn that women maintain friendships by being together and talking together, with incidental activities like having lunch together or shopping together. Men maintain friendships by discussing topics of common interest, but also by *doing things* together, like going hiking, working out, fixing things, participating in active sports, or watching spectator sports together. In *group therapy*, patients also learn to interact with other men in a non-erotic way, to become friends by relating to each other on the basis of equality, honesty, a sharing of common problems, and mutual support.

Three Important Aspects of Reorientation Therapy. When a process is so subtle that it involves the interaction of patient's and therapist's unconscious minds, it is not easy to analyze. Yet there are some clearly identifiable ways in which therapy helps a person who wants to overcome a homosexual habit:

1. Learning to recognize the situations that arouse homosexual cravings. Behavior change may very likely require a change in one's living and work milieu. A patient whose work is in theater, dance, music, dress design, or interior decoration must face up to the fact that he may be working in a homosexual environment. The solution is *not* to change professions but to change jobs. (Hatterer laments the fact that many men have avoided developing their artistic, creative talents because it might cast doubt upon their masculinity.)

2. Learning to cope with life's daily crises (anxieties, disappointments, frustrations, etc.) without looking for homosexual gratification.

[It's very hard] for me to walk by a subway without going down, particularly if I'm low and things are all fucked up for me. I've got to stay away from subways . . . even if it means that I only take buses, 'cause once I hit the subway I head for a john to get a blow job (Hatterer 1970, page 213).

> All I need is three or four drinks and the feeling returns. . . .
> Even after one drink, it makes me feel like going out and getting
> a man. . . . I don't think I've ever had a homosexual orgasm
> without being drunk. When I'm sober I think the worst thing in
> life would be to end up a queer (Hatterer 1970, page 249).

> I think I feel very alone on the road and very anxious to be with
> someone. It would never occur to me to pick up a woman. I'm
> too afraid to do that, and the first time I got involved, actually, I
> was picked up by someone. After I found out what was available
> it always happened at some bar nearby where I stayed, or some-
> how or other I managed to find the gay bar in the city. . . . I can't
> imagine anything like this ever happening to me where I live,
> and yet this thing of picking men up and being picked up seems
> to hang on. You have to help me find out why it just happens
> when I'm not around my family. . . . (Hatterer 1970, page 250)

3. Learning new social skills to help make the transition into the heterosexual world. A person can cut himself off from his old social ties, his little world and its familiar gratifications, only if he can be helped to find his place in another social world. Man is a social animal, and people need people. Undoubtedly, an important ingredient in Nicolosi's reparative therapy program is the group therapy component, discussed in Chapters 17 and 20 of his 1991 book, and summarized below:

> In therapy groups and support groups, the patient learns how to
> get along with other men in a friendly and non-erotic way; what
> men talk about, and what they do together. *When he feels like a
> man among men, then he will be ready to be a man to a woman.*
> Before a patient can cope with rejection by a woman, can [also]
> cope with a woman who is either too aggressive or too passive,
> before he can cope with a failure to gratify a woman, a patient
> must feel some security about his place in the world of men. In
> the past, many therapists failed to understand this, and prema-
> turely pressured their patient into seeking intimacy with a
> woman, with disastrous results.

The Success Rate of Reorientation Therapy

How successful are those therapists who dedicate their career to helping homosexuals find a satisfying and productive place in the straight world? Since 1967, Socarides has treated close to 100 overt homosexuals, and reports (1995, pages 102-104) a success rate, defined as "full heterosexual functioning," of about 35 percent.

A recent survey conducted by NARTH (The National Association for Research and Therapy of Homosexuallity)[11] involved 200 psychologists and other therapists, and 860 patients who wanted to overcome homosexuality. These were not the easiest patients to treat, by the standards of Hatterer or Marmor; their average age was 37, and one-third were married. The group was predominantly (78 percent) but not exclusively male, and almost 90 percent were college graduates. Before treatment, 68 percent of the patients described themselves as exclusively or almost entirely homosexual. After treatment, the percentage of patients who so described themselves fell to 13 percent, and 33 percent described themselves as either exclusively or almost entirely heterosexual. These findings, based on the work of 200 therapists and 860 patients (averaging four patients each), and Socarides' experience with almost 100 patients, come very close to agreeing that about one out of three homosexual patients who enter and stay in therapy[12] eventually join the heterosexual world.

Does therapy merely enable ex-homosexuals to adopt heterosexual behaviors, or does it also enable them to experience heterosexual feelings? This is the kind of question that interested Robert L. Spitzer, professor of psychiatry at Columbia University, who conducted an interview study described in detail in Appendix 1 of this book..

Spitzer issued a call for ex-gay men and women who had been living heterosexual lives for five years or more since they completed therapy. Two hundred and seventy-four people responded. Spitzer spoke to all of them, eliminated 74 as not meeting his strict criteria, giving each of the remaining 200 (143 men and 57 women) a 45-minute interview, guided by a well-structured set of 120 questions that explored their sexual fantasies, feelings, and behavior.

If they were bluffing, Spitzer reasoned, he would get all sorts of stories, and the group wouldn't show any consistency. *But a definite pattern of experience did emerge, and there was a clear-cut gender difference.* Most were about 20 years of age when they entered therapy. First came a reduction of homosexual feelings, and then came a gradual emergence of heterosexual feelings. Women responded to therapy more readily than men. Many of the men reported that they were able to experience heterosexual arousal only after they had become intensely involved with a woman. Most patients were in therapy for about five years. According to their testimony, therapy had changed their emotional life as well as their behavior. Spitzer presented his findings at the 2001 annual convention of the American Psychiatric Association.

The Spitzer study was aimed at offering evidence to the skeptics, but clinicians have known for a long time that some homosexuals can be helped if they are disturbed by their same-sex compulsions. In an interview published in 1971, the psychoanalyst Ovesey averred that therapy can enable a homosexual to find equal pleasure in women. After therapy, *if he marries*, he can stick with heterosexuality because marriage, a family, and the friendship with other marrieds will give him important gratifications that he did not have as a gay man.

> But I've never seen a homosexual who didn't drift back to men
> if he didn't eventually marry, even though he'd managed to
> become [sexually] potent with women. . . . The temptations are
> often too great for a former homosexual without close bonds.
> Often the failure to make such bonds is the greatest problem in a
> homosexual's life (Karlen, pages 436-437).

Reorientation therapy works in a significant but limited way, for a limited portion of those patients who give therapy a serious chance. Our nation spends millions of dollars on research to improve mental health services of all kinds. But no federal dollars are spent to understand, to prevent, and to help reverse *ego-alien* homosexuality, a condition that is accompanied by loneliness, depression, high-risk activity, substance abuse, and disease. Why? Because both the American Psychiatric Association and the American Psychological Association have officially ruled that homosexuality is not an illness, and that reorientation therapy is therefore unethical.

When reorientation therapy is recognized as the legitimate practice that it is, a number of things, all in the public interest, can happen: (1) professional schools (medical, psychological, social work) can train therapists to help those homosexuals who *want* help, (2) funding agencies, public and private, can consider supporting research to enhance the effectiveness of reorientation therapy, and (3) clinics can offer state-of-the art service *coupled with programs of research* on advancing reorientation therapy.

Thousands of people are troubled by homosexual compulsions, and engage hundreds of therapists, who make a serious effort to reorient their patients' sexual lives. There is a sizeable professional literature on this specialty, but the existence of this serious professional specialty is dismissed by too many pro-gay writers as a fraud or a hoax,[13] or its existence is conveniently denied. For example, Socarides (1995, page 104), a leader in the psychoanalytic treatment of homosexuals, and author of half a dozen books on the subject, says he was interviewed for two hours by the science reporter Chandler Burr, a gay man and author of the March 1993 *Atlantic* article on "Homosexuality and Biology," later expanded into the book, *A Separate Creation*. What does Burr say in his *Atlantic* article or book, about his two-hour interview with Socarides? Exactly nothing.

NOTES TO EPILOGUE, PART 1

1. For a history of the struggle on the part of gay activists to persuade the American Psychiatric Asssociation to drop homosexuality from its list of mental disorders, see Marmor's "Epilogue;" also see Bayer. When, in 1974 the entire membership of APA was polled, to ratify their Board of Trustee's action on dropping homosexuality from their list of mental disorders, the decision of the Board was upheld by the slim majority of *58 per cent* of the membership. Opposed were 37.8 per cent, and 3.6 per cent abstained. (Marmor "Epilogue," page 393).

2. For the American Psychological Association's condemnation of reorientation therapy, see endnote 21, page 536.

3. Judd Marmor was a leader among psychoanalysts who sided with gay advocates in the 1973 APA fight to eliminate homosexuality from the Diagnostic Manual. He is the author of the 1965 book, *Sexual Inversion: the Multiple Roots of Homosexuality*, and wrote several chapters of the 1980 book he edited, *Homosexual Behavior, a Modern Reappraisal*, praised as "balanced and comprehensive" in a Foreword to the book written by the gay-friendly psychologist Evelyn Hooker.

4. In 1903, the Vienna newspaper *Die Zeit* published a letter by Freud, saying: "I am . . . of the firm conviction that homosexuals must not be treated as sick people."

In 1930, Freud signed an appeal to the German Reichstag to repeal that part of the German code that since 1871 had made homosexual relations a crime. In part, the petition read:

> Homosexuality has been present throughout history and among
> all peoples. . . . Their sexual orientation is just as inherent to
> them as that of heterosexuals. . . . This law represents an extreme
> violation of human rights. . . . Homosexuals have the same civil
> duties to fulfill as everyone else. In the name of justice, we
> demand that legislators give them the same civil rights by repeal-
> ing the law in question.

The appeal was also signed by Arthur Schnitzler, Stefan Zweig, Franz Werfel, Jakob Wasserman, and Dr. Hermann Eckel, president of the Austrian Bar Association.
[Translation reprinted from "The Gay Rights Freud," by Herbert Spiers and Michael Lynch, in *Body Politic* 33 (1977), pages 8-18.]

5. See Chapter 24, pages 438-446.

6. Lawrence J. Hatterer's experience with distressed homosexuals has not only

been very extensive, but has also spanned an unusually wide socio-economic range. While other psychoanalysts were working only in private practice with well-to-do patients, Hatterer was working for years at an urban mental health walk-in clinic: the Payne Whitney Outpatient Clinic of the New York Presbyterian Hospital.

Hatterer's 1970 book, *Changing Homosexuality in the Male*, summarizes about 20 years' work (1951-1969), and observation of 710 patients, including 200 who received psychotherapy ranging from 1 to 375 hours. Patients were seen at the Payne Whitney Clinic, at Cornell University Medical College, and in the author's private practice.

7. Workshop lecture at 1997 Exodus Convention.

8. Marmor (1980, page 275) agrees: "With appropriate family therapy and guidance, many [effeminate boys] can be helped to achieve more appropriate gender-role patterns, and presumably, in some of them at least, a homosexual life-pattern may be forestalled."

9. Nicolosi argues that the homosexual patient needs to see in his therapist a demonstration of a masculine lifestyle that the patient can learn from, and identify with. The distant style of psychoanalytically oriented therapists, and the nondirective style of Rogerian therapists too closely resembles the feminine tactics of indirection and passivity. This is not what the homosexual client needs to see demonstrated, or to learn from, says Nicolosi. The homosexual patient needs a therapist who is directive, confrontational, and encouraging—a guide and a teacher.

10. This tendency, to push a homosexual patient into heterosexual experience, is expressed in the following quotation, taken from Joseph Epstein's 1970 *Harper's* article (source not given), and attributed to psychoanalyst Allen Wheelis:

> If a homosexual should set out to become heterosexual . . . two things are clear: he should discontinue homosexual relations, however much tempted he may be to continue on a spontaneous basis, and he should undertake, continue, and maintain heterosexual relations, however little heart he may have for girls, however often he fails, and however inadequate and averse he may find himself to be. He would be well advised in reaching for such a goal to anticipate that success, if achieved at all, will require a long time . . . [and] that the effort will be painful and humiliating. . . . [S]ometimes insight will precede and illumine action, and sometimes blind, dogged action must come first, and . . . even so, with the best of will and good faith and determination, he still may fail. . . .

11. The NARTH study was completed in 1997, and released by Executive Director Joseph Nicolosi. Data were tabulated by statisticians at Brigham Young University.

12. Many persons who enter therapy discontinue for one reason or another, and the reported success rate is for those who stayed in therapy. Some quit for financial reasons, some move away because of their job, some are frightened or discouraged or reluctant to change their lifestyle. Similarly, comments Socarides (1995, page 102), many alcoholics would like to give up drinking, but the change would be too dislocating. "If they give up drinking, they have to start looking for a whole new set of friends."

13. Bawer, a voice of homosexual conservatism, warns his readers (page 141): "What has happened to people who claim to have been 'changed' [through psychotherapy] . . . is that these people have returned to a state of denial."

Epilogue, Part 2.

Eighteen More Questions and Answers

1. "Gay advocates define homosexuality as *a lifestyle*. Is this definition consistent with an evolutionary point of view?"

Yes and no. Yes, in the sense that a gay man's life often centers around his sexual orientation: where he lives, who his friends are, which work colleagues and relatives he is close to and which he stays away from, what political activities he participates in, what church he goes to, what charities he contributes to, what books and periodicals he reads, and how he spends his leisure time.

The centrality of his gay identity is sometimes an asset and sometimes a liability. For example, if he is transferred to a new branch of his firm in a new city, he is not a stranger for long. As soon as he finds out who are the gay men at his new work place, as soon as he gets settled into the gay neighborhood, he is among friends. (Because he so easily befriends gay men at work and at home, he is somewhat less likely to befriend colleagues and neighbors who are not gay.)

A gay man whose job as a journalist required a lot of travel discovered that he was meeting gay people everywhere. His interviewer (Kahn, page 29) reports: "He became aware of a community with an emerging culture of its own. '*You have more in common with gay strangers,' [his respondent] says, 'than with straight neighbors.'*"

Nimmons (pages 1101-102) quotes the recollection of a gay man who "tricked [his] way through Europe" enjoying the companionship of gay locals along the way:

> In my twenties I tricked my way through Europe. It was amazing. I got an inside look and participated in all these worlds that were different from mine. It was an important part of my discovering the world, having come from a WASP-y neighborhood where everybody was the same. . . . . I learned a lot about different cultures and customs and ways of living. . . . . When I got home, all I had to show were pictures of people I had met. One of my friends laughed; he said, "I'd have pictures of churches and monuments, you bring home pictures of people."

Homosexuality gives him access to an entirely new social world, a 24-year old gay man reflects (Nimmons, page 102):

> What I really love about [gay men I meet through On Line contact] is I meet men I NEVER would meet in my life. Professors,

515

a sanitation worker, a white guy who's married, a pilot, artists. I love going over to their places—I get to see lives that are totally new to me.

Perhaps we could better understand the homosexual lifestyle if we could compare it with other lifestyles. What other lifestyles come to mind? The "jet setters," the bohemian lifestyle, the lifestyles of religious groups, the criminal lifestyle, the black underclass, and gypsies. Some lifestyle groups, or subcultures (like the Hasidim and gypsies), have little contact with the outside world, others (like most Jews and middle-class blacks) mingle quite freely with the general society. Some gay men live inside a homosexual world: they live in a gay neighborhood, practice a gay occupation (like hairdressing). work for a gay supervisor, eat at gay restaurants, read gay books and newspapers, enjoy gay entertainment (radio, TV, and theater), visit gay bars, shop at gay stores, attend a gay church, belong to gay political organizations, and support gay charities. Many gay men participate in the life of the general society.

From an evolutionary point of view, a full life includes finding a mate and raising a family. Nature has implanted in man powerful drives to fulfill these survival imperatives: a powerful sex drive, a powerful drive to cherish and protect a mate, and to nurture a family. Couples who cannot have children in the usual way often go to considerable lengths to become parents. Childless couples or single persons often develop a quasi-parental relationship with a dog or cat.

From a strictly evolutionary standpoint, a person who cannot or simply has no interest in finding an opposite-sex mate and together raise a family, suffers from a sociopsychological defect.[1] Our theory holds that this defect results from the interaction of genetic and environmental factors. To a significant extent, reorientation therapy makes it a *correctable* defect. It is not as easily correctable as eye-glasses correct a visual defect, but the principle is the same. Better professional training, guided by good research, can improve both preventative and corrective treatment. Meanwhile, persons who must live with a socio-psychological defect deserve all the compassion, understanding, and good will that a decent society extends to persons who must bear a defect of whatever kind.

2. "Homosexuality a *defect*? But gay men are *over-represented* in the arts—from practical arts to fine arts, from hairdressing and window display, to ballet, architecture, the visual arts, poetry, and writing. Doesn't this mean that homosexuals are also a *gifted* population?"

Very true. A low-masculinized brain may be an important component of artistic interest and talent. (Probably, a low-masculinized brain is also characteristic of *heterosexual* men with artistic talent.) To foster artistic talent and potential, a society must value all its potential artists, gay and straight, and help them develop their gifts for all to enjoy.

3. "Is the tendency toward male homosexuality genetic?"

Most gay advocates would answer: *Absolutely*! But the answer offered here, based on substantial evidence, is: *yes, to a degree* homosexuality is based on genetic *tendencies*. In few individuals, the genetic tendency may be very strong, in others just strong enough to tip the balance when facilitated by *environmental*—family or social—factors. With some men, a homosexual adaptation may be based entirely on environmental factors, as portions of Chapters 22 through 25 suggest.

Research in behavioral genetics points to a host of other behavioral tendencies linked to genetic tendencies: aggressiveness, alcoholism, depression, and so on. Scientific and medical advice does not always endorse yielding to genetic tendencies, mild or strong. Sometimes a person seeks help to moderate or even overcome a genetic tendency that is unwanted.

4. "Does upbringing make a difference?"

There are numerous indications—clinical and survey—that for most people, *upbringing probably does indeed make a significant difference.* Parents who want their sons to attain heterosexual maturity will want to make sure their children get plenty of security, affection, attention and guidance from *both* father and mother.

Likewise, boys need plenty of opportunity, from the earliest years of life, to establish stable friendships[2] with other boys, and to enjoy free play time with them. For example, at play time, boys should be wearing clothes that allow for getting dirty or even torn. Another example: an opthamologist of good reputation advises that the majority of boys who need to wear eye-glasses for school work or reading can g*et along* without glasses during play time.

5. "We are advancing beyond the notion that 'all sex play is bad,' and to accept the evidence—from clinical and field observation—that some kinds of sex play are good and perhaps even necessary for normal development. **How can parents decide what kind of sex play is good for their child's development, and what kind to discourage?"**

Unfortunately, research in children's sex play[3] is limited by many factors. (Would schools and parents permit it? Would "one-way-mirror" research violate the children's right to privacy?) What we do know from clinical and comparative studies leads us to advocate that children be raised in an atmosphere of relative freedom. *Generally speaking, parents need not worry about sex play—same-sex or mixed—between children of approximately the same age.* The use of sex by older children (or adults) to abuse or exploit younger children is another matter, and should not be permitted.

6. "Is man-boy sex really so harmful as to justify classifying this activity as criminal conduct?"

Our moral tradition[4] strongly condemns adult-child sex, heterosexual or homosexual. Our laws accordingly term such activity as *child abuse*, and classify it as criminal conduct. A large-scale study (of 4,340 adults drawn from random-probability samples of persons in five large cities) was reported in 1986, asking if the respondent had had sexual contacts with men before the age of 13 (Cameron *et al.*). Seven percent of female respondents answered yes, and three percent of the males answered yes. The man involved was most often identified as a caregiver, someone the child's parents had entrusted with the care of their child. This says something about how often a boy is sexually abused (Not very often, and less than half as often as little girls are sexually abused.) and it does not tell us how damaging, psychologically, the experience was. Nor does it tell us in how many cases the child *invited* the sexual experience (like the cases cited on pages 200-202 and 325-326).

There is strong evidence, statistical as well as clinical, that gay men are more likely to recall childhood molestation, but the cause-effect relationship is not quite clear. A good society protects its most vulnerable members, including minors, oldsters, and the disabled. Minors are too impressionable; they still lack many aspects of common sense: impulse-control, experience, intelligence, and the ability to distinguish between wish and reality. Minors are dependent on the adult world for the basic necessities of life: food, clothing and shelter. Minors also depend on adults for fulfillment of their *psychological* needs for security, approval and love.

Most children *want* to please adults, and the needier a child is, the more desperately he wants to please adults. What does this say about those children whose physical or psychological needs are *not* being met—the neglected, the hungry, the homeless, the fatherless? They cannot say no to a friendly stranger.

So what's the harm in a child's exchanging sexual pleasure for food, or shelter, or emotional support? Some man-boy lovers take pride in the fact that their boy is *better off* than when he was found on the street: homeless and hungry. But a child is entitled to a normal childhood, which prepares him for a normal adulthood. Normally, a child gets his security from his parents (or foster parents), and engages in sexual play with his peers. What kind of a life does man-boy love prepare a child for?

Although one label—child abuse—may cover all adult-child sex, incidents of adult-child sex cover a wide range of situations. One boy may be so vulnerable—neglected, hungry for affection and attention—as to unwittingly *invite* the attention of a boy-lover. Another boy may be so bold and mischievous as to "seduce" and entrap an adult into performing an act that now places the adult at the mercy of the child, who could denounce the adult for committing a crime. (The section on man-boy love in Chapter 11 describes mischievous, daring boys who entrap men into sexual play.)

How harmful is child-adult sex? That depends on whom you listen to. If you listen to psychotherapists, they will tell you that it is very common for patients to tell them they were sexually crippled by childhood experiences of sexual abuse by an older person. If you read the writings of some gay advocates, or some male social workers, you will read about delinquent or homeless boys who were actually helped when they were "adopted" by kindly men (who, incidentally, liked to fondle them).

Does the law punish pedophiles too harshly for their offense? That is a fair question, and one that can be directed against all sorts of crimes (including drug abuse, for example). Justice requires that each case be judged in the light of its circumstances. One punishment does not fit all offenses.

7. "Have you any more thoughts to add to the question of whether adult homosexuality ever results from childhood seduction?"

Unhappy homosexuals frequently report to their therapist that their first homosexual experience was at the invitation of an older and more experienced person.

Back in 1957, my doctoral dissertation explored Alfred Adler's theory that early memories shape the person's *present* attitudes. This theory would suggest that an adult who *now* finds his homosexual habits uncomfortable, will recall his first homosexual experience as abusive.

Ordinarily, a child resists unwelcome physical intimacy with a scream, a fighting gesture, or a shout of No! Go away! or Stop it! In the recollections of men who *claim* to have been abused, one often senses a pre-homosexual vulnerability, a lack of resistance, an acquiescence, or even a hunger for physical contact.

To return to an autobiographical mode, my thesis chairman was E. Lowell Kelly who, by great coincidence, had during the 1930s conducted a pioneer study of male homosexuals in San Francisco, part of a Terman-Miles project. Kelly's core group of respondents were men who were incarcerated for behavior which at that time was illegal. Kelly won their confidence, and they introduced him to some of their buddies on the outside. As part of his study, he wrote up case studies of 18 male homosexuals. A careful reading of these case studies reveals only *one* case in which the experience is described as a seduction, and in that case the respondent said he felt no guilt after the experience (Kelly, page 295).

In just less than half (44 percent) of the cases, the first sexual partner was an older man who "persuaded" or "taught" the neophyte to participate. One respondent recalled (*ibid.*, page 311):

*When we were finished I realized that I had always wanted it and
I have continued to want it.*

8. "Why do certain young men who are not in fact homosexual worry that they might be?"

Because, as Chapter 5 explains, some homosexual potential, large or small, is part of the psychological makeup of virtually every male. We have reviewed (pages 462-464) indications that some "worriers," like gay men, probably have low-masculinized brains. These "worriers" share many of the feelings and inner experiences of females, and this engenders a feeling of masculine deficit. But the "worriers" have a character and personality structure that orients them toward a heterosexual rather than a homosexual life. "Worriers" must learn that for them, homosexual feelings are part of the "storm and stress" of life, rather than an indication of their true sexual orientation.

9. "What about bringing my little boy to a religious congregation led by a minister (or rabbi) who is homosexual?"

One theme of this book is that homosexuality results from an interaction of genetic and environmental factors. A homosexual minister (or rabbi), if he or she is effective, is a significant person in the child's life. A boy who wants to grow up straight would benefit more from association with role models consistent with his own wishes for his future development.

What about the *right* of a gay man to lead a religious congregation? Even if a minister preaches that heterosexuality is the better way for most people, psychological research strongly endorses the common-sense belief that a good example is more effective than fine words, and that practice is more effective than preachment. The world is big enough to provide a job that suits everyone's talents and limitations. Nobody has a right to a job for which he is not well-suited. The public interest comes first.

10. "The Boy Scouts disqualify open homosexuals from serving in leadership roles. Dos this policy make sense?"

How you stand on this question depends on whether you regard homosexuality as a lifestyle and also hold that one lifestyle is as good as another, or that you regard homosexuality as a sociopsychological defect. If it is a defect, then it may be one that is of no consequence for many professional roles, but has serious implications for the role of Boy Scout leader.

The Boy Scout ideology puts certain ideals ahead of others. A gay man may be an admirable person in many ways, but he cannot represent the ideal that is so important to the Boy Scouts: that a boy grows up to be a husband and father (in the traditional sense), a protector and provider for his family, and a full member of the community.

"But scouting has nothing to do with sexual orientation," one may protest. "Are you insinuating that a Boy Scout leader who happens to be gay will flaunt his sexuality?" Scouting is a life experience, and sex is part of life. Sexual matters arise in all kinds of life situations, and where they arise in scouting, they should be dealt with from a *heterosexual*, not a homosexual, point of view.

For example, on overnight camping trips, there is bound to be some same-sex play. Should it be regarded as "fooling around, the kind of thing most kids do, and eventually get over it," or as an indication that "some boys are gay and that's OK." Similarly, gay men and straight men, even the most permissive ones, differ in their attitudes toward masturbation. When the subject emerges in a Boy Scout group, should the topic be dismissed as "something we don't talk about," should it be dealt with from a straight point of view, or from a gay point of view?

One group's standards are not the same as another group's ideals. Does that make all ideals bad? Does it not rather suggest that everyone not only defend his own standards, but respect the legitimate ideals[5] of others? From this perspective, one cannot endorse punitive measures taken against the Boy Scouts (by churches, synagogues, or funding agencies) because they disqualify gay men from leadership roles in their movement.

If we believe that homosexuality results from the interaction of genetic and environmental factors, if in an open and free society the Boy Scout movement is part of a boy's social environment, the group should have the right to favor leaders who are heterosexual.

11. "If my son has a high school teacher who is openly homosexual, would that influence my son's sexual development?"

By the time your son is of high-school age, his sexual orientation has, in all likelihood, been established. Perhaps your question is: "Does a gay male homosexual belong on the teaching staff of a high school?" The answer depends on the *individual* you have in mind: a mediocre teacher who is flamboyantly gay, or an outstandingly good, dedicated and intelligent teacher who keeps his sexual orientation in the background.

A theme of this book is the *diversity* of the male homosexual population. A "male homosexual teacher" is a three-word label that covers an enormous range of personality and character types.

The most important question is: *Is he really a good teacher?* If he is not, he should not be kept on the job simply because this would help to fulfill the school's "commitment to diversity," or because the teacher fills the school's quota of homosexual teachers.

A really good teacher shows a consistent sense of his responsibility toward his students. That was psychoanalyst Judd Marmor's emphasis when he dealt with the question of gay men as teachers, in 1980 (page 268):

> The "dependability" of a [male] homosexual [entrusted with young boys] . . . rests on whether . . . he . . . is a responsible human being with an adequate "superego," and that is the only factor to be evaluated. . . . Individual homosexuals ought to be evaluated on their own merits and not on the basis of a stereo-typed preconception. . . .

An argument can be made about the *priority* given to diversity in school staffing, but there is something to be said for being *open* to diversity. Having a teacher (or neighbor, or coworker) who is homosexual and also a person of good character can be a valuable learning experience; direct evidence that all homo-sexuals are not weird types. A gay man who is an outstanding teacher and also a person of good character might offer a better learning experience than a mediocre teacher who happens to be heterosexual. When a teacher is being hired (or con-sidered for retention), he deserves to be regarded as *an individual*, with *all* his strengths and limitations, and not voted up of down on the basis of one factor alone.

Teaching is both an appealing and difficult career choice for gay men. Whether a teacher is straight or gay, sexual attraction to a student can happen, and complicate (or destroy) the teacher-student relationship. Therapists are trained to anticipate and resolve this intrusion of sexual attraction into their role, but teachers are often quite unprepared for this event.

Sexual attraction to a student is somewhat more difficult for a gay man to resolve for several reasons. First, the gay man is more likely to be unattached. Secondly, a gay attraction is more likely to lead to a secret affair because secre-cy is an everyday tactic in gay life. The sexual pleasure that follows is likely to be mingled with shame, guilt, confusion, risk of blackmail, fear of exposure and dismissal. Monette (pages 195-197) tells of a sexual involvement with a student that was so upsetting, he finally decided to leave the teaching profession alto-gether:

> I racked myself with self-loathing, first to last, a shame that pur-sued me like the Furies from school to school till I finally bailed out of teaching entirely.

12. What about gay marriages: should they be sanctified by the church, and legalized by the government?

A short answer: Gay partnerships, like gay individuals, certainly should be respected. Whether gay partnerships should be applauded, celebrated, sancti-fied, and rewarded is another matter.

Recently, a television station planned to broadcast a panel discussion on the issue of gay marriage, and had no trouble finding three prominent clergymen who said they were opposed to sanctifying gay marriages. *All three* declined to express their opinion on television, however, because they did not want to be labeled "homophobic," and feared the repercussions that would likely follow.

This author does not have a congregation of worshippers to satisfy, and is therefore at liberty to make the following two statements: (1) Gay marriage is an oxymoron if you respect the traditional definition of marriage, which is a permanent and monogamous[6] partnership between a man and a woman. (2) A gay wedding ceremony is also an oxymoron if you acknowledge that a wedding, and the religious ceremony that accompanies it, is a *celebration*, but parents and family—though they may respect the *right* of gay men to live their own lives—usually regard this aspect of their lives with regret. The fact that some men cannot enjoy the role of husband and father—is this a fact we want to celebrate?

Traditionalists argue that we must continue to define marriage as a life partnership *between a man and a woman* because that is the *settled practice* of many cultures, religions, and centuries. In the May 6, 1996 issue of *The New Republic*, Jonathan Rauch successfully argued that *respect for tradition* is not a very persuasive argument against same-sex marriage. Slavery, segregation, and antimiscegenation laws, Rauch pointed out, have also been the settled practice of many generations. The right of women to vote, to charge her husband with rape, to own property, and to obtain a no-fault divorce—all these rights have ended many centuries of settled practice.

Advocates of gay marriage ignore or distort the evidence to support their case. For example, the evidence of both research and field observation indicates that among homosexual men, monogamy is a rarity. Yet, pleas for sanctifying gay marriage insist that gay partnerships are monogamous. For example, L.D. Solomon (pages 51-52) describes homosexual partnerships as "ongoing, loving relationship[s] . . . enduring relationships based on love, support and responsibility . . . monogamous, respectful and supportive . . . [promoting] family stability . . . exclusive, mutually committed . . . unions." (Is he describing most gay partnerships? many gay partnerships? a few gay partnerships? or occasional gay partnerships? Of course, he does not say.) Based on this grossly misleading conception of the gay lifestyle as it is known to exist, Solomon (page 64) argues that homosexual unions deserve the blessing of what he calls Spiritual Judaism:

> [G]ay and lesbian couples, grounded in love and responsibility
> provide a widened choice in the creation and fulfillment of the
> human connection, fostering mutual support and meeting the
> need for companionship and emotional intimacy. These new fam-
> ily arrangements help those who partake of them to realize the
> Devine by enabling them to experience God in their lives and in

intimate relations with one another. If Judaism supports them in
the right way, they can also contribute to the continuity of the
Jewish tradition.

Clearly, the argument for sanctifying and legalizing "gay marriage" is based
on the claim that gay partnerships are stable and monogamous. As chapter 13
amply documents, overwhelmingly the evidence indicates that this is true of only
a very small minority of male homosexual partnerships. Lesbian couples probably match (or even surpass) straight couples in devotion and fidelity, but the evidence—research, clinical and autobiographical—is that the great majority of
male gay couples, even those who live together for many years, do not live a
monogamous married life.[7] If by "marriage" we mean monogamous marriage,
the evidence indicates that "gay marriage" is indeed an oxymoron.

The case for gay marriage also rests heavily on the argument that homosexuals are simply "born that way," and that making the homosexual lifestyle more
attractive, more comfortable, more rewarding will make homosexuality neither
more nor less popular. The facts laid out in this book question that argument, and
indicate quite strongly that the homosexual habit results from an interaction
between genetic and environmental factors. If that is true, redefining marriage to
include a partnership between two men adds a significant environmental factor
favoring the homosexual lifestyle.

Now we must face the really tough question: *Is homosexuality in the public
interest?* Is it in the public interest to make the homosexual lifestyle more attractive, more rewarding to future generations of American men? In this section,
(particularly answers to questions 14 and 15) the author makes no attempt to hide
his belief that in general heterosexuality is better than homosexuality; likelier to
make for a healthier, more productive, and more satisfying life.

Redefining marriage would reward same-sex partnerships with the various
social, legal and financial benefits accorded to a man and wife: tax benefits,
health insurance benefits, pension benefits, the right to bring a person into the
country to live as one's life-partner. Society rewards married couples because
society (governments, employers, families) *favors* marriage, as it is now defined.
But if a college offers an unmarried student a small shared dormitory room, and
gives a gay couple an apartment with facilities for cooking and entertaining, what
is the message?

If it is *not* in the public interest to make homosexuality more rewarding, then
it is not in the public interest to give gay couples all the benefits accorded to married couples. But this does not mean that gay couples should have *none* of the
rights accorded to a married couple.

Should a gay man have the right to visit his partner at the hospital? *Of course.*
Should he have the right to exercise power of attorney if his partner is disabled?
Of course. Should he have the right to inherit his partner's property? *Of course.*

But sanctifying, celebrating and legalizing "gay marriage" is not the only answer. The cohabitation laws of Sweden probably provide a better model for framing appropriate laws for insuring the legal rights of gay couples. *Meanwhile, with good legal guidance[8] gay partners can draw up a document that will secure for them many of the rights (visitation, inheritance, etc.) that are accorded to married couples.*

13. "As a public policy guideline, is there a difference between 'gay rights' and 'gay pride'?"

Yes: men who have become part of the gay community are entitled to all of the rights of citizenship, and deserve the support of all those who believe in the rule of the majority and the rights of the minority. "Gay pride" is a different matter. It is up to gay men themselves to earn, maintain and enhance their pride. It is not the responsibility of the general community to pin a badge of pride on every gay man. One may question the wisdom of a national teacher's union calling for a week of Gay Pride celebrations, or of a state government (such as that of Massachusetts) allocating public funds that are used to build parade floats for Gay Pride Week. It is not in the public interest to glorify, celebrate or elevate the homosexual lifestyle.

At a time when Gay Pride has become a frequently flaunted slogan, it is appropriate to note that heterosexuals may also take pride in their lifestyles—fostering a social environment that favors good family life,[9] finding gratification in raising a new generation, and championing a life that perpetuates and renews the human family. It is also appropriate that this majority respect the rights of *all* law-abiding members of society.

14. "The author clearly implies that an effective reorientation therapy would be a valuable service, and even seems to favor those therapists who work with gender-dysphoric boys, to *prevent* adult homosexuality. **Clearly, the author seems to think that heterosexuality is better than homosexuality. Does not this bias bring into question the author's objectivity, and thus limit the value of this book?**"

Who would dare suggest that a scholar, because he is gay, is disqualified from researching and writing about homosexuality because he is apt to be biased *in favor* of homosexuality?

What makes any book worth-while—fair-minded, factual or objective—is *not* the author's indifference to his topic. *Indifference never produced a book.* What counts is the author's approach to his work: the methods he uses, and the principles of scholarship to which he subscribes. Has he examined enough of the relevant evidence? Does he deal logically with the known facts? Does he distinguish between well-established facts, possibilities and conjectures, between what he knows to be true and what he just wishes were true? Does he understand alternative points of view? Does he want to be recognized as a persuasive advocate or as a respected scholar?

A psychologist who is true to the standards of his profession must adhere to the facts. A sermon may begin, "A gentleman came into my study last week and poured out this tale of woe," and what follows is an imaginary rather than an actual event.[10] A psychologist is expected not to do that; not to invent a story to fit his argument. If he makes a conjecture, he must label it as such. If he invents a composite case history, he must label it as such.

Writing on a controversial topic challenges an author's ability to be logical and honest, and tests his willingness to take an unpopular position, to speak truth to power.[11] How well this author has succeeded is for each reader to decide.

15. "The author admits that he thinks heterosexuality is better (for society, and for most individuals) than homosexuality. Does he regard this as a personal bias ('the author's privilege'), or would he say it is *in the public interest* to favor heterosexuality?"

Author Bruce Bawer (1993, page 48) takes the view that "homosexuality is morally neutral and without interest." Many gay men would not agree with Mr. Bawer, and admit that their life would be more productive, more satisfying, less tension-ridden if they were not homosexual.

Health hazards alone raise serious questions about the acceptability of homosexuality as an "alternative lifestyle." Rotello's book on the HIV-AIDS crisis argues that the gay lifestyle *invited* the AIDS epidemic. Sexual activity involving both oral and anal contact with multiple partners is a risky practice, inviting herpes, hepatitis, syphilis, and gonorrhea, to say nothing of HIV/AIDS.

It is widely believed that gay advocates have discouraged public health officials from warning about the hazards of anal sex and multiple partners. According to Weinrich (page 390 fn.), "Hepatitis B has killed more gay men than [has] AIDS . . . ."

Reverend Howard Bess, who has counseled many gay men and their parents, reflects on the fact that he has *never* met a parent who was glad that his or her son was homosexual. In 1970, a few years before the AIDS crisis broke out, *Harper's* published an article by the noted essayist and onetime editor of *The American Scholar*, Joseph Epstein, in which he expressed how most parents feel about having a son who is homosexual:

> There is much my four sons can do in their lives that might
> cause me to anguish, that might outrage me, that might make me
> ashamed of them and of myself as their father. But nothing they
> could ever do would make me sadder than if any of them were to

become a homosexual.

Epstein's article led to protests and even sit-ins at the offices of *Harper's*, for publishing this common but unpopular point of view. The truth is that not only do many parents of homosexuals feel that way, but many homosexuals themselves privately regret the disturbance of kinship ties and the other social costs of their sexual orientation.[12]

(The gay advocacy group PFLAG, Parents and Friends of Homosexuals, began as a support group to help parents overcome their distress upon learning of their son or daughter's homosexuality. PFLAG started out as a support group and gradually metamorphosed into an advocacy group, arguing that homosexuality is a laudable lifestyle.

A long life of experience as a person, as a husband, as a father, as a psychological counselor and scholar, inclines this author to agree with the silent majority. Life is full of surprises, full of unexpected and undeserved twists and turns, but experience leads me to believe that—for most people, on the average—a heterosexual life is more fulfilling, more complete, more productive and more satisfying, less isolating, less dangerous and less hazardous than a homosexual life. As Joseph Epstein put it in his 1970 *Harper's* article (page 20):

> [T]o be hostage to such a passion as homosexuality seems to me
> to thwart one's ability to live as fully as one might for all else
> that life offers above and beyond sex.

Epstein not only expresses the view that "it would be a great sadness" if any of his children were to grow up homosexual," but adds that "all of the intelligent persons whom I know have feelings about homosexuality similar to my own." He prefaces this statement with the conviction that "only one civilized view of homosexuality [as a civil right] is possible:" a full support for the civil rights of homosexuals, and opposition to all laws penalizing homosexuality between consenting adults.

Homosexuality is an important human rights issue. It is also a medical issue,[13] and a psychological issue. It is also a *public policy* issue, which is to ask, Is homosexuality good for society? It is not a question of who is right, the homosexual community or society in general. *Both* are right to pursue their interests, and in a good society the rights of every minority group must be balanced against the interests of society in general.

Does society have an interest in whether the homosexual community grows? . . . In whether distressed homosexuals have access to reorientation therapy? Is homosexuality good for society? Who would dare raise these questions for public discussion today? Interestingly, these questions were very explicitly raised in a 1971 publication issued by members of the Kinsey research group at Indiana University. In the "Epilogue" of *Human Sexual Behavior*, a book of anthropological studies, editors Marshall and Suggs raise this question (page 236):

> Social approval of active homosexuality is tantamount to declar-
> ing that society has no interest in, or obligation to make well, the
> sociopsychologically deviant[14] so as to prevent a disturbing
> behavior pattern[15] from spreading in its midst—or that the society
> is not concerned with its own survival!

We know that homosexuality results from the interaction of both genetic and environmental (significantly, *social*) factors, but we do not know (except in a very general way) how to identify or deal with these factors, to favor normal sexual development. The ban on reorientation therapy teaching, practice, and research deprives society of potentially good husbands, fathers and members of the community respected by all, and burdens society with millions of dollars in annual health care costs incurred by the homosexual lifestyle.

Mental health workers who are more sensitive to their responsibilities as shapers of public policy, and less concerned with professional politics, or with preventing the disruption of their professional meetings, will ask themselves whether their role as *citizens* should not take priority over their role as members of a professional organization.

The best public policy cannot accommodate every case. A good public policy covers the solid majority of cases, and makes generous allowances for cases that do *not* fit the rule of the majority (just as military draft laws, even in time of war, allow for the humane treatment of conscientious objectors). To repeat: the civil rights of every citizen must be fully protected, regardless of his or her sexual orientation.

16. What do you think the popular newspaper advice columns contribute to an understanding of this issue?

Ann Landers,[16] during her last ten years as an advice columnist, broadcast the "fact" that homosexuals are simply "born that way," although in earlier years she had designated homosexuality as a psychiatric disorder. She probably became uncomfortable with her position for two reasons: (1) it did not fit the official position of the American Psychiatric Association and other mental health groups, and (2) her position, she must have realized, added to the emotional suffering of gay men and their families. Indeed, according to the "social oppression theory" of homosexual suffering, social stigma is the cause of homosexual suffering. If Ann Landers could *prove* that homosexuality was *inborn*, rather than an acquired condition, she would make life easier for gay men and for their loved ones.

How Ann Landers went about *proving* that homosexuality is inborn is a demonstration of her unique "research methodology." In 1982 she published a letter in which a reader informed her of the Bailey-Pillard study offering "scientific evidence that homosexuals are born that way," and expressed the hope that "people will [now] be less hostile to and more tolerant of homosexuals . . . " Ann Landers decided to bolster the Bailey-Pillard findings[17] with some "research" of her own. To "settle the question once and for all," she asked her gay readers to tell her whether they believed their lifestyle was a choice or "the result of genetics." *She received more than 78,000 responses*, and their tone convinced her that homosexuals are indeed "born that way." This point of view made life easier for homosexuals and their loved ones, but also discourged ego-alien homosexuals from seeking reorientation therapy, and discouraged research in reorientation therapy.

For example, consider the following letter published in the Chicago Tribune, January 18, 2002, not in the column of Ann Landers, but in the column of (her sister) Abby Van Buren, who shared the same point of view. The reader wrote that he was gay "but I don't like being gay. . . . I want a wife and children. I also have a career in which further advancement would be very difficult if it becomes known that I am gay. Psychiatrists and other therapists I have consulted have tried to help me adjust to my homosexuality rather than help me change.

"Abby, adjusting to homosexuality is fine for those who have accepted their homosexuality, but I have not. I know I'd be happier straight. Please help me.

--Unhappy"

It is reasonable to suppose that Ann Landers' response would be substantially the same as Abby's, as they shared the same point of view: "Did you choose to be homosexual? If so, you could choose to be 'straight.' But if you have always had erotic feelings for men instead of women, then face it, you are homosexual—and even though you may be able to change your behavior, you will not be able to change your feelings." As for reorientation therapy, Abby warns that the chances of success are slim. She borrows the words of Polonius to conclude: "To thine own self be true. Only then will you find true happiness."

Compare Abby's advice with the words of Richard Isay, gay-affirmative psychoanalyst: Isay writes (page 107) that marriage is *"a worthwhile compromise for some gay men."* They may find a woman they feel a genuine love and affection for, he continues, "even though there is no erotic attraction." They may willingly acquiesce to the value that their family members and friends place on marriage. They may have had a bad homosexual partnership, and vaguely feel that there is something unsatisfying about homosexuality, even though it continues to occupy their fantasies. Isay warns (page 108) that "a functioning homosexual" should not marry "simply for the sake of conforming with the accepted structure of society or in the hope of curing his condition . . . ."

A therapist cannot simplify a human problem like an advice columnist can. A columnist wants to promote the well-being (and contribute to the entertainment) of millions of readers; a therapist tries to help one person at a time.

17. "This book makes some very unflattering statements about some male homosexuals: that theirs is a sociopsychological defect, that their numbers include men who just want to relieve their sexual tensions in the quickest and easiest way possible, that they take life-threatening risks to indulge an empty fantasy, and so on. **Does the author owe the gay community an apology?"**

Yes, to the extent that any portion of this book obscures the fact that many gay men are sane, productive, and happy people. As noted in the section on The Elites (pages 380-385) there are gay men who are leading responsible, productive, socially useful and personally satisfying lives, within the limitations of what a homosexual life can encompass.[20] Before we can construct a theory of male homosexuality, however, we must acquaint ourselves with a representative sample of the *entire* homosexual population, and this scrutiny necessarily brings us face-to-face with some less-than-flattering facts.

The author's attention to the treatment question (although this is not a book about treatment methods) is intended to challenge the widespread "fact" that reorientation therapy doesn't work because it *cannot* work, that reorientation therapy is therefore an unethical practice, and that those who offer it are misguided cranks, quacks, charlatans, or criminals. This egregiously biased attitude (fostered, incredibly, by both the American Psychiatric Association and the American Psychological Association)[21] is an obstruction to research, training, and clinical practice, and wrongly discourages those homosexuals who are miserable about their sexual compulsions and are good candidates (as defined on pages 504-505) for therapy that can help them become good husbands and fathers, as well as full members of the larger society.

The apology the author owes to gay or gay-friendly readers is similar to the apology a dentist owes to his root-canal patient: the dentist's work has brought about a painful experience, but the work has served a positive purpose. Every analogy is limited, and this one breaks down when one responds: "All right—a root canal helps the patient in the long run. Does this book claim to help the gay man cope with his life problems?" In all honesty, the author has to answer: "No, the primary aim of this book was not to help those homosexuals who intend to live out their lives as gay men, but rather to serve the educated general reader who wants to know enough about male homosexuality to make a serious study of an evolutionary puzzle."

This book is also addressed to teachers, researchers, public policy-makers, and to mental-health professionals. This book may not be too helpful to the present generation of gay men (except those who are interested in reorientation therapy), but it is hoped that this book will serve *future generations* of boys and men, that they may live in a world in which advances in scientific knowledge, educational and clinical methods enable them to enjoy a full measure of their potential for intellectual, artistic, spiritual and social experience.

18. Where do we go from here?

While developing a theory on the evolution of male homosexuality, we have encountered some neglected facts and raised some important issues concerning individual welfare and public policy. Most readers, one would hope, will feel that the author has done enough. It is to be hoped that the information offered and the questions raised have made the book worth-while. Other readers may ask, All right: where to we go from here? To that question, the author would reply: The next step is not to legislate or to advocate, except in a way that *advances our knowledge* of sexual orientation, so that policy and practice are moved not by sentiment, by gut feeling, by guess and by hope, but are guided rather by reliable knowledge.

We know that male homosexuality is a very diverse phenomenon, usually resulting from the interaction of genetic and acquired factors, but we do not know the full range of its diversity or how genetic and acquired factors interact to produce a homosexual identity. That is what we stand to gain from well-designed, well-funded programs[18] of longitudinal research (as was suggested in the final paragraphs of Chapter 26), from good research in reorientation therapy, and from good research in the proactive treatment of gender-atypical boys.[19]

19. If you have reached the end of this book, you can call yourself a book reader. And that brings up this final question: **What books can I now read to advance my understanding of evolutionary psychology?** If that is your question, I would like to recommend that you ask your town or college library to order the following two recent books:

If you are looking for a readable college textbook on psychology from the standpoint of Darwinian theory, read *Evolutionary Principles of Human Adolescence*, by Glenn Weisfeld, professor of psychology at Wayne State University, and published in 1999 by Basic Books. An even more recent title by an evolutionary psychologist is *The Blank Slate; The Modern Denial of Human Nature*, by MIT psychology professor Steven Pinker, and published in 2002 by Viking.

Weisfeld addresses the college undergraduate who wants to know what evolutionary psychology is all about. The serious reader's curiosity is both satisfied and sharpened by Weisfeld's presentation. Adolescence is the life stage around which the book is organized, but the subject is human behavior, considered from a biological point of view.

Pinker addresses the topic of evolutionary psychology from a very different point of view. He addresses not only the college student but the educated general reader. Pinker feels driven to advance an understanding of evolutionary psychology (EP), but he also feels passionate about challenging the popular opposing point of view, variously known as environmentalism or cultural determinism.

Pinker acquaints the reader with a fascinating array of recent research findings that support EP (evolutionary psychology), while he hammers away at the
widespread but wrong-headed point of view that blurs the distinction between
objective facts and "social constructs," as if fair-minded thinking required the
egalitarian conviction that every human mind begins as a Blank Slate. In his
Introduction (page xi), Pinker quotes these words of Chekhov: "Man will
become better when you show him what he is like." Pinker goes on to say, ". . .
and so the new sciences of human nature can help lead the way to a realistic, biologically informed humanism."

So this book ends as it began, expressing the conviction that EP opens the
doors and windows of the human mind to a more valid understanding of what
makes us what we are, and how we can fulfill our best potential.

NOTES TO EPILOGUE, PART 2

1. Not long ago, Laura Schlesinger, conservative talk show host, was assailed for
describing homosexuality as a defect. In answer to Question 15, above, we quoted from a 1971 publication published by members of the Kinsey group, in which
homosexuality was characterized as "sociopsychologically deviant." Very recently, commenting on the Herrell study of mental problems in the gay community,
J. Michael Bailey (1999, page 884) suggested the "possibility . . . that homosexuality represents a deviation from normal development and is associated with
other such deviations that may lead to mental illness." Bailey is the co-author of
a number of gay-friendly investigations.

2. In deciding whether to move to a bigger house on the edge of the city or stay
in your present home inside the city; whether to try for rapid promotion by moving to another city or wait for a promotion at your present location; where you
relocate, when you do move, the accessibility of playmates to your children and
the continuity of their friendships always deserves to be considered.

3. John Money discusses this sensitive issue on page 182 of his 1988 book:

> Although [the development of healthy childhood attitudes toward
> sex] ranks with all other aspects of child health in terms of its
> importance, it is virtually the only aspect of child health that is
> totally neglected. Its very existence is indeed denied. There is no
> special clinic anywhere . . . for pediatric sexual health, no text-
> book, not even a chapter of a textbook of pediatric psychology,
> psychiatry, or child development. Juvenile heterosexual rehearsal
> play is widely viewed as an aberration, and a manifestation of
> original sin that evokes abusive punishment, or in some
> instances, exploitation.

4. How universal (or limited) is society's condemnation of man-boy sex? We know of the eranymos-erastes practices by the aristocrats of ancient Athens (described in Chapter 10), but we do not know of any comprehensive survey of this subject.

A survey of child-adult sex play would include an interesting custom of the Cayapas of Ecuador, described by Altschuler (pages 50-51). In that culture, "a common activity that parents and older siblings engage in with young male children [never with girls] is to hold the child overhead, open the mouth, and then close it over the child's genitals. Observation suggests that the experience is not at all frightening to the child." Altschuler reports (page 48) that adult male Capayans are characteristically "marked by anxiety, suspicion, and lack of confidence . . . . extremely heavy and permissive drinking . . . .[and] low male sex drive." "[S]exual intercourse is spoken of as the vagina eating the penis (page 50). Capayan men speak of sexual activity as if they have no control of it: "When the penis wants to bother a woman it erects itself (page 51)." It seems more than possible that a customary mode of 'play' with the infant male influences his adult personality, even though the infant boy seems 'not at all frightened' by the experience.

5. What is "a legitimate ideal?" Simply stated, it is one that is not socially harmful, one that recognizes the rights of others.

6. This is not to suppose that all marriages are 100 percent monogamous, but a habitual practice that would cause a scandal among friends of a married couple, or lead to a bitter divorce, is taken as a matter of course by friends of gay partners.

7. See chapter 13. McWhirter and Mattison, researchers on gay couples, avoid using the word "monogamy," substituting "sexual exclusivity." Martin Duberman has proposed that instead of referring to homosexual promiscuity or "cruising," we adopt the word "adventuring."

8. The Lambda Legal Defense and Education Fund offers the following suggestions for homosexual couples who want legal backing for their relationship: "Joint ownership of stocks, bonds and checking accounts . . . giving each other power of attorney; telling their doctors that the other is to be treated as next of kin; putting both names on the lease of a shared apartment; making wills and leaving instructions with each other for funeral and burial" (Maddox page 209). Outland's *Handbook* recommends a book by Theodore Hughes and David Klein: *Beating the System: The Essential Guide to Personal Finance and Estate Planning for Gay and Lesbian Couples and Individuals.*

9. "Family values" is too important a theme to be monopolized by the political ultra-conservatives or the religious right. "Good family life" is not an altogether subjective concept. If we know what a *dysfunctional* family is, we should also

know what a *functional* family is: one that strengthens the marriage partnership, one that fosters in its members both a sense of security and the feeling of freedom, one that affords pleasure to friends, relatives, grandparents, parents and children alike. Good family life is nurtured not only through individual effort, but through supportive public policy: *e.g.*, tax policy, school policy, and workplace policies, such as family leave privileges.

10. This author once read in a gay-friendly book written by a minister a case history that contained some hard-to-believe details. It was possible to reach the subject of that case history, and he was asked to elaborate on the questionable details. In response to this request, the subject wrote back that the unusual "details" were inventions of the minister-author.

11. In a December, 1992 *Commentary* article, E.L. Pattullo posed the question, Can a social environment become so friendly to homosexuals that "waverers" will be more likely to drift into this lifestyle? The article elicited a storm of angry letters to the editor.

Pattullo is a retired Harvard University professor, not a professional author. Some science writers worry about saying things that may be both important and true but would "get them in trouble." A popular and prolific scientific writer recently said to the book editor of the *Chicago Tribune*: "In general, I feel one should not speak freely about sex, politics or religion because these are subjects which are so often charged with violence and irrational feeling, and you may be in trouble before you know it."

12. Consider, for example, the following statement made by A. Solomon (page 205), gay author of a book that won a 2002 Lambda Literary Award:

> Few people at the age of dawning sexual awareness would
> choose to be gay, and *most people who are gay entertain for*
> *some stretch of time fantasies of conversion.* (Emphasis added.)

13. Homosexuality is a *medical* issue with many ramifications. For example, Should public health agencies responsible for HIV/AIDS prevention openly advise gay men against practicing anal sex, which is known to disproportionately spread HIV?

14. Bear in mind that this statement, that homosexuality is "socio-psychologically deviant" was published in 1971. This language is taboo today, even if the author only meant to state the obvious fact that as socio-psychological behavior, homosexual behavior is *statistically* deviant, that is, practiced by a small minority of the total population.

15. In what ways might homosexuality be *socially disturbing*? Marshall and Suggs (pages 234-235) stress that homosexuals form occupational cliques that

favor their own members and keep others out. They give examples of U.S. Army units that were "captured" by homosexuals, and comment (p. 235) "[W]e believe that when sexual deviation becomes even a partial basis for personnel selection, the results for the larger society cannot but be negative."

In a 1980 *Commentary* article (page 40), Midge Decter asserts that where homosexuals dominate a business or profession (*e.g.*, theater, music, dance, design, fashion, advertising, interior decorating, journalism, publishing), "they themselves have engaged in a good deal of discriminatory practice against others. There are businesses and professions in which it is less than easy for a straight [person]. . . to get ahead." A *Chicago Tribune* article (May 7, 2002, page 21) cites the statement of a former priest that seminarians who were members of a gay clique "were promoted over heterosexuals."

More fundamentally, perhaps, homosexuality weakens family ties, and reduces the portion of men *and women* who are parenting a new generation. To those who believe that society draws its strength from the solidarity of families, and from the dedication of its members to the primary function of the family, homosexuality is not a social asset.

16. The viewpoints of Ann Landers were a significant factor in shaping public opinion since for 46 years she wrote an advice column that, at the time of her death in 2002, was published in more than 1000 newspapers. Her advice was the topic of pulpit sermons and informal conversation everywhere. A 1978 World Almanac survey named her the most influential woman in the United States.

17. Ann Landers' editor, Rick Kogan, credited her with a great "thirst for knowledge and insatiable curiosity." If these traits had led her to read the actual findings of the Bailey-Pillard study, she would have learned that it was based on 56 gay men who were one of a pair of monozygotic (or "identical") twins, and 54 gay men were one of a pair of fraternal twins. In the case of monozygotic twins, 52 per cent were both homosexual or bisexual, and in the case of fraternal twins, only 22 per cent were both homosexual. (This study, and subsequent research on this topic, is discussed in further detail on pages 361-362.) The Bailey-Pillard study does indeed point to a genetic *contribution* to homosexuality, but the fact that only 52 per cent (*not 100 per cent*) of the monozygotic twins were both homosexual, suggests that heredity was not the only determinant of their sexual orientation.

18. The author calls for research *programs*, rather than a single research program. Typically a research program deals with only a limited aspect of a problem. Let different groups compete and collaborate, and replicate each other's findings.

19. At the forefront of bipolar treatment, for example, are children who have been identified as having a high probability of developing bipolar illness at ado-

lescence. They are being medically treated on a *preventative* basis. This tactic parallels the behavioral (not medical) treatment of gender-atypical, or "pre-homosexual" boys, as practiced by Rekers, Zucker & Bradley, and Fitzgibbons.

20. Does this book maintain a *balanced* point of view? As a partial answer to this question, consider the fact that chapter 21, describing *normal* homosexual types, numbers 24 pages, and includes an extensive original case history. Chapter 24, describing *emotionally troubled* types, numbers 9 pages.

21. In a 1998 Chicago newspaper, the executive director of the American Psychological Association, Raymond Fowler, was quoted as saying, "Sexual orientation is not a choice and cannot be altered. . . . Groups who try to change the sexual orientation of people through so-called 'conversion therapy' are misguided and run the risk of causing a great deal of psychological harm to those who they say they are trying to help."

Appendix 1. The Spitzer Report

A Study of 200 Persons' Recollections of Their Sexual Reorientation Experience

At the May 9, 2001 annual meeting of the American Psychiatric Association, Robert L. Spitzer, professor of psychiatry at Columbia University presented the results of an interview study of 200 respondents (143 men and 57 women) who claimed to have changed from homosexual to heterosexual attraction for at least five years.

A total of 274 applicants were recruited from ex-gay religious ministries, from mental health clinicians who practiced reorientation therapy, and from persons who responded to newspaper or radio publicity.

All 274 volunteers were interviewed and 74 were eliminated because they were not predominantly homosexual to begin with, because although they *were* able to change their behavior and self-identity, there was *no* change in sexual attraction, or because their change was of less than five years' duration.

All applicants were asked to give an estimate of their sexual attraction before, during, or after treatment, ranging from 100 per cent (exclusively homosexual) to 0 per cent (exclusively heterosexual). Only those applicants who reported *at least a 10-point gain* from before treatment to after treatment were included in the study population of 200 persons.

Of the 200 respondents, most were Protestant, Caucasion, and had completed college. Before therapy, 53 per cent of the males, and 33 per cent of the females, had never had consensual heterosexual sex. About three-quarters of the men and half of the women were now heterosexually married. About one-fifth had been married before treatment, and their marriage was threatened by homosexual attraction or behavior.

Ony about one-quarter of the subjects had been treated by a mental health professional (23 per cent by a psychologist, three per cent by a psychiatrist). For the majority, the "change effort" was facilitated by a pastoral counselor (12 per cent), by "mentoring" with a heterosexual role model, by self-help reading, or by "spiritual work:" finding a new relationship with God.

Interviews were conducted by telephone by the investigator himself, each was about 45 minutes in duration, and followed a structured interview schedule developed during a pilot study with 40 individuals. (Responses were coded by the interviewer, and audio recordings were made of about one-third of the interviews for documentation purposes.) Of 121 questions asked, 112 were pre-coded, and nine were open-ended.

Sample pre-coded questions

Lustful thoughts or daydreams about having sex with a person of the same sex (during a given year before, during, or after treatment): never, a few times a year, a few times a month, a few times a week, every day.

Same-sex fantasies during masturbation (during a given year before, during, or after treatment): percent of times when masturbating.

Same-sex fantasies during heterosexual sex (same as above).

Yearning for romantic emotional intimacy (same as above).

Homosexual behavior with excitement (same as above).

Why did the subjects want to change? The most commonly reported responses were: (1) negative characteristics of the gay lifestyle: promiscuity, extreme jealousy, stormy and painful relationships, (2) religious conflict, (3) desire to be successfully married. (Male subjects were more likely to express this motivation.)

The therapy experience (or "change effort") varied from person to person, but group trends are discernable and they are about the same for men and for women. The onset of homosexual feelings goes back to about age 12, and therapy begins at about the age of 20. Finding a successful therapeutic relationship often comes after one or more attempts to establish a therapeutic relationship ended in failure. Patients were often advised by their therapist that they had no choice but to accept their homosexuality.

After two years of therapy, the patient gradually begins to feel different sexually. Patients often report a reduction of homosexual feelings and the gradual emergence and intensification of heterosexual feelings. For most of the subjects (79 per cent), therapy ends after five years of therapy. About one-fifth of the subjects (21 per cent) continue to struggle with the issues that they believe caused their homosexuality, or continue to attend ex-gay support groups.

It is commonly reported that attempts to change sexual orientation results in depression. This was not true for this population of 200 subjects, who reported that they were *often* "markedly" or "extremely" depressed before therapy (males 43 per cent, females 47 per cent), and *rarely* so after therapy (males one per cent, females four per cent).

Were the subjects honest and realistic, or were they engaged in self- deception and gross exaggeration? Here are the indications that they were honest and realistic: (1) Very few reported a *total* change in their sexual orientation. Most admitted that the change was limited but significant. (2) Subjects reported a gradual reduction of homosexual feelings followed by more heterosexual feelings. Their therapy experience (or "change effort") followed a predictable course. (3) There were systematic gender differences: women reported more heterosexual experience and feeling before therapy, and made a greater after-therapy change than men.

Comparing sexual feelings before and after therapy, subjects report very high homosexual attraction before therapy, and very high heterosexual attraction after therapy. Heterosexual masturbatory fantasies were unusual before therapy, and quite common after therapy. Many men reported that they were able to experience heterosexual arousal only after they had become intensely emotionally involved with a woman.After therapy, lustful homosexual thoughts continue to be experienced "a few times a year" by 29 per cent of the males, and 63 per cent of the females.

How satisfying was the subjects' post-therapy sex life? A good sex life was defined as (1) being in a loving, emotionally satisfying relationship for the past year, (2) having sex at least once a month, (3) On a 1 to 10 scale (in which 10 is sex as good as it can be, and 1 is sex as bad as it can be), satisfaction with sex is 7 or better, and (3) never or rarely have homosexual thoughts during sex. By these standards, 66 per cent of males, and 44 per cent of females report a good sex life. It should be noted that about half of the females were still unmarried. Many reported that they were dating, and had been sexually aroused.

With those 56 subjects who were married before they went into therapy. a separate analysis was made of the quality of their heterosexual sex life before and after therapy, Using the same 1-10 scale, a rating of seven or better was taken to described an *emotionally* satisfying sex life. Before therapy, this level of satisfaction was claimed by 25 percent, and after therapy by 98 percent. Was their sex life *physically* satisfying? Using the same criterion of a rating of 7 on a 10-point scale, before therapy, 46 percent rated their sex life as physically satisfying, and after therapy, 100 per cent rated their sex life as physically satisfying.

It is quite possible that this study population of 200 is not representative of all homosexuals who try to change their sexual orientation. Those who experience a measure of success are probably more likely to volunteer. We have noted that only three per cent of our subjects had been in therapy with a psychiatrist. The investigator tried to get the help of psychiatrists in asking former patients to volunteer for this study, but found that psychiatrists were reluctant to get in touch with former patients for this purpose. Ex-gay ministers, on the contrary, were eager to cooperate.

Within the practical limitations of this study, it was possible for the investigator to conclude that *"contrary to conventional wisdom, some highly motivated individuals, using a variety of change efforts, can make substantial change in . . . sexual orientation and achieve good heterosexual functioning.* Subjects who made less substantial changes still believed that such changes were extremely beneficial. Complete change (which is generally considered an unrealistic goal in psychotherapy) is uncommon, particularly in male subjects."

In brief, most subjects did not *completely* change their sexual orientation, but reported *diminished* unwanted homosexuality, and reported an *increase* in their heterosexual potential. Even those volunteers who had been rejected because they had changed only their homosexual identity and no longer engaged in homosexual behavior (but still felt homosexual attractions) seemed to find some satisfaction in the attainment of behavioral control and in their shift in identity, though the change was less than they had wished for.

It would be wrong to assume that our subjects are representative of all patients who go into reorientation therapy, and even worse to assume that homosexual orientation is changeable for all or for most highly motivated persons. Worse yet would it be to use this study to justify coercive treatment of homosexuals.

This study should not suggest that homosexuals in general should try to change. Several subjects spontaneously offered variations of the following words: *"I have no problem accepting that most gays have no interest in changing. I wish they could also acknowledge that I had a right to change, and that I have changed."* In other words, "Live and let live."

Critics of The Spitzer Report find fault with Spitzer's sample. This group of volunteers includes very few persons who were treated by a psychiatrist. The group consists mainly of religious ex-gays, who are eager to promote reorientation therapy. The study includes no direct observation of the therapy process, no objective measures of results, and it is based entirely on patient testimony.

Dr. Spitzer would no doubt admit that his study was less than ideal, and would hope that his study would be judged not by its limitations but by its well-controlled methods and positive findings.

. . . . .

Note: Significantly, back in 1973, Dr. Spitzer led the effort to remove homosexuality from APA's official list of psychiatric disorers. "Now, in 2001," he wrote in a guest newspaper editorial (*Wall Street Journal*, May 23, 2001), "I find myself challenging a new orthodoxy." Spitzer explains: "The assumption I am now challenging is this: that every desire for change in sexual orientation is always the result of societal pressure and never the product of a rational, self-directed goal. This new orthodoxy claims that it is impossible for an individual who was predominantly homosexual for many years to change his sexual orientation—not only his sexual behavior, but also in his attraction and fantasies—and to enjoy heterosexuality."

On the basis of the result of his study, Dr. Spitzer suggests: "The mental health professions should stop moving in the direction of banning [reorientation] therapy."

Appendix 2. The story of Bob

A Christian college student is troubled by his homophobia

In the summer of 1997, Bob drove from his home in Ohio to Auburn, Kentucky to attend a Christian conference on recovery from homosexuality, not because he had ever been homosexual but because he thought it might help him shake off the profound feelings of homophobia that, as an adolescent, he had felt so self-righteous about, but were more recently becoming a source of confusion and embarrassment. He had come to the conference to listen, not to speak. I had come as an observer, to take notes for a book on male homosexuality.[1]

Bob unfolded his story to me at lunch one day, at the cafeteria table where by chance we were seated together. Fortunately, I had brought my tape recorder along, and asked Bob for permission to record his story, which he generously granted. What follows is Bob's own story, adapted for readability but true to Bob's own emphasis and message, as spontaneously recalled by him.

"During my junior high school years, teasing and baiting effeminate-looking boys was a favorite sport of mine. About that time, there was a recorded Eddie Murphy gay-bashing comedy routine. I listened to it many times, and it polished up my own style in taunting the sissy-boys at school: 'Where did you learn to lisp like that?' I would ridicule the way they walked and talked, and hoped this would make me popular with those boys I wanted to like me.

"In contrast to the puny little sissy boys, I was tall and husky (and not bad looking). But behind that masculine appearance, I secretly felt inferior and effeminate, as far back as I could remember. As a child I was, and I still am, very much interested in art, literature, and writing. I am also an emotionally expressive person—what is stereotypically described as effeminate in temperament. I grew up in a small town in the Midwest. For a boy to have that temperament and interests was not accepted in that culture.

"Mom was the daughter of a Navy officer. She was a harsh and controlling person, and a depressed person, besides. She would discipline me harshly, and if I cried (as I often did), she would beat me all over again for crying. Boys weren't supposed to cry.

"Home was not a safe place for me. Because of what I regarded as an effeminate temperament, I had very low self-esteem, which must have shaped the homophobic attitudes I would develop later on. Nobody paid attention to my art work or my writing.

"As I grew up, my artistic interests weren't getting me dates or attention from the girls, like being a good athlete would, or being strong. I wasn't popular with

541

the girls, nor did I have any close male friends either. That had been true since early childhood. I had superficial relationships with people on the soccer team that I played on, but I was always a very lonely person.

"During my junior high school years, because of my self-hatred, I followed Eddie Murphy's gay-bashing comedy tapes. Both my self-hatred and my desire to bond with the other boys led me to express a very hateful attitude toward homosexuals.

"I've always been straight. I can't ever remember struggling with homosexual feelings whatsoever. I dated a number of girls, and treated some of them pretty badly. I think I was trying to get even with the way my mother tormented me. A few years ago, I met the girl who is now my wife. What really bowled me over was her incredibly compassionate attitude toward all kinds of people: She was popular around campus, was open about her Christian beliefs, at this public university. She was popular in the gay community, atheist community, as well as with the partying heterosexuals. She had her standards and could still love all those people, not be judgmental about them from a self-righteous, right-wing standpoint. That made her very attractive to me.

"She lovingly confronted my hypocrisy and self-righteousness and said, 'I have gay friends. I don't condone their behavior, but they're human beings, I love their humanity and personhood, and I can make some distinctions without putting my own stamp of approval on their lifestyle.' She extended the same kindness to heterosexual friends who were promiscuous. I had never seen that kind of integrity or character. It's a very rare thing that drew me to her, and made Christianity very attractive and loving to me. Her viewpoint helped me balance my own views, moderated them and brought them in line . . . I saw in her a person I could love and grow with tremendously.

"Anne was a safe person for me, one that I didn't have in my relationship with Mom. Affirming and accepting, Ann was even able to love me, a bigot. I met her at a Christian camp in 1992. We were buddies for a week and then we lost track of each other. The next year, I transferred from a community college to the state university, and was surprised to discover that this was the school Anne was attending too. Our friendship evolved into something more and we were married in July of 1995.

"It wasn't long after I started dating her and having my self-righteousness and hypocrisy challenged that I got a position in campus housing as a resident assistant. I was assigned a partner to work with and share a room with. It turned out that Kevin was gay. At first, he was attracted to me and I was tempted to quit. But I realized how hypocritical I was, and, besides, I needed the job to get through school.

"Kevin turned out to be an incredibly decent person. He was compassionate and charitable and Christ-like in many of his attitudes. I could respect him as a person even though I feel that homosexuality is wrong.

"I could champion the homosexual's civil rights, fight against his harassment even though I don't approve of homosexual behavior. I must face my own sexual sins and my heterosexual acting-out. I have to admit that there is a beam in my own eye.[2]

"I was a graduate student in social work, and was required to take a course in minority group relations. We were taught that since 1973 the American Psychiatric Association did not regard homosexuality as pathological, and that we were to regard homosexuality as an alternative lifestyle. Homosexuals were a minority group, and deserved he same consideration as racial and religious minorities. I couldn't completely agree but neither did I know how to disagree in a calm and logical way.

"I was given an assignment to talk to the class as if I were leading a training session with a group of hospital workers, and help them adopt the correct professional attitudes toward various minority groups: African Americans, Hispanics, Native Americans, women, and gays. I'm afraid I didn't do a very good job of expressing the attitudes we had been taught. Maybe I came across as a real bigot."

Bob says he's changed his mind about going into social work, and is going into teaching instead. Perhaps his social work professors told him they didn't think he was suited for social work, and Bob blamed his unresolved homophobia for ruining his classroom presentation.

"I am the oldest of five children. My dad has worked incredibly hard to support us. He was a loving person. I remember he had a very heavy beard and always had a five o'clock shadow. Part of my going-to-bed ritual was for Dad to give me one of his 'sandpaper hugs.' I always thought that was kind of neat, and hoped someday I would give my kids a sandpaper hug.

"Mom was chronically stressed, and my dad, when he was there, he was a very loving person. I idolized him. He was a safe person. But Mom certainly wore the pants and was the power in the family. When my dad tried to confront her craziness, she threatened him with separation. I watched my dad being emasculated, in a sense, which was hard to take. I was consciously angry with him for not confronting Mom's pathology.

"Two important experiences in overcoming my homophobia were meeting my wife and meeting Kevin, my dorm partner. At first, I thought my wife had just swallowed the ultra-liberal line, but then I realized that her attitude was compassionate and Christian and truly God-like. Meeting Kevin taught me that a gay man could also be more honorable and decent than most of my partying heterosexual friends. Still, I have not altogether overcome my homophobic feelings, and hope that attending this conference will help me adopt a more Christian attitude."

NOTES TO APPENDIX 2

1. Talking across the lunchroom table on a previous day, I told another conference participant that I was there to take notes for a book, and he laughingly replied: "I've heard that before!"

2. Bob's allusion is to Matthew 7:4, How wilt thou say to thy brother, Let me pull out the mote out of thine eye; and, behold, a beam is in thine own eye?

Appendix 3. Summary of Factors Underlying Homosexual Behavior

> It becomes increasingly clear that homosexuality is an extraordinarily complicated phenomenon, in which the causative factors are multiple."—Evelyn Hooker (quoted by Hatterer 1970, page 43)

> As early as 1922, Stekel had reached the conclusion that "a single key does not unlock the riddle of homosexuality" (page 15). "Our investigations have proven that homosexuality has no uniform psychogenesis" (page 296).

Because the basis of homosexual behavior and a homosexual identity are so complex, we are challenged to summarize what is known or conjectured about the basis of this mode of adjustment. The clinical observations of Otto Fenichel and Lawrence Hatterer are preceded here by a review of prenatal factors presented in this book. For convenience in presentation, all these factors are arranged in ten groups.

Of the dozens of factors listed below, some are of critical importance, some may be of moderate importance, and others are of minor significance. It is of course the task of future research to tell us which are which.

1. PRENATAL FACTORS

Genetic factors: low brain-masculinization. Variability is a basic characteristic of all living things. Our by-product theory proposes that just as human males vary in height, weight, etc., they also vary in the extent to which their brains have been masculinized, a process that is generally controlled by genetic factors. Differences in mental life–cognition, emotion, and motivation–ranging from hypermasculinity to gender discordance, stem in significant part from differences in brain masculinization. Our knowledge of brain-masculinization is based on both animal experiments and human studies.

(Genetic factors also determine the degree to which an individual's *physique* is masculinized—ranging from the heavily muscled hypermasculine type, to the androgenous type. This variation is *less* likely to contribute to a homosexual identity than *temperamental* low-masculinization.)

Congenital factors tending toward homosexuality. Nine months of prenatal development elapse between the moment of conception and birth. During

545

these nine months, the development of the embryo (three months after concep-tion, called a fetus) is shaped by all sorts of factors: nutritional, hormonal, drug, etc. Some promote development. while others retard, stunt, or reshape develop-ment.

> Most identical twins are indeed identical in most observable
> ways. Paradoxically, however, some "identical" twins are very
> different from each other (although DNA tests show that they are
> indeed genetically identical). For example, only one may suffer
> from some congenital condition; only one may be left-handed. In
> chapter 19 we examined the evidence regarding homosexuality
> in identical twins. It should come as no surprise that the correla-
> tion is much less than perfect

To a significant extent, outstandingly good looks seems to accompany homo-sexuality. (Why this might be so, is discussed in chapter 12, pages 211-217.) This physical trait is probably the result of both genetic and congenital factors.

LIFE EXPERIENCE

From a non-clinical standpoint, a homosexual identy results when a person discovers that he is sexually attracted to persons of his own sex, and is able to overcome the social obstacles—discouragement, ridicule, threat, ostracism—that would lead him to inhibit or deny his sexual feelings. From a gay-advocate stand-point, a troubled mind—depression, anxiety—and its manifestations—like alco-holism or drug addiction—are the result of social oppression.

Mental health professionals--psychiatrists in general, psychoanalysts, psy-chologists, social case workers—deal with the mentally troubled, whether mod-erately or severely. Most of their patients are not homosexual. The few who are, show that their sexual attitudes are the result of unusual conditions of their upbringing—abnormal parental influences, home influences, peer influences, or cultural influences. *Clinical formulations are derived from the study of mentally troubled patients, and do not always apply to people who feel no need for psy-chological help.* However, these formulations may be of indirect value in help-ing to understand sub-clinical or even ordinary behavior, just as an abnormal physical condition may point to a normal physical requirement.

1. Mother-son relations.

Mother wanted a daughter, and treats son as if he were a girl.

Mother is overly dominant, binding, seductive, overprotective, controlling, or possessive, hypercritical, aggressive, emasculating, demanding, leading to son's repressed hostility toward women.

Mother reacts with hostility toward son who reminds her of hated or feared father or husband; displaced retaliation for past abuse.

> [T]he cold mother who totally lacked physical, emotional, or affectionate contact with her son and who consistently expressed a high degree of hostility, rejection, and domination may have inflicted damage enough to make her son almost untreatable (Hatterer 1970, page 63).

Mother is a punishing person, leading to a fear of women, and avoidance of them as harsh and hostile. Avoidance of mother generalizes to avoidance of women in general and deflects the person's sexual interest to men.

> Patient may deny his fear of women by identifying with women, and adopting a female sex role. Fenichel (page 483) discusses reactive homosexuality.

Mother is fearful of her husband's erotic aggressiveness, and emasculates him in front of her son.

Mother is competitive toward her husband, and attempts to control, dominate, and punish him.

Mother uses son as a substitute-husband, leading to son's fixation on this role. Mother rejects father because she feels ignored or replaced by other women.

Mother exhibits a passivity, anxiety, or fear of men and/or hatred of other women; attitudes adopted by son.

Mother exhibits an inhibited or prohibitive sexual attitude.

> "My mother acts like sex doesn't exist between a man and a woman, and she always made me feel like it was dirty and dangerous. I think she completely denies her own sexual feelings. You know she's never even hugged me or my father, not once in my entire life that I can remember . . . she's obviously afraid of sensual feelings . . . her own and others" (Hatterer 1970, page 73).

A mother can indoctrinate her son, by word or actions, with the rule that "sex" (i.e., heterosexual thoughts) is dirty and dangerous—may prepare the boy for a homosexual adulthood. 1] He avoids contact with girls, and thus never learns to feel comfortable with girls. 2] He avoids contact with boys who talk about girls, and thus does not share heterosexual fantasies with other boys, or profit from their experience. 3] In his masturbatory fantasies he also avoids thinking of girls, and fantasizes male partners instead.

Mother ambivalent about the expression of aggression and dominance; leading to son's emotional, social, and erotic phobic reactions to women.

Mother disappointed over son's emotional or physical weakness, leading to a feeling of rejection by women.

Mother sabotages father-son relationship; son fears, dislikes, disrespects, cannot communicate with father; negative attitudes block male identity.

Son has a strong fixation to the mother, and is unable to leave her.

Son overidentifies with mother, and adopts a feminine passive role.

An absent mother. Wulff describes a homosexual patient whose mother suffered from tuberculosis, was confined to a sanatorium and died when the patient was four years old.

A boy brought up without a mother figure does not develop realistic attitudes toward women. This lack of experience may result instead in distorted attitudes and strange fantasies that women are punishing, castrating creatures, and the person turns to men for expression of his sexual feelings. Freud conjectured (in "Three Essays . . .") that in ancient Greece, noble boys were raised by male slaves, and that this predisposed Greek aristocrats to man-boy love.

2. Father-son relations

Father absence, indifference, emasculation, weakens father-son identification. A homosexual partner may substitute for a non-existent father. The patient seeks an older male whom he can idealize for his status or manly qualities.

Father passivity, dependency, or inadequacy. Father seems emasculated, female-dominated, over-identified with his son; leading to ambiguity of father-son identification.

Father fearful of women, impotent, bisexual, or homosexual.

Fear that father wishes to harm him may be warded off by finding a sexual partner who is a father figure. The person's unconscious says, "I do not need to be afraid of father, since we love each other" (Fenichel, page 334. In Wulff's case, mother was absent and father was brutal and violent.).

> [Homosexual behavior ranges from] the idea of killing the father in order to take his place, and the idea of ingratiation, of being obedient and submissive to such a degree that the father will willingly grant participation (Fenichel, page 334).

Father's excessive aggressiveness, dominance, hostility, or rejection, weakens father-son identification.

Father too competitive with son, to bolster his own ego, leading to an inability to compete with other men.

Father wished for a daughter and related to son accordingly, or father related to son and mother as one and the same; son suffers from a feminized upbringing.

Father rejects son for showing unmasculine traits: small, weak, artistic, or poorly adapted to outdoor sports.

Father uses son for affection normally obtained from his wife, who has rejected him as an erotic partner.

Father narcissistic, not affectionate toward wife or children, and son cannot identify with him.

Son reacts with hostility to father.

3. Other relations with siblings and other members of household (including sexual abuse)

Overwhelmed by too many mother figures or surrogates:older sisters, cousins, aunts, grandparents, servants—a dominating female matriarchal household.

Emasculating brothers and sisters, belittle his malenes.

> "My sisters wanted me to dress up like they did, in dresses and
> high heels. I liked them too much to refuse. But when I first felt
> like having sex with girls, all I could think of was that I was
> doing it with my sisters, and it made me go cold. . . . (Hatterer
> 1970, page 44)."

Statistical data link homosexuality to birth order. Perhaps birth order per se predisposes a boy to homosexuality: he feels inferior to his older siblings, who are bigger and more masculine. Or is homosexuality likely to result when older siblings take unfair advantage of their younger brother, engaging him in aggressive play and forcing him to consistently lose, in competition with them.

Fenichel (pages 336-337) notes that younger brothers may overcompensate for an envious hatred of their older brother by developing an affectionate attitude toward him, and by making a homosexual object choice.

Older siblings (also cousins, uncles, or other familiar older males) may engage a young boy in sexually abusive or seductive behavior. It is a fact that homosexual men are more likely to recall that they were sexually abused during their childhood. What is not clear is the extent to which the abuse experience predisposed the boy toward adult homosexuality, and the extent to which a pre-homosexual boy attracts abusers. (This issue is further discussed on pages 200-202 and 325-326.)

> "My brother masturbated me every night he could," one patient
> will say. "This went on from when I was ten years old and lasted
> until I was sixteen. He forced me to do the same for him . . . yes,
> he also screwed me . . . and then, when he got married, he treat-

ed me with contempt as a fairy. . . ." (Hatterer, page 44).
That cousin who lived with us for a few years took my penis in
his mouth and he really got me started. . . ." (*ibid*).

"I had an unmarried uncle who lived with the family for years.
The folks must have been blind. . . . We had to share the same
room and he began by teaching me how to blow him and everything else just followed. . . . At first I hated it, but then I guess I
grew to love it. . . . Since there was no money for my schooling,
he paid for it. . ." (*ibid*).

4. Peer relations, sexual abuse by older boys

Emasculation by male peers; branded as a sissy boy because of effeminate
appearance, dislike of rough and tumble, aggressive or competitive games; or an
inability to be assertive, aggressive, or appropriately hostile.

Boy's over-identification with female peers, from playing mostly with girls,
with dolls, or by dressing up in girls' clothes.

a one-to-one friendship, promoting premature physical intimacy. "Crush" on
an idealized male figure, to replace an absence of emotional contact with father.

Physically attractive, rejected by his father, and fearful of rejection by his
peers, boy is vulnerable "to erotic exploitation by male peers and/or older males
who wish to be sexually serviced. . . . A mode of gaining status and being valued" (Hatterer 1970, pages 40-41)." (See recollections of Baumann, and Hatterer
patient, page 325 of this book.)

5. Restrictive environments. Normal sexual development requires a relatively normal environment. If the individual is denied ordinary social supports,
he may turn to homosexual behavior as an available outlet for his sexual impulse.

a) All-male environment. Because everyone has a certain amount of sexual feeling toward one's own sex, if females are unavailable, men will be sexually attracted to other men. Military life, prison life, occupations that place men
in all-male societies lead to homosexual behavior. Frequently called situational
homosexuality, Fenichel uses the term accidental homosexuality.

b) When contact with girls is forbidden. Where adolescent boys are
forbidden sexual access to girls, boys engage in "a certain amount of more or less
manifest homosexuality" (Fenichel, page 328).

References

Aaron, W.(1972). *Straight. a Heterosexual Talks About His Homosexual Past.* Garden City, N.Y.: Doubleday.

Abramowitz, S. (1986). Psychosocial outcomes of sex reassignment surgery. *Journal of Consulting and Clinical Psychology,* 54, 183-189.

Adair, N. & Adair, C. (1978). *Word Is Out.* New York: Dell Publishing

Adams, H. E. See Tollison.

Adams, G.R. & Gullotta, T. (1989). *Adolescent Life Experiences.* Pacific Grove, Calif.: Brooks/Cole.

Adler, A. (1938). The inferiority complex. Chapter VI in Social Interest: *A Challenge to Mankind.* London: Faber and Faber.

Albom, M. (1997). *Tuesdays with Morrie.* Doubleday: New York.

Aldridge, R.G. (1983). Sexuality and incarceration. *Corrective and Social Psychiatry,* 29, 74-77.

Allen, L.S., Richey, M.F., Chai, Y.M., & Gorski, R.A. (1991). Sex differences in the corpus collosum of the living human being. *Journal of Neuroscience,* 11, 933-942.

Allen, L.S. & Gorski, R.A. (1991). Sexual dimorphism of the anterior commissure and massa intermedia of the human brain. *Journal of Comparative Neurology,* 312, 97-104.

_____.(1992). Sexual orientation and the size of the anterior commissure in the human brain." *Proceedings of the National Academy of Sciences, USA, 89,* 7199-7202.

_____.(1992a) Sexual orientation and size of anterior commissure in the human brain, *Proceedings of the National Academy of Sciences of the U.S.A., 89,* 7199-7202.

Allyn, D. (2000). Make Love, Not War; *The Sexual Revolution: An Unfettered History.* Boston: Little, Brown & Co.

Alonso, A.M.& Koreck, M.T. (1993). Silences: Hispanics, AIDS, and sexual practices. Ch. 7 in *The Lesbian and Gay Studies Reader,* Abelove, H., et al. (eds.). New York: Routledge.

Altman, D.(1982). *The Homosexualization of America. the Americanization of the Homosexual.* New York: St. Martin's Press.

Altschuler, Milton. (1971). Cayapa personality and sexual motivation. In *Human Sexual Behavior,* Marshall, Donald S. & Suggs, Robert C. (eds.), New York: Basic Books, pages 38-58.

American Psychiatric Association. (1994). *Diagnostic and Statistical Manual of Mental Disorders, Fourth Edition (DSM IV).* Washington, D.C.:American Psychiatric Association.

Andreasen, N.C. (1978). Creativity and psychiatric illness, *Psychiatric Annals 8:3,* 23-45.

_____.(1987 or 1988). Creativity and mental illness: prevalence rates in writers and their first-degree relatives. *American Journal of Psychiatry 144,* 1228-1292.

Anonymous. (1963). Homosexual Fantasies in Heterosexuals. *Journal of the American Medical Association, 183 (7)* 42-43.

Anonymous. (1976). What do you say to a guy after you've blown him in the park? *Body Politic, Oct., no. 27,* 13.

Antill, John K.(1983). Sex role complementarity versus similarity in married couples. *Journal of Personality and Social Psychology, 45,* 145-155.

Antler. See Morse.

Arnold, M. (1998). It's the cachet, not the money. *The New York Times,* May 21, section E, page 3.

Babchuk, W.A., Hames, R.B., & Thompson, R.A. (1985). Sex differences in the recognition of infant facial expressions of emotion: The primary caretaker hypothesis. *Ethology & Sociobiology, 6,* 89-101.

Bailey, J.M. & Pillard, R.C. (1991). A genetic study of male sexual orientation. *Archives of General Psychiatry, 48,* 1089-1096.

_____, Gaulin, S., Agyei, Y., and Gladue, B.A. (1994). Effects of gender and sexual orientation on evolutionarily relevant aspects of human mating psychology. *Journal of Personality and Social Psychology 66 (6),* 1081-1093.

_____. & Martin, N.G. (1995) A twin registry study of sexual orientation. Poster presentation at the *International Academy of Sex Research,* 21st annual meeting, Provincetown, Mass.

_____. (1999) Homosexuality and mental illness. *Archives of General Psychiatry, 56,* 883-884.

Barash, D.P. and Lipton, J.E. (1997). *Making Sense of Sex.* Washington, D.C.: Island Press.

Baron, J. (1996). Some issues in psychotherapy with gay and lesbian clients. *Psychotherapy 33 (4)*, 611-616.

Baumann, R.E. (1986). *The Gentleman from Maryland; The Conscience of a Gay Conservative*. New York: Arbor House.

Bawer, B. (1993). *A Place at the Table; The Gay Individual in American Society*. New York: Poseidon Press.

_____. (1996). *Beyond Queer; Challenging the Gay Left Orthodoxy*. New York: The Free Press.

Bayer, R. (1981). *Homosexuality and American Psychiatry; the Politics of Diagnosis*. New York: Basic Books.

Beach, F. A. (1949). A cross-species survey of mammalian sexual behavior. Paper read at the 38th *Annual Meeting of the American Psychopathological Assn.*, June 1948, and published in *Psychosexual Development in Health and Disease*, P.H. Hoch & J. Zubin, (eds.), New York: Grune & Stratton.

_____. (1978). Human sexuality and evolution. Pages 123-153 in *Human Evolution: Biosocial Perspective*, S.L. Washburn & Elizabeth R. McCown (eds.). Melco Park, Calif.: The Benjamin Cummings.

Beam, J. (1986) Brother to brother: words from the heart. An essay in In the Life: *A Black Gay Anthology*. Boston: Alyson Publications.

Becker, H.S. (1973). *Sociology of Deviance*.

Beiber, Irving et al. (1962). *Homosexuality: A Psychoanalytic Study*. New York: Basic Books.

Bell, A. P. & Weinberg, M.S. (1978). *Homosexualities: A Study of Diversity Among Men and Women*. New York: Simon & Schuster.

_____, Weinberg, M.S. & Hammersmith, S.K. (1981) *Sexual Preference: Its Development in Men and Women*. Bloomington, Ind.: Indiana University Press.

Bem, D. J. (1996). Exotic becomes erotic: a developmental theory of sexual orientation. *Psychological Review, 103*, 320-335.

Bene, E. (1965). On the genesis of male homosexuality: an attempt at clarifying the role of the parents. *British Journal of Psychiatry,* 801-813.

Berenbaum, S.A. (1990) Congenital adrenal hyperplasia: intellectual and psychosexual functioning. Pages 227-260 in *Psychoendocrinology: Brain, Behavior and Hormonal Interactions*, Holmes, C. (ed.). New York: Springer.

_____. & Hines, M. (1992) Early androgens are related to childhood sex-typed toy preferences. *Psychological Science 3*:203-206.

_____. & Snyder, E.(1995). Early hormonal influences on childhood sex-typed activity and playmate preferences: implications for the development of sexual orientation. *Developmental Psychology: 31*, (1), 31-42.

Bergler, E. (1961) *Counterfeit Sex*. New York: Grove Press.

Bergman, D. (1996). Let the living creature lie. In *Boys Like Us, Gay Writers Tell Their Coming Out Stories*. Merla, P. (ed.) Avon Books: New York.

Berman, L. A. (1957). *The Projective Interpretation of Early Recollections*. Doctoral dissertation, University of Michigan.

_____ (1968). *Jews and Intermarriage; A Study in Personality and Culture*. New York: Thomas Yoseloff.

Bernstein, I.S., Gordon, T.P. & Rose, R.M. (1983). The interaction of hormones, behavior, and social context in nonhuman primates. In Svare, B.B. (ed.), *Hormones and Aggressive Behavior*. New York: Plenum.

Bianco, D.(1999). *Gay Essentials; Facts for Your Queer Brain*. Los Angeles: Alyson Books.

Binson, D. et al. (1995). Prevalence and social distribution of men who have sex with men:United States and its urban centers. *Journal of Sex Research, 32 (3)*, 245-254.

Birkby, R.C. (1990). *Boy Scout Handbook, Tenth Edition*. Irving, Texas: Boy Scouts of America.

Blanchard, R. et al. (1983). Measuring physical aggressiveness in heterosexual, homosexual and transsexual males. *Archives of Sexual Behavior, 12 (6)*, 511-524

Blanchard, R. and P. Sheridan. (1992). Sibling size, sibling sex ratio, birth order, and parental age in homosexual and nonhomosexual gender dysphorics. *Journal of Nervous and Mental Disease, 180*: 40-47.

_____ et al. (1995). Birth order and siblilng sex ratio in homosexual male adolescents and probably prehomosexual feminine boys, *Developmental Psychology 31,* 22-30.

_____, Zucker, K.J., Bradley, S.J. & Hume, C.S. (1995). Birth order and sibling sex ratios in homosexual male adolescents and probably prehomosexual feminine boys. *Developmental Psychology 31*:22-30.

_____ and Bogaert, A. (1996). Homosexuality and number of older brothers. *American Journal of Psychiatry*, 153:27-31.

Bloch, I. (1902-3). *Ätiologie der Psychopathia Sexualis.* (2 vols.) Dresden. Bloch's writings have been published in various English editions.

Blum, D. (1997). *Sex on the Brain; The Biological Differences Between Men and Women.* New York: Viking.

Blumstein, P. & Schwartz, P. (1977). Bisexuality: some social psychological issues. *Journal of Social Issues, 33,* 30-44 .

_____ . (1983) *American Couples.* New York: Morrow.

Borgersma, E. (1991). Boy-lovers and their influence on boys: distorted research and anecdotal observations, *Journal of Homosexuality.*

Bouchard, T. Jr., Propping, J. et al. (eds.) (1993). *Twins As a Tool of Behavioral Genetics.* J. Wiley :Chichester, N.Y.

Bourne, K. (1990). *Creating a lesbian identity,* doctoral dissertation in counseling psychology, University of Southern Calif.

Boyer , D. (1989). Male prostitution and homosexual identity. In G. Herdt's (ed.) *Gay and Lesbian Youth.* Binghamton, N.Y.: Harrington Park Press.

Braaten, L. J. & Darling,C.D. (1965). Overt and covert homosexual problems among male college students, *Genetic Psychology Monographs, 71,* 269-310.

Bradbury, T.N., Campbell, S.M., & Fincham, F.D. (1995) Longitudinal and behavioral analysis of masculinity and femininity in marriage. *Journal of Personality & Social Psychology, 68,* 328-41.

Bradley, M. (1965). *Queer St. U.S.A.* Los Angeles: K.D.S..

Brechner, E. M. et al. (1984). *Love, Sex, & Aging: A Consumers Union Report.* Boston: Little Brown.

Brill, A. (1913). The conception of homosexuality. *Journal of the American Medical Association 61(5),* 335-40.

Brown, H.J. (1976). *Familiar Faces, Hidden Lives: the Story of Homosexual Men in America Today.* New York: Harcourt Brace Jovanovich.

Brown, Rita Mae (1976). A stranger in "paradise": Rita Mae Brown goes to the baths. *The Body Politic,* April, pages 15-16.

Brown, Roger (1996). *Against My Better Judgement.* New York: Harrington Pk.

Brownfain, J. J. (1985). A study of the married bisexual male: paradox and resolution. *Journal of Homosexuality, 2,* 173-188.

Browning, F. (1993). *The Culture of Desire: Paradox and Perversity in Gay Lives Today.* New York: Crown Publishers.

Buchan, J. (1919). *Mr. Steadfast.* London: Hodder & Stoughton.

Burdon, W.M. (1996). Deception in intimate relationships: a comparison of heterosexuals and homosexual/bisexuals. *Journal of Homosexuality 32(1),* 77-91.

Burkett, E. & Bruni, F. (1994). *A Gospel of Shame: Children, Sexual Abuse, and the Catholic Church.* New York: Viking.

Burland, C. (1973). Erotic primitive art in North America. Pages 107-126, in Rawson, P. (ed.) *Primitive Erotic Art.* London: Wydenfeld & Nicolson.

Burr, C. (1996). *A Separate Creation; the Search for the Biological Origins of Sexual Orientation.* New York: Hyperion.

Burton, R. V. & Whiting, W.M. (1960). The absent father and cross-sex identity. *Merrill-Palmer Quarterly, 7,* 85-95.

Byrd, A. D. and Nicolosi, J. (2002). A meta-analytic review of treatment of homosexuality. *Psychological Reports, 90*, 1139-1152.

Caird, R. (1994). *Ape Man; the Story of Human Evolution.* New York: Macmillan.

Cameron, P.C., et al. (1986). Child molestation and homosexuality. *Psychological Reports, 38*, 327-337.

Campbell, B.G., editor (1985) *Humankind Emerging, Fourth Edition.* Boston: Little, Brown.

Campbell, JD. (1953). *Manic-Depressive Disease; Clinical and Psychiatric Significance.* Philadelphia: Lippincott.

Cappon, D. (1965). *Toward an Understanding of Homosexuality.* Englewood Cliffs, N.J.: Prentice-Hall.

Carlat, D.J. & C.A.Camargo Jr.(1991). Review of bulimia nervosa in males, *American Journal of Psychiatry,* 148, 831-843.

Carrier, J.M. (1985). Mexican male bisexuality. Pages 75-85 in *Bisexualities: Two Lives to Lead.* Klein, F. & Wolf., T. (eds.) New York: Haworth.

Cassese, J. (editor) (2000). *Gay Men and Childhood Sexual Trauma; Integrating the Shattered Self.* Binghamton, NY: Harrington Park Press.

Chauncey, G. (1994). *Gay New York: Gender, Urban Culture, and the Making of the Gay Male World 1890-1940.* New York: Basic Books.

Chilman, C.S. (1983). The development of adolescent sexuality. *Journal of Research and Development in Education, 16*, 16-26.

Clark, D.(1997). *Loving Someone Gay,* revised edition. Berkeley, Calif. : Celestial Arts Publishing.

Cohen, R, (2000) *Coming Out Straight: Understanding and Healing Homosexuality.* Winchester, VA: Oakhill Press.

Collins, J. (1926) *The Doctor Looks at Love and Life.* New York: George H. Doran.

Comfort, A. (ed.). (1972). *The Joy of Sex: A Gourmet Guide to Lovemaking.* London: Quartet Books.

Consiglio, W. (1991). *Homosexual No More; Practical Strategies for Christians Overcoming Homosexuality.* Wheaton, Ill.: Victor Books.

Cornett, C. (ed.) (1993). *Affirmative Dynamic Psychotheraphy with Gay Men.* Northvale, N.J.: Jason Aronson.

Cory, D. (1951). *The Homosexual in America: A Subjective Approach.* New York: Greenberg.

_____ & LeRoy, J. P. (1963). *The Homosexual and His Society: A View from Within.* New York: Citadel Press.

Cotton, W. L. (1972). Role playing substitutions among homosexuals. *The Journal of Sex Research. 8*, 310-323.

_____(1975). Social and sexual relationships of lesbians. *Journal of Sexual Research 11*, 139-148.

Crenshaw, T.L. (1996). *The Alchemy of Love and Lust.* New York: G.P. Putnam's Sons.

Cupach, W.R. & Metts, S. (1991). Sexuality and communication in close relationships. Pages 93-110 in *Sexuality In Close Relationships,* by McKinney, K. & Sprecher, S. (eds). Hillsdale, N.J.: Lawrence Erlbaum.

Dallas, J. (1991). *Desires in Conflict; Answering the Struggle for Sexual Identity.* Eugene, Oregon: Harvest House.

Davenport, W. (1965). Sexual patterns and their regulation in a society of the Southwest Pacific. In *Sex and Behavior*, F.A. Beach (ed.), New York: Wiley

Davidson, M. (1962). *The World, the Flesh and Myself.* London: GMP Publishers Ltd.

de Lacoste-Utamsing, C. & Holloway, R.L. (1982). Sexual dimorphism in the human corpus callosum. *Science 216*:1431-1432.

Decter, Midge (1980). "The Boys on the Beach," *Commentary*, 35-48.

De Lange, N. (2000). *An Introduction to Judaism.* Cambridge, U.K.: Cambridge University Press.

Devereaux, G. (1937). Institutionalized homosexuality of the Mohave Indians. *Human Biology, 9*, 498-527.

Diagnostic and Statistical Manual of Mental Disorders, Fourth Edition. (DSM-IV) . (1994). Washington, D.C.: American Psychiatric Association.

Diamond, J. (1992). *The Third Chimpanze; the Evolution and Future of the Human Animal.* New

York: HarperCollins.

_____. (1997). *Why is Sex Fun?* New York: Basic Books.

Dickson, G. (1996). Father-son relationships and male sexual development. In J. Nicolosi (Ed.), *Collected Papers from the 1996 NARTH Conference.* Encino, Calif.: National Assn. of Research and Treatment of Homosexuality.

Dimock, P.T. (1988). Adult males sexually abused as children: characteristics & implications for treatment. *Journal of Interpersonal Violence, 3,* 203-221.

Dörner, G. (1980). Prenatal stress and possible aetiogenic factors in homosexuality in human males. *Endokrinologie, 75,* 365-368.

_____. (1980a). Sexual differentiation of the brain, *Vitamins and Hormones, 38,* 325-373.

_____. (1981). Sex hormones and neurotransmitters as mediators for sexual differentiation of the brain, *Endokrinologie, 78,* 129-138.

_____, et al. (1983). Stressful events in prenatal life and bi- and homosexual men. *Experimental & Clinical Endocrinology, 81,* 83-87.

_____. (1985). Sex-specific gonadotrophin secretion, sexual orientation and gender role behavior. Endikronologie, 86, 1-6.

Dover, K. J. (1980) *Greek Homosexuality.* New York: Random House:

DSM-IV. See *Diagnostic . . .*

DuBay, W. H. (1987). *Gay Identity; The Self Under Ban.* Jefferson, N.C.: McFarland & Co., Inc.

Duberman, M. (et al.).(1990). *Hidden from History: Reclaiming the Gay and Lesbian Past.* Meridian: New York.

_____.(1996). *Midlife Queer; Autobiography of a Decade.* New York: Scribner.

Duke, P. & Hochman, G. (1992). *A Brilliant Madness; Living wih Manic-Depressive Illness.* New York: Bantam Books.

Edelstein, L. (trans.) (1943). *The Hippocratic Oath.* Baltimore: Johns Hopkins.

Eichberg, R. (1990). *Coming Out; an Act of Love.* New York: Dutton.

Ellis, H. (1910). Sexual Inversion. In author's *Studies in the Psychology of Sex,* vol.1, part 4. New York: Random House.

Ellis, L. (1995). Sibling sex ratios and birth orders among male and female homosexuals. Poster presentation at *International Behavioral Development Symposium,* Minot State University, May.

_____ & Ames, M.A.. (1987). Neurohormonal functioning and sexual orientation: a theory of homosexuality-heterosexuality. *Psychological Bulletin,* 101, 233-258.

Elson, M. (editor) (1987). *The Kohut Seminars on Self Psychology and Psychotherapy with Adolescents and Young Adults.* New York: Norton.

Epstein, J. (1970). Hetero/homo: the struggle for sexual identity. *Harper's, 241,* 37-51.

Evans, R.I. (November 1974). Lorenz warns: "Man must know that the horse he is riding may be wild and should be bridled. *Psychology Today* 82-93.

Fay, Robert E., et al. (1989). Prevalence and pattern in same-gender contact among men. *Science, 243,* Jan. 20: 334-348.

Feldman, M.P. (1966). Aversion therapy for sex deviations: a critical review. *Psychological Bulletin,* 65, 65-79.

Feldman, S.S., Brown, N.L. & Canning, R.D.(1995). Pathways to early sexual activity: a longitudinal study of the influence of peer status. *Journal of Research in Adolescence, 5,* 387-412.

_____, Aranujo, K. & Winsler, A. (1994). The relationship context of sexual attitudes and behaviors: gender and ethnic differences. Paper presented at the Sexuality Symposium at the biennial meeting of the *Society for Research on Adolescence,* San Diego, Calif.

Fellows, W. (collected and edited by) . (1996). *Farm Boys: Lives of Gay Men from the Rural Midwest.* Madison, Wisc.: University of Wisconsin Press.

Fenichel, O. M. (1945). *The Psychoanalytic Theory of Neurosis.* New York: Norton.

Fergusson, D.M. et al. (1999). Is sexual orientation related to mental health problems and suicidality in young people? *Archives of General Psychiatry,* 56, 876-880.

Finch, F.M. (1967). Sexual activity of children with other children and adults. *Clinical Pediatrics* 6, 267-278.

Finkelhor, D. (1979). *Sexually Victimized Children.* New York: Free Press.

_____. (1981). The sexual abuse of boys. *Victimology: An International Journal*, 6, 76-84.

Finn, R. (1996). Biological determination of sexuality heating up as research field, *The Scientist*, 10, 13,16.

Fisher, P.R. (1972). *The Gay Mystique; the Myth and Reality of Male Homosexuality*. New York: Stein & Day.

Fisher, S. (1989). *Sexual Images of the Self: The Psychology of Erotic Sensations and Illusions*. Hillsdale, N.J.: Lawrence Erlbaum Associates.

Fitzgibbons, R. (1996). Origins and healing of homosexual attractions and behaviors. Appendix I in *The Truth About Homosexuality*, by Harvey, J.F., San Francisco: Ignatius Press.

Ford, C., & Beach, F. (1952). *Patterns of Sexual Behavior*. New York: Harper

Frances, A. & First, M. (1998). *Your Mental Health; A Layman's Guide to the Psychiatric Bible [DSM-IV]*. New York: Scribner.

Freedman, D.G. (1968). Personality development in infancy: a biological approach. Ch. 12 in *Perspectives in Human Evolution*, I., edited by S.L. Washburne and P.C. Jay. New York: Holt, Rinehart & Winston.

Freehof, S. (1973). Judaism and homosexuality, a responsum. *CCAR Journal*, Summer, 31-33,

Freud, S. (1905; revised 1910) Three essays on the theory of sexuality. *Standard Edition of the Complete Psychological Works of Sigmund Freud*, Strachy, J. (ed. and trans.). London: Hogarth Press, 1957, VII, 125-245.

_____. (1910). Leonardo daVinci and a memory of his childhood. *Standard Edition of the Complete Psychological Works of Sigmund Freud*, Strachey, J. (ed. and trans.). London: Hogarth Press, XI, 63-137.

_____. (1914). On narcissism, an introduction. *Standard Edition of the Complete Psychological Works of Sigmund Freud*, Strachey, J. (ed. and trans.). London: Hogarth Press. XIV, 73-102.

_____. (1920). Beyond the pleasure principle. Standard Edition of the Complete Psychological *Works of Sigmund Freud*, Strachey, J. (ed. and trans.). London: Hogarth Press. XVIII, 7-64.

_____. (1940-1962) *Gesammelte Werke*, 18 vols. London: Imago.

Freund, K.W. Sedlácek, F. & Knob, K. (1965). A simple transducor for mechanical plethysmography of the male genital. *Journal of the Experimental Analysis of Behavior 8*:169-170.

Fridell, S.R. et al. (1996). Physical attractiveness of girls with gender identity disorder, Archives of Sexual Behavior 25, 17-30.

Gallup, G.G. & Suarez, S.D. (1983). Homosexuality as a by-product of selection for optimal heterosexual strategies. *Perspectives in Biology and Medicine*, 26 (2) 315-322.

Garber, M. (1995). *Vice Versa: Bisexuality and the Eroticism of Eyeryday Life*. New York: Simon & Schuster.

Garnets, L. & Kimmel, D. (eds.). (1993). *Psychological Perspectives on Lesbian and Gay Male Experiences*. New York: Columbia University Press.

Gaulin, S.J.C. and FitzGerald, R.W. (1986). Sex differences in spatial ability: An evolutionary hypothesis and test. *American Naturalist*, 127, 74-88.

Gerassi, J. (1966) *Boys of Boise; Furor, Vice, and Folly in an American City.* New York: Macmillan.

Gilbert, B.M. (1996). Gays and lesbians under the chupah [marriage canopy]. *Reform Judaism*, 24:4, Summer, 17-21+.

Gilligan, C. (1982). *In a Different Voice: Psychological Theory and Women's Development.* Cambridge, Mass.: Harvard University Press.

Gladue, B. et al. (1984). Neuroendocrine response to estrogen and sexual orientation. *Science*, 225 (4669), 1496=1499.

_____ and Beatty, M. (1990). Sexual orientation and spatial ability in men and women. *Psychobiology, 18*, 101-108.

Glick, B.S. (1959). Homosexual panic: clinical and theoretical considerations. *Journal of Nervous and Mental Disease*, 129 (1), 20-28.

Glueck, S. & Glueck, E. (1950). *Unravelling Juvenile Delinquency*. New York: Commonwealth Fund.

Goldberg, H. (1976). *The Hazards of Being Male; Surviving the Myth of Masculine Privilege.* Plainview, N.Y.: Nash Publishing Corp.

Golden, Carla (1996). "What's in a name? Sexual self-identification among women." In R. Savin-Williams & K. Cohen (eds.), *The Lives of Lesbians, Gays, and Bisexuals: Children to Adults* (pp. 229-249). Fort Worth, Texas: Harcourt Brace & Co.

Goldstone, S.E. (1999). *The Ins and Outs of Gay Sex; A Medical Handbook for Men.* New York: Dell.

Goodheart, Eugene (2001). *Confessions of a Secular Jew; a Memoir.* Woodstock, N.Y.: Overlook Press.

Goodman, P. (1979). "Memoirs of an ancient activist," In *The New Gay Liberation Book . . .* Len Richmond, ed. Palo Alto, Calif.: Ramparts Press. (Originally published in *Win* magazine, 1969.)

Goodwin, F.K. & Jamison, K.R. (1990). *Manic-Depressive Illness.* New York: Oxford University Press.

Gottlieb, David I. (1977). *The Gay Tapes: A Candid Discussion About Male Homosexuality.* Stein & Day: New York.

Gould, R. E. (1979). What we don't know about homosexuality. Pages 36-50 in *Gay Men; The Sociology of Male Homosexuality*, M. P. Levine, ed.). New York: Harper & Row: (Reprinted from The New York Times, Feb. 24, 1974.)

Gould, S. J. (1977a). *Ever Since Darwin.* New York: Norton.

_____. (1977b). *Ontogeny and Phylogeny.* New York: Norton.

_____. (1980). *The Panda's Thumb.* New York: Norton.

_____. (1983). *Hen's Teeth and Horse's Toes; Further Reflections in Natural History.* New York: Norton.

Goy, R.W. et al. (1988). Behavioral masculinization is independent of genital masculinization in prenatally androgenized female rhesus macaques. *Hormones and Behavior, 22*, 552-571.

Gramick, J. et al. (1989). *Homosexuality in the Priesthood and Religious Life.* New York: Crossroad Publishing.

Gravitz, M.A. (1968). Masculinity-femininity orientation on the MMPI and marital status. *Psychological Reports, 23*, 1330.

Green, R. (1975) Sexual identity: research strategies, *Archives of Sexual Behavior, 4*, 337- 352.

_____ , Neuberg, D.S. and Finch, S.J. (1983). Sex-typed motor behaviors of "feminine" boys, conventionally masculine boys, and conventionally feminine girls. *Sex Roles 9*, 571-579.

_____. (1985). Gender identity in childhood and later sexual orientation: follow-up of 78 males. *American Journal of Psychiatry. 142*, 339-341.

_____. (1987). *The "Sissy Boy Syndrome" and the Development of Homosexuality.* New Haven: Yale University Press.

_____ and Fleming, D.T. (1990). Transsexual surgery follow-up: status in the 1990s. *Annual Review of Sex Research, 1*, 163-174.

Greenberg, D. F. (1988). *The Construction of Homosexuality.* Chicago: University of Chicago Press.

Grever,C. (2001). *My husband Is Gay; A Woman's Guide to Surviving the Crisis.* Freedom, Calif.: The Crossing Press.

Grossman, S. (1972). *Sexual knowledge, attitudes and experiences of deaf college students.* Unpublished master's thesis, George Washington University, Washington, D.C.

Gunderson, S. & Morris, R. (1996). *House and Home.* New York: Penguin.

Hall, J. and Kimura, D. (1995). Sexual orientation and performance on sexually dimorphic [throw-to-target] motor tasks. *Archives of Sexual Behavior, 24*, 395-408.

Hamer, D. & Copeland, P. (1994). *The Science of Desire.* New York: Simon & Schuster.

Hamilton, G.V. (1929). *A Research in Marriage.* New York: Boni.

Harlow, H.F. (1962)..The heterosexual affectional system in monkeys. *American Psychologist, 37*, 1-9.

Harris, J.R. (1995). Where is the child's edvironment? A group socialization theory of development. *Psychological Review, 102*, 458-489.

_____. (1998). *The Nurture Assumption: Why Children Turn Out the Way They Do*. New York: Free Press.

_____. (2000). Research on child development: What we can learn from medical research. Paper presented at the *Children's Roundtable*, Brookings Institution, Washington, D.C., September 28.

Harry, J. (1982). *Gay Children Grow Up; Gender, Culture and Gender Deviance*. New York: Praeger Publishers.

Hart, J. (1991). *Gay Sex; A Manual for Men Who Love Men*. Boston: Alyson.

Hathaway, S.R. & McKinley, J.C. (1951). *Minnesota Multiphasic Inventory Manual*.

Hatterer, L. (1965). *The Artist in Society: the Problems and Treatment of the Creative Personality*. New York: Grove Press.

_____. (1970). *Changing Homosexuality in the Male*. New York: McGraw-Hill.

_____. (1980). *The Pleasure Addicts*. Cranbury, N.J.: A.S. Barnes.

Heger, H. (1980). *The Men with the Pink Triangle: the True Life- and-Death Story of Homosexuals in the Nazi Death Camps*. Boston: Alyson.

Helmer, W. J. (1963). New York's middle class homosexuals. *Harper's*, 226 (March), 85-92.

Henry, G. W. (1955). *All the Sexes: A Study of Masculinity and Femininity*. New York: Rinehart & Co.

Herdt, G.H. (1981). *Guardians of the Flutes: Idioms of Masculinity*.: New York: McGraw-Hill.

_____(1997). *Same Sex, Different Cultures; Exploring Gay and Lesbian Lives*. Boulder, Colorado: Westview Press.

Herrell, M.S. et al. (1999). Sexual orientation and suicidality; a co-twin control study in adult men. *Archives of General Psychiatry, 56* (October), 867-874.

Hewitt, C.C. (1961). On the meaning of effeminacy in homosexual men. *American Journal of Psychotherapy, 15 (4)*, 592-602.

Hicks, S. (1980). Relationship and sexual problems of the visually handicapped. *Sexuality and Disability, 2*, 165-176.

Hill, W.W. (1935). The status of the hermaphrodite and transvestite in Navajo culture. *American Anthropologist, 37*, 273-279.

Hippocrates. *Oath of . . . .* See Edelstein.

Hite, S. (1994). *The Hite Report on the Family*. New York: Grove Press.

Hobson, C. (1992). Surviving psychotherapy. Pages 147-157 in *Out of the Closets: Voices of Gay Liberation*, Jay, K. & Young, A. (eds.) New York : New York University Press.

Hochman. See Duke.

Hockenberry, S. & Lieber, F.(1981). *Homosexual Preference in 51 Men*. Term paper done at Indiana University, Kinsey Institute Library item 532.1 H6 8d

Hoffman, M. (1968). *The Gay World: Male Homosexuality and the Social Creation of Evil*. New York: Basic Books.

Hoffman, M. L. (1978). Sex differences in empathy and related behaviors, *Psychological Bulletin, 84*, 712-722.

Holleran, A. (1978). *Dancer from the Dance*. New York: Morrow.

Hooker, E. (1956). A preliminary analysis of group behavior of homosexuals. *The Journal of Psychology. 42*, 217-223.

_____. (1957). The adjustment of the male overt homosexual, *Journal of Projective Techniques, 21*, 19-31. Reprinted in *The Problem of Homosexuality in the Modern World*, edited by H.M. Rutenbeck. New York: Dutton, 1963.

_____. (1963). Male homosexuality, in N.L. Baberow (ed.) *Taboo Topics*. New York: Atherton.

_____. (1965). Male homosexuals and their world. In Marmor, J. (ed.), *Sexual Inversion: The Multiple Roots of Homosexuality*. New York: Basic Books.

_____. (1967). The homosexual community. In John N. Gagnon, et al. (eds.) *Sexual Deviance*. New York: Harper and Row.

Humphrey, M.A. (1990). *My Country, My Right to Serve*. New York: HarperCollins.

Humphreys, L. (1970). *Tea-room Trade: Impersonal Sex in Public Places*. Chicago: Aldine.

_____. (1971). Impersonal sex and perceived satisfaction. Pages 351-374 in *Studies in*

the Sociology of Sex, Henslin,J.M. (ed.). New York: Appleton-Century-Crofts.

_____. (1972). *Out of the Closets: The Sociology of Homosexual Liberation.* Englewood Cliffs, New Jersey: Prentice-Hall.

_____. (1979). Exodus and identity: the emerging gay culture. in Gay Men; *The Sociology of Male Homosexuality*, Levine, M.P. (ed.). New York: Harper & Row.

_____ and Miller, B. (1980) Identities in the emerging gay culture, pages 142-156 in *Homosexual Behavior, a Modern Reappraisal*, edited by J. Marmor. New York: Basic Books.

Isay, R. (1989). *Being Homosexual; Gay Men and Their Development*. New York: Farrar, Straus, Giroux.

Jackson, D. (1979). Testament of a gay militant. Pages. 23-31, in *The New Gay Liberation Book*, Richmond, L. & Noguera, G. (eds.). Palo Alto: Ramparts.

James, W. (1890). *Principles of Psychology*. Harvard University Press: Cambridge, Mass., Reprinted 1981.

Jensen, G. D. (1981). Teenagers' fears that they are homosexual. *Medical Aspects of Human Sexuality*. 15, 47-48.

Johnson, R. and D. Shrier (1985) Sexual victimization of boys, *Journal of Adolescent Health Care, 6*, 352-376.

_____. (1987) Past sexual victimization by females of male patients in an adolescent medicine clinic. *Journal of Adolescent Health Care, 6*, 372-376.

Johnston, M.W. & Bell, A. (1995). Romantic emotional attachment: additional factors in the development of sexual orientation in men. *Journal of Counseling and Development, 73* (6), 621-625.

Jones, E. (1955). *The Life and Work of Sigmund Freud*, 3 volumes. New York: Basic Books.

Jones, J. H. (1997). *Alfred C. Kinsey, a Public/Private Life.* New York: Norton.

Jung, K. G. (1964). *Man and His Symbols*. Garden City, N.Y.: Doubleday & Co.

Kagan, J. & Moss, H. (1962). *Birth to Maturity*. New York: John Wiley.

_____. (1970). The many faces of response. In Cramer, P.(ed.) *Readings in Developmental Psychology Today*. Del Mar, Calif.: CRM Books

Kahn, A.D. (1997). *The Many Faces of Gay; Activists Who Are Changing the Nation.* Westport, Connecticut: Praeger.

Karlen, A. (1971). *Sexuality and Homosexuality; a New View*. New York: Norton.

_____. (1980). Homosexuality in history. Pages 75-99 in *Homosexual Behavior, a Modern Reappraisal*, Marmor, J. (ed.), New York: Basic Books.

Katz, J. N. (1976). *Gay American History; Lesbians and Gay Men in the U.S.A.* New York: Thomas Y. Crowell.

Kaufman, G. & Raphael, L. (1996). *Coming Out of Shame: Transforming Gay and Lesbian Lives*. New York: Doubleday.

Kelly, E.L. and Terman, L. (1936). "A study of male homosexuality." In *Sex and Personality; Studies in Masculinity and Femininity*, by L.M. Terman and C. Cox Miles. New York: McGraw-Hill.

Keneally, T. (2002). Cold sanctuary; how the Church lost its mission. *The New Yorker*, June 17 & 24, 2002. pages 58-66.

Keuls, E.C. (1993). *The Reign of the Phallus*. Berkeley: U. of California Press.

Kimmel, M. S. (1996). *Manhood in America; A Cultural History*. New York: The Free Press.

_____.(2000). *The Gendered Society*. New York: Oxford U. Press.

Kimura, B. (1965) Vergleichende Untersuchungen über depressive Erkrankungen in Japan und in Deutchland. *Fortschrift Neurologishe Psychaitrie 33*, 202-215.

Kimura, D. (September, 1992). Sex differences in the brain. *Scientific American, 283:1*, 119-125.

King, N. See Cassese.

Kinsey, A.C. et al. (1948). *Sexual Behavior in the Human Male*. Philadelphia: Saunders.

Kirk, M. & Madsen, H. (1989). *After the Ball: How America will Conquer Its Fear and Hatred of Gays in the 90's*. New York: Penguin Books. (First   published by Doubleday, 1989.)

Klaich, D. (1974). *Woman Plus Woman*. New York: Morrow.

Klein, F. (1978). *The Bisexual Option: A Concept of One-Hundred Percent Intimacy*. New York: Arbor House.

Kohut. See Elson.

Konner, M. (1982). *The Tangled Wing: Biological Constraints on the Human Spirit*. New York: Holt, Rinehart & Winston.

Kraeplin, E. (1921). *Manic-Depressive Insanity and Paranoia*. (R.M. Barklay, tr., G.M. Robertson, ed.) Edinburgh: Livingstone (Reprinted 1976 in New York by Arno Press.)

Krantz, G.S. (1982). The fossil record of sex, In *Sexual Dimorphism in Homo Sapiens; A Question of Size*, R.L. Hall (ed.), pages 85-105.

Krege, S. et al. (2001). Male-to-female transsexualism: a technique, results and long-term follow-up in 66 patients. *BJU International, 88 (4)*, 396-402.

Kubacki, A. (1986). Male and female mania. *Canadian Journal of Psychiatry 31*, 70-72.

Kulkin, H. et al. (2000). Suicide among gay and lesbian adolescents and young adults: a review of the literature. *Journal of Homosexuality, 40 (1)*, 1-29.

Kurdek, L.A. (1991). Sexuality in homosexual and heterosexual couples. Pages 177-190 in *Sexuality in Close Relationships*. McKinney, K. & Sprecher, S. (eds.). Hillsdale, N..J.: Lawrence Erlbaum.

LaBarre, W. (1955). *The Human Animal*. Chicago: U. of Chicago Press.

_____. (1984). *Muelos: A Stone Age Superstition About Sexuality*. New York: Columbia University Press.

Lalumière, R.B. & Zucker, K. (2000). Sexual orientation and handedness in men and women: a meta-analysis. *Psychological Bulletin, 126(4)*, 575-592.

Larson, R. & Richards, M.H. (1994). *Divergent Realities: The Emotional Lives of Mothers. Fathers. and Adolescents*. New York: Basic Books.

Laumann, E.O. et al. (1994). *The Social Organization of Sexuality*. Chicago: University of Chicago Press.

Layard, J. (1942). *Stone Men of Malekula*. London:Chatto and Windus.

Leakey, R. (1981). *The Making of Mankind*. New York: Dutton.

_____ and Lewin, R. (1992). *Origins Reconsidered; In Search of What Makes Us Human*. New York: Doubleday.

Lefkowitz, B. (1998) *Our Guys*. New York: Vintage Books.

LeVay, S. (1991). A difference in hypothalamic structure between heterosexual and homosexual men. *Science*, 253, 1034-1037.

_____. (1993). *The Sexual Brain*. Cambridge, Mass.: MIT Press.

_____. & Elizabeth Nonas. (1995). *City of Friends; A Portrait of the Gay and Lesbian Community in America*. Cambridge, Mass.: MIT Press.

_____. (1996). *Queer Science; The Use and Abuse of Research Into Homosexuality*. Cambridge, Mass.: MIT Press.

Levine, M. P. (ed.). (1979). *Gay Men; The Sociology of Male Homosexuality*. New York: Harper & Row.

_____. (1990). *Gay Macho: Ethnography of the Homosexual Clone*. New York University doctoral dissertation,.

_____ . (1998). *Gay Macho: the Life and Death of the Homosexual* Clone. New York: New York U. Press.

Leupp, G.P. (1995). *Male Colors; the Construction of Homosexuality in Tokugawa Japan*. Berkeley, Cal.: University of California Press.

Lewes, K. (1988). *The Psychoanalytic Theory of Male Homosexuality*. New York: Simon & Schuster.

Lewis, M. (1975). Early sex differences in the human: studies of socioemotional development. *Archives of Sexual Behavior, 4*, 329-335.

Lewis, O. (1941). The manly-hearted woman among the North Piegan. *American Anthropologist, 43*,173- 87.

Lew-Starowicz, Z. (1992). Problems of homosexual disabled persons. *Sexuality and Disability, 10*, 253. (Abstract)

Lindesay, J. (1987). Laterality shift in homosexual men. *Neuropsychologia, 28 (6)*, 965-969.

Lindholm, C. and C. (1982). The erotic sorcerers. *Science Digest, 90,* Sept. 9.

Liss, J.L. & Welner, A. (1977). Case report: change in homosexual orientation. *American Journal of Psychotherapy. 31,* 102-104.

Loovis, D. (1977). *Straight Answers About Homosexuality for Straight Readers.* Englewood Cliffs, N.J.: Prentiss-Hall.

Lorenz, K. (1966/1963). *On Aggression* (Marjorie Kerr Wilson, trans.). New York: Harcourt, Brace & World.

Lovejoy, J. & Wallen, K. (1968). Sexually dimorphic behavior in group-housed rhesus monkeys at 1 year of age. *Psychobiology, 16,* 348-356.

McCabe, M.P. et al. (1996). Sexuality and quality of life among people with physical disability. *Sexuality and Disability, 18.* 115-123.

Maccoby, E. E. & Jaeklin, C.N. (1974). *The Psychology of Sex Differences.* Stanford, Calif.: Stanford University Press.

_____ (1998). *The Two Sexes; Growing Up Apart. Coming Together.* Cambridge, Mass.: Harvard University Press.

McCormick, C. M.. Witelson, S.F. & Kingstone, E. (1990). Left-handedness in homosexual men and women: neuroendocrine implications. *Psychoneuroendocrinology, 15,* 69-76.

_____ and Witelson, S.F. (1991). A cognitive profile of homosexual men compared to heterosexual men and women. *Psychoneuroendocrinology 16,* 459-473.

_____. (1994). Functional cerebral asymmetry and sexual orientation in men and women. *Behavioral Neuroscience, 28,* 525-531.

McCourt, F. (1996). *Angela's Ashes,* A Memoir. New York: Scribner.

_____ (1999). *'Tis.* New York: Scribner.

McEwen, B.S. (1981). Neural gonadal steroid actions. *Science* 211:1303-1311.

McGrath, T. (a pseudonym) (2000). Doing Time. In *Male Lust; Pleasure, Power, and Transformation.* Edited by K. Kay, J. Nagle, and B. Gould. New York: Harrington Park Press, pages 83-86.

MacLusky, N.J. & Naftolin, F. (1981). Sexual differentiation of the central nervous system. *Science* 211:1294-1303.

McGuire, R.J., Carlisle, J.M., & Young, B.G. (1965) Sexual deviations as conditioned behaviour: a hypothesis. *Behaviour Research and Therapy, 2:* 185-190.

McKirnan, D.J. & Peterson, P.L. (1989). Alcohol and drug use among homosexual men and women: epidemoiology and population characteristics. *Addictive Behaviors, 14,* 545-583.

McNaught, B. (1997). *Now That I'm Out. What Do I Do? Thoughts on Living Deliberately.* New York: St. Martin's Press.

McWhirter, D. P. & Mattison, A.M. (1984). *The Male Couple: How Relationships Develop.* Englewood Cliffs, N.J.: Prentice-Hall.

Maddox, B, (1982). *Married and Gay; An Intimate Look at a Different Relationship.* New York: Harcourt Brace Jovanovich.

Mailer, N. (1959). The homosexual villain, pages. 222-227 in *Advertisements for Myself,* New York: Putnam.

Marcus, E. (1993). *Is It a Choice? Answers to 300 of the Most Frequently Asked Questions about Gays and Lesbians.* San Francisco: HarperSanFrancisco.

Marcuse, H.(1955). *Eros and Civilization.* Boston: Beacon Press.

Margolies, E. (1994). *Undressing the American Male.* New York: Dutton.

Marmor, J. (1965). *Sexual Inversion: the Multiple Roots of Homosexuality.*: New York: Basic Books.

_____. (1980). Clinical aspects of homosexuality. Ch. 15 in *Homosexual Behavior, a Modern Reappraisal,* J. Marmor (ed.). New York: Basic Books.

_____. (1980). Epilogue: Homosexuality and the Issue of Mental Illness. Pages 391-401 in *Homosexual Behavior, a Modern Reappraisal,* J. Marmor (ed.). New York: Basic Books.

Marquis, D.G. (1948). Research planning at the frontiers of science. *American Psychologist, 3,* 430-438.

Marshall, D.S. & Suggs, R.C. (eds.). (1971) *Human Sexual Behavior; Variations in the Ethnographic Spectrum.* New York: Basic Books.

Masters, W. H.& Johnson, V.E. (1970) *Human Sexual Inadequacy*. Boston: Little, Brown & Co._____ (1982). *Homosexuality in Perspective*. New York: Bantam. (First published by Little, Brown in 1979.)
_____ & Kolodny, R.C. (1982). *Masters and Johnson on Sex and Human Loving*. Boston: Little, Brown & Co.

Mayer, J. E. (1961) *Jewish-Gentile Courtship, an Exploratory Study of a Social Process*. New York: Free Press.

Mayr, E. (2001) *What Evolution Is*. New York: Basic Books.

Mazur, A. & Lamb, T.A. (1980). Testosterone, status, and mood in human males. *Hormones & Behavior, 14*, 236-246..

Mead, M. (1963) *Sex and Temperament in Three Primitive Societies*. New York: Morrow Quill Paperbacks. (1950)

Meany, M.J., Stewart, J. & Beatty, W.W. (1985). Sex differences in social play: the socialization of sex roles. Pages 1-58 in Rosenblatt, J.S., Beer, C., Bushnell, M.. & Stater, P. (eds.), *Advances in the Study of Behavior, vol.. 15*. New York: Academic Press.

Meers, D. R. (1975). Sexuality and the ghetto. Pages 411- 438 in *Masturbation: From Infancy to Senescence*, Marcus, I.M. & Frances, J.J.. (eds.). New York: International Universities Press.

Merriam, A.P. (1971). Aspects of sexual behavior among the Bala (Basongye). In *Human Sexual Behavior*, Marshall, Donald S. & Suggs, Robert C. (eds.), New York: Basic Books, pages 71-102.

Miller, Brian. See Humphreys, L. and Miller, B. (1980).

Miller, J.A. et al. (1980). Comparison of family relationships: homosexual vs. heterosexual women. *Psychological Reports* 46, 1127-132.

Miller, M. (1971). What it means to be a homosexual, *The New York Times Magazine, Oct. 10*, 9+

Miller, S. *Men and Friendship*. (1983). San Leandro, Calif.: Gateway Books.

Moberly, E. (1983). *Psychogenesis; The Early Development of Gender Identity*. London: Routledge & Kegan Paul.

Moir, A. & Jessel, D. (1989). *Brain Sex; The Real Difference Between Men & Women*. New York: Lyle Stuart.

Mondimore, F.M. (1996). *A Natural History of Homosexuality*. Baltimore: Johns Hopkins University Press.

_____. (1999). *Bipolar Disorder; A Guide for Patients and Families*. Baltimore: Johns Hopkins University Press.

Monette, P. (1992). *Becoming a Man; Half a Life Story*. New York: Harcourt Brace Javanovich.

Money, J. (1955a). Linguistic resources and psychodynamic theory. *British Journal of Medical Psychology, 20*, 264-266.

_____, J.G. Hampson, & J.L. Hampson (1955b), An examination of some basic sexual concepts: the evdence of human hermaphroditism. *Bulletin of the Johns Hopkins Hosptial, 997*, 301-19.

_____ (1957) Imprinting and the establishment of gender role. *Archives of Neurology and Psychiatry, 77*, 333-336.

_____& Ehrhardt, A.A..(1972). *Man and Woman. Boy and Girl: The Differentiation and Dimorphism of Gender Identity from Conception to Maturity*. Baltimore: The Johns Hopkins University Press.

_____ (1988). *Gay, Straight, and In-Between; the Sexology of Erotic Orientation*. New York: Oxford University Press.

Montserrat, D. (1996). *Sex and Society in Graeco-Roman Egypt*. London: Kegan Paul.

Moore, S. & Rosenthal, D. (1993). *Sexuality in Adolescence*. London: Routledge.

Moore, W. T. (1975). Some economic functions of genital masturbation during adolescent development. Pages 231-276 in *Masturbation: From Infancy to Senescence*, Marcus, I.M. & Frances, J.J. (eds.). New York: International Universities Press.

Mordden, Ethan. (1983). Article in *Christopher Street Reader*, Denneny, M. et al. (eds.). New York: Coward, McCann.

Morse, C. & Larkin, J. (eds.). (1988).*Gay and Lesbian Poetry in Our Time*. New York: St. Martin's Press.

Murphey, M. R., Checkley, S.A., Seckl, J.R. & Lightman, S.L. (1990). Naloxone inhibits oxytosin release at orgasm in man. *Journal of Clinical Endocrinology and Metabolism.* 71, 1056-1058.

Murray, S. 0. (1995). *Latin American Homosexualities.* Albequerque: University of New Mexico Press.

Nanda, S. (1993) Hijras as neither man nor woman. In Abelove, H. et al. (eds.) *The Lesbian and Gay Studies Reader.* New York: Routledge, pages 542-55.

Nardi,P.M. (1999). *Gay Men's Friendships: Invincible Communities.* Chicago: University of Chicago Press.

Nauman et al. See LeVay 1996.

Newton, E. (1972). *Mother Camp: Female Impersonators in America.* Englewood Cliffs, N.J.: Prentice-Hall.

Newton, N. (1978). The role of the oxytocin reflexes in three interpersonal reproductive acts: coitus, birth and breast-feeding. In *Clinical Psychoneuroendocrinology in Reproduction.* L. Carenza et al., editors. New York: Academic Press, 411-18.

Nicolosi, J. (1991). *Reparative Therapy of Male Homosexuality.* New York: Jason Aronson.

_____. (1993). *Healing Homosexuality; Case Stories of Reparative Therapy.* New York: Jason Aronson.

_____ and A.D. Byrd. (2002). A critique of Bem's "Exotic becomes erotic" theory of sexual orientation development. *Psychological Reports,* 90, 931-946.

Nimmons, D. (2002). *The Soul Beneath the Skin; The Unseen Hearts and Habits of Gay Men.* New York: St. Martin's Press.

Nunberg, H. (1938). Homosexuality, magic and aggression. *International Journal of Psychology, 17,* 1-16.

Oates, Joyce Carol (1987). *On Boxing.* Garden City, NY: Dolphin/Doubleday.

Odets, W. (1995). *In the Shadow of the Epidemic; Being HIV-Negative in the Age of AIDS.* Albuquerque: Duke University Press.

Outland, Orland. (2000). *Coming Out; A Handbook for Men.* Los Angeles: Alyson Books.

Owens, R. E. Jr. (1998). *Queer Kids; The Challenges and Promise for Lesbian, Gay, and Bisexual Youth.* Binghampton, N.Y.: Harrington Park Press.

Palmer, C. J. & Tilley, C.F. (1995). Sexual access to females as a motivation for joining gangs: an evolutionary approach. *The Journal of Sex Research, 32,* 213-217.

Pattullo, E.L. (1992). Straight talk about gays. *Commentary,* December, 21-24.

Paulk, J. (1998). *Not Afraid to Change.* Mukilteo, Wash.: WinePress.

Pedersen, L. E. (1991). *Dark Hearts; the Unconscious Forces that Shape Men's Lives.* Boston: Shambala.

Peterson, C. D., Baucom, D.H. & Elliott, M.J.(1989). The relationship between sex-role identity and marital adjustment. *Sex Roles,* 21, 775-787.

Pfeiffer, J.E. (1972). *The Emergence of Man.* New York: Harper & Row.

Phaneuf, J. (1987). Considerations on deafness and homosexuality. *American Annals of the Deaf,* 132 (1)

Phoenix, C.H., Goy, R.W. & Young. W.C. (1967). Sexual behavior: general aspects. In vol. 2 of Martini, I. & Ganong, W.E. (eds.), *Neuroendocrinology.* New York: Academic Press.

Pillard , R.C. (1977). The genetic theory of sexual orientation, In Schneider, R. Jr. (ed.). *The Best of the Harvard Gay and Lesbian Review.* Philadelphia: Temple University Press, 61-67.

_____ & Weinrich, J.D. (1986). Evidence of familial nature of male homosexuality. *Archives of General Psychiatry,* 43, 808.

Pinker, S. (2002). *The Blank Slate; The Modern Denial of Human Nature.* New York: Viking.

Plaut, W.G. (2000) *The Price and Privilege of Growing Old.* New York: CCAR Press.,

Plummer, David (1999). *One of the Boys; Masculinity, Homophobia, and Modern Manhood.* Binghamton, N.Y.: Harrington Park Press.

Pollak, W. (1998). *Real Boys: Rescuing Our Sons from the Myths of Boyhood.* New York: Random House.

Pomeroy, W. B. (1963) *Boys & Sex; A Long-Needed Sexual Guide for Boys.* New York: Delacorte Press.

Ponton, L. (2000). *The Sex Lives of Teenagers.* Dutton: New York.

Posner, R. A. (1992). *Sex and Reason*. Cambridge, Mass.:Harvard University Press.

Potts, M. & Short, R. (1999). *Ever Since Adam and Eve: The Evolution of Human Sexuality*. Cambridge, Eng.: Cambridge University Press.

Prager, D. (1993). Society's needs vs. personal desires; a dialogue with a gay man who was married. *Ultimate Issues*, 9 (4), 15-16.

Prelutsky, J.. (1991). *There'll Be a Slight Delay, And Other Poems for Grown-Ups*. New York: William Morrow & Co.

Rado, S. (1949). An adaptational view of sexual behavior. In Hoch, P.H. & Zubin, J. (eds.), *Psychosexual Development in Health and Disease*. New York: Grune and Stratton, 159-189.

Rainer, J.D. et al. (eds.) (1963). *Family and Mental Health Problems in a Deaf Population*. New York: New York State Psychiatric Institute.

Read, K. E. (1966). *The High Valley*. London: Allen & Unwin.

_____. (1980). *Other Voices: The Style of a Male Homosexual Tavern*. Novato, Calif.: Chandler & Sharp.

Reid, J. (pseud.). (1973) *The Best Little Boy in the World*. (In 1998, author, Andrew Tobias, wrote under his own name, *The Best Little Boy in the World Grows Up*, q.v.)

Reinisch, J. M. (1990). *The Kinsey Institute New Report on Sex*, New York: St. Martin's Press.

Reisman, J. A. (1995). Partner solicitation language as a reflection of male sexual orientation. Encino, Calif.: *Collected Papers of NARTH* (National Association for Research and Therapy of Homosexuals).

Rekers, G.A. (1992). Development of problems in puberty and sex roles in adolescence. In Walker, C.E. & Roberts, M.C. (eds.), *Handbook of Clinical Child Psychology*, Second Edition, New York: Wiley. 606-622.

_____. (1995) *Handbook of Child and Adolescent Sexual Problems*. New York: Lexington Books.

_____. (1996). Gender identity disorder, *The Journal of Human Sexuality*, Carollton, Tex: Lewis & Stanley:

Remafedi, G. (1999) Suicide and sexual orientation; nearing the end of controversy? *Archives of General Psychiatry, 56*, 885-886.

Renaud, H.R. (1950). *Clinical correlates of the masculinity- femininity scale of the MMPI*. Doctoral dissertation, University of Calif. at Berkeley.

Richmond, E. & Noguera, L. (eds.) (1979).*The New Gay Liberation Book*. Palo Alto: Ramparts Press.

Rind, B., Tromovitch, P. & Bauserman, R. (1998). A meta-analytic examination of assumed properties of child sexual abuse using college samples, *Psychological Bulletin*, July.

Rogers, S.M. & Turner, C.F. (1991). Male-male sexual contact in the U.S.A.: findings from five sample surveys, 1970-1990. *Journal of Sex Research*, 28 (4), 491-518.

Ross, H.L. (1971) Modes of adjustment of married homosexuals. *Social Problems*, 18 (3) 385-393.

Ross, J. M. (1992). *The Male Paradox*. New York: Simon & Schuster.

Ross, M. W. (1983). *The Married Homosexual Man: A Psychological Study*. London: Routledge & Kegan Paul.

Rossman, P. (1976). *Sexual Experience Between Men and Boys: Exploring the Pederast Underground*. New York: Association Press.

Rottello, G. (1998). *Sexual Ecology; AIDS and the Destiny of Gay Men*. New York: Penguin. Previously published by Dutton.

Rowe, M. (1999). *Looking for Brothers*. Toronto: Mosaic Press.

Rubin, L. B. (1985). *Just Friends; The Role of Friendship in Our Lives*. New York: Harper & Row.

Rupp, R. (1993). How groups work: coming out of a gay identity, and becoming one of the guys. *NARTH Bulletin 6(3)*, 2+.

Ruse, M. (1988). *Homosexuality, A Philosophical Inquiry*. Oxford, Eng.: Basil Blackwell.

Ryan, C. & Futterman, D. (1998). *Lesbian and Gay Youth; Care and Counseling*. New York: Columbia University Press.

Sackett, G.P. (1968). Abnormal behavior in laboratory-reared rhesus monkeys. In M.W. Ford, *Abnormal Behavior in Animals* (pp. 293-331). Philadelphia: Saunders.

Sagarin, E. (1976). Prison homosexuality and its effect on post-prison sexual behavior. *Psychiatry, 39,* 245-257.

Saghir, M. & Robins, E. (1973). *Male and Female Homosexuality.* Baltimore: Williams & Wilkins.

Sahlins, M. (1959). The social life of monkeys, apes and primitive man. In *Evolution of Man's Capacity for Culture,* J. Spuhler (ed.). Detroit: Wayne State University Press.

Sanders, D.S. (1980). A psychotherapeutic approach to homosexual men. Ch. 19 in *Homosexual Behavior, a Modern Reappraisal,* Marmor, J. (ed.). New York: Basic Books.

Sanders, G. & Ross-Field, L. Sexual orientation and visuo-spatial ability. (1986). *Brain and Cognition, 5,* 280-290.

Sanderson, T. (1992). *How to Be a Happy Homosexual; the Gay Man's Handbook for the 1990s.* London: GMP Publishers Ltd..

Sandfort, T.M.G. et al. (1999) Sexual orientation and mental health: data from the *Netherlands Mental Health Survey and Incidence Study (NEMESIS).* Stony Book, N.Y.: International Academy of Sex Research.

Santrock, J.W. (1966). *Adolescence.* Dubu1que, Iowa: Brown & Benchmark.

Schaefer, S. (1977) Sociosexual behavior in male and female homosexuals: a study of sex differences. *Archives of Sexual Behavior 6,* 355-364.

Schalow, P. G. (1990) Male love in early modern Japan: a literary depiction of the youth, pages 118-128 in *Hidden from History . . . ,* Duberman, M. et al. (eds.) . New York: Meridian.

Schlegel, W.S. (1966). *Die Sexualinstinkte des menschen.* Berne, Switzerland: Spectrum.

Schmidt, G. & Sigusch, V. (1973). Women's sexual arousal. In Zubin, J. & Money, John (eds.), *Contemporary Sexual Behavior: Critical Issues in the 1970s,* chap. 7, pages 117-143. Baltimore: The Johns Hopkins U. Press.

Schwartz, M.F. & Masters, W.H. (1984). The Masters and Johnson treatment program for dissatisfied homosexual men. *American Journal of Psychiatry 141:*173-181.

Sears, P.S. (1951). Doll play aggression in normal young children: influence of sex, age, sibling status, father's absence. *Psychological Monographs 65,* (6) Whole No. 323.

Segal, E. (1981). *Self and World; An Explanation of Aesthetic Realism.* New York: Definition Press.

Seinfeld, J. (1993). *Seinlanguage.* New York: Bantam Books.

Sergios, P. & Cody, J. (1985-6). Importance of physical attractiveness and social assertiveness skills in male homosexual dating behavior and partner selection. *Journal of Homosexuality, 12* (2), 71-84.

Shaywitz, B. A. et al. (1995). Sex differences in the functional organization of the brain for language. *Nature,* 373, 607-609.

Sheldon, W.H. (1936). *Psychology and the Promethean Will: A Constructive Study of the Acute Common Problems of Education, Medicine and Religion,* New York: Harper.

_____. (1942). *The Varieties of Temperament: a Psychology of Constitutional Differences.* New York: Harper.

Sheridan, P.M., Sibship size, sibling sex ratio, birth order, and parental age in homoseual and heterosexual gender dysphorics, *Journal of Nervous and Mental Disease 160,* 49-47.

Shokeid, M. (1995). *A Gay Synagogue in New York.* New York: Columbia University Press.

Shrier, D. & Johnson, R. (1988). Sexual victimization of boys: an ongoing study of an adolescent medicine clinic population. *Journal of the National Medical Association,* 80, 1189-1193.

Siever, M.D. (1994). Sexual orientation and gender as factors in socioculturally acquired vulnerability to body dissatisfaction and eating disorders. *Journal of Consulting and Clinical Psychology, 62,* 252-260.

Signorile, M. (1993). *Queer in America; Sex. the Media. and the Closets of Power.* New York: Random House.

_____. (1995). *Outing Yourself; How to Come Out as Lesbian or Gay to Your Family, Friends and Coworkers.* New York: Random House.

_____. (1997). *Life Outside; The Signorile Report on Gay Men: Sex. Drugs. Muscles. and the Passages of Life.* New York: HarperCollins.

Silber, S.J. (1981). *The Male from Infancy to Old Age.* New York: Scribner's.

Silverstein, C. (1979). Sexual problems of gay men. Pages 179-183 in *The New Gay Liberation Book*, Richmond, L. & Noguera, G. (eds.). Palo Alto, Calif.: Ramparts Press.

_____ and Picano, F. (1992). *The New Joy of Gay Sex*. New York: HarperCollins.

Simms. S.C. (1903). Crow Indian hermaphrodites. *American Anthropology, 5,* 580-581.

Singer, B, (1985). A comparison of evolutionary and environmental theories of erotic response, Part 2: Empirical areas. *J. of Sex Research, 21,* 46-374.

Sipova, I., & Brzek, A. (1983). Parental and interpersonal relationships of transexual and masculine and feminine homosexual men. *Journal of Homosexuality, 9,* 75-85.

Sixty Minutes TV Broadcast. (1995). *The Second Wave*, July 9.

Slater, E.(1962). Birth order and maternal age of homosexuals. *Lancet* 13, 69-71.

Small, M. (1995). *What's Love Got to Do with It? The Evolution of Human Mating*. New York: Anchor Books.

Socarides, C. (1978). *Homosexuality*. Northvale, N.J.: Jason Aronson.

_____. (1995) *Homosexuality: A Freedom Too Far*. Phoenix, Ariz.: Margrave Books:

Solomon, A. (2001). *Noonday Demon: An Atlas of Depression*. New York: Scribner.

Solomon, L.D. (2002). *The Jewish Tradition, Sexuality and Procreation*. Lanham, Md.: University Press of America.

Spiers, H. and Lynch, M. (1977). The gay rights Freud. *Body Politic, No. 33,* 8+.

Spitzer, R.L. Psychiatry and homosexuality. *Wall St. Journal*, May 30, 2001.

Stambolian, G. (1984). *Male Fantasies / Gay Realities; Interviews with Ten Men*. New York: The SeaHorse Press.

Stanford, C. (2001) *Significant Others; The Ape-Human Continuum and the Quest for Human Nature*. New York: Basic Books.

Stearn, J. (1962). *The Sixth Man*. New York: McFadden.

Stekel, Wilhelm. (1922). *The Homosexual Neurosis*. N.Y.: Emerson Books.

Stiller, Richard. (1963). Homosexuality and the American Indian. *Sexology, 29,* 770-772.

Strayer, F.F. & Strayer, J. (1976). An ethological analysis of social agonism and dominance relations among preschool children. *Child Development, 47*: 980-989.

Storms, M.D. (1981). A theory of erotic orientation development. *Psychological Review, 88,* 340-353.

Strean, H. (1993). *Jokes: Their Purpose and Meaning*. Northvale, N.J.: Aronson.

Strong, E.K. (1943). *Vocational Interests of Men and Women*. Stanford, Calif.: Stanford University Press.

Suggs, R.C. & D.S. Marshall. (1971) Anthropological Perspectives on Human Sexual Behavior. In *Human Sexual Behavior*. Marshall, D.S. & Suggs, R.C. (eds.) New York: Basic Books, pages 218-243.

Sullivan, A. (1995). *Virtually Normal: An Argument About Homosexuality*. Alfred A. Knopf.

_____. (1998). *Love Undetectable; Notes on Friendship, Sex and Survival*. New York: Alfred A. Knopf.

Sulloway, F. J. (1996). *Born to Rebel; Birth Order, Family Dynamics and Creative Lives*. New York: Pantheon Books.

Swaab, D.F. & Fliers, E. (1985). A sexually dimorphic nucleus in the human brain. *Science* 228:1112-1115.

Swartz, D.B. (1993) A comparative study of sex knowledge among hearing and deaf college freshmen. *Sexuality and Disability*, 11, 129-147.

Symons, D.(1979). *The Evolution of Human Sexuality*. New York: Oxford University Press.

Tanner, J.M. (1962). *Growth at Adolescence*. Oxford, Eng.: Blackwell Scientific Publications.

Tanner, N.M. and A.L. Zihlman (1976) Women in evolution, part 1: innovation and selection in human origins. *Signs: Journal of Women, Culture, and Society, 1,* 585-608.

Tavis, C. and Wade, C. (1984). *The Longest War: Sex Differences in Perspective*. New York: Harcourt-Brace.

Tenner, Edward. (1996). *Why Things Fight Back; Technology and the Revenge of Unintended Consequences*. New York: Alfred A. Knopf.

Terman, L. M. (1936). *Sex and Personality; Studies in Masculinity and Femininity*. New York: Russell & Russell, 1968.

_____ (1938). *Psychological Factors in Marital Happiness*. New York: McGraw-Hill.

Theilgart, A. et al. (1971). *A Psychological-psychiatric Study of Patients with Klinefelter's Syndrome*. Copenhagen: Universitetsforleget. I Aarhus Ejnar Munksgaard.

Thompson, D. (1994). the sexual experiences of men with learning disabilities having sex with men--issues for HIV prevention. *Sexuality and Disability*, 12, 221-242.

Thompson, W. (2000). Sex, Blindness, and the Way of the Wound, pages 91 94 in *Male Lust; Pleasure, Power, and Transformation*. K. Kay, J.Nagle, and B. Gould, eds. New York: Harrington Park Press.

Thorstad, D. (1990). Man/boy love and the American gay movement. *Journal of Homosexuality*.

Throckmorton, W. (2002). Initial empirical and clinical findings concerning the change process for ex-gays, *Professional Psychology, 33*, 242-248.

Tiger, L. (1984). *Men in Groups*. New York: Marion Boyars. (First published in 1969 by Random House.)

Tobias, A. (1998). *The Best Little Boy in the World Grows Up*. New York: Random House.

Tripp, C.A. (1987). *The Homosexual Matrix*, Second Edition. New York: McGraw-Hill.

Trivers, R.L. (1972). Parental investment and sexual selection. In B. Campbell (ed.), *Sexual Selection and the Descent of Man*, 1871-1971. Chicago: Aldine.

Troiden, R.R. (1979). Becoming homosexual: a model of gay identity acquisition. *Psychiatry, 42*, 362-376.

Updike, J. (1995). The rumor, In *The Afterlife and Other Stories*. N.Y.: Knopf.

Vanggaard, T. (1972). *Phallos: A Symbol and its History in the Male World*. New York: International Universities Press.

Vennard, J.E. (1997). Anger to advocacy: support groups for non-gay spouses. In *Overcoming Heterosexism and Homophobia: Strategies That Work*, edited by J.T. Sears & W.L. Williams. New York: Columbia University Press.

Vicinus, M. (1990). Distance and desire: English boarding school friendships, 1870-1920, In *Hidden from History*, Duberman, M. et al. (eds.). New York: Meridian, 212-229.

Voeller, B. (1980). Society and the gay movement, Ch. 12 in *Homosexual Behavior, a Modern Reappraisal*, Marmor, J. (ed.). New York: Basic Books..

Wah-shan, C. (2000). *Tonzhi; The Politics of Same-sex Eroticism in Chinese Societies*. New York: The Haworth Press.

Washburn, S.L. and R. Moore (1973). *Ape Into Man; a Study of Human Evolution*. Boston: Little Brown.

_____ and Lancaster, C.S. (1966). The evolution of hunting. Ch. 9 in *Perspectives on Human Evolution, vol. 1*, edited by Washburn, S.L. and Jay, P.C. New York: Holt, Rinehart and Winston.

Weinberg, G. (1972). *Society and the Healthy Homosexual*. New York: St. Martin's Press.

Weinberg, M.S. & Bell, A.P. (1978). *Homosexualities: A Study of Diversity Among Men and Women*. New York: Simon & Schuster.

_____, Williams, C.J. & Pryor, D.W. (1994). *Dual Attraction; Understanding Bisexuality*. New York: Oxford University Press.

Weinrich, J.D. (1987). *Sexual Landscapes; Why We Are What We Are, Why We Love Whom We Love*. New York: Macmillan.

Weisfeld, G.(1999). *Evolutionary Principles of Human Adolescence*. New York: Basic Books.

Wellings, K., Field, J., Johnson, P.M. & Woodworth, J. *Sexual Behavior in Britain: The National Survey of Sexual Attitudes and Lifestyles*. London: Penguin.

Wells, J. W. (1990). The sexual vocabularies of heterosexual and homosexual males and females for communicating with a sexual partner. *Archives of Sexual Behavior*, 19, 139-147.

Werner, D. (1979). A cross-cultural perspective on theory and research on male homosexuality. *Journal of Homosexuality* 4:345-362.

Werner, H. (1948). *Comparative Psychology of Mental Development*. New York: International Universities Press.

Westheimer, R.K. (1995). *Heavenly Sex; Sexuality in the Jewish Tradition*. New York University Press: New York, N.Y.

Whitam, F. L. (1977). Childhood indicators of male homosexuality. *Archives of Sexual Behavior,* *6,* 89-96.

_____. (1977). The pre-homosexual male child in three societies: The United States, Guatamala, and Brazil. Paper presented at the *Conference of the American Association of Sex Educators, Therapists & Counselors (Western Division)*, Phoenix, Ariz.

_____. (1983). Culturally invariable properties of male homosexuality: tentative conclusions from cross-cultural research. *Archives of Sexual Behavior, 12*, 207-226.

White, E. (1980). States of Desire New York: E.P. Dutton.

Whitehead, H.(1993). The bow and the burden strap: a new look at institutionalized homosexuality in Native North America. Ch. 33 in *The Lesbian and Gay Studies Reader*, Abelove,H. et al., (eds.). New York: Routledge.

Whiting, B.B. and J.W.M. (1975). *Children of Six Cultures; a Psycho-Cultural Analysis.* Cambridge: Harvard University Press.

Wikan, U. (1977). Man becomes woman: transsexualism in Oman as a key to gender roles. *Man (N.S.) 12*, 304-319.

Will, G. (1996) AIDS: the evolution of an epidemic, in: *The Woven Figure; Conservatism and America's Fabric*. New York: Scribner, 1997.

Williams, G. (1966). *Adaptation and Natural Selection: A Critique of Some Current Evolutionary Thought*. City : Princeton, N.J.: Princeton U. Press.

Williams, W. (1986). *The Spirit and the Flesh: Sexual Diversity in Amrrican Indian Culture.* Boston: Beacon.

Wilmot, M. & Bierley, H. (1984). Cognitive characteristics and homosexuality. *Archives of Sexual Behavior. 13*, 311-319.

Wilson, E.O. (1978). *On Human Nature*. New York: Bantam Books.

Wilson, G.D. & Cox, D.N. (1983). *The Child Lovers: A Study of Paedophiles in Society*. London: Peter Owen.

Wilson, G.T. & Lawson, D.M. (1976). Expectancies, alcohol, and sexual arousal in male social drinkers. *J. of Abnormal Psychology*, 85, 587-594.

Wingfield, J. (1994). Hormone-behavior interactions and mating systems in male and female birds. Pages 303-330 in Short, R.V. & Balaban, E. (eds.) *The Differences Between the Sexes*. New York: Cambridge University Press.

Wittman, C. (1972). A gay manifesto. Pages 330-342 in *Out of the Closets: Voices of Gay Liberation*, Karla, J. & Young, A. (eds.).

Woods, R. (1977). *Another Kind of Love; Homosexuality and Spirituality*. Chicago: Thomas More.

Woog, D. (1995). *School's Out; The Impact of Gay and Lesbian Issues on American Schools*. Boston: Alyson Books.

Wrangham, R.W. & Peterson, D. (1992). *Demonic Males: Apes and the Origins of Human Violence*. Boston: Houghton Mifflin.

Wright, R. (1994). *The Moral Animal . . . The New Science of Evolutionary Psychology*. New York: Pantheon Books.

Wright, W. (1998). *Born That Way: Genes, Behavior, Personality*. New York: Alfred A. Knopf.

Wulff, M. (1942). A case of male homosexuality, International *Journal of Psychoanalysis. 23*, 112-120.

Yalom, I.D. et al. (1973). Prenatal exposure to female hormones, *Archives of General Psvchiatry, 28*, 554- 561.

Young, Goy, R.W. & Phoenix, C.H. (1964). Hormones and sexual behavior. *Science 143*, 212-218.

Zakarewsky, T.T. (1982). Social aspects of deafness. The deaf community and the deaf population. *Collected papers from the conference on the sociology of deafness, vol. 3*. Gallaudent University, Washington, D.C.

Zborowski, M. and E. Herzog. (1952). *Life Is With People*. New York: International Universities Press.

Zucker, K.J. et al. (1993) Physical attractiveness of boys with gender identity disorder, *Archives of Sexual Behavior 22*, 23-36.

Zucker, K.J. & R. Blanchard (1994). Reanalysis of Bieber et al.'s 1962 data on sibling sex ratio and birth order in male homosexuals. *Journal of Nervous and Mental Disease, 182*: 528-530.

_____ & Bradley, S.P. (1995). *Gender Identity Disorder and Psychological Problems in Children and Adolescents*. N.Y.: Guilford Press.

Zuger, B. (1984). Early effeminate behavior in boys: outcome and significance for homosexuality. *Journal of Nervous and Mental Disease*, 172, 90-97.

Subject Index

Authors Index

Index of Cases

This list covers the major respondents and patients mentioned in this book. To find individuals who are not listed here, locate them through the Table of Contents ord Subject Index.

Dear Reader,

If you have any comments, criticisms, or questions you would like to direct to the author, I would appreciate receiving them by letter or e-mail (louisberman@aol.com). I will do my best to acknowledge every communication and to answer your questions.

General readers: let me know about ambiguities, omissions, or other shortcomings in the book. What did you like about the book? What did you dislike about it?

Students:did you find the book instructive, objective, understandable? Did you find any redundancies or omissions, any unaddressed issues, any unanswered questions?

Scholars, instructors, researchers: I would appreciate your advice on errors or omissions. What do you think the book accomplished, or failed to accomplish?

To order a copy of this book online and pay by credit card, log on to barnes&noble.com or amazon.com.

If you would like to order a signed copy of this book, send payment ($19.95 paperback, or $27.50 hardbound) to me, in care of my publisher: Godot Press, 601 Ridge Road, Wilmette, IL 60091.

If you want the book inscribed personally to you (or to a gift recipient), give me the exact wording you would like to see in the signing.

To order online and pay by credit card, log on to amazon.com or barnes&noble.com.

Sincerely,.

Louis A. Berman